ROAD ATLAS
COMPACT EUROPE

T0301067

www.philips-maps.co.uk
First published in 2007 by Philip's,
a division of Octopus Publishing Group Ltd
www.octopusbooks.co.uk
Carmelite House, 50 Victoria Embankment,
London EC4Y 0DZ
An Hachette UK Company
www.hachette.co.uk

Second edition 2023
First impression 2023
ISBN 978-1-84907-648-7

This product includes mapping data licensed from Ordnance Survey®, with the permission of the Controller of His Majesty's Stationery Office © Crown copyright 2023. All rights reserved. Licence number AC0000851689.

is a registered Trade Mark of the Northern Ireland Department of Finance and Personnel. This product includes mapping data licensed from Ordnance Survey of Northern Ireland®, reproduced with the permission of Land and Property Services under delegated authority from the Controller of His Majesty's Stationery Office, © Crown Copyright 2023.

While every reasonable effort has been made to ensure that the information compiled in this atlas is accurate, complete and up-to-date at the time of publication, some of this information is subject to change and the Publisher cannot guarantee its correctness or completeness.

The information in this atlas is provided without any representation or warranty, express or implied and the Publisher cannot be held liable for any loss or damage due to any use or reliance on the information in this atlas, nor for any errors, omissions or subsequent changes in such information.

The representation in this atlas of any road, drive or track is not evidence of the existence of a right of way.

The maps of Ireland on pages 26 to 30 are based upon the Crown Copyright and are reproduced with the permission of Land & Property Services under delegated authority from the Controller of His Majesty's Stationery Office, © Crown Copyright and database right 2023, PMLPA No 100503, and on Ordnance Survey Ireland by permission of the Government © Ordnance Survey Ireland / Government of Ireland Permit number 9274.

Cartography by Philip's
Copyright © Philip's 2023

Front cover photograph:
Prague, Czechia. DaLiu / iStock

Printed in Malaysia

*The UK's best-selling European Atlases.
Data from Nielsen Total Consumer Market 2022.

CONTENTS

II Driving regulations
IX Ski resorts
XII 300 greatest sights of Europe
XXVI **Legend to map symbols**
1 **Key to Route planning map pages**
2 **Route planning maps**
24 **Key to road map pages · Distances**
26 **Road maps of Europe**
201 **Index to road maps**

Driving regulations

The information below is for drivers visiting for fewer than 12 months, as different rules will apply for residents.

Vehicle Fitting headlamp converters or beam deflectors when taking a right-hand-drive car to a country where driving on the right (every country in Europe except the UK and Ireland) is compulsory. A national vehicle plate is required when taking a vehicle abroad. The (GB) identifier was replaced by (UK) in September 2021 and is no longer valid. If you are driving a UK registered vehicle within the EU and its number plate does not include a UK identifier and the Union flag, you will need to attach a UK sticker. Outside the EU and in Cyprus, Malta and Spain, a UK sticker is required even if your number plate includes a UK identifier. A UK sticker isn't required in Ireland.

Vehicle documentation All countries require that you carry a vehicle registration document (V5C), hire certificate (VE103) or letter of authority for the use of someone else's vehicle, full driving licence/International Driving Permit and insurance documentation (and/or green card outside the EU – see also "Insurance" below). Minimum driving ages are often higher for people holding foreign licences. Drivers of vehicles over three years old should ensure that the MOT is up to date and take the certificate with them.

Travel documentation All UK visitors' passports should be valid for at least six months. Some non-EU countries also require a visa. UK nationals may visit the EU Schengen area countries for up to 90 days in a 180-day period without a visa. A UK EHIC (UK European Health Insurance Card) or a UK GHIC (UK Global Health Insurance Card) will allow you to access state provided healthcare when visiting an EU country. They are available from the NHS website https://services.nhsbsa.nhs.uk/cra/start. Not all healthcare in the EU is free so you should also ensure you also have suitable travel insurance. In future, the GHIC card may cover additional countries outside the EU but it is not currently valid in Norway, Iceland, Liechtenstein or Switzerland.

Insurance Third-party cover is compulsory across Europe. Most insurance policies give only basic cover when driving abroad, so you should check that your policy provides at least third-party cover for the countries in which you will be driving and upgrade it to the level that you require. You might be forced to take out extra cover at the frontier if you cannot produce acceptable proof that you have adequate insurance.

Licence A photo licence is preferred. If you have an old-style paper driving licence or are visiting countries outside the EU, you may need to carry an IDP (International Driving Permit). Some non-EU countries may only recognise one of the three available types of IDP (1926, 1949 or 1968) so the correct one should be obtained, see www.gov.uk/driving-abroad/international-driving-permit. If planning to hire a car abroad, you should check in advance if the hire company wish to check your licence for endorsements and permitted vehicles categories. If so, visit www.gov.uk/view-driving-licence to create a digital code (valid for 72 hours) that allows your licence details to be shared. For more information, contact the DVLA (0300 790 6802), www.dft.gov.uk/dvla.

Motorcycles It is compulsory for all motorcyclists and passengers to wear crash helmets in all countries. In France it is compulsory for them to carry reflective jackets.

Other In countries in which reflective jackets are compulsory, one for each person should be carried in the passenger compartment (or motorcycle panniers). Warning triangles should also be carried here. The penalties for infringements of regulations vary considerably between countries. In many, the police have the right to impose on-the-spot fines (ask for a receipt). Serious infringements, such as exceeding the blood-alcohol limit, can result in immediate imprisonment. Please note that driving regulations often change and it has not been possible to include the information for all types of vehicle. The figures given for capitals' populations are for the entire metropolitan area.

Symbols

🏛	Motorway
⚠	Dual carriageway
▲	Single carriageway / expressway
🚗	Surfaced road
🚙	Unsurfaced / gravel road
🏙	Urban area
⊙	Speed limit in kilometres per hour
🖢	Seat belts
👶	Children
⚕	Blood alcohol level
△	Warning triangle
✚	First aid kit
💡	Spare bulb kit
🧯	Fire extinguisher
⊖	Minimum driving age
🛂	Additional documents required
📵	Mobile phones
LEZ	Low Emission Zone
◐	Dipped headlights
❄	Winter driving
★	Other information

Andorra Principat d'Andorra (AND)

Area 468 km² (181 miles²) **Population** 77,500 **Capital** Andorra la Vella (23,000) **Languages** Catalan (official), French, Castilian and Portuguese **Currency** Euro = 100 cents

🏛	⚠	▲	🏙
⊙ n/a	90	60/90	50

🖢 Compulsory
👶 Under 10 and below 150 cm must travel in an EU-approved restraint system adapted to their size in the rear. Airbag must be deactivated if a child is in the front passenger seat.
⚕ 0.05% △ 2 compulsory ✚ Recommended
💡 Compulsory 🧯 Recommended ⊖18
📵 Only allowed with hands-free kit
◐ Compulsory for motorcycles during day and for other vehicles during poor daytime visibility.
❄ Snow chains must be carried or winter tyres fitted 1 Nov–15 May
★ On-the-spot fines imposed
★ Visibility vests compulsory
★ Wearers of contact lenses or spectacles should carry a spare pair

Austria Österreich (A)

Area 83,859 km² (32,377 miles²)
Population 8,913,000 **Capital** Vienna / Wien (2,891,000) **Languages** German (official)
Currency Euro = 100 cents

🏛	⚠	▲	🏙
⊙ 130	100	100	50

If towing trailer under 750kg / over 750 kg
🏛	⚠	▲	🏙
⊙100/80	100/80	100/70	50

Minimum speed on motorways 60 kph

🖢 Compulsory
👶 Under 14 and under 135cm cannot travel as a front or rear passenger unless they use a suitable child restraint; under 14 over 150cm must wear adult seat belt. Airbags must be deactivated if a rear-facing child seat is used in the front.
⚕ 0.049% · 0.01% for professional drivers or if licence held less than 2 years
△ Compulsory ✚ Compulsory
💡 Recommended 🧯 Recommended
⊖ 17 (16 for motorbikes up to 125cc)
🛂 Paper driving licences must be accompanied by photographic proof of identity.
📵 Only allowed with hands-free kit
LEZ Several cities and regions have LEZs affecting HGVs that ban non-compliant vehicles, impose speed restrictions and night-time bans. Trucks in categories N1 to N3 must display an environmental badge (Umwelt-Pickerl) in these areas.
◐ Compulsory for motorcycles and in poor visibility for other vehicles. Headlamp converters compulsory for right-hand drive vehicles
❄ Winter tyres compulsory 1 Nov–15 Apr. Snow chains only permitted if road is fully covered by snow or ice.

★ On-the-spot fines imposed
★ Radar detectors and dashcams prohibited
★ To drive on motorways or expressways, a motorway sticker must be purchased at the border or main petrol station. These are available for 10 days, 2 months or 1 year. Vehicles 3.5 tonnes or over must display an electronic tag.
★ Visibility vests compulsory
★ When traffic flow ceases on a motorway or dual carriageway, vehicles are required to form a corridor between lanes for use by emergency services.

Belarus (BY)

Area 207,600 km² (80,154 miles²)
Population 9,414,000
Capital Minsk (2,256,000)
Languages Belarusian, Russian (both official)
Currency Belarusian ruble = 100 kopek

🏛	⚠	▲	🏙
⊙ 110	90	90	60*

If towing trailer under 750kg
🏛	⚠	▲	🏙
⊙ 90	70	70	50

*In residential areas limit is 20 kph • Vehicle towing another vehicle 50 kph limit • If full driving licence held for less than two years, must not exceed 70 kph

🖢 Compulsory in front seats, and rear seats if fitted
👶 Under 12 not allowed in front seat and must use appropriate child restraint
⚕ 0.00% △ Compulsory
✚ Recommended
💡 Recommended
🧯 Recommended
⊖ 18
🛂 Visa, vehicle technical check stamp, proof of ownership, 1968 International Driving

Permit, green card, local health insurance. Even with a green card, local third-party insurance may be imposed at the border.

- Only allowed with a hands-free kit
- Compulsory during the day in poor visibility or if towing or being towed. Headlamp converters compulsory for right-hand drive vehicles
- Winter tyres compulsory 1 Dec–1 Mar; snow chains recommended
- ★ A temporary vehicle import certificate must be purchased on entry and driver must be registered
- ★ It is illegal for vehicles to be dirty
- ★ Many road signs use only the Cyrillic alphabet
- ★ On-the-spot fines imposed
- ★ Radar-detectors prohibited
- ★ To drive on main motorways an on-board unit must be acquired at the border or a petrol station in order to pay tolls. See www.beltoll.by/index.php/en

Belgium Belgique (B)

Area 30,528 km² (11,786 miles²)
Population 11,847,000
Capital Brussels/Bruxelles (2,500,000)
Languages Dutch, French, German (all official)
Currency Euro = 100 cents

🚗	🚗	🚗	🏙
120[1]	120[1]	90[2]	50[3]
Over 3.5 tonnes			
90	90	70[2]–90	50[3]

[1]Minimum speed of 70 kph may be applied in certain conditions on motorways and some dual carriageways. [2]70 kph in Flanders. [3]20 kph in residential areas, 30 kph near some schools, hospitals and churches, and in designated cycle zones.

- Compulsory
- All under 18s under 135 cm must wear an appropriate child restraint. Airbags must be deactivated if a rear-facing child seat is used in the front
- 0.05% • 0.02% professional drivers
- △ Compulsory Compulsory
- Recommended Compulsory
- 18
- Only allowed with a hands-free kit
- LEZ LEZs in operation in Antwerp, Brussels and areas of Flanders. Preregistration necessary and fees payable for most vehicles.
- Mandatory at all times for motorcycles and during the day in poor conditions for other vehicles
- Winter tyres permitted 1 Oct to 31 Apr. Snow chains only permitted if road is fully covered by snow or ice. Vehicles with spiked tyres restricted to 90 kph on motorways/dual carriageways and 60 kph on other roads.
- ★ Cruise control must be deactivated on motorways where indicated
- ★ If a tram or bus stops to allow passengers on or off, you must not overtake
- ★ Motorcyclists must wear fully protective clothing
- ★ On-the-spot fines imposed
- ★ Radar detectors prohibited
- ★ Sticker indicating maximum recommended speed for winter tyres must be displayed on dashboard if using them
- ★ Visibility vest compulsory
- ★ When a traffic jam occurs on a road with two or more lanes in the direction of travel, motorists should move aside to create a path for emergency vehicles between the lanes.

Bosnia and Herzegovina Bosna i Hercegovina (BIH)

Area 51,197 km² (19,767 mi²)
Population 3,816,000 **Capital** Sarajevo (555,000) **Languages** Bosnian/Croatian/Serbian **Currency** Convertible Marka = 100 convertible pfenniga

🚗	🚗	🚗	🏙
130	100	80	50

- Compulsory if fitted
- Under 12s must sit in rear using an appropriate child restraint. Under-2s may travel in a rear-facing child seat in the front only if the airbags have been deactivated.
- 0.03% • no person under the influence of alcohol may travel in front seats.
- △ 2 compulsory Recommended
- Recommended
- Compulsory for LPG vehicles
- 18
- Original vehicle registration and ownership papers.
- Only allowed with hands-free kit
- Compulsory for all vehicles at all times
- Winter tyres compulsory 15 Nov–15 Apr; the use of snow chains is compulsory in thick snow or if indicated by road signs.
- ★ GPS must have fixed speed camera function deactivated; radar detectors prohibited
- ★ On-the-spot fines imposed
- ★ Visibility vest, tow rope or tow bar recommended
- ★ Spare wheel compulsory, except for two-wheeled vehicles

Bulgaria Bulgariya (BG)

Area 110,912 km² (42,822 miles²)
Population 6,873,000 **Capital** Sofia (1,675,000) **Languages** Bulgarian (official), Turkish **Currency** Lev = 100 stotinki

🚗	🚗	🚗	🏙
140	120	90	50
If towing trailer			
100	90	70	50
Over 3.5 tonnes			
100	90	80	50

- Compulsory in front and rear seats
- Under 3s not permitted in vehicles with no child restraints; 3–10 year olds must sit in rear in an appropriate restraint. Rear-facing child seats may be used in the front only if the airbag has been deactivated
- 0.05% △ Compulsory Recommended
- Recommended Recommended
- 18
- Photo driving licence preferred; a paper licence must be accompanied by an International Driving Permit.
- Only allowed with a hands-free kit
- Compulsory
- Winter tyres compulsory. Snow chains should be carried from 1 Nov–1 Mar. Max speed with chains 50 kph
- ★ Fee at border
- ★ GPS must have fixed speed camera function deactivated; radar detectors prohibited
- ★ On-the-spot fines imposed
- ★ A vignette is required to drive on motorways and main roads. These can be purchased at the border. Digital e-vignettes can be obtained from terminals at border checkpoints or online in advance: https://tollpass.bg/en
- ★ Visibility vest compulsory

Croatia Hrvatska (HR)

Area 56,538 km² (21,829 mi²)
Population 4,189,000 **Capital** Zagreb (1,107,000) **Languages** Croatian
Currency Kuna = 100 lipa

🚗	🚗	🚗	🏙
130	110	90	50
If towing			
90	90	80	50

Lower speed limits for newly qualified drivers; please check before travelling

- Compulsory if fitted
- Children under 12 not permitted in front seat and must use appropriate child seat or restraint in rear. Children under 2 may use a rear-facing seat in the front only if the airbag is deactivated
- 0.05% • 0.00% for drivers under 24 and professional drivers
- △ Compulsory (two if towing)
- Compulsory
- Compulsory except for xenon or LED lights
- Recommended 18
- Only allowed with hands-free kit
- Compulsory in reduced visibility and at all times from the last weekend in October the until last weekend in March
- From 15 Nov to 15 Apr, winter tyres must be fitted, snow chains and shovel must be carried in vehicle. Winter tyres must have minimum tread of 4mm
- ★ Motorway tolls can be paid in cash or by credit or debit card. An electronic toll collection system is also available, for details see www.hac.hr/en
- ★ On-the-spot fines imposed
- ★ Radar detectors prohibited
- ★ Visibility vest compulsory

Czechia Česko (CZ)

Area 78,864 km² (30,449 miles²) **Population** 10,705,000 **Capital** Prague/Praha (2,709,000) **Languages** Czech (official), Moravian **Currency** Czech Koruna = 100 haler

🚗	🚗	🚗	🏙
130	110/80*	90	50
If towing			
80	80	80	50

*80 kph on urban expressways.

- Compulsory in front seats and, if fitted, in rear
- Children under 36 kg and 150 cm must use appropriate child restraint. Only front-facing child restraints are permitted in the front in vehicles with airbags fitted. Airbags must be deactivated if a rear-facing child seat is used in the front.
- 0.00%
- △ Compulsory
- Compulsory
- Recommended
- Recommended
- 18 (17 for motorcycles under 125 cc)
- Licences with a photo preferred. Paper licences should be accompanied by an International Driving Permit.
- Only allowed with a hands-free kit
- LEZ Two-stage LEZ in Prague for vehicles over 3.5 and 6 tonnes. Permit system.
- Compulsory at all times
- Winter tyres compulsory 1 Nov–31 Mar if roads are icy/snow-covered or snow is expected. Also if winter equipment sign (circular blue sign with white car and snowflake) is displayed. Minimum tread depth 4mm.

★ GPS must have fixed speed camera function deactivated; radar detectors prohibited
★ On-the-spot fines imposed
★ Replacement fuses must be carried
★ Spectacles or contact lens wearers must carry a spare pair in their vehicle at all times
★ Vehicles up to 3.5 tonnes require e-vignette for motorway driving, available for 1 year, 60 days, 10 days. https://edalnice.cz/en. Vehicles over 3.5 tonnes are subject to tolls and must carry an electronic tag https://mytocz.eu/en
★ Visibility vest compulsory

Denmark Danmark (DK)

Area 43,094 km² (16,638 miles²) **Population** 5,921,000 **Capital** Copenhagen / København (2,136,000) **Languages** Danish (official)
Currency Krone = 100 øre

⊙			
110-130*	80	80	50**
If towing			
100	80	80	50**

*Over 3.5 tonnes 80 kph
**Central Copenhagen 40 kph

- Compulsory front and rear
- Under 135cm must use appropriate child restraint; in front permitted only in an appropriate rear-facing seat with any airbags disabled.
- 0.05%
- Compulsory / Recommended
- Recommended / Recommended
- 17
- Only allowed with a hands-free kit
- LEZ Aalborg, Aarhus, Copenhagen, Frederiksberg and Odense. Proofs of emissions compliance or compliant filter needed to obtain sticker. Non-compliant vehicles banned. Older diesel-powered trucks, buses and vans may not enter Copenhagen, Aarhus, Odense or Aalborg unless they have been retrofitted with an effective particulate filter.
- Must be used at all times
- Spiked tyres may be fitted 1 Nov–15 April, if used on all wheels

★ On-the-spot fines imposed
★ Radar detectors prohibited
★ Tolls apply on the Storebaeltsbroen and Oresundsbron bridges.
★ Visibility vest recommended

Estonia Eesti (EST)

Area 45,100 km² (17,413 miles²)
Population 1,212,000 **Capital** Tallinn (451,000)
Languages Estonian (official), Russian
Currency Euro = 100 cents

⊙			
n/a	90*	90	50

*In summer, the speed limit on some dual carriageways may be raised to 100/120 kph. The limit on ice roads varies between 10kph and 70 kph according to ice thickness.

- Compulsory if fitted
- Children too small for adult seatbelts must wear a seat restraint appropriate to their size. Rear-facing safety seats must not be used in the front if an air bag is fitted, unless this has been deactivated.
- 0.02%
- 2 compulsory
- Recommended (compulsory for company cars)
- Recommended
- Compulsory ⊝ 18
- Only allowed with a hands-free kit
- Compulsory at all times
- Winter tyres are compulsory from Dec–Mar. Studded winter tyres are allowed from 15 Oct–31 Mar, but this can be extended to start 1 October and/or end 30 April

★ A toll system is in operation in Tallinn
★ On-the-spot fines imposed
★ Radar detectors prohibited
★ Two wheel chocks compulsory
★ Visibility vest compulsory

Finland Suomi (FIN)

Area 338,145 km² (130,557 miles²) **Population** 5,602,000 **Capital** Helsinki (1,537,000)
Languages Finnish, Swedish (both official)
Currency Euro = 100 cents

⊙			
100-120	80-100	80-100*	20/50
Vans, lorries and if towing			
80	80	60	20/50

*100 in summer • If towing a vehicle by rope, cable or rod, max speed limit 60 kph • Maximum of 80 kph for vans and lorries • Speed limits are often lowered in winter

- Compulsory in front and rear
- Below 135 cm must use a child restraint or seat
- 0.05% Compulsory
- Recommended / Recommended
- Recommended ⊝ 18
- Only allowed with hands-free kit
- Must be used at all times
- Winter tyres compulsory Dec–Feb

★ After filling with petrol, it is usual to move the vehicle away from the pump before going to pay.
★ On-the-spot fines imposed
★ Radar-detectors are prohibited
★ Visibility vest compulsory

France (F)

Area 551,500 km² (212,934 miles²) **Population** 68,305,000 **Capital** Paris (13,025,000)
Languages French (official), Breton, Occitan
Currency Euro = 100 cents

⊙			
130	110	80	50
On wet roads or if full driving licence held for less than 3 years			
110	100	70	50
above 3.5 tonnes gross			
90	80	80	50

50kph on all roads if fog reduces visibility to less than 50m

- Compulsory in front seats and, if fitted, in rear
- Children up to age 10 must use suitable child seat or restraint and may only travel in the front if: • the vehicle has no rear seats • no rear seatbelts • the rear seats are already occupied by children up to age 10 • the child is a baby in a rear facing child seat and the airbag is deactivated.
- 0.05% • 0.02% if full driving licence held for less than 3 years • All drivers/motorcyclists are required to carry an unused breathalyser though this rule is not currently enforced.
- Compulsory / Recommended
- Recommended
- ⊝ 18 (16 for motorbikes up to 80cc)
- Passport, UK driving licence, insurance and vehicle registration, ownership and roadworthiness documents.
- Use permitted only with hands-free kit. Must not be used with headphones or earpieces
- LEZ An LEZ operates in the Mont Blanc tunnel and such zones are being progressively introduced across French cities. Non-compliant vehicles are banned during operating hours. Crit'Air stickers must be displayed by compliant vehicles. See http://certificat-air.gouv.fr/en
- Compulsory for poor daytime visibility and at all times for motorcycles
- Snow chains are mandatory on snow covered roads when indicated by local signs. Max speed 50 kph

★ GPS must have fixed speed camera function deactivated; radar-detection equipment is prohibited
★ Headphones or earpieces must not be used for listening to music or making phone calls while driving.
★ Motorcyclists and passengers must have four reflective stickers on their helmets (front, back and both sides) and wear CE-certified gloves.
★ On-the-spot fines imposed
★ Tolls on motorways. Electronic tag needed if using automatic tolls.
★ Visibility vests, to be worn on the roadside in case of emergency or breakdown, must be carried for all vehicle occupants and riders.
★ Wearers of contact lenses or spectacles should carry a spare pair

Germany Deutschland (D)

Area 357,022 km² (137,846 miles²)
Population 84,317,000 **Capital** Berlin (6,145,000) **Languages** German (official)
Currency Euro = 100 cents

⊙			
130*	130*	100	50
If towing			
80	80	80	50

*recommended maximum. • 50kph if visibility below 50m

- Compulsory
- Aged 3-12 and under 150cm must use an appropriate child seat or restraint and sit in the rear. In the front, if child under 3 is in a rear-facing seat, airbags must be deactivated
- 0.05% • 0.00% for drivers 21 or under or with less than two years full licence
- Compulsory / Recommended
- Compulsory except for xenon or LED lights
- Recommended ⊝ 18
- Use permitted only with hands-free kit – also applies to drivers of motorbikes and bicycles
- LEZ Many cities have or are planning LEZs (Umweltzone). Vehicles must display a 'Plakette' sticker, indicating emissions category. Proof of compliance needed to acquire sticker. Non-compliant vehicles banned. www.umwelt-plakette.de/en
- Compulsory during poor daytime visibility and tunnels; recommended at other times. Compulsory at all times for motorcyclists.
- Winter tyres compulsory in all winter weather conditions; snow chains recommended

★ GPS must have fixed speed camera function deactivated; radar detectors prohibited
★ On-the-spot fines imposed
★ Tolls on autobahns for lorries
★ Visibility vest compulsory

Greece Ellas (GR)

Area 131,957 km² (50,948 miles²)
Population 10,534,000 **Capital** Athens /
Athina (3,547,000) **Languages** Greek (official)
Currency Euro = 100 cents

🏛	🛣	⚠	🏭
⊙ 130	110	90	50
If towing			
⊙ 90–100	80–90	80	50

- Compulsory in front seats and,
  if fitted, in rear
- Under 12 or below 135cm must use
  appropriate child restraint. In front if child
  is in rear-facing child seat, any airbags must
  be deactivated.
- 0.05% • 0.02% for drivers with less than
  2 years' full licence
- △ Compulsory ⚏ Compulsory
- ⚐ Recommended 🛑 Compulsory
- ⊖ 17
- 🛢 Only allowed with a hands-free kit
- ⊘ Compulsory during poor daytime visibility
  and at all times for motorcycles
- ❄ Snow chains permitted on ice- or snow-
  covered roads. Max speed 50 kph.
- ★ On-the-spot fines can be imposed but not
  collected by the police
- ★ Radar-detection equipment is prohibited
- ★ Tolls on several newer motorways.

Hungary Magyarorszàg (H)

Area 93,032 km² (35,919 miles²)
Population 9,700,000 **Capital** Budapest
(3,012,000) **Languages** Hungarian (official)
Currency Forint = 100 filler

🏛	🛣	⚠	🏭
⊙ 130	110	90	50*
If towing or if over 3.5 tonnes			
⊙ 80	70	70	50*

*30 kph zones have been introduced in
many cities

- Compulsory
- Under 150cm and over 3 must be seated
  in rear and use appropriate child restraint.
  Under 3 allowed in front only in rear-facing
  child seat with any airbags deactivated.
- 0.00%
- △ Compulsory ⚏ Recommended
- ⚐ Recommended 🛑 Recommended ⊖ 17
- 🛢 Only allowed with a hands-free kit
- LEZ Budapest is divided into zones with varying
  restrictions on HGVs.
- ⊘ Compulsory during the day outside
  built-up areas; compulsory at all times for
  motorcycles
- ❄ Snow chains compulsory where conditions
  dictate. Max speed 50 kph.
- ★ Tolls apply to many motorways and are
  administered through an electronic
  vignette system with automatic number
  plate recognition https://ematrica.
  nemzetiutdij.hu
- ★ On-the-spot fines issued
- ★ Radar detectors prohibited
- ★ Tow rope recommended
- ★ Visibility vest recommended

Iceland Ísland (IS)

Area 103,000 km² (39,768 miles²)
Population 358,000 **Capital** Reykjavik
(233,000) **Languages** Icelandic
Currency Krona = 100 aurar

🏛	🚍	🚗	🏭
⊙ n/a	90	80	50

- Compulsory in front and rear seats
- Children up to 135 cm must use suitable
  child seat or restraint. Up to 150cm
  must not sit in front seat unless airbag is
  deactivated.
- 0.05%
- ⚏ Compulsory 🛑 Recommended
- ⚐ Recommended 🛑 Recommended
- ⊖ 17
- 🛢 Only allowed with a hands-free kit
- ⊘ Compulsory at all times
- ❄ Winter tyres compulsory c. 1 Nov–14 Apr
  (variable). Snow chains may be used
  when necessary.
- ★ Driving off marked roads is forbidden
- ★ Highland roads are not suitable for ordinary
  cars and many are unusable in winter
- ★ On-the-spot fines imposed

Ireland Eire (IRL)

Area 70,273 km² (27,132 miles²)
Population 5,275,000 **Capital** Dublin
(1,418,000) **Languages** Irish, English (both
official) **Currency** Euro = 100 cents

🏛	🛣	⚠	🏭
⊙ 120	100	80	50*
If towing			
⊙ 80	80	80	50*

*Dublin and some other areas have
introduced 30 kph zones

- Compulsory where fitted. Driver
  responsible for ensuring passengers under
  17 comply
- Children 3 and under must be in a suitable
  child restraint system. Airbags must be
  deactivated if a rear-facing child seat is
  used in the front. Those under 150 cm and
  36 kg must use appropriate child restraint.
- 0.05% • 0.02% for novice and professional
  drivers
- △ Recommended (compulsory for HGVs
  and buses)
- ⚏ Recommended
- ⚐ Recommended 🛑 Recommended
- ⊖ 17 (16 for motorbikes up to 125cc;
  18–24 for over 125cc according to power).
- 🛢 Only allowed with a hands-free kit
- ⊘ Compulsory in poor visibility.
- ★ Driving is on the left
- ★ GPS must have fixed speed camera
  function deactivated; radar detectors
  prohibited
- ★ On-the-spot fines imposed
- ★ Tolls are being introduced on some
  motorways; the M50 Dublin has barrier-free
  tolling with number-plate recognition.
  www.etoll.ie/driving-on-toll-roads/
  information-for-visitors

Italy Italia (I)

Area 301,318 km² (116,338 miles²)
Population 61,096,000 **Capital** Rome / Roma
(4,342,000) **Languages** Italian (official)
Currency Euro = 100 cents

🏛	🛣	⚠	🏭
⊙ 130	110	90	50
If towing			
⊙ 80	70	70	50
When wet			
⊙ 110	90	80	50

Some motorways with emergency lanes
have speed limit of 150 kph

- Compulsory in front seats and, if fitted, in
  rear
- Under 12 not allowed in front seats except
  in child safety seat; children under 3 must
  have special seat in the back. For foreign-
  registered cars, the country of origin's
  legislation applies.
- 0.05% • 0.00% for professional drivers or
  with less than 3 years full licence
- △ Compulsory ⚏ Recommended
- ⚐ Recommended 🛑 Recommended
- ⊖ 18 (14 for mopeds, 16 up to 125cc,
  20 up to 350cc)
- 🛢 Only allowed with hands-free kit
- LEZ Italy has many low emission zones with
  varying standards and hours of operation.
  Milan and Palermo operate combined LEZ
  and urban road toll schemes.
- ⊘ Compulsory outside built-up areas,
  in tunnels, on motorways and dual
  carriageways and in poor visibility;
  compulsory at all times for motorcycles
- ❄ Winter tyres or snow chains compulsory
  15 Oct–15 Apr in certain areas where
  signs indicate. Max speed with snow
  chains 50 kph
- ★ On-the-spot fines imposed
- ★ Radar-detection equipment is prohibited
- ★ Tolls on motorways. Blue lanes accept
  credit cards; yellow lanes restricted to
  holders of Telepass pay-toll device.
- ★ Visibility vest compulsory

Kosovo Republika e Kosoves / Republika Kosovo (RKS)

Area 10,887 km² (4203 miles²)
Population 1,935,000 **Capital** Pristina
(162,000) **Languages** Albanian, Serbian
(both official), Bosnian, Turkish, Roma
Currency Euro (Serbian dinar in Serb enclaves)

🏛	🛣	⚠	🏭
⊙ 110–130	100	80	50

- Compulsory
- Under 12 must sit in rear seats in an
  appropriate restraint.
- 0.01%
- △ Compulsory ⚏ Compulsory
- ⚐ Compulsory 🛑 Compulsory
- ⊖ 18
- 🪪 International Driving Permit
  recommended, locally purchased
  third-party insurance (green card is not
  recognised), visa. Visitors from many non-
  EU countries also require documents with
  proof of ability to cover costs and valid
  reason for visiting.
- 🛢 Only allowed with a hands-free kit
- ⊘ Compulsory at all times
- ❄ Winter tyres or snow chains compulsory in
  poor winter weather conditions

Latvia Latvija (LV)

Area 64,589 km² (24,942 miles²)
Population 1,842,000 **Capital** Riga (1,070,000)
Languages Latvian (official), Russian
Currency Euro = 100 cents

🏛	🛣	⚠	🏭
⊙ n/a	90–100*	90**	50
If towing			
⊙ n/a	80	80	50

*100 on designated roads only during
1 Mar–1 Nov. • **80 on gravel roads. In
residential areas limit is 20kph

- Compulsory in front seats and if fitted in
  rear
- If under 12 years and 150cm must use
  suitable child restraint in front and rear
  seats.
- 0.05% • 0.02% with less than 2 years
  experience

△ Compulsory ⊞ Recommended
�! Recommended ⬆Recommended
⊖ 18
▯ Only allowed with hands-free kit
◔ Must be used at all times all year round
❄ Winter tyres compulsory 1 Dec–1 Mar on all vehicles up to 3.5 tonnes. Studded tyres prohibited from 1 May–1 Oct.
★ On-the-spot fines can be imposed but not collected by the police
★ Radar-detection equipment prohibited
★ Visibility vests recommended

Lithuania Lietuva ⓛⓣ

Area 65,200 km² (25,173 miles²)
Population 2,684,000 **Capital** Vilnius (701,000) **Languages** Lithuanian (official), Russian, Polish **Currency** Euro = 100 cents

🜨	⯅	⯅	🏭
⊙130/110*	110/100*	70–90	50
If towing			
⊙ 90	90	70–90	50
If licence held for less than two years			
⊙ 100	90	70–80	50

* Apr–Oct / Nov–Mar

♥ Compulsory
♣ Under 12 or below 135 cm not allowed in front seats unless in suitable restraint; under 3 must use appropriate child seat. A rear-facing child seat may be used in front only if airbags are deactivated.
♈ 0.04% • 0.00% if full licence held less than 2 years
△ Compulsory ⊞ Recommended
�! Recommended ⬆Recommended
⊖ 18
▣ Licences without a photograph must be accompanied by photographic proof of identity, e.g. a passport
▯ Only allowed with a hands-free kit
◔ Must be used at all times
❄ Winter tyres compulsory 10 Nov–10 Apr
★ On-the-spot fines imposed
★ Visibility vest recommended

Luxembourg Ⓛ

Area 2,586 km² (998 miles²)
Population 650,000 **Capital** Luxembourg (129,000) **Languages** Luxembourgian / Letzeburgish (official), French, German
Currency Euro = 100 cents

🜨	⯅	⯅	🏭
⊙130/110*	90	90	50*
If towing			
⊙ 90	75	75	50*

If full driving licence held for less than two years, must not exceed 75 kph • *110 in wet weather • **30 kph zones are progressively being introduced. 20 kph in zones where pedestrians have priority.

♥ Compulsory
♣ Children under 3 must use an appropriate restraint system. Airbags must be disabled if a rear-facing child seat is used in the front. Children 3–18 and/or under 150 cm must use a restraint system appropriate to their size. If over 36kg a seatbelt may be used in the back only
♈ 0.05%, 0.02% for young drivers, drivers with less than 2 years experience and drivers of taxis and commercial vehicles
△ Compulsory
⊞ Recommended, compulsory for buses
�! Recommended
⬆Compulsory (buses, transport of dangerous goods)

⊖ 18
▮ Use permitted only with hands-free kit
◔ Compulsory for motorcyclists and for other vehicles in poor visibility and in tunnels. Outside urban areas, full-beam headlights are compulsory at night and in poor visibility.
❄ Winter tyres compulsory in winter weather
★ On-the-spot fines imposed
★ Visibility vest recommended

North Macedonia
Severna Makedonija ⓃⓂⓀ

Area 25,713 km² (9,927 miles²)
Population 2,131,000 **Capital** Skopje (607,000) **Languages** Macedonian (official), Albanian **Currency** Denar = 100 deni

🜨	⯅	⯅	🏭
⊙ 130	110*	80	50

*if road reserved for motor vehicles, otherwise 80. • Lower limits apply to newly qualified drivers

♥ Compulsory
♣ Under 12 not allowed in front seats
♈ 0.05% • 0.00% for business, commercial and professional drivers and with less than 2 years experience
△ Compulsory ⊞ Recommended
�! Recommended
⬆Recommended; compulsory for LPG vehicles
⊖ 18 (16 with parental supervision, 16 for mopeds)
▣ International Driving Permit; green card
▯ Use not permitted whilst driving
◔ Compulsory at all times
❄ Winter tyres or snow chains compulsory 15 Nov–15 Mar. Max speed 50 kph for vehicles using snow chains
★ GPS must have fixed speed camera function deactivated; radar detectors prohibited
★ Novice drivers may only drive between 11pm and 5am if there is someone over 25 with a valid licence in the vehicle.
★ On-the-spot fines imposed but paid later
★ Tolls apply on many roads
★ Tow rope compulsory
★ Visibility vest recommended and should be kept in the passenger compartment and worn to leave the vehicle in the dark outside built-up areas

Moldova ⓂⒹ

Area 33,851 km² (13,069 miles²)
Population 3,287,000 **Capital** Chisinau (779,000) **Languages** Moldovan / Romanian (official) **Currency** Leu = 100 bani

🜨	⯅	⯅	🏭
⊙ 110	90	90	50
If towing or if licence held under 1 year			
⊙ 70	70	70	50

♥ Compulsory in front seats and, if fitted, in rear seats
♣ Under 12 not allowed in front seats
♈ 0.00%
△ Compulsory
⊞ Recommended
�! Recommended
⬆Recommended
⊖ 18
▣ Car registration document. If not the vehicle owner, written permission from owner (translated into Romanian and legalised); passport; UK driving licence; valid insurance (green card).

⊖ 18
▮ Only allowed with hands-free kit
◔ Must use dipped headlights at all times 1 Nov–31 Mar
❄ Winter tyres recommended 1 Nov–31 Mar
★ On-the-spot-fines imposed
★ Vehicles not registered in Moldova require a vignette. These may be purchased from MAIB (Moldova-Agroindbank) branches or online https://evinieta.gov.md

Montenegro Crna Gora ⓂⓃⒺ

Area 14,026 km², (5,415 miles²) **Population** 605,000 **Capital** Podgorica (250,000)
Languages Serbian (of the Ijekavian dialect)
Currency Euro = 100 cents

🜨	⯅	⯅	🏭
⊙ 100	100	80	50

80kph speed limit if towing a caravan

♥ Compulsory in front and rear seats
♣ Under 12 not allowed in front seats. Under-5s must use an appropriate child seat.
♈ 0.03% • 0.01% if aged up to 24 or licence held for less than 1 year.
△ Compulsory ⊞ Recommended
�! Recommended ⬆Recommended
⊖ 18
▣ Driving licence; 1968 International Driving Permit (1949 IDP my not be recognised); original vehicle registration document; vehicle insurance valid in Montenegro (green card recommended)
▮ Prohibited
◔ Must be used at all times
❄ Driving wheels must be fitted with winter tyres 15 Nov–31 Mar.
★ On-the-spot-fines imposed
★ Tolls in the Sozina tunnel between Lake Skadar and the sea. Toll charged on the open section of new A1 motorway (not yet completed)
★ Visibility vest recommended

Netherlands Nederland ⓃⓁ

Area 41,526 km² (16,033 miles²) **Population** 17,401,000 **Capital** Amsterdam 1,559,000 • administrative capital's-Gravenhage (The Hague) 553,000 **Languages** Dutch (official), Frisian **Currency** Euro = 100 cents

🜨	⯅	⯅	🏭
⊙100–130	80/100	80/100	50

♥ Compulsory
♣ Under 3 must travel in the back, using an appropriate child restraint; 3–18 and under 135cm must use an appropriate child restraint. A rear-facing child seat may only be used in front if airbags are deactivated.
♈ 0.05% • 0.02% if full licence held less than 5 years and for moped riders under 24.
△ Compulsory
⊞ Recommended ♥Recommended
⬆Recommended
⊖ 18
▮ Only allowed with a hands-free kit
LEZ Low emission zones for diesel vehicle operate in Amsterdam, Arnhem, Breda, Delft, Den Haag, Eindhoven, Leiden, Maastricht, Rijswijk, Rotterdam, Tilburg, Utrecht. Restrictions depend on vehicle's Euro emissions standard.
◔ Recommended in poor visibility and on open roads. Compulsory for motorcycles.
★ On-the-spot fines imposed
★ Radar-detection equipment is prohibited
★ Trams have priority over other traffic. You must wait if a bus or tram stops in the middle of the road to allow passengers on or off.

Norway Norge (N)

Area 323,877 km² (125,049 miles²)
Population 5,554,000 **Capital** Oslo (1,558,000)
Languages Norwegian (official), Lappish, Finnish **Currency** Krone = 100 øre

🚗	🛣	▲	🏭
🕐 80–100	80	80	30/50
If towing trailer with brakes			
🕐 80	80	80	50
If towing trailer without brakes			
🕐 60	60	60	50

- 🦺 Compulsory in front seats and, if fitted, in rear
- 👶 Children shorter than 135cm or lighter than 36kg must use appropriate child restraint. Children under 4 must use child safety seat or safety restraint (cot). A rear-facing child seat may be used in front only if airbags are deactivated.
- 🍷 0.02%
- △ Compulsory 🔺 Recommended
- 💡 Recommended 🔦 Recommended
- ⊖ 18 (heavy vehicles 18/21)
- 📱 Only allowed with a hands-free kit
- Qₑ Must be used at all times
- ❄ Winter tyres with at least 3mm tread compulsory during winter. Studded tyres may be used 1 Nov until first Sunday after Easter (15 Oct–1 May in Nordland, Troms, and Finnmark). There is a fee for using studded tyres within city boundaries of Oslo, Bergen and Trondheim. Vehicles under 3.5 tonnes must carry snow chains if snow or ice is expected.
- ★ On-the-spot fines imposed
- ★ Radar-detectors are prohibited
- ★ Tolls apply on some bridges, tunnels and access roads into Bergen, Haugesund, Kristiansand, Oslo, Stavanger, Tønsberg and Trondheim. Several use electronic fee collection www.autopass.no/visitors-payment
- ★ Some of the higher mountain passes can experience snowfall and ice even if conditions are warm at lower altitudes, particularly in spring and autumn.
- ★ Visibility vest compulsory

Poland Polska (PL)

Area 323,250 km² (124,807 miles²)
Population 38,093,000 **Capital** Warsaw / Warszawa (3,101,000) **Languages** Polish (official) **Currency** Zloty = 100 groszy

🚗	🛣	▲	🏭
🕐 140	120*/100	100*/90	20/50/60**
if towing			
🕐 80	80	70	20/50/60**

*expressway, indicated by signs with white car on blue background • **residential / built-up area / built-up area 2300-0500

- 🦺 Compulsory in front seats and, if fitted, in rear
- 👶 Under 12 and below 150 cm must use an appropriate child restraint. Rear-facing child seats not permitted in vehicles with airbags.
- 🍷 0.02%
- △ Compulsory 🔺 Recommended
- 💡 Recommended 🔦 Compulsory
- ⊖ 18 (mopeds and motorbikes under 125cc – 16)
- 📱 Only allowed with a hands-free kit
- Qₑ Compulsory for all vehicles
- ❄ Snow chains permitted only on roads completely covered in snow
- ★ On-the-spot fines imposed

Portugal (P)

Area 88,797 km² (34,284 miles²)
Population 10,242,000 **Capital** Lisbon / Lisboa (2,871,000) **Languages** Portuguese (official) **Currency** Euro = 100 cents

🚗	🛣	▲	🏭
🕐 120*	90/100	90	50/20
If towing			
🕐 100*	80	70	50/20

*50kph minimum; 90kph max if licence less than 1 year

- 🦺 Compulsory in front seats and, if fitted, in rear
- 👶 Under 12 and below 135cm must travel in the rear in an appropriate child restraint; rear-facing child seats permitted in front for under 3s only if airbags deactivated
- 🍷 0.05% • 0.02% if full licence held less than 3 years
- △ Compulsory 🔺 Recommended
- 💡 Recommended 🔦 Recommended
- ⊖ 18
- 📖 MOT certificate for vehicles over 3 years old, photographic proof of identity must be carried at all times. IDP required if you have old-style paper licence, vehicle registrations document, evidence of valid insurance
- 📱 Only allowed with hands-free kit
- LEZ Lisbon's LEZ has a minimum entry requirement of Euro 3 for the central zone and Euro 2 for the outer zone between 0700 and 2100.
- Qₑ Compulsory for motorcycles, compulsory for other vehicles in poor visibility and tunnels
- ★ On-the-spot fines imposed
- ★ Radar detectors and dash-cams prohibited
- ★ Some motorways use traditional toll booths (green lanes are reserved for auto-payment users) but others may only be used by vehicles registered with an automated billing system. www.portugaltolls.com/en
- ★ Visibility vest compulsory
- ★ Wearers of spectacles or contact lenses should carry a spare pair

Romania (RO)

Area 238,391 km² (92,042 miles²) **Population** 18,520,000 **Capital** Bucharest / Bucuresti (2,327,000) **Languages** Romanian (official), Hungarian **Currency** Romanian leu = 100 bani

🚗	🛣	▲	🏭
Cars and motorcycles			
🕐 130	100	90	50
If towing			
🕐 120	90	80	50

If full driving licence has been held for less than one year, speed limits are 20kph lower than those listed above. Tractors and mopeds limited to 45 kph.

- 🦺 Compulsory
- 👶 Under 12s not allowed in front and must use an appropriate restraint in the rear
- 🍷 0.00%
- △ Compulsory 🔺 Compulsory
- 💡 Compulsory 🔦 Compulsory ⊖ 18
- 📖 Green card recommended
- 📱 Only allowed with hands-free kit

- Qₑ Compulsory outside built-up areas, compulsory everywhere for motorcycles
- ❄ Winter tyres compulsory Nov–Mar if roads are snow- or ice-covered, especially in mountainous areas
- ★ Compulsory electronic road tax can be paid for at the border, post offices and some petrol stations and on-line www. roviniete.ro/en
- ★ It is illegal for vehicles to be dirty
- ★ On-the-spot fines imposed
- ★ Visibility vest compulsory

Russia Rossiya (RUS)

Area 17,075,000 km² (6,592,800 miles²)
Population 142,022,000
Capital Moscow / Moskva (12,327,000)
Languages Russian (official), and many others
Currency Russian ruble = 100 kopeks

🚗	🛣	▲	🏭
🕐 110	90	90	60/20
If licence held for under 2 years			
🕐 70	70	70	60/20

- 🦺 Compulsory if fitted
- 👶 Under 8 must use suitable child restraint in front and rear seats; under 12 must use suitable child restraint in front seat
- 🍷 0.03 % △ Compulsory
- 🔺 Compulsory 💡 Compulsory
- 🔦 Compulsory ⊖ 18
- 📖 International Driving Permit with Russian translation, visa, green card endorsed for Russia, International Certificate for Motor Vehicles
- 📱 Only allowed with a hands-free kit
- Qₑ Compulsory during the day outside built-up areas
- ❄ Winter tyres compulsory 1 Dec–1 Mar
- ★ On-the-spot fines imposed but must be paid later
- ★ Picking up hitchhikers is prohibited
- ★ Radar detectors/blockers prohibited
- ★ Road tax payable at the border
- ★ Some toll roads, mainly payable in cash

Serbia Srbija (SRB)

Area 77,474 km², 29,913 miles²
Population 6,739,000 **Capital** Belgrade / Beograd (1,687,000) **Languages** Serbian **Currency** Dinar = 100 paras

🚗	🛣	▲	🏭
🕐 120	100	80	50
If towing			
🕐 80	80	80	50

Speed limits vary so check local signage

- 🦺 Compulsory in front and rear seats
- 👶 Age 3–12 must be in rear seats and wear seat belt or appropriate child restraint; under 3 in rear-facing child seat permitted in front only if airbag deactivated
- 🍷 0.029% • 0.00% for commercial drivers, motorcyclists, or if full licence held less than 1 year
- △ Compulsory 🔺 Recommended
- 💡 Recommended 🔦 Recommended
- ⊖ 18
- 📖 International Driving Permit recommended, insurance that is valid for Serbia or locally bought third-party insurance
- 📱 Only allowed with a hands-free kit
- Qₑ Compulsory
- ❄ Winter tyres compulsory 1 Nov–1 Apr for vehicles up to 3.5 tonnes. Carrying snow chains compulsory in winter as these must be fitted if driving on snow-covered roads when signs indicate.

★ 3-metre tow rope or bar or spare wheel compulsory
★ On-the-spot fines imposed
★ Radar detectors prohibited
★ Tolls on motorways
★ Visibility vest recommended

Slovakia Slovenska Republika (SK)

Area 49,012 km² (18,923 miles²)
Population 5,431,000 **Capital** Bratislava (666,000) **Languages** Slovak (official), Hungarian **Currency** Euro = 100 cents

🕐	🛣	▲	🏘
130/90*	90	90	50

*rural roads / urban roads

🛡 Compulsory
👶 Under 12 or below 150cm must be in rear in appropriate child restraint
🍷 0.00%
△ Compulsory ▯▯ Recommended
🦺 Recommended 🔺Recommended
⊖ 18
📠 Proof of at least third party vehicle insurance
📱 Only allowed with a hands-free kit
⛽ Compulsory at all times
❄ Winter tyres compulsory when snow or ice on the road
★ On-the-spot fines imposed
★ Radar-detection equipment is prohibited
★ Tow rope recommended
★ Electronic vignette required for motorways, validity: 1 year, 30 days, 10 days https://eznamka.sk/en
★ Visibility vests compulsory

Slovenia Slovenija (SLO)

Area 20,256 km² (7,820 miles²)
Population 2,101,000 **Capital** Ljubljana (538,000) **Languages** Slovene
Currency Euro = 100 cents

🕐	🛣	▲	🏘
130	110¹	90¹	50²
If towing			
80	80¹	80¹	50²

¹ 70 kph in urban areas, ² 30 kph and 20 kph zones are increasingly common in cities. 50 kph in poor visibility or with snow chains

🛡 Compulsory
👶 Below 150cm must use appropriate child restraint. A rear-facing baby seat may be used in front only if airbags are deactivated.
🍷 0.05% • 0.00% for commercial drivers, under 21s or with less than one year with a full licence
△ Compulsory ▯▯ Recommended
🦺 Recommended 🔺Recommended
⊖ 18 (motorbikes up to 125cc – 16 ; up to 350cc – 18)
📠 Licences without photographs must be accompanied by an International Driving Permit
📱 Only allowed with hands-free kit
⛽ Must be used at all times
❄ From 15 Nov to 15 Mar winter tyres must be fitted or snow chains must be carried ready for use in icy conditions. Winter tyres also compulsory in wintry conditions beyond those dates.
★ On-the-spot fines imposed
★ Radar detectors prohibited
★ An e-vignette must be purchased before a vehicle can enter a toll road, https://evinjeta.dars.si/en
★ Visibility vest recommended

Spain España (E)

Area 497,548 km² (192,103 miles²) **Population** 47,163,000 **Capital** Madrid (6,792,000)
Languages Castilian Spanish (official), Catalan, Galician, Basque **Currency** Euro = 100 cents

🕐	🛣	▲	🏘
120*	100*	90	50*
Passenger cars & vans with trailers, vehicles below 3.5 t			
90	80	70	50*

*Urban motorways and dual carriageways 80 kph. 20 kph zones are being introduced in many cities

🛡 Compulsory
👶 Under 135cm and below 12 must use appropriate child restraint and sit in rear.
🍷 0.05% • 0.03% if less than 2 years full licence or if vehicle is over 3.5 tonnes or carries more than 9 passengers
△ Two compulsory (one for in front, one for behind) ▯▯ Recommended
🦺 Compulsory 🔺Recommended. Compulsory for buses and LGVs
⊖ 18 (21 for heavy vehicles; 16 for motorbikes up to 125cc)
📱 Only allowed with a hands-free kit. Headphones and earpieces not permitted
⛽ Compulsory for motorcycles and in poor daytime visibility and in tunnels for other vehicles.
❄ Snow chains compulsory in areas indicated by signs
★ Drivers who wear spectacles or contact lenses must carry a spare pair.
★ On-the-spot fines imposed
★ Radar-detection equipment is prohibited
★ Spare wheel compulsory
★ Tolls on motorways
★ Visibility vest compulsory

Sweden Sverige (S)

Area 449,964 km² (173,731 miles²) **Population** 10,484,000 **Capital** Stockholm (2,415,000)
Languages Swedish (official), Finnish
Currency Swedish krona = 100 ore

🕐	🛣	▲	🏘
70–120	70	70	30–50
If towing trailer with brakes			
80	80	70	50

🛡 Compulsory in front and rear seats
👶 Under 15 or below 135cm must use an appropriate child restraint and may sit in the front only if airbag is deactivated; rear-facing baby seat permitted in front only if airbag deactivated.
🍷 0.02% △ Compulsory ▯▯ Recommended
🦺 Recommended 🔺Recommended
⊖ 18
📠 Licences without a photograph must be accompanied by photographic proof of identity, e.g. a passport
📱 Only allowed with hands-free kit
🅻🅴🆉 Gothenberg, Helsingborg, Lund, Malmo, Mölndal, Stockholm, Umeå and Uppsala have LEZs progressively prohibiting older vehicles.
⛽ Must be used at all times
❄ 1 Dec–31 Mar winter tyres, anti-freeze, screenwash additive and shovel compulsory
★ On-the-spot fines imposed
★ Radar-detection equipment is prohibited
★ Tolls on some roads and charges to use some bridges.
★ Tow rope recommended
★ Visibility vest recommended

Switzerland Schweiz (CH)

Area 41,284 km² (15,939 miles²)
Population 8,509,000 **Capital** Bern (134,000) **Languages** French, German, Italian, Romansch (all official)
Currency Swiss Franc = 100 centimes / rappen

🕐	🛣	▲	🏘
120	80–100	80	50
If towing			
80	80	80	50

🛡 Compulsory
👶 Up to 12 years or below 150 cm must use an appropriate child restraint. A rear-facing child seat may only be used in the front if the airbag is deactivated.
🍷 0.05%, but 0.00% for commercial drivers or with less than three years with a full licence
△ Compulsory
▯▯ Recommended
🦺 Recommended
🔺Recommended
⊖ 18 (mopeds up to 50cc – 16)
📱 Only allowed with a hands-free kit
⛽ Compulsory
❄ Winter tyres recommended Nov–Mar; snow chains compulsory in designated areas in poor winter weather
★ All vehicles under 3.5 tonnes must display a vignette on the windscreen. These are valid for one year and can be purchased at border crossings, petrol stations, post offices and online https://shop.post.ch/shop/en/tours-travel/motorway-windscreen-stickers/c/vignette. Vehicles over 3.5 tonnes are subject to a heavy vehicle charge.
★ GPS must have fixed speed camera function deactivated; radar detectors prohibited
★ On-the-spot fines imposed
★ Picking up hitchhikers is prohibited on motorways
★ Spectacles or contact lens wearers must carry a spare pair in their vehicle at all times
★ Visibility vests recommended

Turkey Türkiye (TR)

Area 774,815 km² (299,156 miles²)
Population 83,048,000 **Capital** Ankara (5,157,000) **Languages** Turkish (official), Kurdish **Currency** New Turkish lira = 100 kurus

🕐	🛣	▲	🏘
120	90	90	50
Motorbikes			
80	70	70	50

🛡 Compulsory if fitted
👶 Under 150 cm and below 36kg must use suitable child restraint. Under 3s can only travel in the front in a rear facing seat if the airbag is deactivated. Children 3–12 may not travel in the front seat.
🍷 0.05% immediate confiscation of licence if over limit • 0.00% if towing trailer or caravan
△ Two compulsory (one in front, one behind)
▯▯ Compulsory
🦺 Recommended
🔺Compulsory
⊖ 18
📠 International Driving Permit advised, and required for use with licences without photographs, or UK licence with notarised copy in Turkish; note that Turkey is in both Europe and Asia, green card/UK insurance that covers whole of Turkey or locally bought insurance.
📱 Only allowed with hands-free kit
⛽ Compulsory in poor daytime visibility

★ On-the-spot fines imposed
★ Radar detection equipment prohibited
★ Tolls on several motorways and the Bosphorus bridges; electronic payment required by purchasing HGS vignette or pre-payment card from Post Office or service station.
★ Winter tyres recommended

Ukraine Ukraina (UA)

Area 603,700 km² (233,088 miles²)
Population 43,528,000 **Capital** Kiev / Kyviv (3,475,000) **Languages** Ukrainian (official), Russian **Currency** Hryvnia = 100 kopiykas

⊙	🏛	⚠	🏭
130	110	90	20/50

If driving licence held less than 2 years, must not exceed 70 kph. *50 kph if towing another vehicle.

🚗 Compulsory in front and rear seats
👶 Under 12 and below 145cm must use an appropriate child restraint and sit in rear
🍷 0.02% – if use of medication can be proved. Otherwise 0.00%
△ Compulsory 🧯 Compulsory
💡 Optional 🦺Compulsory
🔞 18
🪪 1968 International Driving Permit, vehicle registration document, ownership documents, green card
📱 Only allowed with a hands-free kit
💡 Compulsory in poor daytime visibility and from 1 Oct–30 Apr
❄ Winter tyres compulsory Nov–Apr in snowy conditions
★ On-the-spot fines imposed
★ Visibility vest, tow rope and tool kit recommended

United Kingdom (GB)

Area 241,857 km² (93,381 miles²)
Population 67,791,000 **Capital** London (14,258,000) **Languages** English (official), Welsh (also official in Wales), Gaelic **Currency** Sterling (pound) = 100 pence

⊙	🏛	⚠	🏭
112	112	96	48

If towing

⊙			
96	96	80	48

Several cities have introduced 32 kph (20 mph) zones away from main roads

🚗 Compulsory in front seats and if fitted in rear seats
👶 Under 3 must use appropriate child restraint in front and rear; 3–12 or under 135cm must use appropriate child restraint in front, in rear must use appropriate child restraint or seat belt if no child restraint is available (e.g. because two occupied restraints prevent fitting of a third).
🍷 0.08% (England, Northern Ireland, Wales) • 0.05% (Scotland)
△ Recommended 🧯 Recommended
💡 Recommended
🦺 Recommended
🔞 17 (16 for mopeds)
📱 Only allowed with hands-free kit
🅛🅔🅩 London's LEZ operates by number-plate recognition; non-compliant vehicles face hefty daily charges. Foreign-registered vehicles must register.
★ Driving is on the left
★ On-the-spot fines imposed
★ Smoking is banned in all commercial vehicles
★ Some toll motorways, bridges and tunnels

The resorts listed are popular ski centres, therefore road access to most is normally good and supported by road clearing during snow falls. However, mountain driving is never predictable and drivers should make sure they take suitable snow chains as well as emergency provisions and clothing. Listed for each resort are: the atlas page and grid square; the resort/minimum piste altitude (where only one figure is shown, they are at the same height) and maximum altitude of its own lifts; the number of lifts and gondolas; the season start and end dates (snow cover allowing); whether snow is augmented by cannon; the nearest town (with its distance in km) and, where available, the website and/or telephone number of the local tourist information centre or ski centre ('00' prefix required for calls from the UK).

The ❄ symbol indicates resorts with snow cannon

Andorra
Pyrenees

Pas de la Casa / Grau Roig 146 B2 ❄
2050–2640m • 31 lifts • Dec–Apr • Andorra La Vella (30km) 🖥 www.pasdelacasa.com •
Access via Envalira Pass (2407m), highest in Pyrenees, snow chains essential.

Austria
Alps

Bad Gastein 109 B4 ❄ 1050/1100–2700m •
42 lifts • Dec–Apr • St Johann im Pongau (45km)
📞+43 6432 3393 0 🖥 www.gastein.com/en

Bad Hofgastein 109 B4 ❄ 860–2295m •
42 lifts • Dec–Apr • St Johann im Pongau (40km)
📞+43 6432 3393 0 🖥 www.gastein.com/en

Bad Kleinkirchheim 109 C4 ❄ 1070–2055m •
24 lifts • Dec–Apr • Villach (35km) 📞+43 4240 8212
🖥 www.badkleinkirchheim.at /en

Ehrwald 108 B1 ❄ 1000–2965m • 24 lifts •
Dec–Mar • Imst (30km) 📞+43 5673 2501
🖥 www.wetterstein-bahnen.at/

Innsbruck 108 B2 ❄ 574/850–3200m •
59 lifts • Dec–Apr • Innsbruck 📞+43 512 5356 0
🖥 www.innsbruck.info/en • *Motorway normally clear. The motorway through to Italy and through the Arlberg Tunnel are both toll roads.*

Ischgl 107 B5 ❄ 1880/1400–2900m • 45 lifts •
Nov–Apr • Landeck (25km) 📞+43 50990 100
🖥 www.ischgl.com/en • *Car entry to resort prohibited between 2200hrs and 0600hrs. Lift linked to Samnaun (Switzerland).*

Kaprun 109 B3 ❄ 800/770–3030m • 25 lifts •
Nov–Apr (glacier skiing Oct–May) • Zell am See (10km) 📞+43 6542 770 🖥 www.zellamsee-kaprun.com

Kirchberg in Tirol 109 B3 ❄ 860–2000m •
56 lifts • Dec–Apr • Kitzbühel (6km)
📞+43 57507 2100 🖥 www.kitzbueheler-alpen.com/en/bri/kirchberg.html • *Easily reached from Munich International Airport (120 km).*

Kitzbühel / Brixen im Thale 109 B3 ❄
800/790–2000m • 90 lifts • Dec–Apr •
Wörgl (40km) 📞+43 57057 2000
🖥 www.kitzbueheler-alpen.com/en

Lech / Oberlech 107 B5 ❄ 1450–2810m • 88 lifts
• Dec–Apr • Bludenz (50km) 📞+43 5583 2161 0
🖥 www.lechzuers.com/en • *Roads normally cleared but keep chains accessible because of altitude. Linked to the other Arlberg resorts.*

Mayrhofen 108 B2 ❄ 630–2500m •
60 lifts • Dec–Apr • Jenbach (35km)
📞+43 5285 6760 🖥 www.mayrhofen.at/en • *Chains rarely required.*

Obertauern 109 B4 ❄ 1740/1640–2350m •
26 lifts • Nov–May • Radstadt (20km)
📞+43 6456 7252 🖥 www.obertauern.com/en •
Roads normally cleared but chain accessibility recommended. Camper vans and caravans not allowed; park these in Radstadt.

Saalbach Hinterglemm 109 B3 ❄
1000/1030–2100m • 52 lifts • Dec–Apr •
Zell am See (19km) 📞+43 6541 6800-68
🖥 www.saalbach.com/home • *Both village centres are pedestrianised and there is a good ski bus service during the daytime.*

St Anton am Arlberg 107 B5 ❄ 1300–2810m •
88 lifts • Dec–Apr • Innsbruck (104km)
📞+43 5446 22690 🖥 www.stantonamarlberg.com/en • *Linked to the other Arlberg resorts.*

Schladming Dachstein 109 B4
❄ 745–1900m • 81 lifts • Dec–Apr •
Schladming 📞+ 43 36 87 233 10
🖥 www.schladming-dachstein.at

Serfaus 108 B1 ❄ 1427/1200–2820m •
68 lifts • Dec–Apr • Landeck (30km)
📞+43 5476 6239 🖥 www.serfaus-fiss-ladis.at/en • *Private vehicles banned from village. Use Dorfbahn Serfaus, an underground funicular that runs on an air cushion.*

Sölden 108 C2 ❄ 1380–3250m, • 32 lifts •
Nov–Apr (glacier Sep–May) • Imst (50km)
📞+43 57200 200 🖥 www.soelden.com • *Roads normally cleared but snow chains recommended because of altitude. The route from Italy and the south over the Timmelsjoch via Obergurgl is closed Oct–May and anyone arriving from the south should use the Brenner Pass motorway.*

Zell am See 109 B3 ❄ 750–1950m •
28 lifts • Dec–Apr (glacier Oct–May) • Zell am See
📞+43 6542 770 🖥 www.zellamsee-kaprun.com •
Low altitude, so good access and no mountain passes to cross.

Zell im Zillertal (Zell am Ziller) 109 B3 ❄
580/930–2410m • 22 lifts • Dec–Apr •
Jenbach (25km) 📞+43 5282 7165–226
🖥 www.zillertalarena.com

Zürs 107 B5 ❄ 1720/1700–2450m •
88 lifts • Dec–Apr • Bludenz (30km)
📞+43 5583 2161 0 🖥 www.lechzuers.com/en •
Roads normally cleared but keep chains accessible because of altitude. Village has garage with 24-hour self-service gas/petrol, breakdown service and wheel chains supply. Linked to the other Arlberg resorts.

France
Alps

Alpe d'Huez 118 B3 ❄ 1860–3330m • 85 lifts •
Dec–Apr • Grenoble (63km) 📞+33 476 11 44 44
🖥 www.alpedhuez.com/en • *Snow chains may be required on access road to resort.*

Avoriaz 118 A3 1800/1100–2280m • 36 lifts • Dec–Apr • Morzine (14km) +33 4 50 74 02 11 www.avoriaz.com/en • *Chains may be required for access road from Morzine. Car-free resort, park on edge of village.*

Chamonix-Mont-Blanc 119 B3 1035–3840m • 49 lifts • Dec–Apr • Martigny (38km) +33 4 50 53 00 24 https://en.chamonix.com • *Linked to Courmayeur*

Chamrousse 118 B2 1700/1420–2250m • 15 lifts • Dec–Apr • Grenoble (30km) +33 4 76 89 92 65 https://en.chamrousse.com • *Roads normally cleared, keep chains accessible because of altitude.*

Châtel 119 A3 1200/1110–2200m • 41 lifts • Dec–Apr • Thonon-Les-Bains (35km) +33 4 50 73 22 44 https://en.chatel.com/ete

Courchevel 118 B3 1300–2470m • 67 lifts • Dec–Apr • Moûtiers (23km) +33 4 79 08 00 29 https://courchevel.com/en/ • *Roads normally cleared but keep chains accessible. Traffic 'discouraged' within the four resort bases.*

Flaine 118 A3 1600–2500m • 24 lifts • Dec–Apr • Cluses (25km) +33 4 50 90 80 01 https://en.flaine.com • *Keep chains accessible for D6 from Cluses to Flaine. Car access for depositing luggage and passengers only. 1500-space car park outside resort. Near Sixt-Fer-á-Cheval.*

La Clusaz 118 B3 1100–2600m • 49 lifts • Dec–Apr • Annecy (32km) https://en.laclusaz.com • *Roads normally clear but keep chains accessible for final road from Annecy.*

La Plagne 118 B3 2500/1250–3250m • 75 lifts • Dec–Apr • Moûtiers (32km) +33 4 79 09 02 01 https://en.la-plagne.com • *Ten different centres up to 2100m altitude. Road access via Bozel, Landry or Aime normally cleared. Linked to Les Arcs by cable car.*

Les Arcs 119 B3 1600/1200–3230m • 77 lifts • Dec–Apr • Bourg-St-Maurice (15km) +33 4 79 07 12 57 https://en.lesarcs.com • *Four base areas up to 2000 metres; keep chains accessible. Pay parking at edge of each base resort. Linked to La Plagne by cable car.*

Les Carroz d'Araches 118 A3 1140–2500m • 80 lifts • Dec–Apr • Cluses (13km) www.lescarroz.com/en/

Les Deux-Alpes 118 C3 1650/1300–3600m • 49 lifts • Dec–Apr & Jun–Aug • Grenoble (75km) +33 4 76 79 22 00 www.les2alpes.com/en • *Roads normally cleared, however snow chains recommended for D213 up from valley road (D1091).*

Les Gets 118 A3 1170/1000–2000m • 47 lifts • Dec–Apr • Cluses (18km) +33 4 50 74 74 74 www.lesgets.com/en

Les Ménuires 118 B3 1815/1850–3200m • 39 lifts • Dec–Apr • Moûtiers (27km) +33 4 79 00 73 00 www.lesmenuires.com • *Keep chains accessible for D117 from Moûtiers.*

Les Sept Laux Prapoutel 118 B3 1350–2400m, • 24 lifts • Dec–Apr • Grenoble (38km) www.les7laux.com/winter • *Roads normally cleared, however keep chains accessible for mountain road up from the A41 motorway. Near St Sorlin d'Arves.*

Megève 118 B3 1100/1050–2350m • 79 lifts • Dec–Apr • Sallanches (12km) +33 4 50 21 27 28 www.megeve.com/en

Méribel 118 B3 1400/1100–2950m • 61 lifts • Dec–Apr • Moûtiers (18km) +33 4 79 08 60 01 www.meribel.net/en • *Keep chains accessible for 18km to resort on D90 from Moûtiers.*

Morzine 118 A3 1000–2460m • 46 lifts • Dec–Apr • Thonon-Les-Bains (30km) +33 4 50 74 72 72 http://en.morzine-avoriaz.com

Pra Loup 132 A2 1500–2600m • 20 lifts • Dec–Apr • Barcelonnette (10km) +33 4 92 84 10 04 www.praloup.com • *Roads normally cleared but chains accessibility recommended.*

Risoul 118 C3 1850/1650–2750m • 59 lifts • Dec–Apr • Briançon (40km) +33 4 92 46 02 60 https://en.risoul.com • *Keep chains accessible. Near Guillestre. Linked with Vars Les Claux.*

St-Gervais Mont-Blanc 118 B3 850/1150–2350m • 27 lifts • Dec–Apr • Sallanches (10km) +33 4 50 93 23 23 www.ski-saintgervais.com/en/

Serre Chevalier 118 C3 1350/1200–2800m • 68 lifts • Dec–Apr • Briançon (10km) www.serre-chevalier.com/en • *Made up of 13 small villages along the valley road, which is normally cleared.*

Tignes 119 B3 2100/1550–3450m • 78 lifts • Jan–Dec • Bourg-St-Maurice (26km) +33 4 79 40 04 40 https://en.tignes.net/ • *Keep chains accessible because of altitude. Linked to Val d'Isère.*

Val d'Isère 119 B3 1850/1550–3450m • 78 lifts • Dec–May, possibly until Jul • Bourg-St-Maurice (30km) +33 4 79 06 06 60 www.valdisere.com/en/ • *Roads normally cleared but keep chains accessible.*

Val Thorens 118 B3 2300/1850–3200m • 31 lifts • Nov–May • Moûtiers (37km) +33 4 79 00 08 08 www.les3vallees.com/en/ski-resort/val-thorens • *Chains mandatory – highest ski resort in Europe. Obligatory paid parking on edge of resort.*

Valloire 118 B3 1430–2750m • 35 lifts • Dec–Apr • Modane (20km) +33 4 79 59 03 96 https://tourism.valloire.net • *Road normally clear up to the Col du Galibier, to the south of the resort, which is closed from 1st November to 1st June. Linked to Valmeinier.*

Valmeinier 118 B3 1500–2750m • 35 lifts • Dec–Apr • St Michel de Maurienne (47km) +33 4 79 59 53 69 www.valmeinier.com/en • *Access from north on D1006 / D902. Col du Galibier, to the south of the resort closed from 1st November to 1st June. Linked to Valloire.*

Valmorel 118 B3 1400–2550m • 50 lifts • Dec–Apr • Moûtiers (15km) +33 4 79 09 85 55 /www.valmorel.com/en/ • *Near St Jean-de-Belleville. Linked with ski areas of Celliers, Doucy and St François-Longchamp.*

Vars Les Claux 118 C3 1850/1650–2750m • 59 lifts • Dec–Apr • Briançon (40km) +33 4 92 46 51 31 www.vars.com • *Four base resorts up to 1850 metres. Keep chains accessible. Linked with Risoul.*

Villard de Lans 118 B2 1050/1160–2170m • 21 lifts • Dec–Apr • Grenoble (32km) +33 4 76 95 10 38 https://uk.villarddelans-correnconenvercors.com

Pyrenees

Font-Romeu 146 B3 1800/1600–2200m • 23 lifts • Nov–Mar • Perpignan (87km) +33 4 68 30 68 30 https://font-romeu.fr/en/ • *Roads normally cleared but keep chains accessible.*

Saint-Lary Soulan 145 B4 830/1650/1700–2515m • 31 lifts • Dec–Apr • Tarbes (75km) +33 5 62 39 50 81 www.saintlary.com • *Access roads constantly cleared of snow.*

Vosges

La Bresse-Hohneck 106 A1 600–1370m • 33 lifts • Dec–Mar • Cornimont (6km) +33 3 29 25 68 78 www.labresse.net

Germany

Alps

Garmisch-Partenkirchen 108 B2 700–2050m • 18 lifts • Nov–Apr • Munich (95km) +49 8821 180 700 www.gapa-tourismus.de/en • *Roads usually clear, chains rarely needed.*

Oberaudorf 108 B3 480–1850m • 30 lifts • Dec–Apr • Kufstein (15km) +49 8033 30120 www.oberaudorf.de (German only) • *Motorway normally kept clear. Near Bayrischzell.*

Oberstdorf 107 B5 820/830–2200m • 26 lifts • Dec–Apr • Sonthofen (15km) +49 8322 7000 www.oberstdorf.de

Rothaargebirge

Winterberg 81 A4 700/620–830m • 19 lifts • Dec–Mar • Brilon (30km) +49 2981 925 00 www.winterberg.de/en • *Roads usually cleared, chains rarely required.*

Greece

Central Greece

Mount Parnassos: Kelaria-Fterolakka 182 E4 1640–2260m • 17 lifts • Dec–Apr • Amfiklia +30 22340 22700 www.parnassos-ski.gr/?lang=en

Mount Parnassos: Gerondovrahos 182 E4 1800–1900m • 3 lifts • Dec–Apr • Amfiklia

Peloponnisos

Mount Helmos: Kalavrita Ski Centre 184 A3 1650–2325m • 8 lifts • Dec–Mar • Kalavrita +30 269202 4451-2 www.kalavrita-ski.gr

Mount Mainalo: Ostrakina 184 B3 1560–1820 • 3 lifts • Dec–Mar • Tripoli www.mainaloski.gr

Macedonia

Mount Falakro: Agio Pnevma 183 B6 1720/1620–2230m • 9 lifts • Dec–Apr • Drama +30 69876 03409 www.falakro.gr (in Greek only)

Mount Vermio: Seli 182 C4 1500–1900m • 9 lifts • Dec–Mar • Kozani +30 23310 49226/49021 www.seli-ski.gr (in Greek)

Mount Vermio: Tria-Pente Pigadia 182 C3 1420–2005m • 7 lifts • Dec–Mar • Ptolemaida +30 23320 44981

Mount Verno: Vigla 182 C3 1650–1900m • 7 lifts • Dec–Mar • Florina +30 23850 45800 www.vigla-ski.com (in Greek)

Mount Vrondous: Lailias 183 B5 1600–1850m • 2 lifts • Dec–Mar • Serres +30 23210 62400 www.lailias.com (in Greek only)

Thessalia

Mount Pelion: Agriolefkes 183 D5 1300–1500m • 5 lifts • Dec–Mar • Volos +30 24280 73719 www.aroundpelion.com/ski-center

Italy

Alps

Bardonecchia 118 B3 1312–2750m • 20 lifts • Dec–Apr • Bardonecchia +39 012 299032 www.bardonecchiaski.com • *Resort reached through the 11km Frejus tunnel from France, roads normally cleared.*

Bórmio 107 C5 1200/1230–3020m • 15 lifts • Dec–Apr • Tirano (40km) www.bormioski.eu/en • *Tolls payable in Munt la Schera Tunnel*

Breuil-Cervinia 119 B4 ❄ 2050–3500m ·
19 lifts · Oct–May · Aosta (54km) ·
☎+39 166 944311 ⌨www.cervinia.it/en ·
*Snow chains strongly recommended. Bus from
Milan airport. Linked to Zermatt.*

Courmayeur 119 B3 ❄ 1200–2760m · 18 lifts ·
Dec–Apr · Aosta (40km) · ☎+39 0165 841612
⌨www.courmayeurmontblanc.it/en · *Linked to
Chamonix. Access through the Mont Blanc tunnel
from France. Roads constantly cleared.*

Limone Piemonte 133 A3 ❄
1000/1050–2050m · 15 lifts · Dec–Apr ·
Cuneo (27km) ☎+39 0171 925281
⌨www.riservabianca.it · *Roads normally cleared, chains rarely required.*

Livigno 107 C5 ❄ 1800–3000m · 32 lifts ·
☎+39 0342 977800 ⌨www.livigno.eu/en ·
*Keep chains accessible. One-way traffic through
Munt la Schera Tunnel, controlled by traffic lights,
toll payable.*

Sestrière 119 C3 ❄ 2035/1840–2840m · 92 lifts ·
Dec–Apr · Oulx (22km) ☎+39 0122 755444
⌨www.sestriere-online.com · *One of Europe's
highest resorts; although roads are normally
cleared keep chains accessible.*

Appennines

Roccaraso – Aremogna 169 B4 ❄ 1285/1240–
2140m · 24 lifts · Dec–Apr · Castel di Sangro (7km)
⌨https://roccaraso.net (Italian only)

Dolomites

Andalo – Fai della Paganella 121 A3 ❄
1042/1050/2125m · 18 lifts · Dec–Apr · Trento
(40km) ☎+39 0461 585588
⌨www.paganella.net/en/paganella-ski

Arabba 108 C2 ❄ 1600/1450–2950m · 26 lifts ·
Dec–Apr · Brunico (45km) ☎+39 436 79130
⌨www.arabba.it · *Roads normally cleared but
keep chains accessible.*

Cortina d'Ampezzo 108 C3 ❄ 1224/1050–
2930m · 36 lifts · Dec–Apr · Belluno (72km)
☎+39 436 869086 ⌨www.dolomiti.org/en/
cortina · *Access from north on route 51 over the
Cimabanche Pass may require chains.*

Corvara (Alta Badia) 108 C2 ❄
1568–2500m · 53 lifts · Dec–Apr · Brunico (38km)
⌨www.altabadia.it/en · *Roads normally clear but
keep chains accessible.*

Madonna di Campiglio 121 A3 ❄ 852–2504m ·
59 lifts · Dec–Apr · Trento (60km) ☎+39 465
447501 ⌨www.ski.it/en · *Roads normally cleared
but keep chains accessible. Linked to Folgarida
and Marilleva.*

Moena di Fassa (Alpe Lusia) 108 C2 ❄
1184/1450–2520m · 8 lifts · Dec–Apr · Bolzano
(40km) ☎+39 0462 573440 ⌨www.fassa.com

Selva di Val Gardena 108 C2 ❄ 1563/1570–
2450m · 78 lifts · Dec–Apr · Bolzano (40km)
☎+39 471 777777 ⌨www.valgardena.it · *Roads
normally cleared but keep chains accessible.*

Norway

Hemsedal 47 B5 ❄ 700/640–1450m ·
20 lifts · Nov–May · Hønefoss (150km)
☎+47 32 055030 ⌨www.hemsedal.com ·
Snow chains recommended.

Slovakia

Chopok (Jasna-Chopok) 99 C3 ❄
900/950–2004m · 22 lifts · Dec–Apr · Jasna
☎+421 907 886644 ⌨www.jasna.sk

Donovaly 99 C3 ❄ 913–1360m · 16 lifts ·
Nov–Apr · Ruzomberok ☎+421 48 4199900
⌨www.parksnow.sk/zima/en

Martinské Hole 98 B2 1250/1150–1456m ·
6 lifts · Nov–May · Zilina ☎+421 43 430 6000
⌨www.martinky.com/en

Strbske Pleso 99 B4 1380–1825m · 7 lifts ·
Dec–Mar · Poprad ☎+421 917 682 260
⌨www.vt.sk

Slovenia
Julijske Alpe

Kanin (Bovec) 122 A2 460/1690–2293m ·
5 lifts · Dec–Apr · Bovec ☎+386 5917 9301
⌨www.kanin.si/en

Kranjska Gora 122 A2 ❄ 800–1210m ·
17 lifts · Dec–Mar · Villach ☎+386 4 5809 440
⌨www.kranjska-gora.si

Vogel 122 A2 570–1800m · 8 lifts · Dec–Apr ·
Bohinjska Bistrica ☎+386 4 5729 712
⌨www.vogel.si

Kawiniške Savinjske Alpe

Krvavec 122 A3 ❄ 1450–1970m · 13 lifts ·
Dec–Apr · Kranj ☎ 386 4 25 25 911
⌨http://www.rtc-krvavec.si/en/

Pohorje

Rogla 123 A4 1517/1050–1500m · 13 lifts ·
Dec–Apr · Slovenska Bistrica ☎+386 3757 6440
⌨www.rogla.eu/en

Spain
Pyrenees

Baqueira-Beret/Bonaigua 145 B4 ❄
1500–2500m · 36 lifts · Dec–Apr · Vielha (15km)
☎+34 973 639 000 ⌨www.baqueira.es ·
*Roads normally clear but keep chains accessible.
Near Salardú.*

Sistema Penibetico

Sierra Nevada 163 A4 ❄ 2100–3300m · 21 lifts ·
Dec–May · Granada (32km) ☎+34 958 70 80 90
⌨http://sierranevada.es · *Access road designed
to be avalanche safe and is snow cleared.*

Sweden

Idre Fjäll 199 D9 ❄ 590–890m · 24 lifts ·
Nov–Apr · Mora (140km) ☎+46 253 41000
⌨www.idrefjall.se

Sälen 49 A5 350–800m · 90 lifts · Nov–Apr ·
Malung (70km) ☎+46 771 84 00 00
⌨www.skistar.com/salen · *Salen consists of
4 linked resorts – Lindvallen, Högfjället,
Tandådalen and Hundfjället.*

Switzerland
Alps

Adelboden 106 C2 1260–2360m · 55 lifts ·
Dec–Apr · Frutigen (15km) ☎+41 33 673 80 80
⌨www.adelboden.ch · *Linked with Lenk.*

Arosa Lenzerheide 107 C4 1230–2865m ·
43 lifts · Dec–Apr · Chur ☎+41 81 378 70 20
⌨https://arosalenzerheide.swiss/en/Ski-Area ·
*Roads cleared but keep chains accessible due to
high altitude.*

Crans Montana 119 A4 ❄ 1500–3000m · 24 lifts ·
Dec–Apr · Sierre (15km) ☎+41 27 485 0404
⌨www.crans-montana.ch · *Roads normally
cleared but keep chains accessible for ascent from
Sierre.*

Davos 107 C4 ❄ 1560/1100–2840m · 55 lifts ·
Nov–Apr · Davos. ☎+41 81 415 21 21
⌨www.davos.ch · *Linked with Klosters.*

Engelberg 106 C3 ❄ 1000/1050–3020m ·
17 lifts · Oct–May · Luzern (39km)
☎+41 41 639 77 77 ⌨www.engelberg.ch ·
Straight access road normally cleared.

Flums (Flumserberg) 107 B4 ❄
1400/1000–2220m · 17 lifts · Dec–Apr · Buchs
(25km) ☎+41 81 720 18 18 ⌨www.flumserberg.
ch · *Roads normally cleared, but 1000-metre
ascent; keep chains accessible.*

Grindelwald 106 C3 ❄ 944–2320m ·
33 lifts · Dec–Apr · Interlaken (20km)
☎+41 33 854 12 12
⌨https://grindelwald.swiss/en ·
Linked with Wengen.

Gstaad – Saanenland 106 C2 ❄
1050/950–3000m · 41 lifts · Dec–Apr
(glacier skiing Nov–Apr) · Gstaad
☎+41 33 748 81 81 ⌨www.gstaad.ch

Klosters 107 C4 ❄ 1191/1110–2840m · 55 lifts ·
Dec–Apr · Davos (10km). ☎+41 81 410 20 20
⌨www.davos.ch/klosters · *Roads normally clear
but keep chains accessible. Linked with Davos.*

Leysin 119 A4 ❄ 2260–2330m · 16 lifts · Dec–Apr
· Aigle (6km) ⌨www.alpesvaudoises.ch/en

Mürren 106 C2 ❄ 1650–2970m · 13 lifts ·
Dec–Apr · Interlaken (18km) ☎+41 33 856 86 86
⌨www.muerren.ch · *No road access. Park in
Strechelberg (1500 free places) and take the
two-stage cable car.*

Nendaz 119 A4 ❄ 1365/1400–3300m · 20 lifts ·
Nov–Apr · Sion (16km) ☎+41 27 289 55 89
⌨www.nendaz.ch · *Roads normally cleared,
however keep chains accessible for ascent from
Sion. Near Vex. Part of 4Vallées ski area.*

Saas-Fee 119 A4 ❄ 1800–3500m · 23 lifts ·
Jan–Dec · Brig (35km) ☎+41 27 958 18 58
⌨www.saas-fee.ch/en/ · *Roads normally cleared
but keep chains accessible because of altitude.*

St Moritz 107 C4 ❄ 1856/1730–3300m · 24 lifts ·
Nov–May · Chur (89km) ☎+41 81 837 33 33
⌨www.stmoritz.ch · *Roads normally cleared but
keep chains accessible.*

Samnaun 107 C5 ❄ 1846/1400–2900m · 45 lifts
· Nov–Apr · Scuol (30km) ☎+41 81 861 88 30
⌨www.samnaun.ch/en/international-ski-resort-
samnaunischgl · *Roads normally cleared but keep
chains acccssible. Lift linked to Ischgl (Austria).*

Verbier 119 A4 ❄ 1500–3330m · 18 lifts ·
Nov–Apr · Martigny (27km) ☎+41 27 775 38 88
⌨www.verbier.ch · *Roads normally cleared. Part
of 4Vallées ski area, with access to Bruson, La
Tzoumaz, Nendaz, Veysonnaz and Thyon.*

Villars-Gryon 119 A4 ❄ 1253/1200–2100m ·
16 lifts · Dec–Apr · Aigle ⌨www.alpesvaudoises.
ch · *Roads normally cleared but keep chains
accessible for ascent from N9. Near Bex.*

Wengen 106 C2 ❄ 944–2320m · 24 lifts ·
Dec–Apr · Interlaken (12km) ☎+41 33 856 85 85
⌨https://wengen.swiss/en · *No road access.
Park at Lauterbrunnen and take mountain
railway. Linked with Grindelwald.*

Zermatt 119 A4 ❄ 1620–3900m · 54 lifts ·
all year · Brig (40km) ☎+41 27 966 81 00
⌨www.zermatt.ch · *Cars not permitted in resort,
park in Täsch (3km) and take shuttle train. Linked
to Breuil-Cervinia.*

Turkey
North Anatolian Mountains

Uludag 186 B4 ❄ 1770–2320m · 15 lifts ·
Dec–Mar · Bursa (36km)
⌨http://skiingturkey.com/resorts/uludag.html ·
Keep chains accessible.

300 greatest sights of Europe

For entries with no website listed, use that given for the national tourist board.

Albania Shqipëria

https://albania.al

Berat

Fascinating old town with picturesque Ottoman Empire buildings and traditional Balkan domestic architecture. **182 C1**

Tirana Tiranë

Capital of Albania. Skanderbeg Square has main historic buildings. Also: 18c Haxhi Ethem Bey Mosque; Art Gallery (Albanian); National Museum of History. Nearby: medieval Krujë; Roman monuments. **182 B1**

Austria Österreich

www.austria.info

Bregenz

Lakeside town bordering Germany, Liechtenstein, Switzerland. Locals, known as Vorarlbergers, have their own dialect. The Martinsturm Roman to 17c tower, 17c town hall and Seekapelle, Kunsthaus modern art museum, Vorarlberger Landesmuseum, Festspielhaus. www.austria.info/uk/where-to-go/cities/bregenz **107 B4**

Graz

University town, seat of imperial court to 1619. Historic centre around Hauptplatz. Imperial monuments: Burg; mausoleum of Ferdinand II; towers of 16c schloss; 17c Schloss Eggengerg (with Old Gallery). Also: 16c Town Hall; Zeughaus; 15c cathedral; New Gallery (good 19–20c); Kunsthaus (modern art). www.graztourismus.at **110 B2**

▼ Majolicahaus, Vienna, Austria

Innsbruck

Old town is reached by Maria-Theresien-Strasse with famous views. Buildings: Goldenes Dachl (1490s); 18c cathedral; remains of Hofburg imperial residence; 16c Hofkirche (tomb of Maximilian I). www.austria.info/us/where-to-go/cities/innsbruck **108 B2**

Krems

On a hill above the Danube, medieval quarter has Renaissance mansions. Also: Gothic Piaristenkirche; Museumkrems; Kunsthalle (modern art). www.krems.at/en/ **97 C3**

Linz

Port on the Danube. Historic buildings are concentrated on Hauptplatz below the imperial 15c schloss. Notable: Baroque Old Cathedral; 16c

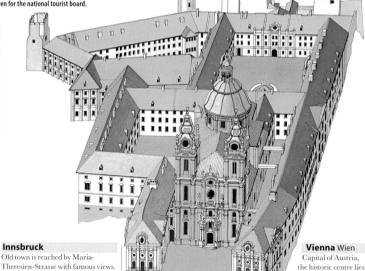

▲ Melk Abbey, Austria

Town Hall; Old Castle Museum; Lentos Art Museum. www.linztourismus.at **96 C2**

Melk

Set on a rocky hill above the Danube, the fortified abbey is the greatest Baroque achievement in Austria – particularly the Grand Library and abbey church. www.stiftmelk.at **110 A2**

Salzburg

Set in subalpine scenery, the town was associated with powerful 16–17c prince-archbishops. The 17c cathedral has a complex of archiepiscopal buildings: the Residence and its gallery (19c); the 13c Franciscan Church (notable altar). Also: Mozart's birthplace; Schloss Mirabell; Salzburg Museum; the Hohensalzburg fortress; the Collegiate Church of St Peter (cemetery, catacombs); Museum of Modern Art at the Mönschberg and Rupertinum. www.austria.info/us/where-to-go/cities/salzburg **109 B4**

Salzkammergut

Natural beauty with 76 lakes (Wolfgangersee, Altersee, Traunsee, Grundlsee) in mountain scenery. Attractive villages (St Wolfgang) and towns (Bad Ischl, Gmunden) include Hallstatt, famous for Celtic remains. www.salzkammergut.at **109 B4**

Vienna Wien

Capital of Austria, the historic centre lies within the Ring. Churches: Gothic St Stephen's Cathedral; 17c Imperial Vault; 14c Augustine Church; 14c Church of the Teutonic Order (treasure); 18c Baroque churches (Jesuit Church, Franciscan Church, St Peter, St Charles). Imperial residences: Hofburg; Schönbrunn. Architecture of Historicism on Ringstrasse (from 1857). Art Nouveau: station pavilions, Secession Building, Postsparkasse, Looshaus, Majolicahaus. Museums: Art History Museum (antiquities, old masters), Cathedral and Diocesan Museum (15c), Albertina (graphic arts), Liechtenstein Museum (old masters), Museum of Applied Arts, Museum of Modern Art (MUMOK), Leopold Museum, Belvedere (Gothic, Baroque, 19–20c); AzW (architecture); Vienna Museum. www.wien.info **111 A3**

Belgium Belgique

http://walloniabelgiumtourism.co.uk

Antwerp Antwerpen

City with many tall gabled Flemish houses on the river. Heart of the city is Great Market with 16–17c guildhouses and Town Hall. Charles Borromeus Church (Baroque). 14–16c Gothic cathedral has Rubens paintings. Rubens also at the Rubens House and his burial place in St Jacob's Church. Excellent museums: Mayer van den Bergh Museum (applied arts); Koninklijk Museum of Fine Arts (Flemish, Belgian); MAS (ethnography, folklore, shipping); Muhka (modern art). www.visitantwerpen.be **79 A4**

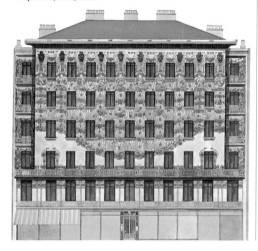

▼ Majolicahaus, Vienna, Austria

Bruges Brugge

Well-preserved medieval town with narrow streets and canals. Main squares: the Market with 13c Belfort and covered market; the Burg with Basilica of the Holy Blood and Town Hall. The collections of Groeninge Museum and Memling museum in St Jans Hospital include 15c Flemish masters. The Onze Lieve Vrouwekerk has a famous *Madonna and Child* by Michelangelo www.visitbruges.be 78 A3

Brussels Bruxelles

Capital of Belgium. The Lower Town is centred on the enormous Grand Place with Hôtel de Ville and rebuilt guildhouses. Symbols of the city include the 'Manneken Pis' and Atomium (giant model of a molecule). The 13c Notre Dame de la Chapelle is the oldest church. The Upper Town contains: Gothic cathedral; Neoclassical Place Royale; 18c King's Palace; Royal Museums of Fine Arts (old and modern masters) Magritte Museum; MRAH (art and historical artefacts); BELvue museum (in the Bellevue Residence). Also: much Art Nouveau (Horta Museum, Hôtel Tassel, Hôtel Solvay); Place du Petit Sablon and Place du Grand Sablon; 19c Palais de Justice. https://visit.brussels/en 79 B4

Ghent Gent

Medieval town built on islands surrounded by canals and rivers. Views from Pont St-Michel. The Graslei and Koornlei quays have Flemish guild houses. The Gothic cathedral has famous Van Eyck altarpiece. Also: Belfort; Cloth Market; Gothic Town Hall; Gravensteen. Museums: STAM Museum in Bijloke Abbey (provincial and applied art); Museum of Fine Arts (old masters). https://visit.gent.be/en 79 A3

Namur

Reconstructed medieval citadel is the major sight of Namur, which also has a cathedral and provincial museums. www.namurtourisme.be/index.php 79 B4

Tournai

The Romanesque-Gothic cathedral is Belgium's finest (much excellent art). Fine Arts Museum has a good collection (15–20c). https://en.visittournai.be 78 B3

▼ Town Hall, Antwerp, Belgium

Bulgaria Bulgariya

http://bulgariatravel.org

Black Sea Coast

Beautiful unspoiled beaches (Zlatni Pyasŭtsi). The delightful resort Varna is popular. Nesebūr is famous for Byzantine churches. Also: Danube Delta in Hungary. 17 D7

Koprivshtitsa

Beautiful village known both for its half-timbered houses and links with the April Rising of 1876. Six house museums amongst which the Lyutov House and the Oslekov House, plus the birthplaces of Georgi Benkovski, Dimcho Debelyanov, Todor Kableshkov, and Lyuben Karavelov. http://bulgariatravel.org/en/object/18/Koprivshtica

Plovdiv

City set spectacularly on three hills. The old town has buildings from many periods: 2c Roman stadium and amphitheatre; 14c Dzumaia Mosque; Archaeological Museum; 19c Ethnographic Museum. Nearby: Bačkovo Monastery (frescoes). http://bulgariatravel.org/en/object/306/plovdiv_grad 183 A6

Rila

Bulgaria's finest monastery, set in the most beautiful scenery of the Rila mountains. The church is richly decorated with frescoes. https://rilskimanastir.org/en/ 183 A5

Sofia Sofiya

Capital of Bulgaria. Sights: exceptional neo-Byzantine cathedral; Church of St Sofia; St Alexander Nevsky Cathedral; Boyana church; 4c rotunda of St George (frescoes); Byzantine Boyana Church (frescoes) on panoramic Mount Vitoša. Museums: National Historical Museum (particularly for Thracian artefacts); National Art Gallery (icons, Bulgarian art). http://bulgariatravel.org/en/object/234/sofia 17 D5

Veliko Tŭrnovo

Medieval capital with narrow streets. Notable buildings: House of the Little Monkey; Hadji Nicoli Inn; ruins of medieval citadel; Baudouin Tower;

churches of the Forty Martyrs and of SS Peter and Paul (frescoes); 14c Monastery of the Transfiguration. http://bulgariatravel.org/en/object/15/veliko_tyrnovo_grad 17 D6

Croatia Hrvatska

http://croatia.hr/en-GB

Dalmatia Dalmacija

Exceptionally beautiful coast along the Adriatic. Among its 1185 islands, those of the Kornati Archipelago and Brijuni Islands are perhaps the most spectacular. Along the coast are several attractive medieval and Renaissance towns, most notably Dubrovnik, Split, Šibenik, Trogir, Zadar. 138 B2

Dubrovnik

Surrounded by medieval and Renaissance walls, the city's architecture dates principally from 15–16c. Sights: many churches and monasteries including Church of St Blaise and Dominican monastery (art collection); promenade street of Stradun, Dubrovnik Museums; Renaissance Rector's Palace; Onofrio's fountain; Sponza Palace. The surrounding area has some 80 16c noblemen's summer villas. 139 C4

Islands of Croatia

There are over 1,000 islands off the coast of Croatia among which there is Brač, known for its white marble and the beautiful beaches of Bol (www.bol.hr); Hvar (www.tzhvar.hr/en/) is beautifully green with fields of lavender, marjoram, rosemary, sage and thyme; Vis (www.tz-vis.hr) has the beautiful towns of Komiža and Vis Town, with the Blue Cave on nearby Biševo. 123 & 137–138

Istria Istra

Peninsula with a number of ancient coastal towns (Rovinj, Poreč, Pula, Piran in Slovene Istria) and medieval hill-top towns (Motovun). Pula has Roman monuments (exceptional 1c amphitheatre). Poreč has narrow old streets; the mosaics in 6c Byzantine basilica of St Euphrasius are exceptional. See also Slovenia. www.istra.hr 122 B2

Plitvička Jezera

Outstandingly beautiful world of water and woodlands with 16 lakes and 92 waterfalls interwoven by canyons. Archaeological museums; art gallery; Gallery of Ivan Meštrović. www.tzplitvice.hr 123 C4

Split

Most notable for the exceptional 4c palace of Roman Emperor Diocletian, elements of which are incorporated into the streets and buildings of the town itself. The town also has a cathedral (11c baptistry) and a Franciscan monastery. www.visitsplit.com/en/1/welcome-to-split 138 B2

Trogir

The 13–15c town centre is surrounded by medieval city walls. Romanesque-Gothic cathedral includes the chapel of Ivan the Blessed. Dominican and Benedictine monasteries house art collections; Ćipiko palace; Lučić palace. www.trogironline.com/tourist_info.html 138 B2

Zagreb

Capital city of Croatia with cathedral and Archbishop's Palace in Kaptol and to the west Gradec with Baroque palaces. Donji Grad – The Lower Town – is home to the Archaeological Museum, Art Pavilion, Museum of Arts and Crafts, Ethnographic Museum, Mimara Museum and National Theatre; Modern Gallery; Museum of Contemporary Art. www.infozagreb.hr/&lang=en 124 B1

Czechia Česka Republica

www.czechtourism.com/home/

Brno

Capital of Moravia. Sights: Vegetable Market and Old Town Hall; Capuchin crypt decorated with bones of dead monks; hill of St Peter with Gothic cathedral; Church of St James; Mies van der Rohe's buildings (Bata, Avion Hotel, Togendhat House). Museums: Moravian Museum; Moravian Gallery; City Art Gallery; Brno City Museum in Spilberk Castle. www.gotobrno.cz/en 97 B4

České Budějovice

Famous for Budvar beer, the medieval town is centred on náměstí Přemysla Otokara II. The Black Tower gives fine views. Nearby: medieval Český Krumlov. www.c-budejovice.cz/en 96 C2

Kutná Hora

A town with strong silver mining heritage shown in the magnificent Cathedral of sv Barbara which was built by the miners. See also the ossuary with 40,000 complete sets of bones moulded into sculptures and decorations. www.czechtourism.com/t/kutna-hora 97 B3

Olomouc

Well-preserved medieval university town of squares and fountains. The Upper Square has the Town Hall. Also: 18c Holy Trinity; Baroque Church of St Michael. http://tourism.olomouc.eu/welcome/en 98 B1

Pilsen Plzeň

Best known for Plzeňský Prazdroj (Pilsener Urquell), beer has been brewed here since 1295. An industrial town with eclectic architecture shown in the railway stations and namesti Republiky (main square). www.czechtourism.com/a/pilsen-area 96 B1

Prague Praha

Capital of Czech Republic and Bohemia. The Castle Quarter has a complex of buildings behind the walls (Royal Castle; Royal Palace;

cathedral). The Basilica of St George has a fine Romanesque interior. The Belvedere is the best example of Renaissance architecture. Hradčani Square has aristocratic palaces and the National Gallery. The Little Quarter has many Renaissance (Wallenstein Palace) and Baroque mansions and the Baroque Church of St Nicholas. The Old Town has its centre at the Old Town Square with the Old Town Hall (astronomical clock), Art Nouveau Jan Hus monument and Gothic Týn church. The Jewish quarter has 14c Staranova Synagogue and Old Jewish Cemetery. The Charles Bridge is famous. The medieval New Town has many Art Nouveau buildings and is centred on Wenceslas Square. www.prague.eu/en **84 B2**

Spas of Bohemia

Spa towns of Karlovy Vary (Carlsbad: www.karlovyvary.cz/en), Márianske Lázně (Marienbad: www.marianskelazne.cz) and Frantiskovy Lázně **83 B4**

Denmark Danmark

www.visitdenmark.co.uk

Aarhus

Second largest city in Denmark with a mixture of old and new architecture that blends well, Aarhus has been dubbed the culture capital of Denmark with the Gothic Domkirke; Latin Quarter; 13th Century Vor Frue Kirke; Den Gamle By, open air museum of traditional Danish life; ARoS (art museum). www.visitaarhus.com **59 B3**

Copenhagen København

Capital of Denmark. Old centre has fine early 20c Town Hall. Latin Quarter has 19c cathedral. 18c Kastellet has statue of the Little Mermaid nearby. The 17c Rosenborg Castle was a royal residence, as was the Christianborg (now government offices). Other popular sights: Nyhavn canal; Tivoli Gardens. Excellent art collections: Ny Carlsberg Glypotek; National Gallery; National Museum. www.visitcopenhagen.com/copenhagen-tourist **61 D2**

Hillerød

Frederiksborg (home of the national history museum) is a fine red-brick Renaissance castle set among three lakes. www.visitnorthsealand.com/ln-int/north-sealand/hillerode **61 D2**

Roskilde

Ancient capital of Denmark. The marvellous cathedral is a burial place of the Danish monarchy. The Viking Ship Museum houses the remains of five 11c Viking ships excavated in the 1960s. www.visitfjordlandet.dk/en/areas/roskilde/ **61 D2**

Estonia Eesti

www.visitestonia.com/en

Kuressaare

Main town on the island of Saaremaa with the 14c Kuressaare Kindlus. **8 C3**

Pärnu

Sea resort with an old town centre. Sights: 15c Red Tower; neoclassical Town Hall; St Catherine's Church. www.visitparnu.com/en **8 C4**

Tallinn

Capital of Estonia. The old town is centred on the Town Hall Square. Sights: 15c Town Hall; Toompea Castle; Three Sisters houses. Churches: Gothic St Nicholas; 14c Church of the Holy Spirit; St Olaf's; Kumu Art Museum; Maritime Museum. www.visittallinn.ee/eng **8 C4**

Tartu

Historic town with 19c university. The Town Hall Square is surrounded by neoclassical buildings. Also: remains of 13c cathedral; Estonian National Museum. http://visittartu.com **8 C5**

Finland Suomi

www.visitfinland.com

Finnish Lakes

Area of outstanding natural beauty covering about one third of the country with thousands of lakes, of which Päijänne and Saimaa are the most important. Tampere, industrial centre of the region, has numerous museums, including the Tampere Art Museum (modern). Savonlinna has the medieval Olavinlinna Castle. Kuopio has the Orthodox and Regional Museums. **8 A5**

Helsinki

Capital of Finland. The 19c neoclassical town planning between the Esplanade and Senate Square includes the Lutheran cathedral. There is also a Russian Orthodox cathedral. The Constructivist Stockmann Department Store is the largest in Europe. The main railway station is Art Nouveau. Gracious 20c buildings in Mannerheimintie avenue include Finlandiatalo by Alvar Aalto. Many good museums: Art Museum of the Ateneum (19–20c); National Museum; Design Museum; Helsinki City Art Museum (modern Finnish); Open Air Museum (vernacular architecture); 18c fortress of Suomenlinna has several museums. www.visitfinland.com/helsinki **8 B4**

Lappland (Finnish)

Vast unspoiled rural area. Lappland is home to thousands of nomadic Sámi living in a traditional way. The capital, Rovaniemi, was rebuilt after WWII; museums show Sámi history and culture. Nearby is the Arctic Circle with the famous Santa Claus Village. Inari is a centre of Sámi culture. See also Norway and Sweden. www.lapland.fi **192–193**

France

https://uk.france.fr/en

Albi

Old town with rosy brick architecture. The vast Cathédrale Ste-Cécile (begun 13c) holds some good art. The Berbie Palace houses the Toulouse-Lautrec Museum. www.albi-tourisme.fr/en **130 B1**

Alps

Grenoble capital of the French Alps, has a good 20c collection in the Museum of Grenoble. The Vanoise Massif has the greatest number of resorts (Val d'Isère, Courchevel). Chamonix has spectacular views of Mont Blanc, France's and Europe's highest peak. www.grenoble-tourisme.com/en **118 B2**

Amiens

France's largest Gothic cathedral has beautiful decoration. The Museum of Picardy has unique 16c panel paintings. www.visit-amiens.com **90 B2**

Arles

Ancient, picturesque town with Roman relics (1c amphitheatre), 11c St Trophime church, Archaeological Museum (Roman art), Van Gogh centre. www.arlestourisme.com/en/ **131 B3**

Avignon

Medieval papal capital (1309–77) with 14c walls and many ecclesiastical buildings. Vast Palace of the Popes has stunning frescoes. The Little Palace has fine Italian Renaissance painting. The 12–13c Bridge of St Bénézet is famous. https://avignon-tourisme.com/en/ **131 B3**

Bourges

The Gothic Cathedral of St Etienne, one of the finest in France, has a superb sculptured choir. Also notable is the House of Jacques Coeur. www.bourgesberrytourisme.com **103 B4**

Brittany Bretagne

Brittany is famous for cliffs, sandy beaches and wild landscape. It is also renowned for megalithic monuments (Carnac) and Celtic culture. Its capital, Rennes, has the Parlement de Bretagne and good collections in the Museum of Brittany (history) and Museum of Fine Arts. Also: Nantes; St-Malo. www.brittanytourism.com **100–101**

Burgundy Bourgogne

Rural wine region with a rich Romanesque, Gothic and Renaissance heritage. The 12c cathedral in Autun and 12c basilica in Vézelay have fine Romanesque sculpture. Monasteries include 11c Abbaye de Cluny (ruins) and Abbaye de Fontenay. Beaune has beautiful Gothic Hôtel-Dieu and 15c Nicolas Rolin hospice. www.burgundy-tourism.com **104 B3**

Caen

City with two beautiful Romanesque buildings: Abbaye aux Hommes; Abbaye aux Dames. The château has

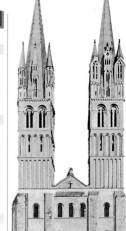

▲ Abbaye aux Hommes, Caen, France

two museums (16–20c painting; history). The *Bayeux Tapestry* is displayed in nearby Bayeux. www.caenlamer-tourisme.com **89 A3**

Carcassonne

Unusual double-walled fortified town of narrow streets with an inner fortress. The fine Romanesque Church of St Nazaire has superb stained glass. www.tourisme-carcassonne.fr/en **130 B1**

Chartres

The 12–13c cathedral is an exceptionally fine example of Gothic architecture (Royal Doorway, stained glass, choir screen). The Fine Arts Museum has a good collection. www.chartres.com **90 C1**

Clermont-Ferrand

The old centre contains the cathedral built of lava and Romanesque basilica. The Puy de Dôme and Puy de Sancy give spectacular views over some 60 extinct volcanic peaks (*puys*). www.clermontauvergnetourisme.com **116 B3**

Colmar

Town characterised by Alsatian half-timbered houses. The Unterlinden Museum has excellent German religious art including the famous Isenheim Altarpiece. Also: Espace André Malraux (contemporary arts). www.tourisme-colmar.com/en/ **106 A2**

Corsica Corse

Corsica has a beautiful rocky coast and mountainous interior. Napoleon's birthplace of Ajaccio has: Fesch Museum with Imperial Chapel and a large collection of Italian art; Maison Bonaparte; cathedral. Bonifacio, a medieval town, is spectacularly set on a rock over the sea. www.visit-corsica.com/en **180**

Côte d'Azur

The French Riviera is best known for its coastline and glamorous resorts. There are many relics of artists who worked here: St-Tropez has Musée de l'Annonciade; Antibes has 12c Château Grimaldi with the Picasso Museum; Cagnes has the Renoir Museum; St-Paul-de-Vence has the excellent Maeght Foundation; and nearby Vence has Matisse's Chapelle du Rosaire. Cannes is famous for its film festival. Also: Marseille, Monaco, Nice. www.provence-alpes-cotedazur.com **133 B3**

Dijon

Great 15c cultural centre. The Palais des Ducs et des Etats is the most notable monument and contains the Museum of Fine Arts. Also: the Charterhouse of Champmol. https://en.destinationdijon.com **105 B4**

Disneyland Paris

Europe's largest theme park follows in the footsteps of its famous predecessors in the United States. www.disneylandparis.com **90 C2**

Le Puy-en-Velay

Medieval town bizarrely set on the peaks of dead volcanoes. It is dominated by the Romanesque cathedral (cloisters). The Romanesque chapel of St-Michel is dramatically situated on the highest rock. www.lepuyenvelay-tourisme.co.uk **117 B3**

Loire Valley

The Loire Valley has many 15–16c châteaux built amid beautiful scenery by French monarchs and members of their courts. Among the most splendid are Azay-le-Rideau, Chambord, Chenonceau and Loches. Also: Abbaye de Fontévraud. www.loirevalley-france.co.uk **102 B2**

Lyon

France's third largest city has an old centre and many museums including the Museum of Fine Arts (old masters) and the modern Musée des Confluences. https://en.lyon-france.co.uk **117 B4**

Marseilles Marseille

Second largest city in France. Spectacular views from the 19c Notre-Dame de la Garde. The Old Port has 11–12c Basilique St Victor (crypt, catacombs). Cantini Museum has major collection of 20c French art, and the Mucem tells the history of Mediterranean civilizations. Château d'If was the setting of Dumas' *The Count of Monte Cristo*. www.marseille-tourisme.com/en/ **131 B4**

Mont-St-Michel

Gothic pilgrim abbey (11–12c) set dramatically on a steep rock island rising from mud flats and connected to the land by a road covered by the tide. The abbey is made up of a complex of buildings. www.ot-montsaintmichel.com/en/ **101 A4**

Nancy

A centre of Art Nouveau. The 18c Place Stanislas was constructed by dethroned Polish king Stanislas. Museums: School of Nancy Museum (Art Nouveau furniture); Fine Arts Museum. www.nancy-tourisme.fr/en/ **92 C2**

Nantes

Former capital of Brittany, with the 15c Château des ducs de Bretagne. The cathedral has a striking interior. www.nantes-tourisme.com/en **101 B4**

Nice

Capital of the Côte d'Azur, the old town is centred on the old castle on the hill. The seafront includes the famous 19c Promenade des Anglais. The aristocratic quarter of the Cimiez Hill has the Marc Chagall Museum and the Matisse Museum. Also: Museum of Modern and Contemporary Art (especially neo-Realism and Pop Art). http://en.nicetourisme.com/ **133 B3**

Paris

Capital of France, one of Europe's most interesting cities. The Île de la Cité area, an island in the River Seine, has the 12–13c Notre Dame, devastated by fire in 2019 and closed for major restoration, and La Sainte Chapelle (1240–48), one of the jewels of Gothic art. The Left Bank area: Latin Quarter with the famous Sorbonne university; Museum of Cluny housing medieval art; the Panthéon; Luxembourg Palace and Gardens; Montparnasse, interwar artistic and literary centre; Eiffel Tower; Hôtel des Invalides with Napoleon's tomb. Right Bank: the great boulevards (Avenue des Champs-Élysées joining the Arc de Triomphe and Place de la Concorde); 19c Opéra Quarter; Marais, former aristocratic quarter of elegant mansions (Place des Vosges); Bois de Boulogne, the largest park in Paris; Montmartre, centre of 19c bohemianism, with the Basilique Sacré-Coeur. The Church of St Denis is the first Gothic church and the mausoleum of the French monarchy. Paris has three of the world's greatest art collections: The Louvre (to 19c, *Mona Lisa*), Musée d'Orsay (19–20c) and National Modern Art Museum in the Pompidou Centre. Other major museums include: Orangery Museum; Paris Museum of Modern Art; Rodin Museum; Picasso Museum; Atelier des Lumières. Notable cemeteries with graves of the famous: Père-Lachaise, Montparnasse. Near Paris are the royal residences of Fontainebleau and Versailles. https://en.parisinfo.com **90 C2**

Pyrenees

Beautiful unspoiled mountain range. Towns include: delightful sea resorts of St-Jean-de-Luz and Biarritz; Pau, with access to the Pyrenees National Park; pilgrimage centre Lourdes. **144–145**

Reims

Together with nearby Épernay, the centre of champagne production. The 13c Gothic cathedral is one of the greatest architectural achievements in France (stained glass by Chagall). Other sights: Palais du Tau with cathedral sculpture, 11c Basilica of St Rémi; cellars on Place St-Niçaise and Place des Droits de l'Homme. https://en.reims-tourisme.com **91 B4**

Rouen

Old centre with many half-timbered houses and 12–13c Gothic cathedral and the Gothic Church of St Maclou with its fascinating remains of a danse macabre on the former cemetery of Aître St-Maclou. The Fine Arts Museum has a good collection. https://en.rouentourisme.com/ **89 A5**

St-Malo

Fortified town (much rebuilt) in a fine coastal setting. There is a magnificent boat trip along the river Rance to Dinan, a splendid well-preserved medieval town. www.saint-malo-tourisme.co.uk **101 A3**

Strasbourg

Town whose historic centre includes a well-preserved quarter of medieval half-timbered Alsatian houses, many of them set on the canal. The cathedral is one of the best in France. The Palais Rohan contains several museums. www.visitstrasbourg.fr/en/welcome-in-strasbourg **93 C3**

Toulouse

Medieval university town characterised by flat pink brick (Hôtel Assézat). The Basilique St Sernin, the largest Romanesque church in France, has many art treasures. Marvellous Church of the Jacobins holds relics of St Thomas Aquinas. www.toulouse-visit.com **129 C4**

▲ Château de Chenonceaux,
Châteaux of the Loire, France

Tours

Historic town centred on Place Plumereau. Good collections in the Guilds Museum and Fine Arts Museum. Also: cathedral (predominantly Gothic). www.tours-tourism.co.uk/en **102 B2**

Versailles

Vast royal palace built for Louis XIV, primarily by Mansart, set in large formal gardens with magnificent fountains. The extensive and much-imitated state apartments include the famous Hall of Mirrors and the exceptional Baroque chapel. http://en.chateauversailles.fr/ **90 C2**

Vézère Valley Caves

A number of prehistoric sites, most notably the cave paintings of Lascaux (some 17,000 years old), now only seen in a duplicate cave, and the cave of Font de Gaume. The National Museum of Prehistory is in Les Eyzies. www.lascaux-dordogne.com/en **129 B4**

Germany Deutschland
www.germany.travel

Northern Germany

Aachen

Once capital of the Holy Roman Empire. Old town around the Münsterplatz with magnificent cathedral. An exceptionally rich treasure is in the Schatzkammer. The Town Hall is on the medieval Market. www.aachen-tourismus.de/en **80 B2**

Berlin

Capital of Germany. Sights include: the Kurfürstendamm avenue; Brandenburg Gate, former symbol of the division between East and West

Germany; Tiergarten; Unter den Linden; 19c Reichstag. Berlin has many excellent art and history collections. Museum Island: Pergamon Musem (classical antiquity, Near and Far East, Islam; Bode Museum (sculpture, Byzantine art); Altes Museum (Greek and Roman); New National Gallery (20th-c European); Old National Gallery (19th-c German); New Museum (Egyptian, prehistoric). Dahlem: Museum of Asian Art; Museum of European Cultures; Museum of Ethnology; Die Brücke Museum (German Expressionism). Tiergarten: Picture Gallery (old masters); Decorative Arts Museum (13–19c); New National

Gothic cathedral, Cologne, Germany

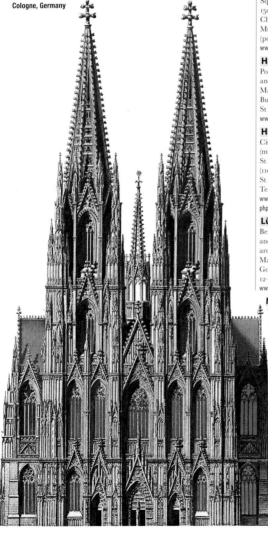

Gallery (19–20c); Bauhaus Archive. Kreuzberg: Gropius Building with Jewish Museum and Berlin Gallery; remains of Berlin Wall and Checkpoint Charlie House. Unter den Linden: German Guggenheim (commissioned contemporary works). http://visitberlin.de **74 B2**

Cologne Köln

Ancient city with 13–19c cathedral (rich display of art). In the old town are the Town Hall and many Romanesque churches (Gross St Martin, St Maria im Kapitol, St Maria im Lyskirchen, St Ursula, St Georg, St Severin, St Pantaleon, St Apostolen). Museums: Diocesan Museum (religious art); Roman-

German Museum (ancient history); Wallraf-Richartz and Ludwig Museum (14–20c art). www.cologne-tourism.com **80 B2**

Dresden

Historic centre with a rich display of Baroque architecture. Major buildings: Castle of the Electors of Saxony; 18c Hofkirche; Zwinger Palace with fountains and pavilions (excellent old masters); Albertinum with excellent Gallery of New Masters; treasury of Grünes Gewölbe. The Baroque-planned New Town contains the Japanese Palace and Schloss Pillnitz. www.dresden.de/en/tourism/tourism.php **84 A1**

Frankfurt

Financial capital of Germany. The historic centre around the Römerberg Square has 13–15c cathedral, 15c Town Hall, Gothic St Nicholas Church, Saalhof (12c chapel). Museums: Museum of Modern Art (post-war); State Art Institute. www.frankfurt-tourismus.de **81 B4**

Hamburg

Port city with many parks, lakes and canals. The Kunsthalle has Old Masters and 19-20c German art. Buildings: 19c Town Hall; Baroque St Michael's Church. www.hamburg-tourism.de **72 A3**

Hildesheim

City of Romanesque architecture (much destroyed). Principal sights: St Michael's Church; cathedral (11c interior, sculptured doors, St Anne's Chapel); superb 15c Tempelhaus on the Market Place. www.hildesheim.de/staticsite/staticsite. php?menuid=1067&topmenu=4 **72 B2**

Lübeck

Beautiful old town built on an island and characterised by Gothic brick architecture. Sights: 15c Holsten Gate; Market with the Town Hall and Gothic brick St Mary's Church; 12–13c cathedral; St Ann Museum. www.luebeck-tourism.de **65 C3**

Mainz

The Electoral Palatinate schloss and Market fountain are Renaissance. Churches: 12c Romanesque cathedral; Gothic St Steven's (with stained glass by Marc Chagall). www.mainz.de **93 A4**

Marburg

Medieval university town with the Market Place and Town Hall, St Elizabeth's Church (frescoes, statues, 13c shrine), 15–16c schloss. **81 B4**

Münster

Historic city with well-preserved Gothic and Renaissance buildings: 14c Town Hall; Romanesque-Gothic cathedral. The Westphalian Museum holds regional art. www.stadt-muenster. de/en/tourismus/home.html **71 C4**

Potsdam

Beautiful Sanssouci Park contains several 18–19c buildings including: Schloss Sanssouci; Gallery (European masters); Orangery; New Palace; Chinese Teahouse. www.potsdam-tourism.com **74 B2**

Rhein Valley Rheintal

Beautiful 80km gorge of the Rhein Valley between Mainz and Koblenz with rocks (Loreley), vineyards (Bacharach, Rüdesheim), white medieval towns (Rhens, Oberwesel) and castles. Some castles are medieval (Marksburg, Rheinfles, island fortress Pfalzgrafenstein) others were built or rebuilt in the 19c (Stolzenfles, Rheinstein). **80 B3**

Weimar

The Neoclassical schloss, once an important seat of government, now houses a good art collection. Church of SS Peter and Paul has a Cranach masterpiece. Houses of famous people: Goethe, Schiller, Liszt. The famous Bauhaus was founded at the School of Architecture and Engineering. www.weimar.de/en/tourism **82 B3**

Southern Germany

Alpine Road
Deutsche Alpenstrasse

German Alpine Road in the Bavarian Alps, from Lindau on Bodensee to Berchtesgaden. The setting for 19c fairy-tale follies of Ludwig II of Bavaria (Linderhof, Hohenschwangau, Neuschwanstein), charming old villages (Oberammergau) and Baroque churches (Weiss, Ottobeuren). Garmisch-Partenkirchen has views on Germany's highest peak, the Zugspitze. **108 B2**

Augsburg

Attractive old city. The Town Hall is one of Germany's finest Renaissance buildings. Maximilianstrasse has several Renaissance houses and Rococo Schaezler Palace (good art collection). Churches: Romanesque-Gothic cathedral; Renaissance St Anne's Church. The Fuggerei, founded 1519 as an estate for the poor, is still in use. www.augsburg-tourismus.de **94 C2**

Bamberg

Well-preserved medieval town. The island, connected by two bridges, has the Town Hall and views of Klein Venedig. Romanesque-Gothic cathedral (good art) is on an exceptional square of Gothic, Renaissance and Baroque buildings – Alte Hofhalttung; Neue Residenz with State Gallery (German masters); Ratstube. http://en.bamberg.info **94 B2**

Black Forest Schwarzwald

Hilly region between Basel and Karlsruhe, the largest and most picturesque woodland in Germany, with the highest summit, Feldberg, lake resorts (Titisee), health resorts (Baden-Baden) and clock craft (Triberg). Freiburg is the regional capital. www.schwarzwald.de **93 C4**

Freiburg

Old university town with system of streams running through the streets. The Gothic Minster is surrounded by the town's finest buildings. Two towers remain of the medieval walls. The Augustine Museum has a good collection. https://visit.freiburg.de/en 106 B2

Heidelberg

Germany's oldest university town, majestically set on the banks of the river and romantically dominated by the ruined schloss. The Gothic Church of the Holy Spirit is on the Market Place with the Baroque Town Hall. Other sights include the 16c Knight's House and the Baroque Morass Palace with the Museum of the Palatinate.
www.tourism-heidelberg.com 93 B4

Lake Constance Bodensee

Lake Constance, with many pleasant lake resorts. Lindau, on an island, has numerous gabled houses. Birnau has an 18c Rococo church. Konstanz (Swiss side) has the Minster set above the Old Town.
www.bodensee.eu/en 107 B4

Munich München

Old town centred on the Marienplatz with 15c Old Town Hall and 19c New Town Hall. Many richly decorated churches: St Peter's (14c tower); Gothic red-brick cathedral; Renaissance St Michael's (royal portraits on the façade); Rococo St Asam's. The Residenz palace consists of seven splendid buildings holding many art objects. Schloss Nymphenburg has a palace, park, botanical gardens and four beautiful pavilions. Superb museums: Old Gallery (old masters), New Gallery (18–19c), Lenbachhaus (modern German). Many famous beer gardens.
www.munich-touristinfo.de 108 A2

Nuremberg Nürnberg

Beautiful medieval walled city dominated by the 12c Kaiserburg. Romanesque-Gothic St Sebaldus Church and Gothic St Laurence Church are rich in art. On Hauptmarkt is the famous 14c Schöner Brunnen. Also notable is 15c Dürer House. The German National Museum has excellent German medieval and Renaissance art.
http://tourismus.nuernberg.de/en 94 B3

Regensburg

Medieval city set majestically on the Danube. Views from 12c Steinerne Brücke. Churches: Gothic cathedral; Romanesque St Jacob's; Gothic St Blaisius; Baroque St Emmeram. Other sights: Old Town Hall (museum); Haidplatz; Schloss Thurn und Taxis; State Museum.
http://tourismus.regensburg.de/en 95 B4

Romantic Road
Romantische Strasse

Romantic route through Aschaffenburg and Füssen, leading through picturesque towns and villages of medieval Germany. The most popular section is the section between Würzburg and Augsburg, centred on Rothenburg ob der Tauber. Also notable are Nördlingen, Harburg Castle, Dinkelsbühl, Creglingen.
www.romantischestrasse.de 94 B2

Rothenburg ob der Tauber

Attractive medieval walled town with tall gabled and half-timbered houses on narrow cobbled streets. The Market Place has Gothic-Renaissance Town Hall, Rattrinke-stubbe and Gothic St Jacob's Church (altarpiece).
www.rothenburg.de/tourismus/willkommen-in-rothenburg 94 B2

Speyer

The 11c cathedral is one of the largest and best Romanesque buildings in Germany. 12c Jewish Baths are well-preserved.
www.speyer.de/sv_speyer/en/Tourism 93 B4

Stuttgart

Largely modern city with old centre around the Old Schloss, Renaissance Alte Kanzlei, 15c Collegiate Church and Baroque New Schloss. Museums: Regional Museum; Old and New State Galleries. The 1930s Weissenhofsiedlung is by several famous architects.
www.stuttgart-tourist.de/en 94 C1

Trier

Superb Roman monuments: Porta Nigra; Aula Palatina (now a church); Imperial Baths; amphitheatre. The Regional Museum has Roman artefacts. Also, Gothic Church of Our Lady; Romanesque cathedral.
www.trier-info.de 92 B2

Ulm

Old town with half-timbered gabled houses set on a canal. Gothic 14–19c minster has tallest spire in the world (161m). www.tourismus.ulm.de 94 C1

Würzburg

Set among vineyard hills, the medieval town is centred on the Market Place with the Rococo House of the Falcon. The 18c episcopal princes' residence (frescoes) is magnificent. The cathedral is rich in art. Work of the great local Gothic sculptor, Riemenschneider, is in Gothic St Mary's Chapel, Baroque New Minster, and the Mainfränkisches Museum. www.wuerzburg.de/en 94 B1

Greece Ellas

www.visitgreece.gr

Athens Athina

Capital of Greece. The Acropolis, with 5c BC sanctuary complex (Parthenon, Propylaia, Erechtheion, Temple of Athena Nike), is the greatest architectural achievement of antiquity in Europe. The Agora was a public meeting place in ancient Athens. Plaka has narrow streets and small Byzantine churches (Kapnikarea). The Olympeum was the largest temple in Greece. Also:

Olympic Stadium; excellent collections of ancient artefacts (Museum of Cycladic and Ancient Greek Art; New Acropolis Museum; National Archeological Museum; Benaki Museum). 185 B4

Corinth Korinthos

Ancient Corinth (ruins), with 5c BC Temple of Apollo, was in 44 BC made capital of Roman Greece by Julius Caesar. Set above the city, the Greek-built acropolis hill of Acrocorinth became the Roman and Byzantine citadel (ruins). 184 B3

Crete Kriti

Largest Greek island, Crete was home to the great Minoan civilization (2800–1100 BC). The main relics are the ruined Palace of Knossos and Malia. Gortys was capital of the Roman province. Picturesque Rethimno has narrow medieval streets, a Venetian fortress and a former Turkish mosque. Matala has beautiful beaches and famous caves cut into cliffs. Iraklio (Heraklion), the capital, has a good Archeological Museum. 185 D6

Delphi

At the foot of the Mount Parnassos, Delphi was the seat of the Delphic Oracle of Apollo, the most important oracle in Ancient Greece. Delphi was also a political meeting place and the site of the Pythian Games. The Sanctuary of Apollo consists of: Temple of Apollo, led to by the Sacred Way; Theatre; Stadium. The museum has a display of objects from the site (5c BC Charioteer). 182 E4

Epidavros

Formerly a spa and religious centre focused on the Sanctuary of Asclepius (ruins). The enormous 4c BC theatre is probably the finest of all ancient theatres. 184 B4

Greek Islands

Popular islands with some of the most beautiful and spectacular beaches in Europe. The many islands are divided into various groups and individual islands: The major groups are the Kiklades and Dodekanisa in the Aegean Sea, the largest islands are Kerkyra (Corfu) in the Ionian Sea and Kriti. 182–185 & 188

Meteora

The tops of bizarre vertical cylinders of rock and towering cliffs are the setting for 14c Cenobitic monasteries, until recently only accessible by baskets or removable ladders. Mega Meteoro is the grandest and set on the highest point. Roussánou has the most extraordinary site. Varlaám is one of the oldest and most beautiful, with the Ascent Tower and 16c church with frescoes. Aghiou Nikolaou also has good frescoes. www.meteora-greece.com 182 D3

Mistras

Set in a beautiful landscape, Mistras

is the site of a Byzantine city, now in ruins, with palaces, frescoed churches, monasteries and houses. 184 B3

Mount Olympus
Oros Olymbos

Mount Olympus, mythical seat of the Greek gods, is the highest, most dramatic peak in Greece. 182 C4

Mycenae Mikines

The citadel of Mycenae prospered between 1950 BC and 1100 BC and consists of the royal complex of Agamemnon: Lion Gate, royal burial site, Royal Palace, South House, Great Court. 184 B3

Olympia

In a stunning setting, the Panhellenic Games were held here for a millennium. Ruins of the sanctuary of Olympia consist of the Doric temples of Zeus and Hera and the vast Stadium. There is also a museum (4c BC figure of Hermes). 184 B2

Rhodes

One of the most attractive islands with wonderful sandy beaches. The city of Rhodes has a well-preserved medieval centre with the Palace of the Grand Masters and the Turkish Süleymaniye Mosque
www.rhodestravels.com 188 C2

Salonica Thessaloniki

Largely modern city with Byzantine walls and many fine churches: 8c Aghia Sofia; 11c Panaghia Halkeo; 14c Dodeka Apostoli; 14c Aghios Nikolaos Orfanos; 5c Aghios Dimitrios (largest in Greece, 7c Mosaics). 183 C5

Hungary Magyarország

https://visithungary.com

Balaton

The 'Hungarian sea', famous for its holiday resorts: Balatonfüred, Tihany, Badasconytomaj, Keszthely. 111 C4

Budapest

Capital of Hungary on River Danube, with historic area centring on the Castle Hill of Buda district. Sights include: Matthias church; Pest district with late 19c architecture, centred on Ferenciek tere; neo-Gothic Parliament Building on river; Millennium Monument. The Royal Castle houses a number of museums: Hungarian National Gallery, Budapest History Museum; Ludwig Collection. Other museums: National Museum of Fine Arts (excellent Old and Modern masters); Hungarian National Museum (Hungarian history). Famous for public thermal baths: Király and Rudas baths, both made under Turkish rule; Gellért baths, the most visited.
www.budapest.com/ 112 B3

Esztergom

Medieval capital of Hungary set in scenic landscape. Sights: Hungary's

largest basilica (completed 1856); royal palace ruins. **112 B2**

Pécs

Attractive old town with Europe's fifth oldest university (founded 1367). Famous for Turkish architecture (Mosque of Gazi Kasim Pasha, Jakovali Hassan Mosque). www.iranypecs.hu/en/index.html **125 A4**

Sopron

Beautiful walled town with many Gothic and Renaissance houses. Nearby: Fertöd with the marvellous Eszergázy Palace. http://portal.sopron.hu/Sopron/portal/english **111 B3**

Ireland

www.ireland.com/en-gb

Aran Islands

Islands with spectacular cliffs and notable pre-Christian and Christian sights, especially on Inishmore. www.aranislands.ie **26 B2**

Cashel

Town dominated by the Rock of Cashel (61m) topped by ecclesiastical ruins including 13c cathedral; 15c Halls of the Vicars; beautiful Romanesque 12c Cormac's Chapel (fine carvings). www.cashel.ie **29 B4**

Connemara

Beautiful wild landscape of mountains, lakes, peninsulas and beaches. Clifden is the capital. www.connemara.ie/en **28 A1**

Cork

Pleasant city with its centre along St Patrick's Street and Grand Parade lined with fine 18c buildings. Churches: Georgian St Anne's Shandon (bell tower); 19c cathedral. www.corkcity.ie/traveltourism **29 C3**

County Donegal

Rich scenic landscape of mystical lakes and glens and seascape of cliffs (Slieve League cliffs are the highest in Europe). The town of Donegal has a finely preserved Jacobean castle. www.govisitdonegal.com **26 B2**

Dublin

Capital of Ireland. City of elegant 18c neoclassical and Georgian architecture with gardens and parks (St Stephen's Green, Merrion Square with Leinster House – now seat of Irish parliament). City's main landmark, Trinity College (founded 1591), houses in its Old Library fine Irish manuscripts (7c Book of Durrow, 8c Book of Kells). Two Norman cathedrals: Christ Church; St Patrick's. Other buildings: originally medieval Dublin Castle with State Apartments; James Gandon's masterpieces: Custom House; Four Courts. Museums: National Museum (archaeology, decorative arts, natural history); National Gallery (old masters, Impressionists); Museum of Modern Art; Dublin Writers' Museum. www.visitdublin.com **30 A2**

Glendalough

Impressive ruins of an important early Celtic (6c) monastery with 9c cathedral, 12c St Kevin's Cross, oratory of St Kevin's Church. www.glendalough.ie **30 A2**

Kilkenny

Charming medieval town, with narrow streets dominated by 12c castle (restored 19c). The 13c Gothic cathedral has notable tomb monuments. www.visitkilkenny.ie **30 B1**

Newgrange

Part of a complex that also includes the sites of Knowth, Dowth, Fourknocks, Loughcrew and Tara, Newgrange is one of the best passage graves in Europe, the massive 4500-year-old tomb has stones richly decorated with patterns. www.knowth.com/newgrange.htm **30 A2**

Ring of Kerry

Route around the Iveragh peninsula with beautiful lakes (Lough Leane), peaks overlooking the coastline and islands (Valencia Island, Skelling). Also: Killarney; ruins of 15c Muckross Abbey. www.theringofkerry.com **29 B2**

Italy Italia
www.italia.it

Northern Italy

Alps

Wonderful stretch of the Alps running from the Swiss and French borders to Austria. The region of Valle d'Aosta is one of the most popular ski regions, bordered by the highest peaks of the Alps. **108–109 & 119–120**

Arezzo

Beautiful old town set on a hill dominated by 13c cathedral. Piazza Grande is surrounded by medieval and Renaissance palaces. Main sight: Piero della Francesca's frescoes in the choir of San Francesco. **135 B4**

Assisi

Hill-top town that attracts crowds of pilgrims to the shrine of St Francis of Assisi at the Basilica di San Francesco, consisting of two churches, Lower and Upper, with superb frescoes. www.assisi-info.com **136 B1**

Bologna

Elegant city with oldest university in Italy. Historical centre around Piazza Maggiore and Piazza del Nettuno with the Town Hall, Palazzo del Podestà, Basilica di San Petronio. Other churches: San Domenico; San Giacomo Maggiore. The two towers (one incomplete) are symbols of the city. Good collection in the National Gallery (Bolognese). www.bolognawelcome.com **135 A4**

Dolomites Dolomiti

Part of the Alps, this mountain range spreads over the region of Trentino-Alto Adige, with the most picturesque scenery between Bolzano and Cortina d'Ampezzo. www.dolomiti.org/en **121 A4**

Ferrara

Old town centre around Romanesque-Gothic cathedral and Palazzo Communale. Also: Castello Estense; Palazzo Schifanoia (frescoes); Palazzo dei Diamanti housing Pinacoteca Nazionale. www.ferraraterraeacqua.it/en **121 C4**

Florence Firenze

City with exceptionally rich medieval and Renaissance heritage. Piazza del Duomo has:13–15c cathedral (first dome since antiquity); 14c campanile; 11c baptistry (bronze doors). Piazza della Signoria has: 14c Palazzo Vecchio (frescoes); Loggia della Signoria (sculpture); 16c Uffizi Gallery with one of the world's greatest collections (13–18c). Other great paintings: Museo di San Marco; Palatine Gallery in 15–16c Pitti Palace surrounded by Boboli Gardens. Sculpture: Cathedral Works Museum; Bargello Museum; Academy Gallery (Michelangelo's *David*). Among many other Renaissance palaces: Medici-Riccardi; Rucellai; Strozzi. The 15c church of San Lorenzo has Michelangelo's tombs of the Medici. Many churches have richly frescoed chapels: Santa Maria

Novella, Santa Croce, Santa Maria del Carmine. The 13c Ponte Vecchio is one of the most famous sights. www.visitflorence.com **135 B4**

Italian Lakes

Beautiful district at the foot of the Alps, most of the lakes with holiday resorts. Many lakes are surrounded by aristocratic villas (Maggiore, Como, Garda). **120–121**

Mantua Mántova

Attractive city surrounded by three lakes. Two exceptional palaces: Palazzo Ducale (Sala del Pisanello; Camera degli Sposi, Castello San Giorgio); luxurious Palazzo Tè (brilliant frescoes). Also: 15c Church of Sant'Andrea; 13c law courts. www.turismo.mantova.it **121 B3**

Milan Milano

Modern city, Italy's fashion and design capital (Corso and Galleria Vittoro Emmanuelle II). Churches include: Gothic cathedral (1386–1813), the world's largest (4c baptistry); Romanesque St Ambrose; 15c San Satiro; Santa Maria delle Grazie with Leonardo da Vinci's *Last Supper* in the convent refectory. Great art collections, Brera Gallery, Ambrosian Library, Museum of Modern Art. Castello Sforzesco (15c, 19c) also has a gallery. The famous La Scala opera house opened in 1778. Nearby: monastery at Pavia. www.turismo.milano.it/wps/portal/tur/en **120 B2**

Padua Pádova

Pleasant old town with arcaded streets. Basilica del Santo is a place of pilgrimage to the tomb of St Anthony. Giotto's frescoes in the Scrovegni chapel are exceptional.

▲ Il Redentore (cutaway), Venice, Italy

Also: Piazza dei Signori with Palazzo del Capitano; vast Palazzo della Ragione; church of the Eremitani (frescoes). www.turismopadova.it 121 B4

Parma

Attractive city centre, famous for Correggio's frescoes in the Romanesque cathedral and church of St John the Evangelist, and Parmigianino's frescoes in the church of Madonna della Steccata. Their works are also in the National Gallery. www.turismo.comune.parma.it 120 C3

Perúgia

Hill-top town centred around Piazza Quattro Novembre with the cathedral, Fontana Maggiore and Palazzo dei Priori. Also: Collegio di Cambio (frescoes); National Gallery of Umbria; many churches. www.perugiaonline.com 136 B1

Pisa

Medieval town centred on the Piazza dei Miracoli. Sights: famous Romanesque Leaning Tower, Romanesque cathedral (excellent façade, Gothic pulpit); 12–13c Baptistry; 13c Camposanto cloistered cemetery (fascinating 14c frescoes). www.turismo.pisa.it/en 134 B3

Ravenna

Ancient town with exceptionally well-preserved Byzantine mosaics. The finest are in 5c Mausoleo di Galla Placidia and 6c Basilica di San Vitale. Good mosaics also in the basilicas of Sant'Apollinare in Classe and Sant'Apollinare Nuovo. www.turismo.ra.it/eng 135 A5

Siena

Outstanding 13–14c medieval town centred on beautiful Piazza del Campo with Gothic Palazzo Publico

(frescoes of secular life). Delightful Romanesque-Gothic Duomo (Libreria Piccolomini, baptistry, art works). Many other richly decorated churches. Fine Sienese painting in Pinacoteca Nazionale and Museo dell'Opera del Duomo. www.sienaonline.com 135 B4

Turin Torino

City centre has 17-18c Baroque layout dominated by twin Baroque churches. Also: 15c cathedral (holds Turin Shroud); Palazzo Reale; 18c Superga Basilica; Academy of Science with rich Egyptian Museum. www.turismotorino.org 119 B4

Urbino

Set in beautiful hilly landscape, Urbino's heritage is mainly due to the 15c court of Federico da Montefeltro at the magnificent Ducal Palace (notable Studiolo), now also a gallery. www.turismo.marche.it/en-us 136 B1

Venice Venezia

Stunning old city built on islands in a lagoon, with some 150 canals. The Grand Canal is crossed by the famous 16c Rialto Bridge and is lined with elegant palaces (Gothic Ca'd'Oro and Ca'Foscari, Renaissance Palazzo Grimani, Baroque Rezzonico). The district of San Marco has the core of the best known sights and is centred on Piazza San Marco with 11c Basilica di San Marco (bronze horses, 13c mosaics); Campanile (exceptional views) and Ducal Palace (connected with the prison by the famous Bridge of Sighs). Many churches (Santa Maria Gloriosa dei Frari, Santa Maria della Salute, Redentore, San Giorgio Maggiore, San Giovanni e Paolo) and scuole (Scuola di San Rocco, Scuola

di San Giorgio degli Schiavoni) have excellent works of art. The Gallery of the Academy houses superb 14–18c Venetian art. The Guggenheim Museum holds 20c art. http://en.turismovenezia.it 122 B1

Verona

Old town with remains of 1c Roman Arena and medieval sights including the Palazzo degli Scaligeri; Arche Scaligere; Romanesque Santa Maria Antica; Castelvecchio; Ponte Scaliger. The famous 14c House of Juliet has associations with *Romeo and Juliet*. Many churches with fine art works (cathedral; Sant'Anastasia; basilica di San Zeno Maggiore). www.visitverona.it 121 B4

Vicenza

Beautiful town, famous for the architecture of Palladio, including the Olympic Theatre (extraordinary stage), Corso Palladio with many of his palaces, and Palazzo Chiericati. Nearby: Villa Rotonda, the most influential of all Palladian buildings. www.vicenzae.org 121 B4

Southern Italy

Naples Napoli

Historical centre around Gothic cathedral (crypt). Spaccanapoli area has numerous churches (bizarre Cappella Sansevero, Gesù Nuovo, Gothic Santa Chiara with fabulous tombs). Buildings: 13c Castello Nuovo; 13c Castel dell'Ovo; 15c Palazzo Cuomo. Museums: National Archeological Museum (artefacts from Pompeii and

Herculaneum); National Museum of Capodimonte (Renaissance painting). Nearby: spectacular coast around Amalfi; Pompeii; Herculaneum. www.visitnaples.eu/en 170 C2

Orvieto

Medieval hill-top town with a number of monuments including the Romanesque-Gothic cathedral (façade, frescoes). www.orvietoviva.com/en 168 A2

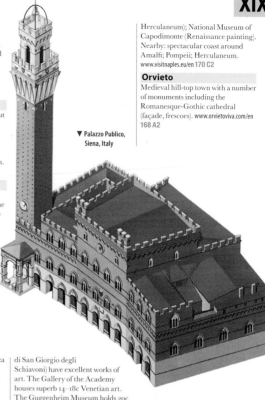

▼ Palazzo Publico, Siena, Italy

Rome Roma

Capital of Italy, exceptionally rich in sights from many eras. Ancient sights: Colosseum; Arch of Constantine; Trajan's Column; Roman and Imperial fora; hills of Palatino and Campidoglio (Capitoline Museum shows antiquities); Pantheon; Castel Sant' Angelo; Baths of Caracalla). Early Christian sights: catacombs (San Calisto, San Sebastiano, Domitilla); basilicas (San Giovanni in Laterano, Santa Maria Maggiore, San Paolo Fuori le Mura). Rome is known for richly decorated Baroque churches: il Gesù, Sant'Ignazio, Santa Maria della Vittoria, Chiesa Nuova. Other churches, often with art treasures: Romanesque Santa Maria in Cosmedin, Gothic Santa Maria Sopra Minerva, Renaissance Santa Maria del Popolo, San Pietro in Vincoli. Several Renaissance and Baroque palaces and villas house superb art collections (Palazzo Barberini, Palazzo Doria Pamphilj, Palazzo Spada, Palazzo Corsini, Villa Giulia, Galleria Borghese) and are beautifully frescoed (Villa Farnesina). Fine Baroque public spaces with fountains: Piazza Navona; Piazza di Spagna with the Spanish Steps; also Trevi Fountain. Nearby: Tivoli; Villa Adriana. Rome also contains the Vatican City (Città del Vaticano). www.turismoroma.it/?lang=en 168 B2

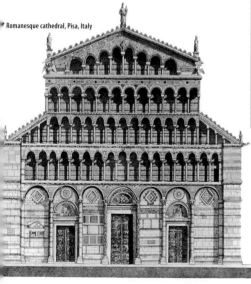

◀ Romanesque cathedral, Pisa, Italy

Volcanic Region
Region from Naples to Sicily. Mount Etna is one of the most famous European volcanoes. Vesuvius dominates the Bay of Naples and has at its foot two of Italy's finest Roman sites, Pompeii and Herculaneum, both destroyed by its eruption in 79AD. Stromboli is one of the beautiful Aeolian Islands.

Sardinia Sardegna
Sardinia has some of the most beautiful beaches in Italy (Alghero). Unique are the nuraghi, some 7000 stone constructions (Su Nuraxi, Serra Orios), the remains of an old civilization (1500–400 BC). Old towns include Cagliari and Sàssari. www.sardegnaturismo.it/en 178–179

Sicily Sicilia
Surrounded by beautiful beaches and full of monuments of many periods, Sicily is the largest island in the Mediterranean. Taormina with its Greek theatre has one of the most spectacular beaches, lying under the mildly active volcano Mount Etna. Also: Agrigento; Palermo, Siracusa. www.sicilytourism.com 176–177

Agrigento
Set on a hill above the sea and famed for the Valley of the Temples. The nine originally 5c BC Doric temples are Sicily's best-preserved Greek remains. www.agrigento-sicilia.it 176 B2

Palermo
City with Moorish, Norman and Baroque architecture, especially around the main squares (Quattro Canti, Piazza Pretoria, Piazza Bellini). Sights: remains of Norman palace (12c Palatine Chapel); Norman cathedral; Regional Gallery (medieval); some 8000 preserved bodies in the catacombs of the Cappuchin Convent. Nearby: 12c Norman Duomo di Monreale. www.palermotourism.com 176 A2

Syracuse Siracusa
Built on an island connected to the mainland by a bridge, the old town has a 7c cathedral, ruins of the Temple of Apollo; Fountain of Arethusa; archaeological museum. On the mainland: 5c BC Greek theatre with seats cut out of rock; Greek fortress of Euralus; 2c Roman amphitheatre; 5–6c Catacombs of St John. 177 B4

Latvia Latvija
www.latvia.travel/en

Riga
Well-preserved medieval town centre around the cathedral. Sights: Riga Castle; medieval Hanseatic houses; Great Guild Hall; Gothic Church of St Peter; Art Nouveau buildings in the New Town. Nearby: Baroque Rundale Castle. www.latvia.travel/en/discover-riga-capital-latvia 8 D4

Lithuania Lietuva
www.lithuania.travel/en/

Vilnius
Baroque old town with fine architecture including: cathedral; Gediminas Tower; university complex; Archbishop's Palace; Church of St Anne. Also: remains of Jewish life; Vilnius Picture Gallery (16–19c regional); Lithuanian National Museum. http://vilnius.com 13 A6

Luxembourg
www.visitluxembourg.com/en

Luxembourg
Capital of Luxembourg, built on a rock with fine views. Old town is around the Place d'Armes. Buildings: Grand Ducal Palace; fortifications of Rocher du Bock; cathedral. Museum of History and Art holds an excellent regional collection. 92 B2

Malta
http://www.visitmalta.com/en/home

Valletta
Capital of Malta. Historic walled city, founded in 16c by the Maltese Knights, with 16c Grand Master's Palace and a richly decorated cathedral; fine arts museum – Muża. 175 C3

Monaco
www.visitmonaco.com

Monaco
Major resort area in a beautiful location. Sights include: Monte Carlo casino, Prince's Palace at Monaco-Ville; 19c cathedral; oceanographic museum. 133 B3

Netherlands
Nederland
www.holland.com

Amsterdam
Capital of the Netherlands. Old centre has picturesque canals lined with distinctive elegant 17–18c merchants' houses. Dam Square has 15c New Church and Royal Palace. Other churches include Westerkerk. The Museumplein has three world-famous museums: the Rijksmuseum (several art collections including 15–17c painting); Van Gogh Museum; Municipal Museum (art from 1850 on). Other museums: Anne Frank House; Jewish Historical Museum; Rembrandt House; Hermitage Museum (exhibitions). 70 B1

Delft
Well-preserved old Dutch town with gabled red-roofed houses along canals. Gothic churches: New Church; Old Church. Famous for Delftware (two museums). www.delft.nl 70 B1

Haarlem
Many medieval gabled houses centred on the Great Market with 14c Town Hall and 15c Church of St Bavon. Museums: Frans Hals Museum; Teylers Museum. www.visithaarlem.com/en/ 70 B1

The Hague Den Haag
Seat of Government and of the royal house of the Netherlands. The 17c Mauritshuis houses the Royal Picture Gallery (excellent 15–18c Flemish and Dutch). Other museums: Escher Museum; Meermanno Museum (books); Municipal Museum. 70 B1

Het Loo
Former royal palace and gardens set in a vast landscape (commissioned by the future King and Queen of England, William and Mary). www.paleishetloo.nl 70 B2

Keukenhof
In spring, landscaped gardens, planted with bulbs of many varieties, are the largest flower gardens in the world. www.keukenhof.nl 70 B1

Leiden
University town of beautiful gabled houses set along canals. The Rijksmuseum Van Oudheden is Holland's most important home to archaeological artefacts from the Antiquity. The 16c Hortus Botanicus is one of the oldest botanical gardens in Europe. The Cloth Hall with van Leyden's *Last Judgement*. http://leidenholland.com 70 B1

Rotterdam
The largest port in the Europe. The Boymans-van Beuningen Museum has a huge and excellent decorative and fine art collection (old and modern). Nearby: 18c Kinderdijk with 19 windmills. https://en.rotterdam.info 79 A4

Utrecht
Delightful old town centre along canals with the Netherlands' oldest university and Gothic cathedral. Good art collections: Central Museum; National Museum. www.utrecht.nl 70 B2

North Macedonia
Severna Makedonija
www.macedonia-timeless.com

Ohrid
Old town, beautifully set by a lake, with houses of wood and brick, remains of a Turkish citadel, many churches (two cathedrals; St Naum south of the lake). 182 B2

Skopje
Historic town with Turkish citadel, fine 15c mosques, oriental bazaar, ancient bridge. Superb Byzantine churches nearby. 182 A3

▼ Westerkerk, Amsterdam, Netherlands

Norway Norge
www.visitnorway.com

Bergen
Norway's second city in a scenic setting. The Quay has many painted wooden medieval buildings. Sights: 12c Romanesque St Mary's Church; Bergenhus fortress with 13c Haakon's Hall; Rosenkrantz Tower; Grieghallen; Bergen Art Museum (Norwegian art); Bryggens Museum. https://en.visitbergen.com 46 B2

Lappland (Norwegian)
Vast land of Finnmark is home to the Sámi. Nordkapp is the northern point of Europe. Also Finland, Sweden. 192–193

Norwegian Fjords
Beautiful and majestic landscape of deep glacial valleys filled by the sea. The most thrilling fjords are between Bergen and Ålesund. www.fjords.com 46 & 198

Oslo
Capital of Norway with a modern centre. Buildings: 17c cathedral; 19c city hall, 19c royal palace; 19c Stortinget (housing parliament); 19c University; 13c Akershus (castle); 12c Akerskirke (church). Museums: National Gallery; Munch Museum; Viking Ship Museum; Folk Museum (reconstructed buildings). www.visitoslo.com 48 C2

Stavkirker
Wooden medieval stave churches of bizarre pyramidal structure, carved with images from Nordic mythology. Best preserved in southern Norway.

Tromsø
Main arctic city of Norway with a university and two cathedrals. www.visittromso.no/en 192 C3

Trondheim
Set on the edge of a fjord, a modern city with the superb Nidaros cathedral (rebuilt 19c). Also: Stiftsgaard (royal residence); Applied Arts Museum. www.trondheim.com 199 B7

Poland Polska
https://poland.travel/en-gb

Częstochowa
Centre of Polish Catholicism, with the 14c monastery of Jasna Góra a pilgrimage site to the icon of the Black Madonna for six centuries. http://jci.jasnagora.pl/?lng=en 86 B3

Gdańsk
Medieval centre with: 14c Town Hall (state rooms); Gothic brick St Mary's Church, Poland's largest; Long Market has fine buildings (Artus Court); National Museum. www.gdansk.pl/en 69 A3

Kraków
Old university city, rich in architecture, centred on superb 16c Marketplace with Gothic-Renaissance Cloth Hall containing the Art Gallery (19c Polish), Clock Tower, Gothic red-brick St Mary's Church (altarpiece). Czartoryski Palace has city's finest art collection. Wawel Hill has the Gothic cathedral and splendid Renaissance Royal Palace. The former Jewish ghetto in Kazimierz district has 16c Old Synagogue, now a museum. www.krakow.pl/english 99 A3

Poznań
Town centred on the Old Square with Renaissance Town Hall and Baroque mansions. Also: medieval castle; Gothic cathedral; National Museum (European masters). 76 B1

Tatry
One of Europe's most delightful mountain ranges with many beautiful ski resorts (Zakopane). Also in Slovakia. 99 B3

Warsaw Warszawa
Capital of Poland, with many historic monuments in the Old Town with the Royal Castle (museum) and Old Town Square surrounded by reconstructed 17–18c merchants' houses. Several churches including: Gothic cathedral; Baroque Church of the Nuns of Visitation. Richly decorated royal palaces and gardens: Neoclassical Łazienki Palace; Baroque palace in Wilanów. The National Museum has Polish and European art. https://warsawtour.pl/en 77 C6

Wrocław
Historic town centred on the Market Square with 15c Town Hall and mansions. Churches: Baroque cathedral; St Elizabeth; St Adalbert. National Museum displays fine art. Vast painting of Battle of Racławice is specially housed. http://visitwroclaw.eu/en 85 A5

Portugal
www.visitportugal.com/en

Alcobaça
Monastery of Santa Maria, one of the best examples of a Cistercian abbey, founded in 1147 (exterior 17–18c). The church is Portugal's largest (14c tombs). www.mosteiroalcobaca.gov.pt/en 154 A1

Algarve
Modern seaside resorts among picturesque sandy beaches and rocky coves (Praia da Rocha). Old towns: Lagos; Faro. www.visitalgarve.pt/en/Default.aspx 160 B1

Batalha
Abbey is one of the masterpieces of French Gothic and Manueline architecture (tombs, English Perpendicular chapel, unfinished pantheon). www.mosteirobatalha.gov.pt/en 154 A2

Braga
Historic town with cathedral and Baroque staircase of Bom Jesus do Monte. 148 A1

Coimbra
Old town with narrow streets set on a hill. The Romanesque Old Cathedral is particularly fine (portal). The university (founded 1290) has a fascinating Baroque library. Also: Museum of Machado de Castro; many monasteries and convents. www.coimbraportugaltourism.com 148 B1

Évora
Centre of the town, surrounded by walls, has narrow streets of Moorish character and medieval and Renaissance architecture. Churches: 12–13c Gothic cathedral; São Francisco with a chapel decorated with bones of some 5000 monks; 15c Convent of Dos Lóis. The Jesuit university was founded in 1559. Museum of Évora holds fine art (particularly Flemish and Portuguese). Also: well-preserved remains of Roman temple. www.evora-portugal.com 154 C3

Guimarães
Old town with a castle with seven towers or vast keep. Churches: Romanesque chapel of São Miguel; São Francisco. Alberto Sampaio Museum and Martins Sarmento Museum are excellent. www.visitportugal.com/en/content/guimaraes 148 A1

Lisbon Lisboa
Capital of Portugal. Baixa is the Neoclassical heart of Lisbon with the Praça do Comércio and Rossio squares. São Jorge castle (Visigothic, Moorish, Romanesque) is surrounded by the medieval quarters. Bairro Alto is famous for *fado* (songs). Monastery of Jerónimos is exceptional. Churches: 12c cathedral; São Vicente de Fora; São Roque (tiled chapels); Torre de Belém. Museums: Gulbenkian Museum (ancient, oriental, European, Modern Art Centre); National Museum of Ancient Art; Design Museum; National Tile Museum (housed in Convento da Madre de Deus). Nearby: palatial monastic complex Mafra; royal resort Sintra. www.visitlisboa.com 154 B1

Porto
Historic centre with narrow streets. Views from Clérigos Tower. Churches: São Francisco; cathedral. Soares dos Reis Museum holds fine and decorative arts (18–19c). The suburb of Vila Nova de Gaia is the centre for port wine. https://visitporto.travel/en-GB/home#/ 148 A1

Tomar
Attractive town with the Convento de Cristo, founded in 1162 as the headquarters of the Knights Templar (Charola temple, chapter house, Renaissance cloisters). 154 A2

Romania
http://romaniatourism.com

Bucovina
Beautiful region in northern Romanian Moldova renowned for a number of 15–16c monasteries and their fresco cycles. Of particular note are Moldovita, Voroneţ and Suceviţa. 17 B6

Bucharest Bucureşti
Capital of Romania with the majority of sites along the Calea Victoriei and centring on Piaţa Revoluţei with 19c Romanian Athenaeum and 1930s Royal Palace housing the National Art Gallery. The infamous 1980s Civic Centre with People's Palace is a symbol of dictatorial aggrandisement. 17 C7

Carpathian Mountains Carpaţii
The beautiful Carpathian Mountains have several ski resorts (Sinaia) and peaks noted for first-rate mountaineering (Făgă raşuiui, Rodnei). Danube Delta Europe's largest marshland, a spectacular nature reserve. Travel in the area is by boat, with Tulcea the starting point for visitors. The Romanian Black Sea Coast has a stretch of resorts (Mamaia, Eforie) between Constanţa and the border, and well-preserved Roman remains in Histria. 17 B6

Transylvania Transilvania
Beautiful and fascinating scenic region of medieval citadels (Timişoara, Sibiu) provides a setting for the haunting image of the legendary Dracula (Sighişoara, Braşov, Bran Castle). Cluj-Napoca is the main town. 17 B5

Russia Rossiya
www.visitrussia.com/

Moscow Moskva
Capital of Russia, with many monuments. Within the Kremlin's red walls are: 15c Cathedral of the Dormition; 16c Cathedral of the Archangel; Cathedral of the Annunciation (icons), Armour Palace. Outside the walls, Red Square has the Lenin Mausoleum and 16c St Basil's Cathedral. There are a number of monasteries (16c Novodevichi). Two superb museums: Tretiakov Art Gallery (Russian); Pushkin Museum of Fine Art (European); also State Historical Museum. Kolomenskoe, once a royal summer retreat, has the Church of the Ascension. 9 E10

Novgorod
One of Russia's oldest towns, centred on 15c Kremlin with St Sophia Cathedral (iconostasis, west door). Two other cathedrals: St Nicholas; St George. Museum of History, Architecture and Art has notable icons and other artefacts. http://visitnovgorod.com 9 C7

Peterhof (Petrovdorets)
Also known as Petrovdorets, Peterhof is a grand palace with numerous pavilions (Monplaisir) set in beautiful parkland interwoven by a system of fountains, cascades and waterways connected to the sea. http://en.peterhofmuseum.ru 9 C6

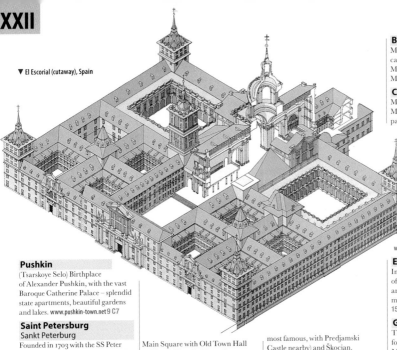

▼ El Escorial (cutaway), Spain

Burgos
Medieval town with Gothic cathedral, Moorish-Gothic Royal Monastery and Charterhouse of Miraflores. **143 B3**

Cáceres
Medieval town with originally Moorish walls and several aristocratic palaces with solar chambers. **155 A4**

Córdoba
Capital of Moorish Spain with a labyrinth of streets and houses with tile-decorated patios. The 8–10c Mezquita is the finest mosque in Spain. A 16c cathedral was added at the centre of the building and a 17c tower replaced the minaret. The old Jewish quarter has 14c synagogue. www.turismodecordoba.org/cordoba-world-heritage-site **156 C3**

El Escorial
Immense Renaissance complex of palatial and monastic buildings and mausoleum of the Spanish monarchs. www.patrimonionacional.es/en/ **151 B3**

Granada
The Alhambra was hill-top palace-fortress of the rulers of the last Moorish kingdom and is the most splendid example of Moorish art and architecture in Spain. The complex has three principal parts: Alcazaba fortress (11c); Casa Real palace (14c, with later Palace of Carlos V); Generalife gardens. Also: Moorish quarter; gypsy quarter; Royal Chapel with good art in the sacristy. www.turgranada.es/en/ **163 A4**

León
Gothic cathedral has notable stained glass. Royal Pantheon commemorates early kings of Castile and León. **142 B1**

Madrid
Capital of Spain, a mainly modern city with 17–19c architecture at its centre around Plaza Mayor. Sights: Royal Palace with lavish apartments and Royal Armoury museum; Descalzas Reales Convent (tapestries and other works). Spain's three leading galleries: Prado (15–18c); Queen Sofia Centre (20c Spanish, Picasso's *Guernica*); Thyssen-Bornemisza Museum (medieval to modern). http://turismomadrid.es/en/ **151 B4**

Oviedo
Gothic cathedral with 12c sanctuary. Three Visigothic (9c) churches: San Julián de los Prados, Santa María del Naranco, San Miguel de Lillo. **141 A5**

Palma
Situated on Mallorca, the largest and most beautiful of the Balearic islands, with an impressive Gothic cathedral and the Sert Studios with works by Miró. www.palma.com **166 B2**

Pushkin
(Tsarskoye Selo) Birthplace of Alexander Pushkin, with the vast Baroque Catherine Palace – splendid state apartments, beautiful gardens and lakes. www.pushkin-town.net **9 C7**

Saint Petersburg
Sankt Peterburg
Founded in 1703 with the SS Peter and Paul Fortress and its cathedral by Peter the Great, and functioning as seat of court and government until 1918. Many of the most famous sights are around elegant Nevski Prospekt. The Hermitage, one of the world's largest and finest art collections is housed in several buildings including the Baroque Winter and Summer palaces. The Mikhailovsky Palace houses the Russian Museum (Russian art). Other sights: neoclassical Admiralty; 19c St Isaac's Cathedral and St Kazan Cathedral; Vasilievsky Island with 18c Menshikov Palace; Alexander Nevsky Monastery; 18c Smolny Convent. www.saint-petersburg.com **9 C7**

Sergiev Posad
(Zagorsk) Trinity St Sergius monastery with 15c cathedral. **9 D11**

Serbia Srbija
www.serbia.travel

Belgrade Beograd
Capital of Serbia. The largely modern city is set between the Danube and Sava rivers. National Museum; Museum of Contemporary Art. To the south there are numerous fascinating medieval monasteries, richly embellished with frescoes. www.tob.rs **127 C2**

Slovakia
Slovenska Republika
http://slovakia.travel/en

Bratislava
Capital of Slovakia, dominated by the castle (Slovak National Museum, good views). Old Town centred on the Main Square with Old Town Hall and Jesuit Church. Many 18–19c palaces (Mirbach Palace, Pálffy Palace, Primate's Palace), churches (Gothic cathedral, Corpus Christi Chapel) and museums (Slovak National Gallery). www.visitbratislava.com **111 A4**

Košice
Charming old town with many Baroque and neoclassical buildings and Gothic cathedral. **12 D4**

Spišské Podhradie
Region, east of the Tatry, full of picturesque medieval towns (Levoča, Kežmarok, Prešov) and architectural monuments (Spišský Castle). **99 B4**

Tatry
Beautiful mountain region. Poprad is an old town with 19c villas. Starý Smokovec is a popular ski resort. See also Poland. **99 B3**

Slovenia Slovenija
www.slovenia.info/en

Istria Istra
Two town centres, Koper and Piran, with medieval and Renaissance squares and Baroque palaces. See also Croatia. **122 B2**

Julian Alps Julijske Alpe
Wonderfully scenic section of the Alps with lakes (Bled, Bohinj), deep valleys (Planica, Vrata) and ski resorts (Kranjska Gora, Bohinjska Bistrica). **122 A2**

Karst Caves
Numerous caves with huge galleries, extraordinary stalactites and stalagmites, and underground rivers. The most spectacular are Postojna (the most famous, with Predjamski Castle nearby) and Škocjan. www.postojnska-jama.eu/en **123 B3**

Ljubljana
Capital of Slovenia. The old town, dominated by the castle (good views), is principally between Prešeren Square and Town Hall (15c, 18c), with the Three Bridges and colonnaded market. Many Baroque churches (cathedral, St Jacob, St Francis, Ursuline) and palaces (Bishop's Palace, Seminary, Gruber Palace). Also: 17c Križanke church and monastery complex; National Gallery and Modern Gallery show Slovene art. www.visitljubljana.com/en/visitors **123 A3**

Spain España
www.spain.info/en_GB/

Ávila
Medieval town with 2km-long 11c walls and 12c cathedral. Pilgrimage site to shrines to St Teresa of Ávila (Convent of Santa Teresa, Convent of the Incarnation). www.avilaturismo.com/en **150 B3**

Barcelona
Showcase of Gothic ('Barri Gòtic': cathedral; Santa María del Mar; mansions on Carrer de Montcada) and *modernista* architecture ('Eixample' area with Manzana de la Discòrdia; Sagrada Familia, Güell Park, La Pedrera). Many elegant boulevards (La Rambla, Passeig de Gràcia). Museums: National Art Museum of Catalonia, Catalan Archaeology, Picasso Museum, Miró Museum, Tàpies Museum. Nearby: monastery of Montserrat (Madonna); Figueres (Dali Museum). www.barcelonaturisme.com/wv3/en **147 C3**

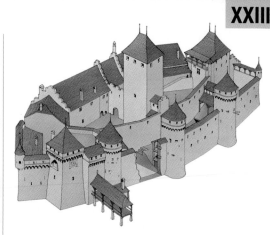

Picos de Europa
Mountain range with river gorges and peaks topped by Visigothic and Romanesque churches. 142 A2

Pyrenees
Unspoiled mountain range with beautiful landscape and villages full of Romanesque architecture (cathedral of Jaca). The Ordesa National Park has many waterfalls and canyons. 144–145

Salamanca
Delightful old city with some uniquely Spanish architecture: Renaissance Plateresque is famously seen on 16c portal of the university (founded 1218); Baroque Churrigueresque on 18c Plaza Mayor; both styles at the Convent of San Esteban. Also: Romanesque Old Cathedral; Gothic-Plateresque New Cathedral; House of Shells. www.salamanca.es/en 150 B2

Santiago di Compostela
Medieval city with many churches and religious institutions. The famous pilgrimage to the shrine of St James the Apostle ends here in the magnificent cathedral, originally Romanesque with many later elements (18c Baroque façade). www.santiagoturismo.com 140 B2

Segovia
Old town set on a rock with a 1c Roman aqueduct. Also: 16c Gothic cathedral; Alcázar (13–15c, rebuilt 19c); 12-sided 13c Templar Church of Vera Cruz. 151 B3

Seville Sevilla
City noted for festivals and flamenco. The world's largest Gothic cathedral (15c) retains the Orange Court and minaret of a mosque, which became its bell tower. The Alcázar is a fine example of Moorish architecture. The massive 18c tobacco factory, now part of the university, was the setting for Bizet's *Carmen*. Barrio de Santa Cruz is the old Jewish quarter with narrow streets and white houses. Casa de Pilatos (15–16c) has a fine domestic patio. The Museum of Fine Arts is in a former convent. Nearby: Roman Italica with amphitheatre. www.visitasevilla.es/en 162 A2

Tarragona
The city and its surroundings have some of Spain's best-preserved Roman heritage, including amphitheatre and Praetorium tower. Also: Gothic cathedral (cloister). www.tarragonaturisme.cat/en 147 C2

Toledo
Historic city with Moorish, Jewish and Christian sights. The small 11c mosque of El Cristo de la Luz is one of the earliest in Spain. Two synagogues have been preserved: Santa María la Blanca; El Tránsito. Churches: San Juan de los Reyes; Gothic cathedral (good artworks). El Greco's *Burial of the Count of Orgaz* is in the Church of Santo Tomé. More of his works are in

the El Greco house and, with other art, in Hospital de Santa Cruz. 151 C3

Valencia
The old town has houses and palaces with elaborate façades. Also: Gothic cathedral and Lonja de la Seda (Silk Exchange). www.visitvalencia.com/en 159 B3

Zaragoza
Town notable for Moorish architecture (11c Aljafería Palace). The Basilica de Nuestra Señora del Pilar, one of two cathedrals, is highly venerated. www.zaragoza.es/turismo 153 A3

Sweden Sverige
https://visitsweden.com

Abisko
Popular resort in the Swedish part of Lapland set in an inspiring landscape of lakes and mountains. www.visitabisko.com 194 B9

Gothenburg Göteborg
Largest port in Sweden, the historic centre has 17–18c Dutch architectural character (Kronhuset). The Art Museum has interesting Swedish works. www.goteborg.com/en 60 B1

Gotland
Island with Sweden's most popular beach resorts (Ljugarn) and unspoiled countryside with churches in Baltic Gothic style (Dahlem, Bunge). Visby is a pleasant walled medieval town. http://gotland.com/en 57 C4

Lappland (Swedish)
Swedish part of Lappland with 18c Arvidsjaur the oldest preserved Sámi village. Jokkmokk is a Sámi cultural centre, Abisko a popular resort in fine scenery. Also Finland, Norway. www.kirunalapland.se 192–193

Lund
Charming university city with medieval centre and a fine 12c Romanesque cathedral (14c astronomical clock, carved tombs). www.visitlund.se/en 61 D3

Malmö
Old town centre set among canals and parks dominated by a red-brick castle (museums) and a vast market square with Town Hall and Gothic Church of St Peter. www.malmotown.com/en 61 D3

Mora
Delightful village on the shores of Siljan Lake in the heart of the Dalarna region, home to folklore and traditional crafts. 50 A1

Stockholm
Capital of Sweden built on a number of islands. The Old Town is largely on three islands with 17–18c houses, Baroque Royal Castle (apartments and museums), Gothic cathedral, parliament. Riddarholms church has tombs of the monarchy. Museums include: National Museum; Modern Museum (one of world's best modern collections); Nordiska Museet (cultural history); open-air Skansen

(Swedish houses). Baroque Drottningholm Castle is the residence of the monarchy. www.visitstockholm.com 57 A4

Swedish Lakes
Beautiful region around the Vättern and Vänern Lakes. Siljan Lake is in the Dalarna region where folklore and crafts are preserved (Leksand, Mora, Rättvik). 55 B4

Uppsala
Appealing university town with a medieval centre around the massive Gothic cathedral. www.destinationuppsala.se/en 51 C4

Switzerland Schweiz
www.myswitzerland.com/en-gb/home.html

Alps
The most popular Alpine region is the Berner Oberland with the town of Interlaken a starting point for exploring the large number of picturesque peaks (Jungfrau). The valleys of the Graubünden have famous ski resorts (Davos, St Moritz). Zermatt lies below the most recognizable Swiss peak, the Matterhorn. 119 A4

Basle Basel
Medieval university town with Romanesque-Gothic cathedral (tomb of Erasmus). Superb collections: Art Museum; Museum of Contemporary Art. www.basel.com/en 106 B2

Bern
Capital of Switzerland. Medieval centre has fountains, characteristic streets (Spitalgasse) and tower-gates. The Bärengraben is famed for its bears. Also: Gothic cathedral; good Fine Arts Museum. www.bern.com/en 106 C2

Geneva Genève
The historic area is centred on the Romanesque cathedral and Place du Bourg du Four. Excellent collections: Art and History Museum; new Museum of Modern and Contemporary Art. On the lake shore: splendid medieval Château de Chillon. www.geneve.com 118 A3

▲ Château de Chillon, Switzerland

Interlaken
Starting point for excursions to the most delightful part of the Swiss Alps, the Bernese Oberland, with Grindelwald and Lauterbrunnen – one of the most thrilling valleys leading up to the ski resort of Wengen with views on the Jungfrau. www.interlaken.ch 106 C2

Lucerne Luzern
On the beautiful shores of Vierwaldstättersee, a charming medieval town of white houses on narrow streets and of wooden bridges (Kapellbrücke, Spreuerbrücke). It is centred on the Kornmarkt with the Renaissance Old Town Hall and Am Rhyn-Haus (Picasso collection). www.luzern.com/en 106 C1

Zürich
Set on Zürichsee, the old quarter is around Niederdorf with 15c cathedral. Gothic Fraumünster has stained glass by Chagall. Museums: Swiss National Museum (history); Art Museum (old and modern masters); Rietberg Museum (non-European cultures). www.zuerich.com/en 107 B3

Turkey Türkiye
www.goturkeytourism.com

Istanbul
Divided by the spectacular Bosphorus, the stretch of water that separates Europe from Asia, the historic district is surrounded by the Golden Horn, Sea of Marmara and the 5c wall of Theodosius. Major sights: 6c Byzantine church of St Sophia (converted first to a mosque in 1453 and then a museum in 1934); 15c Topkapi Palace; treasury and Archaeological Museum; 17c Blue Mosque; 19c Bazaar; 16c Süleymaniye Mosque; 12c Kariye Camii; European district with Galata Tower and 19c Dolmabahçe Palace. http://en.istanbul.com 186 A3

Ukraine Ukraina
www.ukraine.com

Kiev Kyïv
Capital of Ukraine, known for its cathedral (11c, 17c) with Byzantine frescoes and mosaics. The Monastery of the Caves has churches, monastic buildings and catacombs.
www.kiev.info **13 C9**

United Kingdom
www.visitbritain.com

England
www.visitengland.com

Bath
Elegant spa town with notable 18c architecture: Circus, Royal Crescent, Pulteney Bridge, Assembly Rooms, Pump Room. Also: well-preserved Roman baths; superb Perpendicular Gothic Bath Abbey. Nearby: Elizabethan Longleat House; exceptional 18c landscaped gardens at Stourhead. https://visitbath.co.uk **43 A4**

Brighton
Resort with a sea-front of Georgian, Regency and Victorian buildings, Palace Pier, i360 observation tower, and old town of narrow lanes. The main sight is the Oriental-style Royal Pavilion. Nearby: South Downs National Park.
www.visitbrighton.com **44 C3**

Bristol
Old port city with the fascinating Floating Harbour. Major sights include Gothic 13–14c Church of St Mary Redcliffe, SS Great Britain and 19c Clifton Suspension Bridge. http://visitbristol.co.uk **43 A4**

Cambridge
City with university founded in the early 13c. Peterhouse (1284) is the oldest college. Most famous colleges were founded in 14–16c: Queen's, King's (with the superb Perpendicular Gothic 15–16c King's College Chapel), St John's (with famous 19c Bridge of Sighs), Trinity, Clare, Gonville and Caius, Magdalene. Museums: excellent Fitzwilliam Museum (classical, medieval, old masters). Kettle's Yard (20c British). www.visitcambridge.org **45 A4**

Canterbury
Medieval city and old centre of Christianity. The Norman-Gothic cathedral has many sights and was a major medieval pilgrimage site (as related in Chaucer's *Canterbury Tales*). St Augustine, sent to convert the English in 597, founded St Augustine's Abbey, now in ruins.
www.canterbury.co.uk **45 B5**

Chatsworth
One of the richest aristocratic country houses in England (largely 17c) set in a large landscaped park. The palatial interior has some 175 richly furnished rooms and a major art collection. www.chatsworth.org **40 B2**

Chester
Charming medieval city with complete walls. The Norman-Gothic cathedral has several abbey buildings. www.visitcheshire.com **38 A4**

Cornish Coast
Scenic landscape of cliffs and sandy beaches with picturesque villages (Fowey, Mevagissey). St Ives has the Tate Gallery with work of the St Ives Group. St Michael's Mount is reached by causeway at low tide. www.visitcornwall.com **42 B1**

Dartmoor
Beautiful wilderness area in Devon with tors and its own breed of wild pony as well as free-ranging cattle and sheep. www.dartmoor.co.uk **42 B3**

Durham
Historic city with England's finest Norman cathedral and a castle, both placed majestically on a rock above the river.
www.thisisdurham.com **37 B5**

Eden Project
Centre showing the diversity of plant life on the planet, built in a disused clay pit. Two biomes, one with Mediterranean and Southern African focus and the larger featuring a waterfall, river and tropical trees plants and flowers. Outdoors also features plantations including bamboo and tea. www.edenproject.com **42 B2**

Hadrian's Wall
Built to protect the northernmost border of the Roman Empire in the 2c AD, the walls originally extended some 120km with castles every mile and 16 forts. Best-preserved walls around Hexam; forts at Housesteads and Chesters.
http://hadrianswallcountry.co.uk **37 A4**

Lake District
Beautiful landscape of lakes (Windermere, Coniston) and England's high peaks (Scafell Pike, Skiddaw, Old Man), famous for its poets, particularly Wordsworth.
www.lakedistrict.gov.uk **36 B3**

Leeds Castle
One of the oldest and most romantic English castles, standing in the middle of a lake. Most of the present appearance dates from 19c.
www.leeds-castle.com **45 B4**

Lincoln
Old city perched on a hill with narrow streets, majestically dominated by the Norman-Gothic cathedral and castle.
www.visitlincolnshire.com **40 B3**

Liverpool
City on site of port founded in 1207 and focused around 1846 Albert Dock, now a heritage attraction. Croxteth Hall and Country Park; Speke Hall; Sudley House; Royal Liver Building; Liverpool Cathedral; Walker Art Gallery; Tate Liverpool; University of Liverpool Art Gallery. www.visitliverpool.com **38 A4**

London
Capital of UK and Europe's largest city. To the east of the medieval heart of the city – now the largely modern financial district and known as the City of London – is the Tower of London (11c White Tower, Crown Jewels) and 1880s Tower Bridge. The popular heart of the city and its entertainment is the West End, around Piccadilly Circus, Leicester Square and Trafalgar Square (Nelson's Column). Many sights of political and royal power: Whitehall (Banqueting House, 10 Downing Street, Horse Guards); Neo-Gothic Palace of Westminster (Houses of Parliament) with Big Ben; The Mall leading to Buckingham Palace (royal residence, famous ceremony of the Changing of the Guard). Numerous churches include: 13–16c Gothic Westminster Abbey (many tombs, Henry VII's Chapel); Wren's Baroque St Paul's Cathedral, St Mary-le-Bow, spire of St Bride's, St Stephen Walbrook. Museums of world fame: British Museum (prehistory, oriental and classical antiquity, medieval); Victoria and Albert Museum (decorative arts); National Gallery (old masters to 19c); National Portrait Gallery (historic and current British portraiture); Tate – Britain and Modern; Science Museum; Natural History Museum. Madame Tussaud's waxworks museum is hugely popular. Other sights include: London Eye, Kensington Palace; Greenwich with Old Royal Observatory (Greenwich meridian), Baroque Royal Naval College, Palladian Queen's House; Tudor Hampton Court Palace; Syon House. Nearby: Windsor Castle (art collection, St George's Chapel). www.visitlondon.com **44 B3**

Longleat
One of the earliest and finest Elizabethan palaces in England. The palace is richly decorated. Some of the grounds have been turned into a

◀ Salisbury Cathedral, England

pleasure park, with the Safari Park, the first of its kind outside Africa. www.longleat.co.uk **43 A4**

Manchester

Founded on a Roman settlement of 79AD and a main player in the Industrial Revolution. Victorian Gothic Town Hall; Royal Exchange; Cathedral. Many museums including Imperial War Museum North, Lowry Centre and Manchester Art Gallery. www.visitmanchester.com **40 B1**

Newcastle upon Tyne

A key player in the Industrial Revolution with 12th century cathedral and many museums as well as strong railway heritage. www.newcastlegateshead.com **37 B5**

Norwich

Medieval quarter has half-timbered houses. 15c castle and gallery. Many medieval churches include the Norman-Gothic cathedral. www.visitnorwich.co.uk **41 C5**

Oxford

Old university city. Earliest colleges date from 13c: University College; Balliol; Merton. 14–16c colleges include: New College; Magdalen; Christ Church (perhaps the finest). Other buildings: Bodleian Library; Radcliffe Camera; Sheldonian Theatre; cathedral. Good museums: Ashmolean Museum (antiquity to 20c); Museum of the History of Science; Museum of Modern Art; Christ Church Picture Gallery (14–17c). Nearby: outstanding 18c Blenheim Palace. www.experienceoxfordshire.org **44 B2**

▼ Radcliffe Camera, Oxford, England

Petworth

House (17c) with one of the finest country-house art collections (old masters), set in a huge landscaped park. www.nationaltrust.org.uk **44 C3**

Salisbury

Pleasant old city with a magnificent 13c cathedral built in an unusually unified Gothic style. Nearby: Wilton House. www.visitwiltshire.co.uk **44 B2**

Stonehenge

Some 4000 years old, one of the most famous and haunting Neolithic monuments in Europe. Many other Neolithic sites are nearby. www.english-heritage.org.uk **44 B2**

Stourhead

Early 18c palace famous for its grounds, one of the finest examples of neoclassical landscaped gardening, consisting of a lake surrounded by numerous temples. www.nationaltrust.org.uk **43 A4**

Stratford-upon-Avon

Old town of Tudor and Jacobean half-timbered houses, famed as the birth and burial place of William Shakespeare and home of the Royal Shakespeare Company. www.visitstratforduponavon.co.uk/visitors-guide **44 A2**

Wells

Charming city with beautiful 12–16c cathedral (west facade, scissor arches, chapter house, medieval clock). Also Bishop's Palace; Vicar's Close. www.wellssomerset.com **43 A4**

Winchester

Historic city with 11–16c cathedral. Also: 13c Great Hall, Winchester College, St Cross almshouses. Western gateway to the South Downs National Park. www.visitwinchester.co.uk **44 B2**

York

Attractive medieval city surrounded by well-preserved walls with magnificent Gothic 13–15c Minster. Museums: York City Art Gallery (14–19c); Jorvik Viking Centre. Nearby: Castle Howard. www.visityork.org **40 B2**

Antrim Coast

Spectacular coast with diverse scenery of glens (Glenarm, Glenariff), cliffs (Murlough Bay) and the famous Giant's Causeway, consisting of some 40,000 basalt columns. Carricke-fergus Castle is the largest and best-preserved Norman castle in Ireland. http://antrimcoastandglensaonb.ccght.org http://causewaycoastaonb.ccght.org **27 A4**

Belfast

Capital of Northern Ireland. Sights: Donegall Square with 18c Town Hall; neo-Romanesque Protestant cathedral; University Square; Ulster Museum (European painting). https://visitbelfast.com **27 B5**

Giant's Causeway

Spectacular and unique rock formations in the North Antrim coast, formed by volcanic activity 50–60 million years ago. World Heritage Site. www.nationaltrust.org.uk **27 A4**

Edinburgh

Capital of Scotland, built on volcanic hills. The medieval Old Town is dominated by the castle set high on a volcanic rock (Norman St Margaret's Chapel, state apartments, Crown Room). Holyrood House (15c and 17c) has lavishly decorated state apartments and the ruins of Holyrood Abbey (remains of Scottish mon-archs). The 15c cathedral has the Crown Spire and Thistle Chapel. The New Town has good Georgian architecture (Charlotte Square, Georgian House). Excellent mus-eums: Scottish National Portrait Gallery, National Gallery of Scotland; Scottish National Gallery of Modern Art. **35 C4**

▼ The facade of Basilica San Pietro, Vatican City

Glamis Castle

In beautiful, almost flat landscaped grounds, 14c fortress, rebuilt 17c, gives a fairy-tale impression. www.glamis-castle.co.uk **35 B5**

Glasgow

Scotland's largest city, with centre around George Square and 13–15c Gothic cathedral. Fine art collections: Glasgow Museum and Art Gallery; Hunterian Gallery; Burrell Collection; Kelvingrove Art Gallery and Museum. **35 C3**

Loch Ness

In the heart of the Highlands, the lake forms part of the scenic Great Glen running from Inverness to Fort William. Famous as home of the fabled Loch Ness Monster (exhibition at Drumnadrochit). Nearby: ruins of 14–16c Urquhart Castle. www.lochness.com **32 D2**

Caernarfon

Town dominated by a magnificent 13c castle, one of a series built by Edward I in Wales (others include Harlech, Conwy, Beaumaris, Caerphilly). www.caernarfon.com **38 A2**

Cardiff

Capital of Wales, most famous for its medieval castle, restored 19c in Greek, Gothic and Oriental styles. Also: National Museum and Gallery. www.visitcardiff.com **39 C3**

Vatican City Città del Vaticano

Independent state within Rome. On Piazza San Pietro is the 15–16c Renaissance-Baroque Basilica San Pietro (Michelangelo's dome and *Pietà*), the world's most important Roman Catholic church. The Vatican Palace contains the Vatican Museums with many fine art treasures including Michelangelo's frescoes in the Sistine Chapel. www.museivaticani.va **168 B2**

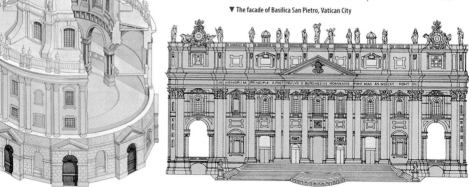

Legend to road maps
pages 26–200

⑦ ⑧	Motorway with junctions – full, restricted access
◇ ◇	services, rest or parking area
	tunnel
	under construction
	Toll motorway – with toll barrier
	Pre-pay motorway – 'Vignette' must be purchased before travel
	Principal trunk highway – single / dual carriageway
	Tunnel
	Under construction
	Other main highway – single / dual carriageway
	Other important road
	Other road
E25	European road number
A49	Motorway number
135	National road number
	Distances – in kilometres
143	major
28	minor
Col Bayard 1248	Mountain pass
	Scenic route, gradient – arrow points uphill
	Principal railway
	tunnel
	Ferry route
	Short ferry route
	International boundary
	National boundary
	National park
	Natural park
ORLY ✈	Airport
AQUEDUC ROMAINE	Ancient monument
⚐	Beach
CHÂTEAU DU LUDE	Castle or house
GROTTE DU GRAND ROC	Cave
VULCANIA	Other place of interest
GIVERNY	Park or garden
ST CHRISTOL	Religious building
	Ski resort
DISNEYLAND PARIS	Theme park
VERSAILLES	World Heritage site
1754	Spot height
Bordeaux	World Heritage town
Toulouse	Town of tourist interest
■ ●	Town with Low Emission Zone

Route planning maps
pages 2–23

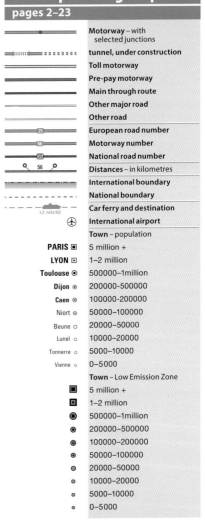

	Motorway – with selected junctions
	tunnel, under construction
	Toll motorway
	Pre-pay motorway
	Main through route
	Other major road
	Other road
25	European road number
56	Motorway number
55	National road number
56	Distances – in kilometres
	International boundary
	National boundary
LE HAVRE	Car ferry and destination
✈	International airport
	Town – population
PARIS ■	5 million +
LYON ▣	1–2 million
Toulouse ◉	500000–1million
Dijon ⊙	200000-500000
Caen ◎	100000-200000
Niort ⊙	50000–100000
Beune ○	20000–50000
Lunel ○	10000–20000
Tonnerre ○	5000–10000
Vienne ○	0–5000
	Town – Low Emission Zone
■	5 million +
▣	1–2 million
◉	500000–1million
◉	200000–500000
◎	100000–200000
◉	50000–100000
○	20000–50000
○	10000–20000
○	5000–10000
○	0–5000

Scale · pages 2–23
1:4 526 000, 1 cm = 45.3 km, 1 in = 71.4 miles

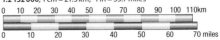

0 20 40 60 80 100 120 140 160 180 200 km

0 20 40 60 80 100 120 140 mile

Scale · pages 26–181
1:1 066 000, 1 cm = 10.7 km, 1 in = 16.8 miles

0 10 20 30 40 50 km

0 5 10 15 20 25 30 miles

Scale · pages 182–200
1:2 132 000, 1 cm = 21.3 km, 1 in = 33.7 miles

0 10 20 30 40 50 60 70 80 90 100 110km

0 10 20 30 40 50 60 70 miles

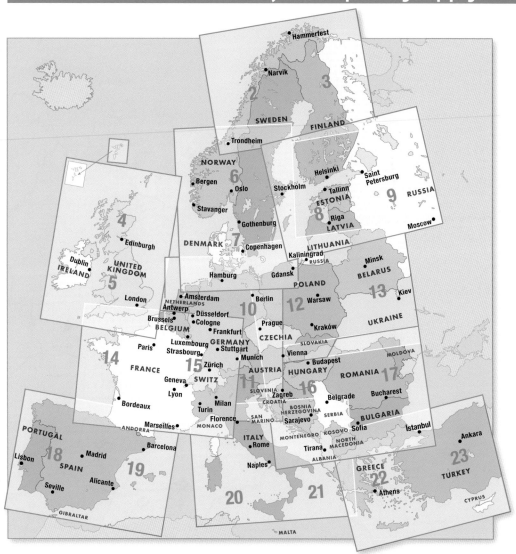

Top tips for staying safe

1 Plan your route before you go.
That includes the journey you make to reach your destination and any excursions or local journeys you make while you're there.

2 Take extra care at junctions when you're driving on the 'right side' of the road. Be careful if you are reversing out of a parking space on the street, as things will feel in the wrong place. If driving in a group, involve everybody in a quick 'junction safety check'. Having everyone call out a catchphrase such as "DriLL DriLL DriLL" (Driver Look Left) at junctions

and roundabouts is a small but potentially life-saving habit.

3 Remember that you will be subject to the same laws as local drivers. Claiming ignorance will not be accepted as an excuse.

4 Take fatigue seriously. The European motorway network makes it easy to cover big distances but you should also make time for proper breaks (15 minutes every two hours). If possible, share the driving and set daily limits for driving hours.

5 Expect the unexpected. Styles of driving in your destination country are likely to be very different from those you know in the UK. Drive defensively and certainly don't get involved in any altercations on the road.

6 Drink-driving limits across Europe are generally lower than those in the UK.
Bear this in mind if you're flying to a destination before hiring a car and plan to have a drink on the plane. Drivers who cause collisions due to drinking are likely to find their insurance policy will not cover them.

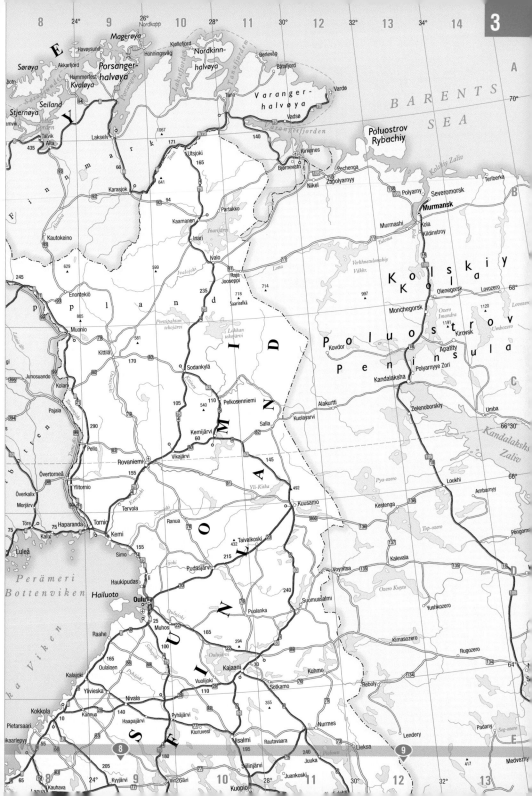

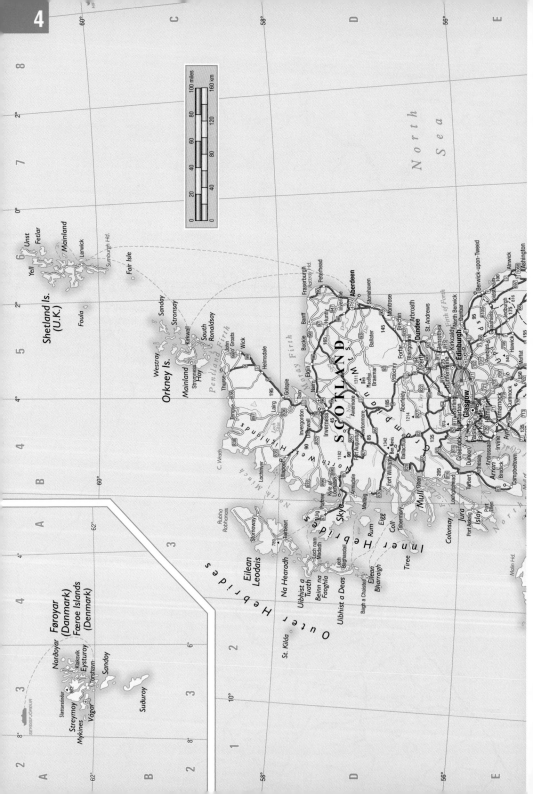

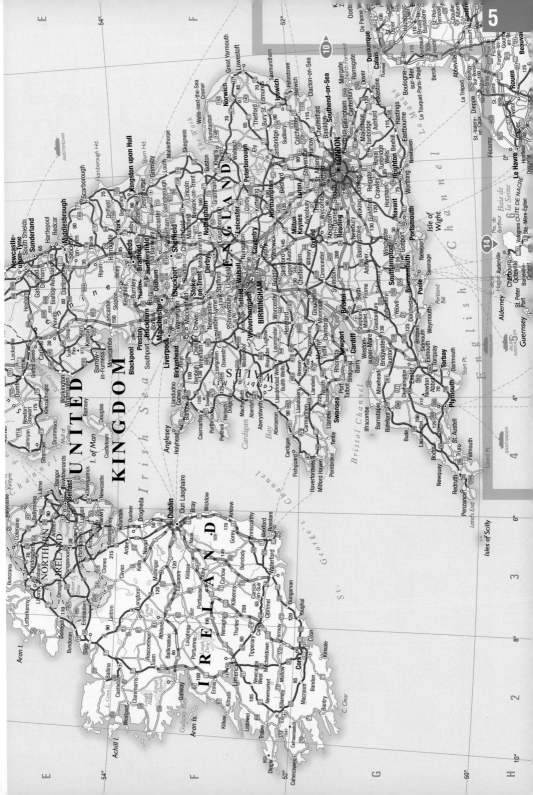

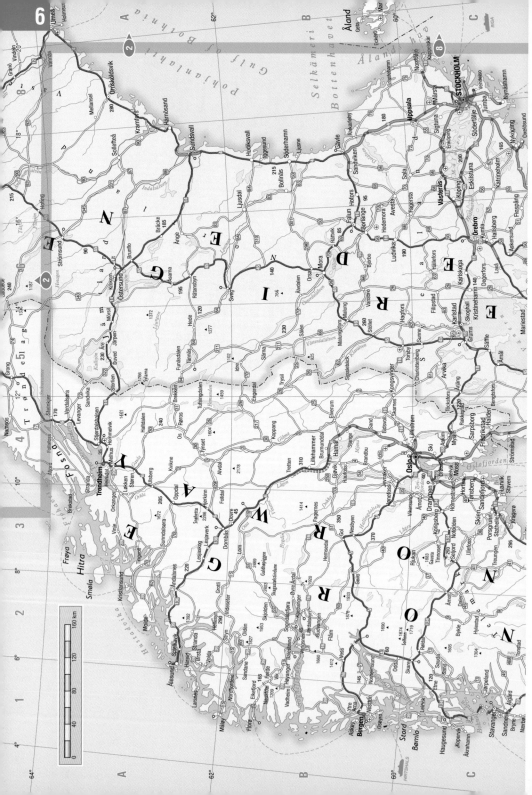

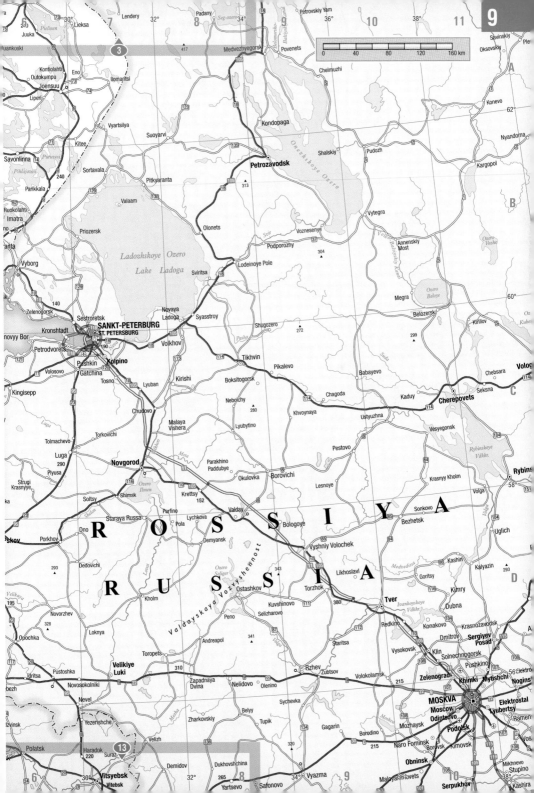

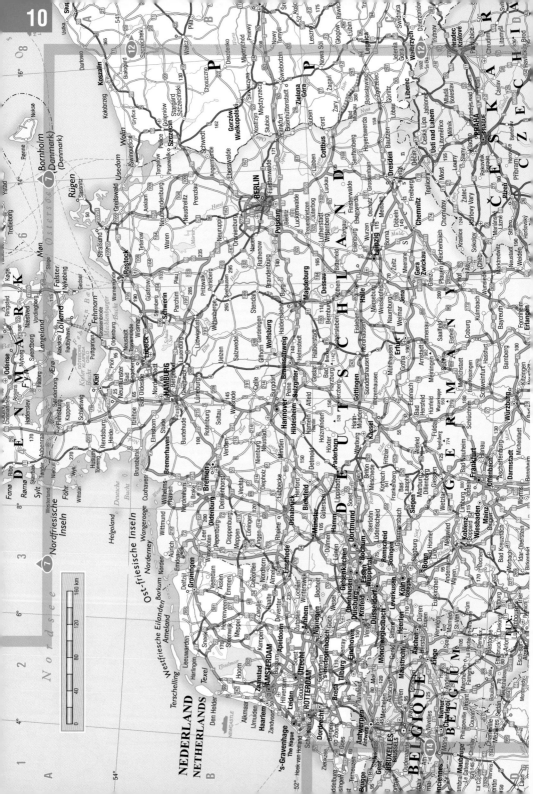

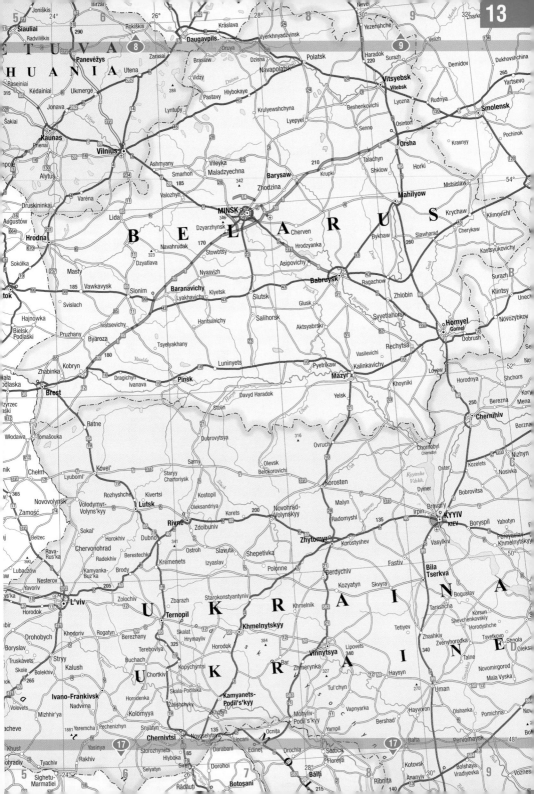

COSTA VERDE

COSTA MONTAÑESA

A Coruña · Ferrol · Ortigueira · Ribadeo · Luarca · **Gijón** · **Xixón** · Villaviciosa · Llanes · San Vicente de la Barquera · **Santander** · C. de Ajo · Castro Urdiales · Getxo · **Bilbao**

Vimianzo · C. Touriñán · Carballo · Betanzos · Baamonde · Mondoñedo · Tineo · Salas · **Oviedo** · Pola de Siero · Mieres · Picos de Europa · 2648 · Torrelavega · **Barakaldo** · Amurrio · Durango

Corcubión · C. Fisterra · **Santiago de Compostela** · Ordes · Lugo · Cangas de Narcea · Grado · Pola de Lena · Langreo · Riaño · Potes · Reinosa · 105 · Oña · Orduña

Muros · Noia · Padrón · Melide · Becerreá · Sarria · Villablino · Villafranca del Bierzo · La Pola de Gordón · Cervera de Pisuerga · Osorno · Briviesca · Miranda de Ebro · Santo Domingo de la Calzada

Vilagarcía de Arousa · A Estrada · Lalín · Chantada · **León** · La Robla · Saldaña · **Burgos** · Salas de los Infantes

Marín · Pontevedra · O Carballiño · Monforte de Lemos · Ponferrada · Astorga · Sahagún · Palencia · Aranda de Duero · Burgo de Osma · **Soria** · Picos de Urbión · 2228

Vigo · Redondela · Celanova · **Ourense** · Pobra de Trives · La Bañeza · Benavente · Valencia de Don Juan · Villalón de Campos · Medina de Rioseco · Santo Domingo de Silos

Baiona · Ponteareas · Tui · Valença · Xinzo de Limia · Verín · A Gudiña · Bragança · Alcañices · Zamora · Toro · **Valladolid** · Cuéllar · San Esteban de Gormaz · Medinaceli

Caminha · Viana do Castelo · Chaves · Vila Pouca de Aguiar · Mirandela · Miranda do Douro · Medina del Campo · Olmedo · Segovia · Villacastín · 2430 · El Molar · **Guadalajara** · Brihuega

Braga · Guimarães · Murça · Vila Real · Fermoselle · Ledesma · **Salamanca** · Arévalo · Peñaranda de Bracamonte · **Ávila** · **MADRID** · **Alcalá de Henares**

Porto · Vila Nova de Gaia · Amarante · Peso da Régua · Lamego · Vitigudino · La Fuente de San Esteban · Alba de Tormes · El Escorial · **Legañés** · **Getafe** · Arganda

Ovar · Oliveira de Azeméis · São João da Madeira · Abergaria-a-Velha · Viseu da Beira · Celorico da Beira · Pinhel · Ciudad Rodrigo · Béjar · El Barco de Ávila · San Martín de Valdeiglesias · **Parla** · Aranjuez · Tarancón

Aveiro · Águeda · Tondela · Mangualde · Guarda · Vilar Formoso · Fuentes de Oñoro · Pico Almanzor · 2592 · Arenas de San Pedro · Navalcarnero · Illescas · **Toledo** · Ocaña

Mira · Mealhada · Belmonte · Fundão · Penamacôr · Plasencia · Coria · Navalmoral de la Mata · Talavera de la Reina · Maqueda · Madridejos · La Almarcha

Coimbra · Figueira da Foz · Miranda do Corvo · Penacova · Hoyos · Belvis de la Jara · Navahermosa · Orgaz · Quintanar de la Orden · Pedro Muñoz

Leiria · Pombal · Proença-a-Nova · Castelo Branco · Alcántara · Trujillo · Guadalupe · Logrosán · Malagón · Alcázar de San Juan · Tomelloso

Peniche · Caldas da Rainha · Tomar · Abrantes · Gavião · Nisa · Valencia de Alcántara · Arronches · **Cáceres** · Zorita · Miajadas · Ciudad Real · Daimiel · Manzanares

Torres Vedras · Santarém · Almeirim · Portalegre · Ponte de Sor · Monforte · Campo Maior · Almendralejo · Villanueva de la Serena · Almadén · Valdepeñas · Villahermosa

C. Carvoeiro · Torres Novas · Estremoz · Elvas · **Badajoz** · **Mérida** · Don Benito · Castuera · Almodóvar del Campo · **Puertollano** · Villanueva de los Infantes

Mafra · Sintra · C. da Roca · **LISBOA** / **LISBON** · Vendas Novas · Montemor-o-Novo · **Évora** · Olivenza · Villafranca de los Barros · Hinojosa del Duque · Pozoblanco · Andújar · Bailén · Linares · La Carolina

Estoril · Cascais · COSTA DO SOL · Almada · Barreiro · Setúbal · Alcácer do Sal · Viana do Alentejo · Reguengos de Monsaraz · Jerez de los Caballeros · Zafra · Los Santos de Maimona · Llerena · Fuente Obejuna · Espiel · Montoro · **Úbeda** · Villacarrillo

C. Espichel · B. de Setúbal · Grândola · Ferreira do Alentejo · Beja · Moura · Barrancos · Fregenal de la Sierra · Azuaga · Peñarroya-Pueblonuevo · **Córdoba** · Baeza · **Jaén** · Huelma · Cúllar de Baza

Santiago do Cacém · Sines · C. de Sines · Aljustrel · Mértola · Cortegana · Aracena · Posadas · Castro del Río · Martos · Alcalá la Real · **Granada** · Mulhacén · 3478

Cercal · Odemira · Monchique · Vila Real de Santo António · Valverde del Camino · Nerva · Lora del Río · La Carlota · Montilla · Baena · Priego de Córdoba · Santa Fe · Guadix

Vila do Bispo · C. de São Vicente · Sagres · Lagos · Portimão · Albufeira · Loulé · Faro · Olhão · Tavira · Ayamonte · **Huelva** · La Palma del Condado · Almonte · Sanlúcar la Mayor · Carmona · Écija · Lucena · Loja · Alcalá la Real · Archidona · Antequera · Alhama de Granada · Órgiva · Berja · **Almería**

G. de Cádiz · COSTA DE LA LUZ · Dos Hermanas · **Sevilla** / **Seville** · Utrera · Morón de la Frontera · Osuna · Estepa · Campillos · Vélez Málaga · Motril · Adra

Lebrija · Arcos de la Frontera · Ronda · **Málaga** · Torremolinos · Fuengirola

Sanlúcar de Barrameda · El Puerto de Santa María · **Jerez de la Frontera** · Medina Sidonia · Coín · Marbella · COSTA DEL SOL

Cádiz · San Fernando · Puerto Real · Chiclana de la Frontera · Vejer de la Frontera · San Roque · Estepona

ISLAS CANARIAS · C. Trafalgar · Tarifa · **Algeciras** · La Línea de la Concepción · Gibraltar (U.K.) · Ceuta (Esp.) (Spain) · Alborán

Str. of Gibraltar · C. Spartel · **Tanger** · Tangier · Pico de Europa

MELILLA · AL HOCEIMA · NADOR · TANGER

0 · 40 · 80 · 120 · 160 km

POR TU GAL · **ESPAÑA** · **ESPAÑA** · **CASTILLA** · **Castilla y León** · **Cordillera Cantábrica**

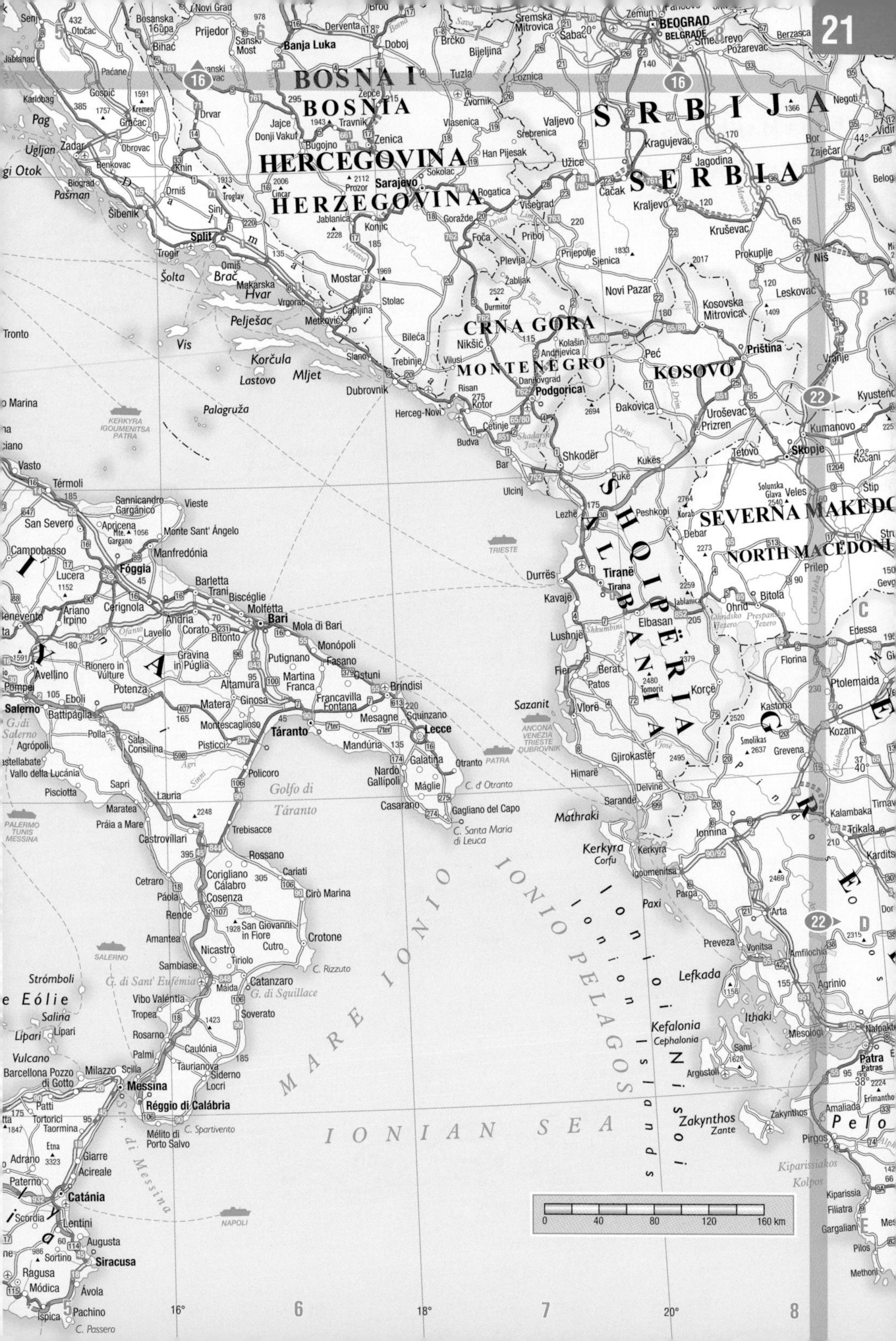

BOSNA I HERCEGOVINA
BOSNIA HERZEGOVINA
SRBIJA
SERBIA
CRNA GORA
MONTENEGRO
KOSOVO
SHQIPËRIA
ALBANIA
SEVERNA MAKEDONIJA
NORTH MACEDONIA
MARE IONIO
IONIO PELAGOS
IONIAN SEA
Ionioi Nisoi
Ionian Islands
Golfo di Táranto
Str. di Messina
G. di Sant' Eufémia
G. di Squillace
G. di Salerno
Kiparissiakos Kolpos
Dalmacija
Novi Grad
Senj
Otočac
Bosanska Krupa
Bihać
Prijedor
Sanski Most
Banja Luka
Derventa
Doboj
Brčko
Bijeljina
Sremska Mitrovica
Šabac
Zemun
BEOGRAD
BELGRADE
Smederevo
Požarevac
Berzasca
Jablanac
Pag
Gospić
Karlobag
Gračac
Zadar
Ugljan
Dugi Otok
Obrovac
Benkovac
Biograd
Pašman
Knin
Drniš
Šibenik
Sinj
Split
Trogir
Šolta
Brač
Omiš
Makarska
Hvar
Vis
Pelješac
Korčula
Lastovo
Mljet
Palagruža
Drvar
Jajce
Donji Vakuf
Bugojno
Travnik
Zenica
Žepce
Tuzla
Zvornik
Vlasenica
Srebrenica
Han Pijesak
Sokolac
Sarajevo
Prozor
Jablanica
Konjic
Mostar
Stolac
Čapljina
Metković
Vrgorac
Bileća
Trebinje
Slano
Dubrovnik
Herceg-Novi
Rogatica
Goražde
Foča
Višegrad
Priboj
Prijepolje
Pljevlja
Žabljak
Durmitor
Nikšić
Vilusi
Risan
Kotor
Cetinje
Budva
Bar
Ulcinj
Podgorica
Danilovgrad
Kolašin
Andrijevica
Sjenica
Novi Pazar
Peć
Đakovica
Prizren
Uroševac
Priština
Kosovska Mitrovica
Loznica
Valjevo
Užice
Čačak
Kraljevo
Kragujevac
Jagodina
Kruševac
Prokuplje
Niš
Leskovac
Vranje
Bor
Zaječar
Negotin
Kyustendil
Kumanovo
Skopje
Tetovo
Kočani
Štip
Veles
Solunska Glava
Prilep
Bitola
Ohrid
Ohridsko Jezero
Prespansko Jezero
Debar
Korab
Edessa
Florina
Ptolemaida
Kastoria
Kozani
Grevena
Smolikas
Kalambaka
Trikala
Karditsa
Ioannina
Arta
Preveza
Vonitsa
Amfilochia
Agrinio
Lefkada
Ithaki
Kefalonia
Cephalonia
Argostoli
Sami
Mesologi
Nafpaktos
Patra
Patras
Erimantho
Amaliada
Pirgos
Zakynthos
Zante
Kiparissia
Filiatra
Gargaliani
Pilos
Methoni
Peloponnisos
Kerkyra
Corfu
Igoumenitsa
Parga
Paxi
Mathraki
Sarandë
Delvinë
Gjirokastër
Himarë
Vlorë
Sazanit
Fier
Patos
Berat
Tomorit
Korçë
Lushnjë
Elbasan
Kavajë
Durrës
Tiranë
Tirana
Lezhë
Shkodër
Skadarsko Jezero
Kukës
Pukë
Peshkopi
Librazhd
Tronto
San Marina
Vasto
Térmoli
San Severo
Campobasso
Lucera
Fóggia
Benevento
Ariano Irpino
Avellino
Pompei
Salerno
Eboli
Battipáglia
Agrópoli
Castellabate
Vallo della Lucánia
Pisciotta
Sannicandro Gargánico
Vieste
Apricena
Mte. Gargano
Monte Sant' Ángelo
Manfredónia
Cerignola
Barletta
Trani
Bisceglie
Molfetta
Bari
Mola di Bari
Monópoli
Andria
Corato
Bitonto
Lavello
Ofanto
Rionero in Vúlture
Potenza
Gravina in Púglia
Altamura
Putignano
Fasano
Martina Franca
Ostuni
Brindisi
Francavilla Fontana
Mesagne
Squinzano
Lecce
Matera
Ginosa
Montescaglioso
Pisticci
Táranto
Mandúria
Nardò
Gallipoli
Galatina
Otranto
Máglie
Casarano
Gagliano del Capo
C. d' Otranto
C. Santa Maria di Leuca
Policoro
Sala Consilina
Polla
Sapri
Lauria
Maratea
Práia a Mare
Castrovillari
Trebisacce
Rossano
Cariati
Corigliano Cálabro
Cirò Marina
Cetraro
Páola
Rende
Cosenza
San Giovanni in Fiore
Crotone
C. Rizzuto
Cutro
Amantea
Nicastro
Tiriolo
Sambiase
Catanzaro
Maida
Vibo Valéntia
Tropea
Soverato
Rosarno
Palmi
Caulónia
Taurianova
Siderno
Locri
Scilla
Messina
Réggio di Calábria
Mélito di Porto Salvo
C. Spartivento
Strómboli
Isole Eólie
Salina
Lípari
Vulcano
Barcellona Pozzo di Gotto
Milazzo
Patti
Tortorici
Taormina
Etna
Giarre
Acireale
Adrano
Paternò
Catánia
Scordia
Lentini
Augusta
Siracusa
Sortino
Ragusa
Módica
Ávola
Ispica
Pachino
C. Passero
Sicilia
Italia
KERKYRA IGOUMENITSA PATRA
TRIESTE
ANCONA VENEZIA TRIESTE DUBROVNIK
PATRA
PALERMO TUNIS MESSINA
SALERNO
NAPOLI
0 40 80 120 160 km
16°
18°
20°
6
7
8
A
B
C
D
E
16
22

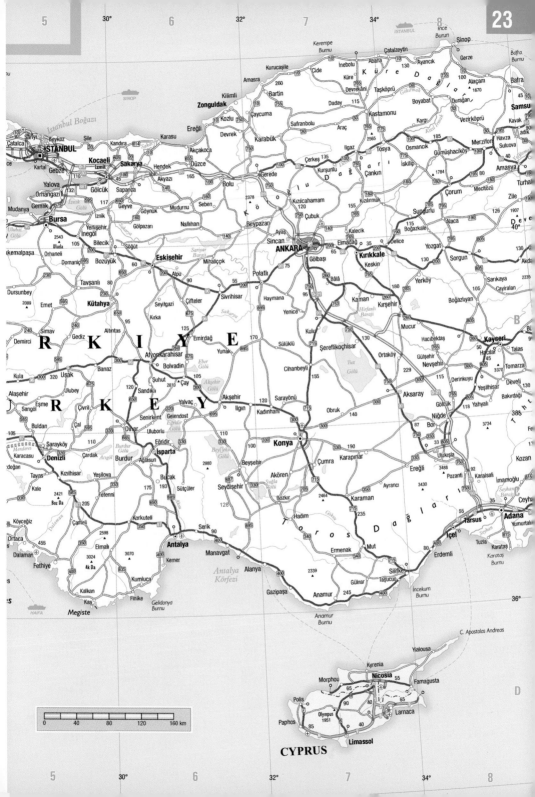

97 Map pages at 1:1 066 000
182 Map pages at 1:2 132 000

ICELAND
ÍSLAND

Reykjavik

Hammerfest
192 193
Tromsö
194 Narvik
196 197
195 FINLAND
SUOMI
Oulu

198 199 200
Trondheim
NORWAY Umeå
NORGE SWEDEN Vaasa
SVERIGE

Gävle
46 47 48 49 50 51 Turku Helsinki Saint Petersburg
Bergen Oslo Stockholm Tallinn Sankt Peterburg
52 53 54 55 56 57 ESTONIA RUSSIA
Stavanger Örebro EESTI ROSSIYA
Kristiansand

58 Gothenburg Göteborg Riga LATVIA
60 62 LATVIJA
DENMARK 61 Copenhagen LITHUANIA
DANMARK 59 63 LIETUVA Vilnius
Esbjerg Køibenhavn Minsk
Malmö Kaliningrad RUSSIA
64 65 66 67 Gdansk ROSSIYA BELARUS
Kiel 68 69
Hamburg Szczecin Warsaw Brest
70 71 72 73 Berlin 76 77 Warszawa
NETHERLANDS Bremen Poznan POLAND UKRAINE
NEDERLAND Hanover 74 75 POLSKA UKRAINA
Amsterdam Hannover
GERMANY 84 85 86 87
Rotterdam 80 DEUTSCHLAND Dresden Wroclaw Kraków Lviv
Antwerp 81 Leipzig MOLDOVA
Düsseldorf 82 83 Prague
78 Calais Cologne Frankfurt CZECHIA
Brussels Köln ČESKÁ REPUBLIKA
BELGIUM 79 Nuremberg 96 97 SLOVAKIA
Le Havre BELGIQUE Luxembourg Nürnberg Brno SLOVENSKÁ REP.
88 89 90 91 LUXEMBOURG 93 94 95 98 99
Brest Paris Luxembourg Vienna Wien Bratislava
101 Strasbourg Stuttgart Munich AUSTRIA Budapest
Rennes 102 103 104 105 106 107 München ÖSTERREICH HUNGARY MAGYARORSZAG
100 Dijon Salzburg 108 109 110 111 112 113
Nantes Tours LIECHTENSTEIN Innsbruck Graz Szeged RROMÂNIA
114 115 116 117 Geneva SWITZERLAND SLOVENIA 124 125 126
FRANCE Basel Zürich SCHWEIZ Ljubljana Zagreb CROATIA Timişoara
Clermont- Lyon 118 119 120 121 SLOVENIJA HRVATSKA Belgrade Bucharest
Ferrand Milan Venice 122 123 Beograd București
Bordeaux Turin Milano Venezia BOSNIA 127 BULGARIA
128 129 130 131 Torino Bologna HERZEGOVINA SERBIA BULGARIYA
A Coruña Nice Genoa SAN Split Sarajevo SRBIJA Sofia
140 141 Toulouse Marseilles Génova MARINO 136 137 138 139 Sofiya
Vigo 132 133 MONACO Florence KOSOVO
142 143 144 145 146 Marseille Firenze ITALY MONTENEGRO Skopje
Porto Bilbao ANDORRA 134 135 ITALIA CRNA GORA NORTH
PORTUGAL Valladolid 147 180 170 171 MACEDONIA
148 149 150 151 152 153 SPAIN Ajaccio Rome Bari Tirana SEVERNA
Madrid ESPAÑA Barcelona Roma Naples MAKEDONIJA
154 155 Zaragoza 168 169 Napoli 172 173 Salonica
Lisbon 156 157 158 159 Valencia 178 Táranto ALBANIA Thessaloníki
Lisboa 166 167 Palma 174 SHQIPËRIA 182 183
160 162 163 164 165 179 175 GREECE
161 Seville Cordoba Alicante Cagliari ELLAS
Sevilla Granada Palermo Catània Patras Athens
GIBRALTAR Málaga 176 177 Patra Athína
184 185

MALTA

Amsterdam
2945 **Athina**
1505 3192 **Barcelona**
1484 3742 2803 **Bergen**
650 2412 1863 1309 **Berlin**
197 2895 1308 1506 764 **Bruxelles**
2245 1219 2644 3037 1707 2181 **Bucuresti**
1420 1530 1999 2212 882 1358 852 **Budapest**
367 3100 1269 1783 956 215 2398 1573 **Calais**
533 3630 1817 270 1504 763 3021 2196 548 **Dublin**
1093 3826 1995 175 1695 941 3124 2299 725 346 **Edinburgh**
441 2499 1313 1506 550 383 1804 979 575 1123 1301 **Frankfurt**
1029 3080 2362 819 668 1145 1734 1550 1342 477 176 1067 **Göteborg**
447 2719 1780 1023 286 563 2014 1189 760 477 1486 485 582 **Hamburg**
1560 2539 2338 1063 475 1239 1834 1069 1431 1318 1236 1588 505 1113 **Helsinki**
2756 1145 2990 3653 2223 2706 690 1341 2911 3537 3657 2314 2891 2530 2350 **İstanbul**
965 2782 2090 1103 370 1081 2077 1252 1278 752 479 795 284 518 803 2593 **København**
256 2684 1376 1427 566 198 1983 1158 390 338 1116 180 986 404 1517 2499 714 **Köln**
2331 4460 1268 3723 2869 3141 3917 3222 2069 2417 2795 2400 3282 2700 3817 4342 3014 2339 **Lisboa**
480 3210 1387 458 1074 333 2591 1766 118 430 608 695 122 678 1991 3107 1188 508 2187 **London**
406 2661 1190 1613 749 209 2052 1227 424 572 1150 240 1172 590 1703 2472 900 186 2160 542 **Luxembourg**
1790 3809 617 3183 2364 1600 3262 2622 1528 1634 2254 1930 2742 2160 3276 3589 2174 1798 651 1646 1628 **Madrid**
1210 2683 509 2436 1541 1030 2154 1505 1063 1588 1789 1023 1994 1412 2525 2479 2172 1006 1777 1182 822 1126 **Marseille**
1085 2182 1038 2141 1060 890 1668 992 1072 1620 1798 683 1700 1118 1535 1993 1230 868 2315 1190 679 1655 538 **Milano**
2457 2930 3655 2229 1821 2585 1761 2099 2800 3348 3526 2312 1665 2115 1160 2605 2325 2387 4875 2918 2852 4224 3270 3027 **Moskva**
839 2106 1340 1738 594 789 1497 672 994 1524 1720 398 1247 765 1069 1907 969 580 2545 1094 555 2010 1011 473 2305 **München**
1347 3372 2680 503 981 1463 2667 1842 1660 773 729 1385 316 900 697 3089 1390 1304 3604 1778 1490 3063 2312 2018 1823 1559 **Oslo**
510 2917 988 1922 1051 320 2307 1482 281 829 1007 591 1481 899 2012 2727 1209 495 1821 399 351 1280 782 857 2903 810 1799 **Paris**
950 2067 1750 1675 345 888 1362 537 1097 1635 1816 512 1013 652 770 1878 715 690 2870 1205 753 2329 1399 853 1853 388 1305 1061 **Praha**
1691 1140 1385 2706 1502 1520 1904 1263 1678 2226 2404 1289 2265 1683 1977 2237 1993 1474 2653 1736 1285 2002 876 606 3362 918 2583 1389 1309 **Roma**
2347 4223 1031 3736 2894 2150 3709 3010 2078 2626 2804 2344 3296 2713 3826 4034 3023 2318 401 2196 2178 550 1540 2078 4774 2371 3613 1830 2781 2446 **Sevilla**
2206 828 2453 3101 1673 2156 391 790 2361 2891 3087 1764 2341 1980 1800 550 2041 1949 3706 2461 1922 3037 1929 1443 2252 1367 2632 2177 1328 1687 3484 **Sofia**
1399 3418 2726 1063 1006 1509 2713 1886 1673 2264 1069 1431 505 946 167 3165 590 1380 3650 1824 1536 3109 2358 2064 1228 1600 530 1845 1351 2629 3059 2679 **Stockholm**
1256 2128 2366 1909 606 1350 1473 648 1542 2110 2268 1136 1274 886 361 1989 956 1152 3480 1840 1345 2960 2015 1469 1245 996 1506 1677 616 1853 3397 1439 1612 **Warszawa**
1168 1772 1856 1970 640 1114 1067 242 1308 1954 2694 731 1308 947 1088 1583 1010 916 3100 1524 993 2473 1353 818 2137 430 1600 1240 295 1126 2876 1033 1646 727 **Wien**
816 2426 1030 1938 863 619 1810 985 804 1352 1530 464 1497 915 2164 2323 1433 589 2296 922 410 1647 699 292 2552 303 1815 592 691 898 2061 1173 1861 1307 743 **Zürich**

Legend / example:

548 **Dublin**   **Dublin ▶ Göteborg = 477 km**
726 346 **Edinburgh**
575 1123 1301 **Frankfurt**
1342 477 176 1067 **Göteborg**
760 477 1486 485 582 **Hamburg**

Distances shown in blue involve at least one ferry journey

km

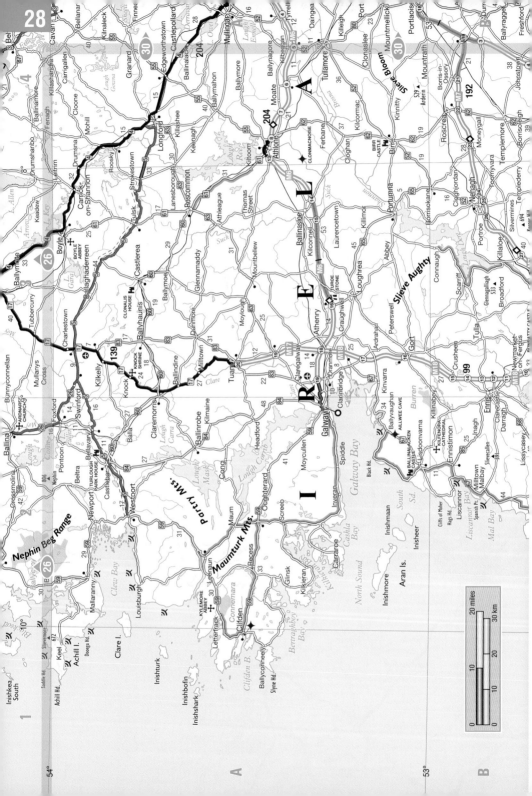

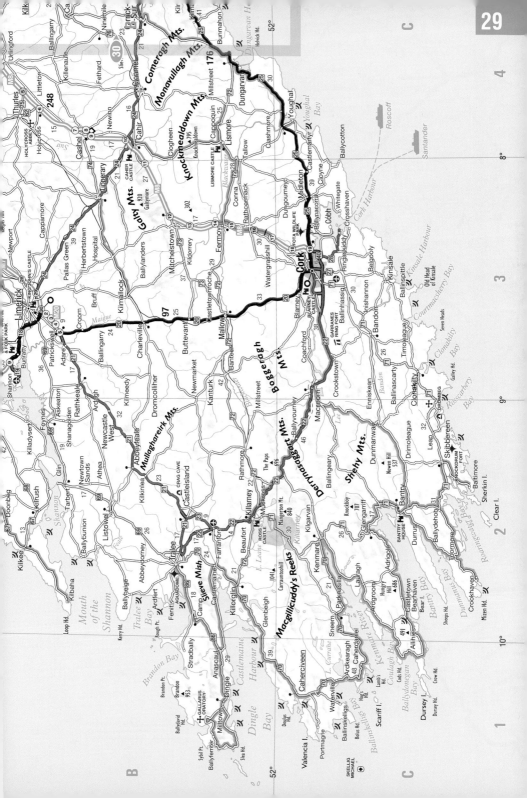

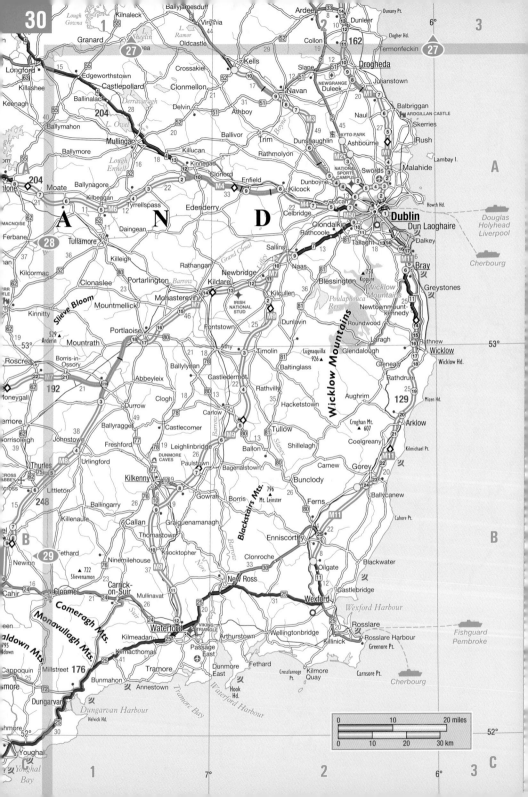

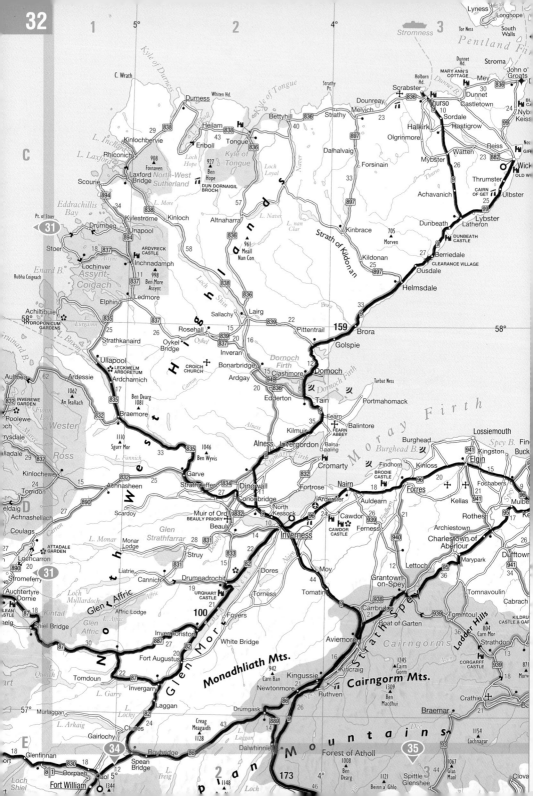

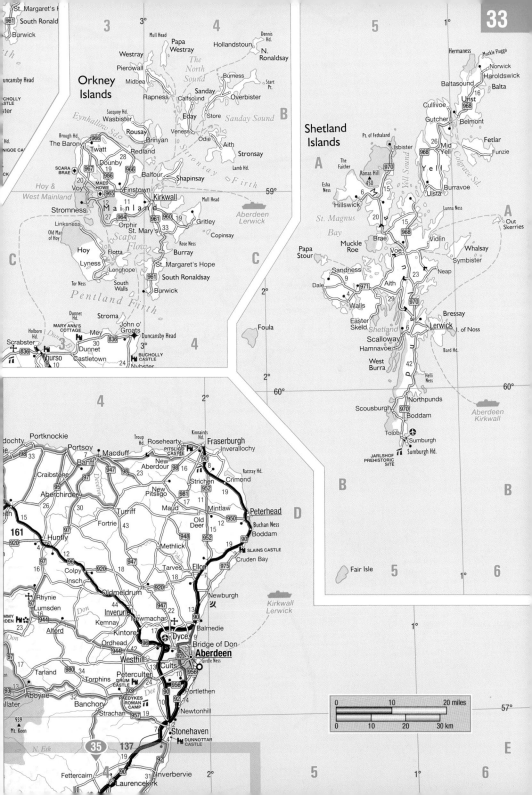

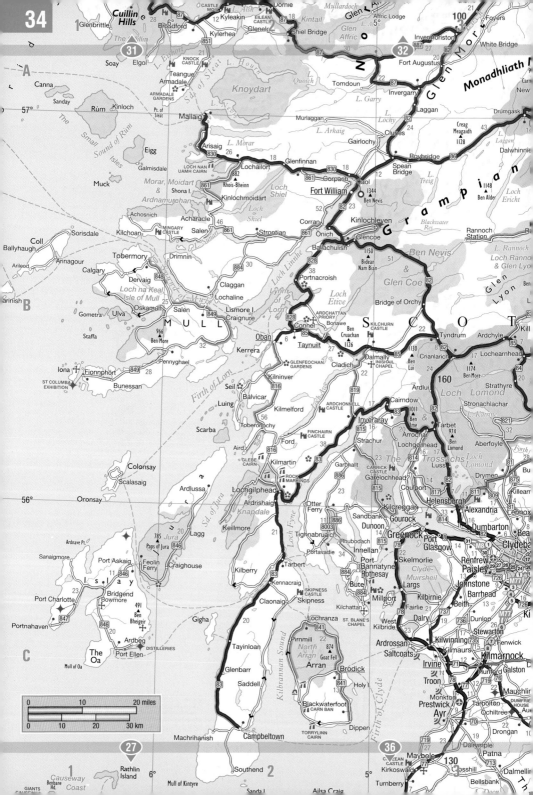

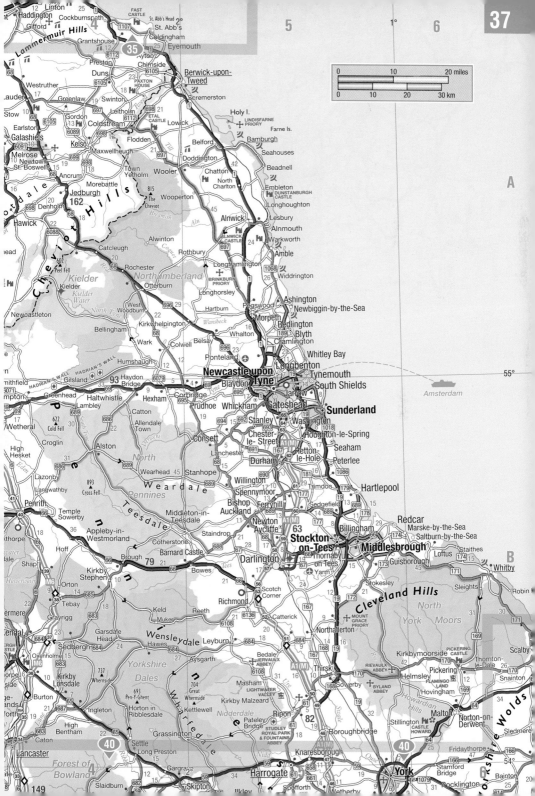

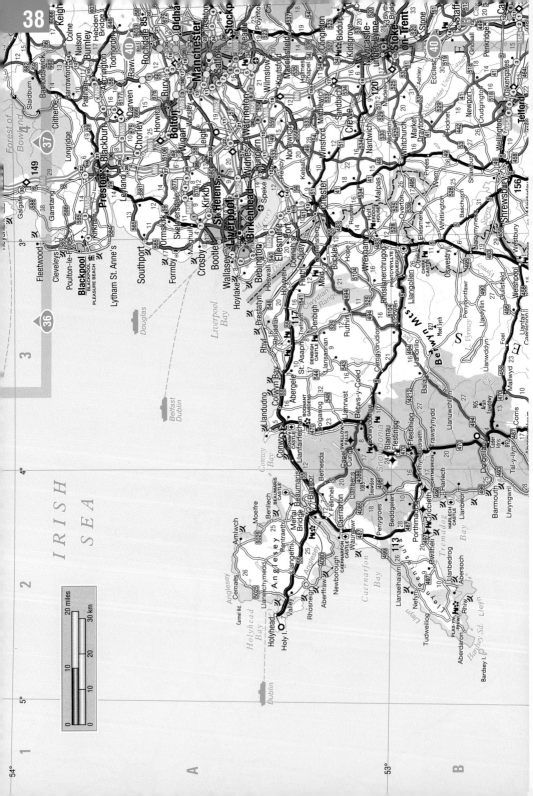

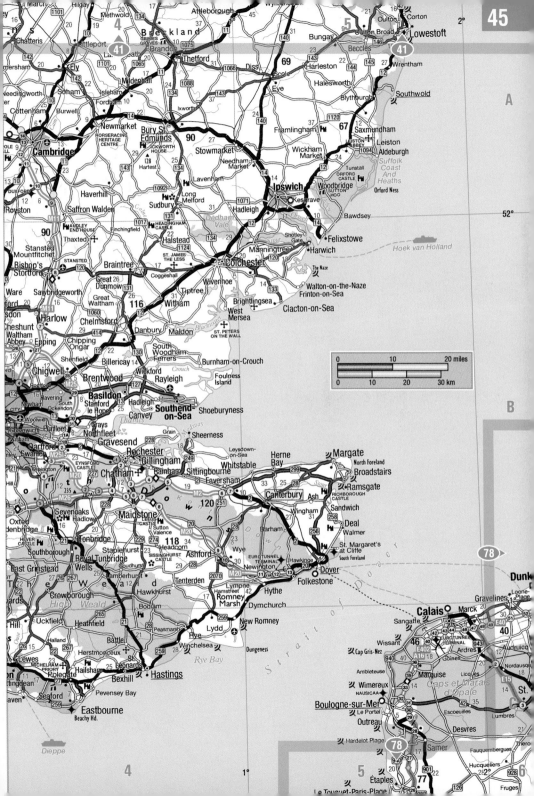

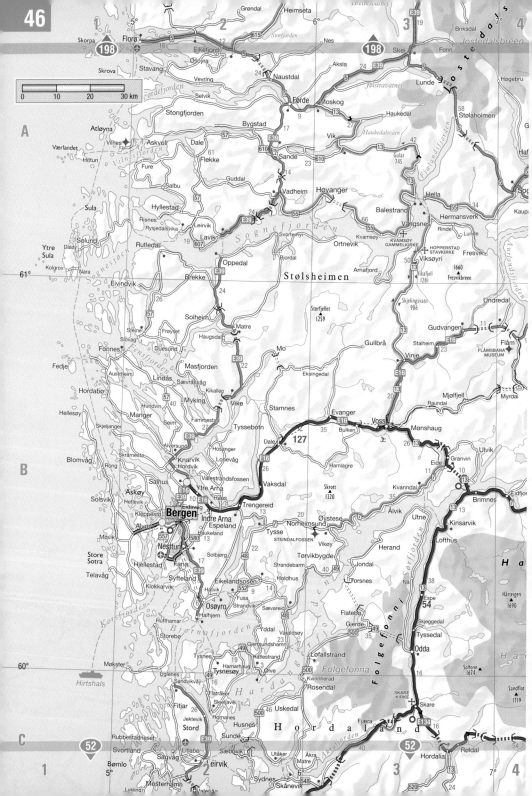

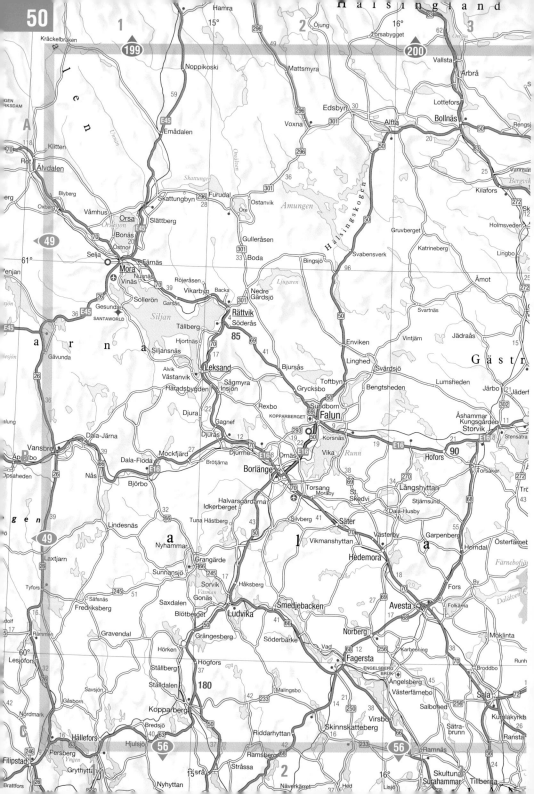

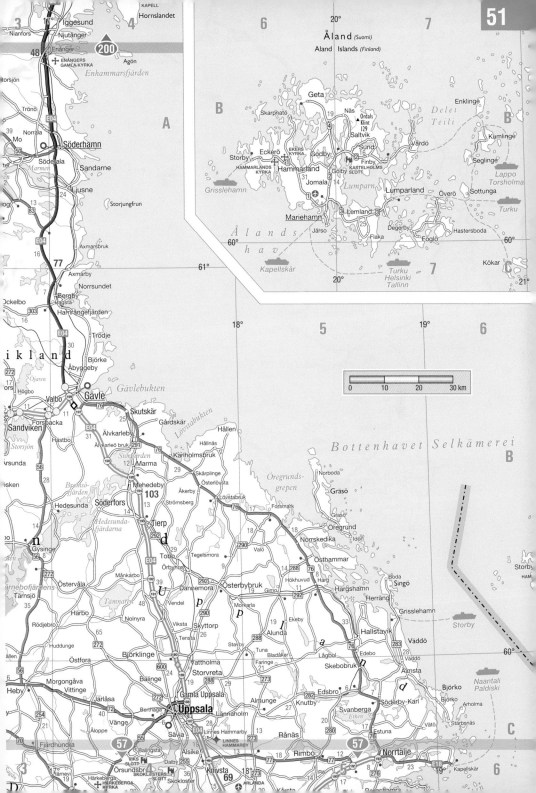

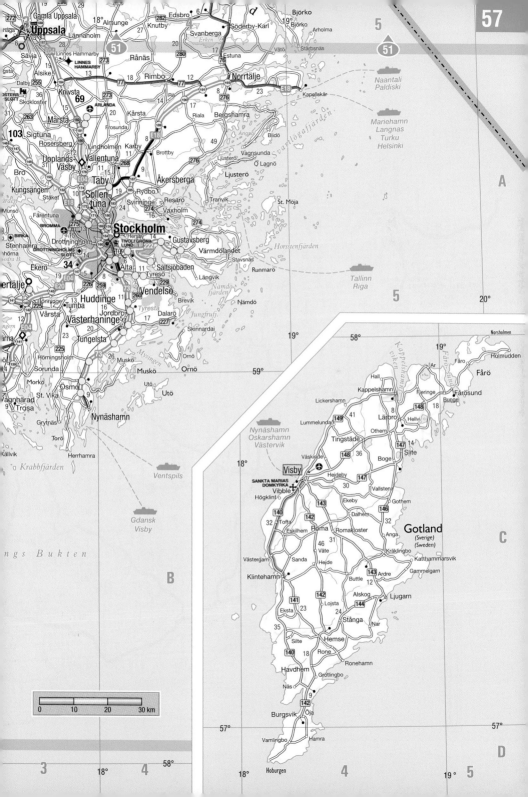

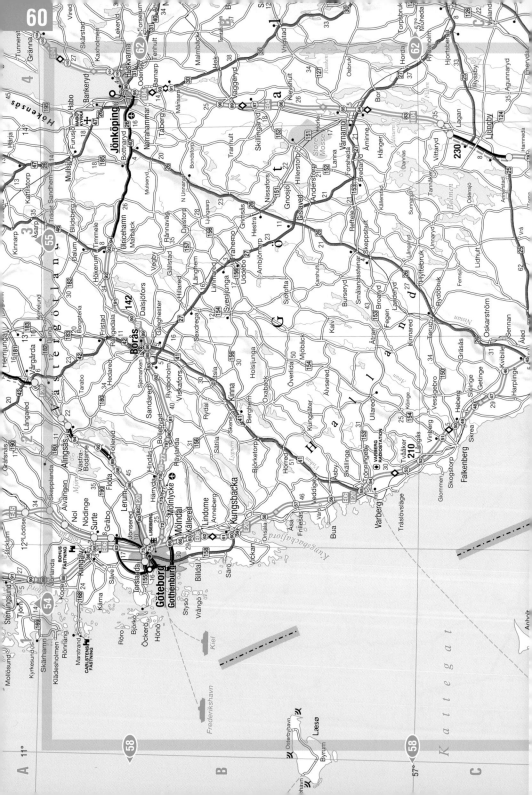

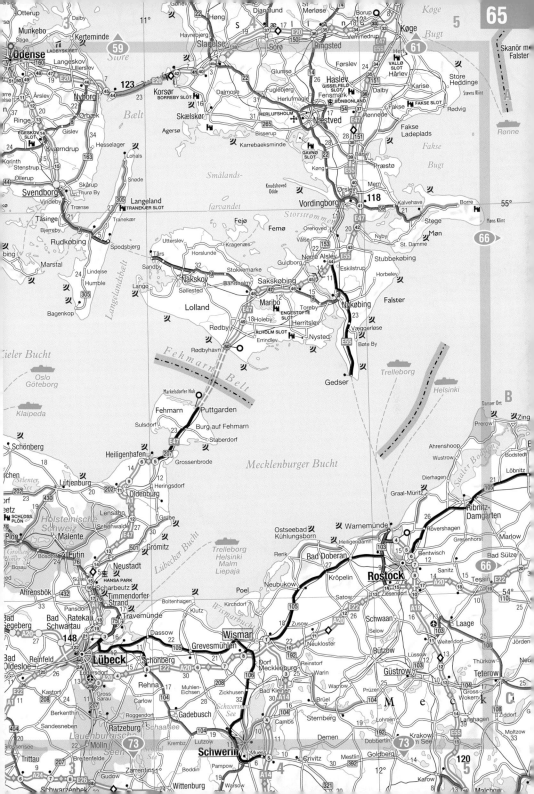

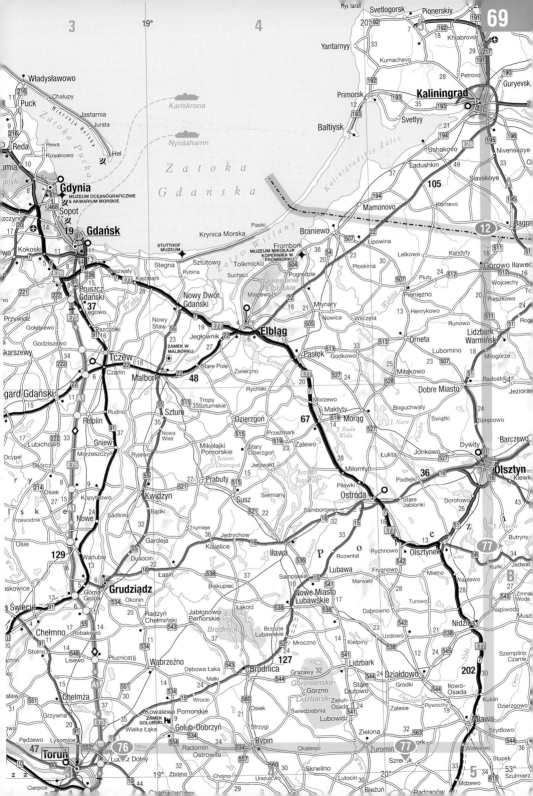

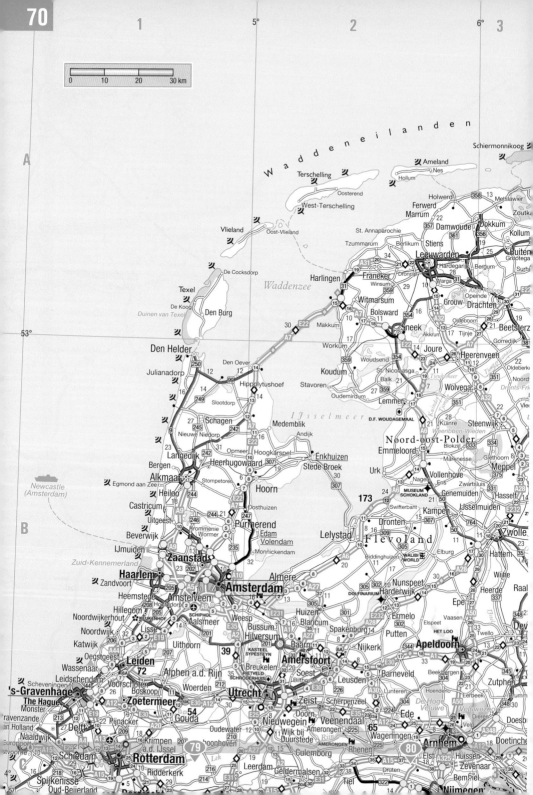

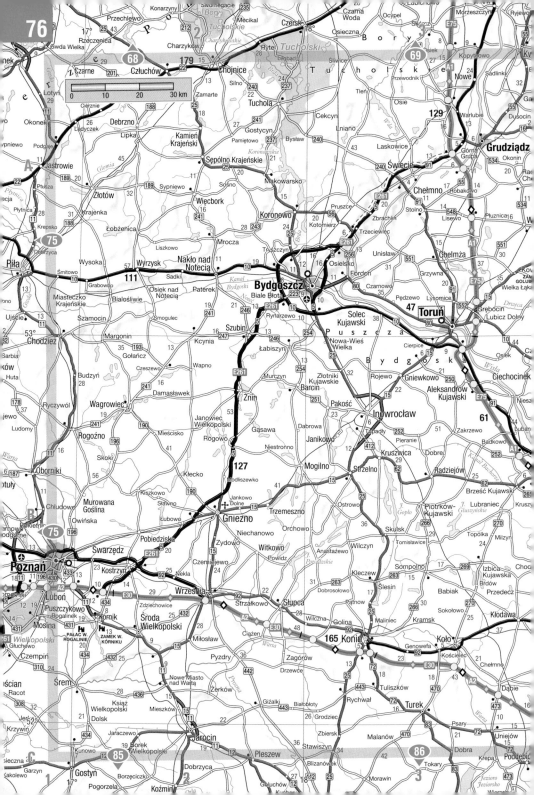

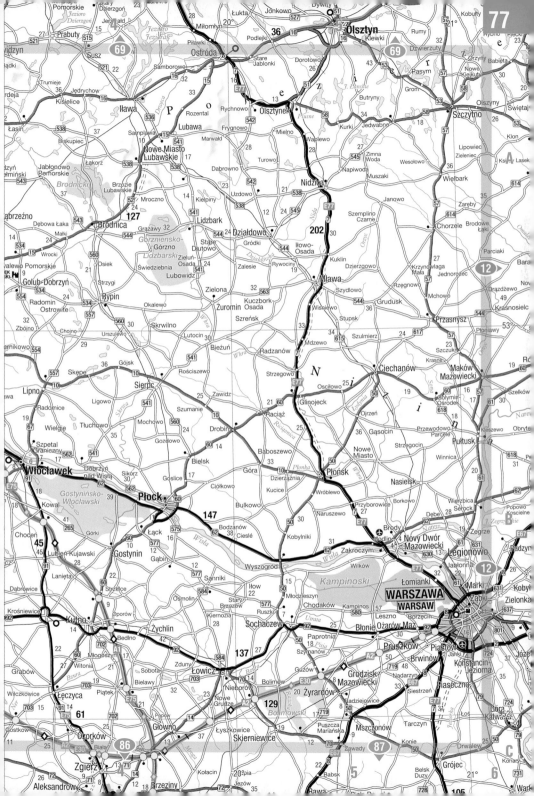

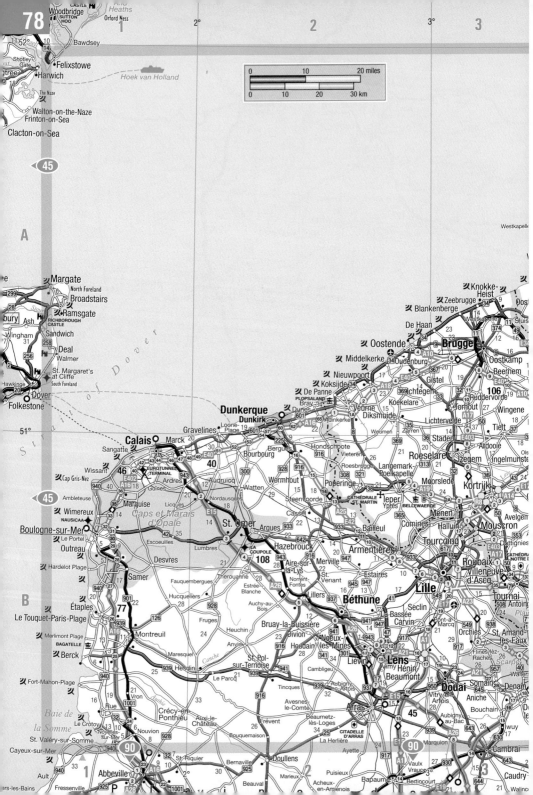

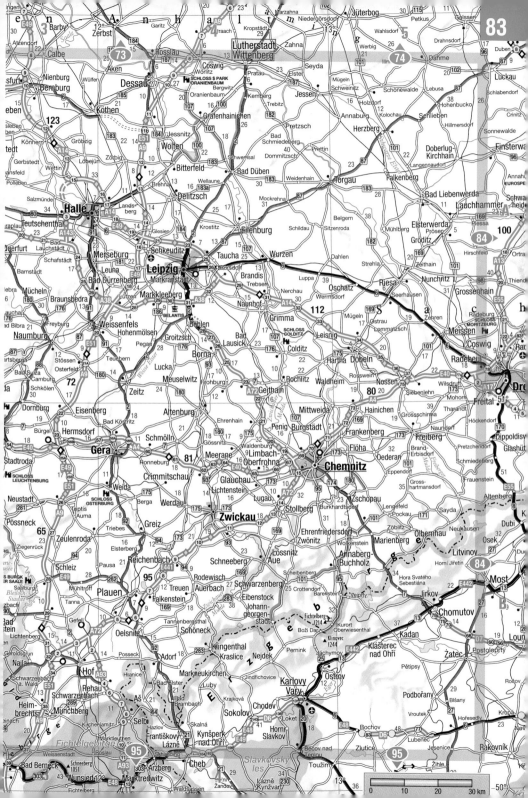

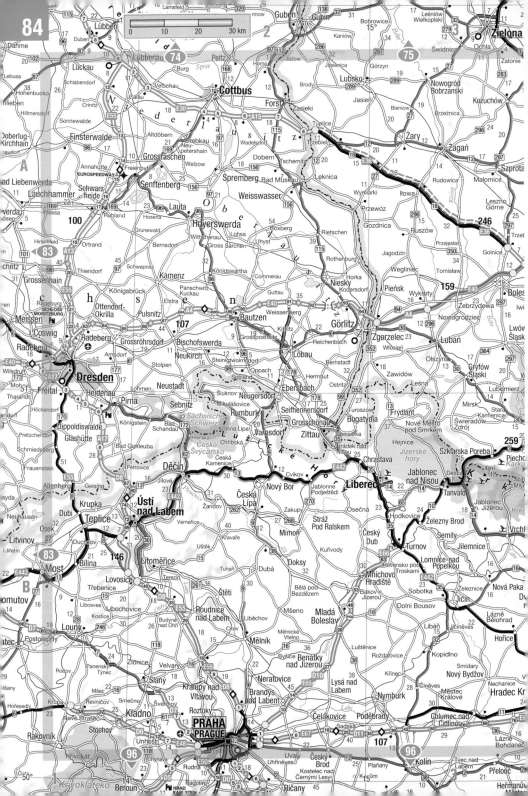

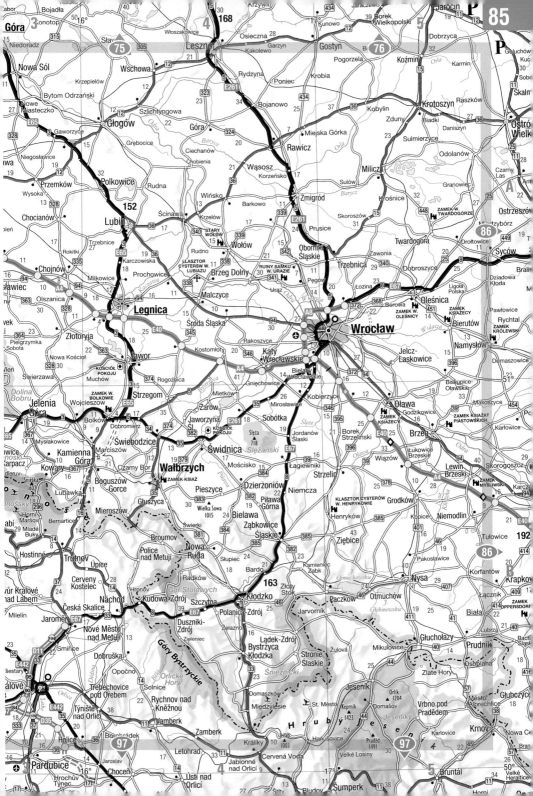

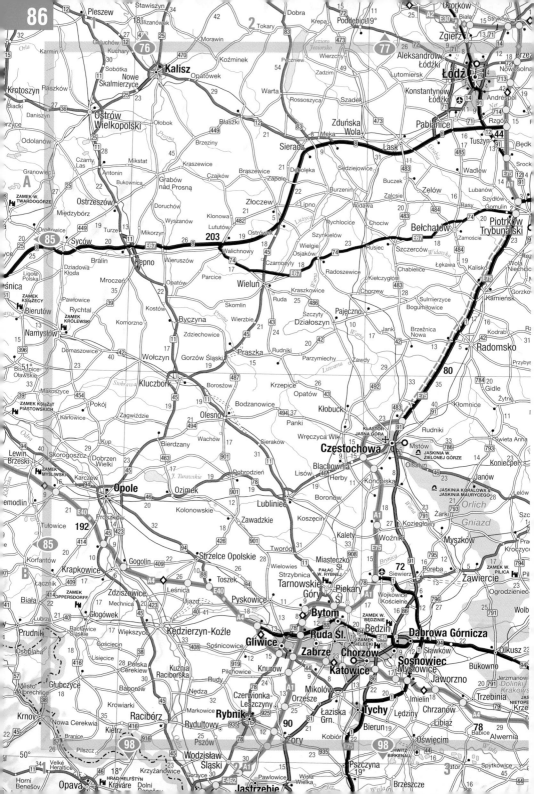

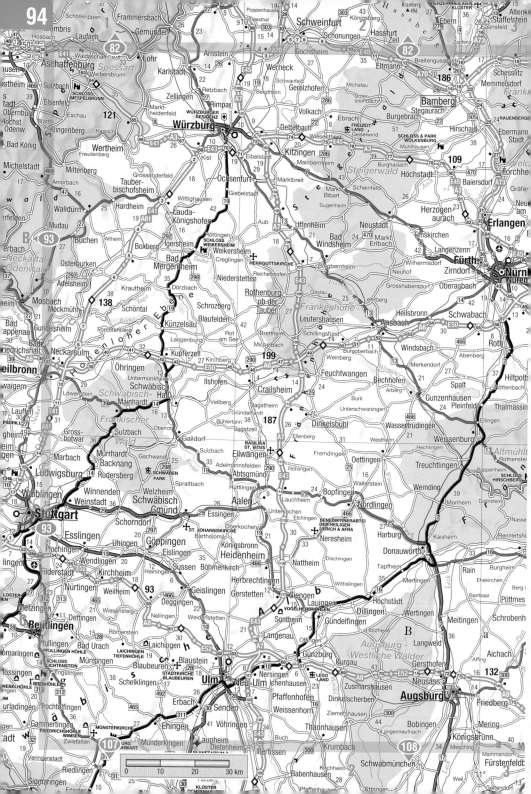

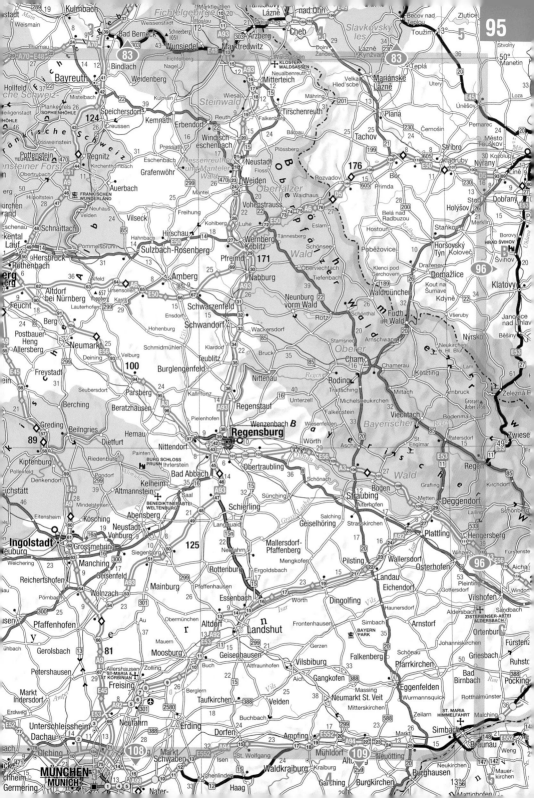

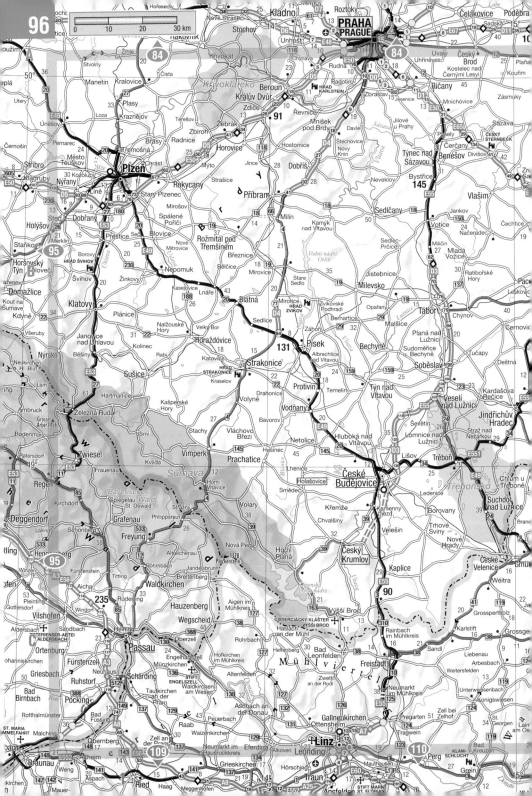

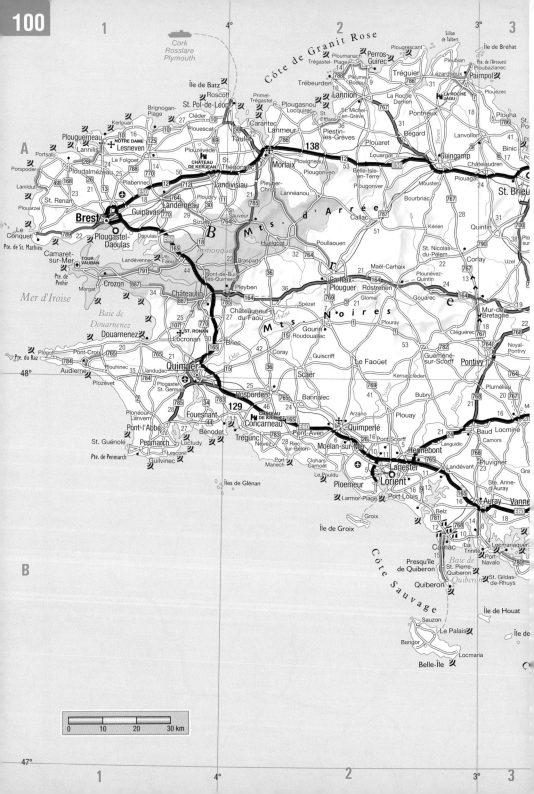

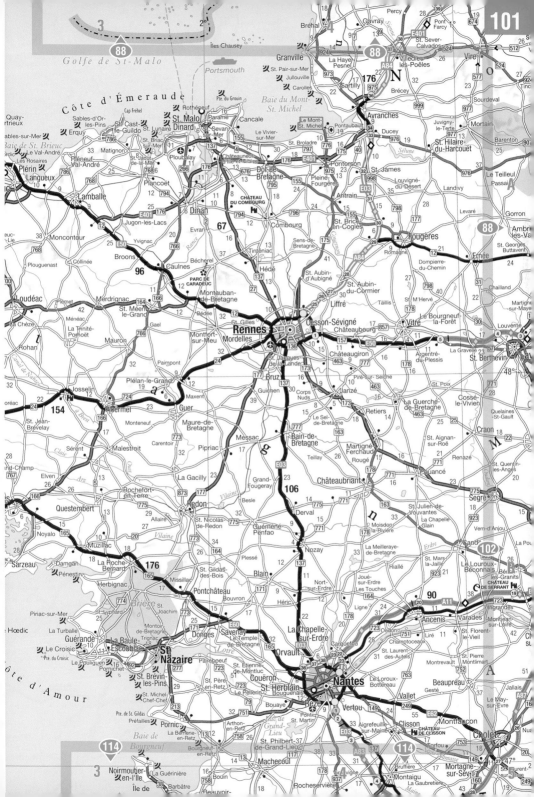

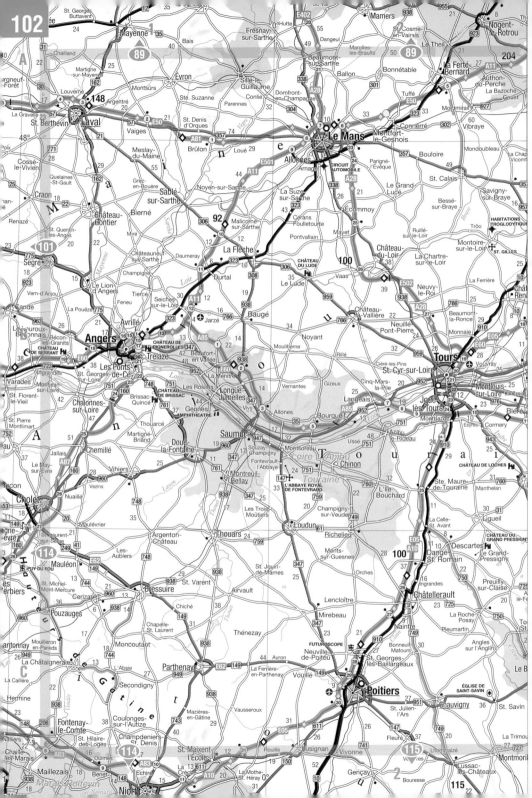

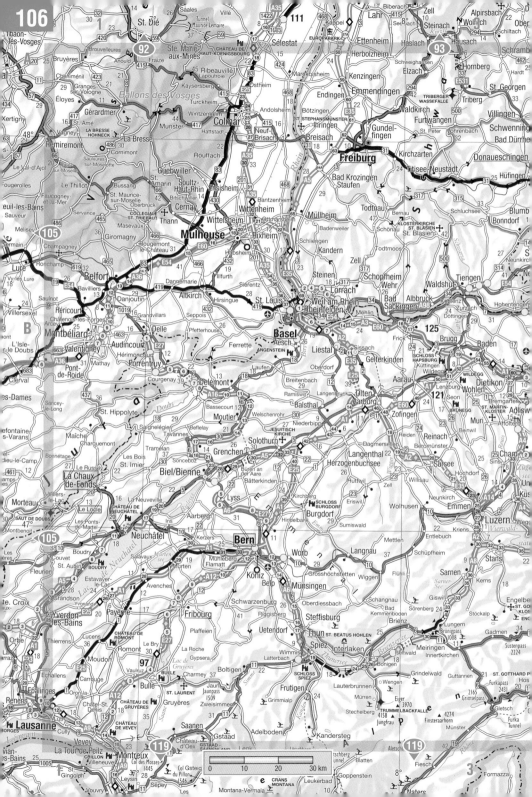

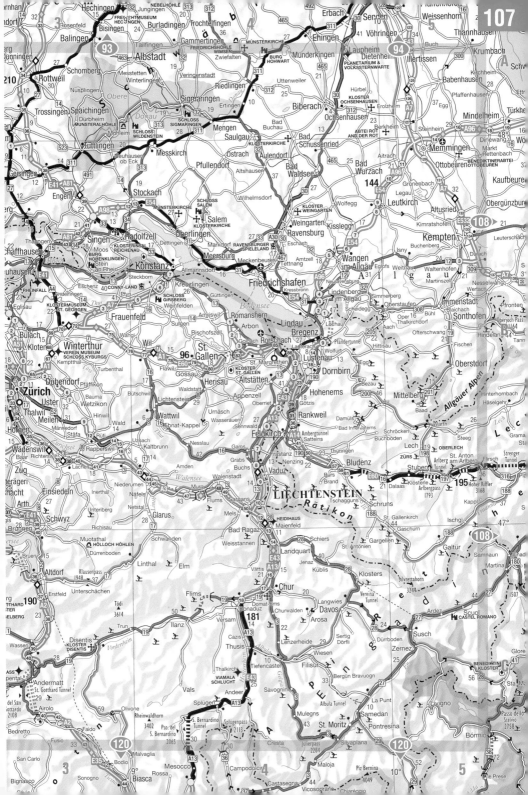

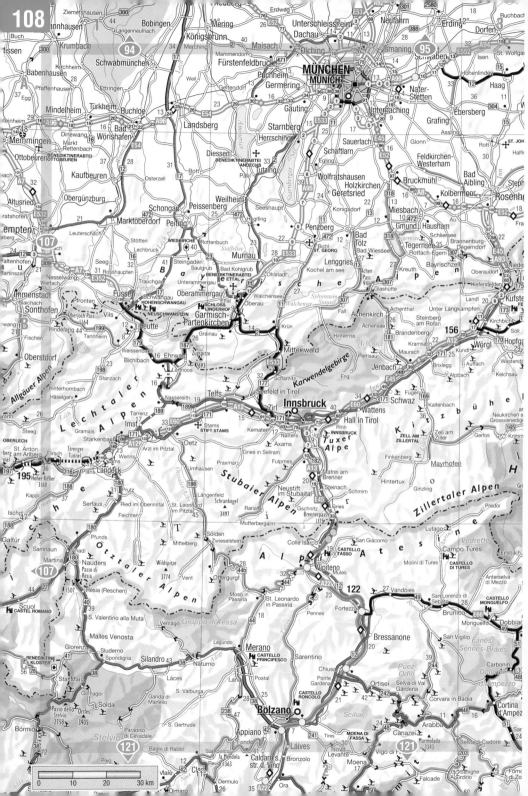

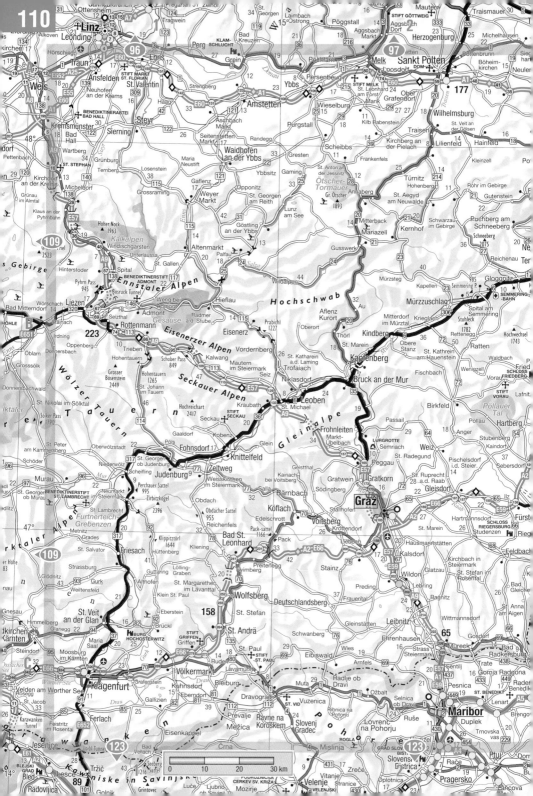

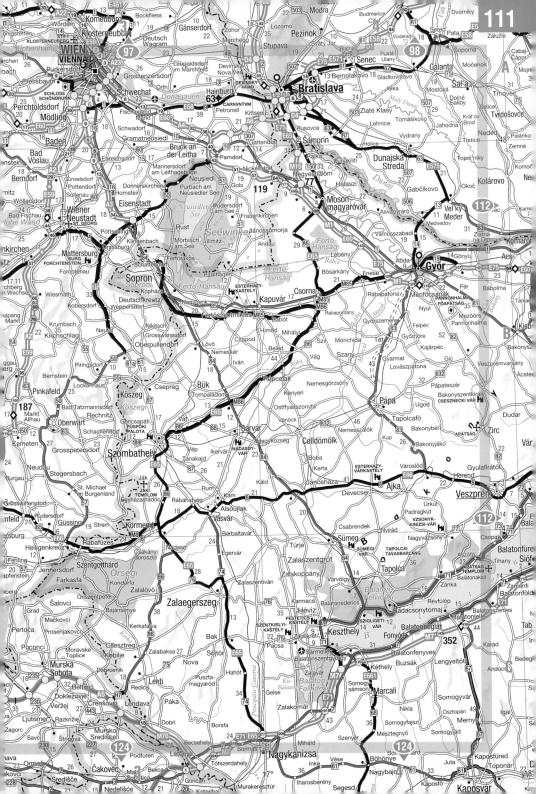

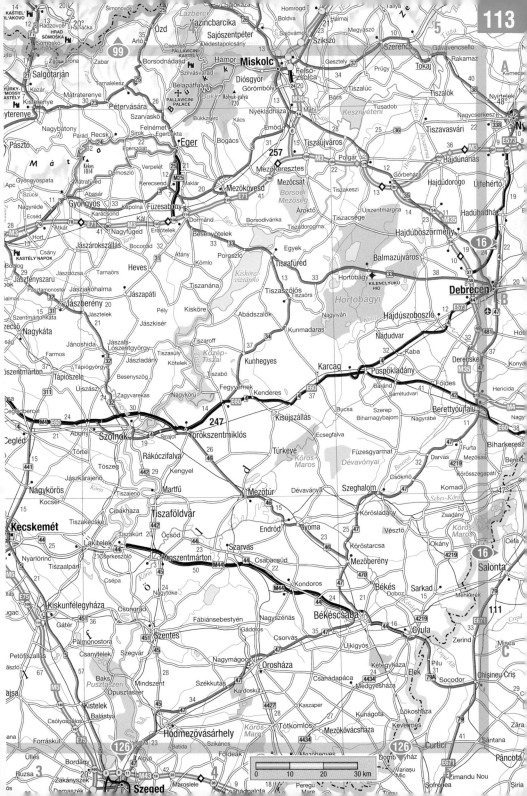

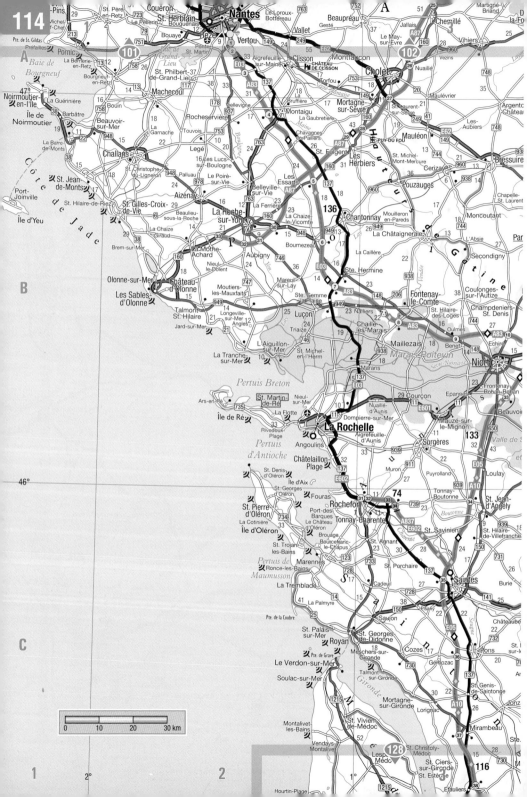

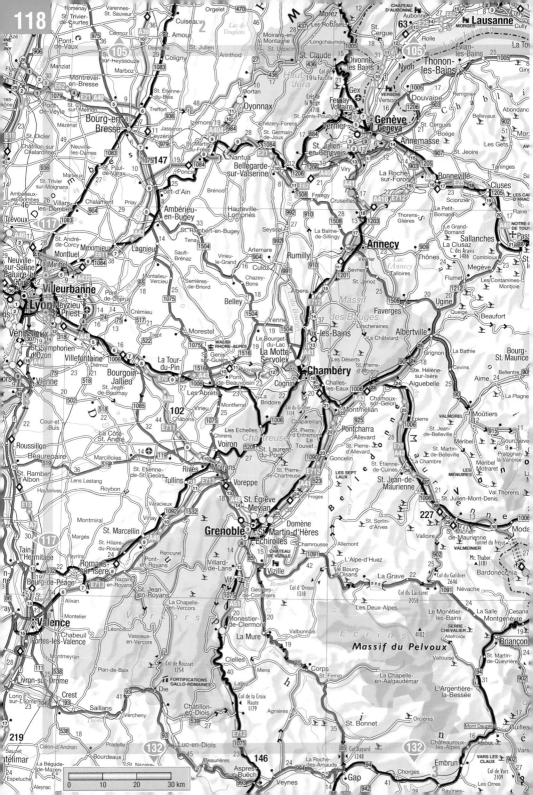

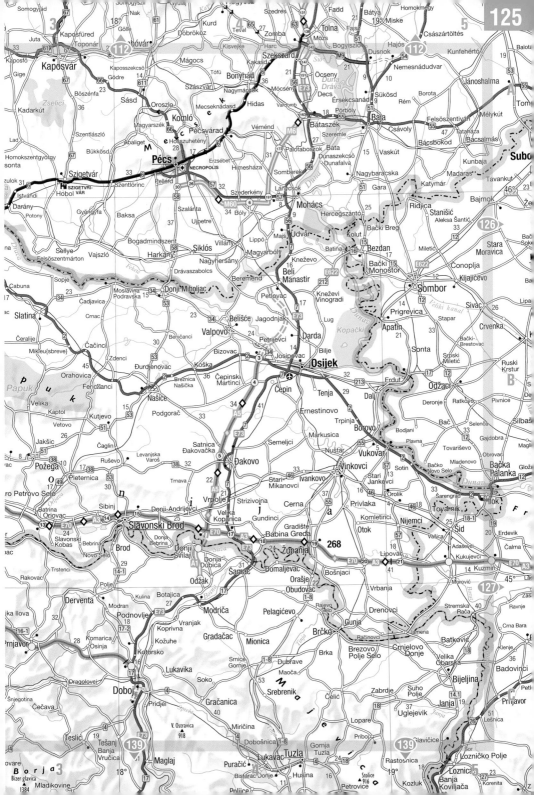

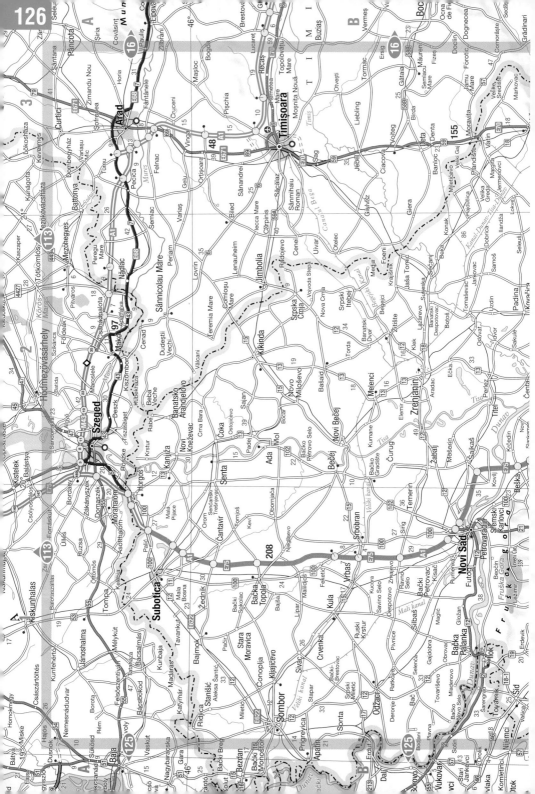

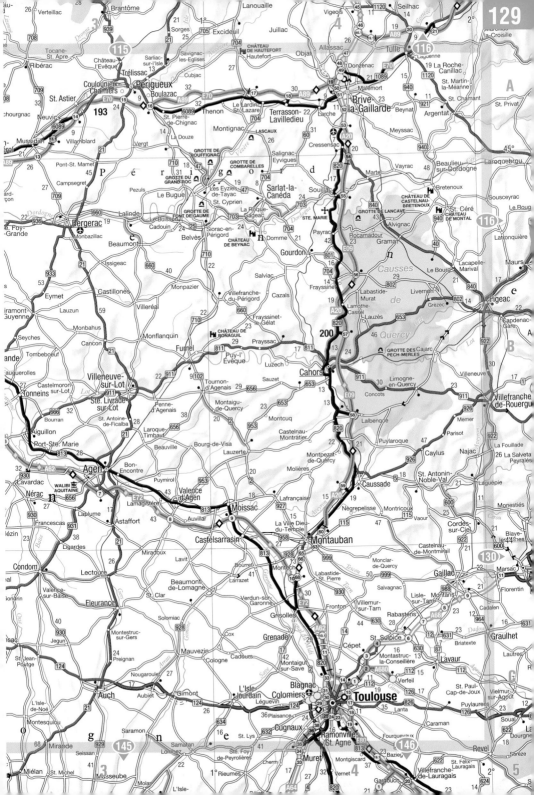

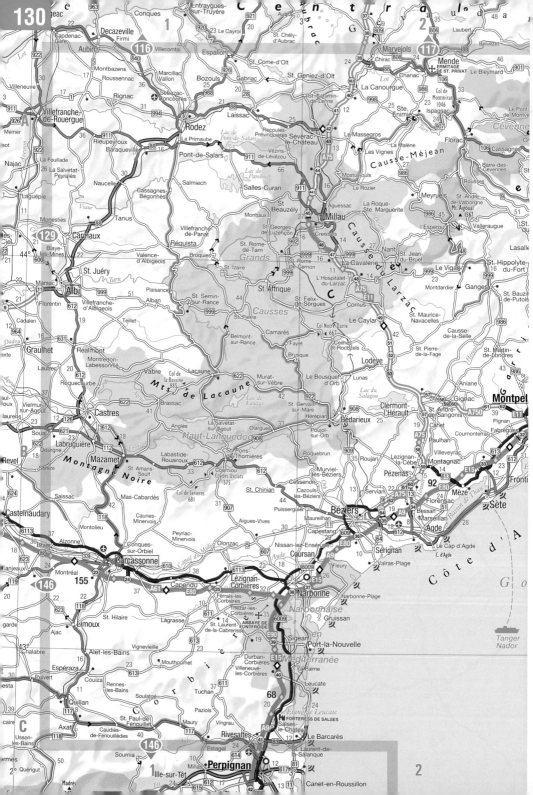

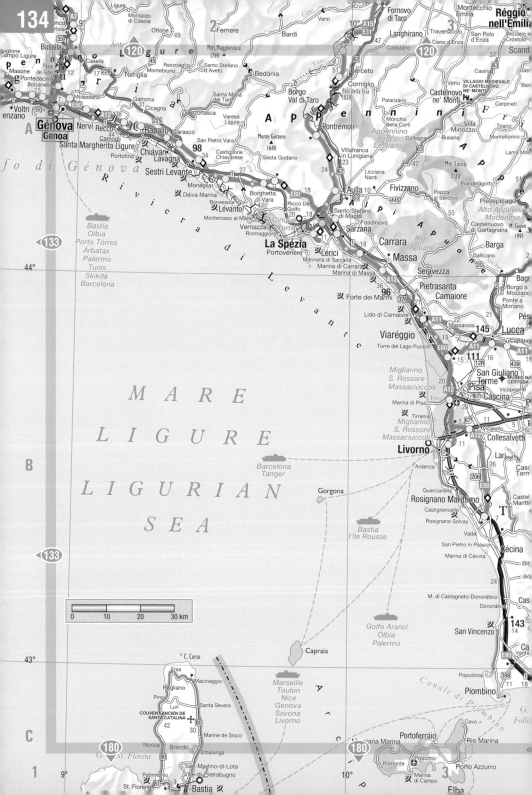

Unije   Nerezine

Čunski   **3**

Mali Lošinj   **123**
Veli Lošinj

Susak

Silba   Olib

Premuda

Ist

Virsko more

Ancona

Zadar
Split
Starigrad
Durrès
Zadar
Trieste

Prizna
Stara Novalja
Novalja   Cesarica   Ostarijska Vrata
Karlobag
Pag   Metajna

Pag   AENONA
Gorica

Lukovo Šugorje

Vir   Povljana
Vir   Privlaka
Vrsi
AENONA   Nin
Sestrunj   Petrčane
Božava   Brbinj
Ugljan   Preko
TVRĐAVA SV. MIHOVILA
Kali   Sukošan
Kukljica

Dugi Otok

Klanac
Lički Osik   Podlapača
Gospić   **4**
Brušane   Vrebac   Udbina   **123**
Bilaj   **389**
Medak   Gornja Ploča
Vaganski vrh   Sveti Rok
Barić Draga   Radúc   A1
Tribanj   Starigrad-   Paklenica
Kruščica   Paklenica
Ražanac   Velebit   Gračac

Poličnik   E65
Posedarje
Novigrad   Obrovac
Murvica   Medvide
Zadar   Zemunik Donji
Bibinje   Benkovac   ASSERIA   BURNUM   **138**
Sukošan
Miranje   Krka
Turanj   Đevrske
Pašman   Biograd na Moru   MANASTIR KRKA
Zaglav   Sali   Pašman   Pakoštane   Stankovci   Skradin
Tkon   Vransko Jezero
Telašćica   Zut   Pirovac   Prokljansko Jezero
Murter   Šibenik
Kornati   Kornat   Tisno   Vodice
Žirje   KATEDRALA SV. JAKOVA
Zablaće
Krapanj
Primošten

Jabucka

Svetac

Rogoznica

138

Biševo

I Tronto

degli Abruzzi   **3**   15°   **4**

0   10   20   30 km

A D R I A T I C   S E A

A

B

C

43°

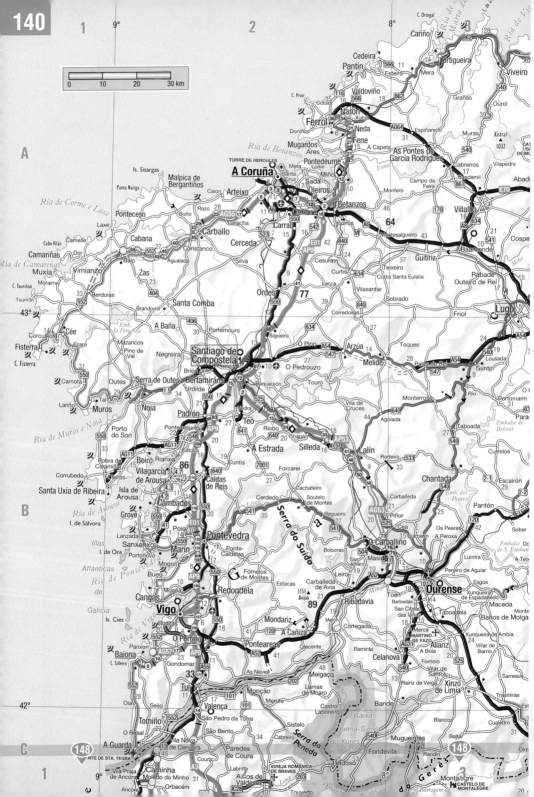

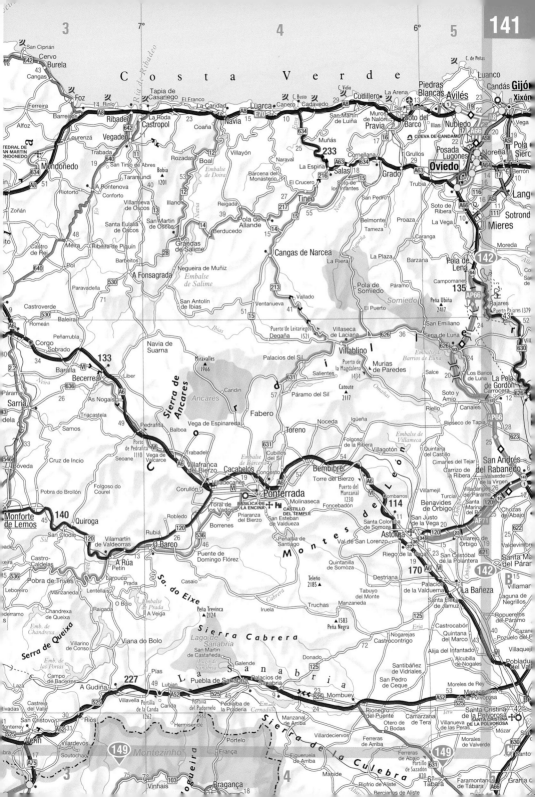

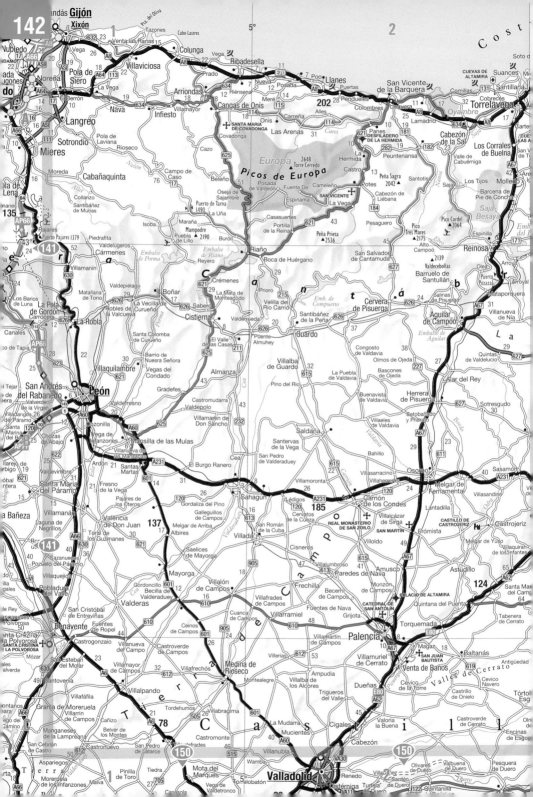

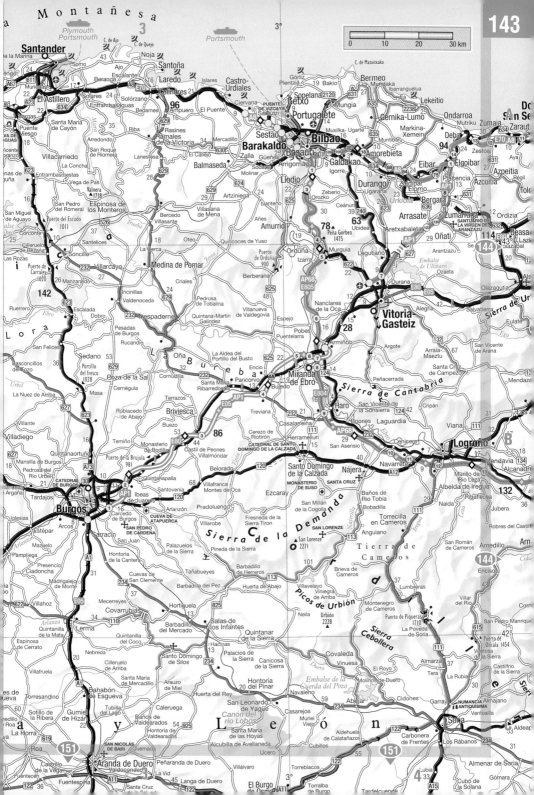

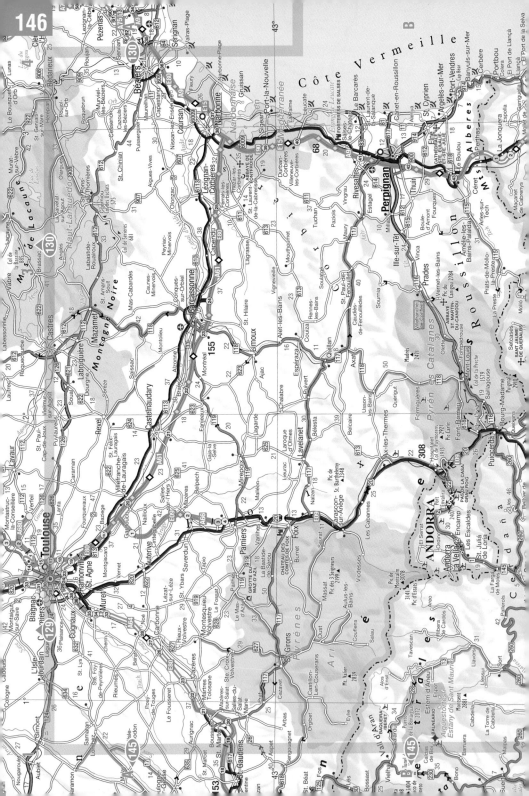

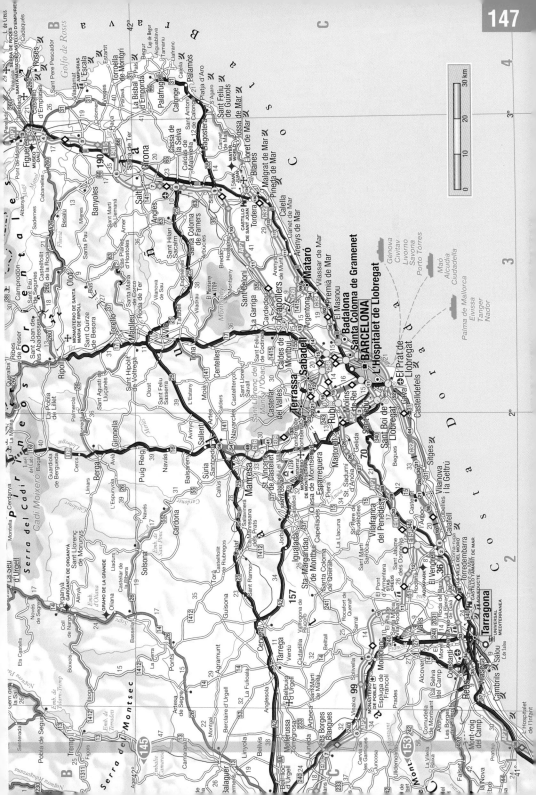

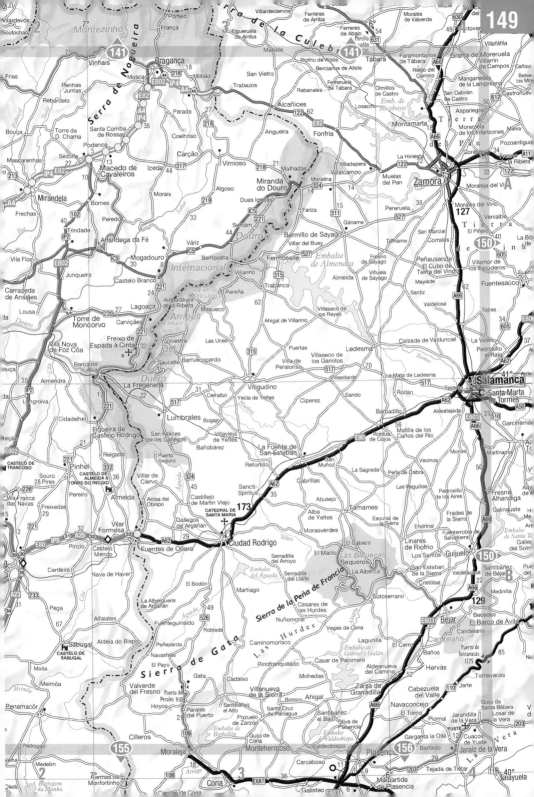

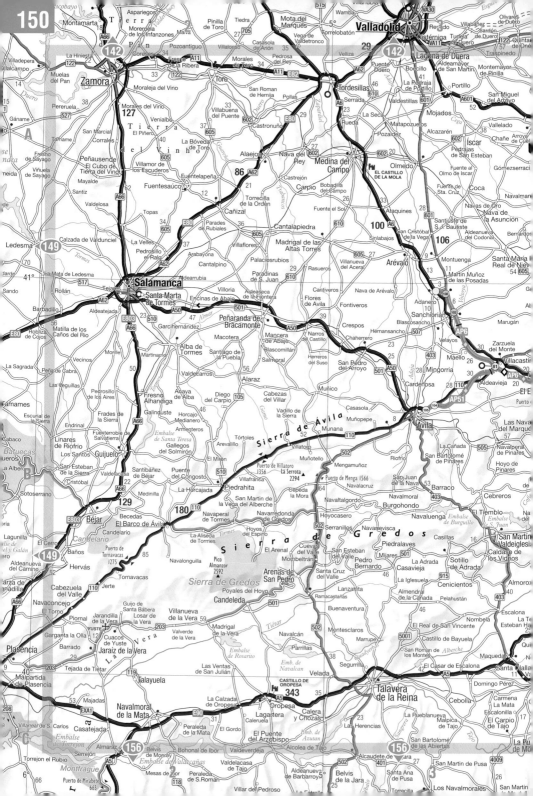

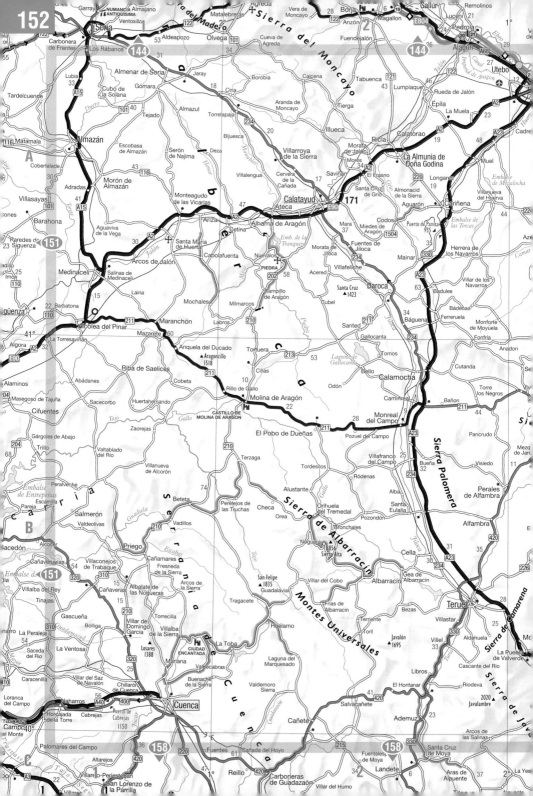

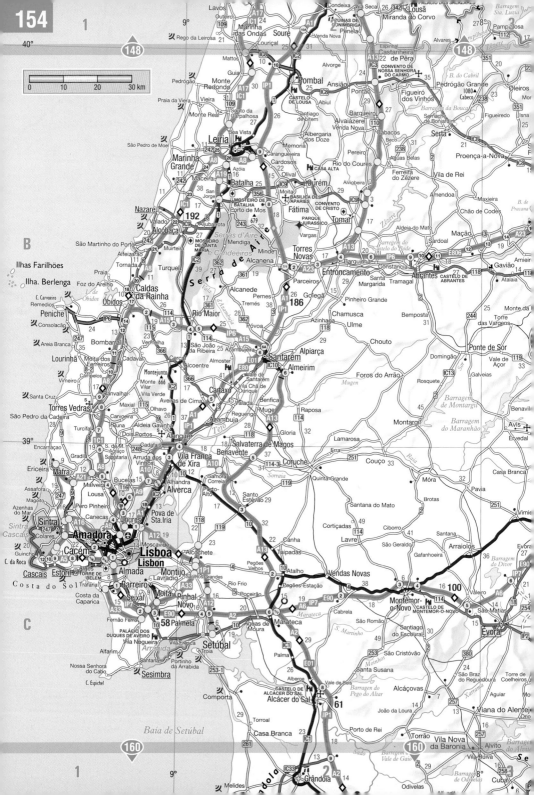

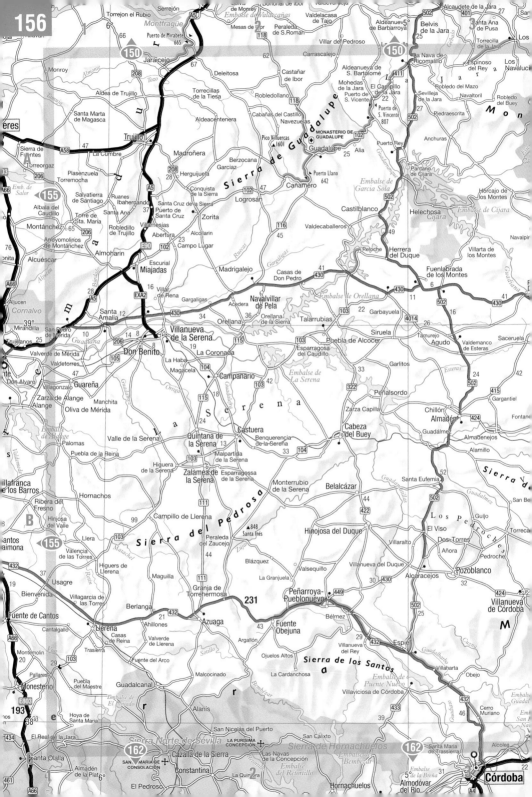

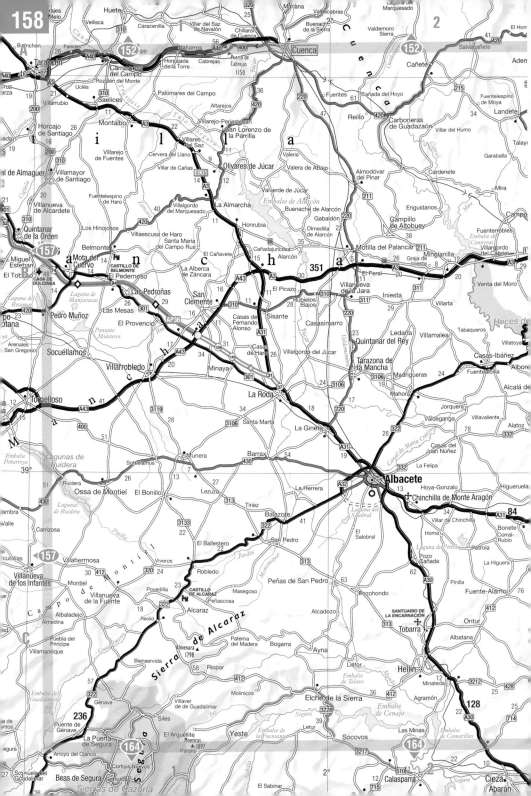

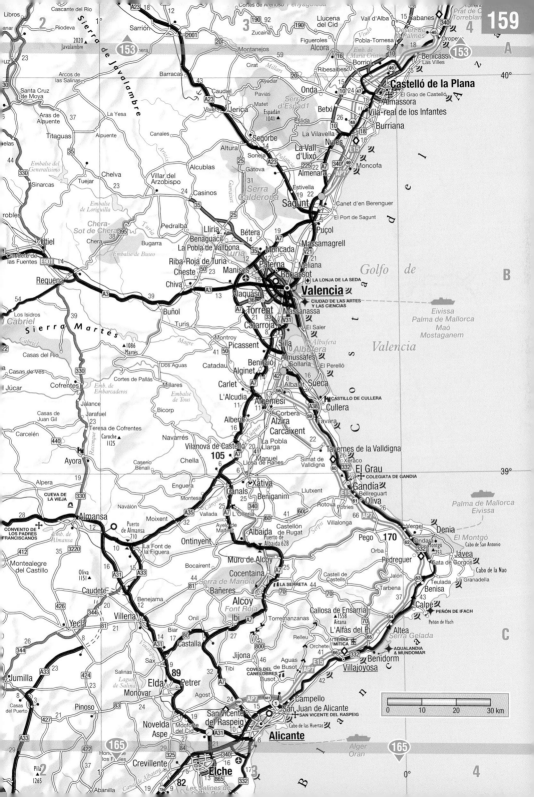

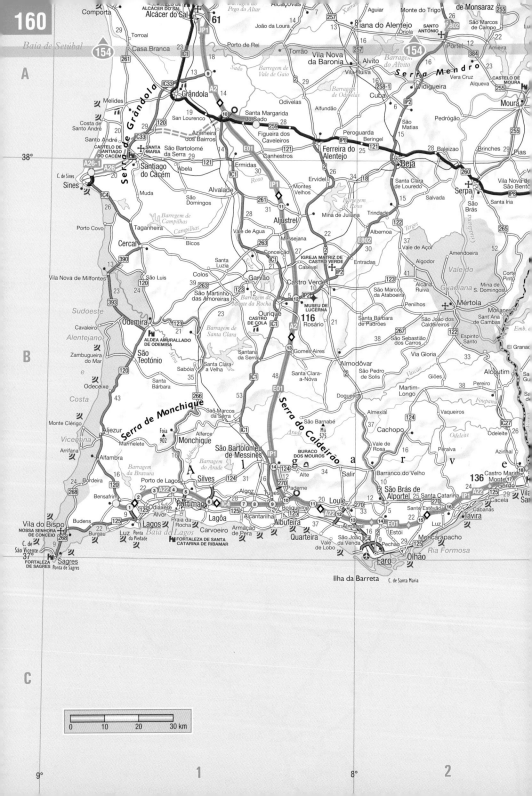

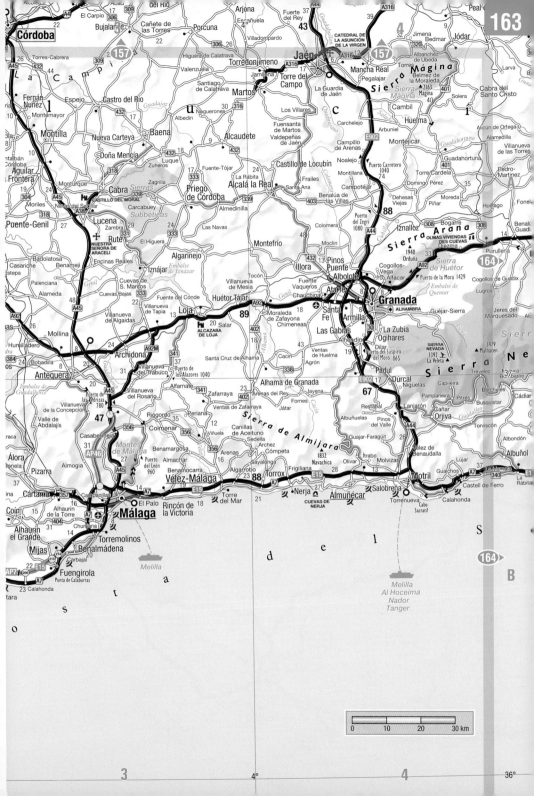

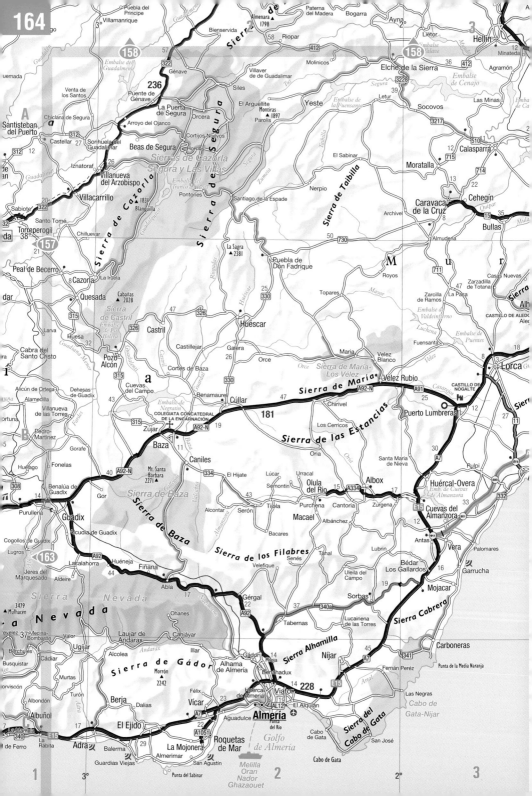

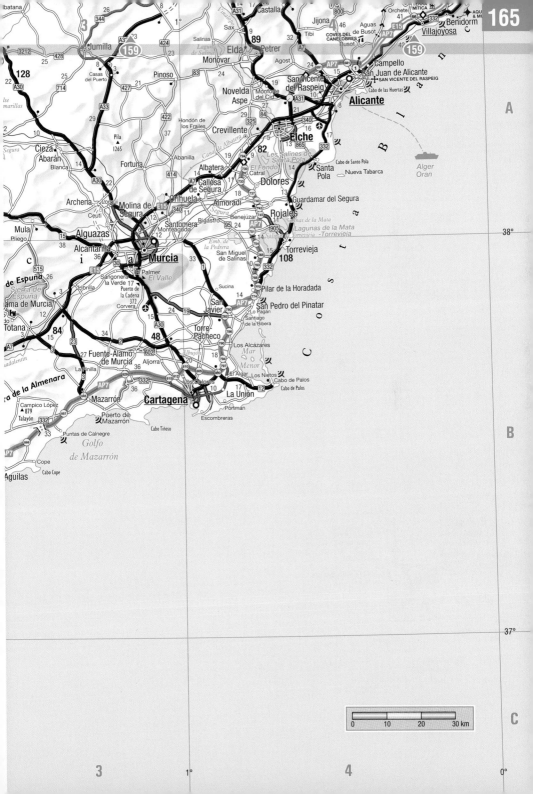

1   2°   2

A

40°

40°

Islas
Columbretes
(España)
(Spain)

○ ○ Is. Columbretes
○ ○ *Islas Columbretes*

1°

ISLAS
BALEARES

BALEARIC
ISLANDS

Port de Sóller   For
Deià   **Sóller**
Tunel de
Sóller
Valldemossa   Alar
Banyalbufar   25   Bunyola
Estellencs   39   Espòrles   **Marratxi**
Puigpunyent   12
Sa Dragonera   **10**   **Palma de**   **8** MA
Andratx   **Mallorca**
Port d'Andratx   Calvià   MAT   **6**   **10**
Peguera   15   13   **6**
Santa Ponça   17 14   Palma   13
Magaluf   Nova   Can
Cap de Cala Figuera   Cala Pastilla
Cap Enderrocat   S'Arenal   13
Bahía   Maó
Barcelona   **de Palma**

Valencia   **Mallorca**
Majorca
Eivissa   Cap I
Denia

B

Portinatx

Eivissa
Ibiza   8   Sant Joan Baptista
Sant Miquel   Pta. Grossa
Santa Agnès   12   Sant Carlos
300   Tagomago
39ª Conillera   Sant Antoni   Es Canà
de Portmany   Santa Eulàlia des Riu
Sant   16   11   Cala Llonga
Rafel   **600**   *Palma de Mallorca*
Sant Josep   8   *Barcelona*
de sa Talaia   **20**   **Eivissa**
Ibiza
Es Vedrà   Sant Francesc
Cap   de ses Salines
Llentrisca   Punta Portàs
S'Espardell
Denia   S'Espalmador
Valencia

Formentera
Sa Savina   Es Pujols
C Sant Francesc de Formentera   Sant Ferran
Nuestra Señora
Sa Verge des Pilar
C. de Barbària   Pta. Rotja

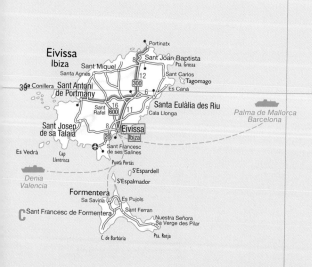

1   2°   2

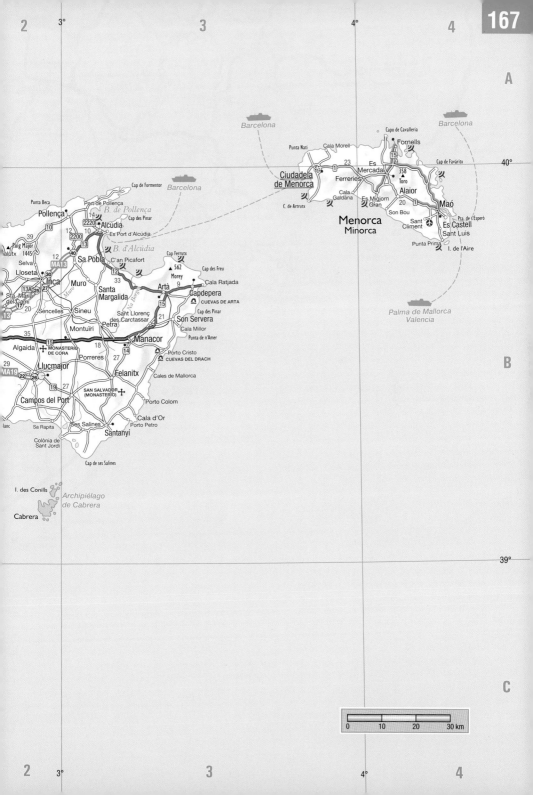

A

2 3° 3 4° 4

Barcelona

Capo de Cavalleria

Punta Nati   Cala Morell   Fornells

Cap de Favàritx

Cap de Formentor   Barcelona

Ciudadela   23   Es
de Menorca   Mercadal   358   40°
Ferreries   Toro

Cala   Es Migjorn   Alaior   Maó
Galdana   Gran   20

Menorca   Son Bou   Sant   Es Castell
Minorca   Climent   Sant Luis

Cap de Formentor

Punta Beca
Pollença   Port de Pollença   Cap des Pinar
B. de Pollença   Punta Prima   I. de l'Aire

2220   Alcúdia   Cap des Pinar
39   2200   10   Es Port d'Alcúdia
Puig Major   14   13
1445   B. d'Alcúdia   Cap Ferrutx
Selva   12   Sa Pobla   C'an Picafort
Lloseta   MA13   12   562   Cap des Freu
30   Inca   12   Morey   Cala Ratjada
13A   27   33   Artà   9   Capdepera
Sta. Maria   Santa   CUEVAS DE ARTA
del Camí   Sencelles   Sineu   Margalida   Cap des Pinar
13   Sant Llorenç   21
Montuïri   Petra   des Carctassar   Son Servera
35   Cala Millor
15   18   14   Punta de n'Amer
Algaida   MONASTERIO   Porto Cristo
DE CORA   27   CUEVAS DEL DRACH
29   Porreres
MA19   Llucmajor   Felanitx   Cales de Mallorca
22   26
19   27   SAN SALVADOR
(MONASTERIO)   Porto Colom
Campos del Port
Porto Petro
Sa Rapita   Cala d'Or
Ses Salines   Santanyí
Colònia de
Sant Jordi
Cap de ses Salines

Palma de Mallorca
Valencia

B

I. des Conills
Archipiélago
de Cabrera
Cabrera

C

0   10   20   30 km

2 3° 3 4° 4

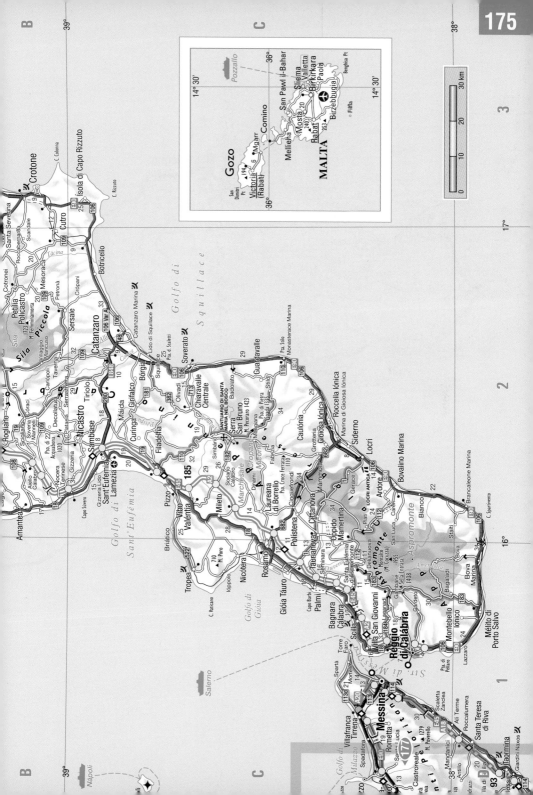

3

4

Canneto

Lípari 15°

Lípari

Vulcano

A

Salerno

Golfo di Milazzo

Capo di Milazzo

Villafranca
Tirrena 113d Sparta Torre
Faro Scilla

Milazzo A20 13 Villa San
Spadafora

Capo Calavà Golfo di Patti 113 Messina
Gioiosa Marea 22 Barcellona-
Brolo Pozzo di Gotto Rometta 114 A2 Reggio
di Caláb
Cefalù C. d'Orlando Patti Falcone Santa Lucia 184
del Mela E45 Villa San

Sant'Ágata 26 Mazzarrà 13 Castroreale M. Poverello Scaletta
Militello Naso S. Andrea 1279 Zanclea E45 Pta. di 106
Santo Stéfano 15 19 Ucria Montalbano 30 Ali Terme A18 Péllaro Mont
25 di Camastra Caterina Longi 116 Elicona Novara Mandanici E90
113 San Alcara di Sicilia Roccalumera Mé
E90 Fratello il Fùsi Floresta Antillo Santa Teresa Porto S
A20 Tortorici 185 di Riva
13 Tusa 176 289 M. Soro Santa Doménica Pila. d'Zoppo Ali Terme 175
Castelbuono 117 1847 Vittória 1264 Pila. Mandrazzi Monti
Nébrodi Randazzo 1125 Francavilla di Sicilia
1979 Mistretta Nébrodi 120 Castiglione 93
Pzo. Carbonara 286 di Sicilia Taormina
Geraci Siculo Capizzi Ledi Ancipa Rassopisciaro Linguaglossa
Petralia Colle del Cesarò 120 6 Giardini Naxos
Sottana Contrasto 35 Maletto Etna 114
120 Gangi 18 1107 Cerami Troina 25 Piedimonte Etneo
Sperlinga 29 Bronte 7 Fiumefreddo di Sicilia
120 Pella Madonnuzza Gagliano 284 Etna Máscali
29 1147 Nicosia Castelferrato 575 3323 Riposto
Alimena CASTELLO 11 E45
21 DI ADRANO Zafferana Giarre
Leonforte Regalbuto 25 Adrano Etnea 31
Agira Centúripe 17 Nicolosi Acireale
Villarosa 14 Assoro 28 Santa Maria Biancavilla Trecastagni Napoli
Calascibetta di Licodia Belpasso Aci Catena
121 156 Catenanuova Paternò 121 11 Aci Castello
Enna 192 A19 33 6
117b Pergusa E932 Misterbianco Catánia
122 Raddusa Gerbini 114
Caltanissetta 117b 16 Valguarnera Castel Simeto Golfo di
626 Caropepe di Iùdica 417 Catánia
Pietraperzia Pila Grottacalda Ramacca 2
191 647 Aidone 28 417
Barrafranca 288 Mirabella Imbáccari Lago di
VILLA ROMANA Lentini
Riesi DEL CASALE 117b San Michele di Ganzaria 24 385 A18
Piazza Armerina 417 Lentini E45
Mazzarino Palagonia
Caltagirone 194 Villasmundo Capo S. Croce
Butera 190 124 Grammichele Francofonte 114 Augusta
Niscemi 417 Mineo 194 Melilli Priolo
E931 12 Vizzini Gargallo
Falconara 117b 10 Licodia Bùccheri Sortino 21 Golfo di Augusta
115 Eubea 124 Ferla
Gela San Pietro 514 Monterosso Solarino 124 Floridia Siracusa
Almo M. Lauro 32 Canicattini
E45 Giarratana 986 Bagni 28 A18 37°
Golfo di Gela Acate Chiaramonte Palazzolo 9 C. Murro
Gulfi Acréide 287 di Porco
115 Vittória Cómiso 194 115 Cassibile
Scoglitti 8 5 Ragusa Noto 45
16 11 Módica Ávola Golfo di
Santa Croce 17 13 A18 Noto
Camerina 115 E45
C. Scarámia Rosolini ELORO ANTICA
Scicli 20
194 5 115
Marina di Ragusa 1 Ispica Marzamemi
Donnalucata 66 Pachino
Sampieri Pozzallo C. Passero
Portopalo di
C. Passero

B

C

3

4

15°

Valletta

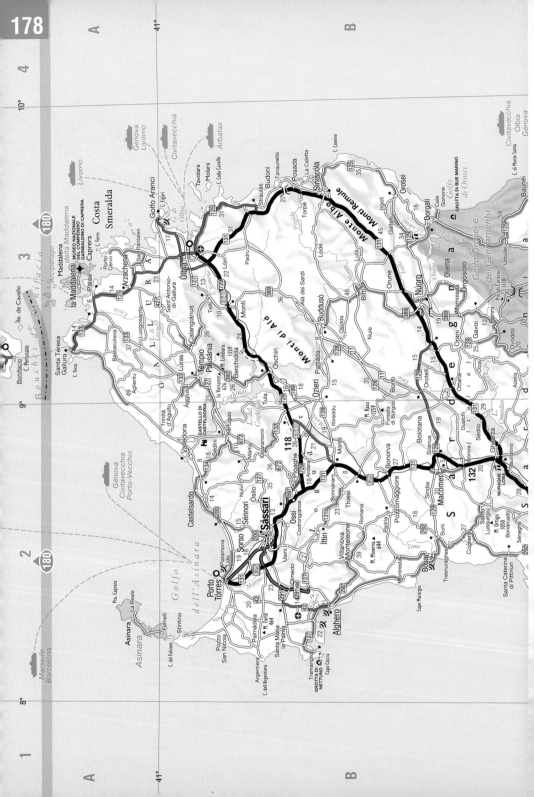

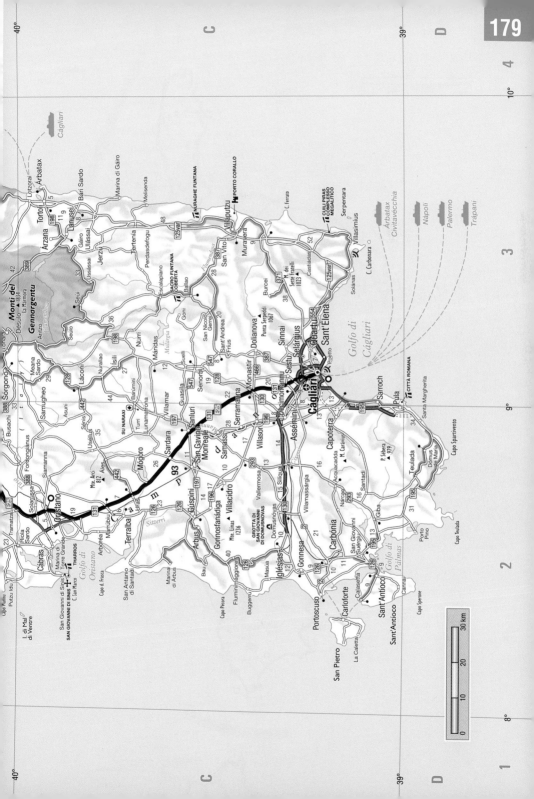

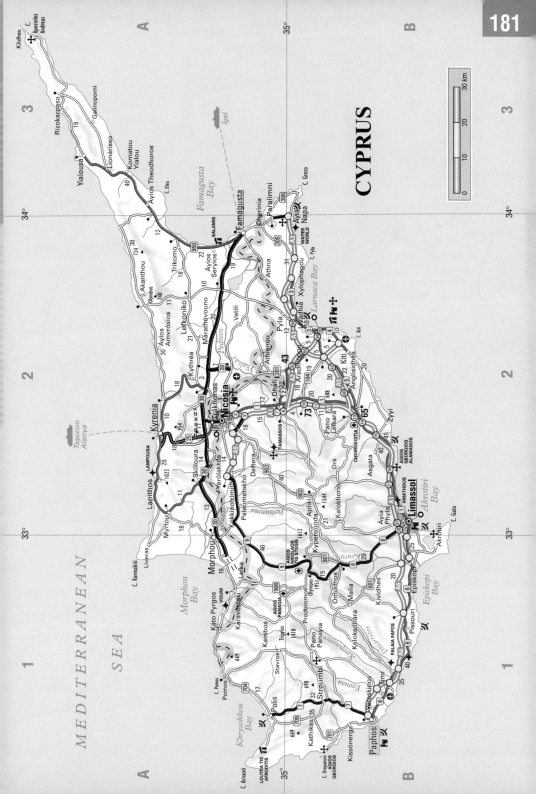

CYPRUS

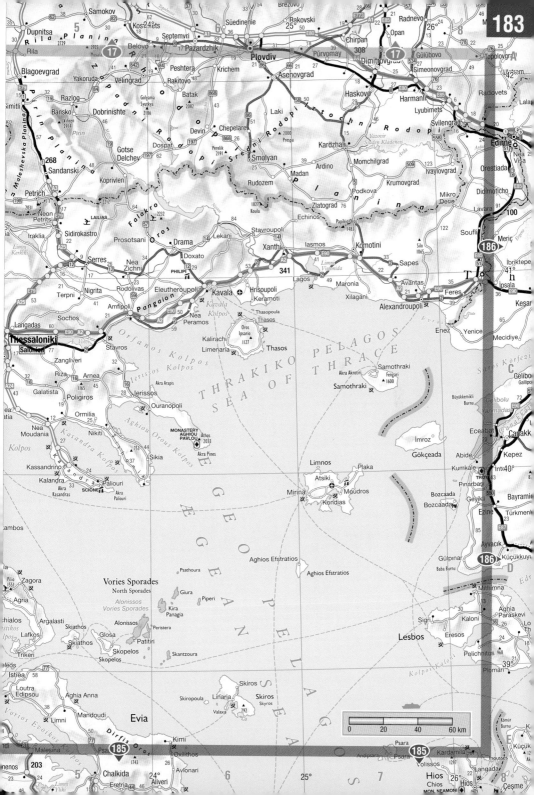

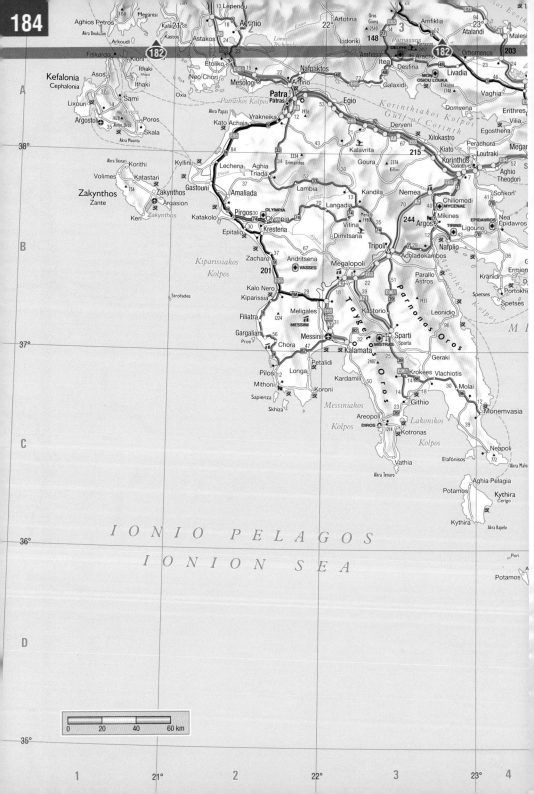

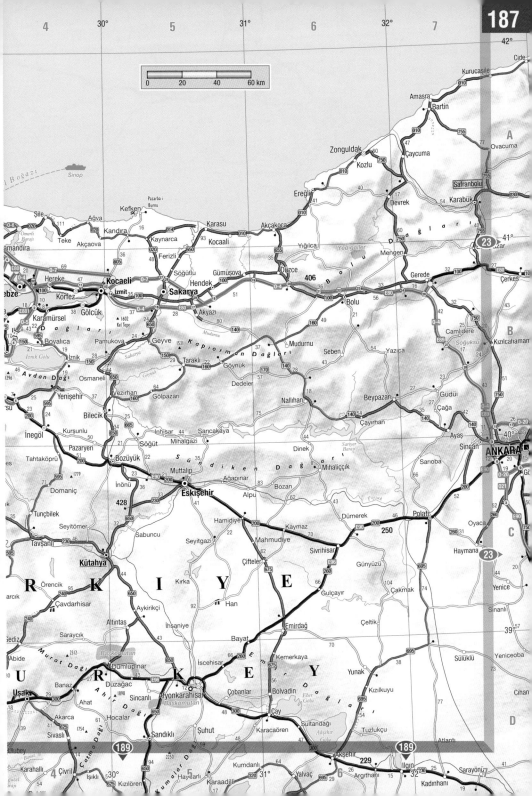

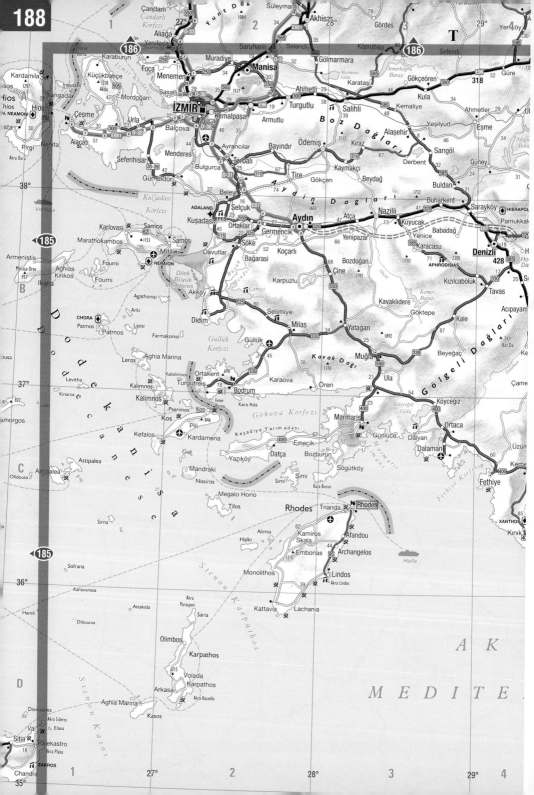

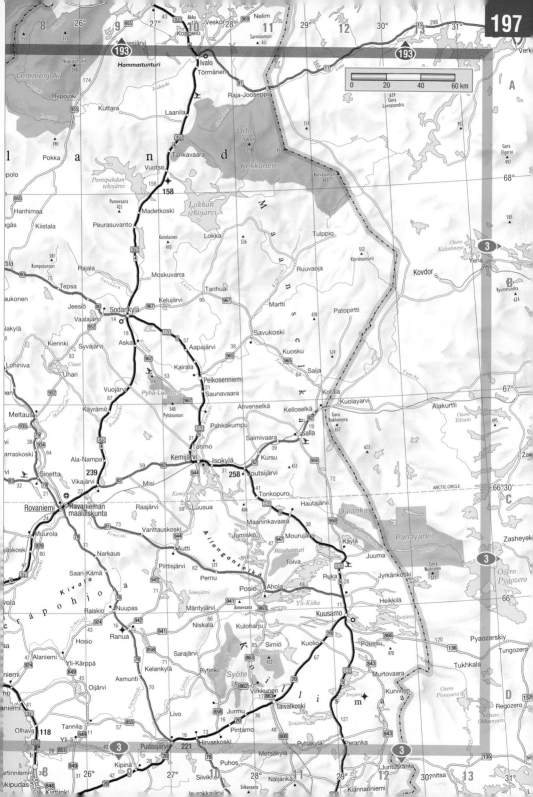

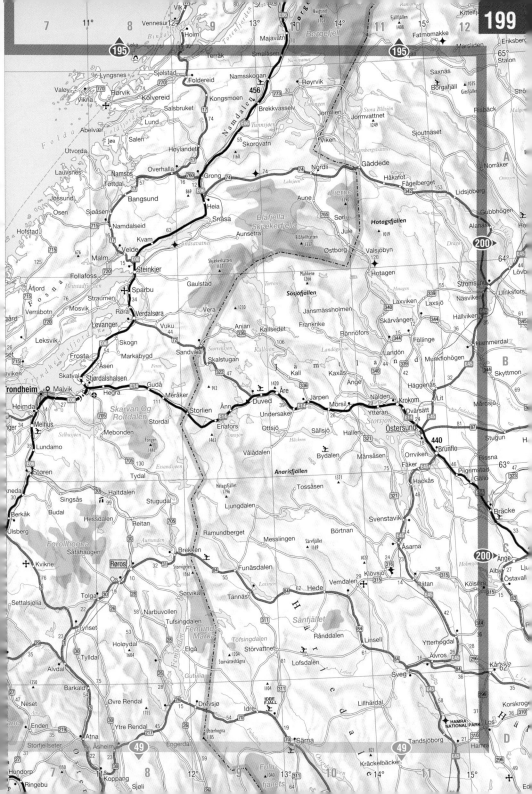

	English	French	German	Italian
(A)	Austria	Autriche	Österreich	Austria
(AL)	Albania	Albanie	Albanien	Albania
(AND)	Andorra	Andorre	Andorra	Andorra
(B)	Belgium	Belgique	Belgien	Belgio
(BG)	Bulgaria	Bulgarie	Bulgarien	Bulgaria
(BIH)	Bosnia-Herzegovin	Bosna-Herzegovine	Bosnien-Herzegowina	Bosnia-Herzogovina
(BY)	Belarus	Belarus	Weissrussland	Bielorussia
(CH)	Switzerland	Suisse	Schweiz	Svizzera
(CY)	Cyprus	Chypre	Zypern	Cipro
(CZ)	Czechia	République Tchèque	Tschechische Republik	Repubblica Ceca
(D)	Germany	Allemagne	Deutschland	Germania
(DK)	Denmark	Danemark	Dänemark	Danimarca
(E)	Spain	Espagne	Spanien	Spagna
(EST)	Estonia	Estonie	Estland	Estonia
(F)	France	France	Frankreich	Francia
(FIN)	Finland	Finlande	Finnland	Finlandia
(FL)	Liechtenstein	Liechtenstein	Liechtenstein	Liechtenstein
(FO)	Faeroe Islands	Îles Féroé	Färoër-Inseln	Isole Faroe
(GBZ)	Gibraltar	Gibraltar	Gibraltar	Gibilterra
(GR)	Greece	Grèce	Griechenland	Grecia
(H)	Hungary	Hongrie	Ungarn	Ungheria
(HR)	Croatia	Croatie	Kroatien	Croazia
(I)	Italy	Italie	Italien	Italia
(IRL)	Ireland	Irlande	Irland	Irlanda
(IS)	Iceland	Islande	Island	Islanda
(KOS)	Kosovo	Kosovo	Kosovo	Kosovo
(L)	Luxembourg	Luxembourg	Luxemburg	Lussemburgo
(LT)	Lithuania	Lituanie	Litauen	Lituania
(LV)	Latvia	Lettonie	Lettland	Lettonia
(M)	Malta	Malte	Malta	Malta
(MC)	Monaco	Monaco	Monaco	Monaco
(MD)	Moldova	Moldavie	Moldawien	Moldavia
(MNE)	Montenegro	Monténégro	Montenegro	Montenegro
(N)	Norway	Norvège	Norwegen	Norvegia
(NL)	Netherlands	Pays-Bas	Niederlande	Paesi Bassi
(NMK)	North Macedonia	Macédoine du Nord	Nordmakedonien	Macedonia del Nord
(P)	Portugal	Portugal	Portugal	Portogallo
(PL)	Poland	Pologne	Polen	Polonia
(RO)	Romania	Roumanie	Rumänien	Romania
(RSM)	San Marino	Saint-Marin	San Marino	San Marino
(RUS)	Russia	Russie	Russland	Russia
(S)	Sweden	Suède	Schweden	Svezia
(SK)	Slovakia	République Slovaque	Slowak Republik	Repubblica Slovacca
(SLO)	Slovenia	Slovénie	Slowenien	Slovenia
(SRB)	Serbia	Serbie	Serbien	Serbia
(TR)	Turkey	Turquie	Türkei	Turchia
(UA)	Ukraine	Ukraine	Ukraine	Ucraina
(UK)	United Kingdom	Royaume Uni	Grossbritannien und Nordirland	Regno Unito

Aab – Aho

A

Aabenraa DK...64 A2
Aabybro DK....58 A2
Aach D........107 B4
Aachen D......80 B2
Aalborg DK...58 A2
Aalen D........94 C2
Aalestrup DK..58 B2
Aalsmeer NL...70 B1
Aalst B.........79 B4
Aalten NL.....71 C3
Aalter B.......79 A3
Äänekoski FIN..8 A4
Aapajärvi
FIN.......197 B10
Ağapınar TR..187 C5
Aarau CH.....106 B3
Aarberg CH...106 B2
Aarburg CH...106 B2
Aardenburg NL.79 A3
Aarhus DK....59 B3
Aars DK.......58 B2
Aarschot B....79 B4
Aarup DK.....59 C3
Aba H.........113 C3
Abádánes E...152 B1
Abades E......151 A3
Abadin E.....141 A3
Abádszalók H. 113 B4
Abana TR......23 A8
A Baña E.....140 B2
Abanilla E....165 A3
Abano Terme
I...........121 B4
Abarán E.....165 A3
Abasár H.....113 B4
Abbadia San
Salvatore I...135 C4
Abbaue D......74 A2
Abbehausen D.72 A1
Abbekäs S.....66 A2
Abbeville F....90 A1
Abbey IRL.....28 A3
Abbeydorney
IRL...........29 B2
Abbeyfeale IRL..29 B2
Abbeyleix IRL...30 B1
Abbey Town
UK..........36 B3
Abbiategrasso
I............120 B1

Abborrträsk
S............196 D2
Abbots Bromley
UK...........40 C2
Abbotsbury UK .43 B4
Abda H........111 B4
Abejar E.....143 C4
Abela P.......160 B1
Abelvær N....199 A8
Abenberg D....94 B2
Abenójar E...157 B3
Abensberg D...95 C3
Aberaeron UK...39 B2
Abercarn UK....39 C3
Aberchirder UK 33 D4
Aberdare UK...39 C3
Aberdaron UK..38 B2
Aberdeen UK ..33 D4
Aberdulais UK ..39 C3
Aberdyfi UK....39 B2
Aberfeldy UK...32 D4
Aberffraw UK..38 A2
Aberfoyle UK ..34 B3
Abergavenny
UK...........39 C3
Abergele UK...38 A3
Abergynolwyn
UK...........38 B3
Aberporth UK...39 B2
Abersoch UK...38 B2
Abertillery UK ..39 C3
Abertura E....156 A2
Aberystwyth
UK...........39 B2
Abetone I.....135 A3
Abfaltersbach
TR...........186 B1
Abide
Çanakkale
TR.........187 A7
Abiego E.....145 B3
Abild D........64 B1
Abingdon-on-
Thames UK....44 B2
Abington UK...36 A3
Abisko S......194 B9
Abiul P........154 B2
Abla E.........164 B2
Ablis F........90 C1
A Bola E.....140 B3
Abondance F..118 A3
Abony H......113 B4
Aboyne UK....33 D4

Abrantes P... 154 B2
Abreiro P ... 148 A2
Abreschviller
F...........92 C3
Abrest F......117 A3
Abriès F......119 C3
Abrud RO 17 B5
Absdorf A......97 C3
Abtenau A 109 B4
Abtsgmünd D..94 C1
Abusejo E.....149 B3
Åby
Kronoberg S ... 62 A2
Östergötland S..56 B2
Åbyggeby S....51 B4
Åbytorp S......55 A6
A Cañiza E.... 140 B2
A Capela E ... 140 A2
Acate I........177 B3
Accadia I......171 B3
Accéglio I 132 A2
Accettura I ...172 B2
Acciaroli I 170 C3
Accous F......145 A3
Accrington UK ..40 B1
Accúmoli I 169 A3
Acedera E.....156 A2
Acehúche E ...155 B4
Acered E......152 A2
Acerenza I 172 B1
Acerno I.......170 C3
Acerra I.......170 C2
Aceuchal E....155 C4
Acharacle UK ..34 B2
Acharnes GR ..185 A4
Achavanich UK..32 C3
Achladokambos
GR.........184 B3
Achnasheen
UK...........32 D1
Achnashellach
UK...........32 D1
Achosnich UK ..34 B1
Aci Castello I .. 177 B4

Aci Catena I ... 177 B4
Acilia I 168 B2
Acıpayam TR.. 189 B4
Acireale I...... 177 B4
Acle UK.......41 C5
A Coruña E ... 140 A2
Acquacadda I .179 C2
Acqua Doria F. 180 B1
Acquanegra sul
Chiese I 121 B3
Acquapendente
I 168 A1
Acquasanta Terme
I 136 C2
Acquasparta I. 168 A2
Acquaviva I ... 135 B4
Acquaviva delle
Fonti I 171 C4
Acquaviva Picena
I 136 C2
Acquigny F 89 A5
Àcqui Terme I . 119 C5
Acri I 174 B2
Acs H......... 112 B2
Ácsteszér H ... 112 B1
Acy-en-Multien
F..........90 B2
Ada SRB...... 126 B2
Adak S........195 E9
Ådalsbruk N ...48 B3
Adamas GR... 185 C5
Adamsfjord
N...........193 B10
Adamuz E..... 157 B3
Adana TR......23 C8
Ádánd H...... 112 C2
Adanero E 150 B3
Adare IRL......29 B3
Adaševci SRB . 125 B5
Adeanueva de Ebro
E........... 144 B2
Adelboden
CH......... 106 C2
Adelebsen D...82 A1
Adélfia I....... 173 A2
Adelmannsfelden
D............94 C2
Adelsheim D...94 B1
Adelsö S......57 A3
Ademuz E..... 152 B2
Adenau D......80 B2
Adendorf D....72 A3
Adinkerke B ...78 A2

Adjud RO.......17 B7
Adliswil CH ... 107 B3
Admont A..... 110 B1
Ådneram N 52 A2
Adolfsström
S........... 195 D7
Adony H...... 112 B2
Adorf
Hessen D 81 A4
Sachsen D 83 B4
Adra E........ 164 C1
Adradas E..... 152 A1
Adrall E...... 147 B2
Adrano I...... 177 B3
Ádria I........ 121 B5
Adrigole IRL...29 C2
Adwick le Street
UK...........40 B2
Adzaneta E ... 153 B3
Aesch CH..... 106 B2
A Estrada E... 140 B2
Afandou GR... 188 C3
Áfarnes N..... 198 C4
Affi I...........121 B3
Affing D........94 C2
Affoltern CH.. 106 B3
Affric Lodge
UK........... 32 D1
Áfjord N...... 199 B7
Aflenz Kurort
A........... 110 B2
A Fonsagrada
E........... 141 A3
Afragóla I..... 170 C2
Afritz A....... 109 C4
Afyonkarahisar
TR......... 187 D5
Ágasegyháza
H........... 112 C3
Agay F........ 132 B2
Agazzano I.... 120 C2
Agde F........ 130 B2
Agdenes N.... 198 B6
Agen F........ 129 B3
Ager E........ 145 C4
Agerbæk DK ...59 C1
Agerskov DK...64 A2
Agger DK......58 B1
Aggersund DK .58 A2
Ággius I....... 178 B3
Aggsbach Dorf
A............97 C3
Aggsbach Markt
A............97 C3
Aggtelek H.....99 C4

Aghalee UK 27 B4
Aghia GR..... 182 D4
Aghia Anna
GR.......... 183 E5
Aghia Galini
GR.......... 185 D5
Aghia Marina
GR.......... 188 D1
Aghia Paraskevi
GR.......... 186 C1
Aghia Pelagia
GR.......... 184 C3
Aghia Triada
GR.......... 184 B2
Aghiokambos
GR.......... 182 D4
Aghios Efstratios
GR.......... 183 D6
Aghios Kirikos
GR.......... 185 B7
Aghios Matheos
GR.......... 182 D1
Aghios Mironas
GR.......... 185 D6
Aghios Nikolaos
GR.......... 185 D6
Aghios Petros
GR.......... 182 E2
Aghio Theodori
GR.......... 184 B4
Agiči BIH..... 124 C2
Agira I........ 177 B3
Aglientu I..... 178 A3
Agnières F 118 C2
Agno CH...... 120 B1
Agnone I...... 170 B2
Agolada E.... 140 B2
Agon Coutainville
F............88 A2
Ágordo I...... 121 A5
Agost E....... 165 A4
Agramón E.... 158 C2
Agramunt E... 147 C2
Agreda E...... 144 C2
Agria GR..... 183 D5
Agrigento I ... 176 B2
Agrinio GR... 182 E3
Agrón E....... 163 A4
Agrópoli I.... 170 C2
Aguadulce
Almería E 164 C2
Sevilla E 162 A3
Agualada E ... 140 A2
Agua Longa P. 148 A1

A Guarda E... 140 C2
Aguarón E 152 A2
Aguas E....... 145 B3
Aguas Belas P. 154 B2
Aguas de Busot
E........... 159 C3
Aguas de Moura
P........... 154 C2
Águas Frias P . 148 A2
Aguas Santas
P........... 148 A1
Aguaviva E.... 153 B3
Aguaviva de la
Vega E...... 152 A1
A Gudiña E... 141 B3
Agudo E...... 156 B3
Águeda P..... 148 B1
Aguessac F... 130 A2
Agugliano I... 136 B2
Aguiar P...... 154 C3
Aguiàr da Beira
P........... 148 B2
Aguilafuente
E........... 151 A3
Aguilar de Campóo
E........... 142 B2
Aguilar de la
Frontera E ... 163 A3
Aguilas E..... 164 B3
Agunnaryd S...60 C4
Ahat TR...... 187 D4
Ahaus D........71 B3
Åheim N...... 198 C2
Ahigal E...... 149 B3
Ahigal de Villarino
E........... 149 A3
Ahillones E... 156 B2
Ahlbeck
Mecklenburg-
Vorpommern
D............66 C3
Mecklenburg-
Vorpommern
D............74 A3
Ahlen D........81 A3
Ahlhorn D.....71 B5
Ahmetbey TR . 186 A2
Ahmetler TR .. 188 A4
Ahmetli TR... 188 A2
Ahoghill UK....27 B4
Ahola FIN.... 197 C11

Ahrensbök D ...65 B3
Ahrensburg D .72 A3
Ahrenshoop D ..66 B1
Ahun F 116 A2
Åhus S 63 C2
Ahvenselkä
  FIN........197 C11
Aibar E........144 B2
Aich D 95 C4
Aicha D 96 C1
Aichach D......94 C3
Aidone I.......177 B3
Aiello Cálabro
  I.............175 B2
Aigen im Mühlkreis
  A..............96 C1
Aigle CH 119 A3
Aignan F 128 C3
Aignay-le-Duc
  F.............104 B3
Aigre F........115 C4
Aigrefeuille-
  d'Aunis F....114 B3
Aigrefeuille-sur-
  Maine F......101 B4
Aiguablava E .147 C4
Aiguebelle F ..118 B3
Aigueperse F .116 A3
Aigues-Mortes
  F.............131 B3
Aigues-Vives
  F.............130 B1
Aiguilles F 119 C3
Aiguillon F 129 B3
Aigurande F ..103 C3
Ailefroide F ...118 C3
Aillant-sur-Tholon
  F.............104 B2
Ailly-sur-Noye
  F..............90 B2
Ailly-sur-Somme
  F..............90 B2
Aimargues F ..131 B3
Aime F.........118 B3
Ainaži LV........8 D4
Ainet A........109 C3
Ainhoa F 144 A2
Ainsa E........145 B4
Airaines F 90 B1
Aird UK 34 B2
Aird Asaig
  Tairbeart UK ..31 B2
Airdrie UK.....35 C4
Aire-sur-l'Adour
  F.............128 C2
Aire-sur-la-Lys
  F..............78 B2
Airole I........133 B3
Airolo CH 107 C3
Airvault F 102 C1
Aisey-sur-Seine
  F.............104 B3
Aissey F 105 B5
Aisy-sur-Armançon
  F.............104 B3
Aiterhofen D...95 C4
Aith
  Orkney UK....33 B4
  Shetland UK ..33 A5
Aitona E.......153 A4
Aitrach D 107 B5
Aiud RO........17 B5
Aix-en-Othe F. 104 A2
Aix-en-Provence
  F.............131 B4
Aixe-sur-Vienne
  F.............115 C5
Aix-les-Bains
  F.............118 B2
Aizenay F 114 B2
Aizkraukle LV...8 D4
Aizpute LV......8 D2
Ajac F.........146 A3
Ajaccio F 180 B1
Ajain F........116 A1
Ajaureforsen
  S............195 E6
Ajdovščina
  SLO 122 B2
Ajka H 111 B4
Ajo E..........143 A3
Ajofrin E 157 A4
Ajos FIN.......196 D7
Ajuda P 155 C3
Akanthou CY ..181 A2
Akarca TR.....189 A4
Akasztó H......112 C3
Akçakoca TR..187 A6
Akçaova TR...187 A4
Akçay TR......189 C4

Aken D.........83 A4
Åkerby S........51 B4
Åkernes N 52 B3
Åkersberga S ..57 A4
Åkers styckebruk
  S.............56 A3
Åkervik N.....195 E4
Akhisar TR 186 D2
Åkirkeby DK....67 A3
Akköy TR 188 B2
Akkrum NL......70 A2
Ákören TR 189 B7
Åkra N 52 A2
Akranes IS 190 C3
Åkrehamn N...52 A1
Akrotiri CY 181 B1
Aksaray TR 23 B8
Akşehir TR 189 A6
Akseki TR 189 B6
Aksla N 46 A3
Aksu TR 189 C5
Aktsyabrski
  BY.............13 B8
Akureyri IS 191 B7
Åkvåg N 53 B5
Akyazı TR 187 B5
Ål N.............47 B5
Ala I...........121 B4
Alaca TR........23 A8
Alacaatlı TR ...186 C3
Alaçam TR......23 A8
Alaçatı TR 188 A1
Aladağ TR.....189 C7
Aladžari I.....178 B3
Ala di Stura I ..119 B4
Alaejos E 150 A2
Alagna
  Valsésia I 119 B4
Alagón E 144 C2
Alaior E.......167 B4
Alájar E.......161 B3
Alakurtti
  RUS 197 C13
Alakylä FIN ...196 B7
Alameda I......163 A3
Alameda de la
  Sagra E 151 B4
Alamedilla E ..163 A4
Alaminos E....156 B3
Alaminos E....151 B5
Ala-Nampa
  FIN..........197 C9
Alanäs S 199 A12
Alandroal P ...155 C3
Alange E 156 B1
Alaniemi FIN...197 D8
Alanís E 156 B2
Alanno I.......169 A3
Ålansbro S....200 D3
Alanya TR 189 C7
Alap H 112 C2
Alaquáso E....159 B3
Alaraz E.......150 B2
Alarcón E......158 B1
Alar del Rey E .142 B2
Alaró E........167 B2
Alaşehir TR....188 A3
Alássio I.......133 A4
Åglasun TR....189 B5
Alatoz E.......159 B2
Alatri I........169 B3
Alavus FIN.......8 A3
Alba
  E............152 B2
  I............119 C5
Alba Adriática
  I............136 C2
Albacete E 158 C2
Alba de Tormes
  E............150 B2
Alba de Yeltes
  E............149 B3
Albaida E......159 C3
Alba-Iulia RO ...17 B5
Albæk DK......58 A3
Albaladejo E ..158 C1
Albala del
  Caudillo E ...156 A1
Albalat E......159 B3
Albalate de
  Cinca E......145 C4
Albalate del
  Arzobispo E .153 A3
Albalate de las
  Nogueras E ..152 B1
Albalete de
  Zorita E 151 B5
Alban F 130 B1
Albánchez E ..164 B2
Albanchez de
  Úbeda E.....163 A4
Albano Laziale
  I............168 B2
Albanyà E.....147 B3

Albaredo d'Adige
  I............121 B4
Albares E 151 B4
Albarracin E ..152 B2
Albatarrec E ..153 A4
Albatera E 165 A4
Albbruck D 106 B3
Albedin E......163 A3
Albelda de Iregua
  E............143 B4
Albenga I 133 A4
Albens F 118 B2
Alberga
  Södermanland
  S............56 A2
  Södermanland
  S............56 B2
Albergaria-a-Nova
  P............148 B1
Albergaria-a-Velha
  P............148 B1
Albergaria dos
  Doze P 154 B2
Alberge P 154 C2
Alberic E 159 B3
Albernoa P....160 B2
Alberobello I..173 B3
Alberoni I......122 B1
Albersdorf D...66 B2
Albersloh D.....81 A3
Albert F........90 A2
Albertirsa H....112 B3
Albertville F....118 B3
Alberuela de Tubo
  E............145 C3
Albi F.........130 B1
Albidona I 174 B2
Albínia I.......168 A1
Albino I.......120 B2
Albinshof D....66 C2
Albires E......142 B1
Albisola Marina
  I............133 A4
Albocácer E ..153 B4
Albolote E 163 A4
Albondón E ...164 C1
Alborea E 158 B2
Albox E 164 B2
Albrechtice nad
  Vitavou CZ....96 B2
Albstadt D 107 A4
Albufeira P....160 B1
Albuñol E 164 C1
Albuñuelas E .163 B4
Alburquerque
  E............155 B3
Alby
  Öland S 63 B4
  Västernorrland
  S...........200 D1
Alcácer do Sal
  P............154 C2
Alcáçovas P ...154 C2
Alcadozo E 158 C2
Alcafoces P....155 B3
Alcains P 155 B3
Alcaláde Guadaira
  E............162 A2
Alcaláde Gurrea
  E............144 B3
Alcalá Henares
  E............151 B4
Alcalá de la Selva
  E............153 B3
Alcalá del Júcar
  E............158 B2
Alcalá de los
  Gazules E ...162 B2
Alcaláde Río
  E............162 A2
Alcaláde Valle
  E............162 B2
Alcaláde Xivert
  E............153 B4
Alcalála Real
  E............163 A4
Álcamo I.......176 B1
Alcampell E ...145 C4
Alcanadre E ..143 B4
Alcanar E 153 B4
Alcanede P....154 B2
Alcanena P....154 B2
Alcañices E ...149 A3
Alcántara E ...155 B4
Alcantarilha P .160 B1
Alcantarilla E .165 B3
Alcañz E 153 A3
Alcaracejos E .156 B3
Alcara il Fusi I .177 A3
Alcaraz E 158 C1
Alcaria Ruiva
  P............160 B2

Alcarraz E 153 A4
Alcaudete E ...163 A3
Alcaudete de la
  Jara E 150 C3
Alcázar de San
  Juan E.......157 A4
Alcazarén E ...150 A3
Alcester UK 44 A2
Alcoba E.......157 A3
Alcobaça P....154 B1
Alcobendas E .151 B4
Alcocer E......151 B5
Alcochete P....154 C2
Alcoentre P....154 B2
Alcolea
  Almería E ...164 C2
  Córdoba E ..156 C3
Alcolea de
  Calatrava E .157 B3
Alcolea de Cinca
  E............145 C4
Alcolea del Pinar
  E............152 A1
Alcolea del Río
  E............162 A2
Alcolea de Tajo
  E............150 C2
Alcollarín E ...156 A2
Alconchel E ...155 C3
Alconera E 155 C4
Alcontar E 164 B2
Alcora E.......153 B3
Alcorcón E 151 B4
Alcorisa E 153 B3
Alcossebre E .153 B4
Alcoutim P....160 B2
Alcover E......147 C2
Alcoy E 159 C3
Alcsútdoboz
  H............112 B2
Alcubierre E ..145 C3
Alcubilla de
  Avellaneda
  E............143 C3
Alcubilla de
  Nogales E ...141 B5
Alcubillas E ...157 B4
Alcublas E 159 B3
Alcúdia E 167 B3
Alcudia de Guadix
  E............164 B1
Alcuéscar E ..155 A4
Aldbrough UK ..41 B3
Aldeacentenera
  E............156 A2
Aldeadávila de la
  Ribera E 149 A3
Aldea del Cano
  E............155 B4
Aldea del Fresno
  E............151 B3
Aldea del Obispo
  E............149 B3
Aldea del Rey
  E............157 B4
Aldea de Trujillo
  E............156 A2
Aldealcorvo E .151 A4
Aldealuenga de
  Santa Maria
  E............151 A4
Aldeamayor de San
  Martin E 150 A3
Aldeanueva de
  Barbarroya
  E............150 C2
Aldeanueva del
  Camino E 149 B4
Aldeanueva del
  Codonal E....150 A3
Aldeanueva de San
  Bartolomé E .156 A2
Aldeapozo E ..144 C1
Aldeaquemada
  E............157 B4
Aldearrubia E .150 A2
Aldeaseca de la
  Frontera E ...150 B2
Aldeasoña E ..151 A3
Aldeatejada E .150 B2
Aldeavieja E ..150 B3
Aldeburgh UK .45 A5
Aldehuela E ..152 B2
Aldehuela de
  Calatañazor
  E............143 C4
Aldeia da Serra
  P............155 C3
Aldeia do Bispo
  P............149 B3
Aldeia do Mato
  P............154 B2

Aldeia Gavinha
  P............154 B1
Aldeire E 164 B1
Aldenhoven D .80 B2
Aldersbach D...95 C5
Aldershot UK ..44 B3
Aludes F.......144 A2
Åled S..........60 C2
Aldea E........165 B3
Alegria E 143 B4
Aleksandrovac
  SRB 127 C3
Aleksandrów
  Kujawski PL...76 B3
Aleksandrów
  Łódzki PL.....86 A3
Aleksa Šantić
  SRB 126 B1
Ålem S.........62 B4
Alençon F......89 B4
Alenquer P....154 B1
Alenya F 146 B3
Aléria F 180 A2
Alès F 131 A3
Áles I..........179 C2
Alessándria I..120 C1
Alessándria della
  Rocca I......176 B2
Alessano I.....173 C4
Ålesund N.....198 C3
Alet-les-Bains
  F............146 B3
Alexandria
  GR 182 C4
  RO 17 D6
  UK 34 C3
Alexandroupoli
  GR 183 C7
Aleyrac F 131 A3
Alézio I.......173 B4
Alfacar E 163 A4
Alfaiates P ...149 B3
Alfajarin E 153 A3
Alfambra
  E............152 B2
  P............160 B1
Alfândega da Fé
  P............149 A3
Alfarela de Jafes
  P............148 A2
Alfarelos P....148 B1
Alfarim P......154 C1
Alfarnate E ...163 B3
Alfaro E 144 B2
Alfarrás E 145 C4
Alfaz del Pi E .159 C3
Alfedena I.....169 B4
Alfeizarão P ..154 B1
Alfeld
  Bayern D.....95 B3
  Niedersachsen
  D............72 C2
Alfena P.......148 A1
Alferce P......160 B1
Alfhausen D...71 B4
Alfonsine I....135 A5
Alford
  Aberdeenshire
  UK 33 D4
  Lincolnshire
  UK 41 B4
Alforja E 147 C1
Alfoz E........141 A3
Alfreton UK....40 B2
Alfta S.........50 A3
Alfundão P....160 A1
Algaida E......167 B2
Algar E........162 B2
Algarås S......55 B5
Ågård N........52 A2
Algarinejo E ..163 A3
Algarrobo E ..163 B3
Algatocin E ...162 B2
Algeciras E....162 B2
Algemesí E....159 B3
Algés P........154 C1
Algete E.......151 B4
Alghero I......178 B2
Älghult S......62 A3
Alginet E......159 B3
Algodonales
  E............162 B2
Algodor
  P............154 C2
Algora E.......151 B5
Algoso P 149 A3
Algoz P 160 B1
Ålgsjö S.......200 B3
Algutsrum S ...63 B4
Algyö H 126 A2

Alhama de Almería
  E............164 C2
Almázan E 152 A1
Alhama de Aragón
  E............152 A2
Alhama de Granada
  E............163 B4
Alhama de Murcia
  E............165 B3
Alhambra E ...157 B4
Alhandra P....154 C1
Alhaurin de la Torre
  E............163 B3
Alhaurín el Grande
  E............163 B3
Alhendin E....163 A4
Alhóndiga E ..151 B5
Alia E 156 A2
Ália I..........176 B2
Aliaga TR 186 D1
Aliaga E.......153 B3
Alibunar SRB..127 B2
Alicante E.....165 A4
Alicún de Ortega
  E............164 B1
Alife I.........170 B2
Almería E 164 C2
Alimena I......177 B3
Alingsås S......60 B2
Alinyà E.......147 B2
Aliseda E......155 B4
Ali Terme I....177 A4
Aliveri GR.....185 A5
Alixan F 117 C5
Aljaraque E ...161 B2
Aljezur P......160 B1
Aljorra E 165 B3
Aljubarrota P .154 B2
Aljucen E......155 B4
Aljustrel P 160 B1
Alken B 79 B5
Alkmaar NL....70 B1
Alkoven A 96 C2
Allaines F 103 A3
Allaire F.......101 B3
Allanche F 116 B2
Alland A 111 A3
Allariz E.......140 B3
Allassac F 129 A4
Allauch F......131 B4
Alleen N........52 B3
Allègre F 117 B3
Allemont F....118 B3
Allendale Town
  UK 37 B4
Allendorf D....81 B4
Allentsteig A...97 C3
Allepuz E 153 B3
Allersberg D...95 B3
Allershausen D .95 C3
Alles E 142 A2
Allevard F 118 B3
Allgunnen S ...62 A3
Allihies IRL....29 C1
Allingåbro DK..58 B3
Allmannsdorf
  D............107 B4
Allo E.........144 B1
Alloa UK 35 B4
Allogny F 103 B4
Ållohuokta S .196 B2
Allones
  Eure et Loir
  F............90 C1
  Maine-et-Loire
  F............102 B2
Allonnes F 128 B2
Allons F 128 B2
Allos F 132 A2
Ållsa K........55 B5
Allstedt D......82 A3
Alltwalis UK...39 C2
Allumiere I....168 A1
Almaceda P ..155 B3
Almacelles E .145 C4
Almáchar E ...163 B3
Almada P......154 C1
Almadén E 156 B3
Almadén de la Plata
  E............161 B3
Almadenejos
  E............156 B3
Almadrones E .151 B5
Almagro E.....157 B4
Almajano E ...144 C1
Almansa E.....159 C2
Almansil P 160 B2
Almanza E.....142 B1
Almaraz E.....150 C2
Almarza E.....143 C4
Almásfüzitö
  H............112 B2

Almassora E ...159 B3
Almedina E ...158 C1
Almazul E 152 A1
Alme D..........81 A4
Almedina E ...158 C1
Almedinilla E .163 A3
Almeida
  E............149 A3
  P............149 B3
Almeirim P....154 B2
Almelo NL......71 B3
Almenar E 145 C4
Almenara E ...159 B3
Almenar de Soria
  E............152 A1
Almendra P ...149 B2
Almendral E ..155 C4
Almendral de la
  Cañada E ...150 B3
Almendralejo
  E............155 C4
Almenno San
  Bartolomeo I. 120 B2
Almere NL......70 B2
Almería E 164 C2
Almerimar E ..164 C2
Almese I.......119 B4
Almexial P 160 B2
Álmhult S......63 B2
Almiropotamos
  GR 185 A5
Almiros GR....182 D4
Almodôvar P...160 B1
Almodóvar del
  Campo E 157 B3
Almodóvar del
  Pinar E 158 B2
Almodóvar del Río
  E............162 A2
Almofala P 148 B2
Almogia E 163 B3
Almoharin E ..156 A1
Almonacid de la
  Sierra E 152 A2
Almonacid de
  Toledo E 157 A4
Almonaster la Real
  E............161 B3
Almondsbury
  UK 43 A4
Almonte E 161 B3
Almoradí E 165 A4
Almoraima E .162 B2
Almoster P 154 B2
Almsele S 200 B3
Ålmsta S.......51 C5
Almudévar E ..145 B3
Almudéjar E ..163 A4
Almuñécar E ..163 B4
Almunge S 51 C5
Almuradiel E ..157 B4
Almussafes E .159 B3
Almvik S.......62 A4
Alness UK 32 D2
Almvarth UK...37 A5
Alnwick UK ...37 A5
Åloppe S.......51 C4
Álora E 163 B3
Alos d'Ensil E .146 B2
Alosno E 161 B2
Alozaina E 163 B3
Alpbach A.....108 B2
Alpedrete de la
  Sierra E 151 B4
Alpedrinha P .148 B2
Alpen D........80 A2
Alpera E 159 C2
Alphen aan de Rijn
  NL...........70 B1
Alpiarça P 154 B2
Alpignano I ...119 B4
Alpirsbach D...93 C4
Alpu TR 187 C5
Alpuente E 159 B2
Alquézar E 145 B4
Als DK.........58 B3
Alsasua E 144 B1
Alsdorf D......80 B2
Alselv DK......59 C1
Alsfeld D.......81 B5
Alsike S........57 A3
Alskog S.......57 C4
Alsleben D.....83 A3
Alsónémedi H 112 B3
Alsótold H 113 B3
Alsóújlak H ...111 B3
Alstad N......194 C6
Alstätte D......71 B3
Alsterbro S....62 B3
Alstermo S....62 B3
Alston UK......37 B4

Alsvåg N...... 194 B6
Alsvik N...... 194 C5
Alta N..... 192 C7
Ålta S..... 57 A4
Altamura I... 172 B2
Altarejos E... 158 B1
Altaussee A... 109 B4
Altavilla Irpina
I..... 170 B2
Altavilla Silentina
I..... 170 C3
Altdöbern D....84 A2
Altdorf
CH..... 107 C3
D..... 95 C4
Altdorf bei
Nürnberg D...95 B3
Alte P..... 160 B1
Altea E..... 159 C3
Altedo I..... 121 C4
Altena D.....81 A3
Altenau D....82 A2
Altenberg D....84 B1
Altenberge D..71 B4
Altenbruch D...64 C1
Altenburg D....83 B4
Altenfelden A..96 C1
Altengronau D..82 B1
Altenheim D...93 C3
Altenhundem
D..............81 A4
Altenkirchen
Mecklenburg-Vorpommern
D...............66 B2
Radom D....81 B3
Altenkunstadt
D..............82 B3
Altenmarkt
A.............. 110 B1
D............. 109 A3
Altenmarkt im
Pongall A... 109 B4
Altensteig D...93 C4
Altentreptow
D...............74 A2
Altenwalde D...64 C1
Alten-weddingen
D...............73 B4
Alter do Chão
P............. 155 B3
Altfraunhofen
D...............95 C4
Altheim
A............. 109 A4
D............. 109 A4
Althofen A... 110 C1
Altınoluk TR.. 186 C1
Altınova TR... 186 C1
Altıntaş TR... 187 C5
Altınyaka TR.. 189 C5
Altınyayla TR . 189 B4
Altkirch F... 106 B2
Altlandsberg D .74 B2
Altlewin D....74 B3
Altmannstein
D...............95 C3
Altmorschen D..82 A1
Altmunster A . 109 B4
Altnaharra UK..32 C2
Alto Campóo
E............. 142 A2
Altofonte I... 176 A2
Altomonte I... 174 B2
Alton
Hampshire
UK..............44 B3
Staffordshire
UK.............. 40 C2
Altopáscio I... 135 B3
Altötting D... 109 A3
Altreichenau D .96 C1
Alt Ruppin D...74 B1
Altshausen D. 107 B4
Altstätten CH . 107 B4
Altura E..... 159 B3
Altusried D... 107 B5
Alūksne LV.....8 D5
Alunda S.....51 B5
Alustante E... 152 B2
Alva UK.....35 B4
Alvaiázere P... 154 B2
Alvalade P... 160 B1
Älvängen S....60 B2
Alvarenga P... 148 B1
Alvares P..... 154 B2
Alvdal N... 199 C7
Älvdalen S... 49 A6
Alverca P... 154 C1
Åversund N... 46 B2
Alvesta S.....62 B2
Alvignac F... 129 B4
Alvignano I... 170 B2

Ålvik N.......46 B3
Alvik S..........50 B1
Alvimare F.....89 A4
Alviobeira P . 154 B2
Alvito P..... 160 A2
Älvkarleby S....51 B4
Älvkarleöbruk
S..............51 B4
Alvor P..... 160 B1
Alvorge P... 154 B2
Alvøy N.......46 B2
Älvros S..... 199 C11
Alvsbacka S....55 A4
Älvsbyn S... 196 D4
Älvsered S....60 B2
Alwernia PL....86 B3
Alwinton UK...37 A4
Alvik UK.....35 B4
Alytus LT..... 13 A6
Alzénau D....93 A5
Alzey D..... 93 B4
Alzira E..... 159 B3
Alzonne F... 146 A3
Amadora P... 154 C1
Åmål S..........55 A3
Amalfi I..... 170 C2
Amaliada GR . 184 B2
Amance F... 105 B5
Amancey F... 105 B5
Amándola I ... 136 C2
Amantea I..... 175 B2
Amarante P . 148 A1
Amareleja P... 161 A2
Amares P..... 148 A1
Amaseno I... 169 B3
Amasra TR... 187 A7
Amatrice I... 169 A3
Amay B..........79 B5
Ambarnyy RUS..3 D13
Ambazac F... 115 C5
Ambelonas
GR..........182 D4
Amberg D.....95 B3
Ambérieu-en-
Bugey F... 118 B2
Ambérieux-en-
Dombes F . 117 A4
Ambert F... 117 B3
Ambés F... 128 A2
Ambjörby S...49 B5
Ambjörnarp S..60 B3
Amble UK.....37 A5
Ambleside UK . 36 B4
Ambleteuse F . 78 B1
Amboise F... 102 B2
Ambrières-les-
Vallées F....88 B3
Amden CH... 107 B4
Amel B..........80 B2
Amélia I..... 168 A2
Amélie-les-Bains-
Palalda F... 146 B3
Amelinghausen
D...............72 A3
Amendoa P... 154 B2
Amendoeira P 160 B2
Améndola I... 171 B3
Amendolara I . 174 B2
Amer E..... 147 B3
A Merca E... 140 B3
Amerongen NL .70 B2
Amersfoort NL . 70 B2
Amersham UK . 44 B3
Amesbury UK . 44 B2
Amfikli:a GR . 182 E4
Amfilochia GR . 182 D3
Ämfipoli GR . 183 C5
Amfissa GR . 184 A3
Amièira P... 155 C3
Amieira F... 171 B4
Amieiro P... 148 B1
Amiens F......90 B2
Amindeo GR . 182 C3
Åminne S.....60 B3
Åmli N...........53 B4
Amlwch UK....38 A2
Ammanford UK .39 C3
Ammarnäs S... 195 E7
Åmmeberg S...55 B5
Amorbach D... 94 B1
Amorebieta E . 143 A4
Amorgos GR . 185 C6
Amorosa P... 148 A1
Amot
Buskerud N ... 48 C1
Telemark N . 53 A3
S...........50 B3
Åmotfors S....54 A3
Åmotsdal N... 53 A4
Amou F... 128 C2
Ampezzo I... 122 A1
Ampfing D.....95 C4

Ampflwang A. 109 A4
Amplepuis F .. 117 B4
Amposta E... 153 B4
Ampthill UK....44 A3
Ampudia E... 142 C2
Ampuero E... 143 A3
Amriswil CH . 107 B4
Åmsele S..... 200 B5
Amstelveen NL .70 B1
Amsterdam NL .70 B1
Amstetten A . 110 A1
Amtzell D.... 107 B4
Amulree UK....35 B4
Amurrio E..... 143 A4
Amusco E... 142 B2
Anacapri I... 170 C2
Anadia P..... 148 B1
Anadon E... 152 B2
Anafi GR..... 185 C6
Anagni I..... 169 B3
Anamur TR.... 23 C7
Ananyiv UA... 17 B8
Anascaul IRL... 29 B1
Ånäset S........2 D7
Ana-Sira N....52 B2
Anastázewo PL .76 B3
Anaya de Alba
E............. 150 B2
Ança P..... 148 B1
Ancaster UK....40 C3
Ancede P..... 148 A1
Ancenis F... 101 B4
Ancerville F...91 C5
Anchuras E... 156 A3
Ancona I..... 136 B2
Ancora P..... 148 A1
Ancrum UK....35 C5
Ancy-le-Franc
F............. 104 B3
Andalo I..... 121 A3
Åndalsnes N . 198 C4
Andance F... 117 B4
Andau A..... 111 B4
Andebu N.....53 A6
Andeer CH... 107 C4
Andelfingen
CH...........107 B3
Andenes N... 194 A7
Andenne B....79 B5
Anderlues B....79 B4
Andermatt
CH...........107 C3
Andernach D... 80 B3
Andernos-les-Bains
F............. 128 B1
Anderslöv S....66 A2
Anderstorp S...60 B3
Andijk NL......70 B2
Andoain E... 144 A1
Andocs H..... 112 C1
Andolsheim F . 106 A2
Andorra E... 153 B3
Andorra La Vella
AND.........146 B2
Andosilla E... 144 B2
Andover UK....44 B2
Andratx E... 166 B2
Andreapol RUS ..9 D8
Andreas UK....36 B2
Andréspol PL ..86 A3
Andrest F... 145 A4
Andretta I... 172 B1
Andrezieux-
Bouthéon F . 117 B4
Andria I..... 171 B4
Andrijevica
MNE......... 16 D3
Andritsena GR 184 B2
Andros GR... 185 B5
Andrychów PL . 99 B3
Andselv N... 194 A9
Anduze F... 131 A2
Åneby N.......48 B2
Aneby S........62 A2
Anet F..........90 C1
Anfo I..... 121 B3
Ånge S........62 A2
Änge S........199 B11
Angeja P... 148 B1
Ängelholm S...61 C2
Angeli FIN... 193 D9
Ängelsberg S...50 C3
Anger A..... 110 B2
Angera I..... 120 B1

Angermünde
D...............74 A3
Angern A......97 C4
Angers F... 102 B1
Angerville F...90 C2
Anghiari I... 135 B5
Angle UK.......39 C1
Anglès E..... 147 C3
Anglés F... 130 B1
Anglès F... 114 B2
Anglesola E... 147 C2
Angles sur l'Anglin
F............. 115 B4
Anglet F... 128 C1
Anglisidhes
CY........... 181 B2
Anglure F......91 C3
Angoulême F . 115 C4
Angoulins F... 114 B2
Angsö S........56 A2
Angueira P... 149 A3
Angües E... 145 B3
Anguiano E... 143 B4
Anguillara Sabazia
I............. 168 A2
Anguillara Véneta
I............. 121 B4
Anhée B........79 B4
Anholt DK......60 C1
Aniane F......130 B2
Aniche F.......78 B3
Ånimskog S....54 B3
Anina RO......16 C4
Anixi GR..... 182 D3
Anizy-le-Château
F...............91 B3
Anjalankoski FIN. 8 B5
Anjan S..... 199 B9
Ankara TR... 187 C7
Ankaran SLO... 122 B2
Ankarsrum S...62 A4
Ankerlia N... 192 C4
Anklam D......66 C2
Ankum D......71 B4
Anlauftal A... 109 B4
Anlezy F... 104 C2
Ånn S..... 199 B9
Annaberg A... 110 B2
Annaberg-
Buchholz D....83 B5
Annaberg im
Lammertal A . 109 B4
Annaburg D....83 A5
Annahütte D...84 A1
Annalong UK...27 B5
Annan UK......36 B3
Anndalsvågen
N...........195 E3
Anneberg
Halland S......60 B2
Jönköping S . 62 A2
Annecy F... 118 B3
Annelund S....60 B3
Annemasse F . 118 A3
Annenskiy Most
RUS.........9 C10
Annerstad S....60 C3
Annestown IRL.30 B1
Annevoie-Rouillon
B...............79 B4
Annonay F... 117 B4
Annot F... 132 B2
Annweiler D...93 B3
Ano Poroia GR 183 B5
Añora E..... 156 B3
Ano Siros GR . 185 B5
Anould F... 106 A1
Anquela del
Ducado E... 152 B1
Anröchte D....81 A4
Ans DK........59 B2
Ansager DK... 59 C1
Ansbach D....94 B2
Anseroeul B....79 B3
Ansfelden A... 110 A1
Ansião P... 154 B2
Ansó E..... 144 B3
Ansoain E... 144 B2
Anstruther UK . 35 B5
Antalya TR... 189 C5
Antas E..... 164 B3
Antegnate I... 120 B2
Antequera E... 163 A3
Anterselva di
Mezzo I..... 108 C3
Antibes F... 132 B3
Antigüedad E . 142 C2
Antillo I..... 177 B4
Antirio GR... 184 A2
Antnäs S... 196 D4
Ant-Ob UK....31 B1
Antoing B......79 B3

Antonin PL.....86 A1
Antrain F... 88 B2
Antrim UK......27 B4
Antrodoco I... 169 A3
Antronapiana
I............. 119 A5
Antuzede P... 148 B1
Antwerp =
Antwerpen B..79 A4
Antwerpen =
Antwerpen B..79 A4
Anversa d'Abruzzi
I............. 169 B3
Anvin F........78 B2
Anzat-le-Luguet
F............. 116 B3
Anzi I..... 172 B1
Ånzio I..... 168 B2
Anzola d'Emilia
I............. 135 A4
Anzón E... 144 C2
Aoiz E..... 144 B2
Aosta I..... 119 B4
Apalhão P... 155 B3
Apatin SRB... 125 B5
Apatity RUS.... 3 C13
Apc H..... 112 B3
Apécchio I... 136 B1
Apeldoorn NL...70 B2
Apen D........71 A4
Apenburg D....73 B4
Apensen D....72 A2
A Peroxa E... 140 B3
Apiro I..... 136 B2
Apolda D......82 A3
Apolonia GR . 185 C5
Apostag H... 112 C2
Appelbo S.....49 B6
Appennino I... 136 C2
Appenzell CH . 107 B4
Appiano I... 121 A4
Appignano I... 136 B2
Appingedam
NL............71 A3
Appleby-in-
Westmorland
UK............37 B4
Applecross UK .31 B3
Appledore UK . 42 A2
Appoigny F... 104 B2
Apremont-la-Forêt
F...............92 C1
Aprica I..... 120 A3
Apricena I... 171 B3
Aprigliano I... 174 B2
Aprília I..... 168 B2
Apt F..... 131 B4
Apta E..... 143 C3
Aquiléia I... 122 B2
Aquilónia I... 172 B1
Aquino I..... 169 B3
Ar S..........57 C4
Arabayona E . 150 A2
Aracena E... 161 B3
Arachova GR . 184 A3
Aračinovo
NMK........182 A3
Arad RO......126 A3
Aradac SRB... 126 B2
Aradhippou
CY........... 181 B2
Aragnouet F . 145 B3
Aragona I... 176 B2
Arahal E..... 162 A2
Aramits F... 144 A3
Aramon F... 131 B3
Aranda de Duero
E............. 143 C3
Aranda de
Moncayo E . 152 A2
Arandelovac
SRB......... 127 C2
Aranjuez E... 151 B4
Arantzazu E . 143 B4
Aranzueque E . 151 B4
Aras de Alpuente
E............. 159 B2
Arauzo de Miel
E............. 143 C3
Arazede P... 148 B1
Arbas F... 145 B4
Arbatax I... 179 C3
Arbeca E... 147 C1
Arberg D......94 B2
Arbesbach A . 96 C3
Arboga S......56 A1
Arbois F... 105 C4

Arbon CH.... 107 B4
Arboréa I..... 179 C2
Arborio I..... 119 B5
Årbostad N... 194 B8
Arbråth UK....35 B5
Arbucies E... 147 C3
Arbuniel E... 163 A4
Arbus I..... 179 C2
Arcachon F... 128 B1
Arcar I... 169 B3
Arcen NL......80 A2
Arcévia I... 136 B1
Arcey F... 106 B1
Archanes GR . 185 D6
Archangelos
GR........... 188 C3
Archena E... 165 A3
Archez E... 163 B4
Archiac F... 115 C3
Archidona E... 163 A3
Archiestown
UK............ 32 D3
Archivel E... 164 A3
Arcidosso I... 135 C4
Arcille I..... 135 C4
Arcis-sur-Aube
F...............91 C4
Arc-lès-Gray F . 105 B4
Arco I..... 121 B3
Arcones E... 151 A4
Arcos E... 143 B3
Arcos de Jalón
E............. 152 A1
Arcos de la
Frontera E . 162 B2
Arcos de la Sierra
E............. 152 B1
Arcos de las Salinas
E............. 159 B2
Arcos de Valdevez
P............. 148 A1
Arcozelo P... 148 B1
Arc-sur-Tille F . 105 B4
Arcy-sur-Cure
F............. 104 B2
Ardagh IRL....29 B2
Årdal N......52 A2
Ardala S......55 B4
Ardales E... 162 B3
Ardara I..... 178 B2
IRL...........26 B2
Ardarroch UK . 31 B3
Ardbeg UK....34 C1
Ardcharnich
UK............ 32 D1
Ardchyle UK...34 B3
Ardee IRL......27 C4
Ardentes F... 103 C3
Ardersier UK . 32 D2
Ardes F... 116 B3
Ardessie UK... 32 D1
Ardez CH... 107 C5
Ardfert IRL....29 B2
Ardgay UK....32 D2
Ardglass UK...27 B5
Ardgroom IRL .29 C2
Ardhasig UK...31 B2
Ardino BG......31 B2
Ardisa E..... 144 B3
Ardkearagh
IRL...........29 C1
Ardlui UK......34 B3
Ardlussa UK...34 B2
Ardón E......34 B1
Ardooie B......78 B3
Ardore I..... 175 C2
Ardrahan IRL . 28 A3
Ardre S........57 C4
Ardres F......78 B1
Ardrishaig UK . 34 B2
Ardrossan UK . 34 C3
Åre S........199 B10
Areia Branca
P............. 154 B1
Aremark N....54 A2
Arenales de San
Gregorio E . 157 A4
Arenas E... 163 B3

Arenas del Rey
E............. 163 B4
Arenas de
San Juan E... 157 A4
Arenas de San
Pedro E... 150 B2
Arendal N... 53 B4
Arendonk B....79 A5
Arengosse F . 128 B2
Arentorp S....55 B3
Arenys de Mar
E............. 147 C3
Arenys de Munt
E............. 147 C3
Arenzano I... 133 A4
Areo E..... 146 B2
Areópoli GR . 184 C3
Ares E..... 140 A2
Arès F..... 128 B1
Ares del Maestrat
E............. 153 B3
Aresvika N... 198 B5
Arette F... 144 A3
Aretxabaleta
E............. 143 A4
Arevalillo E... 150 B2
Arévalo E... 150 A3
Arez P..... 155 B3
Arezzo I..... 135 B4
Arfeuilles F... 117 A3
Argalasti GR . 183 D5
Argallón E... 156 B2
Argamasilla de
Alba E..... 157 A4
Argamasilla de
Calatrava E . 157 B3
Arganda E... 151 B4
Arganil P... 148 B1
Argasion GR . 184 B1
Argegno I... 120 B2
Argelès-Gazost
F............. 145 A3
Argelès-sur-Mer
F............. 146 B4
Argenta I... 121 C4
Argentan F... 89 B3
Argentat F... 116 B1
Argentera I... 132 A2
Argenteuil F...90 C2
Argenthal D...93 B3
Argentiera I... 178 B2
Argenton-
Château F... 102 C1
Argenton-sur-
Creuse F... 103 C3
Argentré F... 102 A1
Argentré-
du-Plessis F . 101 A4
Argent-sur-
Sauldre F... 103 B4
Argirades
GR........... 182 D1
Argithani TR . 189 A6
Argos GR... 184 B3
Argos Orestiko
GR........... 182 C3
Argostoli GR . 184 A1
Argote E... 143 B4
Arguedas E... 144 B2
Argueil F......90 B1
Arholma S....51 C6

Ariano Irpino
I............. 170 B3
Ariano nel
Polésine I... 121 C5
Aribe E..... 144 B2
Aridea GR... 182 C4
Arienzo I... 170 B2
Arild S........61 C2
Arileod UK....34 B1
Arilje SRB... 127 D2
Arinagour UK . 34 B1
Ariño E..... 153 A3
Arinthod F... 118 A2
Arisaig UK....34 B2
Arisgotas E... 157 A4
Aritzo I..... 179 C3
Ariza E..... 152 A1
Årjäng S......54 A3
Arjeplog S... 195 D8
Arjona E... 157 C3
Arjonilla E... 157 C3
Arkasa GR... 188 D2
Arkelstorp S...63 B2
Arklow IRL....30 B2
Arkösund S....56 B2
Ärla S........56 A2
Arlanc F... 117 B3
Arlanzón E... 143 B3
Arlebosc F... 117 B4

Arlena di Castro I 168 A1
Arles F 131 B3
Arles-sur-Tech F 146 B3
Arló H 113 A4
Arlon B 92 B1
Armação de Pera P 160 B1
Armadale
Highland UK 31 B3
West Lothian UK 35 C4
Armagh UK 27 B4
Armamar P 148 A2
Armenistis GR 185 B7
Armeno I 119 B5
Armenteros E 150 B2
Armentières F 78 B2
Armilla E 163 A4
Armiñón E 143 B4
Armoy UK 27 A4
Armuña de Tajuña E 151 B4
Armutlu
Bursa TR 186 B3
İzmir TR 188 A2
Arnac-Pompadour F 115 C5
Arnafjord N 46 A3
Arnage F 102 B2
Arnas F 117 A4
Årnäs S 55 B4
Arnay-le-Duc F 104 B3
Arnborg DK 59 B2
Arnbruck D 95 B4
Arnea GR 183 C5
Arneberg
Hedmark N 48 A2
Hedmark N 49 B4
Arneburg D 73 B5
Arnedillo E 144 B1
Arnedo E 144 B1
Arneguy F 144 A2
Arnés E 153 B4
Árnes IS 190 A4
Årnes
Akershus N 48 B3
Troms N 194 A9
Arnfels A 110 C2
Arnhem NL 70 C2
Arnissa GR 182 C3
Arno S 56 B3
Arnold UK 40 B2
Arnoldstein A 109 C4
Arnsberg D 81 A4
Arnschwang D 95 B4
Arnsdorf D 84 A1
Årnset N 198 B6
Arnside UK 37 B4
Arnstadt D 82 B2
Arnstein D 94 B1
Arnstorf D 95 C4
Arnum DK 59 C1
Aroche E 161 B3
Ároktő H 113 B4
Arolla CH 119 A4
Arolsen D 81 A5
Arona I 119 B5
Åros N 54 A1
Arosa
CH 107 C4
P 148 A1
Ærøskøbing DK 65 B3
Arøsund DK 59 C2
Arouca P 148 B1
Årøysund N 54 A1
Arpajon F 90 C2
Arpajon-sur-Cère F 116 C2
Arpela FIN 196 C7
Arpino I 169 B3
Arquata del Tronto I 136 C2
Arques F 78 B2
Arques-la-Bataille F 89 A5
Arquillos E 157 B4
Arraia-Maeztu E 143 B4
Arraiolos P 154 C2
Arrancourt F 92 C2
Arras F 78 B2
Arrasate E 143 A4
Årre DK 59 C1
Arreau F 145 B4
Arredondo E 143 A3
Arrens-Marsous F 145 B3
Arriate E 162 B2
Arrifana P 160 B1
Arrigorriaga E 143 A4
Arriondas E 142 A1
Arroba de los Montes E 157 A3
Arrochar UK 34 B3
Arromanches-les-Bains F 88 A3
Arronches P 155 B3
Arroniz E 144 B1
Arrou F 103 A3
Arroya E 142 B2
Arroya de Cuéllar E 150 A3
Arroyal E 142 B2
Arroyo de la Luz E 155 B4
Arroyo del Ojanco E 164 A2
Arroyo de San Servan E 155 C4
Arroyomolinos de León E 161 A3
Arroyomolinos de Montánchez E 156 A1
Arruda dos Vinhos P 154 C1
Arsac F 128 B2
Ars-en-Ré F 114 B2
Arsiè I 121 B4
Arsiero I 121 B4
Årslev DK 59 C3
Ársoli I 169 A3
Ars-sur-Moselle F 92 B2
Årsunda S 50 B3
Artà E 167 B3
Arta GR 182 D3
Artajona E 144 B2
Artegna I 122 A2
Arteixo E 140 A2
Artemare F 118 B2
Arten I 121 A4
Artena I 169 B2
Artenay F 103 A3
Artern D 82 A3
Artés E 147 C2
Artesa de Segre E 147 C2
Arth CH 107 B3
Arthez-de-Béarn F 145 A3
Arthon-en-Retz F 101 B4
Arthurstown IRL 30 B2
Artieda E 144 B3
Artix F 145 A3
Artotina GR 182 E4
Artsyz UA 17 B8
Artziniega E 143 A3
A Rúa E 141 B3
Arudy F 145 A3
Arundel UK 44 C3
Arveyres F 128 B2
Arvidsjaur S 196 D2
Arvieux F 118 C3
Arvika S 54 A3
Åryd
Blekinge S 63 B3
Kronoberg S 62 B2
Arzachena I 178 A3
Arzacq-Arraziguet F 128 C2
Árzana I 179 C3
Arzano F 100 B2
Aržano HR 138 B2
Arzberg D 95 A4
Arzignano I 121 B4
Arzila P 148 B1
Arzl im Pitztal A 108 B1
Arzúa E 140 B2
As B 80 A1
Aš CZ 83 B4
Ås N 54 A1
Åsa S 60 B2
Asaa DK 58 A3
Aşağıçiğil TR 189 A6
Ašanja SRB 127 C2
Åsarna S 199 C11
Åsarøy N 52 A2
Åsarp S 55 B4
Asasp F 145 A3
Åsbro S 55 A6
Åsby S 60 B2
Asby S 62 A3
Asbygri IS 191 A9
Ascain F 144 A2
Ascea I 172 B1
Ascha D 95 B4
Aschach an der Donau A 96 C2
Aschaffenburg D 93 B5
Aschbach Markt A 110 A1
Ascheberg
Nordrhein-Westfalen D 81 A3
Schleswig-Holstein D 65 B3
Aschendorf D 71 A4
Aschersleben D 82 A3
Asciano I 135 B4
Ascó E 153 A4
Asco F 180 A2
Áscoli Piceno I 136 C2
Áscoli Satriano I 171 B3
Ascona CH 120 A1
Ascot UK 44 B3
Ascoux F 103 A4
Åse N 194 A6
Åseda S 62 A3
Åsele S 200 B3
Åsen
N 199 B8
S 49 A5
Asendorf D 72 B2
Asenovgrad BG 183 A6
Åsensbruk S 54 B3
Åseral N 52 B3
Asfeld F 91 B4
Åsgårdstrand N 54 A1
Ásgarður IS 190 B1
Asgate CY 181 B2
Ash
Kent UK 45 B5
Surrey UK 44 B3
Åshammar S 50 B3
Ashbourne
IRL 30 A2
UK 40 B2
Ashburton UK 43 B3
Ashby-de-la-Zouch UK 40 C2
Ashchurch UK 44 B1
Åsheim N 199 D8
Ashford UK 45 B4
Ashington UK 37 A5
Ashley UK 38 B4
Ashmyany BY 13 A6
Ashton-under-Lyne UK 40 B1
Ashwell UK 44 A3
Asiago I 121 B4
Asipovichy BY 13 B8
Aska FIN 197 B9
Askam-in-Furness UK 36 B3
Askeaton IRL 29 B3
Asker N 48 C2
Askersund S 55 B5
Åskilje S 200 B3
Askim N 54 A2
Askland N 53 B4
Äsköping S 56 A2
Askvoll N 46 A2
Åsljunga S 61 C3
Asmunti FIN 197 D9
Asnæs DK 61 D1
As Neves E 140 B2
As Nogaís E 141 B3
Ásola I 120 B3
Asolo I 121 B4
Asos GR 184 A1
Asotthalom H 126 A1
Aspach A 109 A4
Aspang Markt A 111 B3
Aspariegos E 149 A4
Asparn an der Zaya A 97 C4
Aspatria UK 36 B3
Aspberg S 55 A4
Aspe E 165 A4
Aspet F 145 A4
Äspö S 63 B3
As Pontes de García Rodríguez E 140 A3
Aspres-sur-Buëch F 132 A1
Aspsele S 200 C4
Assafora P 154 C1
Asse B 79 B4
Assebakte N 193 C9
Assel D 72 A2
Asselborn L 92 A1
Assémini I 179 C2
Assen NL 71 B3
Assenede B 79 A3
Assens
Aarhus Amt. DK 58 B3
Fyns Amt. DK 59 C2
Assesse B 79 B5
Assisi I 136 B1
Åsskard N 198 B5
Assling D 108 B3
Asso I 120 B2
Asson F 145 A3
Ássoro I 177 B3
Assumar P 155 B3
Åsta N 48 A3
Astaffort F 129 B3
Astakos GR 184 A2
Asten NL 80 A1
Asti I 119 C5
Astipalea GR 188 C1
Astorga E 141 B4
Åstorp S 61 C2
Åsträsk S 200 B5
Astudillo E 142 B2
Asuni I 179 C2
Asványráró H 111 B4
Aszód H 112 B3
Aszófő H 111 C4
Atabey TR 189 B5
Atalaia P 154 B3
Atalandi GR 182 E4
Atalho P 154 C2
Átány H 113 B4
Atanzón E 151 B4
Ataquines E 150 A3
Atarfe E 163 A4
Atça TR 188 B3
Ateca E 152 A2
A Teixeira E 141 B3
Atella I 172 B1
Atessa I 169 A4
Ath B 79 B3
Athboy IRL 30 A2
Athea IRL 29 B2
Athenry IRL 28 A3
Athens = Athina GR 185 B4
Atherstone UK 40 C2
Athienou CY 181 A2
Athies F 90 B2
Athies-sous-Laon F 91 B3
Athina = Athens GR 185 B4
Athleague IRL 28 A3
Athlone IRL 28 A4
Athna CY 181 A2
Athy IRL 30 B2
Atienza E 151 A5
Atina I 169 B3
Atkár H 113 B3
Atlantı TR 189 A7
Atna N 199 D7
Åtorp S 55 A5
Atrå N 47 C5
Ätran S 60 B2
Atri I 169 A3
Atripalda I 170 C2
Atsiki GR 183 D7
Attendorn D 81 A3
Attichy F 90 B3
Attigliano I 168 A2
Attigny F 91 B4
Attleborough UK 41 C5
Åtvidaberg S 56 B1
Atzendorf D 73 C4
Au
Steiermark A 110 B2
Vorarlberg A 107 B4
Bayern D 95 C3
Bayern D 108 B2
Aub D 94 B2
Aubagne F 132 B1
Aubange B 92 B1
Aubel B 80 B1
Aubenas F 117 C4
Aubenton F 91 B4
Auberive F 105 B4
Aubeterre-sur-Dronne F 128 A3
Aubiet F 129 C3
Aubigné F 115 B3
Aubigny F 114 B2
Aubigny-au-Bac F 78 B3
Aubigny-en-Artois F 78 B2
Aubigny-sur-Nère F 103 B4
Aubin F 130 A1
Aubonne CH 105 C5
Aubrac F 116 C2
Aubusson F 116 B2
Auch F 129 C3
Auchencairn UK 36 B3
Auchinleck UK 36 A2
Auchterarder UK 35 B4
Auchtermuchty UK 35 B4
Auchtertyre UK 31 B3
Auchy-au-Bois F 78 B2
Audenge F 128 B1
Auderville F 88 A2
Audierne F 100 A1
Audincourt F 106 B1
Audlem UK 38 B4
Audruicq F 78 B2
Audun-le-Roman F 92 B1
Audun-le-Tiche F 92 B1
Aue
Nordrhein-Westfalen D 81 A4
Sachsen D 83 B4
Auerbach
Bayern D 95 B3
Sachsen D 83 B4
Auffach A 108 B3
Augher UK 27 B3
Aughnacloy UK 27 B4
Aughrim IRL 30 B2
Augignac F 115 C4
Augsburg D 94 C2
Augusta I 177 B4
Augusten-borg DK 64 B2
Augustfehn D 71 A4
Augustów PL 12 B5
Aukrug D 64 B2
Auktsjaur S 196 D2
Auldearn UK 32 D3
Aulendorf D 107 B4
Auletta I 172 B1
Aulla I 134 A2
Aullène F 180 B2
Aulnay F 115 B3
Aulnoye-Aymeries F 79 B3
Ault F 90 A1
Aultbea UK 31 B3
Aulum DK 59 B1
Aulus-les-Bains F 146 B2
Auma D 83 B3
Aumale F 90 B1
Aumetz F 92 B1
Aumont-Aubrac F 116 C3
Aunay-en-Bazois F 104 B2
Aunay-sur-Odon F 88 A3
Aune N 199 A10
Auneau F 90 C1
Auneuil F 90 B1
Auning DK 58 B3
Aunsetra N 199 A9
Aups F 132 B2
Aura D 82 B1
Auray F 100 B3
Aurdal N 47 B6
Aure N 198 B5
Aurich D 71 A4
Aurignac F 145 A4
Aurillac F 116 C2
Auriol F 132 B1
Auritz-Burguette E 144 B2
Aurlandsvangen N 47 B4
Auronzo di Cadore I 109 C3
Auros F 128 B2
Auroux F 117 C3
Aurskog N 48 C3
Aursmoen N 48 C3
Ausónia I 169 B3
Ausservillgraton A 109 C3
Austad N 52 B3
Austbygda N 47 B5
Aústis I 178 B3
Austmarka N 49 B4
Austre Moland N 53 B4
Austre Vikebygd N 52 A1
Austrheim N 46 B1
Auterive F 146 A2
Autheuil-Authouillet F 89 A5
Authon F 132 A2
Authon-du-Perche F 102 A2
Autol E 144 B2
Autreville F 92 C1
Autrey-lès-Gray F 105 B4
Autti FIN 197 C10
Autun F 104 C3
Auty-le-Châtel F 103 B4
Auvelais B 79 B4
Auvillar F 129 B3
Auxerre F 104 B2
Auxi-le-Château F 78 B2
Auxon F 104 A2
Auxonne F 105 B4
Auxy F 104 C3
Auzances F 116 A2
Auzon F 117 B3
Ağva TR 187 A4
Availles-Limouzine F 115 B4
Avaldsnes N 52 A1
Avallon F 104 B2
Avantas GR 183 C7
Avaviken S 195 E9
Avebury UK 44 B2
A Veiga E 141 B3
Aveiras de Cima P 154 B2
Aveiro P 148 B1
Avelgem B 79 B3
Avellino I 170 C2
Avenches CH 106 C2
A-Ver-o-Mar P 148 A1
Aversa I 170 C2
Avesnes-le-Comte F 78 B2
Avesnes-sur-Helpe F 91 A3
Avesta S 50 B3
Avetrana I 173 B3
Avezzano I 169 A3
Avià E 147 B2
Aviano I 122 A1
Aviemore UK 32 D3
Avigliana I 119 B4
Avigliano I 172 B1
Avignon F 131 B3
Ávila E 150 B3
Avilés E 141 A5
Avilley F 105 B5
Avintes P 148 A1
Avinyo E 147 C2
Àvio I 121 B3
Avioth F 92 B1
Avis P 154 B3
Avize F 91 C4
Avlonari GR 185 A5
Ávola I 177 C4
Avon F 90 C2
Avonmouth UK 43 A4
Avord F 103 B4
Avranches F 88 B2
Avril F 92 B1
Avrillé F 102 B1
Avtovac BIH 139 B4
Awans B 79 B5
Axams A 108 B2
Axat F 146 B3
Axbridge UK 43 A4
Axel NL 79 A3
Ax-les-Thermes F 146 B2
Axmarby S 51 B4
Axmarsbruk S 51 A4
Axminster UK 43 B3
Axvall S 55 B4
Ay F 91 B4
Aya E 144 A1
Ayamonte E 161 B2
Ayancık TR 23 A8
Ayaş TR 187 B7
Aydın TR 188 B2
Ayelo de Malferit E 159 C3
Ayer CH 119 A4
Ayerbe E 144 B3
Ayette F 78 B2
Ayia Napa CY 181 B2
Áyia Phyla CY 181 B2
Áyios Amvrósios CY 181 A2
Áyios Seryios CY 181 A2
Áyios Theodhoros CY 181 A3
Aykirikçi TR 187 C5
Aylesbury UK 44 B3
Ayllón E 151 A4
Aylsham UK 41 C5
Ayna E 158 C1
Ayódar E 159 B3
Ayora E 159 B2
Ayr UK 36 A2
Ayrancı TR 23 C7
Ayrancılar TR 188 A2
Ayron F 115 B4
Aysgarth UK 37 B4
Ayton UK 35 C5
Aytos BG 17 D7
Ayvacık TR 186 C1
Ayvalık TR 186 C1
Aywaille B 80 B1
Azaila E 153 A3
Azambuja P 154 B2
Azambujeira P 154 B2
Azanja SRB 127 C2
Azannes-et-Soumazannes F 92 B1
Azanúy-Alins E 145 C4
Azaruja P 155 C3
Azay-le-Ferron F 115 B5
Azay-le-Rideau F 102 B2
Azcoitia E 143 A4
Azé F 117 A4
Azeiteiros P 155 B3
Azenhas do Mar P 154 C1
Azinhaga P 154 B2
Azinhal P 160 B2
Azinheira dos Bairros P 160 A1
Aznalcázar E 161 B3
Aznalcóllar E 161 B3
Azóia P 154 B2
Azpeitia E 144 A1
Azuaga E 156 B2
Azuara E 153 A3
Azuqueca de Henares E 151 B4
Azur F 128 C1
Azzano Décimo I 122 B1

B

Baad A 107 B5
Baamonde E 140 A3
Baar CH 107 B3
Bağarasi TR 188 B2
Baarle-Nassau B 79 A4
Baarn NL 70 B2
Babadağ TR 188 B3
Babadag RO 17 C8
Babaeski TR 186 A2
Babayevo RUS 9 C9
Babenhausen
Bayern D 107 A5
Hessen D 93 B4
Babiak PL 76 B3
Babice PL 86 B3
Babigoszcz PL 75 A3
Babimost PL 75 B4
Babina Greda HR 125 B4
Babócsa H 124 A3
Bábolma H 112 B1
Baborów PL 86 B1
Baboszewo PL 77 B5
Babót H 111 B4
Babruysk BY 13 B8
Babsk PL 87 A4
Bač SRB 125 B5
Bac UK 31 A2
Bacares E 164 B2
Bacău RO 17 B7
Baccarat F 92 C2
Bacharach D 93 A3
Backa S 50 B2
Bačka Palanka SRB 126 B1
Backaryd S 63 B3
Bačka Topola SRB 126 B1
Backe S 200 C2
Bäckebo S 62 B4
Bäckefors S 54 B3
Bäckhammar S 55 A5
Bački Breg SRB 125 B4

Bački-Brestovac SRB 126 B1
Bački Monoštor SRB 125 B4
Bački Petrovac SRB 126 B1
Bački Sokolac SRB 126 B1
Backnang D....94 C1
Bačko Gradište SRB 126 B2
Bačko Novo Selo SRB 125 B5
Bačko Petrovo Selo SRB 126 B2
Bácoli I....... 170 C2
Bacqueville-en-Caux F 89 A5
Bácsalmás H . . 126 A1
Bácsbokod H . 125 A5
Bad Abbach D. ..95 C4
Badacsonytomaj H.......... 111 C4
Bad Aibling D. 108 B3
Badajoz E.... 155 C4
Badalona E ... 147 C3
Badalucco I.... 133 B3
Bad Aussee A . 109 B4
Bad Bederkesa D............72 A1
Bad Bentheim D............71 B4
Bad Bergzabern D............93 B3
Bad Berka D...82 B3
Bad Berleburg D............81 A4
Bad Berneck D .95 A3
Bad Bevensen D............73 A3
Bad Bibra D....82 A2
Bad Birnbach D .95 C5
Bad Blankenburg D............82 B3
Bad Bleiberg A.......... 109 C4
Bad Brambach D............83 B4
Bad Bramstedt D............64 C2
Bad Breisig D...80 B3
Bad Brückenau D............82 B1
Bad Buchau D. 107 A4
Bad Camberg D 81 B4
Badderen N.... 192 C6
Bad Doberan D .65 B4
Bad Driburg D .81 A5
Bad Düben D...83 A4
Bad Dürkheim D............93 B4
Bad Dürrenberg D............83 A4
Bad Dürrheim D............107 A3
Bad Elster D...83 B4
Bad Ems D....81 B3
Baden A.......... 111 A3
CH 106 B3
Bádenas E ... 152 A2
Baden-Baden D............93 C4
Bad Endorf D 108 B3
Badenweiler D............106 B2
Baderna HR ... 122 B2
Bad Essen D...71 B5
Bad Fischau A. 111 B3
Bad Frankenhausen D............82 A3
Bad Freienwalde D............74 B3
Bad Friedrichshall D............93 B5
Bad Füssing D. .96 C1
Bad Gandersheim D............82 A2
Bad Gastein A. 109 B4
Bad Gleichenberg A.......... 110 C2
Bad Goisern A. 109 B4
Bad Gottleuba D............84 B1
Bad Grund D...82 A2
Bad Hall A.... 110 A1
Bad Harzburg D............82 A2
Bad Herrenalb D............93 C4
Bad Hersfeld D. .82 B1
Bad Hofgastein A.......... 109 B4

Bad Homburg D............81 B4
Bad Honnef D...80 B3
Bad Hönningen D............80 B3
Badia Calavena I.......... 121 B4
Badia Polésine I.......... 121 B4
Badia Pratáglia I.......... 135 B4
Badia Tedalda I.......... 135 B5
Bad Iburg D....71 B5
Bad Innerlaterns A.......... 107 B4
Bad Ischl A 109 B4
Bad Karlshafen D............81 A5
Bad Kemmeriboden CH 106 C2
Bądki PL 69 B3
Bad Kissingen D............82 B2
Bad Kleinen D. .65 C4
Bad Kohlgrub D............108 B2
Bad König D...93 B5
Bad Königshofen D............82 B2
Bad Köstritz D .83 B4
Badkowo PL ...76 B3
Bad Kreuzen A.......... 110 A1
Bad Kreuznach D............93 B3
Bad Krozingen D............106 B2
Bad Laasphe D..81 B4
Bad Langensalza D............82 A2
Bad Lauchstädt D............83 A3
Bad Lausick D..83 A4
Bad Lauterberg D............82 A2
Bad Leonfelden A.........96 C2
Bad Liebenwerda D............83 A5
Bad Liebenzell D.........93 C4
Bad Lippspringe D............81 A4
Badljevina HR. 124 B3
Bad Meinberg D............81 A4
Bad Mergentheim D.........94 B1
Bad Mitterndorf A.......... 109 B4
Bad Münder D .72 B2
Bad Münstereifel D............80 B2
Bad Muskau D .84 A2
Bad Nauheim D 81 B4
Bad Nenndorf D............72 B2
Bad Neuenahr-Ahrweiler D....80 B3
Bad Neustadt D............82 B2
Bad Oeynhausen D............72 B1
Badolato I 175 C2
Badolatosa E.. 163 A3
Bad Oldesloe D .65 C3
Badonviller F ..92 C2
Bad Orb D....81 B5
Badovinci SRB 127 C1
Bad Peterstal D .93 C4
Bad Pyrmont D .72 C2
Bad Radkersburg A.......... 110 C2
Bad Ragaz CH. 107 C4
Bad Rappenau D............93 B5
Bad Reichenhall D............109 B3
Bad Saarow-Pieskow D....74 B3
Bad Sachsa D..82 A2
Bad Säckingen D............106 B2
Bad Salzdetfurth D............72 B3
Bad Salzig D...81 B3
Bad Salzuflen D............72 B2
Bad Salzungen D............82 B2
Bad Sankt Leonhard A.. 110 C1

Bad Sassendorf D............81 A4
Bad Schandau D............84 B2
Bad Schmiedeberg D............83 A4
Bad Schönborn D............93 B4
Bad Schussenried D............107 A4
Bad Schwalbach D............81 B4
Bad Schwartau D............65 C3
Bad Segeberg D............64 C3
Bad Soden D...81 B4
Bad Soden-Salmünster D. .81 B5
Bad Sooden-Allendorf D....82 A1
Bad Sulza D....83 A3
Bad Tatzmannsdorf A.......... 111 B3
Bad Tennstedt D............82 A2
Bad Tölz D ... 108 B2
Badules E 152 A2
Bad Urach D....94 C1
Bad Vellach A. 110 C1
Bad Vilbel D....81 B4
Bad Vöslau A.. 111 B3
Bad Waldsee D............107 B4
Bad Wiessee D............108 B2
Bad Wildungen D............81 A5
Bad Wilsnack D............73 B4
Bad Windsheim D.........94 B2
Bad Wörishafen D............108 A1
Bad Wurzach D............108 B1
Bad Zwesten D. .81 A5
Bad Zwischenahn D............71 A5
Baells E 145 C4
Baena E ... 163 A3
Baeza E ... 157 C4
Baflo NL 71 A3
Baga E ... 147 B2
Bagaladi I 175 C1
Bagenkop DK ..65 B3
Baggetorp S ...56 A2
Bagh a Chaisteil UK 31 C1
Bagheria I.... 176 A2
Bagn N.........47 B6
Bagnacavallo I.... 135 A4
Bagnái I 135 A4
Bagnara Cálabra I.... 175 C1
Bagnasco I.... 133 A4
Bagnères-de-Bigorre F ... 145 A4
Bagnères-de-Luchon F ... 145 B4
Bagni del Másino I.... 120 A2
Bagni di Lucca I.... 134 A3
Bagni di Rabbi I.... 121 A3
Bagni di Tívoli I.... 168 B2
Bagno di Romagna I.... 135 B4
Bagnoles-de-l'Orne F ... 132 B2
Bagnols-sur-Cèze F ... 131 A3
Bagnorégio I ... 168 A2
Bagolino I.... 121 B3
Bagrationovsk RUS 12 A4
Bağrdan SRB . 127 C3
Báguena E ... 152 A2

Bahabón de Esgueva E.... 143 C3
Bahillo E 142 B2
Báia delle Zágare I....... 171 B4
Báia Domizia I.......... 169 B3
Baia Mare RO ...17 B5
Baiano I 170 C2
Baião P 148 A1
Baiersbronn D ..93 C4
Baiersdorf D....94 B3
Baignes-Ste Radegonde F 115 C3
Baigneux-les-Juifs F 104 B3
Baildon UK.......40 B2
Bailén E ... 157 B4
Băileşti RO ...17 C5
Baileux B.......91 A4
Bailieborough IRL 27 C4
Bailleul F......78 B2
Baillonville B . . .79 B5
Bailó E 144 B3
Bain-de-Bretagne F 101 B4
Bains F 117 B3
Bains-les-Bains F 105 A5
Bainton UK.......40 B3
Baio E 140 A2
Baiona E 140 B2
Bais F 89 B3
Baiso I 134 A3
Baiuca P 148 B2
Bajánsenye H . 111 C3
Bajina Bašta SRB 127 D1
Bajmok SRB .. 126 B1
Bajna H 112 B2
Bajovo Polje MNE 139 B4
Bajša SRB .. 126 B1
Bak H 111 C3
Bakar HR.... 123 B3
Bakewell UK 40 B2
Bakio E 143 A4
Bakka N.......47 C6
Bakkafjörður IS 191 A11
Bakkagerði IS 191 B12
Bække DK......59 C2
Bakken N..... 48 B3
Baklan TR.... 189 B4
Bākmarksbro DK 58 B1
Bakonybél H... 111 B4
Bakonycsernye H 112 B2
Bakonyjákó H 111 B4
Bakonyszentkirály H 111 B4
Bakonyszombathely H 112 B1
Bakov nad Jizerou CZ...........84 B2
Bąkowiec PL ...87 A5
Baks H 113 C4
Baksa H 125 B4
Bakum D.......71 B5
Bālā TR.......23 B7
Bala UK.......38 B3
Balaguer E ... 145 C4
Balassagyarmat H 112 A3
Balástya H ... 113 C4
Balatonakali H 111 C4
Balatonalmádi H 112 C1
Balatonboglár H 111 C4
Balatonbozsok H 112 C2
Balatonederics H 111 C4
Balatonfenyves H 111 C4
Balatonföldvár H 112 C1
Balatonfüred H 112 C1
Balatonfüzfö H 112 B2
Balatonkenese H 112 B2
Balatonkiliti H 112 C2

Balatonlelle H 111 C4
Balatonszabadi H. 112 C2
Balatonszemes H. 111 C4
Balatonszentgyörgy H. 111 C4
Balazote E ... 158 C1
Balbeggie UK ..35 B4
Balbigny F ... 117 B4
Balboa E 141 B4
Balbriggan IRL.30 A2
Balchik BG ...17 D8
Balçova TR... 188 A2
Baldock UK.......44 B3
Bale HR 122 B2
Baleira E 141 A3
Baleizao P ... 160 A2
Balen B 79 A5
Balerma E.... 164 C2
Balestrand N. .46 A3
Balestrate I ... 176 A2
Balfour UK.......33 B4
Bálganet S.......63 B3
Bálgari BG 17 D7
Balıkesir TR .. 186 C2
Balıklıçeşme TR. 186 B2
Bälinge S.......51 C4
Balingen D... 107 A3
Balingsta S....56 A3
Balintore UK ...32 D3
Balizac F 128 B2
Balk NL.......70 B2
Balkbrug NL ...71 B3
Balla IRL.......28 A2
Ballachulish UK 34 B2
Ballaghaderreen IRL 26 C2
Ballancourt-sur-Essonne F.....90 C2
Ballantrae UK....36 A2
Ballao I..... 179 C3
Ballasalla UK....36 B2
Ballater UK.....32 D3
Ballen DK......59 C3
Ballenstedt D..82 A3
Balleroy F......88 A3
Ballerup DK....61 D2
Ballesteros de Calatrava E .. 157 B4
Balli TR..... 186 B2
Ballina IRL....26 B1
Ballinalack IRL .30 A1
Ballinamore IRL.... 26 B3
Ballinascarty IRL 29 C3
Ballinasloe IRL .28 A3
Ballindine IRL ..28 A3
Balling DK......58 B1
Ballingarry Limerick IRL...29 B3
Tipperary IRL...30 B1
Ballingeary IRL .29 C2
Ballinhassig IRL .29 C3
Ballinluig UK ...35 B4
Ballino I 121 B3
Ballinrobe IRL ..28 A2
Ballinskelligs IRL 29 C1
Ballinspittle IRL 29 C3
Ballintra IRL 26 B2
Ballivor IRL....30 A2
Ballobar E ... 153 A4
Ballon F 102 A2
IRL 30 B2
Ballószög H... 112 C3
Ballsh AL......182 C1
Ballstad N. 194 B4
Ballum DK......64 A1
Ballybay IRL....27 B4
Ballybofey IRL ..26 B3
Ballybunion IRL 29 B2
Ballycanew IRL .30 B2
Ballycarry UK ...27 B5
Ballycastle IRL .26 B1
UK 27 A4
Ballyclare UK ...27 B5
Ballyconneely IRL 28 A1
Ballycotton IRL .29 C3
Ballycroy IRL ...26 B1
Ballydehob IRL .29 C2
Ballyferriter IRL 29 B1
Ballygawley UK .27 B3
Ballyhaunis IRL 28 A3
Ballyheige IRL ..29 B2
Ballyjamesduff IRL 27 C3

Ballylanders IRL 29 B3
Ballylynan IRL...30 B1
Ballymahon IRL 28 A4
Ballymena UK...27 B4
Ballymoe IRL....28 A3
Ballymoney UK 27 A4
Ballymote IRL ..26 B2
Ballynacorra IRL 29 C3
Ballynahinch UK 27 B5
Ballynure UK....27 B5
Ballyragget IRL .30 B1
Ballysadare IRL .26 B2
Ballyshannon IRL 26 B2
Ballyvaughan IRL 28 A2
Ballyvourney IRL 29 C2
Ballywalter UK .27 B5
Balmaclellan UK 36 A2
Balmaseda E .. 143 A3
Balmazújváros H. 113 B5
Balme I 119 B4
Balmedie UK ...33 D4
Balmuccia I ... 119 B5
Balna-paling UK 32 D2
Balneário de Panticosa E . 145 B3
Balotaszállás H. 126 A1
Balsa P 148 A2
Balsareny E ... 147 C2
Balsorano-Nuovo I 169 B3
Bålsta S.......57 A3
Balsthal CH ... 106 B2
Balta UA......17 A8
Baltanás E ... 142 C2
Baltar E 140 C3
Baltasound UK .33 A6
Bălţi MD 17 B7
Baltimore IRL ..29 C2
Baltinglass IRL .30 B2
Baltiysk RUS ...69 A4
Baltów PL......87 A5
Balugães P ... 148 A1
Bælum DK......58 B3
Balve D........81 A3
Balvi LV........8 D5
Balvicar UK 34 B2
Balya TR..... 186 C2
Balzo I 136 C2
Bamberg D....94 B2
Bamburgh UK...37 A5
Banatska Palanka SRB 127 C3
Banatski Brestovac SRB 127 C2
Banatski Despotovac SRB 126 B2
Banatski Dvor SRB 126 B2
Banatski-Karlovac SRB 127 B3
Banatsko Arandjelovo SRB 126 A2
Banatsko-Novo Selo SRB 127 C2
Banaz TR.... 187 D4
Banbridge UK ..27 B4
Banbury UK....44 A2
Banchory UK ...33 D4
Bande B.........79 B5
E 140 B3
Bandholm DK ..65 B4
Bandırma TR.. 186 B2
Bandol F 132 B1
Bandon IRL 29 C3
Baneasa RO ...17 C7
Bañeres E 159 C3
Banff UK......33 D4
Bangor F 100 B2
UK 38 A2
Down UK 27 B5
Gwynedd UK ..38 A2
Bangsund N ... 199 A8
Banie PL 74 A3
Banja Koviljača SRB 127 C1
Banjaloka SLO 123 B3

Banja Luka BIH........... 124 C3
Banjani SRB ... 127 C1
Banja Vrućica BIH........... 125 C3
Banka SK......98 C1
Bankekind S ...56 B1
Bankend UK....36 A3
Bankeryd S 62 A2
Bankfoot UK ...35 B4
Bankso BG ... 183 B5
Banloc RO.... 126 B3
Bannalec F.... 100 B2
Bannes F.......91 C3
Bannockburn UK 35 B4
Bañobárez E .. 149 B3
Bañon E..... 152 B2
Banon F 132 A1
Baños E 149 B4
Baños de Gigonza E 162 B2
Baños de la Encina E 157 B4
Baños de Molgas E 140 B3
Baños de Rio Tobia E 143 B4
Baños de Valdearados E 143 C3
Bánov CZ......98 C1
Banova Jaruga HR........... 124 B2
Bánovce nad Bebravou SK ..98 C2
Banovići BIH... 139 A4
Banovići Selo BIH........... 139 A4
Bánréve H......99 C4
Bansin D........66 C3
Banská Belá SK...........98 C2
Banská Bystrica SK...........99 C3
Banská Štiavnica SK...........98 C2
Bansko BG ... 183 B5
Banstead UK ...44 B3
Banteer IRL 29 B3
Bantheville F ...91 B5
Bantry IRL.....29 C2
Bantzenheim F 106 B2
Banyalbufar E 166 B2
Banyoles E ... 147 B3
Banyuls-sur-Mer F 146 B4
Bapaume F 90 A2
Bar MNE 16 D3
UA 13 D7
Barabhas UK ...31 A2
Baracal P 148 B2
Baracska H ... 112 B2
Barahona E ... 151 A5
Barajes de Melo E 151 B5
Barakaldo E... 143 A4
Baralla E 141 B3
Barañain E ... 144 B2
Baranavichy BY 13 B7
Báránd H 113 B5
Baranda SRB . 127 B2
Baranello I ... 170 B2
Baranów Sandomierski PL...........87 B5
Baraqueville F 130 A1
Barasoain E .. 144 B2
Barbacena P .. 155 C3
Barbadás E ... 140 B3
Barbadillo E .. 149 B4
Barbadillo de Herreros E .. 143 B3
Barbadillo del Mercado E .. 143 B3
Barbadillo del Pez E 143 B3
Barban HR ... 123 B3
Barbaros TR .. 186 B2
Barbastro E .. 145 B4
Barbate E 162 B2
Barbatona E .. 152 A1
Barbâtre F ... 114 B1

Barbazan F..... 145 A4
Barbeitos E.... 141 A3
Barbentane F. 131 B3
Barberino di Mugello I..... 135 A4
Barbezieux-St Hilaire F...... 115 C3
Barbonne-Fayel F............91 C3
Barbotan-les-Thermes F... 128 C2
Barby D........73 C4
Bárcabo E..... 145 B4
Barca de Alva P............. 149 A3
Barcarrota E.. 155 C4
Barcellona-Pozzo di Gotto I...... 177 A4
Barcelona E... 147 C3
Barcelonette F............ 132 A2
Barcelos P.... 148 A1
Bárcena del Monasterio E............. 141 A4
Barcena de Pie de Concha E.... 142 A2
Barchfeld D.....82 B2
Barcin PL......76 B2
Barcino PL.....68 A1
Bárcis I....... 122 A1
Barco P....... 148 B2
Barcones E.... 151 A5
Barcs H....... 124 B3
Barcus F...... 144 A3
Bardejov SK... 12 D4
Bárdesø DK..... 59 C3
Bardi I....... 120 C2
Bardney UK.....40 B3
Bardo PL.......85 B4
Bardolino I... 121 B3
Bardonécchia I............. 118 B3
Bardoňovo SK 112 A2
Baréges F..... 145 B4
Barenstein D....83 B5
Barentin F......89 A4
Barenton F.....88 B3
Barevo BIH.... 138 A3
Barfleur F......88 A2
Barga I....... 134 A3
Bargas E...... 151 C3
Barge I....... 119 C4
Bargemon F... 132 B2
Barghe I...... 120 B3
Bargoed UK.....39 C3
Bargrennan UK..36 A2
Bargteheide D..64 C3
Barham UK......45 B5
Baril I....... 173 A2
Barić Draga HR........... 137 A4
Barilović HR.. 123 B4
Bari Sardo I.. 179 C3
Barisciano I.. 169 A3
Barjac F...... 131 A3
Barjols F..... 132 B1
Barjon F...... 105 B3
Bârkåker N....54 A1
Barkald N..... 199 D7
Barkowo
  Dolnośląskie PL........... 85 A4
  Pomorskie PL ..68 B2
Bårlad RO......17 B7
Bar-le-Duc F ...91 C5
Barles F...... 132 A2
Barletta I..... 171 B4
Barlinek PL....75 B4
Barmouth UK ..38 B2
Barmstedt D...64 C2
Barnard Castle UK........... 37 B5
Barnarp S......62 A2
Bärnau D......95 B4
Bärnbach A ... 110 B2
Barneberg D...73 B4
Barnenitz D....74 B1
Barnet UK......44 B3
Barnetby le Wold UK........... 40 B3
Barneveld NL...70 B2
Barneville-Carteret F............88 A2
Barnoldswick UK........... 40 B1
Barnowko PL...75 B3
Barnsley UK....40 B2
Barnstädt D....83 A3
Barnstaple UK .42 A2

Barnstorf D.....72 B1
Barntrup D.....72 C2
Baron F.......90 B2
Baronissi I.... 170 C2
Baroncourt P... 170 C2
Barqueiro P... 154 B2
Barquinha P .. 154 B2
Barr
  F.............93 C3
  UK........... 36 A2
Barra P....... 148 B1
Barracas E.... 159 A3
Barraco E..... 150 B3
Barrado E..... 150 B2
Barrafranca I.. 177 B3
Barranco do Velho P............. 160 B2
Barrancos P... 161 A3
Barrax E...... 158 B1
Barrbaar D.....94 C2
Barre-des-Cevennes F .. 130 A2
Barreiro P.... 154 C1
Barreiros E... 141 A3
Barrême F 132 B2
Barret-le-Bas F............ 132 A1
Barrhead UK.. 34 C3
Barrhill UK.....36 A2
Barrio de Nuesra Señora E.... 142 B1
Barrowford UK..40 B1
Barrow-in-Furness UK........... 36 B3
Barrow upon Humber UK ...40 B3
Barruecopardo E............. 149 A3
Barruelo de Santullán E .. 142 B2
Barruera E.... 145 B4
Barry UK...... 39 C3
Bårse DK......65 A4
Barsinghausen D............. 72 B2
Barssel D......71 A4
Bar-sur-Aube F............ 104 A3
Bar-sur-Seine F............ 104 A3
Barth D........66 B1
Bartholomä D ..94 C1
Bartin TR..... 187 A7
Barton-upon-Humber UK ...40 B3
Barúmini I.... 179 C2
Baruth D.......74 B2
Barvaux B......80 B1
Barver D.......72 B1
Barwatd PL....99 B3
Barwice PL....68 B1
Barysaw BY ... 13 A8
Barzana E..... 141 A5
Bârzava RO ...16 B4
Bárzio I...... 120 B2
Bas E......... 147 B3
Bašaid SRB.... 126 B2
Basaluzzo I... 120 C1
Basarabeasca MD........... 17 B8
Basauri E..... 143 A4
Baschi I...... 168 A2
Baschurch UK ..38 B4
Basconcillos del Tozo E...... 143 B3
Bascones de Ojeda E............. 142 B2
Basécles B.....79 B3
Basel CH...... 106 B2
Basélice I..... 170 B2
Basildon UK....45 B4
Basingstoke UK 44 B2
Baška
  CZ........... 98 B2
  HR........... 123 C3
Baška Voda HR........... 138 B2
Bäsksjö S..... 200 B3
Baslow UK......40 B2
Başmakçı TR .. 189 B5
Basovizza I... 122 B2
Bassacutena I.. 178 A3
Bassano del Grappa I............. 121 B4
Bassano Romano I............. 168 A2
Bassecourt CH 106 B2
Bassella E.... 147 B2
Bassevuovdde N............. 193 D9
Bassou F...... 104 B2
Bassoues F.... 128 C3
Bassum D......72 B1
Båstad S......61 C2

Bastardo I..... 136 C1
Bastelica F.... 180 A2
Bastelicaccia F............. 180 B1
Bastia
  F............. 180 A2
  I............. 136 B1
Bastogne B....92 A1
Baston UK......40 C3
Bastuträsk S .. 200 B6
Bata H....... 125 A4
Batajnica SRB. 127 C2
Batak BG..... 183 B6
Batalha P..... 154 B2
Bátaszék H.... 125 A4
Batea E....... 153 A4
Batelov CZ.....97 B3
Bath UK....... 43 A4
Bathgate UK .. 35 C4
Batida H...... 126 A2
Batignano I... 135 C4
Batina HR..... 125 B4
Bátka SK......99 C4
Batković BIH . 125 C5
Batley UK......40 B2
Batnfjordsøra N............. 198 C4
Batočina SRB . 127 C3
Bátonyterenye H............. 113 B3
Batrina HR.... 125 B3
Båtsfjord N .. 193 B13
Båtskärsnäs S............. 196 D6
Battaglia Terme I............. 121 B4
Bätterkinden CH........... 106 B2
Battice B.......80 B1
Battipáglia I.. 170 C2
Battle UK...... 45 C4
Battonya H ... 126 A3
Batuša SRB.... 127 C3
Bátya H....... 112 C2
Bau I......... 179 C2
Baud F........ 100 B2
Baudour B......79 B3
Baugé F....... 102 B1
Baugy F....... 103 B4
Baume-les-Dames F............. 105 B5
Baumholder D..93 B3
Baunatal D.....81 A5
Baunei I...... 178 B3
Bauska LV......8 D4
Bautzen D......84 A2
Bavanište SRB.......... 127 C2
Bavay F....... 79 B3
Bavilliers F... 106 B1
Bavorov CZ.....96 B2
Bawdsey UK ...45 A5
Bawinkel D....71 B4
Bawtry UK......40 B2
Bayat TR...... 187 D5
Bayel F....... 105 A3
Bayındır TR... 188 A2
Bayon F.......92 C2
Bayonne F.... 128 C1
Bayons F..... 132 A2
Bayramiç TR .. 186 C1
Bayreuth D.....95 B3
Bayrischzell D 108 B3
Baza E....... 164 B2
Bazas F....... 128 B2
Baziege F..... 146 A2
Bazoches-les-Gallerandes F............. 103 A4
Bazoches-sur-Hoëne F......89 B4
Bazzano I..... 135 A4
Beaconsfield UK........... 44 B3
Beade E....... 140 B2
Beadnell UK...37 A5
Beaminster UK..43 B4
Bearsden UK ..34 C3
Beas E........ 161 B3
Beasain E..... 144 A1
Beas de Segura E............. 164 A2
Beattock UK...36 A3
Beaubery F.... 117 A4
Beaucaire F... 131 B3
Beaufort
  F............. 118 B3
  IRL.......... 29 B2
Beaufort-en-Vallée F............. 102 B1

Beaujeu
  Alpes-de-Haute-Provence F .. 132 A2
  Rhône F...... 117 A4
Beaulac F..... 128 B2
Beaulieu
  F............. 103 B4
  UK........... 44 C2
Beaulieu-sous-la-Roche F...... 114 B2
Beaulieu-sur-Dordogne F.. 129 B4
Beaulieu-sur-Mer F............. 133 B3
Beaulon F..... 104 C2
Beauly UK..... 32 D2
Beaumaris UK...38 A2
Beaumesnil F ..89 A4
Beaumetz-lès-Loges F.......78 B2
Beaumont
  B............. 79 B4
  F............. 129 B3
Beaumont-de-Lomagne F... 129 C3
Beaumont-du-Gâtinais F... 103 A4
Beaumont-en-Argonne F....91 B5
Beaumont-Hague F............. 88 A2
Beaumont-la-Ronce F............. 102 B2
Beaumont-le-Roger F............. 89 A4
Beaumont-sur-Oise F............. 90 B2
Beaumont-sur-Sarthe F..... 102 A2
Beaune F..... 105 B3
Beaune-la-Rolande F............. 103 A4
Beaupréau F... 101 B5
Beauraing B....91 A4
Beaurepaire F. 117 B5
Beaurepaire-en-Bresse F..... 105 C4
Beaurières F . 132 A1
Beauvais F.....90 B2
Beauval F......90 A2
Beauville F... 129 B3
Beauvoir-sur-Mer F............. 114 B1
Beauvoir-sur-Niort F............. 114 B3
Beba Veche RO........... 126 A2
Bebertal D.....73 B4
Bebra D........82 B1
Bebrina HR.... 125 B3
Beccles UK.....45 A5
Becedas E..... 150 B2
Beceite E..... 153 B4
Bečej SRB.... 126 B2
Becerreá E.... 141 B3
Becerril de Campos E............. 142 B2
Bécherel F.... 101 A4
Bechhofen D...94 B2
Bechyně CZ.....96 B2
Becilla de Valderaduey E............. 142 B1
Beckfoot UK ...36 B3
Beckingham UK........... 40 B3
Beckum D......81 A4
Beco P........ 154 B2
Bécon-les-Granits F............. 102 B1
Bečov nad Teplou CZ........... 83 B4
Becsehely H... 111 C3
Bedale UK......37 B5
Bédar E....... 164 B3
Bédarieux F... 130 B2
Bédarrides F . 131 A3
Bedburg D.....80 B2
Beddgelert UK..38 A2
Beddingestrand S............. 66 A2
Bédée F....... 142 B1
Bedford UK....44 A3
Bedlington UK..37 A5
Bedmar E..... 163 A4
Bédoin F..... 131 A4
Bedónia I..... 134 A2

Bedretto CH .. 107 C3
Bedsted DK.....58 B1
Bedum NL......71 A3
Bedwas UK.....39 C3
Bedworth UK ...40 C2
Będzin PL......86 B3
Beekbergen NL.70 B2
Beek en Donk NL........... 80 A1
Beelen D.......71 C5
Beelitz D......74 B1
Beer UK........43 B3
Beerfelde D....74 B3
Beerfelden D ..93 B4
Beernem B......78 A3
Beeskow D.....74 B3
Beetsterzwaag NL........... 70 A3
Beetzendorf D .73 B4
Beflelay CH ... 106 B2
Begaljica SRB . 127 C2
Bégard F..... 100 A2
Begejci SRB... 126 B2
Begijar E..... 157 C4
Begijnendijk B ..79 A4
Begndal N.....48 B1
Begues E..... 147 C2
Beguildy UK ...39 B3
Begur E....... 147 C4
Beho B........ 80 B1
Behringen D ...82 A2
Beilen NL......71 B3
Beilngries D ...95 B3
Beine-Nauroy F 91 B4
Beinwil CH.... 106 B3
Beiseförth D...82 A1
Beith UK...... 34 C3
Beitostølen N .47 A5
Beius RO......16 B5
Beja P....... 160 A2
Béjar E....... 149 B4
Bekçiler TR... 189 C4
Békés H...... 113 C5
Békéscsaba H. 113 C5
Bekilli TR.... 189 A4
Bekkarfjord N............. 193 B11
Bela SK....... 98 B2
Bélâbre F..... 115 B5
Bela Crkva SRB.......... 127 C3
Belalcázar E.. 156 B2
Belá nad Radbuzou CZ........... 95 B4
Belanovica SRB.......... 127 C2
Bélapátfalva H............. 113 A4
Belá pod Bezdězem CZ........... 84 B2
Belcaire F.... 146 B2
Bełchatów PL...86 A3
Belchite E.... 153 A3
Bělčice CZ.....96 B1
Belcoo UK......26 B3
Belecke D......81 A4
Beled H....... 111 B4
Belej HR...... 123 C3
Beleño E..... 142 A1
Bélesta F..... 146 B2
Belevi TR..... 188 A2
Belfast UK.....27 B5
Belford UK.....37 A5
Belfort F..... 106 B1
Belgentier F . 132 B1
Belgern D......83 A5
Belgioioso I... 120 B2
Belgodère F... 180 A2
Belgooly IRL...29 C3
Belgrade = Beograd SRB.......... 127 C2
Belica HR..... 124 A2
Beli Manastir HR........... 125 B4
Belin-Béliet F. 128 B2
Belinchón E... 151 B4
Belišće HR.... 125 B4
Bělkovice-Lašťany CZ........... 98 B1
Bella I....... 172 B1
Bellac F...... 115 B5
Bellágio I.... 120 B2
Bellananagh IRL.......... 27 C3
Bellano I..... 120 A2
Bellária I..... 136 A1
Bellavary IRL...26 C1
Belleau F......90 B3
Belleek UK.....26 B2
Bellegarde
  Gard F....... 131 B3
  Loiret F..... 103 B4

Bellegarde-en-Diois F............. 132 A1
Bellegarde-en-Marche F.... 116 B2
Bellegarde-sur-Valserine F .. 118 A2
Belle-Isle-en-Terre F............. 100 A2
Bellême F......89 B4
Bellenaves F .. 116 A3
Bellentre F... 118 B3
Bellevaux F... 118 A3
Bellevesvre F . 105 C4
Belleville F... 117 A4
Belleville-sur-Vie F............. 114 B2
Bellevue-la-Montagne F . 117 B3
Belley F...... 118 B2
Bellheim D.....93 B4
Bellinge DK.....59 C3
Bellingham UK........... 37 A4
Bellinzago Novarese I... 120 B1
Bellinzona CH. 120 A2
Bellizzi I.... 170 C2
Bello E....... 152 B2
Bellpuig d'Urgell E............. 147 C2
Bellreguart E . 159 C3
Bellsbank UK ..36 A2
Belltall E..... 147 C2
Belluno I..... 121 A5
Bellvís E...... 147 C1
Bélmez E..... 156 B2
Belmez de la Moralada E .. 163 A4
Belmont UK....33 A6
Belmont-de-la-Loire F...... 117 A4
Belmonte
  Asturias E .. 141 A4
  Cuenca E .. 158 B1
  P............. 148 B2
Belmonte de San José E....... 153 B3
Belmonte de Tajo E............. 151 B4
Belmont-sur-Rance F............. 130 B1
Belmullet IRL...26 B1
Belobreşca RO........... 127 C3
Beloeil B......79 B3
Belogradchik BG........... 16 D5
Belokorovichi UA........... 13 C8
Belorado E.... 143 B3
Belotić SRB... 127 C1
Bělotin CZ.....98 B1
Belovo BG.... 183 A6
Belozersk RUS .9 C10
Belp CH...... 106 C2
Belpasso I.... 177 B3
Belpech F.... 146 A2
Belper UK......40 B2
Belsay UK......37 A5
Belsk Duzy PL..87 A4
Beltinci SLO... 111 C3
Beltra IRL......26 C1
Belturbet IRL...27 B3
Beluša SK......98 B2
Belvedere Maríttimo I.. 174 B1
Belvès F...... 129 B3
Belvès-de-Razès F...... 130 B1
Belvezet F.... 130 A2
Belvis de la Jara E............. 150 C3
Belvis de Monroy E............. 150 C2
Belyy RUS......9 E8
Belz F....... 100 B2
Belzig D.......73 B5
Bembibre E.... 141 B4
Bembridge UK..44 C2
Bemmel NL.....80 A1
Bemposta
  Bragança P . 149 A3
  Santarém P . 154 B2
Benabarre E... 145 B4
Benacazón E .. 161 B3
Benaguacil E . 159 B3
Benahadux E... 164 C2

Benalmádena E............. 163 B3
Benalúa de Guadix E............. 164 B1
Benalúa de las Villas E..... 163 A4
Benalup E.... 162 B2
Benamargosa E............. 163 B3
Benamaurel E. 164 B2
Benameji E... 163 A3
Benamocarra E............. 163 B3
Benaocaz E... 162 B2
Benaoján E... 162 B2
Benarrabá E . 162 B2
Benasque E... 145 B4
Benátky nad Jizerou CZ....84 B2
Benavente
  E............. 142 B1
  P............. 154 C2
Benavides de Órbigo E.... 141 B5
Benavila P.... 154 B3
Bendorf D......81 B3
Benedikt SLO . 110 C2
Benejama E... 159 C3
Benejúzar E... 165 A4
Benešov CZ.....96 B2
Bénestroff F ...92 C2
Benet F....... 114 B3
Bene Vagienna I............. 133 A3
Bénévent-l'Abbaye F............. 116 A1
Benevento I... 170 B2
Benfeld F......93 C3
Benfica P..... 154 B2
Bengtsfors S ...54 A3
Bengtsheden S .50 B2
Beničanci HR... 125 B4
Benicarló E... 153 B4
Benicàssim E . 153 B4
Benidorm E... 159 C3
Benifaió E.... 159 B3
Beniganim E . 159 C3
Benington UK..41 B4
Benisa E...... 159 C4
Benkovac HR . 137 A4
Benllech UK....38 A2
Benneckenstein D............. 82 A2
Bénodet F.... 100 B1
Benquerencia de la Serena E.... 156 B2
Bensafrim P... 160 B1
Bensbyn S.... 196 D5
Bensdorf D.....73 B5
Benshausen D .82 B2
Bensheim D....93 B4
Bentley UK.....44 B3
Bentwisch D...65 B5
Beočin SRB... 126 B1
Beograd = Belgrade SRB.......... 127 C2
Beragh UK.....27 B3
Beranga E..... 143 A3
Berat AL...... 182 C1
Bérat F....... 146 A2
Beratzhausen D............. 95 B3
Bérbaltavár H. 111 B3
Berbegal E.... 145 C3
Berbenno di Valtellina I.. 120 A2
Berberana E .. 143 B3
Bercedo E..... 143 A3
Bercel H...... 112 B3
Bercenay-le-Hayer F............. 91 C3
Berceto I..... 134 A2
Berchem B.....79 B3
Berchidda I... 178 B3
Berching D.....95 B3
Berchtesgaden D............. 109 B4
Bérchules E... 163 B4
Bercianos de Aliste E............. 149 A3
Berck F........ 78 B1
Berclaire d'Urgell E............. 147 C1
Berdoias E.... 140 A1
Berdún E...... 144 B3
Berdychiv UA.. 13 D8
Bere Alston UK .42 B2
Bere Regis UK.43 B4
Berehove UA.. 16 A5
Berek BIH.... 124 B3

Beremend H .. 125 B4
Bere Regis UK . .43 B4
Berestechko
UA 13 C6
Berettyóújfalu
H............. 113 B5
Berezhany UA . . 13 D6
Berezivka UA ... 17 B9
Berezna UA 13 C9
Berg
D 95 B3
N............. 195 E3
S.............56 B2
Berga
Sachsen-Anhalt
D............. 82 A3
Thüringen D ..83 B4
E 147 B2
S.............62 A4
Bergama TR... 186 C2
Bérgamo I 120 B2
Bergara E 143 A4
Bergby S......51 B4
Berge
Brandenburg
D.............74 B1
Niedersachsen
D.............71 B4
Telemark N 53 A4
Telemark N 53 A4
Bergeforsen
S 200 D3
Bergen
Mecklenburg-
Vorpommern
D.............66 B2
Niedersachsen
D.............72 B2
Niedersachsen
D.............73 B3
N.............46 B2
NL 70 B1
Bergen op Zoom
NL 79 A4
Bergerac F ... 129 B3
Bergères-
lés-Vertus F ...91 C4
Bergeyk NL 79 A5
Berghausen D ..93 C4
Bergheim D....80 B2
Berghem S....60 B2
Berg im Gau D ..95 C3
Bergisch Gladbach
D.............80 B3
Bergkamen D...81 A3
Bergkvara S....63 B4
Berglern D....95 C3
Bergnäset S... 196 D5
Bergneustadt
D.............81 A3
Bergsäng S....49 B5
Bergshamra S...57 A4
Bergsjö S 200 E3
Bergs slussar
S..............56 B1
Bergsviken S. 196 D4
Bergtheim D...94 B2
Bergues F 78 B2
Bergum NL....70 A2
Bergün Bravuogn
CH 107 C4
Bergwitz D....83 A4
Berhida H.... 112 B2
Beringel P 160 A2
Beringen D....79 A5
Berja E...... 164 C2
Berkåk N 199 C7
Berkeley UK....43 A4
Berkenthin D ..65 C3
Berkhamsted
UK 44 B3
Berkheim D .. 107 A5
Berkhof D....72 B2
Berkovići BIH . 139 B4
Berkovitsa
BG 17 D5
Berlanga E ... 156 B2
Berlanga de Duero
E 151 A5
Berlevåg N .. 193 B13
Berlikum NL 70 A2
Berlin D......74 B2
Berlstedt D....82 A3
Bermeo E 143 A4
Bermillo de Sayago
E 149 A3
Bern CH...... 106 C2
Bernalda I 174 A2
Bernardos E... 150 A3
Bernartice
Jihočeský CZ....96 B2
Východočeský
CZ 85 B3

Bernau
Baden-Württemberg
D........... 106 B3
Bayern D 109 B3
Brandenburg
D.............74 B2
Bernaville F .. 90 A2
Bernay F......89 A4
Bernburg D 83 A3
Berndorf A.... 111 B3
Berne D.......72 A1
Bernecebaráti
H............ 112 A2
Bernhardsthal
A.............97 C4
Bernkastel-Kues
D.............92 B3
Bernolákovo
SK.......... 111 A4
Bernsdorf D...84 A2
Bernstadt D...84 A2
Bernstein A .. 111 B3
Bernués E 145 B3
Beromünster
CH 106 B3
Beroun CZ 96 B2
Berovo NMK .. 182 B4
Berre-l'Étang
F 131 B4
Berriedale UK. .32 C3
Berriew UK.....39 B3
Berrocal E.... 161 B3
Bersenbrück D. .71 B4
Bershad' UA ... 13 D8
Bertamiráns E 140 B2
Berthåga S....51 C4
Berthelming F ..92 C2
Bertincourt F ...90 A2
Bertinoro I ... 135 A5
Bertogne B 92 A1
Bertrix B 91 B5
Berufjörður
IS 191 C11
Berville-sur-Mer
F 89 A4
Berwick-upon-
Tweed UK 37 A4
Berzasca RO ...16 C4
Berzence H ... 124 A3
Berzocana E .. 156 A2
Besalú E.... 147 B3
Besançon F ... 105 B5
Besenfeld D....93 C4
Besenyötelek
H............ 113 B4
Besenyszög
H............ 113 B4
Beshenkovichi
BY............13 A8
Besigheim D ...93 C5
Běšiny CZ.....96 B1
Beška SRB.... 126 B2
Beşkonak TR . 189 B6
Besle F...... 101 B4
Besnyő H 112 B2
Bessais-le-
Fromental F .. 103 C4
Bessan F 130 B2
Besse-en-
Chandesse F . 116 B2
Bessèges F .. 131 A3
Bessé-sur-Braye
F 102 B2
Bessines-sur-
Gartempe F . 115 B5
Best NL 79 A5
Bestorp S....56 B1
Betanzos E.... 140 A2
Betelu E.... 144 A2
Bétera E...... 159 B3
Beteta E.... 152 B1
Béthenville F ..91 B4
Bethesda UK ..38 A2
Béthune F....78 B2
Beton-Bazoches
F 90 C3
Bettembourg L .92 B2
Betterdorf L ...92 B2
Bettna S.....56 B2
Béttola I 120 C2
Bettona I 136 B1
Bettyhill UK....32 C2
Betws-y-Coed
UK 38 A3
Betxí E...... 159 B3
Betz F........90 B2
Betzdorf D 81 B3
Beuil F...... 132 A2
Beulah UK 39 B3
Beuzeville F....89 A4
Bevagna I 136 C1
Bevens-bruk S .56 A1
Beveren B.....79 A4

Beverley UK.....40 B3
Bevern D......81 A5
Beverstedt D...72 A1
Beverungen D .81 A5
Beverwijk NL ...70 B1
Bex CH 119 A4
Bexhill UK......45 C4
Beyazköy TR . 186 A2
Beychevelle
F 128 A2
Beydağ TR ... 188 A3
Beyeğaç TR ... 188 B3
Beykoz TR..... 186 A4
Beynat F 129 A4
Beyoğlu TR ... 186 A4
Beypazarı TR . 187 B6
Beyşehir TR . 189 B6
Bezas E...... 152 B2
Bezdan SRB .. 125 B4
Bèze F...... 105 B4
Bezenet F 116 A2
Bezhetsk RUS ..9 D10
Béziers F 130 B2
Bezzecca I 121 B3
Biadki PL.....85 A5
Biała
Łódzkie PL 77 C4
Opolskie PL .. 85 B5
Białaczów PL...87 A4
Biała Podlaska
PL 13 B5
Biała Rawska
PL............87 A4
Białobłoty PL...76 B2
Białobrzegi PL .87 A4
Białogard PL...67 C4
Białośliwie PL...76 A2
Białowąs PL....68 B1
Biały Bór PL....68 B1
Białystok PL ...13 B5
Biancavilla I... 177 B3
Bianco I..... 175 C2
Biandrate I ... 119 B5
Biar E...... 159 C3
Biarritz F 144 A2
Bias F...... 128 B1
Biasca CH.... 120 A1
Biatorbágy H . 112 B2
Bibbiena I... 135 B4
Bibbona I 134 B3
Biberach
Baden-Württemberg
D 93 C4
Baden-Württemberg
D 107 A4
Bibione I... 122 B2
Biblis D......93 B4
Bibury UK.....44 B2
Bicaj AL..... 182 B2
Biccari I..... 171 B3
Bicester UK....44 B2
Bichl D...... 108 B2
Bichlbach A... 108 B1
Bicorp E...... 159 B3
Bicos P...... 160 B1
Bicske H..... 112 B2
Bidache F 128 C1
Bidart F 144 A2
Biddinghuizen
NL 70 B2
Biddulph UK ...40 B1
Bideford UK....42 A2
Bidford-on-Avon
UK 44 A2
Bidjovagge N . 192 C6
Bie S........56 A2
Bieber D......81 B5
Biebersdorf D...74 C2
Biebesheim D...93 B4
Biel E....... 144 B3
Bielany
Wrocławskie
PL............85 A4
Bielawa PL....85 B4
Bielawy PL....77 B4
Biel / Bienne
CH 106 B2
Bielefeld D....72 B1
Bielica PL.....13 B6
Biella I...... 119 B5
Bielsa E..... 145 B4
Bielsk PL.....77 B4
Bielsko-Biała
PL............99 B3
Bielsk Podlaski
PL.............13 B5
Bienenbuttel
D.............72 A3
Bieniow PL....84 A3
Bienservida E . 158 C1
Bienvenida E . 156 B1

Bierdzany PL...86 B2
Bierné F..... 102 B1
Biersted DK....58 A2
Bierun PL.....86 B3
Bierutów PL....85 A5
Bierwart B 79 B5
Bierzwina PL...75 A4
Bierzwnik PL...75 A4
Biescas E.... 145 B3
Biesenthal D...74 B2
Biesiekierz PL...67 B5
Bietigheim-
Bissingen D .. 93 C5
Bièvre B......91 B5
Bieżuń PL.....77 B4
Biga TR..... 186 B2
Bigadiç TR ... 186 C3
Biganos F 128 B2
Bigas P...... 148 B2
Bigastro E.... 165 A4
Bigbury UK 42 B3
Biggar UK.....36 A3
Biggleswade
UK 44 A3
Bignasco CH .. 119 A5
Biguglia F 180 A2
Bihać BIH 124 C1
Biharnagybajom
H 113 B5
Bijeljani BIH .. 139 B4
Bijeljina BIH .. 125 C5
Bijuesca E.... 152 A2
Bilaj HR..... 137 A4
Bila Tserkva
UA 13 D9
Bilbao E..... 143 A4
Bilcza PL.....87 B4
Bildudalur IS . . 190 B2
Bileća BIH.... 139 C4
Bilecik TR.... 187 B4
Biled RO..... 126 B2
Bilgoraj PL.....12 C5
Bilhorod-
Dnistrovskyy
UA 17 B9
Bilina CZ......84 B1
Bilisht AL.... 182 C2
Bilje HR..... 125 B4
Billdal S......60 B1
Billerbeck D ...71 C4
Billesholm S ...61 C2
Billingborough
UK 40 C3
Billinge S.....61 D3
Billingham UK ..37 B5
Billinghay UK ..41 B3
Billingsfors S ...54 B3
Billingshurst
UK 44 B3
Billom F..... 116 B3
Billsta S..... 200 C4
Billund DK....59 C2
Bilovec CZ....98 B2
Bílovice CZ....98 C1
Bilstein D.....81 A4
Bilthoven NL...70 B2
Bilto N...... 192 C5
Bilzen B......80 B1
Bíña Sk...... 112 B2
Binaced E.... 145 C4
Binasco I..... 120 B2
Binbrook UK ...41 B3
Binche B......79 B4
Bindlach D....95 B3
Bindslev DK....58 A3
Binéfar E.... 145 C4
Bingen D......93 B3
Bingham UK ...40 C3
Bingsjö S.....50 A2
Binic F...... 100 A3
Binz D.......66 B2
Biograd na Moru
HR 137 B4
Bionaz I..... 119 B4
Bioska SRB.... 127 D1
Birda RO..... 126 B3
Birdlip UK.....44 B1
Biri N........48 B2
Birkeland N....53 B4
Birkenfeld
Baden-Württemberg
D 93 C4
Rheinland-Pfalz
D 92 B3
Birkenhead
UK 38 A3
Birkerød DK....61 D2
Birkfeld A.... 110 B2
Birkirkara M . 175 C3
Birmingham
UK 40 C2

Birr IRL.......28 A4
Birresborn D...80 B2
Birstein D.....81 B5
Biržai LT.......8 D4
Birzebbugia
M 175 C3
Bisáccia I 172 A1
Bisacquino I .. 176 B2
Bisbal de Falset
E 153 A4
Biscarrosse F . 128 B1
Biscarrosse Plage
F 128 B1
Biscarrués E .. 144 B3
Biscéglie I.... 171 B4
Bischheim F....93 C3
Bischofsheim D 82 B1
Bischofshofen
A 109 B4
Bischofswerda
D.............84 A2
Bischofswiesen
D............ 109 B3
Bischofszell
CH 107 B4
Bischwiller F ...93 C3
Bisenti I..... 169 A3
Bishop Auckland
UK 37 B5
Bishop's Castle
UK 39 B3
Bishops Lydeard
UK 43 A3
Bishop's Stortford
UK 45 B4
Bishop's Waltham
UK 44 C2
Bisignano I ... 174 B2
Bisingen D....93 C4
Biskupice-
Oławskie PL ...85 A5
Biskupiec PL...69 B4
Bismark D....73 B4
Bismo N..... 198 D5
Bispgården S . 200 C2
Bispingen D ...72 A2
Bissen L......92 B2
Bissendorf D...71 B5
Bisserup DK....65 A4
Bistango I.... 119 C5
Bistarac Donje
BIH 139 A4
Bistret RO.....17 C6
Bistrica BIH .. 124 C3
Bistrica ob Sotli
SLO 123 A4
Bistrița RO....17 B6
Bitburg D......92 B2
Bitche F......93 B3
Bitetto I..... 171 B4
Bitola NMK... 182 B3
Bitonto I..... 171 B4
Bitschwiller F . 106 B2
Bitterfeld D...83 A4
Bitti I....... 178 B3
Biville-sur-Mer
F 89 A5
Bivona I..... 176 B2
Biwer L......92 B2
Bizeljsko SLO . 123 A4
Bizovac HR.... 125 B4
Bjåen N......52 A3
Bjärnum S....61 C3
Bjärred S.....61 D3
Bjästa S..... 200 C4
Bjelland
Vest-Agder N ..52 B3
Vest-Agder N ..52 B3
Bjelovar HR ... 124 B2
Bjerkreim N ...52 B2
Bjerkvik N 194 B8
Bjerreby DK....65 B3
Bjerregård DK .59 B1
Bjerringbro DK .58 B2
Bjøberg N.....47 B5
Bjøllånes N .. 195 D5
Björbo S......50 B1
Bjordal N.....46 A2
Björg IS...... 191 B8
Bjørkåsen N . 194 B7
Björke
Gävleborg S ...51 B4
Östergötland
S 56 B1
Bjørkelangen
N.............48 C3
Björketorp S...60 B2
Bjørkholmen
S 196 C2
Bjørklidèn S . 194 B9
Björkö S......57 B4
Björköby S....62 A2

Björkvik S......56 B2
Bjørn N 195 D3
Bjørna S 200 C4
Björneborg S . 55 A5
Bjørnerod S ...54 A2
Bjørnevatn
N............ 193 C13
Björnlunda S...56 A3
Bjørnstad N . 193 C14
Bjuråker S....51 A3
Björsäter S....56 B2
Bjurberget S ...49 B4
Bjurholm S... 200 C5
Bjursås S.....50 B2
Bjurtjärn S....55 A5
Bjuv S.......61 C2
Blachownia PL .86 B2
Blackburn UK ..38 A4
Blackpool UK ..38 A3
Blackstad S....62 A4
Blackwater IRL . .30 B2
Blackwaterfoot
UK 34 C2
Blacy F.......91 C4
Bládåker S....51 B5
Blaenau Ffestiniog
UK 38 B3
Blaenavon UK . .39 C3
Blaengarw UK . .39 C3
Blagaj
BIH 124 B2
BIH 139 B3
Blagdon UK....43 A4
Blagnac F 129 C4
Blagoevgrad
BG 183 A5
Blaichach D . . 107 B5
Blain F...... 101 B4
Blainville-sur-l'Eau
F 92 C2
Blair Atholl UK . .35 B4
Blairgowrie UK. .35 B4
Blajan F..... 145 A4
Blakeney UK ...39 C4
Blakstad N....53 B4
Blåmont F.....92 C2
Blanca E..... 165 A3
Blancos E.... 140 C3
Blandford Forum
UK 43 B4
Blanes E.... 147 C3
Blangy-sur-Bresle
F 90 B1
Blankaholm S . .62 A4
Blankenberge
B 79 A3
Blankenburg D .82 A2
Blankenfelde D .74 B2
Blankenhain D .82 B3
Blankenheim D .80 B2
Blankenhout D .81 B3
Blanquefort F . 128 B2
Blansko CZ....97 B4
Blanzac F 115 C4
Blanzy F..... 104 C3
Blaricum NL....70 B2
Blarney IRL....29 C3
Blascomillán
E 150 B2
Blascosancho
E 150 B3
Błaszki PL.....86 A2
Blatná CZ......96 B1
Blatné SK.... 111 A4
Blatnice CZ....98 C1
Blatnika BIH . 139 A3
Blato HR..... 138 C2
Blato na Cetini
HR 138 B2
Blatten CH... 119 A4
Blaubeuren D ..94 C1
Blaufelden D...94 B1
Blaustein D....94 C1
Blaydon UK....37 B5
Blaye F...... 128 A2
Blaye-les-Mines
F 130 A1
Blázquez E... 156 B2
Bleckede D....73 A3
Blecua E..... 145 B3
Bled SLO.... 123 A3
Bleiburg A ... 110 C1
Bleicherode D .82 A2
Bleik N...... 194 A6
Bleikvassli N . 195 E4
Bléneau F.... 104 B1
Blentarp S....61 D3
Blera I...... 168 A2
Bléré F...... 102 B2
Blesle F..... 116 B3

Blessington IRL .30 A2
Blet F...... 103 C4
Bletchley UK...44 B3
Bletterans F .. 105 C4
Blidö S.......57 A4
Blidsberg S....60 B3
Blieskastel D...92 B3
Bligny-sur-Ouche
F 104 B3
Blikstorp S....55 B5
Blinisht AL.... 182 B1
Blinja HR.... 124 B2
Blizanówek PL . .76 C3
Bliżyn PL......87 A4
Blois F...... 103 B3
Blokhus DK....58 A2
Blokzijl NL.....70 B2
Blombacka S...55 A4
Blomberg D....72 C2
Blomskog S....54 A3
Blomstermåla
S 62 B4
Blomvåg N....46 B1
Blönduós IS . . 190 B5
Błonie PL......77 B5
Blonville-sur-Mer
F 89 A4
Blötberget S...50 B2
Blovice CZ....96 B1
Bloxham UK ...44 A2
Blšany CZ.....83 B5
Bludenz A.... 107 B4
Bludov CZ....97 B4
Blumberg D . . 107 B3
Blyberg S.....49 A6
Blyth
Northumberland
UK 37 A5
Nottinghamshire
UK 40 B2
Blyth Bridge
UK 35 C4
Blythburgh UK. .45 A5
Blythe Bridge
UK 40 C1
Bø
Nordland N . . 194 B5
Telemark N 53 A5
Boal E...... 141 A4
Boan MNE.... 139 C5
Boario Terme
I........... 120 B3
Boat of Garten
UK 32 D3
Boa Vista P... 154 B2
Bobadela TR ..23 A8
Bobalna TR .. 111 B4
Bobadilla
Logroño E ... 143 B4
Málaga E ... 163 A3
Bobadilla del
Campo E ... 150 A2
Bobadilla del
Monte E.... 151 B4
Bóbbio I..... 120 C2
Bóbbio Péllice
I........... 119 C4
Bobigny F.....90 C2
Bobingen D....94 C2
Böblingen D...93 C5
Bobolice PL....68 B1
Boboras E.... 140 B2
Boboshevo
BG 182 A4
Bobowa PL....99 B4
Bobrová UA ...13 C9
Bobrovica UA . .13 C9
Bobrowice PL .75 C4
Bobrówko PL . .75 B4
Boca de Huérgano
E 142 B2
Bocairent E ... 159 C3
Bočar SRB.... 126 B2
Bocchigliero I . 174 B2
Boceguillas E . 151 A4
Bochnia PL....99 B4
Bocholt
B 80 A1
D 80 A2
Bochov CZ....83 B5
Bochum D.....80 A3
Bockara S.....62 A4
Bockenem D...72 B3
Bockfliess A ...97 C4
Bockhorn D....71 A5
Bočna SLO... 123 A3
Bocognano F . 180 A2
Boconád H.... 113 B4
Bőcs H...... 113 A4

Boczów PL 75 B3
Boda S 50 A2
Böda S 62 A5
Boda
  Stockholm S . . .51 B5
  Värmland S . . . 55 A4
  Västernorrland
  S 200 D2
Bodafors S 62 A2
Boda Glasbruk
  S 63 B3
Bodajk H 112 B2
Boddam
  Aberdeenshire
  UK 33 D5
  Shetland UK . . . 33 B5
Boddin D 73 A4
Bödefeld-Freiheit
  D 81 A4
Boden S 196 D4
Bodenmais D . . .95 B5
Bodenteich D . . .73 B3
Bodenwerder
  D 72 C2
Bodiam UK 45 B4
Bodinnick UK . . .42 B2
Bodio CH 120 A1
Bodjani SRB . . . 125 B5
Bodmin UK 42 B2
Bodø N 194 C5
Bodonal de la
  Sierra E 161 A3
Bodrum TR 188 B2
Bodstedt D 66 B1
Bodträskfors
  S 196 C3
Bodzanów PL . . .77 B5
Bodzanowice
  PL 86 B2
Bodzechów PL . .87 B5
Bodzentyn PL . . .87 B4
Boecillo E 150 A3
Boëge F 118 A3
Boën F 117 B3
Bogács H 113 B4
Bogadmindszent
  H 125 B4
Bogajo E 149 B3
Bogarra E 158 C1
Bogarre E 163 A4
Bogatić SRB . . . 127 C1
Bogatynia PL . . .84 B2
Bogda RO 126 B3
Bogdaniec PL . . .75 B4
Boge S 57 C4
Bogen
  D 95 C4
  Nordland N . . . 194 B7
  Nordland N . . 194 C6
  S 49 B4
Bogense DK 59 C3
Bognanco Fonti
  I 119 A5
Bognelv N 192 B6
Bognes N 194 B7
Bogno CH 120 A2
Bognor Regis
  UK 44 C3
Bogoria PL 87 B5
Bogorangen S . . .49 B4
Boguchwaly PL .69 B5
Bogumiłowice
  PL 86 A3
Boguslav UA . . . 13 D9
Boguszów-Gorce
  PL 85 B4
Bogyiszló H . . . 112 C2
Bohain-en-
  Vermandois F . .91 B3
Böheimkirchen
  A 110 A2
Bohinjska Bistrica
  SLO 122 A2
Böhlen D 83 A4
Böhmenkirch
  D 94 C1
Bohmte D 71 B5
Bohonal de Ibor
  E 150 C2
Böhönye H 124 A3
Bohumin CZ 98 B2
Boiro E 140 B2
Bois-d'Amont
  F 105 C5
Boisseron F . . . 131 B3
Boitzenburg D . .74 A2
Boixols E 147 B2
Boizenburg D . . .73 A3
Bojadła PL 75 C4
Bojano I 170 B2

Bojanowo PL . . .85 A4
Bøjden DK 64 A3
Bojkovice CZ . . .98 B1
Bojná SK 98 C2
Bojnice SK 98 C2
Boka SRB 126 B2
Böklund D 64 B2
Bokod H 112 B2
Böksholm S 62 A2
Boksitogorsk
  RUS 9 C8
Bol HR 138 B2
Bolaños de
  Calatrava E . . 157 B4
Bolayır TR 186 B1
Bolbec F 89 A4
Bölcske H 112 C2
Boldekow D 64 B2
Boldog H 112 B3
Boldva H 113 A4
Bőle S 196 D4
Bolekhiv UA . . 13 D5
Bolesławiec PL . .84 A3
Boleszkowice
  PL 74 B3
Bolewice PL 75 B5
Bólgheri I 134 B3
Bolhrad UA 17 C8
Boliden S 200 B6
Bolimów PL 77 B5
Boliqueime P . 160 B1
Boljevci SRB . . 127 C2
Boljkovci SRB . 127 C2
Bolków PL 85 B4
Bollebygd S 60 B2
Bollène F 131 A3
Bólliga E 152 B1
Bollnäs S 50 A3
Bollstabruk S . 200 D3
Bollullos E 161 B3
Bollullos par del
  Condado E . . 161 B3
Bologna I 135 A4
Bologne F 105 A4
Bolognetta I . . 176 B2
Bolognola I . . . 136 C2
Borðeyri IS . . . 190 B4
Bolótana I 178 B2
Bolsena I 168 A1
Bolshaya
  Vradiyevka
  UA 17 B9
Bolsover UK 40 B2
Bolstad S 54 B3
Bolsward NL . . .70 A2
Boltaña E 145 B4
Boltenhagen D .65 C4
Boltigen CH . . . 106 C2
Bolton UK 38 A4
Bolu TR 187 B6
Bolungarvik
  IS 190 A2
Bolvadin TR . . . 187 D6
Bóly H 125 B4
Bolzaneto I . . . 133 A4
Bolzano I 108 C2
Bomba I 169 A4
Bombarral P . . 154 B1
Bömenzien D . . .73 B4
Bomlitz D 72 B2
Bømlo N 52 A1
Bøn N 48 B3
Bona F 104 B2
Bonaduz CH . . 107 C4
Bonanza E 161 C3
Boñar E 142 B1
Bonarbridge
  UK 32 D2
Bonárcado I . . . 178 B2
Bonares E 161 B3
Bonäs S 50 A1
Bonassola I . . . 134 A2
Bonawe UK 34 B2
Bondal N 53 A4
Bondeno I 121 C4
Bondorf D 93 C4
Bondstorp S 60 B3
Bon-Encontre
  F 129 B3
Bo'ness UK 35 B4
Bonete E 158 C2
Bonifacio F . . . 180 B2
Bonigen CH . . . 106 C2
Bonin PL 67 B5
Bonn D 80 B3
Bonnánaro I . . . 178 B2
Bonnásjøen
  N 194 C6
Bonnat F 116 A1
Bonndorf D . . . 106 B3
Bonnétable F . 102 A2
Bonnétage F . . 106 B1

Bonneuil-les-Eaux
  F 90 B2
Bonneuil-Matours
  F 115 B4
Bonneval F . . . 103 A3
Bonneval-sur-Arc
  F 119 B4
Bonneville F . . 118 A3
Bonnières-sur-
  Seine F 90 B1
Bonnieux F . . . 131 B4
Bönnigheim D . .93 B5
Bonnyrigg UK . .35 C4
Bonny-sur-Loire
  F 103 B4
Bono
  E 145 B4
  I 178 B3
Bonorva I 178 B2
Bønsnes N 48 B2
Bonyhád H 125 A4
Boom B 79 A4
Boos F 89 A5
Boostedt D 64 B3
Bootle
  Cumbria UK . . .36 B3
  Merseyside UK . 38 A3
Bopfingen D . . .94 C2
Boppard D 81 B3
Boqueixón E . 140 B2
Bor
  CZ 95 B4
  S 62 A2
  SRB 16 C5
  TR 23 C8
Boran-sur-Oise
  F 90 B2
Borås S 60 B2
Borba P 155 C3
Borbona I 169 A3
Borča SRB 127 C2
Borci BIH 139 B4
Borculo NL 71 B3
Bordány H 126 A1
Bordeaux F . . . 128 B2
Bordeira P 160 B1
Bordesholm D . .64 B2
Borðeyri IS . . . 190 B4
Bordighera I . . 133 B3
Bording DK 59 B2
Bordón E 153 B3
Bore I 120 C2
Borehamwood
  UK 44 B3
Borek Strzeliński
  PL 85 B5
Borek Wielkopolski
  PL 76 C2
Boreland UK . . .36 A3
Borello I 135 A5
Borensberg S . . .56 B1
Borgafjäll S . . 199 A12
Borgarnes IS . 190 C4
Borgentreich
  D 81 A5
Börger D 71 B4
Borger NL 71 B3
Borggård S 56 B1
Borgholm S 62 B4
Borghetto
  d'Arróscia I . 133 A3
Borghetto Santo
  Spírito I 133 A4
Borgholz S 62 B4
Borghorst D 71 B4
Bórgia I 175 C2
Borgloon B 79 B5
Børglum DK 58 A2
Borgo F 180 A2
Borgo alla Collina
  I 135 B4
Borgo a Mozzano
  I 134 B3
Borgoforte I . . 121 B3
Borgofranco
  d'Ivrea I 119 B4
Borgomanero
  I 119 B5
Borgomasino
  I 119 B4
Borgonovo Val
  Tidone I 120 B2
Borgo Pace I . 135 B5
Borgorose I . . . 169 A3
Borgo San
  Dalmazzo I . . 133 A3
Borgo San Lorenzo
  I 135 B4
Borgosésia I . . 119 B5
Borgo Val di Taro
  I 134 A2

Borgo Valsugana
  I 121 A4
Borgo Vercelli
  I 119 B5
Borgstena S 60 B3
Borgue UK 36 B2
Borgund N 47 A4
Borgvik S 55 A3
Borja E 144 C2
Bork D 80 A3
Borken D 80 A2
Borkenes N . . . 194 B7
Børkop DK 59 C2
Borkowice PL . . .87 A4
Borkowo PL 77 B5
Borkum D 71 A3
Borlänge S 50 B2
Borlu TR 186 D3
Bormes-les-
  Mimosas F . . 132 B2
Bórmio I 107 C5
Bormujos E . . . 161 B3
Borna D 83 A4
Borne NL 71 B3
Bornes P 149 A2
Borne Sulinowo
  PL 68 B1
Bornheim D 80 B2
Bornhöved D . . .64 B3
Börnicke D 74 B1
Bornos E 162 B2
Borobia E 152 A2
Borodino RUS . . .9 E9
Borohrádek CZ .85 B4
Boronów PL 86 B2
Bórore I 178 B2
Borosław PL 86 B2
Borota H 126 A1
Borovany CZ . . .96 C2
Borovichi RUS . . .9 C8
Borovnica
  SLO 123 B3
Borovo HR . . . 125 B4
Borovsk RUS . . .9 E10
Borovy CZ 96 B1
Borowa PL 85 A5
Borox E 151 B4
Borrby S 66 A3
Borre
  DK 65 B5
  N 54 A1
Borredá E 147 B2
Borrenes E . . . 141 B4
Borriol E 159 A3
Borris
  DK 59 C1
  IRL 30 B2
Borris-in-Ossory
  IRL 28 B4
Borrisokane IRL 28 B3
Borrisoleigh
  IRL 28 B4
Borrowdale UK .36 B3
Børrud N 49 C4
Borşa RO 17 B6
Borsdorf D 83 A4
Børselv N 193 B9
Borsfa H 111 C3
Borský Mikuláš
  SK 98 C1
Borsodivánka
  H 113 B4
Borsodnádasd
  H 113 A4
Börte N 53 A3
Borth UK 39 B2
Bort-les-Orgues
  F 116 B2
Börtnan S . . . 199 C10
Børtnes N 47 B6
Borup DK 61 D1
Boryslav UA . . 13 D5
Boryspil UA . . . 13 C9
Boryszyn PL 75 B4
Borzęciczki PL . .85 A5
Borzęcin PL 77 B5
Borzonasca I . . 134 A2
Borzyszkowy
  PL 68 A2
Borzytuchom
  PL 68 A2
Bosa I 178 B2
Bošáca SK 98 C1
Bosanci HR . . . 123 B4
Bosanska Krupa
  BIH 124 C2
Bosanski Petrovac
  BIH 124 C2
Bosansko Grahovo
  BIH 138 A2
Bošany SK 98 C2

Bósárkány H . . 111 B4
Bosau D 65 B3
Bósca h 112 C3
Boscastle UK . . .42 B2
Bosco I 120 C1
Bosco Chiesanuova
  I 121 B4
Bösdorf D 65 B3
Bösel D 71 A4
Bosham UK 44 C3
Bösingfeld D . . .72 B2
Bosjön S 49 C5
Boskoop NL 70 B1
Boskovice CZ . . .97 B4
Bošnjaci HR . . . 125 B4
Bošnjane SRB . 127 D3
Bossast E 145 B4
Bossolasco I . . 133 A4
Boštanj SLO . . 123 A4
Boston UK 41 C3
Bostrak N 53 A4
Böszénfa H . . . 125 A3
Bot E 153 A4
Botajica BIH . . 125 C4
Bøte By DK 65 B4
Bothel UK 36 B3
Boticas P 148 A2
Botilsäter S 55 A4
Botngård N . . . 198 B6
Botoš SRB 126 B2
Botoşani RO . . .17 B7
Botricello I . . . 175 C2
Botsmark S . . . 200 B6
Bottendorf D . . .81 A4
Bottesford UK . .40 C3
Bottnaryd S 60 B3
Bottrop D 80 A2
Botunje SRB . . 127 C3
Bötzingen D . . 106 A2
Bouaye F 101 B4
Bouça P 149 A2
Boucau F 128 C1
Bouchain F 78 B3
Bouchoir F 90 B2
Boudreville F . 105 B3
Boudry CH 106 C1
Bouesse F 103 C3
Bouguenais F . 101 B4
Bouhy F 104 B2
Bouillargues
  F 131 B3
Bouillon B 91 B5
Bouilly F 104 A2
Bouin F 114 B2
Boulay-Moselle
  F 92 B2
Boulazac F . . . 129 A3
Boule-d'Amont
  F 146 B3
Bouligny F 92 B1
Boulogne-sur-
  Gesse F 145 A4
Boulogne-sur-Mer
  F 78 B1
Bouloire F 102 B2
Bouquemaison
  F 78 B2
Bourboule F 89 A4
Bourbon-Lancy
  F 104 C2
Bourbon-
  l'Archambault
  F 104 C2
Bourbonne-les-
  Bains F 105 B4
Bourbourg F . . .78 B2
Bourbriac F . . . 100 A2
Bourcefranc-le-
  Chapus F . . . 114 C2
Bourdeaux F . . 131 A4
Bouresse F . . . 115 B4
Bourg F 128 A2
Bourg-Achard
  F 89 A4
Bourganeuf F . 116 B1
Bourg-Argental
  F 117 B4
Bourg-de-Péage
  F 117 B5
Bourg-de-Thizy
  F 117 A4
Bourg-de-Visa
  F 129 B3
Bourg-en-Bresse
  F 118 A2
Bourges F 103 B4
Bourg-et-Comin
  F 91 B3
Bourg-Lastic F 116 B2
Bourg-Madame
  F 146 B2
Bourgneuf-en-Retz
  F 114 A2
Bourgogne F . . .91 B4

Bourgoin-Jallieu
  F 118 B2
Bourg-St Andéol
  F 131 A3
Bourg-St Maurice
  F 119 B3
Bourgtheroulde
  F 89 A4
Bourgueil F . . . 102 B2
Bourmont F . . . 105 A4
Bourne UK 40 C3
Bournemouth
  UK 43 B5
Bourneville F . . .89 A4
Bournezeau F . 114 B2
Bourran F 129 B3
Bourret F 129 C4
Bourron-Marlotte
  F 90 C2
Bourton-on-the-
  Water UK 44 B2
Boussac F 116 A2
Boussens F . . . 145 A4
Boutersem B . . .79 B4
Bouttencourt F .90 B1
Bouvières F . . . 131 A4
Bouvron F 101 B4
Bouxwiller F . . .93 C3
Bouzas E 140 B2
Bouzonville F . .92 B2
Bova I 175 D1
Bovalino Marina
  I 175 C2
Bovallstrand S .54 B2
Bova Marina I . 175 D1
Bovec SLO . . . 122 A2
Bóvegno I 120 B3
Bovenden D 82 A1
Boverdal N . . . 198 D5
Boves F 90 B2
Bóves I 133 A3
Bovey Tracey
  UK 43 B3
Bovino I 171 B3
Bøvlingbjerg
  DK 58 B1
Bovolenta I . . . 121 B4
Bovolone I 121 B4
Bowes UK 37 B5
Bowmore UK . . .34 C1
Bowness-on-
  Windermere
  UK 36 B4
Box UK 43 A4
Boxberg
  Baden-Württemberg
  D 94 B1
  Sachsen D 84 A2
Boxholm S 55 B6
Boxmeer NL 80 A1
Boxtel NL 79 A5
Boyabat TR 23 A8
Boyalıca TR . . . 187 B4
Boyle IRL 26 C2
Bozan TR 187 C6
Božava HR . . . 137 A3
Bozburun TR . . 188 C3
Bozcaada TR . . 186 C1
Bozdoğan TR . . 188 B3
Božec TR 186 B2
Bożepole Wielkie
  PL 68 A2
Boževac SRB . . 127 C3
Božice CZ 97 C4
Bozkır TR 189 B7
Bozouls F 130 A1
Bozova TR 189 B5
Bozüyük TR . . . 187 C5
Bózzolo I 121 B3
Bra I 119 C4
Braås S 62 A3
Brabrand DK . . .59 B3
Bracadale UK . . .31 B2
Bracciano I . . . 168 A2
Bracieux F 103 B3
Bräcke S 199 C12
Brackenheim
  D 93 B5
Brackley UK 44 A2
Bracklin IRL 27 C4
Bracknell UK . . .44 B3
Brackwede D . . .72 C1
Braco UK 35 B4
Brad RO 16 B5
Bradford UK 40 B2
Bradford on Avon
  UK 43 A4
Brădina BIH . . . 139 B4
Brådland N 52 B2
Bradwell-on-Sea
  UK 45 B4
Bradworthy UK .42 B2
Brae UK 33 A5

Braemar UK . . . 32 D3
Braemore UK . . 32 D1
Braga P 148 A1
Bragança P . . . 149 A3
Bräila RO 17 C7
Braine F 91 B3
Braine-le-Comte
  B 79 B4
Braintree UK . . .45 B4
Braives B 79 B5
Brake D 72 A1
Brakel
  B 79 B3
  D 81 A5
Bräkne-Hoby S .63 B3
Brålanda S 54 B3
Bralin PL 86 A1
Brallo di Pregola
  I 120 C2
Bram F 146 A3
Bramafan F . . . 132 B2
Bramberg am
  Wildkogel A . 109 B3
Bramdrupdam
  DK 59 C2
Bramming DK . .59 C1
Brampton UK . . .37 B4
Bramsche D 71 B4
Branca I 136 B1
Brancaleone
  Marina I 175 D2
Brancaster UK . .41 C4
Brand
  Nieder Österreich
  A 96 C3
  Vorarlberg A . 107 B4
Brandbu N 48 B2
Brande DK 59 C2
Brande-
  Hornerkirchen
  D 64 C2
Brandenberg
  A 108 B2
Brandenburg D .73 B5
Brand-Erbisdorf
  D 83 B5
Brandis D 83 A4
Brando F 180 A2
Brandomil E . . 140 A2
Brandon UK 45 A4
Brandshagen D .66 B2
Brandval N 49 B4
Brandýs nad Labem
  CZ 84 B2
Branice PL 98 A1
Braničevo
  SRB 127 C3
Braniewo PL . . .69 A4
Branik SLO . . . 122 B2
Brankovina
  SRB 127 C1
Branky CZ 98 B1
Branne F 128 B2
Brannenburg-
  Degerndorf
  D 108 B3
Brantôme F . . . 115 C4
Branzi I 120 A2
Bras d'Asse F . 132 B2
Braskereidfoss
  N 48 B3
Braşov RO 17 C6
Brasparts F . . . 100 A2
Brassac F 130 B1
Brassac-les-Mines
  F 116 B3
Brasschaat B . . .79 A4
Brastad S 54 B2
Břasy CZ 96 B1
Braszewice PL . .86 A2
Bratislava SK . . 111 A4
Brattfors S 55 A5
Brattvåg N . . . 198 C3
Bratunac BIH . . 127 C1
Braubach D 81 B3
Braunau A 95 C5
Braunfels D 81 B4
Braunlage D 82 A2
Braunsbedra D .83 A3
Braunschweig

Brdani SRB 127 D2
Brdów PL 76 B3
Brea de Tajo E . 151 B4
Brécey F 88 B2
Brechen D 81 B4
Brechin UK 35 B5
Brecht B 79 A4
Brecketfeld D . .80 A3
Břeclav CZ 97 C4
Brecon UK 39 C3
Brécy F 103 B4
Breda
    E 147 C3
    NL 79 A4
Bredaryd S 60 B3
Bredbyn S 200 C4
Breddin D 73 B5
Bredebro DK 64 A1
Bredelar D 81 A4
Bredenfelde D .74 A2
Bredsjö S 50 C1
Bredstedt D 64 B1
Bredsten DK 59 C2
Bredträsk S . . . 200 C4
Bredviken S . . . 195 D5
Bree B 80 A1
Bregana HR 123 B4
Breganze I 121 B4
Bregenz A 107 B4
Bréhal F 88 B2
Brehna D 83 A4
Breiðdalsvík
    IS 191 C11
Breidenbach F . .93 B3
Breil-sur-Roya
    F 133 B3
Breisach D 106 A2
Breitenbach
    CH 106 B2
    D 81 B5
Breitenberg D . .96 C1
Breitenfelde D . .73 A3
Breitengussbach
    D 94 B2
Breivikbotn N . 192 B6
Brejning DK 59 C2
Brekke N 46 A2
Brekken N 199 C8
Brekkestø N . . .53 B4
Brekkvasselv
    N 199 A10
Brekstad N 198 B6
Breland N 53 B3
Bremanger N . 198 D1
Bremen D 72 A1
Bremerhaven
    D 72 A1
Bremervörde
    D 72 A2
Bremgarten
    CH 106 B3
Bremsnes N . . . 198 B4
Brem-sur-Mer
    F 114 B2
Brenderup DK . .59 C2
Brenes E 162 A2
Brengova
    SLO 110 C2
Brenna PL 98 B2
Breno I 120 B3
Brénod F 118 A2
Brensbach D . . .93 B4
Brentwood UK .45 B4
Brescello I 121 C3
Bréscia I 120 B3
Breskens NL . . .79 A3
Bresles F 90 B2
Bresnica SRB . . 127 D2
Bressana I 120 B2
Bressanone I . . 108 C2
Bressuire F . . . 102 C1
Brest
    BY 13 B5
    F 100 A1
    HR 122 B2
Brestač SRB . . . 127 C1
Brestanica
    SLO 123 A4
Brestova HR . . 123 B3
Brestovac HR . 125 B3
Bretenoux F . . 129 B4
Breteuil
    Eure F 89 B4
    Oise F 90 B2
Brétigny-
    sur-Orge F . . .90 C2
Bretten D 93 B4
Bretteville-sur-
    Laize F 89 A3
Brettheim D . . .94 B2
Breuil-Cervínia
    I. 119 B4
Breukelen NL . .70 B2

Brevik
    N 53 A5
    Stockholm S . . . 57 A4
    Västra Götaland
    S 55 B5
Breza BIH 139 A4
Brežice SLO . . . 123 B4
Bréziers F 132 A2
Breznica HR . . . 124 A2
Breznica Našička
    HR 125 B4
Březnice CZ 96 B1
Brezolles F 89 B5
Březovánad
    Svitavou CZ . . .97 B4
Brezovápol
    Bradlom SK . . .98 C1
Brezovica
    SK 99 B4
    SLO 123 B3
Brezový Polje Selo
    BIH 125 C4
Briançon F 118 C3
Brianconnet
    F 132 B2
Briare F 103 B4
Briatexte F 129 C4
Briático I 175 C2
Briaucourt F . . 105 A4
Bribir HR 123 B3
Bricquebec F . . .88 A2
Bridgend
    Argyll & Bute
    UK 34 C1
    Bridgend UK . . 39 C3
Bridge of Cally
    UK 35 B4
Bridge of Don
    UK 33 D4
Bridge of Earn
    UK 35 B4
Bridge of Orchy
    UK 34 B3
Bridgnorth UK . .39 B4
Bridgwater UK .43 A4
Břidličná CZ 98 B1
Bridlington UK .41 A3
Bridport UK 43 B4
Briec F 100 A1
Brie-Comte-Robert
    F 90 C2
Brienne-le-Château
    F 91 C4
Brienon-sur-
    Armançon F . . 104 B2
Brienz CH 106 C3
Brienza I 172 B1
Briesen D 74 B3
Brieskow
    Finkenheerd
    D 74 B3
Brietlingen D . .72 A3
Brieva de Cameros
    E 143 B4
Briey F 92 B1
Brig CH 119 A5
Brigg UK 40 B3
Brighouse UK . .40 B2
Brightlingsea
    UK 45 B5
Brighton UK . . .44 C3
Brignogan-Plage
    F 100 A1
Brignoles F . . . 132 B2
Brigstock UK . . .40 C3
Brihuega E 151 B5
Brijuni HR 122 C2
Brillon-en-Barrois
    F 91 C5
Brilon D 81 A4
Brimnes N 46 B3
Brinches P 160 A2
Bríndisi I 173 B3
Brinje HR 123 B4
Brinon-sur-Beuvron
    F 104 B2
Brinon-sur-Sauldre
    F 103 B4
Brinyan UK 33 B3
Brión E 140 B2
Briones E 143 B4
Brionne F 89 A4
Brioude F 117 B3
Brioux-sur-
    Boutonne F . 115 B3
Briouze F 89 B3
Briscous F 144 A2
Brisighella I . . . 135 A4
Brissac-Quincé
    F 102 B1
Brissago CH . . . 120 A1
Bristol UK 43 A4

Brive-la-Gaillarde
    F 129 A4
Briviesca E 143 B3
Brixham UK 43 B3
Brixlegg A 108 B2
Brjánslækur IS 190 B2
Brka BIH 125 C4
Brnaze HR 138 B2
Brněnec CZ 97 B4
Brno CZ 97 B4
Bro S 57 A3
Broadclyst UK . .43 B3
Broadford
    IRL 28 B3
    UK 31 B3
Broad Haven
    IRL 26 B1
Broadstairs UK .45 B5
Broadstone UK .43 B4
Broadway UK . . .44 A2
Broager DK 64 B2
Broaryd S 60 B3
Broby S 61 C4
Brobyværk DK .59 C3
Bročanac BIH . . 138 B3
Brocas F 128 B2
Brock D 71 B4
Brockel D 72 A2
Brockenhurst
    UK 44 C2
Broczyno PL . . .75 A5
Brod
    BIH 125 B3
    NMK 182 B3
Brodalen S 54 B2
Broddbo S 50 C3
Brodek u Přerova
    CZ 98 B1
Broden-bach D .80 B3
Brodick UK 34 C2
Brod na Kupi
    HR 123 B3
Brodnica PL 69 B4
Brodnica Graniczna
    PL 68 A3
Brodowe Łąki
    PL 77 A6
Brody
    Lubuskie PL 75 B4
    Lubuskie PL . . . 84 A2
    Mazowieckie
    PL 77 B5
Broglie F 89 B4
Brójce PL 75 B4
Brokind S 56 B1
Brolo I 177 A3
Brome D 73 B3
Bromley UK 45 B4
Bromölla S 63 B2
Bromont-Lamothe
    F 116 B2
Brömsebro S . . .63 B3
Bromsgrove
    UK 44 A1
Bromyard UK . .39 B4
Bronchales E . . 152 B2
Bronco E 149 B3
Brønderslev
    DK 58 A2
Broni I 120 B2
Brønnøysund
    N 195 E3
Brøns DK 59 C1
Bronte I 177 B3
Bronzani Mejdan
    BIH 124 C2
Bronzolo I 121 A4
Broons F 101 A3
Broquies F 130 A1
Brora UK 32 C3
Brørup DK 59 C2
Brösarp S 63 C2
Brossac F 115 C3
Brostrud N 47 B5
Brotas P 154 C2
Brötjärna S 50 B2
Broto E 145 B3
Brottby S 57 A4
Brøttum N 48 A2
Brou F 103 A3
Brouage F 114 C2
Brough UK 37 B4
Broughshane
    UK 27 B4
Broughton UK . .35 C4
Broughton-in-
    Furness UK . . .36 B3
Broumov CZ 85 B4
Broût-Vernet
    F 116 A3
Brouvelieures
    F 106 A1

Brouwershaven
    NL 79 A3
Brovary UA 13 C9
Brovst DK 58 A2
Brownhills UK . .40 C2
Brozas E 155 B4
Brozzo I 120 B3
Brtnice CZ 97 B3
Brtonigla HR . . 122 B2
Bruay-la-Buissière
    F 78 B2
Bruchhausen-
    Vilsen D 72 B2
Bruchsal D 93 B4
Bruck D 95 B4
Brück D 74 B1
Bruck an der
    Grossglockner-
    strasse A 109 B3
Bruck an der Leitha
    A 111 A3
Bruck an der Mur
    A 110 B2
Brückl A 110 C1
Bruckmühl D . . 108 B2
Brue-Auriac F . 132 B1
Brüel D 65 C4
Bruen CH 107 C3
Bruère-Allichamps
    F 103 C4
Bruff IRL 29 B3
Bruflat N 47 B6
Brugg CH 106 B3
Brugge B 78 A3
Brüggen D 80 A2
Brühl D 80 B2
Bruinisse NL . . .79 A4
Brûlon F 102 B1
Brumano I 120 B2
Brumath F 93 C3
Brummen NL . . .70 B3
Brumov-Bylnice
    CZ 98 B2
Brumunddal N .48 B2
Brunau D 73 B4
Brunehamel F . .91 B4
Brünen D 80 A2
Brunete E 151 B3
Brunflo S 199 B11
Brunico I 108 C2
Brunkeberg N . .53 A4
Brunn D 74 A2
Brunnen CH . . . 107 C3
Brunsbüttel D . .64 C2
Brunssum NL . . .80 B1
Bruntál CZ 98 B1
Brušane HR . . . 137 A4
Brusasco I 119 B5
Brusio CH 120 A3
Brusno SK 99 C3
Brusque F 130 B1
Brussels = Bruxelles
    B 79 B4
Brüssow D 74 A3
Brusy PL 68 B2
Bruton UK 43 A4
Bruvno HR 138 A1
Bruvoll N 48 B3
Bruxelles = Brussels
    B 79 B4
Bruyères F 106 A1
Bruz F 101 A4
Bruzaholm S . . .62 A3
Brwinów PL 77 B5
Brynamman UK .39 C3
Bryncrug UK . . .39 B2
Bryne N 52 B1
Brynmawr UK . .39 C3
Bryrup DK 59 B2
Brzeg PL 85 B5
Brzeg Dolny PL .85 A4
Brześć Kujawski
    PL 76 B3
Brzesko PL 99 B4
Brzeszcze PL . . .99 B3
Brzezie PL 68 B1
Brzeziny
    Łódzkie PL 87 A3
    Wielkopolskie
    PL 86 A2
Brzeźnica PL . . .84 A3
Brzeźnica Nowa
    PL 86 A3
Brzeźno PL 75 A4
Brznik SLO 98 C4
Brzotín SK 99 C4
Brzozie Lubawskie
    PL 69 B4
Bua S 60 B2
Buarcos P 148 B1
Buaveng N 52 A1
Bubbio I 119 C5
Bubry F 100 B2

Buca TR 188 A2
Bucak TR 189 B5
Bučany SK 98 C1
Buccheri I 177 B3
Buccino I 172 B1
Bucelas P 154 C1
Buch
    Bayern D 94 C2
    Bayern D 95 C4
Buchach UA 13 D6
Bucharest =
    Bucureşti RO . .17 C7
Buchbach D 95 C4
Buchboden A . 107 B4
Buchen D 94 B1
Büchen D 73 A3
Buchenberg
    D 107 B5
Buchères F 104 A3
Buchholz D 72 A2
Buchloe D 108 A1
Buchlovice CZ . .98 B1
Buchs CH 107 B4
Buchy F 89 A5
Bückeburg D . . .72 B2
Buckfastleigh
    UK 42 B3
Buckhaven UK . .35 B4
Buckie UK 33 D4
Buckingham
    UK 44 A3
Buckley UK 38 A3
Bückwitz D 73 B5
Bučovice CZ 97 B5
Bucsa H 113 B5
Bucureşti =
    Bucharest RO . .17 C7
Bucy-lés-Pierreport
    F 91 B3
Buczek PL 86 A3
Bud N 198 C3
Budakalasz H . 112 B3
Budakeszi H . . . 112 B2
Budal N 199 C7
Budaörs H 112 B2
Budapest H . . . 112 B3
Búðardalur IS . 190 B4
Budča SK 99 C3
Buddusò I 178 B3
Bude UK 42 B2
Budeč CZ 97 B3
Büdelsdorf D . . .64 B2
Budens P 160 B1
Budia E 151 B5
Budimlić-Japra
    BIH 124 C2
Büdingen D 81 B5
Budinšćina
    HR 124 A2
Budišov CZ 98 B1
Budleigh Salterton
    UK 43 B3
Budmerice SK . .98 C1
Budoni I 178 B3
Búdrio I 135 A4
Budva MNE . . . 16 D3
Budyněnad Ohří
    CZ 84 B2
Budziszewice
    PL 87 A3
Budzyń PL 76 B1
Bue N 52 B1
Bueña E 152 B2
Bueu E 140 B2
Buezo E 143 B3
Bugac H 112 C3
Bugarra E 159 B3
Bugeat F 116 B1
Buggerru I 179 C2
Bugojno BIH . . . 138 A3
Bugøyfjord
    N 193 C13
Bugøynes N . . 193 C13
Bugyi H 112 B3
Buharkent TR . 188 B3
Bühl
    Baden-Württemberg
    D 93 C4
    Bayern D 94 C2
Bühlertal D 93 C4
Bühlertann D . . .94 B1
Buia I 122 A2

Builth Wells UK .39 B3
Buin N 47 B6
Buis-les-Baronnies
    F 131 A4
Buitenpost NL . .70 A3
Buitrago del
    Lozoya E 151 B4
Bujalance E . . . 157 C3
Bujaraloz E . . . 153 A3
Buje HR 122 B2
Bujedo E 143 B3
Bük H 111 B3
Buk PL 75 B5
Bükkösd H 125 A3
Bükkzsérc H . . 113 B4
Bukovci SLO . . 124 A1
Bukowiec PL . . .75 B5
Bukowina
    Tatrzańska PL . .99 B4
Bukowno PL . . .86 B3
Bülach CH 107 B3
Büland IS 191 D7
Buldan TR 188 A3
Bulgnéville F . . 105 A4
Bulgurca TR . . . 188 A2
Bülkau D 64 C1
Bulken N 46 B3
Bullas E 164 A3
Bulle CH 106 C2
Büllingen B 80 B2
Bullmark S 200 B6
Bulqizë AL 182 B2
Buna BIH 139 B3
Bunahowen IRL 26 B1
Bunbeg IRL 26 A2
Bunclody IRL . . .30 B2
Buncrana IRL . . .27 A3
Bunde D 71 A4
Bünde D 72 B1
Bundoran IRL . . .26 B2
Bunessan UK . . .34 B1
Bungay UK 45 A5
Bunge S 57 C5
Bunić HR 123 C4
Bunmahon IRL . .30 B1
Bunnyconnellan
    IRL 26 B1
Buño E 140 A2
Buñol E 159 B3
Bunratty IRL 29 B3
Bunsbeek B 79 B4
Buñuel E 144 C2
Bunyola E 166 B2
Buonabitácolo
    I. 172 B1
Buonalbergo I 170 B2
Buonconvento
    I 135 B4
Buonvicino I . . 174 B1
Burano I 122 B1
Burbach D 81 B4
Burcei I 179 C3
Burdons-sur-
    Rognon F . . . 105 A4
Burdur TR 189 B5
Bureå S 2 D7
Burela E 141 A3
Büren D 81 A4
Büren an der Aare
    CH 106 B2
Burford UK 44 B2
Burg
    Cottbus D 84 A2
    Magdeburg D . .73 B4
    Schleswig-Holstein
    D 64 B2
Burgas BG 17 D7
Burgau
    A 111 B3
    D 94 C2
    P 160 B1
Burg auf Fehmarn
    D 65 B4
Burgbernheim
    D 94 B2
Burgdorf
    CH 106 B2
    D 72 B3
Burgebrach D . .94 B2
Bürgel D 83 B3
Burgess Hill UK .44 C3
Burghaslach D .94 B2
Burghausen
    D 109 A3
Burghead UK . . .32 D3
Burghule Marsh
    UK 41 B4
Búrgio I 176 B2
Burgkirchen
    D 109 A3

Brd – Bus 209

Burgkunstadt
    D 82 B3
Burglengenfeld
    D 95 B4
Burgo P 148 B1
Burgoberbach
    D 94 B2
Burgohondo
    E 150 B3
Burgos E 143 B3
Burgsinn D 82 B1
Burgstädt D 83 B4
Burgstall D 73 B4
Burg Stargard
    D 74 A2
Burgsvik S 57 C4
Burgui E 144 B3
Burguillos E . . . 162 A2
Burguillos del Cerro
    E 155 C4
Burguillos de
    Toledo E 151 C4
Burhaniye TR . 186 C1
Burhave D 71 A5
Burie F 114 C3
Burjassot E . . . 159 B3
Burk D 94 B2
Burkhardtsdorf
    D 83 B4
Burlada E 144 B2
Burladingen
    D 107 A4
Burlage D 71 A4
Burness UK 33 B4
Burnham UK . . .44 B3
Burnham Market
    UK 41 C4
Burnham-on-
    Crouch UK . . .45 B4
Burnham-on-Sea
    UK 43 A4
Burniston UK . . .40 A3
Burnley UK 40 B1
Burntisland UK .35 B4
Burón E 142 A1
Buronzo I 119 B5
Burovac SRB . . 127 C3
Burow D 74 A2
Burravoe UK . . .33 A5
Burrel AL 182 B2
Burret F 146 B2
Burriana E 159 B3
Burry Port UK . .39 C2
Bürs A 107 B4
Bursa TR 186 B4
Burseryd S 60 B3
Bürstadt D 93 B4
Burton UK 37 B4
Burton Agnes
    UK 41 A3
Burton Bradstock
    UK 43 B4
Burton Latimer
    UK 44 A3
Burton upon
    Stather UK . . .40 B3
Burton upon Trent
    UK 40 C2
Burträsk S 200 B6
Burujón E 151 C3
Burwell UK 45 A4
Burwick UK 33 C4
Bury UK 40 B1
Bury St Edmunds
    UK 45 A4
Burzenin PL 86 A2
Busachi I 179 B2
Busalla I 134 A1
Busana I 134 A3
Busano I 119 B4
Busca I 133 A3
Busch D 73 B4
Buševec HR . . . 124 B2
Bushat AL 182 B1
Bushey UK 44 B3
Bushmills UK . . .27 A4
Bušince SK 112 A3
Buskhyttan S . . .56 B2
Busko-Zdrój PL .87 B4
Busot E 159 C3
Busovača BIH . 139 A3
Busquistar E . . 163 B4
Bussang F 106 B1
Busseto I 120 C3
Bussière-Badil
    F 115 C4
Bussière-Poitevine
    F 115 B4
Bussolengo I . . 121 B3
Bussoleno I . . . 119 B4

Bussum NL......70 B2
Busto Arsízio I 120 B1
Büsum D......64 B1
Butera I......177 B3
Butgenbach B...80 B2
Butler's Bridge
  IRL......27 B3
Butryny PL.....77 A5
Bütschwil CH . 107 B4
Buttermere UK..36 B3
Buttevant IRL...29 B3
Buttle S......57 C4
Buttstädt D 82 A3
Butzbach D 81 B4
Bützfleth D 72 A2
Bützow D 65 C4
Buxières-les-Mines
  F......104 C1
Buxtehude D ...72 A2
Buxton UK 40 B2
Buxy F......104 C3
Büyükçekmece
  TR......186 A3
Büyükkarıştıran
  TR......186 A2
Büyükorhan
  TR......186 C3
Buzançais F ...103 C3
Buzancy F.....91 B4
Bužau RO 17 C7
Buzet HR......122 B2
Buzias RO 126 B3
Buzsák H.....111 C4
Buzy F......145 A3
By S......50 B3
Byala BG 17 D6
Byaroza BY....13 B6
Byczyna PL.....86 A2
Bydalen S 199 B10
Bydgoszcz PL ..76 A3
Bygdin N......47 A5
Bygdsiljum S . 200 B6
Bygland N 53 B3
Byglandsfjord
  N......53 B3
Bygstad N 46 A2
Bykhaw BY....13 B9
Bykle N......52 A3
Bylderup-Bov
  DK......64 B2
Byrkjedal N ...52 B2
Byrkjelo N ...198 D3
Byrum DK.....58 A3
Býšice CZ 84 B2
Byske S......2 D7
Byškovice CZ ..98 B1
Bysław PL.....76 A2
Bystré CZ 97 B4
Bystrice CZ.....96 B2
Bystrice CZ.....98 B2
Bystřice nad
  Pernštejnem
  CZ......97 B4
Bystřice pod
  Hostýnem CZ . 98 B1
Bystrzyca Kłodzka
  PL......85 B4
Bytča SK 98 B2
Bytnica PL.....75 B4
Bytom PL......86 B2
Bytom Odrzański
  PL......85 A3
Bytów PL......68 A2
Byxelkrok S....62 A5
Bzenec CZ 98 C1
Bzince SK 98 C1

C

Çağa TR......187 B7
Cabacos P 154 B2
Cabaj-Čápor
  SK......98 C2
Cabana E 140 A2
Cabanac-et-
  Villagrains F . 128 B2
Cabañaquinta
  E......142 A1
Cabanas P 160 B2
Cabañas del
  Castillo E ...156 A2
Cabañas de Yepes
  E......151 C4
Cabanelles E ..147 B3
Cabanes E 153 B4
Cabanillas E...154 A2
Čabar HR......123 B3
Cabasse F 132 B2
Cabdella E ...146 B2

Cabeceiras de
  Basto P......148 A1
Cabeço de Vide
  P......155 B3
Cabella Ligure
  I......120 C2
Cabeza del Buey
  E......156 B2
Cabeza la Vaca
  E......161 A3
Cabezamesada
  E......151 C4
Cabezarados
  E......157 B3
Cabezarrubias del
  Puerto E 157 B3
Cabezas del Villar
  E......150 B2
Cabezas Rubias
  E......161 B2
Cabezón E 142 C2
Cabezón de la Sal
  E......142 A2
Cabezón de
  Liébana E ...142 A2
Cabezuela E ...151 A4
Cabezuela del Valle
  E......149 B4
Cabo de Gata
  E......164 C2
Cabo de Palos
  E......165 B4
Cabolafuente
  E......152 A1
Cabourg F 89 A3
Cabra
  E......163 A3
  P......148 B2
Cabra del Santo
  Cristo E 163 A4
Cábras I......179 C2
Cabreiro P 140 C2
Cabreiros E ...140 A3
Cabrejas E ...152 A1
Cabrela P 154 C2
Cabrillas E ...149 B3
Cabuna HR....125 B3
Cacabelos E ...141 B4
Čačak SRB.....127 D2
Cáccamo I....176 B2
Caccuri I......174 B2
Cacela P 160 B2
Cacém P 154 C1
Cáceres E 155 A4
Cachafeiro E ..140 B2
Cachopo P 160 B2
Cachtice SK ...98 C1
Čačinci HR 125 B3
Cadafais P 154 C1
Cadalen F 129 C5
Cadalso E 149 B3
Cadaqués E ...147 B4
Cadaval P 154 B1
Cadavedo E ..141 A4
Čađavica BIH..138 A2
Čadca SK.....98 B2
Cadéac F 145 B4
Cadelbosco di
  Sopra I......121 C3
Cadenazzo
  CH......120 A1
Cadenberge D ..64 C2
Cadenet F 131 B4
Cadeuil F 114 C3
Cádiar E 164 C1
Cadillac F 128 B2
Cádiz E 162 B1
Čadjavica HR...125 B3
Cadouin F 129 B3
Cadours F 129 C4
Cadrete E 152 A3
Caen F 89 A3
Caerleon UK ...39 C4
Caernarfon UK ..38 A2
Caerphilly UK ..39 C3
Caersws UK ...39 B3
Cefedë P 154 B2
Caggiano I 172 B1
Cágli I......136 B1
Cágliari I 179 C3
Čaglin HR 125 B3
Cagnano Varano
  I......171 B3
Cagnes-sur-Mer
  F......132 B3
Caher IRL 29 B4
Caherciveen
  IRL......29 C1
Caherdaniel
  IRL......29 C1
Cahors F 129 B4

Cahul MD 17 C8
Caiazzo I.....170 B2
Caion E 140 A2
Cairndow UK...34 B3
Cairnryan UK ..36 B1
Cairo Montenotte
  I......133 A4
Caister-on-Sea
  UK......41 C5
Caistor UK 41 B3
Caivano I.....170 C2
Cajarc F 129 B4
Čajniče BIH....139 B5
Çakırlar TR ...189 C5
Çakmak TR....187 C6
Čakovec HR ...124 A2
Çal TR......189 A4
Cala E 161 B3
Calabritto I....172 B1
Calaceite E ...153 B4
Calacuccia F ..180 A2
Cala d'Or E ...167 B3
Calaf E 147 C2
Calafat RO 17 C5
Calafell E 147 C2
Cala Galdana
  E......167 B3
Cala Gonone I . 178 B3
Calahonda
  E......163 B4
  Granada E ...163 B4
  Málaga E ...163 B3
Calahorra E ...144 B2
Calais F 78 B1
Cala Llonga E . 166 C1
Calalzo di Cadore
  I......109 C3
Cala Millor E ..167 B3
Calamocha E ..152 B2
Calamonte E ..155 C4
Cala Morell E ..167 A3
Calanais UK ...31 A2
Calañas E 161 B3
Calangiánus I . 178 B3
Calanais RO ...17 C7
Cala Ratjada E 167 B3
Calascibetta I . 177 B3
Calasetta I 179 C2
Calasparra E ..164 A3
Calatafimi I...176 B1
Calatayud E ...152 A2
Calatorao E ...152 A2
Calau D 84 A1
Calbe D 73 C4
Calcena E 152 A2
Calcinelli I....136 B1
Calco I......120 B2
Caldarola I 136 B2
Caldas da Rainha
  P......154 B1
Caldas de Boi
  E......145 B4
Caldas de Malavella
  E......147 C3
Caldas de Reis
  E......140 B2
Caldas de San Jorge
  P......148 A1
Caldas de Vizela
  P......148 A1
Caldaso de los
  Vidrios E 150 B3
Caldbeck UK...36 B3
Caldearenas E .145 B3
Caldelas P 148 A1
Calders E 147 C2
Caldes de Montbui
  E......147 C3
Caldicot UK ...39 C4
Caldirola I....120 C2
Caledon UK ...27 B4
Calella
  Barcelona E . 147 C3
  Girona E 147 C4
Calenzana I ...180 A1
Calera de León
  E......161 A3
Calera y Chozas
  E......150 C3
Caleruega E ...143 C3
Caleruela E ...150 C2
Cales de Mallorca
  E......167 B3
Calestano I....134 A1
Calfsound UK ..33 B4
Calgary UK....34 B1
Calimera I 173 B4
Calitri I......172 B1
Calizzano I....133 A4
Callac F 100 A2
Callan IRL 30 B1

Callander UK...35 B3
Callas F 132 B2
Calliano
  Piemonte I...119 B5
  Trentino Alto Adige
  I......121 B4
Callington UK...42 B2
Callosa de Ensarriá
  E......159 C3
Callosa de Segura
  E......165 A4
Çalma SRB 127 B1
Calmbach D....93 C4
Calne UK......43 A5
Calolziocorte
  I......120 B2
Calonge E 147 C4
Čalovec SK....112 B1
Calpe E 159 C4
Caltabellotta I 176 B2
Caltagirone I...177 B3
Caltanissetta I 177 B3
Caltavuturo I . 176 B2
Çaltılıbük TR . . 186 C3
Caltojar E 151 A5
Caluire-et-Cuire
  F......117 B4
Caluso I......119 B4
Calvello I.....172 B1
Calvi F 180 A1
Calviá E 166 B2
Calvinet F 116 C2
Calvisson F ...131 B3
Calvörde D....73 B4
Calw D......93 C4
Calzada de
  Calatrava E . 157 B4
Calzada de
  Valduncie E . 150 A2
Calzadilla de los
  Barros E 155 C4
Cam UK 43 A4
Camaiore I 134 B3
Camarasa E ...145 C4
Camarena E ...151 B3
Camarès F 130 B1
Camaret-sur-
  Aigues F 131 A3
Camaret-sur-Mer
  F......100 A1
Camarillas E ..153 B3
Camariñas E ..140 A1
Camarma E ...151 B4
Camarzana de Tera
  E......141 B4
Camas E 161 B3
Cambados E ..140 B2
Camberley UK ..44 B3
Cambil E 163 A4
Cambligeu F...78 B2
Cambo-les-Bains
  F......144 A2
Camborne UK...42 B1
Cambrai F 78 B3
Cambre E 140 A2
Cambridge UK .45 A4
Cambrils E 147 C2
Camburg D 83 A3
Camden UK ...44 B3
Cameleño E ...142 A2
Camelford UK ..42 B2
Çameli TR 189 B4
Camelle E 140 A1
Camerano I ...136 B2
Camerino I 136 B2
Camerota I....172 B1
Camigliatello
  Silano I......174 B2
Caminha P 148 A1
Caminomorisco
  E......149 B3
Cammarata I...176 B2
Camogli I 134 A2
Camors F 100 B3
Camp IRL 29 B2
Campagna I ...172 B1
Campagnano di
  Roma I......168 A2
Campagnático
  I......135 C4
Campan F 145 A4
Campana I 174 B2
Campanario E .156 B2
Campanillas E .163 B3
Campano E 162 B1

Campaspero
  E......151 A3
Campbeltown
  UK......34 C2
Campello E ...165 A4
Campelos P ...154 B1
Campi Bisénzio
  I......135 B4
Campico López
  E......165 B3
Campíglia
  Maríttima I...134 B3
Campillo de
  Altobuey E...158 B2
Campillo de
  Aragón E.....152 A2
Campillo de Arenas
  E......163 A4
Campillo de Llerena
  E......156 B2
Campillos E ...162 A3
Câmpina RO ...17 C6
Campi Salentina
  I......173 B4
Campli I......136 C2
Campo E 145 B4
Campobasso I . 170 B2
Campobello di
  Licata I......176 B2
Campobello di
  Mazara I 176 B1
Campo da Feira
  E......140 A3
Campodársego
  I......121 B4
Campodolcino
  I......120 A2
Campofelice di
  Roccella I ...176 B2
Campofiorito
  I......176 B2
Campofórmido
  I......122 A2
Campofranco
  I......176 B2
Campofrio E ...161 B3
Campogalliano
  I......121 C3
Campo Ligure
  I......133 A4
Campolongo I 109 C3
Campo Lugar
  E......156 A2
Campo Maior
  P......155 B3
Campomanes
  E......141 A5
Campomarino
  I......170 B3
Campo Molino
  I......133 A3
Campomono
  F......180 B1
Campo Real E ..151 B4
Camporeale I . 176 B2
Camporeggiano
  I......136 B1
Camporrells E . 145 C4
Camporrobles
  E......158 B2
Campos E 167 B3
Camposa P 148 A1
Camposampiero
  I......121 B4
Camposanto I . 121 C4
Campos del Port
  E......167 B3
Campotéjar E ..163 A4
Campotosto I . . 169 A3
Campo Túres
  I......108 C2
Camprodón E ..147 B3
Campsegret F . 129 B3
Camrose UK....39 C1
Camuñas E ...157 A4
Çamyolu TR ...189 C7
Çan TR 186 B2
Cana I......135 C4
Cañada del Hoyo
  E......158 B2
Cañadajuncosa
  E......158 B1
Cañada Rosal
  E......162 A2
Čanak HR 123 C4
Çanakkale TR . 186 B1

Canale I 119 C2
Canales
  Asturias E ...141 B5
  Castellón de la
  Plana E 159 B3
Canals E 159 C3
Canal San Bovo
  I......121 A4
Cañamares E . . 152 B1
Cañamares E . . 156 A2
Cañar E 163 B4
Cañate la Real
  E......162 B2
Cañaveral E ..155 B4
Cañaveral de León
  E......161 A3
Cañaveras E ...152 B1
Cañaveruelas
  E......151 B5
Caol UK 34 B2
Caórle I......122 B1
Caorso I......120 B2
Cáparde BIH...139 A4
Caparroso E ..144 B2
Capbreton F...128 C1
Capdenac-Gare
  F......116 C2
Capdepera E ..167 B3
Cap-de-Pin F ..128 B2
Capel Curig UK .38 A3
Capellades E ..147 C2
Capena I 168 A2
Capendu F 146 A3
Capestang F ..130 B2
Capestrano I...169 A3
Cap Ferret F...128 B1
Capileira E ...163 B4
Capinha P 148 B2
Ca'Pisani I....122 C1
Capistrello I...169 B3
Capizzi I......177 B3
Čaplje BIH 124 C2
Čapljina BIH ...139 B3
Capo di Ponte
  I......120 A3
Caposile I 122 B1
Capoterra I....179 C2
Cappamore IRL .29 B3
Cappeln D 71 B5
Cappoquin IRL ..29 B4
Capracotta I ...169 B4
Capránica I ...168 A2
Caprarola I....168 A2
Capretta I 135 C5
Capri I......170 C2
Capriati a Volturno
  I......170 B2
Caprino Veronese
  I......121 B3
Captieux F 128 B2
Cápua I......170 B2
Capurso I 173 A2
Capvern F 145 A4
Carabaña E ...151 B4
Carabias E 151 A4
Caracal RO 17 C6
Caracenilla E . 152 B1
Caráglio I.....133 A3
Caraman F 146 A2
Caramánico Terme
  I......169 A4
Caranga E 141 A4
Caranguejeira
  P......154 B2
Caransebeş RO . . 16 C5
Carantec F 100 A2
Carapelle I 171 B3
Carasco I 134 A2
Carate Brianza
  I......120 B2
Caravaca de la Cruz
  E......164 A3
Caravággio I ...120 B2
Carbajal E 163 B3
Carbajo E 155 B3
Carballeda E ..140 B3
Carballeda de Avia
  E......140 B2
Carballo E 140 A2
Carbis Bay UK ..42 B1
Carbon-Blanc
  F......128 B2
Carbonera de
  Frentes E 143 C4
Carboneras E ..164 C3
Carboneras de
  Guadazón
  E......158 B2
Carbonero el Mayor
  E......151 A3

Carboneros E . 157 B4
Carbónia I 179 C2
Carbonin I 108 C3
Carbonne F . . . 146 A2
Carbost
 Highland UK 31 B2
 Highland UK 31 B2
Carcaboso E . . 149 B3
Carcabuey E . . 163 A3
Carcaixent E . . 159 B3
Carcans F 128 A1
Carcans-Plage
 F 128 A1
Carção P 149 A3
Carcar E 144 B2
Cárcare I 133 A4
Carcassonne
 F 146 A3
Carcastillo E . . 144 B2
Carcedo de Burgos
 E 143 B3
Carcelén E . . . 159 B2
Carcès F 132 B2
Carchelejo E . . 163 A4
Çardak
 Çanakkale
 TR. 186 B1
 Denizli TR. 189 B4
Cardedeu E . . . 147 C3
Cardeña E . . . 157 B3
Cardenete E . . 158 B2
Cardeñosa E . . 150 B3
Cardeto I 175 C1
Cardiff UK 39 C3
Cardigan UK . . .39 B2
Cardona E . . . 147 C2
Cardosos P. . . 154 B2
Carei RO 16 B5
Carentan F. 88 A2
Carentoir F . . . 101 B3
Careri I 175 C2
Carevdar HR . . 124 A2
Cargèse F 180 A1
Carhaix-Plouguer
 F 100 A2
Caria P 148 B2
Cariati I 174 B2
Carignan F 91 B5
Carignano I . . . 119 C4
Cariñena E . . . 152 A2
Carini I 176 A2
Cariño E 140 A3
Carínola I 170 B1
Carisbrooke UK 44 C2
Carlabhagh UK .31 A2
Carlepont F 90 B3
Carlet E 159 B3
Carlingford IRL . .27 B4
Carlisle UK 36 B4
Carloforte I . . . 179 C2
Carlópoli I . . . 175 B2
Carlow
 D 65 C3
 IRL 30 B2
Carlton UK 40 C2
Carluke UK 35 C4
Carmagnola I . . 119 C4
Carmarthen UK .39 C2
Carmaux F . . . 130 A1
Carmena E . . . 150 C3
Cármenes E . . . 142 B1
Carmine I 133 A3
Carmona E . . . 162 A2
Carmonita E . . 155 B4
Carmyllie UK . . .35 B5
Carnac F 100 B2
Carndonagh
 IRL 27 A3
Carnew IRL 30 B2
Carnforth UK . . .37 B4
Cárnia I 122 A2
Carnlough UK . . .27 B5
Carno UK 39 B3
Carnon Plage
 F 131 B2
Carnota E 140 B1
Carnoustie UK . .35 B5
Carnwath UK . . .35 C4
Carolei I 174 B2
Carolinensiel D .71 A4
Carolles F 88 B2
Caronal 120 A2
Caronía I 177 A3
Carovigno I . . . 173 B3
Carovilli I 170 B2
Carpaneto
 Piacentino I . . 120 C2
Carpegna I . . . 135 B5
Carpenédolo I . 121 B3
Carpentras F . . 131 A4
Carpi I 121 C3
Carpignano Sésia
 I 119 B5

Carpineti I 134 A3
Carpineto Romano
 I 169 B2
Cărpiniş RO . . . 126 B2
Carpino I 171 B3
Carpinone I . . . 170 B2
Carpio E 150 A2
Carquefou F . . 101 B4
Carqueiranne
 F 132 B2
Carral E 140 A2
Carranque E . . 151 B4
Carrapichana
 P 148 B2
Carrara I 134 A3
Carraroe IRL 28 A2
Carrascalejo E 156 A2
Carrascosa del
 Campo E . . . 151 B5
Carratraca E . . 162 B3
Carrazeda de
 Ansiães P . . . 148 A2
Carrazedo de
 Montenegro
 P 148 A2
Carrbridge UK . 32 D3
Carregal do Sal
 P 148 B1
Carreña E 142 A2
Carrick IRL 26 B2
Carrickart IRL . . .26 A3
Carrickfergus
 UK 27 B5
Carrickmacross
 IRL 27 C4
Carrick-on-
 Shannon IRL . .26 C2
Carrick-on-Suir
 IRL 30 B1
Carrigallen IRL . .27 C3
Carrión E 161 B3
Carrión de
 Calatrava E . . 157 A4
Carrión de los
 Condes E . . . 142 B2
Carrizo de la Ribera
 E 141 B5
Carrizosa E . . . 157 B5
Carro F 131 B4
Carros F 133 B3
Carrouge CH . . 106 C1
Carrouges F 89 B3
Carrù I 133 A3
Carryduff UK . . .27 B5
Carry-le-Rouet
 F 131 B4
Carsóli I 169 A3
Carsphairn UK . .36 A2
Cartagena E . . 165 B4
Cártama E . . . 163 B3
Cartaxo P 154 B2
Cartaya E 161 B2
Carteret F 88 A2
Cartes E 142 A2
Carúnchio I . . . 170 B2
Carviçães P . . . 149 A3
Carvin F 78 B2
Carvoeiro P . . . 154 B1
Carvoeiro P . . . 160 B1
Casabermeja
 E 163 B3
Casa Branca
 Portalegre P . . 154 C3
 Setúbal P 154 C2
Casacalenda I . 170 B2
Casa Castalda
 I 136 B1
Casaio E 141 B4
Casa l'Abate I . 173 B4
Casalarreina E 143 B4
Casalbordino
 I 169 A4
Casalborgone
 I 119 B4
Casalbuono I . . 174 A1
Casalbuttano ed
 Uniti I 120 B2
Casàl di Principe
 I 170 B2
Casalécchio di Reno
 I 135 A4
Casale Monferrato
 I 119 B5
Casalina I 136 C1
Casalmaggiore
 I 121 C3
Casalnuovo
 Monterotaro
 I 170 B3
Casaloldo I . . . 121 B3
Casalpusterlengo
 I 120 B2

Casamássima
 I 173 B2
Casamicciola Terme
 I 170 C1
Casamozza F . . 180 A2
Casarabonela
 E 162 B3
Casarano I . . . 173 B4
Casar de Cáceres
 E 155 B4
Casar de Palomero
 E 149 B3
Casarejos E . . . 143 C3
Casares E 162 B2
Casares de las
 Hurdes E . . . 149 B3
Casariche E . . . 163 A3
Casarrubios del
 Monte E 151 B3
Casas de Don Pedro
 E 156 A2
Casas de Fernando
 Alonso E 158 B1
Casas de Haro
 E 158 B1
Casas de Juan Gil
 E 159 B2
Casas del Juan
 Núñez E 158 B2
Casas del Puerto
 E 159 C2
Casas del Río
 E 159 B2
Casas de Millán
 E 155 B4
Casas de Reina
 E 156 B2
Casas de Ves
 E 159 B2
Casas-Ibáñez
 E 158 B2
Casasimarro E 158 B1
Casas Nuevas
 E 164 B3
Casasola E . . . 150 B3
Casasola de Arión
 E 150 A2
Casasuertes E . 142 A2
Casatejada E . . 150 C2
Casavieja E . . . 150 B3
Casazza I 120 B2
Cascais P 154 C1
Cascante E . . . 144 C2
Cascante del Rio
 E 152 B2
Cáscia I 169 A3
Casciana Terme
 I 134 B3
Cáscina I 134 B3
Cáseda E 144 B2
Casekow D 74 A3
Casella I 134 A2
Caselle Torinese
 I 119 B4
Casemurate I . . 135 A5
Casenove I . . . 136 C1
Caseres E 153 A4
Caserío Benali
 E 159 B3
Caserta I 170 B2
Casével P 160 B1
Cashel IRL 29 B4
Casillas E 150 B3
Casillas de Coria
 E 155 B4
Casina I 134 A3
Casinos E 159 B3
Čáslav CZ 97 B3
Cásola Valsénio
 I 135 A4
Cásole d'Elsa
 I 135 B4
Cásoli I 169 A4
Casória I 170 C2
Caspe E 153 A3
Cassà de la Selva
 E 147 C3
Cassagnas F . . 130 A2
Cassagnes-
 Bégonhès F . . 130 A1
Cassano allo Iónio
 I 174 B2
Cassano d'Adda
 I 120 B2
Cassano delle
 Murge I 171 C4
Cassano Magnago
 I 120 B1
Cassano Spinola
 I 120 C1
Cassel F 78 B2
Cássibile I 177 C4
Cassine I 119 C5

Cassino I 169 B3
Cassis F 132 B1
Cassolnovo I . . 120 B1
Cassuéjouls F . 116 C2
Častá SK 98 C1
Castagnaro I . . 121 B4
Castagneto
 Carducci E . . 134 B3
Castagnola
 CH 120 A1
Castalla E 159 C3
Castañar de Ibor
 E 156 A2
Castanheira de
 Pêra P 154 A2
Cástano Primo
 I 120 B1
Castasegna
 CH 120 A2
Castéggio I . . . 120 B2
Casteição P . . . 148 B2
Castejón E . . . 144 B2
Castejón de
 Monegros E . . 153 A3
Castejón de Sos
 E 145 B4
Castejón de
 Valdejasa E . . 144 C3
Castèl Bolognese
 I 135 A4
Castelbuono I . 177 B3
Casteldáccia I . 176 A2
Castel d'Aiano
 I 135 A3
Castel d'Ario I . 121 B3
Castel de Cabra
 E 153 B3
Casteldelfino
 I 132 A3
Castél del Monte
 I 169 A3
Castel del Piano
 I 135 C4
Castel di lúdica
 I 177 B3
Castel di Río I . 135 A4
Castèl di Sangro
 I 169 B4
Castél di Tora
 I 169 A2
Castelfidardo
 I 136 B2
Castelfiorentino
 I 135 B3
Castelforte I . . 169 B3
Castelfranco Emília
 I 121 C4
Castelfranco in
 Miscano I . . . 170 B3
Castelfranco
 Véneto I 121 B4
Castèl Frentano
 I 169 A4
Casteljaloux
 F 128 B3
Castellabate I . 170 C2
Castellammare del
 Golfo I 176 A1
Castellammare
 di Stábia I . . 170 C2
Castellamonte
 I 119 B4
Castellana Grotte
 I 173 B3
Castellane F . . 132 B2
Castellaneta
 Marina I 173 B2
Castellar E . . . 157 B4
Castellarano I . 135 A3
Castellar de la
 Frontera E . . . 162 B2
Castellar de la
 Ribera E 147 B2
Castellar de
 Santiago E . . 157 B4
Castell Arquato
 I 120 C2
Castell'Azzara
 I 135 C4
Castellbell i Villar
 I 147 C2
Castelldans E . 153 A4
Castell de Cabres
 E 153 B4
Castell de Castells
 E 159 C3
Castelldefels
 E 147 C2

Castell de Ferro
 E 163 B4
Castelleone I . . 120 B2
Castellet E . . . 147 C2
Castelletto di
 Brenzone I . . 121 B3
Castellfollit de la
 Roca E 147 B3
Castellfollit de
 Riubregos E . . 147 C2
Castellfort E . . 153 B3
Castellina in Chianti
 I 135 B4
Castellina
 Marittima I . . 134 B3
Castellóde Farfaña
 E 145 C4
Castellóde la Plana
 E 159 B3
Castél Madama
 I 169 B2
Castello
 d'Empúries
 E 147 B4
Castello di Fiemme
 I 121 A4
Castelli I 147 C2
Castellón de Rugat
 E 159 C3
Castellote E . . 153 B3
Castello Tesino
 I 121 A4
Castellterçol E 147 C3
Castellúcchio
 I 121 B3
Castellúccio
 de'Sáuri I . . . 171 B3
Castelluccio
 Inferiore I . . . 174 B1
Castelmássa I . 121 B4
Castelmáuro I . 170 B2
Castelmoron-sur-
 Lot F 129 B3
Castelnaudary
 F 146 A2
Castelnau-de-
 Médoc F 128 A2
Castelnau-de-
 Montmirail F . 129 C4
Castelnau-Magnoac
 F 145 A4
Castelnau-
 Montratier F . 129 B4
Castelnou E . . 153 A3
Castelnovo
 ne'Monti I . . . 134 A3
Castelnuovo
 Berardenga I . 135 B4
Castelnuovo della
 Dáunia I 170 B3
Castelnuovo di
 Garfagnana
 I 134 A3
Castelnuovo di Val
 di Cécina I . . 135 B3
Castelnuovo Don
 Bosco I 119 B4
Castelnuovo Scrivia
 I 120 C1
Castelo Branco
 Bragança P . . 149 A3
 Castelo Branco
 P 155 B3
Castelo de Paiva
 P 148 A1
Castelo de Vide
 P 155 B3
Castelo do Neiva
 P 148 A1
Castelo Mendo
 P 149 B3
Castelraimondo
 I 136 B2
Castél San
 Gimignano I . 135 B4
Castèl San Giovanni
 I 120 B2
Castèl San Pietro
 Terme I 135 A4
Castelsantángelo
 I 136 C2
Castelsaraceno
 I 174 A1
Castelsardo I . . 178 B2
Castelserás E . 153 A3

Castél Volturno
 I 170 B1
Castenédolo I . . 120 B3
Castets F 128 C1
Castiádas I . . . 179 C3
Castiglioncello
 I 134 B3
Castiglione I . . 169 A3
Castiglione
 Chiavarese I . 134 A2
Castiglione d'Adda
 I 120 B2
Castiglione dei
 Pepoli I 135 A4
Castiglione della
 Pescáia I . . . 135 C3
Castiglione delle
 Stiviere I . . . 121 B3
Castiglione di
 Sicília I 177 B4
Castiglione d'Órcia
 I 135 B4
Castiglion
 Fiorentino I . . 135 B4
Castilblanco E 156 A2
Castilblanco de los
 Arroyos E . . . 161 B4
Castil de Peones
 E 143 B3
Castilfrio de la
 Sierra E 144 C1
Castilgaleu E . 145 B4
Castilisar E . . . 144 B2
Castilleja E . . . 161 B3
Castillejar E . . 164 B2
Castillejo de Martin
 Viejo E 149 B3
Castillejo de
 Mesleón E . . . 151 A4
Castillejo de
 Robledo E . . . 151 A4
Castillo de Bayuela
 E 150 B3
Castillo de Locubín
 E 163 A3
Castillon-la-Bataille
 F 128 B2
Castillon-Len-
 Couserans F . 146 B2
Castillonroy E . 145 C4
Castilruiz E . . . 144 C1
Castione I 120 A2
Castions di Strada
 I 122 B2
Castirla F 180 A2
Castlebar IRL . . .28 A2
Castlebellingham
 IRL 27 C4
Castleblaney
 IRL 27 B4
Castlebridge
 IRL 30 B2
Castle Cary UK . .43 B4
Castlecomer
 IRL 30 B1
Castlederg UK . .27 B3
Castledermot
 IRL 30 B2
Castle Douglas
 UK 36 B3
Castleford UK . . .40 B2
Castleisland IRL 29 B2
Castlemaine
 IRL 29 B2
Castlemartyr
 IRL 29 C3
Castlepollard
 IRL 30 A1
Castlerea IRL . . .28 A3
Castleton UK . . .40 B2
Castletown
 Highland UK . .32 C3
 Isle of Man UK .36 B2
Castletown
 Bearhaven
 IRL 29 C2
Castletownroche
 IRL 29 B3
Castlewellan
 UK 27 B5
Casto I 120 B3
Castrejón E . . . 150 A2
Castrelo del Valle
 E 141 B3

Castres F 130 B1
Castricum NL . . .70 B1
Castries F 131 B2
Castrignano del
 Capo I 173 C4
Castril E 164 B2
Castrillo de Duero
 E 151 A4
Castrillo de la Vega
 E 143 C3
Castrillo de Onielo
 E 142 C2
Castro
 E 142 A2
 I 173 B4
Castrocabón
 E 141 B5
Castro-Caldelas
 E 141 B3
Castrocaro Terme
 I 135 A4
Castro del Río
 E 163 A3
Castro de Rey
 E 141 A3
Castrofilippo I . 176 B2
Castrogonzalo
 E 142 B1
Castrojeriz E . . 142 B2
Castro Laboreiro
 P 140 B2
Castro Marim
 P 160 B2
Castromonte
 E 142 C1
Castromudarra
 E 142 B1
Castronuevo
 E 142 C1
Castronuño E . 150 A2
Castropol E . . . 141 A3
Castroreale I . . 177 A4
Castroserracin
 E 151 A4
Castro-Urdiales
 E 143 A3
Castroverde E . 141 A3
Castro Verde
 P 160 B1
Castroverde de
 Campos E . . . 142 C1
Castroverde de
 Cerrato E . . . 142 C2
Castrovillari I . . 174 B2
Castuera E . . . 156 B2
Catadau E . . . 159 B3
Cataéggio I . . . 120 A2
Çatalca TR . . . 186 A3
Catallar TR . . . 189 C5
Çatalzeytin TR . .23 A8
Catánia I 177 B4
Catanzaro I . . . 175 C2
Catanzaro Marina
 I 175 C2
Catarroja E . . . 159 B3
Catarruchos P . 148 B1
Catcleugh UK . . .37 A4
Catenanuova
 I 177 B3
Caterham UK . . .44 B3
Cati E 153 B4
Čatići BIH 139 A4
Catignano I . . . 169 A3
Catillon F 91 A3
Catoira E 140 B2
Caton UK 37 B4
Catral E 165 A4
Catterick UK . . .37 B5
Cáttolica I . . . 136 B1
Cáttolica Eraclea
 I 176 B2
Catton UK 37 B4
Caudebec-en-Caux
 F 89 A4
Caudete E 159 C3
Caudete de las
 Fuentes E . . . 159 B2
Caudiel E 159 B3
Caudiès-de-
 Fenouillèdes
 F 146 B3
Caudry F 91 A3
Caulkerbush
 UK 36 B3
Caulnes F 101 A3

Caulónia I....175 C2
Caumont-l'Evente F....88 A3
Caunes-Minervois F....146 A3
Cauro F....180 B1
Caussade F....129 B4
Causse-de-la-Selle F....130 B2
Cauterets F....145 B3
Cava de Tirreni I....170 C2
Cavaglià I....119 B5
Cavaillon F....131 B4
Cavalaire-sur-Mer F....132 B2
Cavaleiro P....160 B1
Cavalese I....121 A4
Cavallermaggiore I....119 C4
Cavallino I....122 B1
Cavan IRL....27 C3
Cavárzere I....121 B5
Çavdarhisar TR....187 C4
Çavdır TR....189 B4
Cavernães P....148 B2
Cavezzo I....121 C4
Čavle HR....123 B3
Cavo I....134 C3
Cavour I....119 C4
Cawdor UK....32 D3
Çay TR....187 D6
Çaycuma TR....187 A7
Cayeux-sur-Mer F....78 B1
Cayiralan TR....23 B8
Çayırhan TR....187 B6
Caylus F....129 B4
Cayres F....117 C3
Cazalilla E....157 C4
Cazalla de la Sierra E....156 C2
Cazals F....129 B4
Cazanuecos E....142 B1
Cazaubon F....128 C2
Cazaux F....128 B1
Cazères F....146 A2
Cazin BIH....124 C1
Cazis CH....107 C4
Čazma HR....124 B2
Cazo E....142 A1
Cazorla E....164 B2
Cazouls-lès-Béziers F....130 B2
Cea
León E....142 B1
Orense E....140 B3
Ceánuri E....143 A4
Ceauce F....88 B3
Cebolla E....150 C3
Čebovce SK....112 A3
Cebreros E....150 B3
Čečava BIH....125 C3
Ceccano I....169 B3
Cece H....112 C2
Cecenowo PL....68 A2
Cechtice CZ....96 B3
Čechtín CZ....97 B3
Cécina I....134 B3
Ceclavín E....155 B4
Cedégolo I....120 A3
Cedeira E....140 A2
Cedillo E....155 B3
Cedillo del Condado E....151 B4
Cedrillas E....153 B3
Cedynia PL....74 B3
Cée E....140 B1
Cefalù I....177 A3
Céggia I....122 B1
Cegléd H....113 B3
Céglédbercel H....112 B3
Céglie Messápica I....173 B3
Cehegín E....164 A3
Ceilhes-et-Rocozels F....130 B2
Ceinos de Campos E....142 B1
Ceira P....148 B1
Čejč CZ....97 C4
Cekcyn PL....76 A3
Cela BIH....124 C2
Čelákovice CZ....84 B2
Celano I....169 A3
Celanova E....140 B3

Celbridge IRL....30 A2
Čelebić BIH....138 B2
Celenza Valfortore I....170 B2
Čelić BIH....125 C4
Čelinac BIH....124 C3
Cella E....152 B2
Celldömölk H....111 B4
Celle D....72 B3
Celle Ligure I....133 A4
Celles B....79 B4
Celles-sur-Belle F....115 B3
Cellino San Marco I....173 B3
Celorico da Beira P....148 B2
Celorico de Basto P....148 A1
Çeltik TR....187 C6
Çeltikçi TR....189 B5
Cemaes UK....38 A2
Cembra I....121 A4
Čemerno BIH....139 B4
Cenad RO....126 A2
Cenei RO....126 B2
Ceneselli I....121 B4
Cenicero E....143 B4
Cenicientos E....150 B3
Censeau F....105 C5
Čenta SRB....126 B2
Centallo I....133 A3
Centelles E....147 C3
Cento I....121 C4
Centúripe I....177 B3
Cepeda la Mora E....150 B2
Cépet F....129 C4
Čepin HR....125 B4
Čepinski Martinci HR....125 B4
Cepovan SLO....122 A2
Ceprano I....169 B3
Čeralije HR....125 B3
Cerami I....177 B3
Cerano I....120 B1
Cérans Foulletourte F....102 B2
Ceraso I....172 B1
Cerbaia I....135 B4
Cerbère F....146 B4
Cercal
Lisboa P....154 B1
Setúbal P....160 B1
Čerčany CZ....96 B2
Cerceda E....151 B4
Cercedilla E....151 B3
Cercemaggiore I....170 B2
Cercs E....147 B2
Cercy-la-Tour F....104 C2
Cerda I....176 B2
Cerdedo E....140 B2
Cerdeira P....149 B2
Cerdon F....103 B4
Cère I....121 B4
Ceres UK....35 B5
Ceresole-Reale I....119 B4
Cereste F....132 B1
Cerezo de Abajo E....151 A4
Cerezo de Riotirón E....143 B3
Cerfontaine B....79 B4
Cergy F....90 B2
Cerignola I....171 B3
Cérilly F....104 C1
Cerisiers F....104 A2
Cerizay F....114 B3
Çerkeş TR....23 A7
Çerkezköy TR....186 A3
Cerkije SLO....123 A3
Cerknica SLO....123 B3
Cerkno SLO....122 A2
Cerkwica PL....67 B4
Cerna HR....125 B4
Černá Hora CZ....97 B4
Cernavodă RO....17 C8
Cernay F....106 B2
Cerne Abbas UK....43 B4
Cernégula E....143 B3
Cernik HR....124 B3

Cernóbbio I....120 B2
Černošin CZ....95 B4
Cernovice CZ....96 B2
Cérons F....128 B2
Cerovlje HR....123 B3
Cerovo SK....99 C3
Cerqueto I....135 C5
Cerralbo E....149 B3
Cerreto d'Esi I....136 B1
Cerreto Sannita I....170 B2
Cerrigydrudion UK....38 A3
Cërrik AL....182 B1
Cerro Muriano E....156 B3
Certaldo I....135 B4
Certosa di Pésio I....133 A3
Cerva P....148 A2
Cervaro I....169 B3
Cervatos de la Cueza E....142 B2
Červená Řečice CZ....97 B3
Červená-Skala SK....99 C4
Cervená Voda CZ....97 A4
Cerveny Kostelec CZ....85 B4
Cervera E....147 C2
Cervera de la Cañada E....152 A2
Cervera del Llano E....158 B1
Cervera del Río Alhama E....144 B2
Cervera de Pisuerga E....142 B2
Cervéteri I....168 B2
Cérvia I....135 A5
Cervià de les Garrigues E....147 C1
Cervignano del Friuli I....122 B2
Cervinara I....170 B2
Cervione F....180 A2
Cervon F....104 B2
Cesana Torinese I....119 C3
Cesarica HR....137 A4
Cesarò I....177 B3
Cesena I....135 A5
Cesenático I....135 A5
Cësis LV....8 D4
Česká Belá CZ....97 B3
Česká Kamenice CZ....84 B2
Česká Lípa CZ....84 B2
Česká Skalice CZ....85 B4
Česká Třebová CZ....96 B2
České Budějovice CZ....96 C2
České Velenice CZ....96 C2
Český Brod CZ....96 A2
Český Dub CZ....84 B2
Český Krumlov CZ....96 C2
Český Těšín CZ....98 B2
Češljeva Bara SRB....127 C3
Çeşme TR....188 A1
Cessenon F....130 B2
Cesson-Sévigné F....101 A4
Cestas F....128 B2
Čestobrodica SRB....127 C2
Cesuras E....140 A2
Cetina E....152 A2
Cetin Grad HR....123 B4
Cetinje MNE....16 D3
Cetraro I....174 B1
Ceuti E....165 A3
Ceva I....133 A4
Cevico de la Torre E....142 C2
Cevico Navero E....142 C2
Cevins F....118 B3
Cévio CH....119 A5
Cevizli TR....189 B6
Cewice PL....68 A2
Ceylan TR....189 C4
Ceyrat F....116 B3
Ceyzériat F....118 A2
Cézens F....116 B2
Chaam NL....79 A4
Chabanais F....115 C4

Chabeuil F....117 C5
Chabielice PL....86 A3
Chablis F....104 B2
Chabons F....118 B2
Chabówka PL....99 B3
Chabreloche F....117 B3
Chabris F....103 B3
Chagford UK....42 B3
Chagny F....105 C3
Chagoda RUS....9 C9
Chaherrero E....150 B3
Chailland F....88 B3
Chaillé-les-Marais F....114 B2
Chailles F....103 B3
Chailley F....104 A2
Chalabre F....146 B3
Chalais F....128 A3
Chalamont F....118 B2
Chalampé F....106 B2
Châlette-sur-Loing F....103 A4
Chalindrey F....105 B4
Chalkida GR....185 A4
Challacombe UK....42 A3
Challans F....114 B2
Challes-les-Eaux F....118 B2
Chalmazel F....117 B3
Chalmoux F....104 C2
Chalonnes-sur-Loire F....102 B1
Châlons-en-Champagne F....91 C4
Chalon-sur-Saône F....105 C3
Chalupy PL....69 A3
Châlus F....115 C4
Cham
CH....106 B3
D....95 B4
Chamberet F....116 B1
Chambéry F....118 B2
Chambilly F....117 A4
Chambley F....92 B1
Chambly F....90 B2
Chambois F....89 B4
Chambon-sur-Lac F....116 B2
Chambon-sur-Voueize F....116 A2
Chambord F....103 B3
Chamborigaud F....131 A2
Chamboulive F....116 B1
Chamerau D....95 B4
Chamonix-Mont Blanc F....119 B3
Chamoux-sur-Gelon F....118 B3
Champagnac-le-Vieux F....117 B3
Champagney F....106 B1
Champagnole F....105 C4
Champagny-Mouton F....115 B4
Champaubert F....91 C3
Champdeniers-St Denis F....114 B3
Champdieu F....117 B4
Champdôtre F....105 B4
Champeix F....116 B3
Champéry CH....119 A3
Champigne F....102 B1
Champignelles F....104 B2
Champigny-sur-Veude F....102 B2
Champlitte-et-le-Prelot F....105 B4
Champoluc I....119 B4
Champoly F....117 B3
Champorcher I....119 B4
Champrond-en-Gâtine F....89 B5
Champs-sur-Yonne F....104 B2
Champtoceaux F....101 B4
Chamrousse F....118 B2
Chamusca P....154 B2
Chanac F....130 A2
Chanaleilles F....117 C3
Chandler's Ford UK....44 B2
Chandra GR....185 D7

Chandrexa de Queixa E....141 B3
Chañe E....150 A3
Changy F....117 A3
Chania GR....185 D5
Channes F....104 B3
Chantada E....140 B3
Chantelle F....116 A3
Chantenay-St Imbert F....104 C2
Chanteuges F....117 B3
Chantilly F....90 B2
Chantonnay F....114 B2
Chão de Codes P....154 B2
Chaource F....104 A3
Chapa E....140 B2
Chapareillan F....118 B2
Chapel en le Frith UK....40 B2
Chapelle Royale F....103 A3
Chapelle-St Laurent F....102 C1
Charbonnat F....104 C3
Chard UK....43 B4
Charenton-du-Cher F....104 C1
Charlbury UK....44 B2
Charleroi B....79 B4
Charlestown IRL....26 C2
Charlestown of Aberlour UK....32 D3
Charleville IRL....29 B3
Charleville-Mézières F....91 B4
Charlieu F....117 A4
Charlottenberg S....49 C4
Charlton Kings UK....44 B1
Charly F....90 C3
Charmes F....92 C2
Charmes-sur-Rhône F....117 C4
Charmey CH....106 C2
Charminster UK....43 B4
Charmont-en-Beauce F....103 A4
Charny F....104 B2
Charolles F....117 A4
Chârost F....103 C4
Charquemont F....106 B1
Charrin F....104 C2
Charroux F....115 B4
Chartres F....90 C1
Charzykow PL....68 B2
Chasseneuil-sur-Bonnieure F....115 C4
Chassigny F....105 B4
Château-Arnoux F....132 A2
Châteaubernard F....115 C3
Châteaubourg F....101 A4
Châteaubriant F....101 B4
Château-Chinon F....104 B2
Château-d'Oex CH....106 C2
Château-d'Olonne F....114 B2
Château-du-Loir F....102 B2
Châteaudun F....103 A3
Châteaugiron F....101 A4
Château-Gontier F....102 B1
Château-Landon F....103 A4
Château-la-Vallière F....102 B2
Château-l'Evêque F....129 A3
Châteaulin F....100 A1
Châteaumeillant F....103 C4
Châteauneuf
Nièvre F....104 B2
Saône-et-Loire F....117 A4
Châteauneuf-de-Randon F....117 C3

Châteauneuf-d'Ille-et-Vilaine F....88 B2
Châteauneuf-du-Faou F....100 A2
Châteauneuf-du-Pape F....131 A3
Châteauneuf-en-Thymerais F....89 B5
Châteauneuf-la-Forêt F....116 B1
Châteauneuf-le-Rouge F....132 B1
Châteauneuf-sur-Charente F....115 C3
Châteauneuf-sur-Cher F....103 C4
Châteauneuf-sur-Loire F....103 B4
Châteauneuf-sur-Sarthe F....102 B1
Châteauponsac F....115 B5
Château-Porcien F....91 B4
Châteauredon F....132 A2
Châteaurenard
Bouches du Rhône F....131 B3
Loiret F....104 B1
Château-Renault F....102 B2
Châteauroux F....103 C3
Châteauroux-les-Alpes F....118 C3
Château-Salins F....92 C2
Château-Thierry F....91 B3
Châteauvillain F....105 A3
Châtel F....119 A3
Châtelaillon-Plage F....114 B2
Châtelaudren F....100 A3
Châtel-Censoir F....104 B2
Châtel-de-Neuvre F....116 A3
Châtelet B....79 B4
Châtel-Guyon F....116 B3
Châtellerault F....115 B4
Châtel-Montagne F....117 A3
Châtel-St Denis CH....106 C1
Châtel-sur-Moselle F....92 C2
Châtelus-Malvaleix F....116 A2
Châtenois F....105 A4
Châtenois-les-Forges F....106 B1
Chatham UK....45 B4
Châtillon I....119 B4
Châtillon-Coligny F....103 B4
Châtillon-en-Bazois F....104 B2
Châtillon-en-Diois F....118 C2
Châtillon-sur Chalaronne F....117 A4
Châtillon-sur-Indre F....103 C3
Châtillon-sur-Loire F....103 B4
Châtillon-sur-Marne F....91 B3
Châtillon-sur-Seine F....104 B3
Châtres F....91 C3
Chatteris UK....45 A4
Chatton UK....37 A5
Chauchina E....163 A4
Chaudes-Aigues F....116 C2
Chaudrey F....91 C4
Chauffailles F....117 A4
Chaulnes F....90 B2
Chaumergy F....105 C4
Chaumont F....105 A4
Chaumont-en-Vexin F....90 B1
Chaumont-Porcien F....91 B4

Chaumont-sur-Aire F....91 C5
Chaumont-sur-Loire F....103 B3
Chaunay F....115 B4
Chauny F....90 B3
Chaussin F....105 C4
Chauvigny F....115 B4
Chavagnes-en-Paillers F....114 B2
Chavanges F....91 C4
Chaves P....148 A2
Chavignon F....91 B3
Chazelles-sur-Lyon F....117 B4
Chazey-Bons F....118 B2
Cheadle
Greater Manchester UK....40 B1
Staffordshire UK....40 C2
Cheb CZ....83 B4
Chebsara RUS....9 C11
Checa E....152 B2
Checiny PL....87 B4
Cheddar UK....43 A4
Cheddleton UK....40 B1
Chef-Boutonne F....115 B3
Cheles E....155 C3
Chella E....159 B3
Chelles F....90 C2
Chelm PL....13 C5
Chełmno
Kujawsko-Pomorskie PL....76 A3
Wielkopolskie PL....76 B3
Chelmsford UK....45 B4
Chelmuzhi RUS....9 A9
Chełmża PL....76 A3
Cheltenham UK....44 B1
Chelva E....159 B2
Chémery F....103 B3
Chemery-sur-Bar F....91 B4
Chemillé F....102 B1
Chemin F....105 C4
Chemnitz D....83 B4
Chénerailles F....116 A2
Cheniménil F....105 A5
Chenonceaux F....103 B3
Chenôve F....105 B3
Chepelare BG....183 B6
Chepstow UK....39 C4
Chera E....159 B3
Cherasco I....119 C4
Cherbonnières F....115 C3
Cherbourg F....88 A2
Cherchiara di Calábria I....174 B2
Cherepovets RUS....9 C10
Cherni Vrah UK....13 C9
Chernivtsi UA....17 A6
Chernobyl = Chornobyl UA....13 C9
Chernyakhovsk RUS....12 A4
Chéroy F....104 A1
Cherven BY....13 B8
Chervonohrad UA....13 C6
Cherykaw BY....13 B9
Chesham UK....44 B3
Cheshunt UK....44 B3
Chessy-lès-Pres F....104 A2
Cheste E....159 B3
Chester UK....38 A4
Chesterfield UK....40 B2
Chester-le-Street UK....37 B5
Chevagnes F....104 C2
Chevanceaux F....115 C3
Chevillon F....91 C5
Chevilly F....103 A3
Chew Magna UK....43 A4
Chézery-Forens F....118 A2
Chialamberto I....119 B4
Chiampo I....121 B4
Chianale I....119 C4
Chianciano Terme I....135 B4

Chiaramonte Gulfi
I. 177 B3
Chiaramonti I. . 178 B2
Chiaravalle I . . 136 B2
Chiaravalle
   Centrale I 175 C2
Chiaréggio I . . 120 A2
Chiari I 120 B2
Chiaromonte
   I. 174 A2
Chiasso CH. . . . 120 B2
Chiávari I 134 A2
Chiavenna I. . . . 120 A2
Chichef F 102 C1
Chichester UK. . .44 C3
Chiclana de la
   Frontera E . . . 162 B1
Chiclana de Segura
   E. 164 A1
Chiddingfold
   UK 44 B4
Chieri I 119 B4
Chiesa in
   Valmalenco
   I. 120 A2
Chieti I 169 A4
Chieti Scalo I. . 169 A4
Chiéuti I. 171 B3
Chigwell UK. . . .45 B4
Chíliomodi
   GR 184 B3
Chillarón de
   Cuenca E. . . . 152 B1
Chillarón del Rey
   E. 151 B5
Chilleurs-aux-Bois
   F. 103 A4
Chillón E 156 B3
Chilluevar E. . . 164 B1
Chiloeches E . . 151 B4
Chimay B 91 A4
Chimeneas E . . 163 A4
Chinchilla de Monte
   Aragón E. . . . 158 C2
Chinchón E . . . 151 B4
Chingford UK . . .45 B4
Chinon F 102 B2
Chióggia I 122 B1
Chiomonte I . . 119 B3
Chipiona E . . . 161 C3
Chippenham
   UK 43 A4
Chipping Campden
   UK 44 A2
Chipping Norton
   UK 44 B2
Chipping Ongar
   UK 45 B4
Chipping Sodbury
   UK 43 A4
Chirac F 130 A2
Chirbury UK. . . .39 B3
Chirens F 118 B2
Chirivel E 164 B2
Chirk UK 38 B3
Chirnside UK. . .35 C5
Chişinău =
   Khisinev MD . .17 B8
Chişineu Criş
   RO 113 C5
Chíssey-en-Morvan
   F. 104 B3
Chiusa I. 108 C2
Chiusa di Pésio
   I. 133 A3
Chiusaforte I. . 122 A2
Chiusa Scláfani
   I. 176 B2
Chiusi I. 135 B4
Chiva E. 159 B3
Chivasso I. 119 B4
Chlewiska PL. . .87 A4
Chludowo PL. . .75 B5
Chlumec nad
   Cidlinou CZ . . .84 B3
Chlum u Třeboně
   CZ 96 C2
Chmielnik PL. . .87 B4
Chobienia PL . . .85 A4
Chobienice PL. . .75 B4
Choceň CZ. 97 A4
Choceň PL 77 B4
Chochołow PL. . .99 B3
Chocianów PL. . .85 A3
Choctaw PL. 86 A3
Chociwel PL. . . .75 A4
Choczewo PL . . .68 A2
Chodaków PL. . . .77 B5
Chodecz PL 77 B4
Chodov CZ. 83 B4
Chodzież PL. 75 B5
Chojna PL. 74 B3
Chojnice PL. 68 B2

Chojno
   Kujawsko-
   Pomorskie PL . .77 B4
Chojno
   Wielkopolskie
   PL. 75 B5
Chojnów PL. 85 A3
Cholet F. 114 A3
Chomérac F . . . 117 C4
Chomutov CZ. . .83 B5
Chop UA 12 D5
Chora GR. 184 B2
Chora Sfakion
   GR 185 D5
Chorges F. 132 A2
Chorley UK. 38 A4
Chornobyl =
   Chernobyl UA. .13 C9
Chortkiv UA. . . 13 D6
Chorzele PL. . . .77 A5
Chorzew PL. 86 A2
Chorzów PL. 86 B2
Choszczno PL. . .75 A4
Chotěboř CZ. . . .97 B3
Chouilly F 91 B4
Chouto P. 154 B2
Chouzy-sur-Cisse
   F. 103 B3
Chozas de Abajo
   E. 142 B1
Chrast CZ. 97 B3
Chrast CZ 96 B1
Chrastava CZ . . .84 B2
Chřibská CZ. 84 B2
Christchurch
   UK 44 C2
Christiansfeld
   DK 59 C2
Chroberz PL. . . .87 B4
Chropyně CZ. . . .98 B1
Chrudim CZ 97 B3
Chrzanów PL. . . .86 B3
Chtelnica SK . . .98 C1
Chudovo RUS . . .9 C7
Chueca E. 157 A4
Chulmleigh UK. .42 B3
Chur CH. 107 C4
Church Stretton
   UK 39 B4
Churriana E . . . 163 B3
Churwalden
   CH 107 C4
Chvalšiny CZ. . .96 C2
Chwaszczyno
   PL. 69 A3
Chynava CZ. 96 A2
Chýnov CZ. 96 B2
Ciacova RO. . . . 126 B3
Ciadîr-Lunga
   MD. 17 B8
Ciadoncha E . . 143 B3
Cianciana I. . . . 176 B2
Ciano d'Enza I. 134 A3
Ciążeń PL. 76 B2
Cibakháza H . . 113 C4
Ciborro P 154 C2
Cicagna I. 134 A2
Cicciano I 170 C2
Ciciliano I. 169 B2
Cicognolo I. . . 120 B3
Cidadelhe P. . . 149 B2
Cide TR. 23 A7
Cidones E. 143 C4
Ciechanów
   Dolnośląskie
   PL. 85 A4
Ciechanów
   Mazowieckie
   PL. 77 B5
Ciechocinek PL .76 B3
Cielądz PL. 87 A4
Ciemnik PL. 75 A4
Ciempozuelos
   E. 151 B4
Ciepielów PL. . .87 A5
Cierny Balog
   SK. 99 C3
Cierge-Gaud F. 145 B4
Cierpice PL. 76 B3
Cieszanów E . . 146 A3
Cierznie PL. 68 B2
Cieszyn PL. 98 B2
Cieutat F. 145 A4
Cieza E. 165 A3
Cifer SK 98 C1
Çifteler TR 187 C6
Cifuentes E . . . 151 B5
Cigales E 142 C2
Cigliano I. 119 B5
Çihanbeyli TR . 23 B7
Cilavegna I. . . . 120 B1
Cilleros E 149 B3
Cilleruelo de Arriba
   E. 143 C3

Cilleruelo de
   Bezana E. 143 B3
Cimalmotto
   CH 119 A5
Cimanes del Tejar
   E. 141 B5
Ciminna I 176 B2
Cimişlia MD. . . .17 B8
Cimoláis I. 122 A1
Cîmpulung RO . .17 C6
Çınarcık TR. . . . 186 B4
Cinctorres E. . . 153 B3
Cinderford UK . .39 C4
Çine TR. 188 B3
Çınevès CZ. 84 B3
Ciney B 79 B5
Cinfães P. 148 A1
Cingia de Botti
   I. 120 B3
Cíngoli I. 136 B2
Cinigiano I 135 C4
Cinobaña SK 99 C3
Cinq-Mars-la-Pile
   F. 102 B2
Cinquefrondí
   I. 175 C2
Cintegabelle
   F. 146 A2
Cintruénigo E. 144 B2
Ciółkowo PL. . . .77 B4
Ciperez E. 149 B3
Cirat E 153 B3
Cirella I 174 B1
Cirencester UK. .44 B2
Cirey-sur-Vezouze
   F. 92 C2
Ciria E. 152 A2
Ciriè I 119 B4
Cirigliano I 174 A2
Cirò I. 174 B2
Cirò Marina I . . 174 B3
Ciry-le-Noble
   F. 104 C3
Cisláu RO. 17 C7
Cismon del Grappa
   I. 121 B4
Cisneros E 142 B2
Cissac-Médoc
   F. 128 A2
Čista CZ 96 A1
Cisterna di Latina
   I. 169 B2
Cisternino I . . . 173 B3
Cisternino I . . . 173 B3
Čitluk BIH 139 B3
Cítov CZ. 84 B2
Cittadella I 121 B4
Cittádella Pieve
   I. 135 C5
Cittá del Vaticano =
   Vatican City
   I. 168 B2
Cittá di Castello
   I. 135 B5
Cittaducale I. . . 169 A2
Cittanova I 175 C2
Cittá Sant'Angelo
   I. 169 A4
Ciudadela de
   Menorca E. . . 167 B4
Ciudad Real E. 157 B4
Ciudad Rodrigo
   E. 149 B3
Ciutadilla E . . . 147 C2
Cividale del Friuli
   I. 122 A2
Cívita I 169 A3
Cívita Castellana
   I. 168 A2
Civitanova Alta
   I. 136 B2
Civitanova Marche
   I. 136 B2
Civitavécchia
   I. 168 A1
Civitella di
   Romagna I. . . 135 A4
Civitella di Tronto
   I. 136 C2
Civitella Roveto
   I. 169 B3
Civray F 115 B4
Çivril TR 189 A4
Cizur Mayor E . 144 B2
Clabhach UK . . .34 B1
Clachan na Luib
   UK 31 B1
Clacton-on-Sea
   UK 45 B5
Cladich UK 34 B2
Claggan UK. 34 B2

Clairvaux-les-Lacs
   F. 105 C4
Clamecy F. 104 B2
Claonaig UK 34 C2
Clarecastle IRL . .28 B3
Claregalway
   IRL 28 A3
Claremorris IRL .28 A2
Clarinbridge
   IRL 28 A3
Clashmore
   I. 178 B2
Claudy UK 27 B3
Claudy UK 27 B3
Clausthal-Zellerfeld
   D. 82 A2
Cláut I. 122 A1
Clay Cross UK . . .40 B2
Claye-Souilly F. .90 C2
Cléder F. 100 A1
Cleethorpes UK 41 B3
Clefmont F 105 A4
Cléguérec F . . . 100 A2
Clelles F. 118 C2
Clenze D. 73 B3
Cleobury Mortimer
   UK 39 B4
Cléon-d'Andran
   F. 117 C4
Cléré-les-Pins
   F. 102 B2
Clères F. 89 A5
Clermont F. 90 B2
Clermont-en-
   Argonne F 91 B5
Clermont-Ferrand
   F. 116 B3
Clermont-l'Hérault
   F. 130 B2
Clerval F 105 B5
Clervaux L. 92 A2
Cléry-St André
   F. 103 B3
Cles I. 121 A4
Clevedon UK. . . .43 A4
Cleveleys UK. . . .38 A3
Cley UK 41 C5
Clifden IRL 28 A1
Clifford UK. 39 B3
Clisson F 101 B4
Clitheroe UK. . . .40 B1
Clogh IRL. 30 B1
Cloghan
   Donegal IRL . .26 B3
   Offaly IRL. 28 A4
Clogheen IRL. . .29 B4
Clogher UK 27 B3
Cloghjordan
   IRL 28 B3
Clohars-Carnoët
   F. 100 B2
Clonakilty IRL. . .29 C3
Clonaslee IRL. . .30 A1
Clondalkin IRL . .30 A2
Clones IRL. 27 B3
Clonmany IRL. . .27 A3
Clonmel IRL. 29 B4
Clonmellon IRL. .30 A1
Clonord IRL. 30 A1
Clonroche IRL. . .30 B2
Cloone IRL 26 C3
Cloppenburg D. 71 B5
Closeburn UK. . .36 A3
Clough UK. 27 B5
Clova UK 35 B4
Clovelly UK 42 B2
Clowne UK 40 B2
Cloyes-sur-le-Loir
   F. 103 B3
Cloyne IRL. 29 C3
Cluis F 103 C3
Cluj-Napoca RO 17 B5
Clun UK 39 B3
Clunes UK 34 B3
Cluny F. 105 C3
Cluses F 118 A3
Clydach UK 39 C3
Clydebank UK . . .34 C3
Coachford IRL. . .29 C3
Coagh UK. 27 B4
Coalisland UK . . .27 B4
Coalville UK 40 C2
Coca E 150 A3
Cocentaina E . . 159 C3

Cochem D. 80 B3
Cockburnspath
   UK 35 C5
Cockermouth
   UK 36 B3
Codigoro I 121 C5
Codogno I. 120 B2
Codos E 152 A2
Codróipo I. . . . 122 B1
Codrongianos
   I. 178 B2
Coelhoso P. . . . 149 A3
Coesfeld D. 71 C4
Coevorden NL . .71 B3
Cofrentes E . . . 159 B2
Cogeces del Monte
   E. 150 A3
Coggeshall UK. .45 B4
Cognac F. 115 C3
Cogne I 119 B4
Cogolin F 132 B2
Cogollos de Guadix
   E. 164 B1
Cogollos-Vega
   E. 163 A4
Cogolludo E . . . 151 B4
Coimbra P 148 B1
Coín E. 163 B3
Coirós E 140 A2
Čoka SRB. 126 B2
Col SLO 123 B3
Colares P. 154 C1
Cölbe D 81 B4
Colbitz D. 73 B4
Colchester UK. . .45 B4
Coldingham
   UK 35 C5
Colditz D. 83 A4
Coldstream UK. .35 C5
Colebrooke UK. .43 B3
Colera E. 146 B4
Coleraine UK. . . .27 A4
Colfiorito I 136 B1
Cólico I. 120 A2
Coligny F 118 A2
Colindres E . . . 143 A3
Collado-Mediano
   E. 151 B3
Collado Villalba
   E. 151 B4
Collagna I. 134 A3
Collanzo E 142 A1
Collat F. 117 B3
Coll de Nargó
   E. 147 B2
Colléccchio I . . 120 C3
Colledimezzo
   I. 169 B4
Colle di Val d'Elsa
   I. 135 B4
Colleferro I. . . . 169 B3
Colle Isarco I . . 108 C2
Collelongo I. . . 169 B3
Collepasso I. . . 173 B4
Collepepe I . . . 136 C1
Collesalvetti I . 134 B3
Colle Sannita
   I. 170 B2
Collesano I. . . . 176 B2
Colli a Volturno
   I. 169 B4
Collin UK. 36 A3
Collinée F 101 A3
Collingham
   Nottinghamshire
   UK 40 B2
Collingham
   West Yorkshire
   UK 40 B2
Collinghorst D . .71 A4
Cóllio I 120 B3
Collobrières F. 132 B2
Collon IRL. 27 C4
Collooney IRL. . .26 B2
Colmar F. 106 A2
Colmars F 132 A2
Colmenar E . . . 163 B3
Colmenar de la
   Sierra E 151 A4
Colmenar de Oreja
   E. 151 B4
Colmenar Viejo
   E. 151 B4
Colne UK 40 B1
Colobraro I . . . 174 A2
Cologna Véneta
   I. 121 B4
Cologne = Köln
   D. 80 B2
Cologne al Serio
   I. 120 B2

Colombey-les-
   Belles F 92 C1
Colombey-les-deux-
   Églises F 105 A3
Colombres E . . 142 A2
Colomera E . . . 163 A4
Colomers E . . . 147 B3
Colòmbia de Sant
   Jordi E 167 B3
Colorno I. 120 C3
Colos P. 160 B1
Cölpin D 74 A2
Colpy UK 33 D4
Colsterworth
   UK 40 C3
Coltishall UK. . . .41 C5
Colunga E. 142 A1
Colwell UK 37 A4
Colwyn Bay UK .38 A3
Colyford UK. 43 B3
Comácchio I . . . 121 C5
Coma-ruga E . . 147 C2
Combarros E . . 141 B4
Combeaufontaine
   F. 105 B4
Comber UK 27 B5
Comblain-au-Pont
   B. 80 B1
Combloux F . . . 118 B3
Combourg F 88 B2
Combronde F . 116 B3
Comeglians L. . 109 C3
Comillas E 142 A2
Comines F 78 B3
Cómiso I 177 C3
Comloşu Mare
   RO 126 B2
Commensacq
   F. 128 B2
Commentry F . 116 A2
Commerau D . . .84 A2
Commercy F 92 C1
Como I. 120 B2
Cómpeta E 163 B4
Compiègne F . . .90 B2
Comporta P. . . 154 C2
Comps-sur-Artuby
   F. 132 B2
Comrat MD 17 B8
Comrie UK. 35 B4
Comunanza I . . 136 C2
Cona
   Emilia Romagna
   I. 121 C4
   Veneto I 121 B5
Concarneau F . 100 B2
Conceição P. . . 160 B1
Conches-en-Ouche
   F. 89 B4
Concordia
   Sagittária I. . . 122 B1
Concordia sulla
   Sécchia I 121 C3
Concots F 129 B4
Condat F 116 B2
Condé-en-Brie
   F. 91 C3
Condeixa P . . . 148 B1
Condemios de
   Abajo E 151 A4
Condemios de
   Arriba E 151 A4
Condé-sur-l'Escaut
   F. 79 B3
Conde-sur-Marne
   F. 91 B4
Condé-sur-Noireau
   F. 88 B3
Condino I 121 B3
Condofuri I . . . 175 D1
Condom F 129 C3
Condove I 119 B4
Condrieu F 117 B4
Conegliano I. . . 122 B1
Conflans-sur-
   Lanterne F . . . 105 B5
Confolens F . . . 115 B4
Conforto E 141 A3
Cong IRL 28 A2
Congleton UK. . .40 B1
Congosto de
   Valdavia E . . . 142 B2
Congostrina E . 151 A4
Conil de la Frontera
   E. 162 B1
Coningsby UK. . .41 B3
Conlie F. 102 A1
Conliège F 105 C4
Connah's Quay
   UK 38 A3

Connantre F . . .91 C3
Connaugh IRL. . .28 B3
Connaux F 131 A3
Connel UK 34 B2
Connerré F. 102 A2
Cononbridge
   UK 32 D2
Čonoplja SRB . 126 B1
Conques F 116 C2
Conques-sur-Orbiel
   F. 146 A3
Conquista E. . . 157 B3
Conquista de la
   Sierra E 156 A2
Consándolo I . . 121 C4
Consélice I. . . . 135 A4
Conselve I 121 B4
Consenvoye F. . .91 B5
Consett UK. 37 B5
Consolação P . 154 B1
Constancia P. . 154 B2
Constância RO . .17 C8
Constanţa RO. . 17 C8
Constanti E . . . 147 C2
Constantina E. 162 A2
Consuegra E . . 157 A4
Consuma I. 135 B4
Contarina I . . . 122 B1
Contay F. 90 B2
Conthey CH. . . 119 A4
Contigliano I. . 168 A2
Contis-Plage
   F. 128 B1
Contrada I 170 C2
Contres F 103 B3
Contrexéville
   F. 105 A4
Controne I 172 B1
Contursi Termi
   I. 172 B1
Conty F 90 B2
Conversano I . . 173 B3
Conwy UK 38 A3
Cookstown UK . .27 B4
Coole F 91 C4
Coolgreany IRL .30 B2
Cooneen UK 27 B3
Cootehill IRL . . .27 B3
Cope E. 165 B3
Copenhagen =
   København
   DK 61 D2
Copertino I . . . 173 B4
Copparo I 121 C4
Coppenbrugge
   D. 72 B2
Corabia RO. . . . 17 D6
Córaci I 175 B2
Coralici BIH . . . 124 C1
Corato I 171 B4
Coray F 100 A2
Corbeil-Essonnes
   F. 90 C2
Corbeny F. 91 B3
Corbera E 159 B3
Corbie F 90 B2
Corbigny F 104 B2
Corbie F. 90 B2
Corbridge UK . . .37 B4
Corby UK. 40 C3
Corconte E . . . 143 A3
Corcubión E. . . 140 B1
Corcumello I. . . 169 A3
Cordenòns I. . . 122 B1
Cordes-sur-Ciel
   F. 129 B4
Córdoba E 156 C3
Cordobilla de
   Lácara E. 155 B4
Cordovado I . . . 122 B1
Coreses E 150 A2
Corfe Castle
   UK 43 B4
Corga de Lobão
   P. 148 B1
Cori I 169 B2
Coria E. 155 B4
Coria del Río
   E. 162 A1
Corigliano Cálabro
   I. 174 B2
Corinaldo I 136 B1
Corinth = Korinthos
   GR 184 B3
Cório I 119 B4
Coripe E 162 B2
Coristanco E . . 140 A2
Cork IRL. 29 C3
Corlay F. 100 A2
Corleone I. 176 B2

Corleto Monforte
I............172 B1
Corleto Perticara
I............174 A2
Çorlu TR......186 A2
Cormainville
F............103 A3
Cormatin F....104 C3
Cormeilles F...89 A4
Cormery F....102 B2
Cormòns I.....122 B2
Cormoz F.....118 A2
Cornago E....144 B1
Cornberg D....82 A1
Cornellana E..141 A4
Corneşti MD...17 B8
Corníglio I....134 A3
Cornimont F...106 B1
Corniolo I....135 B4
Cornuda I....121 B5
Cornudella de
Montsant E...147 C1
Cornudilla E..143 B3
Cornus F.....130 B2
Çorovodë AL..182 C2
Corpach UK...34 B2
Corps F......118 C2
Corps Nuds F..101 B4
Corral de Almaguer
E...........157 A4
Corral de Ayllon
E...........151 A4
Corral de Calatrava
E...........157 B3
Corrales F....149 A4
Corral-Rubio
E...........158 C2
Corran UK....34 B2
Corredoiras
E...........140 A2
Corréggio I...121 C3
Corrèze F....116 B1
Corridónia I...136 B2
Corris UK.....38 B3
Corrubedo E..140 B1
Córsico I.....120 B2
Corsock UK...36 A3
Corte F......180 A2
Corteconcepción
E...........161 B3
Corte de Peleas
E...........155 C4
Cortegaca P..148 B1
Cortegada E..148 B3
Cortegana E..161 B3
Cortemaggiore
I............120 B2
Cortemilia I..133 A4
Corte Pinto P.160 B2
Cortes E.....144 C2
Cortes de Aragón
E...........153 B3
Cortes de Arenoso
E...........153 B3
Cortes de Baza
E...........164 B2
Cortes de la
Frontera E...162 B2
Cortes de Pallás
E...........159 B3
Cortiçadas P..154 C2
Cortico P....148 A2
Cortijo de Arriba
E...........157 A3
Cortijos Nuevos
E...........164 A2
Cortina d'Ampezzo
I............108 C3
Corton UK....41 C5
Cortona I....135 B4
Coruche P....154 C2
Corullón E...141 B4
Çorum TR.....23 A8
Corvara in Badia
I............108 C2
Cörvera E....165 B3
Corwen UK....38 B3
Cosenza I....174 B2
Cosham UK...44 C2
Coslada E....151 B4
Cosne-Cours-sur-
Loire F.....104 B1
Cosne d'Allier
F...........104 C1
Cospeito E...140 A3
Cossato I....119 B5
Cossaye F....104 C2
Cossé-le-Vivien
F...........101 B5
Cossonay CH..106 C1

Costa da Caparica
P...........154 C1
Costa de Santo
André P.....160 A1
Costalpino I...135 B4
Costa Nova P..148 B1
Costaros F....117 C3
Costeşti RO....17 C6
Costigliole d'Asti
I............119 C5
Costigliole Saluzzo
I............133 A3
Coswig
Sachsen D....83 A5
Sachsen-Anhalt
D...........83 A4
Cotherstone
UK.........37 B5
Cotronei I....175 B2
Cottbus D....84 A2
Cottenham UK..45 A4
Cottingham UK .40 B3
Coublanc F...105 B4
Couches F....104 C3
Couço P.....154 C2
Coucouron F..117 C3
Coucy-le-Château-
Auffrique F...90 B3
Couëron F....101 B4
Couflens F....146 B2
Couhé F.....115 B4
Couiza F.....146 B3
Coulags UK....31 B3
Coulanges F..104 C2
Coulanges-la-
Vineuse F...104 B2
Coulanges-sur-
Yonne F....104 B2
Couleuvre F..104 C1
Coulmier-le-Sec
F...........104 B3
Coulommiers
F...........90 C3
Coulonges-sur-
l'Autize F...114 B3
Coulounieix-
Chamiers F..129 A3
Coulport UK...34 B3
Coupar Angus
UK.........35 B4
Coupéville F...91 C4
Couptrain F...89 B3
Coura P.....140 C2
Courcelles B...79 B4
Courcelles-Chaussy
F...........92 B2
Courchevel F..118 B3
Cour-Cheverny
F...........103 B3
Courçôme F...115 C4
Courçon F....114 B3
Cour-et-Buis F.117 B4
Courgenay CH 106 B2
Courmayeur I..119 B3
Courniou F...130 B1
Cournon-
d'Auvergne
F...........116 B3
Cournonterral
F...........130 B2
Courpière F...117 B3
Coursan F....130 B2
Courseulles-sur-
Mer F......89 A3
Cours-la-Ville
F...........117 A4
Courson-les-
Carrières F..104 B2
Courtalain F..103 A3
Courtenay F..104 A2
Courtomer F..89 B4
Courville
Eure-et-Loire
F...........89 B5
Marne F.....91 B3
Coussac-Bonneval
F...........115 C5
Coutances F..88 A2
Couterne F...89 B3
Coutras F....128 A2
Couvet CH....106 C1
Couvin B.....91 A4
Couzon F....104 C2
Covadonga E.142 A1
Covaleda E...143 C4
Covarrubias E.143 B3
Covas F.....148 A1
Cove UK.....31 B3
Coventry UK...44 A2
Coverack UK...42 B1
Covigliáio I...135 A4
Covilhã P....148 B2
Cowbridge UK..39 C3

Cowdenbeath
UK.........35 B4
Cowes UK....44 C2
Cox F.......129 C4
Cózar E.....157 B4
Cozes F.....114 C3
Cozzano F....180 B2
Cracol F....174 A2
Cracow = Kraków
PL.........99 A3
Craibstone UK .33 D4
Craighouse UK .34 C2
Craignure UK ..34 B2
Crail UK......35 B5
Crailsheim D...94 B2
Craiova RO....17 C5
Cramlington
UK.........37 A5
Cranleigh UK...44 B3
Craon F.....101 B5
Craonne F....91 B3
Craponne F...117 B4
Craponne-sur-
Arzon F....117 B3
Crathie UK....32 D3
Crato P.....155 B3
Craughwell IRL .28 A3
Craven Arms
UK.........39 B4
Crawford UK...36 A3
Crawinkel D...82 B2
Crawley UK...44 B3
Creag Ghoraidh
UK.........31 B1
Crecente E...140 B2
Crèches-sur-Saône
F...........117 A4
Crécy-en-Ponthieu
F...........78 B1
Crécy-la-Chapelle
F...........90 C2
Crécy-sur-Serre
F...........91 B3
Crediton UK...43 B3
Creeslough IRL .26 A3
Creetown UK...36 B2
Creeve UK....27 B4
Creglingen D..94 B2
Creil F......90 B2
Creissels F...130 A2
Crema I.....120 B2
Cremeaux F..117 B3
Crémenes E...142 B1
Crémieu F....118 B2
Cremlingen D..73 B3
Cremona I....120 B3
Creney F....91 C4
Črenšovci
SLO.......111 C3
Créon F.....128 B2
Crepaja SRB..127 B2
Crépey F....92 C1
Crépy F.....91 B3
Crépy-en-Valois
F...........90 B2
Cres HR.....123 C3
Crescentino I..119 B5
Crespino I....121 C4
Crespos E....150 B3
Cressage UK...39 B4
Cressensac F..129 A4
Cressia F....105 C4
Crest F......117 C5
Cresta CH....107 C4
Créteil F.....90 C2
Creully F....88 A3
Creussen D...95 B3
Creutzwald F..92 B2
Creuzburg D..82 A2
Crevalcore I..121 C4
Crèvecoeur-le-
Grand F.....90 B2
Crevillente E..165 A4
Crévola d'Ossola
I............119 A5
Crewe UK....38 A4
Crewkerne UK..43 B4
Criales E....143 B3
Crianlarich UK .34 B3
Criccieth UK...38 B2
Crickhowell UK .39 C3
Cricklade UK...44 B2
Crieff UK.....35 B4
Criel-sur-Mer F.90 A1
Crikvenica HR. 123 B3
Crillon F.....90 B1
Crimmitschau
D...........83 B4
Crimond UK...33 D5
Crinitz D.....84 A1
Cripán E....143 B4
Criquetot-l'Esneval
F...........89 A4

Crispiano I....173 B3
Crissolo I....119 C4
Cristóbal E...149 B4
Crivitz D.....73 A4
Črna SLO....110 C1
Crna Bara
Srbija SRB...127 C1
Vojvodina
SRB.......126 B2
Crnac HR....125 B3
Crnča SRB....127 C1
Crni Lug
BIH.........138 A2
HR.........123 B3
Črni Vrh SLO..123 B3
Crnjelovo Donje
BIH.........125 C5
Črnomelj SLO. 123 B4
Crocketford UK .36 A3
Crocq F.....116 B2
Crodo I.....119 A5
Croglin UK...37 B4
Crolly IRL....26 A2
Cromarty UK...32 D2
Cromer UK...41 C5
Cronat F.....104 C2
Crookhaven
IRL.........29 C2
Crookstown
IRL.........29 C3
Croom IRL....29 B3
Cropalati I....174 B2
Crópani I....175 C2
Crosbost UK...31 A2
Crosby UK....38 A3
Crosía I.....174 B2
Crossakiel IRL..27 C3
Cross-Hands
UK.........39 C2
Crosshaven IRL .29 C3
Crosshill UK...36 A2
Crossmolina
IRL.........26 B1
Crotone I....175 B3
Crottendorf D..83 B4
Crouy F.....90 B3
Crowborough
UK.........45 B4
Crowland UK..41 C3
Crowthorne UK .44 B3
Croyde UK....42 A2
Croydon UK...44 B3
Crozon F....100 A1
Cruas F.....117 C4
Crucoli RO...126 A3
Crúcoli I....174 B3
Cruden Bay UK .33 D5
Crudgington
UK.........38 B4
Cruis F......132 A1
Crumlin UK...27 B4
Cruseilles F...118 A3
Crusheen IRL..28 B3
Cruz de Incio
E...........141 B3
Crvenka SRB .126 B1
Červený Kamen
SK.........98 B2
Csabacsüd H..113 C4
Csabrendek H 111 B4
Csákánydoroszló
H..........111 C3
Csákvár H....112 B2
Csanádapáca
H..........113 C4
Csanádpalota
H..........126 A2
Csány H.....113 B3
Csanytelek H .113 C4
Csapod H....111 B3
Császár H....112 B2
Császártöltés
H..........112 C3
Csávoly H....125 A5
Csemő H....113 B3
Csengőd H....112 C3
Csépa H.....113 C4
Csepreg H....111 B3
Cserkeszölö
H..........113 C4
Csernely H....113 A4
Csesztreg H...111 C3
Csökmö H....113 B5
Csököly H....124 A3
Csokonyavisonta
H..........124 A3
Csólyospálos
H..........113 C3

Cuacos de Yuste
E...........150 B2
Cualedro E...140 C3
Cuanca de Campos
E...........142 B1
Cuba P.....160 A2
Cubel E.....152 A2
Cubelles E...147 C2
Cubillos E...143 C4
Cubillos del Sil
E...........141 B4
Cubjac F....129 A3
Cubo de la Solana
E...........152 A1
Çubuk TR....23 A7
Cuckfield UK...44 B3
Cucuron F....131 B4
Cudillero E...141 A4
Cuéllar E....151 A3
Cuenca E....152 B1
Cuers F.....132 B2
Cuerva E....157 A3
Cuevas Bajas
E...........163 A3
Cuevas del
Almanzora E. 164 B3
Cuevas del Becerro
E...........162 B2
Cuevas del Campo
E...........164 B2
Cuevas del Valle
E...........150 B2
Cuevas de San
Clemente E..143 B3
Cuevas de San
Marcos E...163 A3
Cuges-les-Pins
F...........132 B1
Cúglieri I....178 B2
Cugnaux F...129 C4
Cuijk NL.....80 A1
Cuinzier F....117 A4
Cuiseaux F...105 C4
Cuisery F....105 C4
Culan F.....103 C4
Culemborg NL .79 A5
Cúllar E.....164 B2
Cullaville UK...27 B4
Cullera E....159 B3
Cullivoe UK...33 A5
Cullompton UK .43 B3
Cully CH.....106 C1
Culoz F.....118 B2
Cults UK.....33 D4
Cumbernauld
UK.........35 C4
Cumbres de San
Bartolomé E. 161 A3
Cumbres Mayores
E...........161 A3
Cumiana I....119 C4
Čumić SRB...127 C2
Cumnock UK...36 A2
Çumra TR....23 C7
Cúneo I.....133 A3
Cunlhat F....117 B3
Čunski HR....123 C3
Cuntis E....140 B2
Cuorgnè I....119 B4
Cupar UK....35 B4
Cupello I....170 A2
Cupra Marittima
I............136 B2
Cupramontana
I............136 B2
Ćuprija SRB..127 D3
Curinga I....175 C2
Currelos E...140 B3
Currie UK....35 C4
Curtea de Argeş
RO.........17 C6
Curtici RO...126 A3
Curtis E.....140 A2
Curtis Santa Eulalia
E...........140 A2
Čurug SRB...126 B2
Cusano Mutri
I............170 B2
Cushendall UK .27 A4
Cusset F....117 A3
Cussy-les-Forges
F...........104 B3
Custines F....92 C2
Cutanda E...152 B2
Cutro I......175 B2
Cutrofiano I..173 B4
Cuts F......90 B3
Cuvilly F.....90 B2
Cuxhaven D...64 C1
Cvikov CZ....84 B2
Cwmbran UK..39 C3

Cybinka PL....75 B3
Czacz PL.....75 B5
Czajków PL...86 A2
Czaplinek PL...75 A5
Czarlin PL....69 A3
Czarna-Dąbrówka
PL.........68 A2
Czarna Woda
PL.........68 B3
Czarnca PL...87 B3
Czarne PL....68 B1
Czarnków PL...75 B5
Czarnowo PL..76 A3
Czarnozyly PL..86 A2
Czarny Bór PL..85 B4
Czarny-Dunajec
PL.........99 B3
Czarny Las PL..86 A1
Czchow PL....99 B4
Czechowice-
Dziedzice PL..98 B2
Czempiń PL...75 B5
Czermno PL...87 A4
Czernichow PL .99 B3
Czerniejewo PL .76 B2
Czernikowo PL .76 B3
Czersk PL....68 B2
Czerwieńsk PL .75 B4
Czerwionka-
Leszczyny PL..86 B2
Częstochowa
PL.........86 B3
Czeszewo PL...76 B2
Człopa PL....75 A5
Człuchów PL...68 B2
Czołpino PL...68 A2

D

Dağ TR.....189 B5
Daaden D....81 B3
Dabas H.....112 B3
Dąbie PL.....76 B3
Dąbki PL.....67 B5
Dabo F......92 C3
Dąbrowa PL...76 B3
Dąbrowa Górnicza
PL.........86 B3
Dąbrowa
Tarnowska PL .87 B4
Dąbrowice PL..77 B4
Dabrowno PL..77 A5
Dachau D....108 A2
Dačice CZ....97 B3
Daday TR....23 A7
Dagali N.....47 B5
Dägebüll D....64 B1
Dagmarsellen
CH.........106 B2
Dahlen D....83 A4
Dahlenburg D .73 A3
Dahme D....83 A5
Dahn D......93 B3
Dähre D.....73 B3
Daikanvik S...195 E7
Dail bho Dheas
UK.........31 A2
Dailly UK....36 A2
Daimiel E....157 A4
Daingean IRL..30 A1
Đakovica KOS. 16 D4
Đakovo HR...125 B4
Dal
Akershus N....48 B3
Telemark N...47 C5
Dalaas A....107 B5
Dalabrog UK...31 B1
Dalane N....53 B3
Dalarö S.....57 A4
Dalbeattie UK .36 B3
Dalby
DK.........61 D3
Skåne S....61 D3
Uppsala S....57 A3
Värmland S...54 A3
Dale
Hordaland N..46 B2
Sogn og Fjordane
N..........46 A2
Pembrokeshire
UK.........39 C1
Shetland UK..33 A5
Dalen
Akershus N....48 B3
Telemark N...53 A4
Dalbnaig UK...32 C2
Daleszyce PL..87 B4
Dalhalvaig UK .32 C3
Dalheim L....92 B2
Dalhem S....57 C4

Dalias E.....164 C2
Dalj HR.....125 B4
Dalkeith UK...35 C4
Dalkey IRL....30 A2
Dalmally UK...34 B3
Dalmellington
UK.........36 A2
Dalmose DK...65 A4
Daløy N.....46 A1
Dalry
Dumfries &
Galloway UK.. 34 C3
North Ayrshire
UK.........36 A2
Dalrymple UK..36 A2
Dalseter N...47 A6
Dalsjöfors S...60 B3
Dalskog S....54 B3
Dals Långed S..54 B3
Dals Rostock S .54 B3
Dalston UK...36 B4
Dalstorp S...60 B3
Dalton-in-Furness
UK.........36 B3
Daluis F.....132 A2
Dalum
D...........71 B4
S...........60 B3
Dalvík IS.....191 B7
Dalyan TR....188 C3
Damasi GR...182 D4
Damaskawek
PL.........76 B2
Damazan F...129 B3
Damgan F....101 B3
Dammarie-les-Lys
F...........90 C2
Dammartin-en-
Goële F.....90 B2
Damme D....71 B5
Damnica PL...68 A2
Dampierre F..105 B4
Dampierre-sur-
Salon F.....105 B4
Damüls A....107 B4
Damville F....89 B5
Damvillers F..92 B1
Damwoude NL .70 A2
Danasjö S...195 E7
Danbury UK...45 B4
Dångebo S...63 B3
Dangers F....89 B5
Dangé-St Romain
F...........102 C2
Dangeul F....89 B4
Danilovgrad
MNE.......16 D3
Danischenhagen
D...........64 B3
Daniszyn PL...85 A5
Danjoutin F...106 B1
Dannas S....60 B3
Dannemarie F 106 B2
Dannemora S .51 B4
Dannenberg D .73 A4
Dánszentmiklós
H..........112 B3
Dány H.....112 B3
Daoulas F....100 A1
Darabani RO...17 A7
Darány H....125 B3
Darda HR....125 B4
Dardesheim D .73 C3
Darfield UK...40 B2
Darfo I......120 B3
Dargin PL....68 A1
Dargun D....66 C1
Darlington UK .37 B5
Darlowo PL...68 A1
Darmstadt D...93 B4
Darney F....105 A5
Daroca E....152 A2
Darragh IRL...28 B2
Dartford UK...45 B4
Dartington UK .43 B3
Dartmouth UK .43 B3
Darton UK....40 B2
Daruvar HR...124 B3
Darvas H....113 B5
Darvel UK....36 A2
Darwen UK...38 A4
Dassel D.....82 A1
Dassow D....65 C3
Datça TR....188 C2
Datteln D....80 A3
Dattenfeld D...81 B3
Daugard DK...59 C2
Daugavpils LV .8 E5
Daun D......80 B2
Daventry UK...44 A2

Davle CZ 96 B2
Davor HR 124 B3
Davos CH 107 C4
Davutlar TR . . . 188 B2
Davyd Haradok BY 13 B7
Dawlish UK 43 B3
Dax F 128 C1
Dazkırı TR 189 B4
Deal UK 45 B5
Deauville F 89 A4
Deba E 143 A4
Debar NMK . . . 182 B2
Dębe PL 77 B5
Dębica PL 87 B5
Dębnica Kaszubska PL 68 A2
Dębno PL 74 B3
Dębołęka PL . . . 86 A2
Dębowa Łąka PL 69 B4
Debrc SRB 127 C1
Debrecen H . . 113 B5
Debrznica PL . . . 75 B4
Debrzno PL 68 B2
Debstedt D 72 A1
Decazeville F . 130 A1
Dechtice SK 98 C1
Decima I 168 B2
Decimomannu I 179 C2
Děčín CZ 84 B2
Decize F 104 C2
De Cocksdorp NL 70 A1
Decollatura I . 175 B2
Decs H 125 A4
Deddington UK 44 B2
Dedeler TR 187 B5
Dedelow D 74 A2
Dedemli TR . . . 189 B7
Dedemsvaart NL 71 B3
Dédestapolcsány H 113 A4
Dedovichi RUS . . 9 D6
Deeping St Nicholas UK 41 C3
Deftera CY 181 A2
Dég H 112 C2
Degaña E 141 B4
Degeberga S . . 61 D4
Degerby FIN . . . 51 B7
Degerfors S 55 A5
Degerhamn S . . 63 B4
Degernes N 54 A2
Deggendorf D . . 95 C4
Deggingen D . . 94 C1
Dego I 133 A4
Degolados P . . 155 B3
De Haan B 78 A3
Dehesas de Guadix E 164 B1
Dehesas Viejas E 163 A4
Deia E 166 B2
Deining D 95 B3
Deinze B 79 B3
Déiva Marina I 134 A2
Dej RO 17 B5
Deje S 55 A4
De Koog NL 70 A1
Delabole UK . . . 42 B2
Delary S 61 C3
Delbrück D 81 A4
Delčevo NMK . 182 B4
Delden NL 71 B3
Deleitosa E . . . 156 A2
Delekovec HR . 124 A2
Delémont CH . 106 B2
Delft NL 70 B1
Delfzijl NL 71 A3
Délia I 176 B2
Delianuova I . 175 C1
Deliblato SRB . 127 C3
Delice TR 23 B7
Deliceto I 171 B3
Delitzsch D 83 A4
Dellach D 109 C4
Delle F 106 B2
Delme F 92 C2
Delmen-horst D 72 A1
Delnice HR 123 B3
Delsbo S 200 E2
Delvin IRL 30 A1
Delvinë AL . . . 182 D2
Demandice SK 112 A2
Demen D 73 A4
Demidov RUS . . 13 A9
Demigny F 105 C3

Demirci TR 186 C3
Demirköy TR . . . 186 A2
Demirtaş TR . . . 186 B4
Demmin D 66 C2
Demonte I 133 A3
Demyansk RUS . . . 9 D8
Denain F 78 B3
Denbigh UK 38 A3
Den Burg NL . . . 70 A1
Dender-monde B 79 A4
Denekamp NL . . 71 B4
Den Ham NL . . . 71 B3
Den Helder NL . . 70 B1
Denholm UK . . . 35 C5
Denia E 159 C4
Denizli TR 188 B4
Derecske H . . . 113 B5
Dereköy TR . . . 186 A2
Derenberg D . . . 82 A2
Dermbach D . . . 82 B2
Dermulo I 121 A4
Deronje SRB . . 125 B5
Derrygonnelly UK 26 B3
Derrylin UK 27 B3
Derry/Londonderry UK 27 B3
Dersingham UK 41 C4
Deruta I 136 C1
Dervaig UK 34 B1
Derval F 101 B4
Derveni GR . . . 184 A3
Derventa BIH . . 125 C3
Dervock UK 27 A4
Desana I 119 B5
Descartes F . . . 102 C2
Desenzano del Garda I 121 B3
Deset N 48 A3
Deševa BIH . . . 139 B4
Desford UK 40 C2
Desimirovac SRB 127 C2
Désio I 120 B2
Deskati GR . . . 182 D3
Deskle SLO . . . 122 A2
Desná CZ 84 B3
Dešov CZ 97 C3
Despotovac SRB 127 C3
Despotovo SRB 126 B1
Dessau D 83 A4
Deštná CZ 96 B2
Destriana E . . . 141 B4
Désulo I 179 B3
Desvres F 78 B1
Deszk H 126 A2
Deta RO 126 B3
Detmold D 72 C1
Dětřichov CZ . . . 97 B3
Dettelbach D . . 94 B2
Dettingen
Baden-Württemberg D 94 C1
Dettingen
Baden-Württemberg D 107 B4
Dettwiller F 93 C3
Detva SK 99 C3
Deurne NL 80 A1
Deutschkreutz A 111 B3
Deutschlandsberg A 110 C2
Deutsch Wagram A 111 A3
Deva RO 17 B5
Dévaványa H . 113 B4
Devecikonağı TR 186 C3
Devecser H 111 B3
Develi TR 23 B8
Deventer NL . . . 70 B3
Devil's Bridge UK 39 B3
Devin BG 183 B6
Devinska Nova Ves SK 111 A3
Devizes UK 43 A5

Devonport UK . . 42 B2
Devrek TR 187 A6
Devrekâni TR . . . 23 A7
Ðevrske HR . . . 137 B4
De Wijk NL 71 B3
Deza E 152 A1
Dežanovac HR 124 B3
Dezzo I 120 B3
Dhali CY 181 A2
Dherinia CY . . . 181 A2
Diamante I . . . 174 B1
Dianalund DK . . 61 D1
Diano d'Alba I . 119 C5
Diano Marina I 133 B4
Dicomano I . . . 135 B4
Didcot UK 44 B2
Didim TR 188 B2
Didimoticho GR 186 A1
Die F 118 C2
Diebling F 92 B2
Dieburg D 93 B4
Diego del Carpio E 150 B2
Diekirch L 92 B2
Diélette F 88 A2
Diemelstadt D . 81 A5
Diémoz F 118 B2
Dienten am Hochkönig A 109 B3
Diepenbeek B . . 79 B5
Diepholz D 71 B5
Dieppe F 89 A5
Dierberg D 74 A1
Dierdorf D 81 B3
Dieren NL 70 B3
Dierhagen D . . . 66 B1
Diesdorf D 73 B3
Diessen D 108 B2
Diest B 79 B5
Dietenheim D . . 94 C2
Dietfurt D 95 B3
Dietikon CH . . . 106 B3
Dietzenbach D . 93 A4
Dieue-sur-Meuse F 92 B1
Dieulefit F . . . 131 A4
Dieulouard F . . . 92 C2
Dieuze F 92 C2
Diever NL 71 B3
Diez D 81 B4
Diezma E 163 A4
Differdange L . . . 92 B1
Digermulen N . 194 B6
Dignac F 115 C4
Dignano I 122 A1
Digne-les-Bains F 132 A2
Digny F 89 B5
Digoin F 104 C2
Dikanäs S 195 E7
Dikili TR 186 C1
Diksmuide B . . . 78 A2
Dilar E 163 A4
Dillenburg D . . 81 B4
Dillingen
Bayern D 94 C2
Saarland D . . . 92 B2
Dilsen B 80 A1
Dimaro I 121 A3
Dimitrovgrad BG 183 B5
Dimitsana GR . 184 B3
Dinami I 175 C2
Dinan F 101 A3
Dinant B 79 B4
Dinar TR 189 A5
Dinard F 101 A3
Dinek TR 187 C6
Dingden D 80 A2
Dingelstädt D . 82 A2
Dingle
IRL 29 B1
S 54 B2
Dingolfing D . . . 95 C4
Dingtuna S 56 A2
Dingwall UK . . . 32 D2
Dinkelsbühl D . 94 B2
Dinkelscherben D 94 C2
Dinklage D 71 B5
Dinslaken D . . . 80 A2
Dinxperlo NL . . 80 A2
Diö S 63 B2
Diósgyőr H . . . 113 A4
Diósjenő H . . . 112 B3
Diou F 104 C2
Dippen UK 34 C2

Dipperz D 82 B1
Dippoldiswalde D 84 B1
Dirdal N 52 B2
Dirksland NL . . . 79 A4
Dirlewang D . . 108 B1
Dischingen D . . 94 C2
Disentis CH . . . 107 C3
Diso I 173 B4
Diss UK 45 A5
Dissen D 71 B5
Distington UK . . 36 B3
Ditzingen D 93 C5
Ditzum D 71 A4
Divača SLO . . . 122 B2
Dives-sur-Mer F 89 A3
Divín SK 99 C3
Divion F 78 B2
Divišov CZ 96 B2
Divonne les Bains F 118 A3
Dixmont F 104 A2
Dizy-le-Gros F . 91 B4
Djúpivogur IS 191 C11
Djupvasshytta N 198 C4
Djura S 50 B1
Djurås S 50 B2
Djurmo S 50 B2
Djursdala S 62 A3
Dlouhá Loucka CZ 98 B1
Długowola PL . . 87 A5
Dmitrov RUS . . . 9 D10
Dno RUS 9 D6
Doade E 141 B3
Doğanhisar TR 189 A6
Dobanovci SRB 127 C2
Dobbertin D . . . 73 A5
Dobbiaco I . . . 108 C3
Dobczyce PL . . . 99 B4
Dobele LV 8 D3
Döbeln D 83 A5
Doberlug-Kirchhain D 83 A5
Dobern D 84 A2
Dobersberg A . . 97 C3
Dobiegniew PL . 75 B4
Dobieszyn PL . . 87 A5
Doboj BIH 125 C4
Dobošnica BIH 125 C4
Dobre PL 77 B6
Dobřany CZ 96 B1
Dobre Miasto PL 69 B5
Dobreta-Turnu-Severin RO . . . 16 C5
Dobri H 111 C3
Dobrica SRB . . . 126 B2
Dobrin BG . . . 17 D7
Dobřichovice CZ 96 B2
Dobrinishte BG 183 B5
Dobříš CZ 96 B2
Dobrna SLO . . . 123 A4
Dobrodzień PL . 86 B2
Döbrököz H . . . 112 C2
Dobromani BIH 139 B3
Dobromirești PL 85 A5
Dobrosołowo PL 76 B3
Dobroszyce PL . 85 A5
Dobrovnik SLO 111 C3
Dobrush BY . . . 13 B9
Dobruška CZ . . . 85 B4
Dobrzany PL . . . 75 A4
Dobrzeń Wielki PL 86 B1
Dobrzyca
Wielkopolskie PL 75 A5
Dobrzyca
Wielkopolskie PL 85 A5
Dobrzyń nad Wisłą PL 77 B4
Dobšiná SK 99 C4

Dochamps B . . . 80 B1
Docking UK 41 C4
Docksta S 200 C4
Doddington UK 37 A4
Döderhult S 62 A4
Doesburg NL . . . 70 B3
Doetinchem NL 71 C3
Dogliani I 133 A3
Dogueno P . . . 160 B2
Doische B 91 A4
Dois Portos P . 154 B1
Dojč SK 98 C1
Dokka N 48 B2
Dokkedal DK . . . 58 B3
Dokkum NL 70 A2
Doł SK 99 C3
Doksy CZ 84 B2
Dokuz TR 189 A7
Dolancourt F . . 104 A3
Dolceácqua I . . 133 B3
Dol-de-Bretagne F 88 B2
Dole F 105 B4
Dølemo N 53 B4
Dolenja vas SLO 123 B3
Dolenjske Toplice SLO 123 B4
Dolfor UK 39 B3
Dolgarrog UK . . 38 A3
Dolgellau UK . . 38 B3
Doliana GR . . . 182 D2
Dolianova I . . . 179 C3
Dolice PL 75 A4
Doljani HR . . . 138 A2
Döllach im Mölltal A 109 C3
Dollnstein D . . . 94 C3
Dolle D 73 B4
Dollot F 104 A2
Döllstädt D 82 A2
Dolná Strehová SK 99 C3
Dolné Saliby SK 111 A4
Dolni Benešov CZ 98 B2
Dolni Bousov CZ 84 B3
Dolni Kounice CZ 97 B4
Dolni Kralovice CZ 96 B3
Dolní Újezd CZ . 97 B4
Dolni Žandov CZ 95 A4
Dolný Kubín SK . 99 B3
Dolo I 121 B5
Dolores E 165 A4
Dolovo SRB . . 127 C2
Dölsach A 109 C3
Dolsk PL 76 B2
Dolwyddelan UK 38 A3
Domaljevac BIH 125 B4
Domanic TR . . . 187 C4
Domaniža SK . . 98 B2
Domanovići BIH 139 B3
Domašov CZ . . 98 B1
Domažlice CZ . . 95 B4
Dombås N 198 C6
Dombasle-sur-Meurthe F . . . 92 C2
Dombegyház H 126 A3
Dombóvár H . 112 C2
Domène F 118 B2
Domérat F . . . 116 A2
Domfessel F . . . 92 C3
Domfront F 88 B3
Domfront-en-Champagne F 102 A2
Domingão P . 154 B2
Domingo Pérez
Granada E . 163 A4
Toledo E . . . 150 C3
Dömitz D 73 A4
Dommartin-le-Franc F 91 C4
Dommartin F 91 B5
Domme F 129 B4
Dommitzsch D . 83 A4

Domodóssola I 119 A5
Domokos GR . . 182 D4
Domoszló H . . . 113 B4
Dompaire F . . . 105 A5
Dompierre-du-Chemin F 88 B2
Dompierre-sur-Besbre F 104 C2
Dompierre-sur-Mer F 114 B3
Domrémy-la-Pucelle F 92 C1
Dömsöd H . . . 112 B3
Domsure F . . . 118 A2
Dómus de Maria I 179 D2
Domusnóvas I 179 C2
Domvena GR . 184 A3
Domžale SLO . 123 A3
Donado E 141 B4
Donaghadee UK 27 B5
Don Álvaro E . . 155 C4
Doña Mencía E 163 A3
Donaueschingen D 106 B3
Donawörth D . 94 C2
Don Benito E . 156 B2
Doncaster UK . 40 B2
Donegal IRL . . . 26 B2
Donestebe-Santesteban E 144 A2
Donges F 101 B3
Dongo I 120 A2
Donington UK . 41 C3
Doniños E 140 A2
Donja Bebrina HR 125 B4
Donja Brela HR 138 B2
Donja Dubica BIH 125 B4
Donja Dubrava HR 124 A2
Donja Kupčina HR 123 B4
Donja Šatornja SRB 127 C2
Donja Stubica HR 124 B1
Donje Brišnik BIH 138 B3
Donje Stative HR 123 B4
Donji-Andrijevci HR 125 B4
Donji Kazanci BIH 138 B2
Donji Koričáni BIH 138 A3
Donji Lapac HR 124 C1
Donji Malovan BIH 138 B3
Donji Miholjac HR 125 B4
Donji Mosti HR 124 B2
Donji Poloj HR 123 B4
Donji-Rujani BIH 138 B2
Donji Srb HR . 138 A2
Donji Svilaj BIH 125 B4
Donji Tovarnik SRB 127 C1
Donji Vakuf BIH 138 A3
Donja SLO . . . 109 C4
Donnalucata I 177 C3
Donnemarie-Dontilly F 90 C3
Donnersbach A 110 B1
Donnersbachwald A 109 B5
Donnerskirchen A 111 B3
Donorático I . 134 B3
Donostia-San Sebastián E . 144 A2
Donovaly SK . . . 99 C3
Donzenac F . . 129 A4
Donzère F 131 A3
Donzy F 104 B2
Doonbeg IRL . . . 29 B2
Dor E 140 A1
Dorchester UK . 43 B4
Dørdal N 53 A5

Dordrecht NL . . 79 A4
Dörentke D 71 B4
Dores UK 32 D2
Dorfen D 95 C4
Dorfgastein A . 109 B4
Dorfmark D 72 B2
Dorf Mecklenburg D 65 C4
Dorgali I 178 B3
Dorking UK 44 B3
Dormagen D . . . 80 A2
Dormánd H . . . 113 B4
Dormans F 91 B3
Dornava SLO . 124 A1
Dornbirn A 107 B4
Dornburg D 83 A3
Dorndorf D 82 B2
Dornecy F 104 B2
Dornes F 104 C2
Dornhan D 93 C4
Dornie UK 31 B3
Dornoch UK . . . 32 D2
Dornum D 71 A4
Dorog H 112 B2
Dorohoi RO . . . 17 B7
Dorotea S 200 B2
Dorotowo PL . . 69 B5
Dörpen D 71 B4
Dorsten D 80 A2
Dortan F 118 A2
Dortmund D . . . 80 A3
Doruchów PL . . 86 A2
Dorum D 64 C1
Dörverden D . . . 72 B2
Dörzbach D 94 B1
Dos Aguas E . . 159 B3
Dosbarrios E . 151 C4
Döşemealtı TR 189 B5
Dos Hermanas E 162 A2
Dospat BG . . . 183 B6
Dos-Torres E . 156 B3
Dötlingen D . . . 72 B1
Dottignies B . . . 78 B3
Döttingen CH . 106 B3
Douai F 78 B3
Douarnenez F . 100 A1
Douchy F 104 B2
Douchy-les-Mines F 78 B3
Doucier F 105 C4
Doudeville F . . . 89 A4
Doué-la-Fontaine F 102 B1
Douglas
Isle of Man
UK 36 B2
South Lanarkshire
UK 36 A3
Doulaincourt-Saucourt F . . . 91 C5
Doulevant-le-Château F 91 C4
Doullens F 90 A2
Dounby UK 33 B3
Doune UK 35 B3
Dounreay UK . . 32 C3
Dour B 79 B3
Dourdan F 90 C2
Dourgne F . . . 146 A3
Dournazac F . . 115 C4
Douro Calvo P 148 B2
Douvaine F . . . 118 A3
Douvres-la-Délivrande F . . . 89 A3
Douzy F 91 B5
Dover UK 45 B5
Dovje SLO 109 C4
Dovre N 198 D6
Downham Market UK 41 C4
Downhill UK . . . 27 A4
Downpatrick UK 27 B5
Dowra IRL 26 B2
Doxato GR . . . 183 B6
Doyet F 116 A2
Dozule F 89 A3
Draá F 91 B3
Drača SRB . . . 127 C2
Dračevo
BIH 139 C4
NMK 182 B3
Drachten NL . . 70 A3
Draga SLO . . . 123 B3
Drăgăşani RO . 17 C6
Dragaš SRB . . 123 B3
Dragatuš SLO . 123 B4
Dragichyn BY . 13 B6
Draginja SRB . 127 C1

Dragocvet
  SRB 127 D3
Dragolovci
  BIH...........125 C3
Dragoni I......170 B2
Dragør DK 61 D2
Dragotina HR . 124 B2
Dragotinja
  BIH...........124 B2
Dragozetići
  HR 123 B3
Draguignan F . 132 B2
Drahnsdorf D . .74 C2
Drahonice CZ . .96 B2
Drahovce SK ...98 C1
Drama GR.....183 B6
Drammen N.....54 A1
Drangedal N ...53 A5
Drangsnes IS . . 190 B4
Dransfeld D.....82 A1
Dranske D 66 B2
Draperstown
  UK 27 B4
Drassburg A . 111 B3
Dravaszabolcs
  H.............125 B4
Dravograd
  SLO 110 C2
Drawno PL.....75 A4
Drawsko Pomorskie
  PL............75 A4
Drayton UK ...41 C5
Draženov CZ ...95 B4
Draževac SRB . 127 C2
Dražice HR 123 B3
Drebkau D.....84 A2
Dreieich D 93 A4
Dreisen D 93 B4
Drenovci HR . . 125 C4
Drensteinfurt
  D............81 A3
Dresden D 84 A1
Dretyń PL.....68 A1
Dreux F 89 B5
Dřevohostice
  CZ 98 B1
Drevsjø N ... 199 D9
Drewitz D......73 B5
Drezdenko PL. .75 B4
Drežnica HR... 123 B4
Drežnik-Grad
  HR 123 C4
Drietoma SK ...98 C1
Driffield UK 40 A3
Drimnin UK ...34 B2
Drimoleague
  IRL...........29 C2
Dringenberg D .81 A5
Drinić BIH 138 A2
Drinjača BIH . . 139 A5
Drinovci BIH . . 138 A3
Driopida GR... 185 B5
Drivstua N ... 198 C6
Drlače SRB ... 127 C1
Drnholec CZ ...97 C4
Drniš HR 138 B2
Drnje HR 124 A2
Drnovice CZ ...97 B4
Dro I 121 B3
Drøbak N.....54 A1
Drobin PL.....77 B5
Drochia MD ...17 A7
Drochtersen D .64 C2
Drogheda IRL . .30 A2
Drohobych UA . 13 D5
Droitwich Spa
  UK 29 A6
Drołtowice PL...85 A5
Dromahair IRL . 26 B2
Dromcolliher
  IRL...........29 B3
Dromore
  Down UK 27 B4
  Tyrone UK 27 B3
Dromore West
  IRL............26 B2
Dronero I 133 A3
Dronfield UK . .40 B2
Drongan UK ...36 A2
Dronninglund
  DK 58 A3
Dronrijp NL 70 A2
Dronten NL 70 B2
Drosendorf A ..97 C3
Drösing A......97 C4
Drottningholm
  S.............57 A3
Droué F 103 A3
Drulingen F....92 C3

Drumbeg UK 32 C1
Drumcliff IRL....26 B2
Drumgask UK . .32 D2
Drumkeeran
  IRL 26 B2
Drummore UK . .36 B2
Drumnadrochit
  UK 32 D2
Drumquin UK ...27 B3
Drumshanbo
  IRL............26 B2
Drumsna IRL ...26 C2
Drunen NL 79 A5
Druskininkai
  LT.............13 A5
Druten NL......80 A1
Druya BY.......13 A7
Družetići SRB . 127 C2
Drvar BIH 138 A2
Drvenik HR ... 138 B3
Drwalew PL....77 C6
Drymen UK 34 B3
Drynoch UK ...31 B2
Drzewce PL....76 B2
Drzewiany PL ..68 B1
Drzewica PL...87 A4
Dualchi I.......178 B2
Duas Igrejas P. 149 A3
Dub SRB 127 D1
Dubá CZ 84 B2
Dubăsari MD....17 B8
Duben D.......74 C2
Dübendorf
  CH 107 B3
Dubi CZ......84 B1
Dubica HR 124 B2
Dublin IRL......30 A2
Dubna RUS.....9 D10
Dubňany CZ ...98 C1
Dubnica nad
  Váhom SK 98 C2
Dubník SK 112 B2
Dubno UA 13 C6
Dubodiel SK ...98 C2
Dubona SRB ... 127 C2
Dubovac SRB . 127 C3
Dubovic BIH ...124 C2
Dubranec HR . 124 B1
Dubrava HR ...124 B2
Dubrava BIH . . 125 C4
Dubravica
  HR 123 B4
  SRB 127 C3
Dubrovnik HR . 139 C4
Dubrovytsya
  UA 13 C7
Ducey F 88 B2
Duchcov CZ ...84 B1
Ducherow D ...74 A2
Dučina SRB.... 127 C2
Duclair F 89 A4
Dudar H.......112 B1
Duddington UK .40 C3
Duderstadt D ..82 A2
Dudeştii Vechi
  RO 126 A2
Dudley UK 40 C1
Dueñas E 142 C2
Duesund N 46 B2
Dueville I 121 B4
Duffel B.......79 A4
Duffield UK....40 C2
Dufftown UK ...32 D3
Duga Resa HR . 123 B4
Dugi Rat HR ...138 B2
Dugny-sur-Meuse
  F.............92 B1
Dugopolje HR. 138 B2
Dugo Selo HR . 124 B2
Duino I 122 B2
Duisburg D 80 A2
Dukat AL......182 C1
Dukovany CZ ...97 B4
Duleek IRL.....30 A2
Dülken D 80 A2
Dülmen D......80 A3
Dulovo BG 17 D7
Dulpetorpet N .49 B4
Dulverton UK ..43 A3
Dumbarton UK .34 C3
Dümerek TR ...187 C6
Dumfries UK ...36 A3
Dumlupınar
  TR 187 D4
Dümpelfeld D...80 B2
Dunaalmás H . 112 B2
Dunabogdány
  H.............112 B3
Dunafalva H . . 125 A4
Dunaföldvár
  H.............112 C2
Dunaharaszti
  H.............112 B3

Dunajská Streda
  SK............111 B4
Dunakeszi H . . 112 B3
Dunakiliti H... 111 B4
Dunakömlöd
  H.............112 C2
Dunapataj H . . 112 C2
Dunaszekcsö
  H.............125 A4
Dunaszentgyorgy
  H.............112 C2
Dunatetétlen
  H.............112 C3
Dunaújváros
  H.............112 C2
Dunavecse H . . 112 C2
Dunbar UK 35 B5
Dunbeath UK . .32 C3
Dunblane UK ..35 B4
Dunboyne IRL . .30 A2
Dundalk IRL....27 B4
Dundee UK 35 B5
Dundrennan
  UK 36 B3
Dundrum UK ...27 B5
Dunfanaghy
  IRL............26 A3
Dunfermline
  UK 35 B4
Dungannon UK .27 B4
Dungarvan IRL . .29 B4
Dungiven UK ...27 B4
Dunglow IRL ...26 B2
Dungourney
  IRL............29 C3
Duninowo PL ..68 A1
Dunkeld UK ...35 B4
Dunker S 56 A2
Dunkerque =
  Dunkirk F.....78 A2
Dunkineely IRL .26 B2
Dunkirk =
  Dunkerque F. .78 A2
Dun Laoghaire
  IRL............30 A2
Dunlavin IRL ...30 A2
Dunleer IRL....27 C4
Dun-le-Palestel
  F............116 A1
Dun-les-Places
  F............104 B3
Dunlop UK 36 A2
Dunloy UK 27 A4
Dunmanway
  IRL............29 C2
Dunmore IRL...28 A3
Dunmore East
  IRL............30 B2
Dunmurry UK ..27 B4
Dunnet UK 32 C3
Dunningen D . 107 A3
Dunoon UK 34 C3
Dunscore UK ..36 A3
Dunsford UK ...43 B3
Dunshaughlin
  IRL............30 A2
Dunstable UK . .44 B3
Dunster UK 43 A3
Dun-sur-Auron
  F............103 C4
Dun-sur-Meuse
  F.............91 B5
Dunvegan UK . .31 B2
Duplek SLO ...110 C2
Dupnitsa BG ...17 D5
Durağan TR ...23 A8
Durach D 107 B5
Durak TR......186 C3
Durana E 143 B4
Durance F 128 B3
Durango E 143 A4
Durankulak
  BG 17 D8
Duras F 128 B3
Durban-Corbières
  F............146 B3
Dürbheim D . 107 A3
Durbuy B 79 B5
Dúrcal E 163 B4
Đurđenovac
  HR 125 B4
Đurđevac HR ..124 A3
Đurđevik BIH . 139 A4
Düren D.......80 B2
Durham UK 37 B5
Đurinci SRB ...127 C2
Durlach D......93 C4
Durmanec HR . 124 A1
Durness UK 32 C2
Dürnkrut A 97 C4
Dürrboden

CH 107 C3
Durrës AL.....182 B1
Durrow IRL.....30 B1
Durrus IRL.....29 C2
Dursunbey TR . 186 C3
Durtal F 102 B1
Durup DK 58 B1
Durusu TR 186 A3
Dusina BIH ...139 B3
Dusnok H......112 C2
Dusocin PL.....69 B3
Düsseldorf D ...80 A2
Dusslingen D ..93 C5
Duszniki PL....75 B5
Duszniki-Zdrój
  PL.............85 B4
Dutovlje SLO . 122 B2
Duvebo S 55 B5
Duved S 199 B9
Düzağac TR ...187 D5
Düzce TR......187 B6
Dvärsätt S ... 199 B11
Dvor HR 124 B2
Dvorce CZ 98 B1
Dvorníky SK ...98 C1
Dvory nad Žitavou
  SK............112 B2
Dvůr Králové nad
  Labem CZ.....85 B3
Dybvad DK.....58 A3
Dyce UK.......33 D4
Dygowo PL.....67 B4
Dykehead UK . .35 B4
Dymchurch UK .45 B5
Dymer UA 13 C9
Dyrnes N......198 B4
Dywity PL......69 B5
Džanići BIH ...139 B3
Dziadowa Kłoda
  PL.............86 A1
Działdowo PL . .77 A5
Działoszyce PL .87 B4
Działoszyn PL . .86 A2
Dziemiany PL ..68 A2
Dzierzążnia PL .77 B5
Dzierzgoń PL...69 B4
Dzierzgowo PL .77 A5
Dzierżoniów
  PL.............85 B4
Dzisna BY......13 A8
Dziwnów PL....67 B3
Dźwierzuty PL .77 A5
Dzyarzhynsk
  BY............13 B7
Dzyatlava BY...13 B6

E

Ea E 143 A4
Eaglesfield UK .36 A3
Ealing UK 44 B3
Eardisley UK ...39 B3
Earls Barton UK .44 A3
Earl Shilton UK .40 C2
Earlston UK 35 C5
Easington UK ..41 B4
Easky IRL......26 B2
Eastbourne UK .45 C4
East Calder UK .35 C4
East Dereham
  UK 41 C4
Easter Skeld
  UK 33 A5
East Grinstead
  UK 45 B4
East Ilsley UK . .44 B2
East Kilbride
  UK 36 A2
Eastleigh UK ...44 C2
East Linton UK .35 C5
East Markham
  UK 40 B3
Easton UK.....43 B4
East Wittering
  UK 44 C3
Eaton Socon
  UK 44 A3
Eaux-Bonnes
  F.............145 B3
Eauze F 128 C3
Ebberup DK....59 C2
Ebbw Vale UK .39 C3
Ebelsbach D ...94 A2
Ebeltoft DK 59 B3
Ebene Reichenau
  A 109 C4
Eben im Pongau
  A 109 B4
Ebensee A 109 B4
Ebensfeld D ...94 A2

Eberbach D 93 B4
Ebergötzen D . .82 A2
Ebermann-Stadt
  D.............94 B3
Ebern D.......82 B2
Eberndorf A . . 110 C1
Ebersbach D ...84 A2
Ebersberg D . . 108 A2
Ebersdorf
  Bayern D 82 B3
  Niedersachsen
  D.............72 A2
Eberstein A . . 110 C1
Eberswalde D . .74 B2
Ebnat-Kappel
  CH 107 B4
Éboli I 170 C3
Ebrach D......94 B2
Ebreichsdorf
  A 111 B3
Ebreuil F 116 A3
Ebstorf D......72 A3
Ecclefechan UK .36 A3
Eccleshall UK ..40 C1
Eceabat TR ...186 B1
Echallens CH ..106 C1
Echauri E 144 B2
Echinos GR....183 B7
Echiré F 114 B3
Échirolles F ... 118 B2
Echourgnac F . 128 A3
Echt NL.......80 A1
Echte D 82 A2
Echternach L ...92 B2
Ecija E 162 A2
Ečka SRB 126 B2
Eckartsberga D .82 A3
Eckelshausen D 81 B4
Eckental D 94 B3
Eckernförde D . .64 B2
Eckerö FIN 51 B6
Eckington UK ..40 B2
Éclaron F 91 C4
Écommoy F ... 102 B2
Écouché F 89 B3
Ecouis F 90 B1
Ecséd H 113 B3
Ecsegfalva H ..113 B4
Écueillé F 103 B3
Ed S 54 B2
Eda glasbruk S .49 C4
Edam NL 70 B2
Edane S 55 A3
Edderton UK ...32 D2
Ede NL........70 B2
Edebäck S 49 B5
Edebo S.......51 B5
Edelény H......99 C4
Edelschrott A . 110 B2
Edemissen D . .72 B3
Edenbridge UK .45 B4
Edenderry IRL . .30 A1
Edenkoben D . .93 B4
Edersleben D . .82 A3
Edessa GR....182 C4
Edewecht D 71 A4
Edgeworthstown
  IRL............30 A1
Edinburgh UK . .35 C4
Edinet MD 17 A7
Edirne TR.....186 A1
Edland N 52 A3
Edolo I 120 A3
Edøy N........198 B5
Edremit TR ...186 C2
Edsbro S 51 C5
Edsbruk S 56 B2
Edsbyn S 50 A2
Edsele S 200 C2
Edsleskog S ...54 A3
Edsvalla S 55 A4
Eekloo B 79 A3
Eemshaven NL .71 A3
Eerbeek NL....70 B3
Eersel NL 79 A5
Eferding A 96 C2
Effiat F 116 A3
Efteløt N 53 A5
Egeln D 73 C4
Eger H 113 B4
Egerbakta H ..113 B4
Egersund N 52 B2
Egerszólát H . 113 B4
Egervár H.....111 C3
Egg
  A 107 B4
  D.............94 C2
Eggby S 55 B4
Eggedal N 48 B6
Eggenburg A ...97 C3
Eggenfelden D .95 C4

Eggesin D......74 A3
Eggum N 194 B4
Egham UK.....44 B3
Éghezée B 79 B4
Egiertowo PL . .68 A3
Egilsstaðir IS . 191 B11
Egina GR......185 B4
Eginio GR 182 C4
Egio GR 184 A3
Égletons F 116 B2
Egling D 108 B2
Eglinton UK ...27 A3
Eglisau CH ... 107 B3
Égliseneuve-
d'Entraigues
  F 116 B2
Eglofs D 107 B4
Egmond aan Zee
  NL 70 B1
Egna I 121 A4
Egosthena GR . 184 A4
Egremont UK ..36 B3
Egtved DK 59 C2
Eguilles F 131 B4
Eguilly-sous-Bois
  F 104 A3
Éguzon-Chantôme
  F 103 C3
Egyek H 113 B4
Egyházasrádóc
  H 111 B3
Ehekirchen D ..94 C3
Ehingen D 94 C1
Ehra-Lessien D .73 B3
Ehrang D 92 B2
Ehrenfriedersdorf
  D.............83 B4
Ehrenhain D ...83 B4
Ehrenhausen
  A 110 C2
Ehringshausen
  D.............81 B4
Ehrwald A 108 B1
Eibar E 143 A4
Eibelstadt D ...94 B2
Eibenstock D ..83 B4
Eibergen NL ...71 B3
Eibiswald A ... 110 C2
Eichenbarleben
  D.............73 B4
Eichendorf D ...95 C4
Eichstätt D 95 C3
Eickelborn D ...81 A4
Eide
  Hordaland N . .46 B2
  Møre og Romsdal
  N 198 C4
Eidet N 194 A9
Eidfjord N 46 B4
Eidsberg N 54 A2
Eidskog N 49 B4
Eidsvåg
  Hordaland N . .46 B2
  Møre og Romsdal
  N 198 C5
Eidsvoll N 48 B3
Eikefjord N 46 A2
Eikelandsosen
  N.............46 B2
Eiken N 52 B3
Eikesdal N 198 C5
Eikstrand N ...53 A5
Eilenburg D ...83 A4
Eilsleben D 73 B4
Eina N 48 B2
Einbeck D 82 A1
Eindhoven NL .79 A5
Einsiedeln CH . 107 B3
Einville-au-Jard
  F 92 C2
Eisenach D 82 B2
Eisenberg
  Rheinland-Pfalz
  D.............93 B4
  Thüringen D ...83 B3
Eisenerz A 110 B1
Eisenhüttenstadt
  D.............74 B3
Eisenkappel A 110 C1
Eisenstadt A . 111 B3
Eisentratten
  A 109 C4
Eisfeld D 82 B2
Eisleben D 82 A3
Eislingen D 94 C1
Eitensheim D ..95 C3
Eiterfeld D 82 B1
Eitorf D 80 B3
Eivindvik N 46 B2

Eivissa = Ibiza
  E 166 C1
Eixo P 148 B1
Ejby DK 59 C2
Eje de los
  Caballeros E . 144 B2
Ejstrupholm
  DK 59 C2
Ejulve E 153 B3
Eke B 79 B3
Ekeby
  Gotland S 57 C4
  Skåne S 61 D2
  Uppsala S 51 B5
Ekeby-Almby S .56 A1
Ekenäs S 55 B4
Ekenässjön S ...62 A3
Ekerö S 57 A3
Eket S 61 C3
Eketorp S 63 B4
Ekevik S 56 B2
Ekkerøy N ... 193 B14
Eksingedal N . .46 B2
Eksjö S 62 A2
Eksta S 57 C4
Ekträsk S 200 B5
El Álamo
  Madrid E..... 151 B4
  Sevilla E 161 B3
El Algar E 165 B4
El Almendro E . 161 B2
El Aquián E ...164 C2
Élancourt F 90 C1
El Arenal E ... 150 B2
El Arguellite E . 164 A2
Elassona GR . . 182 D4
El Astillero E . . 143 A3
Elati GR 182 D3
El Ballestero E . 158 C1
El Barco de Ávila
  E 150 B2
Elbasan AL ...182 B2
El Berrón E ...142 A1
El Berrueco E . 151 B4
Elbeuf F 89 A4
El Bingarrode D .82 A2
Elblag PL......69 A4
El Bodón E ... 149 B3
El Bonillo E ...158 C1
El Bosque E ...162 B2
El Bullaque E . 157 A3
Elburg NL 70 B2
El Burgo E 162 B3
El Burgo de Ebro
  E 153 A3
El Burgo de Osma
  E 151 A4
El Burgo Ranero
  E 142 B1
El Buste E 144 C2
El Cabaco E ...149 B3
El Callejo E ...143 A3
El Campillo E . 161 B3
El Campillo de la
  Jara E 156 A2
El Cañavete E . 158 B1
El Carpio E ...157 C3
El Carpio de Tajo
  E 150 C3
El Casar E 151 B4
El Casar de
  Escalona E ... 150 B3
El Castillo de las
  Guardas E ... 161 B3
El Centenillo E 157 B4
El Cerro E 149 B4
El Cerro de
  Andévalo E . . 161 B3
Elche E 165 A4
Elche de la Sierra
  E 158 C1
Elchingen D ...94 C2
El Comenar E . 162 B2
El Coronil E ...162 A2
El Crucero E ...141 A4
El Cubo de Tierra
  del Vino E ... 149 A4
El Cuervo E ...162 B1
Elda E 159 C3
Eldena D 73 A4
Eldingen D 72 B3
Elefsina GR ...185 A4
Elek H 113 C5
Elena BG 17 D6
Eleutheroupoli
  GR 183 C6
El Frago E 144 B3
El Franco E ... 141 A4

El Frasno E 152 A2
Elgå N......... 199 C8
El Garrobo E ... 161 B3
El Gastor E 162 B2
Elgin UK....... 32 D3
Elgoibar E 143 A4
Elgol UK....... 31 B2
El Gordo E..... 150 C2
El Grado E..... 145 B4
El Granado E ... 161 B2
El Grao de Castelló
E........... 159 B4
El Grau E 159 C3
Elgshøa N......49 A4
El Higuera E... 163 A3
El Hijate E.... 164 B2
El Hontanar E . 152 B2
Elhovo BG...... 17 D7
El Hoyo E...... 157 B4
Elie UK........35 B5
Elizondo E 144 A2
Elk PL 12 B5
Ellenberg D....94 B2
Ellesmere UK....38 B4
Ellesmere Port
UK..........38 A4
Ellezelles B....79 B3
Ellingen D 94 B2
Ellmau A 109 B3
Ellon UK....... 33 D4
Ellös S........54 B2
Ellrich D.......82 A2
Ellwangen D ...94 C2
Elm
CH 107 C4
D 72 A2
Elmadağ TR...23 B7
El Madroño E.. 161 B3
El Maillo E..... 149 B3
Elmalı TR..... 189 C4
El Masnou E... 147 C3
El Mirón E..... 150 B2
El Molar E.... 151 B4
El Molinillo E.. 157 A3
El Morell E.... 147 C2
Elmshorn D....64 C2
Elmstein D.....93 B3
El Muyo E..... 151 A4
Elne F 146 B3
Elnesvågen N. 198 C4
El Olmo E..... 151 A4
Elorrio E 143 A4
Előszállás H... 112 C2
Elouda GR.... 185 D6
Éloyes F...... 105 A5
El Palo E...... 163 B3
El Pardo E.... 151 B4
El Payo E..... 149 B3
El Pedernoso
E........... 158 B1
El Pedroso E.. 162 A2
El Peral E..... 158 B2
El Perelló
Tarragona E .. 153 B4
Valencia E ... 159 B3
Elphin UK....32 C1
El Picazo E ... 158 B1
El Pinell de Bray
E........... 153 A4
El Piñero E.... 150 A2
El Pla de Santa
Maria E 147 C2
El Pobo E..... 153 B3
El Pobo de Dueñas
E........... 152 B2
El Pont
d'Armentera
E........... 147 C2
El Port de la Selva
E........... 147 B4
El Port de Llançà
E........... 146 B4
El Port de Sagunt
E........... 159 B3
El Prat de Llobregat
E........... 147 C3
El Provencio E. 158 B1
El Puente E.... 143 A3
El Puente del
Arzobispo E.. 150 C2
El Puerto E.... 141 A4
El Puerto de Santa
María E 162 B1
El Real de la Jara
E........... 161 B3
El Real de San
Vicente E 150 B3
El Robledo E .. 157 A3
El Rocio E 161 B3
El Rompido E.. 161 B2
El Ronquillo E. 161 B3
El Royo E..... 143 C4
El Rubio E 162 A3

El Sabinar E ... 164 A2
El Saler E..... 159 B3
El Salobral E .. 158 C2
El Saucejo E .. 162 A2
Els Castells E .. 147 B2
Elsdorf D.......80 B2
Elsenfeld D ...93 B5
El Serrat AND . 146 B2
Elsfleth D 72 A1
Elspeet NL.....70 B2
Elst NL 70 C2
Elstead UK.....44 B3
Elster D.......83 A4
Elsterberg D ..83 B4
Elsterwerda D .83 A5
Elstra D.......84 A2
El Temple E ... 144 C3
El Tiemblo E... 150 B3
Eltmann D 94 B2
El Toboso E ... 157 A5
El Tormillo E .. 145 C3
El Torno E 149 B4
Eltville D......93 A4
El Valle de las Casas
E........... 142 B1
Elvas P 155 C3
Elvebakken N . 192 C7
El Vellón E.... 151 B4
Elven F....... 101 B3
El Vendrell E .. 147 C2
Elverum N 48 B3
El Villar de Arnedo
E........... 144 B1
Elvington UK...40 B3
El Viso E...... 156 B3
El Viso del Alcor
E........... 162 A2
Elxleben D.....82 A2
Ely UK........45 A4
Elzach D...... 106 A3
Elze D........72 B2
Emådalen S...50 A1
Embleton UK... 37 A5
Embonas GR .. 188 C2
Embrun F..... 132 A2
Embún E 144 B3
Emden D......71 A4
Emecik TR.... 188 C2
Emet TR...... 186 C4
Emirdağ TR ... 187 C6
Emlichheim D..71 B3
Emmaboda S ..63 B3
Emmaljunga S .61 C3
Emmeloord NL..70 B2
Emmen
CH 106 B3
NL 71 B3
Emmendingen
D 106 A2
Emmer-
Compascuum
E............ 71 B4
Emmerich D...80 A2
Emmern D 72 B2
Emöd H....... 113 B4
Émpoli I...... 135 B3
Emsbüren D ..71 B4
Emsdetten D...71 B4
Emsfors S.....62 A4
Emskirchen D..94 B2
Emstek D......71 B5
Emsworth UK...44 B3
Emyvale IRL....27 B4
Enafors S ... 199 B9
Enånger S.....51 A4
Encamp AND... 146 B2
Encarnação P . 154 C1
Encinas de Abajo
E........... 150 B2
Encinas de Esgueva
E........... 142 C2
Encinasola E .. 161 A3
Encinas Reales
E........... 163 A3
Encio E....... 143 B3
Enciso E...... 144 B1
Enden N...... 199 D7
Endingen D ... 106 A2
Endrinal E.... 149 B4
Endröd H 113 C4
Enebakk N.....54 A2
Eneryda S.....63 B2
Enese H....... 111 B4
Enez TR...... 183 C8
Enfield IRL....30 A2
Engelberg CH. 106 C3
Engelhartszell
A............96 C1
Engelskirchen
D............80 B3
Engen D...... 107 B3
Enger N.......48 B2

Engerdal N.... 199 D8
Engerneset N ..49 A4
Enge-sande D..64 B1
Engesvang DK .59 B2
Enghien B......79 B4
Engstingen D ..94 C1
Engter D......71 B5
Enguera E.... 159 C3
Enguidanos E . 158 B2
Enkenbach D ..93 B3
Enkhuizen NL...70 B2
Enklinge FIN ...51 B7
Enköping S....56 A3
Enna I....... 177 B3
Ennezat F.... 116 B3
Ennigerloh D ..81 A4
Enningdal N....54 B2
Ennis IRL......28 B3
Enniscorthy IRL .30 B2
Enniskean IRL..29 C3
Enniskillen UK ..27 B3
Ennistimon
IRL 28 B2
Enns A 110 A1
Eno FIN 9 A7
Enontekiö
FIN 196 A6
Ens NL........70 B2
Enschede NL...71 B3
Ensdorf D.....95 B3
Ensisheim F ...106 B2
Enstaberga S ..56 B2
Enstone UK 44 B2
Entlebuch CH . 106 B3
Entrácque I .. 133 A3
Entradas P ... 160 B1
Entrains-sur-
Nohain F 104 B2
Entrambasaguas
E........... 143 A3
Entrambasmestas
E........... 143 A3
Entraygues-sur-
Truyère F ... 116 C2
Entre-os-Rios
P........... 148 A1
Entrevaux F... 132 B2
Entrin Bajo E .. 155 C4
Entroncamento
P........... 154 B2
Entzheim F....93 C3
Envermeu F...89 A5
Enviken S.....50 B2
Enying H...... 112 C2
Enzingerboden
A........... 109 B3
Enzklösterle D .93 C4
Épagny F.....90 B2
Epalinges CH . 106 C1
Epannes F.....114 B3
Epanomí GR .. 182 C4
Epe
D............71 B4
NL 70 B2
Épernay F.....91 B3
Épernon F.....90 C1
Epfig F........93 C3
Epierre F..... 118 B3
Épila E....... 152 A2
Épinac F..... 104 C3
Épinal F...... 105 A5
Episcopía I ... 174 A2
Episkopi CY ... 181 B1
Epitálio GR... 184 B2
Epoisses F.... 104 B3
Eppenbrunn D .93 B3
Eppendorf D...83 B5
Epping UK 45 B4
Eppingen D...93 B4
Epsom UK.....44 B3
Epworth UK....40 B3
Eraclea I..... 122 B1
Eraclea Mare I. 122 B1
Erba I........ 120 B2
Erbach
Baden-Württemberg
D............94 C1
Hessen D 93 B4
Erbalunga F... 180 A2
Erbendorf D ...95 B4
Érchie I...... 173 B3
Ercolano I.... 170 C2
Ercsi H....... 112 B2
Érd H........ 112 B2
Erdek TR..... 186 B2
Erdemli TR....23 C8
Erdevik SRB .. 126 B1
Erdut HR..... 125 B5
Erdweg D.....95 C3
Ereğli
Konya TR 23 C8

Ereğli continued
Zonguldak
TR......... 187 A6
Erenkaya TR .. 189 B7
Eresfjord N ... 198 C5
Eresos GR.... 183 D7
Eretria GR.... 185 A4
Erfde D.......64 B2
Erfjord N......52 A2
Erfstadt D.....80 B2
Erfurt D.......82 B3
Érgli LV........8 D4
Ergoldsbach D .95 C4
Eriboll UK.....32 C2
Érice I....... 176 A1
Ericeira P.... 154 C1
Égridir TR.... 189 B5
Eriksberg S .. 195 E6
Eriksmåla S ...62 B3
Eringsboda S ..63 B3
Eriswil CH.... 106 B2
Erithres GR... 185 A4
Erkelenz D.....80 A2
Erkner D.......74 B2
Erkrath D......80 A2
Erla E....... 144 B3
Erlangen D....94 B3
Erli I........ 133 A4
Erlsbach A ... 109 C3
Ermelo NL.....70 B2
Ermenak TR....23 C7
Ermezinde P . 148 A1
Ermidas P ... 160 A1
Ermioni GR... 184 B4
Ermoupoli GR. 185 B5
Ermsleben D ..82 A3
Erndtebrück D .81 B4
Ernée F.......88 B3
Ernestinovo
HR 125 B4
Ernstbrunn A ..97 C4
Erolzheim D ... 107 A5
Erquelinnes B ..79 B4
Erquy F...... 101 A3
Erra P....... 154 C2
Erratzu E.... 144 A2
Errindlev DK ...65 B4
Erro E....... 144 B2
Ersa F....... 180 A2
Érsekcsanád
H........... 125 A4
Ersekë AL.... 182 C2
Érsekvadkert
H........... 112 B3
Ersmark S ... 200 C6
Erstein F......93 C3
Erstfeld CH... 107 C3
Ertebølle DK...58 B2
Ertingen D ... 107 A4
Ervedal
Coimbra P ... 148 B1
Portalegre P . 154 B3
Ervenik HR.... 138 A1
Ervidel P.... 160 B1
Ervy-le-Châtel
F........... 104 A2
Erwitte D.....81 A4
Erxleben D....73 B4
Erzsébet H ... 125 A4
Esbjerg DK....59 C1
Esbly F.......90 C2
Escacena del
Campo E 161 B3
Escalada E ... 143 B3
Escalante E ... 143 A3
Escalaplano I . 179 C3
Escalona E ... 150 B3
Escalona del Prado
E........... 151 A3
Escalonilla E .. 150 C3
Escalos de Baixo
P........... 155 B3
Escalos de Cima
P........... 155 B3
Escamilla E... 152 B1
Es Caná E.... 166 B1
Escañuela E .. 157 C3
Es Castell E ... 167 B4
Escatrón E.... 153 A3
Eschach D.....94 B1
Eschau D......93 B5
Eschede D.....72 B3
Eschenau D....95 B3
Eschenbach D..95 B3
Eschenz CH... 107 B3
Eschershausen
D............72 C2
Esch-sur-Alzette
L............92 B1
Esch-sur-Sûre L .92 B1
Eschwege D...82 A2

Eschweiler D...80 B2
Escobasa de
Almazán E ... 152 A1
Escoeuilles F...78 B1
Escombreras
E........... 165 B4
Escos F...... 144 A2
Escource F.... 128 B1
Escragnolles F 132 B2
Escrick UK.....40 B2
Escucha E.... 153 B3
Escurial E.... 156 A2
Escurial de la Sierra
E........... 149 B4
Esens D.......71 A4
Esgos E...... 140 B3
Esher UK......44 B3
Eskdalemuir
UK...........36 A3
Eskifjörður
IS 191 B12
Eskilsater S....55 A4
Eskilstrup DK ...65 B4
Eskilstuna S....56 A2
Eskipazar TR .. 187 B7
Eskişehir TR.. 187 C5
Eslarn D......95 B4
Eslava E..... 144 B2
Eslida E..... 159 B3
Eslohe D......81 A4
Eslöv S....... 61 D3
Eşme TR..... 188 A3
Es Mercadal E. 167 B4
Es Migjorn Gran
E........... 167 B4
Espalion F.... 130 A1
Esparragalejo
E........... 155 C4
Esparragosa del
Caudillo E ... 156 B2
Esparragosa de la
Serena E ... 156 B2
Esparreguera
E........... 147 C2
Esparron F.... 132 B1
Espe N.......46 B3
Espedal N.....52 B2
Espejo
Álava E 143 B3
Córdoba E ... 163 A3
Espeland N ...46 B2
Espelkamp D ..72 B1
Espeluche F... 131 A3
Espera E..... 162 B2
Esperança P . 155 B3
Espéria I..... 169 B3
Espevær N....52 A1
Espiel E...... 156 B2
Espinama E .. 142 A2
Espiñaredo E.. 140 A3
Espinasses F .. 132 A2
Espinelves E .. 147 C3
Espinhal P ... 154 A2
Espinho P.... 148 A1
Espinosa de Cerrato
E........... 143 C3
Espinosa de los
Monteros E .. 143 A3
Espinoso del
Rey E...... 156 A3
Espírito Santo
P........... 160 B2
Espluga de
Francolí E ... 147 C2
Esplús E..... 145 C4
Espolla E..... 146 B3
Espoo FIN..... 8 B4
Esporles E.... 166 B2
Es Port d'Alcúdia
E........... 167 B3
Esposende P . 148 A1
Espot E...... 146 B2
Es Pujols E... 166 C1
Esquedas E ...145 B3
Esquivias E .. 151 B4
Essay F.......89 B4
Essen
B........... 79 A4
Niedersachsen
D........... 71 B4
Nordrhein-
Westfalen D... 80 A3
Essenbach D...95 C4
Essertaux F...90 B2
Essingen D....94 C2
Es Soleràs E .. 153 A4
Essoyes F.... 104 A3
Estacas E.... 140 B2

Estadilla E 145 B4
Estagel F..... 146 B3
Estaires F......78 B2
Estang F..... 128 C2
Estarreja P... 148 B1
Estartit E..... 147 B4
Estavayer-le-Lac
CH 106 C1
Este I....... 121 B4
Esteiro E..... 140 A2
Estela P..... 148 A1
Estella E..... 144 B1
Estellencs E .. 166 B2
Estepa E..... 162 A3
Estépar E.... 143 B3
Estepona E... 162 B2
Esternay F....91 C3
Esterri d'Aneu
E........... 146 B2
Esterwegen D ..71 B4
Estissac F.... 104 A2
Estivadas E .. 140 B3
Estivareilles F. 116 A2
Estivella E.... 159 B3
Estói P....... 160 B2
Estopiñán E .. 145 C4
Estoril P..... 154 C1
Estoublon F... 132 B2
Estrée-Blanche
F............78 B2
Estrées-St Denis
F............90 B2
Estrela P..... 155 C3
Estremera E .. 151 B4
Estremoz P... 155 C3
Estuna S..... 51 C5
Esyres F..... 102 B2
Esztergom H.. 112 B2
Étables-sur-Mer
F........... 100 A3
Étain F.......92 B1
Étalans F.... 105 B5
Étalle B.......92 B1
Étampes F....90 C2
Étang-sur-Arroux
F........... 104 C3
Étaples F......78 B1
Etauliers F... 128 A2
Etili TR...... 186 C1
Etna N.......52 A1
Etne N.......52 A1
Etoges F......91 C3
Etoliko GR.... 184 A2
Eton UK......44 B3
Étréaupont F...91 B3
Étréchy F.....90 C2
Étrépagny F...90 B1
Étretat F......89 A4
Étroeungt F...91 A3
Étroubles I... 119 B4
Ettal D...... 108 B2
Ettelbruck L...92 B2
Etten UK......79 A4
Ettenheim D . 106 A2
Ettington UK...44 A2
Ettlingen D ...93 C4
Ettringen D ... 108 A1
Etuz F....... 105 B4
Etxarri-Aranatz
E........... 144 B1
Etyek H...... 112 B2
Eu F.........90 A1
Euerdorf D....82 B2
Eulate E..... 144 B1
Eupen B......80 B2
Europoort NL ..79 A4
Euskirchen D...80 B2
Eutin D....... 65 B3
Evanger N....46 B3
Évaux-les-Bains
F........... 116 A2
Evciler
Afyon TR..... 189 A4
Çanakkale TR. 186 C1
Evenskjær N .. 194 B7
Evenstad N....48 A3
Evercreech UK .43 A4
Everöd S......61 D4
Everswinkel D .71 C4
Evertsberg S ..49 A5
Evesham UK ..44 A2
Évian-les-Bains
F........... 118 A3
Evisa F...... 180 A1
Evje N........53 B3
Evolène CH ... 119 A4
Évora P..... 154 C3
Evoramonte P 155 C3
Evran F...... 101 A4
Evrecy F......89 A3
Evron F......89 B3
Évreux F......90 B1

Évron F 102 A1
Évry F........90 C2
Ewell UK......44 B3
Ewersbach D...81 B4
Excideuil F ... 115 C5
Exeter UK.....43 B3
Exmes F......89 B4
Exminster UK ..43 B3
Exmouth UK ...43 B3
Eydehamn N ...53 B4
Eye
Peterborough
UK 41 C3
Suffolk UK ... 45 A5
Eyemouth UK...35 C5
Eyguians F... 132 A1
Eyguières F ... 131 B4
Eygurande F . 116 B2
Eylie F...... 145 B4
Eymet F..... 129 B3
Eymoutiers F . 116 B1
Eynsham UK...44 B2
Eyrarbakki IS . 190 D4
Eystrup D 72 B2
Ezaro E...... 140 B1
Ezcaray E.... 143 B4
Ezcároz E.... 144 B2
Ezine TR..... 186 C1
Ezmoriz P.... 148 B1

F

Fabara E..... 153 A4
Fábbrico I.... 121 C3
Fåberg N......48 A2
Fabero E..... 141 B4
Fábiánsebestyén
H........... 113 C4
Fåborg DK.....64 A3
Fabrèques F . 130 B2
Fabriano I.... 136 B1
Fabrizia I.... 175 C2
Facha P..... 148 A1
Facinas E.... 162 B2
Fačkov SK.....98 B2
Fadagosa P .. 155 B3
Fadd H...... 112 C2
Faédis I..... 122 A2
Faenza I..... 135 A4
Fafe P....... 148 A1
Fagagna I.... 122 A2
Făgăras RO...17 C6
Fågelberget
S.......... 199 A11
Fågelfors S....62 A3
Fågelmara S ..63 B3
Fågelsta S.....55 B6
Fagerås S.....55 A4
Fagerheim N ..47 B4
Fagerhøy N...48 A1
Fagerhult S....62 A3
Fagerlund N...48 B2
Fagernes
Oppland N 47 B6
Troms N 192 C3
Fagersanna S ..55 B5
Fagersta S....50 B2
Fåglavik S.....55 B4
Fagnano Castello
I........... 174 B2
Fagnières F ...91 C4
Faido CH..... 107 C3
Fains-Véel F...91 C5
Fairford UK....44 B2
Fairlie UK.....34 C3
Fajsz H...... 112 C2
Fakenham UK..41 C4
Fåker S...... 199 B11
Fakse DK......65 A5
Fakse Ladeplads
DK...........65 A5
Falaise F......89 B3
Falcade I..... 121 A4
Falcarragh IRL ..26 A2
Falces E..... 144 B2
Fălciu RO.....17 B8
Falconara I... 177 B3
Falconara
Marittima I... 136 B2
Falcone I..... 177 A4
Faldingworth
UK...........40 B3
Falerum S.....56 B2
Falkenberg
Bayern D 95 B4
Bayern D 95 C4
Brandenburg
D........... 83 A5

Falkenberg
continued
S 60 C2
Falkensee D 74 B2
Falkenstein
Bayern D 95 B4
Sachsen D 83 B4
Falkenthal D 74 B2
Falkirk UK 35 B4
Falkland UK 35 B4
Falköping S 55 B4
Fall D 108 B2
Falla S 56 B1
Fallingbostel D 72 B2
Falmouth UK 42 B1
Falset E 147 C1
Fălticeni RO 17 B7
Falun S 50 B2
Famagusta CY 181 A2
Fammestad N 46 B2
Fana N 46 B2
Fanano I 135 A3
Fanari GR 182 D3
Fanjeaux F 146 A3
Fano I 136 B2
Fântânele RO 126 A3
Fão P 148 A1
Fara in Sabina
I 168 A2
Faramontanos de
Tábara E 149 A4
Fara Novarese
I 119 B5
Farasdues E 144 B2
Fårbo S 62 A4
Fareham UK 44 C2
Färentuna S 57 A3
Färgelanda S 54 B2
Färila S 200 E1
Faringdon UK 44 B2
Faringe S 51 C5
Farini I 120 C2
Fariza E 149 A3
Färjestaden S 63 B4
Farkadona GR 182 D4
Farkasfa H 111 C3
Farlete E 153 A3
Färlöv S 61 C4
Farmos H 113 B3
Farnă SK 112 B2
Färnäs S 50 B1
Farnborough
UK 44 B3
Farnese I 168 A1
Farnham UK 44 B3
Farnroda D 82 B2
Faro P 160 B2
Fåro S 57 C5
Fårösund S 57 C5
Farra d'Alpago
I 122 A1
Farranfore IRL 29 B2
Farre DK 59 B2
Farsala GR 182 D4
Farsø DK 58 B2
Farsund N 52 B2
Farum DK 61 D2
Fårup DK 58 B2
Fasana I 172 B1
Fasano I 173 B3
Fáskrúðsfjörður
IS 191 C11
Fassberg D 72 B3
Fastiv UA 13 C8
Fastnäs S 49 B5
Fátima P 154 B2
Fatmomakke
S 195 E6
Fättjaur S 195 E6
Faucogney-et-la-
Mer F 105 B5
Fauguerolles
F 128 B3
Faulenrost D 74 A1
Faulquemont F 92 B2
Fauquembergues
F 78 B2
Fauske N 194 C6
Fauville-en-Caux
F 89 A4
Fauvillers B 92 B1
Fåvang N 48 A2
Favara
E 159 B3
I 176 B2
Faverges F 118 B3
Faverney F 105 B5
Faversham UK 45 B4
Favignana I 176 B1
Fawley UK 44 C2
Fay-aux-Loges
F 103 B4
Fayence F 132 B2
Fayet F 130 B1
Fayl-Billot F 105 B4
Fayón E 153 A4
Fearn UK 32 D3
Fécamp F 89 A4
Feda N 52 B2
Fedje N 46 B1
Feeny UK 27 B3
Fegen S 60 B3
Fegyvernek H 113 B4
Fehrbellin D 74 B1
Fehring A 111 C3
Feichten A 108 B1
Feiring N 48 B3
Feistritz im
Rosental A 110 C1
Feketić SRB 126 B1
Felanitx E 167 B3
Feld am See A 109 C4
Feldbach A 110 C2
Feldberg D 74 A2
Feldkirch A 107 B4
Feldkirchen in
Kärnten A 109 C5
Feldkirchen-
Westerham
D 108 B2
Felgueiras P 148 A1
Felitto I 172 B1
Félix E 164 C2
Felixstowe UK 45 B5
Felizzano I 119 C5
Felletin F 116 B2
Fellingsbro S 56 A1
Felnac RO 126 A3
Felnémet H 113 B4
Felpéc H 111 B4
Fels am Wagram
A 97 C3
Felsberg D 81 A5
Felsönyék H 112 C2
Felsöszentiván
H 126 A1
Felsöszentmárton
H 125 B3
Felsözsolca H 113 A4
Felsted DK 64 B2
Feltre I 121 A4
Femsjö S 60 C3
Fenagh IRL 26 B3
Fene E 140 A2
Fenestrelle I 119 B4
Fénétrange F 92 C3
Feneu F 102 B1
Fengersfors S 54 B3
Fenit IRL 29 B2
Fensmark DK 65 A4
Fenwick UK 36 A2
Feolin Ferry UK 34 C1
Ferbane IRL 28 A4
Ferdinandovac
HR 124 A3
Ferdinandshof
D 74 A2
Fère-Champenoise
F 91 C3
Fère-en-Tardenois
F 91 B3
Ferentillo I 168 A2
Ferentino I 169 B3
Feres GR 183 C8
Feria E 155 C4
Feričanci HR 125 B3
Ferizli TR 187 B5
Ferla I 177 B3
Ferlach A 110 C1
Ferleiten A 109 B3
Fermil P 148 A2
Fermo I 136 B2
Fermoselle E 149 A3
Fermoy IRL 29 B3
Fernancabellero
E 157 A4
Fernán Nuñéz
E 163 A3
Fernán Peréz
E 164 C2
Fernão Ferro
P 154 C1
Fernay-Voltaire
F 118 A3
Ferndown UK 43 B5
Ferness UK 32 D3
Fernhurst UK 44 B3
Ferns IRL 30 B2
Ferpécle CH 119 A4
Ferrals-les-
Corbières F 146 A3
Ferrandina I 172 B2
Ferrara I 121 C4
Ferrara di Monte
Baldo I 121 B3
Ferreira E 141 A3
Ferreira do
Alentejo P 160 A1
Ferreira do Zêzere
P 154 B2
Ferreras de Abajo
E 141 C4
Ferreras de Arriba
E 141 C4
Ferreries E 167 B4
Ferreruela E 152 A2
Ferreruela de
Tabara E 149 A3
Ferret CH 119 B4
Ferrette F 106 B2
Ferriere I 120 C2
Ferrière-la-Grande
F 79 B3
Ferrières
Hautes-Pyrénées
F 145 A3
Loiret F 103 A4
Oise F 90 B2
Ferrières-sur-
Sichon F 117 A3
Ferrol E 140 A2
Ferryhill UK 37 B5
Fertörakos H 111 B3
Fertöszentmiklós
H 111 B3
Ferwerd NL 70 A2
Festieux F 91 B3
Festøy N 198 C3
Festvåg N 194 C5
Feteşti RO 17 C7
Fethard
Tipperary IRL 29 B4
Wexford IRL 30 B2
Fethiye TR 188 C4
Fetsund N 48 C3
Fettercairn UK 35 B5
Feucht D 95 B3
Feuchtwangen
D 94 B2
Feudingen D 81 B4
Feuges F 91 C4
Feuquières F 90 B1
Feurs F 117 B4
Fevik N 53 B4
Ffestiniog UK 38 B3
Fiamignano I 169 A3
Fiano I 119 B4
Ficarazzi I 176 A2
Ficarolo I 121 C4
Fichtelberg D 95 A3
Ficulle I 135 C5
Fidenza I 120 C3
Fidjeland N 52 B2
Fieberbrunn
A 109 B3
Fier AL 182 C1
Fiera di Primiero
I 121 A4
Fiesch CH 119 A5
Fiesso Umbertiano
I 121 C4
Figari F 180 B2
Figeac F 116 C2
Figeholm S 62 A4
Figgjo N 52 B1
Figline Valdarno
I 135 B4
Figols E 145 B4
Figueira da Foz
P 148 B1
Figueira de Castelo
Rodrigo P 149 B3
Figueira dos
Caveleiros P 160 A1
Figueiredo P 154 B3
Figueiredo de Alva
P 148 B2
Figueiródos Vinhos
P 154 B2
Figueres E 147 B3
Figueroles E 153 B3
Figueruela de
Arriba E 141 C4
Filadélfia I 175 C2
Fil'akovo SK 99 C3
Filderstadt D 94 C1
Filey UK 41 A3
Filiaşi RO 17 C5
Filiates GR 182 D2
Filiatra GR 184 B2
Filipstad S 55 A5
Filisur CH 107 C4
Fillan N 198 B5
Filotio GR 185 B6
Filottrano I 136 B2
Filskov DK 59 C2
Filton UK 43 A4
Filtvet N 54 A1
Filzmoos A 109 B4
Finale Emília I 121 C4
Finale Lígure I 133 A4
Fiñana E 164 B2
Finby FIN 51 B7
Fincham UK 41 C4
Finchingfield
UK 45 B4
Findhorn UK 32 D3
Findochty UK 33 D4
Finike TR 189 C5
Finkenberg A 108 B2
Finnea IRL 27 C3
Finneidfjord
N 195 D4
Finnerödja S 55 B5
Finnskog N 49 B4
Finnsnes N 194 A9
Finntorp S 54 A3
Finócchio I 168 B2
Finsjö S 62 A4
Finsland N 52 B3
Finspång S 56 B1
Finsterwalde D 84 A1
Finsterwolde
NL 71 A4
Finstown UK 33 B3
Fintona UK 27 B3
Fionnphort UK 34 B1
Fiorenzuola d'Arda
I 120 C2
Firenze = Florence
I 135 B4
Firenzuola I 135 A4
Firmi F 130 A1
Firminy F 117 B4
Firmo I 174 B2
Fischamend Markt
A 111 A3
Fischbach
A 110 B2
D 93 B3
Fischbeck D 73 B5
Fischen D 107 B5
Fishbourne UK 44 C2
Fishguard UK 39 C2
Fiskardo GR 184 A1
Fiskebäckskil S 54 B2
Fiskebøl N 194 B5
Fismes F 91 B3
Fisterra E 140 B1
Fitero E 144 B2
Fitjar N 46 C2
Fiuggi I 169 B3
Fiumata I 169 A3
Fiumefreddo
Brúzio I 174 B2
Fiumefreddo di
Sicília I 177 B4
Fiumicino I 168 B2
Fivemiletown
UK 27 B3
Fivizzano I 134 A3
Fjälkinge S 63 B2
Fjällåsen S 196 B3
Fjällbacka S 54 B2
Fjæra N 46 C3
Fjärdhundra S 56 A2
Fjellerup DK 58 B3
Fjerritslev DK 58 A2
Fjordgard N 194 A8
Fjugesta S 55 A5
Flå N 47 B6
Flåbygd N 53 A4
Flaça E 147 B3
Flace F 117 A4
Fladungen D 82 B2
Flaine F 118 A3
Flaka FIN 51 B7
Flåm N 46 B4
Flamatt CH 106 C2
Flamborough
UK 41 A3
Flammersfeld
D 81 B3
Flassans-sur-Issole
F 132 B2
Flatdal N 53 A4
Flatebø N 46 B3
Flateby N 48 C3
Flateland N 52 A3
Flateyri IS 190 A2
Flatøydegard
N 47 B6
Flatråker N 46 C2
Flattach A 109 C4
Flatvarp S 62 A4
Flauenskjold
DK 58 A3
Flavigny-sur-
Moselle F 92 C2
Flavy-le-Martel
F 90 B3
Flawil CH 107 B4
Flayosc F 132 B2
Flechtingen D 73 B4
Fleckeby D 64 B2
Fleet UK 44 B3
Fleetmark D 73 B4
Fleetwood UK 38 A3
Flehingen D 93 B4
Flekke N 46 A2
Flekkefjord N 52 B2
Flen S 56 A2
Flensburg D 64 B2
Fleringe S 57 C4
Flerohopp S 62 B3
Flers F 88 B3
Flesberg N 47 C6
Fleurance F 129 C3
Fleuré F 115 B4
Fleurier CH 105 C5
Fleurus B 79 B4
Fleury
Hérault F 130 B2
Yonne F 104 B2
Fleury-les-Aubrais
F 103 B3
Fleury-sur-Andelle
F 89 A5
Fleury-sur-Orne
F 89 A3
Flieden D 81 B5
Flimby UK 36 B3
Flims CH 107 C4
Flines-lèz-Raches
F 78 B3
Flint UK 38 A3
Flirey F 92 C1
Flirsch A 108 B1
Flisa N 49 B4
Flisby S 62 A2
Fliseryd S 62 A4
Flix E 153 A4
Flixecourt F 90 A2
Flize F 91 B4
Flobecq B 79 B3
Floby S 55 B4
Floda S 60 B2
Flodden UK 37 A4
Flogny-la-Chapelle
F 104 B2
Flöha D 83 B5
Flonheim D 93 B4
Florac F 130 A2
Floreffe B 79 B4
Florence = Firenze
I 135 B4
Florennes B 79 B4
Florensac F 130 B2
Florentin F 129 C5
Florenville B 91 B5
Flores de Avila
E 150 B2
Floresta I 177 B3
Floreşti MD 17 B8
Florídia I 177 B4
Florina GR 182 C3
Florø N 46 A2
Flörsheim D 93 A4
Floss D 95 B4
Fluberg N 48 B2
Flúðir IS 190 C5
Flühli CH 106 C3
Flumet F 118 B3
Fluminimaggiore
I 179 C2
Flums CH 107 B4
Flyeryd S 63 B3
Flygsfors S 62 B3
Foča BIH 139 B4
Foça TR 186 D1
Fochabers UK 32 D3
Focşani RO 17 C7
Foel UK 38 B3
Foeni RO 126 B2
Fogdö S 56 A2
Fóggia I 171 B3
Foglianise I 170 B2
Föglö FIN 51 B7
Fohnsdorf A 110 B1
Foiano della Chiana
I 135 B4
Foix F 146 B2
Fojnica
BIH 139 B3
BIH 139 B4
Fokstua N 198 C6
Földeák H 126 A2
Foldereid N 199 A9
Főldes H 113 B5
Folegandros
GR 185 C5
Folelli F 180 A2
Folgaria I 121 B4
Folgosinho P 148 B2
Folgoso de la
Ribera E 141 B4
Folgoso do Courel
E 141 B3
Foligno I 136 C1
Folkärna S 50 B3
Folkestad N 198 C3
Folkestone UK 45 B5
Follafoss N 199 B8
Folldal N 198 C6
Follebu N 48 A2
Follina I 121 B5
Föllinge S 199 B11
Follónica I 135 C3
Fölsbyn S 54 A3
Foncebadón
E 141 B4
Foncine-le-Bas
F 105 C5
Fondevila E 140 C2
Fondi I 169 B3
Fondo I 121 A4
Fonelas E 164 B1
Fonfría
Teruel E 152 B2
Zamora E 149 A3
Fonn N 46 A3
Fonnes N 46 B1
Fonni I 178 B3
Fontaine F 91 C4
Fontainebleau
F 90 C2
Fontaine de
Vaucluse F 131 B4
Fontaine-Française
F 105 B4
Fontaine-le-Dun
F 89 A4
Fontan F 133 A3
Fontanarejo E 157 A3
Fontane I 133 A3
Fontanélice I 135 A4
Fontanières F 116 A2
Fontanosas E 157 B3
Fonteblanda I 168 A1
Fontenay-le-Comte
F 114 B3
Fontenay-Trésigny
F 90 C2
Fontevrault-
l'Abbaye F 102 B2
Fontiveros E 150 B3
Fontoy F 92 B1
Fontpédrouse
F 146 B3
Font-Romeu F 146 B3
Fontstown IRL 30 A2
Fonyód H 111 C4
Fonz E 145 B4
Fonzaso I 121 A4
Fóppolo I 120 A2
Föra S 62 A4
Forbach
D 93 C4
F 92 B2
Forcall E 153 B3
Forcalquier F 132 B1
Forcarei E 140 B2
Forchheim D 94 B3
Forchtenau A 111 B3
Forchtenberg
D 94 B1
Ford UK 34 B2
Førde
Hordaland N 52 A1
Sogn og Fjordane
N 46 A2
Förderstedt D 83 A3
Førdesfjorden
N 52 A1
Fordham UK 45 A4
Fordingbridge
UK 44 C2
Fordon PL 76 A3
Fordongiánus
I 179 C2
Forenza I 172 B1
Foresta di Búrgos
I 178 B2
Forfar UK 35 B5
Forges-les-Eaux
F 90 B1
Foria I 172 B1
Forío I 170 C1
Forjães P 148 A1
Førland N 52 B3
Forlì I 135 A5
Forlimpopoli I 135 A5
Formazza I 119 A5
Formby UK 38 A3
Formerie F 90 B1
Fórmia I 169 B3
Formígine I 135 A3
Formigliana I 119 B5
Formiguères
F 146 B3
Fornalutx E 166 B2
Fornåsa S 56 B1
Fornelli I 178 B2
Fornells E 167 A4
Fornelos de Montes
E 140 B2
Fornes E 163 B4
Forneset N 192 C3
Forni Avoltri I 109 C3
Forni di Sopra
I 122 A1
Forni di Sotto
I 122 A1
Forno
Piemonte I 119 B4
Piemonte I 119 B5
Forno Alpi-Gráie
I 119 B4
Forno di Zoldo
I 121 A5
Fornos de Algodres
P 148 B2
Fornovo di Taro
I 120 C3
Foros do Arrão
P 154 B2
Forráskút H 126 A1
Forres UK 32 D3
Forriolo E 140 B3
Fors S 50 B3
Forsand N 52 B2
Forsbacka S 51 B3
Forserum S 62 A2
Forshaga S 55 A4
Forsheda S 60 B3
Forsinain UK 32 C3
Førslev DK 65 A4
Förslöv S 61 C2
Forsmark
Uppsala S 51 B5
Västerbotten
S 195 E6
Forsmo S 200 C3
Forsnäs S 195 D9
Forsnes N 198 B5
Forssa FIN 8 B3
Forssjöbruk S 56 B2
Forst D 84 A2
Forsvik S 55 B5
Fortanete E 153 B3
Fort Augustus
UK 32 D2
Forte dei Marmi
I 134 B3
Fortezza I 108 C2
Forth UK 35 C4
Fort-Mahon-Plage
F 78 B1
Fortrie UK 33 D4
Fortrose UK 32 D2
Fortun N 47 A4
Fortuna E 165 A3
Fortuneswell
UK 43 B4
Fort William UK 34 B2
Forvik N 195 E3
Fos F 145 B4
Fosdinovo I 134 A3
Foss N 47 B6
Fossacésia I 169 A4
Fossano I 133 A3
Fossato di Vico
I 136 B1
Fossbakken N 194 B8
Fosse-la-Ville B 79 B4
Fossombrone
I 136 B1
Fos-sur-Mer F 131 B3
Fot H 112 B3
Fouchères F 104 A3
Fouesnant F 100 B1
Foug F 92 C1
Fougères F 88 B2
Fougerolles F 105 B5
Foulain F 105 A4
Fountainhall
UK 35 C5
Fouras F 114 C2
Fourchambault
F 104 B2
Fourmies F 91 A4
Fourna GR 182 D3
Fournels F 116 C3
Fourni GR 188 B1
Fournols F 117 B3
Fourques F 146 B3
Fourquevaux
F 146 A2

Fours F........ 104 C2
Fowey UK 42 B2
Foxdale UK 36 B2
Foxford IRL 26 C1
Foyers UK...... 32 D2
Foynes IRL 29 B2
Foz E........... 141 A3
Foza I 121 B4
Foz do Arelho
P.............. 154 B1
Foz do Giraldo
P.............. 155 B3
Frabosa Soprana
I............... 133 A3
Frades de la Sierra
E.............. 149 B4
Fraga E......... 153 A4
Fragagnano I . 173 B3
Frailes E........ 163 A4
Fraire B 79 B4
Fraize F 106 A1
Framlingham
UK 45 A5
Frammersbach
D.............. 94 A1
Framnes N 54 A1
França P 148 B2
Francaltroff F ...92 C2
Francavilla al Mare
I............... 169 A4
Francavilla di Sicilia
I............... 177 B4
Francavilla Fontana
I............... 173 B3
Francavilla in Sinni
I............... 174 A2
Francescas F . 129 B3
Franco P 148 A2
Francofonte I . 177 B3
Francos E....... 151 A4
Frändefors S ...54 B3
Franeker NL.....70 A2
Frangy F 118 A2
Frankenau D....81 A4
Frankenberg
Hessen D 81 A4
Sachsen D 83 B5
Frankenburg
A.............. 109 A4
Frankenfels A. 110 B2
Frankenmarkt
A.............. 109 B4
Frankenthal D . 93 B4
Frankfurt
Brandenburg
D.............. 74 B3
Hessen D 81 B4
Frankrike S . 199 B10
Fränsta S 200 D2
Františkovy Lázně
CZ 83 B4
Franzburg D 66 B1
Frascati I...... 168 B2
Frasdorf D 109 B3
Fraserburgh
UK 33 D4
Frashër AL.... 182 C2
Frasne F 105 C5
Frasnes-lez-
Anvaing B......79 B3
Frasseto F..... 180 B2
Frastanz A 107 B4
Fratel P 155 B3
Fratta Todina
I............... 135 C5
Frauenau D.... 95 B5
Frauenfeld CH 107 B3
Frauenkirchen
A.............. 111 B3
Frauenstein D . .83 B5
Frauental A ... 110 C2
Frayssinet F .. 129 B4
Frayssinet-le-Gélat
F.............. 129 B4
Frechas P 149 A2
Frechen D.......80 B2
Frechilla E 142 B2
Freckenhorst D .71 C4
Fredeburg D ...81 A4
Fredelsloh D ...82 A1
Fredeng N 48 B2
Fredensborg
DK 61 D2
Fredericia DK .57 C2
Frederiks DK...59 B2
Frederikshavn
DK 58 A3
Frederikssund
DK 61 D2
Frederiksværk
DK 61 D2
Fredrika S 200 B4
Fredriksberg S . 50 B1
Fredriksdal S ...62 A2
Fredrikstad N...54 A1
Fregenal de la
Sierra E 161 A3
Fregene I 168 B2
Freiberg D 83 B5
Freiburg
Baden-Württemberg
D.............. 106 B2
Niedersachsen
D.............. 64 C2
Freienhagen D.81 A5
Freienhufen D..84 A1
Freiensteinau
D.............. 81 B5
Freihung D 95 B3
Freilassing D. 109 B3
Freisen D 92 B3
Freising D.......95 C3
Freistadt A 96 C2
Freital D 84 A1
Freixedas P ... 149 B2
Freixo de Espada à
Cinta P 149 A3
Fréjus F 132 B2
Fremdingen
D.............. 94 C2
Frenštát pod
Radhoštěm
CZ 98 B2
Freren D 71 B4
Freshford IRL ...30 B1
Freshwater
UK 44 C2
Fresnay-sur-Sarthe
F...............89 B4
Fresneda de la
Sierra E 152 B1
Fresneda de la
Sierra Tiron
E.............. 143 B3
Fresnedillas
E.............. 151 B3
Fresnes-en-Woevre
F...............92 B1
Fresne-St Mamès
F.............. 105 B4
Fresno Alhandiga
E.............. 150 B2
Fresno de la Ribera
E.............. 150 A2
Fresno de la Vega
E.............. 142 B1
Fresno de Sayago
E.............. 149 A4
Fresnoy-Folny
F...............90 B1
Fresnoy-le-Grand
F...............91 B3
Fressenville F . .90 A1
Fresvik N 46 A3
Frétigney F ... 105 B4
Freudenberg
Baden-Württemberg
D.............. 94 B1
Nordrhein-
Westfalen D. . 81 B3
Freudenstadt
D.............. 93 C4
Freux B 92 B1
Frévent F 78 B2
Freyburg D 83 A3
Freyenstein D .73 A5
Freyming-
Merlebach F ...92 B2
Freystadt D 95 B3
Freyung D 96 C1
Frias de
Albarracin E . 152 B2
Fribourg CH .. 106 C2
Frick CH...... 106 B3
Fridafors S 63 B2
Fridaythorpe
UK 40 A3
Friedberg
Bayern D 94 C2
Hessen D 81 B4
Friedeburg D . .71 A4
Friedewald D ..82 B1
Friedland
Brandenburg
D.............. 74 B3
Mecklenburg-
Vorpommern
D.............. 74 A2
Niedersachsen
D.............. 82 A1
Friedrichroda
D.............. 82 B2
Friedrichsdorf
D.............. 81 B4
Friedrichshafen
D.............. 107 B4
Friedrichskoog
D.............. 64 B1
Friedrichstadt
D.............. 64 B2
Friedrichswalde
D.............. 74 A2
Friesach A 110 C1
Friesack D 73 B5
Friesenheim D. 93 C3
Friesoythe D ...71 A4
Friggesund S . 200 E2
Frigliana E 163 B4
Frihetsli N ... 192 D3
Frillesås S 60 B2
Frinnaryd S 62 A2
Frinton-on-Sea
UK 45 B5
Friockheim UK .35 B5
Friol E......... 140 A3
Fristad S 60 B2
Fritsla S.........60 B2
Fritzlar D 81 A5
Frizington UK . .36 B3
Frödinge S 62 A4
Froges F 118 B2
Frohburg D 83 A4
Frohnhausen D .81 B4
Frohnleiten A. 110 B2
Froissy F 90 B2
Frombork PL...69 A4
Frome UK 43 A4
Frómista E 142 B2
Fröndenberg
D.............. 81 A3
Fronsac F 128 B2
Front I 119 B4
Fronteira P ... 155 B3
Frontenay-Rohan-
Rohan F...... 114 B3
Frontenhausen
D.............. 95 C4
Frontignan F . 130 B2
Fronton F 129 C4
Fröseke S 62 B3
Frosinone I ... 169 B3
Frosolone I ... 170 B2
Frosta N 199 B7
Frøstrup DK....58 A1
Frosunda S 57 A4
Frouard F 92 C2
Frövi S..........56 A1
Frøyset N 46 B2
Fruges F 78 B2
Frutigen CH... 106 C2
Frýdek-Místek
CZ 98 B2
Frýdlant D 84 B3
Frydlant nad
Ostravicí CZ. .98 B2
Frygnowo PL...77 A5
Fryšták CZ 98 B1
Fucécchio I... 135 B3
Fuencaliente
Ciudad Real
E.............. 157 A4
Ciudad Real E. 157 B3
Fuencemillán
E.............. 151 B4
Fuendejalón
E.............. 144 C2
Fuengirola E . 163 B3
Fuenlabrada
E.............. 151 B4
Fuenlabrada de los
Montes E..... 156 A3
Fuensalida E . 151 B3
Fuensanta E . 164 B3
Fuensanta de
Martos E..... 163 A4
Fuente-Alamo
E.............. 158 C2
Fuente-Álamo de
Murcia E..... 165 B3
Fuentealbilla
E.............. 158 B2
Fuente al Olmo de
Iscar E....... 150 A3
Fuentecén E... 151 A4
Fuente Dé E ... 142 A2
Fuente de Cantos
E.............. 155 C4
Fuente del Arco
E.............. 156 B2
Fuente del Conde
E.............. 163 A3
Fuente del Maestre
E.............. 155 C4
Fuente de Santa
Cruz E....... 150 A3
Fuente el Fresno
E.............. 157 A4
Fuente el Saz de
Jarama E..... 151 B4
Fuente el Sol
E.............. 150 A3
Fuenteguinaldo
E.............. 149 B3
Fuentelapeña
E.............. 150 A2
Fuentelcésped
E.............. 151 A4
Fuentelespino de
Haro E 158 B1
Fuentelespino de
Moya E 158 B2
Fuentenovilla
E.............. 151 B4
Fuente Obejuna
E.............. 156 B2
Fuente Palmera
E.............. 162 A2
Fuentepelayo
E.............. 151 A3
Fuentepinilla
E.............. 151 A5
Fuenterroble de
Salvatierra E . 150 B2
Fuenterrobles
E.............. 158 B2
Fuentes E 158 B1
Fuentes de
Andalucía E . 162 A2
Fuentes de Ebro
E.............. 153 A3
Fuentes de Jiloca
E.............. 152 A2
Fuentes de la
Alcarria E.... 151 B5
Fuentes de León
E.............. 161 A3
Fuentes de Nava
E.............. 142 B2
Fuentes de Oñoro
E.............. 149 B3
Fuentes de Ropel
E.............. 142 B1
Fuentespalda
E.............. 153 B4
Fuentespina E 151 A4
Fuente-Tójar
E.............. 163 A3
Fuente Vaqueros
E.............. 163 A4
Fuentidueña
E.............. 151 A4
Fuentidueña de
Tajo E 151 B4
Fuerte del Rey
E.............. 157 C4
Fügen A....... 108 B2
Fuglebjerg DK . 65 A4
Fuglevik N 54 A1
Fuhrberg D 72 B2
Fulda D 82 B1
Fulgatore I ... 176 B1
Fully CH....... 119 A4
Fulnek CZ 98 B1
Fülöpszállás
H............. 112 C3
Fulpmes A.... 108 B2
Fulunäs S 49 A5
Fumay F 91 B4
Fumel F 129 B3
Funäsdalen S . 199 C9
Fundão P 148 B2
Funzie UK 33 A6
Furadouro P .. 148 B1
Fure N 46 A2
Fürstenau D ...71 B4
Furstenau D ...81 A4
Fürstenberg D .74 A2
Fürstenfeld A . 111 B3
Fürstenfeldbruck
D.............. 108 A2
Fürstenstein D. 96 C1
Fürstenwalde
D.............. 74 B3
Fürstenwerder
D.............. 74 A2
Fürstenzell D ..96 C1
Furta H........ 113 B5
Fürth
Bayern D 94 B2
Hessen D 93 B4
Furth im Wald
D.............. 95 B4
Furtwangen
D.............. 106 A3
Furuby S 62 B3
Furudal S.......50 A2
Furuflaten N . . 192 C4
Furulund S 61 D3
Furusjö S........60 B3
Fusa N 46 B2
Fuscaldo I.... 174 B2
Fusch an der
Grossglockner-
strasse A 109 B3
Fushë Arrëz
AL 182 A2
Fushë-Krujë
AL 182 B1
Fusina I....... 122 B1
Fusio CH 107 C3
Füssen D...... 108 B1
Fustiñana E... 144 B2
Futog SRB 126 B1
Futrikelv N ... 192 C3
Füzesabony H 113 B4
Füzesgyarmat
H............. 113 B5
Fužine HR 123 B3
Fylling S 61 C2
Fynshav DK 64 B2
Fyresdal N 53 A4

G

Gaaldorf A 110 B1
Gabaldón E... 158 B2
Gabarret F ... 128 C2
Gabčíkovo SK. 111 B4
Gąbin PL........77 B4
Gabriac F..... 130 A1
Gabrovo BG... 17 D6
Gaby I......... 119 B4
Gacé F..........89 B4
Gacko BIH.... 139 B4
Gäddede S ... 199 A11
Gadebusch D . . 65 C4
Gadmen CH.. 106 C3
Gádor E....... 164 C2
Gádoros H ... 113 C4
Gael F........ 101 A3
Găeşti RO 17 C6
Gaeta I........ 169 B3
Gafanhoeira P 154 C2
Gaflenz A..... 110 B1
Gagarin RUS ... 9 E9
Gaggenau D...93 C4
Gagliano
Castelferrato
I............... 177 B3
Gagliano del Capo
I............... 173 C4
Gagnet S 50 B2
Gaibanella I . 121 C4
Gaildorf D 94 B1
Gaillac F 129 C4
Gaillefontaine
F...............90 B1
Gaillon F 89 A5
Gainsborough
UK 40 B3
Gairloch UK ...31 B3
Gairlochy UK . . 34 B3
Gáiro I........ 179 C3
Gaj
HR 124 B3
SRB 127 C3
Gaja-la-Selve
F............. 146 A2
Gajanejos E.. 151 B5
Gajary SK......97 C4
Gajdobra SRB. 126 B1
Galan F 145 A4
Galanta SK.... 111 A4
Galapagar E.. 151 B3
Galápagos E . 151 B4
Galaroza E.... 161 B3
Galashiels UK . . 35 C5
Galatas GR.... 185 B4
Galati RO 17 C8
Galatina I 173 B4
Galatista GR . 183 C5
Galátone I 173 B4
Galaxidi GR . 184 A3
Galdakao E... 143 A4
Galeata I...... 135 B4
Galende E..... 141 B4
Galera E....... 164 B2
Galéria F...... 180 A1
Galgamácsa
H............. 112 B3
Galgate UK 38 A4
Galgon F 128 B2
Galinduste E... 150 B2
Galinoporni
CY 181 A3
Galisteo E.... 155 B4
Galizes P 62 B3
Galków PL......87 A3
Gallarate I 120 B1
Gallardon F 90 C1
Gallegos de
Argañán E ... 149 B3
Gallegos del
Solmirón E... 150 B2
Galleguillos de
Campos E ... 142 B1
Galleno I...... 135 B3
Galliate I...... 120 B1
Gallicano I.... 134 A3
Gállio I........ 121 B4
Gallipoli I 173 B3
Gallipoli = Gelibolu
TR............ 186 B1
Gällivare S ... 196 B3
Gallizien A.... 110 C1
Gallneukirchen
A.............. 96 C2
Gallocanta E . 152 B2
Gällstad S 60 B3
Gallur E....... 144 C2
Galmisdale UK .31 C2
Galmpton UK ..43 B3
Galston UK 36 A2
Galta N 52 A1
Galtelli I...... 178 B3
Galten DK......59 B2
Galtür A....... 107 C5
Galve de Sorbe
E.............. 151 A4
Galveias P ... 154 B2
Gálvez E 157 A3
Galway IRL 28 A2
Gamaches F....90 B1
Gámbara I.... 120 B3
Gambárie I... 175 C1
Gambassi Terme
I............... 135 B3
Gambatesa I . 170 B2
Gambolò I.... 120 B1
Gaming A..... 110 B2
Gamla Uppsala
S.............. 51 C4
Gamleby S 62 A4
Gamlingay UK . . 44 A3
Gammelgarn S. 57 C4
Gammelstad
S.............. 196 D5
Gammertingen
D.............. 107 A4
Gams CH 107 B4
Gamvik
Finnmark N . . 192 B6
Finnmark N . . 193 A12
Gan F......... 145 A3
Gáname E.... 149 A3
Ganda di Martello
I............... 108 C1
Gandarela P . 148 A1
Ganddal N 52 B1
Ganderkesee D. 72 A1
Gandesa E.... 153 A4
Gandia E...... 159 C3
Gandino I..... 120 B2
Gandrup DK ...38 A3
Ganges F 130 B2
Gånghester S ...60 B3
Gangi I........ 177 B3
Gangkofen D . . 95 C4
Gannat F 116 A3
Gannay-sur-Loire
F.............. 104 C2
Gänserndorf A ..97 C4
Ganzlin D 73 A5
Gap F 132 A2
Gara H 125 A5
Garaballa E... 158 B2
Garaguso I ... 172 B2
Garbayuela E . 156 A2
Garbhall UK ...34 B2
Garbsen D 72 B2
Garching D ... 109 A3
Garciaz E..... 156 A2
Garcihernández
E.............. 150 B2
Garcillán E ... 151 B3
Garcinarro E.. 151 B5
Garciosobaco E 162 B2
Gárdal 181 C4
Gardanne F .. 131 B4
Gárdárslõ S 49 B5
Gárdby S 63 B4
Gardelegen D ..73 B4
Gardermoen N .48 B3
Gardiki GR ... 182 E3
Garding D 64 B1
Gardone Riviera
I............... 121 B3
Gardone Val
Trómpia I ... 120 B3
Gárdony H 112 B2
Gardouch F .. 146 A2
Gårdsjö S 55 B5
Gårdskär S 51 B4
Gards Köpinge
S.............. 63 C2
Garein F 128 B2
Garelochhead
UK 34 B3
Garéoult F ... 132 B1
Gareśnica HR . 124 B2
Garéssio I 133 A4
Garforth UK ...40 B2
Gargaliani GR 184 B2
Gargaligas E . 156 A2
Gargallo E ... 153 B3
Garganta la Olla
E.............. 150 B2
Gargantiel E . 156 B3
Gargellen A... 107 C4
Gargilesse-
Dampierre F . 103 C3
Gargnano I... 121 B3
Gargnäs S.... 195 E8
Gárgoles de Abajo
E.............. 152 B1
Gargrave UK ...40 B1
Garitz D........73 C5
Garlasco I.... 120 B1
Garlieston UK . . 36 B2
Garlin F 128 C2
Garlitos E 156 B2
Garmisch-
Partenkirchen
D.............. 108 B2
Garnat-sur-
Engièvre F .. 104 C2
Garpenberg S . . 50 B3
Garphyttan S . .55 A5
Garray F 143 C4
Garrel D........71 B5
Garriguella E . 146 B4
Garrison UK ...26 B2
Garrovillas E . 155 B4
Garrucha E... 164 B3
Gars-am-Kamp
A.............. 97 C3
Gârsås S 50 B1
Garstang UK ...38 A4
Gartow D 73 A4
Gartz D.........74 A3
Gærum DK 58 A3
Garvagh UK ...27 B4
Garvão P 160 B1
Garve UK 32 D2
Garwolin PL...12 C4
Garz D..........66 B2
Garzyn PL......85 A4
Gąsawa PL 76 B2
Gåsborn S......49 C6
Gaschurn A ... 107 C5
Gascueña E .. 152 B1
Gasny F 90 B1
Gąsocin PL.....77 B5
Gastes F 128 B1
Gastouni GR . 184 B2
Gastouri GR . . 182 D1
Gata
E.............. 149 B3
HR 138 B2
Gata de Gorgos
E.............. 159 C4
Gătaia RO 16 B4
Gatchina RUS ... 9 C7
Gatehouse of Fleet
UK 36 B2
Gátér H 113 C3
Gateshead UK . . 37 B5
Gátova E...... 159 B3
Gattendorf A . 111 A3
Gatteo a Mare
I............... 136 A1
Gattinara I ... 119 B5
Gattorna I.... 134 A2
Gaucín E...... 162 B2
Gaulstad N... 199 B9
Gaupne N 47 A4
Gautefall N 53 A4
Gauting D 108 A2
Gauto S...... 195 D7
Gava E........ 147 C3
Gávavencsello
H............. 113 A5
Gavi I......... 120 C1
Gaviãn P 154 B3

Gavirate I 120 B1
Gävle S 51 B4
Gavoi I 178 B3
Gavorrano I... 135 C3
Gavray F 88 B2
Gavrio GR..... 185 B5
Gävunda S..... 49 B6
Gaweinstal A ..97 C4
Gaworzyce PL...85 A3
Gawroniec PL...75 A5
Gaydon UK.....44 A2
Gayton UK.....41 C4
Gazipaşa TR... 189 C7
Gazoldo degli
Ippoliti I 121 B3
Gazzuolo I 121 B3
Gbelce SK 112 B2
Gdańsk PL 69 A3
Gdinj HR 138 B2
Gdov RUS 8 C5
Gdów PL 99 B4
Gdynia PL 69 A3
Gea de Albarracin
E 152 B2
Geary UK...... 31 B2
Géaudot F 91 C4
Geaune F 128 C2
Gebesee D 82 A2
Gebiz TR 189 B5
Gebze TR..... 187 B4
Géderlak H 112 C2
Gedern D 81 B5
Gedinne B 91 B4
Gediz TR 187 D4
Gèdre F 145 B4
Gedser DK 65 B4
Gedsted DK.... 58 B2
Geel B......... 79 A4
Geesthacht D .. 72 A3
Geetbets B..... 79 B5
Gefell D........ 83 B3
Gehrden D 72 B2
Gehren D 82 B3
Geilenkirchen
D............. 80 B2
Geilo N........47 B5
Geinsheim D .. 93 B4
Geisa D 82 B1
Geiselhöring D .95 C4
Geiselwind D .. 94 B2
Geisenfeld D .. 95 C3
Geisenhausen
D............. 95 C4
Geisenheim D.. 93 B4
Geising D 84 B1
Geisingen D . 107 B3
Geislingen D ..94 C1
Geistthal A.. 110 B2
Geiterygghytta
N............. 47 B4
Geithain D 83 A4
Geithus N...... 48 C1
Gela I........ 177 B3
Geldermalsen
NL 79 A5
Geldern D..... 80 A2
Geldrop NL ... 80 A1
Geleen NL..... 80 B1
Gelembe TR.. 186 C2
Gelendost TR . 189 A6
Gelibolu = Gallipoli
TR........... 186 B1
Gelida E...... 147 C2
Gelnhausen D ..81 B5
Gelnica SK 99 C4
Gelsa E....... 153 A3
Gelse H 111 C3
Gelsenkirchen
D............. 80 A3
Gelsted DK..... 59 C2
Geltendorf D . 108 A2
Gelterkinden
CH 106 B2
Gelting D 64 B2
Gelu RO 126 A3
Gelves E 162 A1
Gembloux B ...79 B4
Gemeaux F 105 B4
Gémenos F.... 132 B1
Gemerská Poloma
SK........... 99 C4
Gemerská Ves
SK........... 99 C4
Gemert NL.....80 A1
Gemla S........62 B2
Gemlik TR.... 186 B4
Gemmenich B...80 B1
Gemona del Friuli
I............. 122 A2
Gémozac F.... 114 C3

Gemund D......80 B2
Gemünden
Bayern D 94 A1
Hessen D 81 B4
Rheinland-Pfalz
D.............93 B3
Genappe B 79 B4
Génave E 164 A2
Genazzano I.. 169 B2
Gençay F..... 115 B4
Gencsapáti H . 111 B3
Gendringen NL.80 A2
Genelard F.... 104 C3
Genemuiden
NL 70 B3
Generalski Stol
HR 123 B4
Geneva = Genève
CH 118 A3
Genevad S......61 C3
Genève = Geneva
CH 118 A3
Genevrières F . 105 B4
Gengenbach D..93 C4
Genillé F 103 B3
Genk B........80 B1
Genlis F...... 105 B4
Gennep NL.....80 A1
Genner DK..... 64 A2
Gennes F 102 B1
Genoa = Génova
I............. 134 A1
Genola I...... 133 A3
Génova = Genoa
I............. 134 A1
Genowefa PL...76 B3
Gensingen D...93 B3
Gent = Ghent B..79 A3
Genthin D..... 73 B5
Gentioux F 116 B1
Genzano di
Lucánia I 172 B2
Genzano di Roma
I............. 168 B2
Georgenthal D..82 B2
Georgsmarienhütte
D............. 71 B5
Gera D........ 83 B4
Geraards-bergen
B.............79 B3
Gerace I...... 175 C2
Geraki GR.... 184 C3
Gérardmer F . 106 A1
Geras A........97 C3
Gerbéviller F...92 C2
Gerbini I 177 B3
Gerbstedt D ...83 A3
Gerði IS 191 C9
Gerede TR.... 187 B7
Gerena E...... 161 B3
Geretsried D . 108 B2
Gérgal E 164 B2
Gergy F 105 C3
Gerindote E... 150 C3
Gerjen H 112 C2
Gerlos A 108 B3
Germay F......92 C1
Germencik TR. 188 B2
Germering D.. 108 A2
Germersheim
D.............93 B4
Gernika-Lumo
E............ 143 A4
Gernrode D ...82 A3
Gernsbach D ..93 C4
Gernsheim D ..93 B4
Geroda D...... 82 B1
Gerola Alta I . 120 A2
Geroldsgrun D ..83 B3
Gerolsbach D ...95 C3
Gerolstein D ...80 B2
Gerolzhofen D ..94 B2
Gerovo HR.... 123 B3
Gerpinnes B ...79 B4
Gerrards Cross
UK 44 B3
Gerri de la Sal
E............ 147 B2
Gersfeld D.....82 B1
Gerstetten D...94 C2
Gersthofen D..94 C2
Gerstungen D..82 B2
Gerswalde D...74 A2
Gerzat F...... 116 B3
Gerze TR.......23 A8
Gerzen D.......95 C4
Gescher D......71 C4
Geseke D...... 81 A4
Geslau D.......94 B2
Gespunsart F...91 B4
Gesté F 101 B4
Gestorf D......72 B2

Gesualda I 170 C3
Gesunda S..... 50 B1
Gesztely H 113 A4
Geta FIN 51 B6
Getafe E 151 B4
Getinge S......60 C2
Getxo E 143 A4
Geversdorf D ..64 C2
Gevgelija
NMK 182 B4
Gevora del
Caudillo E... 155 C4
Gevrey-
Chambertin F 105 B3
Gex F 118 A3
Gey D.........80 B2
Geyikli TR.... 186 C1
Geysir IS 190 C5
Geyve TR..... 187 B5
Gföhl A........97 C3
Ghedi I....... 120 B3
Ghent = Gent B..79 A3
Gheorgheni RO . 17 B6
Ghigo I....... 119 C4
Ghilarza I 178 B2
Ghisonaccia F . 180 A2
Ghisoni F 180 A2
Gialtra GR.... 182 E4
Gianitsa GR.. 182 C4
Giardinetto
Vécchio I.... 171 B3
Giardini
Naxos I...... 177 B4
Giarratana I.. 177 B3
Giarre I....... 177 B4
Giat F 116 B2
Giaveno I..... 119 B4
Giazza I...... 121 B4
Giba I 179 C2
Gibellina
Nuova I 176 B1
Gibostad N.. 194 A9
Gibraleón E... 161 B3
Gibraltar GBZ. 162 B2
Gic H 111 B4
Gideå S 200 C5
Gideåkroken
S 200 B3
Gidle PL......86 B3
Giebelstadt D...94 B1
Gieboldehausen
D............. 82 A2
Gielniów PL....87 A4
Gielow D......74 A1
Gien F 103 B4
Giengen D 94 C2
Giens F 132 B2
Giera RO 126 B2
Gieselwerder D..81 A5
Giessen D......81 B4
Gieten NL......71 A3
Giethoorn NL ..70 B3
Giffaumont-
Champaubert
F.............91 C4
Gifford UK.....35 C5
Gifhorn D 73 B3
Gige H 125 A3
Gignac F 130 B2
Gijón = Xixón
E............ 142 A1
Gilena E 162 A3
Gilford UK.....27 B4
Gillberga S.....55 A3
Gilleleje DK.....61 C2
Gilley F 105 B5
Gilley-sur-Loire
F............ 104 C2
Gillingham
Dorset UK 43 A4
Medway UK.... 45 B4
Gilocourt F....90 B2
Gilserberg D...81 B5
Gilsland UK....37 B4
Gilze NL.......79 A4
Gimåt S 200 C4
Gimo S........51 B5
Gimont F 129 C3
Ginasservis F . 132 B1
Gingelom B....79 B5
Gingst D.......66 B2
Ginosa I 171 C4
Ginzling A 108 B2
Gióes P....... 160 B2
Gióia dei Marsi
I............. 169 B3
Gióia del Colle
I............. 173 B2
Gióia Sannitica
I............. 170 B2
Gióia Táuro I . 175 C1
Gioiosa Iónica
I............. 175 C2

Gioiosa Marea
I............. 177 A3
Giosla UK......31 A2
Giovinazzo I .. 171 B4
Girifalco I 175 C2
Giromagny F . 106 B1
Girona E 147 C3
Gironcourt-sur-
Vraine F...... 92 C1
Gironella E ... 147 B2
Gironville-sous-
les-Côtes F....92 C1
Gisburn UK....40 B1
Giske N....... 198 C2
Gislaved S..... 60 B3
Gisley DK 59 C3
Gisors F....... 90 B1
Gissi I 170 A2
Gistad S....... 56 B1
Gistel B....... 78 A2
Gistrup DK 58 B3
Giswil CH 106 C3
Githio GR 184 C3
Giugliano in
Campania I .. 170 C2
Giulianova I.. 136 C2
Giulvăz RO... 126 B2
Giurgiu RO... 17 D6
Give DK 59 C2
Givet F....... 91 A4
Givors F...... 117 B4
Givry
B............. 79 B4
F............ 104 C3
Givry-en-
Argonne F 91 C4
Givskud DK 59 C2
Gizalki PL.....76 B2
Gizeux F 102 B2
Gizycko PL.....12 A4
Gizzeria I 175 C2
Gizzeria Lido I. 175 C2
Gjedved DK ...59 C2
Gjegjan AL.. 182 B2
Gjendesheim N.47 A5
Gjerde N......46 B3
Gjerlev DK.....58 B3
Gjermundshamn
N............. 46 B2
Gjerrild DK.... 58 B3
Gjerstad N 53 B5
Gjesås N 49 B4
Gjesvær N ... 193 A9
Gjirokastër AL 182 C2
Gjøfjell N 54 A1
Gjøl DK 58 A2
Gjøra N 198 C6
Gjøvik N...... 48 B2
Gladbeck D ...80 A2
Gladenbach D ..81 B4
Gladstad N... 195 E2
Glamis UK.....35 B4
Glamoč BIH .. 138 A2
Glamsbjerg DK. 59 C3
Gland CH 105 C5
Glandorf D 71 B4
Glanegg A ... 110 C1
Glanshammar
S.............56 A1
Glarus CH 107 B4
Glasgow UK...35 C3
Glashütte
Bayern D ... 108 B2
Sachsen D 84 B1
Glastonbury
UK 43 A4
Glatzau A 110 C2
Glauchau D ...83 B4
Glava S........54 A3
Glavatičevo
BIH.......... 139 B4
Glavičice BIH . 127 C1
Gŭlŭbovo BG. 183 A7
Glein
A............. 110 B1
N............ 195 D3
Gleinstätten
A............. 110 C2
Gleisdorf A .. 110 B2
Glenamoy IRL..26 B1
Glenarm UK...27 B5
Glenavy UK....27 B4
Glenbarr UK...34 C2
Glenbeigh IRL..29 B2
Glenbrittle UK. 31 B2
Glencoe UK....34 B2
Glencolumbkille
IRL.......... 26 B2
Glendalough
IRL.......... 30 A2
Glenealy IRL...30 B2
Glenelg UK.... 31 B3
Glenfinnan UK. 34 B2
Glengarriff IRL .29 C2

Glenluce UK.....36 B2
Glennamaddy
IRL.......... 28 A3
Glenrothes UK. 35 B4
Glenties IRL....26 B2
Glesborg DK....58 B3
Glesien D......83 A4
Gletsch CH ... 106 C3
Glewitz D......66 B1
Glifada GR ... 185 B4
Glimåkra S.....63 B2
Glin IRL 29 B2
Glina HR 124 B2
Glinde D.......72 A3
Glinojeck PL ...77 B5
Glinsk IRL 28 A2
Gliwice PL.....86 B2
Glödnitz A ... 109 C5
Gloggnitz A .. 110 B2
Głogów SRB.. 127 C2
Głogów PL.....85 A4
Głogówek PL...86 B1
Glomel F..... 100 A2
Glomfjord N .. 195 D4
Glommen S....60 C2
Glommersträsk
S 196 D2
Glonn D...... 108 B2
Glorenza I.... 108 C1
Gloria P...... 154 B2
Glosa GR..... 183 D5
Glossop UK....40 B2
Gloucester UK .39 C4
Głowaczów PL .87 A5
Głowczyce PL..68 A2
Głowen D......73 B5
Głowno PL.....77 C4
Głożan SRB... 126 B1
Głubczyce PL..86 B1
Głuchołazy PL .85 B5
Głuchów PL....87 A4
Głuchowo PL...75 B5
Glücksburg D...64 B2
Glückstadt D...64 C2
Glumina BIH .. 139 A5
Glumsø DK.....65 A4
Gluofci SRB... 127 C1
Glusk BY 13 B8
Głuszyca PL...85 B4
Glyngøre DK...58 B1
Glyn Neath UK .39 C3
Gmünd
Karnten A ... 109 C4
Nieder Österreich
A 96 C2
Gmund D..... 108 B2
Gmunden A... 109 B4
Gnarp S...... 200 D3
Gnarrenburg D .72 A2
Gnesau A 109 C4
Gnesta S.......56 A3
Gnięchowice
PL............85 A4
Gniew PL......69 B3
Gniewkowo PL .76 B3
Gniezno PL.....76 B2
Gnoien D......66 C1
Gnojnice BIH.. 139 B3
Gnojno PL.....87 B4
Gnosall UK.....40 C1
Gnosjö S.......60 B3
Göbel TR..... 186 B3
Göçbeyli TR.. 186 C2
Goch D........80 A2
Gochsheim D ..94 A2
Göd H 112 B3
Godalming UK .44 B3
Godby FIN 51 B6
Goddelsheim D 81 A4
Gödenroth D ..93 C3
Goderville F....89 A4
Godiasco I.... 120 C2
Godič SLO.... 123 A3
Godkowo PL...69 A4
Godmanchester
UK 44 A3
Gödöllő H 112 B3
Gödre H 125 A3
Godshill UK....44 C2
Godzikowice
PL............85 B5
Godziszewo PL.69 A3
Goes NL.......79 A3
Goetzenbrück
F.............93 C3
Góglio I 119 A5

Gogolin PL.....86 B2
Göhren D......66 B2
Goirle NL......79 A5
Góis P 148 B1
Góito I 121 B3
Goizueta E ... 144 A2
Gojna Gora
SRB 127 D2
Gójsk PL...... 77 B4
Gökçedağ TR. 186 C3
Gökçen TR ... 188 A2
Gökçeören
TR........... 188 A3
Gökçeyazı TR . 186 C2
Göktepe TR .. 188 B3
Gol N........47 B5
Gola
HR 124 A3
N............. 48 A1
Gołańcz PL....76 B2
Gölby FIN 51 B6
Gölcük
Kocaeli TR . 187 B4
Niğde TR 23 B8
Golčův Jenikov
CZ............97 B3
Gölcük
S 196 D2
Goldach CH ... 107 B4
Goldbach D....93 A5
Goldberg D ...73 B4
Goldberg D ...73 B5
Goldelund D ...64 B2
Goldenstedt D .72 B1
Gołębiewo PL..69 A3
Golega P 154 B2
Goleniów PL...75 A3
Golfo Arancí I . 178 B3
Gölhisar TR .. 189 B4
Golina PL......76 B3
Gölle H 112 C2
Göllersdorf A ..97 C4
Golling an der
Salzach A ... 109 B4
Gölmarmara
TR........... 186 D2
Golnice PL.....84 A3
Golnik SLO... 123 A3
Gölova TR.... 189 C5
Gölpazari TR . 187 B5
Gols A 111 B3
Golspie UK.... 32 D3
Golssen D......74 C2
Golub-Dobrzyń
PL............77 B4
Golubinci SRB. 127 C2
Goluchów PL...86 A1
Golymin-Ośrodek
PL............77 B5
Golzow D......73 B5
Gomagoi I ... 108 C1
Gómara E 152 A1
Gomaringen D .93 C5
Gömbe TR.... 189 C4
Gömeç TR.... 186 C1
Gomel = Homyel
BY........... 13 B9
Gomes Aires P 160 B1
Gómezserracin
E............ 150 A3
Gommern D...73 B4
Gomunice PL..86 A3
Gonäs S.......50 B2
Goncelin F.... 118 B2
Gończyce PL...87 A5
Gondomar
E............ 140 B2
P............ 148 A1
Gondrecourt-le-
Château F....92 C1
Gondrin F.... 128 C3
Gönen
Balikesir TR . 186 B2
Isparta TR ... 189 B5
Gonfaron F .. 132 B2
Goni E....... 179 C3
Goni
GR 182 D4
I............ 179 C3
Gonnesa I 179 C2
Gonnosfanádiga
I............ 179 C2
Gönyü H 111 B4
Gonzaga I.... 121 C3
Goodrich UK...39 C4
Goodwick UK..39 C1
Goole UK...... 40 B3
Goor NL.......71 B3

Göppingen D ..94 C1
Gor E....... 164 B2
Góra
Dolnośląskie
PL........... 85 A4
Mazowieckie
PL........... 77 B5
Gorafe E 164 B1
Gorawino PL...67 C4
Goražde BIH .. 139 B4
Görbeháza H.. 113 B5
Gordaliza del Pino
E............ 142 B1
Gördes TR.... 186 D3
Gørding DK....59 C1
Górdola CH... 120 A1
Gordon UK....35 C5
Gordoncillo E . 142 B1
Gorebridge UK.35 C4
Gorenja Vas
SLO 123 A3
Gorenje Jelenje
HR 123 B3
Gorey
IRL.......... 30 B2
UK 88 A1
Gorgonzola I . 120 B2
Gorica HR.... 137 A4
Gorican HR... 124 A2
Gorinchem NL .79 A4
Goring UK.....44 B2
Goritsy RUS ...9 D10
Göritz D.......74 A2
Gorízia I..... 122 B2
Górki PL.......77 B4
Gorleben D ...73 A4
Gorleston-on-sea
UK 41 C5
Gørlev DK.....61 D1
Görlitz D 84 A2
Görlzig D..... 143 A4
Görmin D 66 C2
Górna Grupa
PL............69 B3
Gorna Oryahovitsa
BG 17 D6
Gorna Gorevnica
SRB 127 D2
Gornja Ploča
HR 137 A4
Gornja Radgona
SLO 110 C2
Gornja Sabanta
SRB 127 D3
Gornja Trešnjevica
SRB 127 C2
Gornja Tuzla
BIH.......... 125 C4
Gornje Polje
MNE 139 C4
Gornje Ratkovo
BIH.......... 124 C2
Gornji Grad
SLO 123 A3
Gornji Humac
HR 138 B2
Gornji Jasenjani
BIH.......... 139 B3
Gornji Kamengrad
BIH.......... 124 C2
Gornji Kneginec
HR 124 A2
Gornji Kosinj
HR 123 C4
Gornji Milanovac
SRB 127 C2
Gornji Podgradci
BIH.......... 124 B3
Gornji Ravno
BIH.......... 138 B3
Gornji Sjenicak
HR 124 B1
Gornji Vakuf
BIH.......... 138 B3
Górno PL......87 B4
Görömböly
H............ 113 A4
Górowo Iławeckie
PL............69 A5
Gorran Haven
UK 42 B2
Gorredijk NL...70 A3
Gorron F...... 88 B3
Gorseinon UK.39 C2
Gort IRL...... 28 A3
Gortin UK.....27 B3
Görzke D......73 B5
Gorzkowice PL .86 A3
Górzno
Kujawsko-
Pomorskie PL . 77 A4
Zachodnio-
Pomorskie PL . 75 A4

Gorzów Śląski PL 86 A2
Gorzów Wielkopolski PL 75 B4
Górzyca PL . . . 74 B3
Gorzyce PL 98 B2
Górzyn PL 84 A2
Gorzyń PL 75 B4
Gorzyno PL . . . 68 A2
Gosaldo I 121 A4
Gosau A 109 B4
Gosberton UK . . 41 C3
Gościcino PL . . . 68 A3
Gościęcin PL . . . 86 B2
Gościm PL 75 B4
Gościno PL 67 B4
Gosdorf A 110 C2
Gosforth UK . . . 36 B3
Goslar D 82 A2
Goslice PL 77 B4
Gospić HR 137 A4
Gosport UK 44 C2
Gössäter S 55 B4
Gossau CH 107 B4
Goss Ilsede D . . 72 B3
Gössnitz D 83 B4
Gössweinstein D 95 B3
Gostivar NMK . 182 B2
Gostkow PL 77 C4
Göstling an der Ybbs A 110 B1
Gostomia PL . . . 75 A5
Gostycyn PL . . . 76 A2
Gostyń PL 85 A5
Gostynin PL . . . 77 B4
Goszczyn PL . . . 87 A4
Göta S 54 B3
Göteborg = Gothenburg S . . 60 B1
Götene S 55 B4
Gotha D 82 B2
Gothem S 57 C4
Gothenburg = Göteborg S 60 B1
Gotse Delchev BG 183 B5
Gottersdorf D . . . 95 C4
Göttingen D . . . 82 A1
Gottne S 200 C4
Götzis A 107 B4
Gouarec F 100 A2
Gouda NL 70 B1
Goudhurst UK . . 45 B4
Goumenissa GR 182 C4
Goura GR 184 B3
Gourdon F 129 B4
Gourgançon F . . 91 C4
Gourin F 100 A2
Gournay-en-Bray F 90 B1
Gourock UK 34 C3
Gouveia P 148 B2
Gouvy B 80 B1
Gouzeacourt F 90 A3
Gouzon F 116 A2
Govedari HR . . 138 C3
Govérnolo I . . . 121 B3
Gowarczów PL . . 87 A4
Gowerton UK . . 39 C2
Gowidlino PL . . . 68 A2
Gowran IRL 30 B1
Goyatz D 74 B3
Göynük TR 187 B5
Antalya TR . . . 189 C5
Gozdnica PL . . . 84 A3
Gozdowo PL . . . 77 B4
Gozee B 79 B4
Graal-Müritz D . . 65 B5
Grabenstätt D 109 B3
Grabhair UK . . . 31 A2
Gråbo S 60 B2
Grabovac HR 138 B2
SRB 127 C2
Grabovci SRB . 127 C1
Grabow D 73 A4
Grabów PL 77 B4
Grabow nad Pilicą PL 87 A5
Grabów nad Prosna PL 86 A2
Grabowno PL . . . 76 A2
Grabs CH 107 B4
Gračac CH 138 A1
Gračanica BIH . 125 C4
Graçay F 103 B3
Grad SLO 111 C3

Gradac BIH 139 C4
HR 138 B3
MNE 139 B5
Gradačac BIH . 125 C4
Gradec HR 124 B2
Gradefes E 142 B1
Grades A 110 C1
Gradil P 154 C1
Gradina HR 124 B3
MNE 139 B5
Gradisca d'Isonzo I 122 B2
Gradiška BIH . . 124 B3
Gradište HR . . . 125 B4
Grado E 141 A4
I 122 B2
Grafenau D 96 C1
Gräfenberg D . . 95 B3
Gräfenhainichen D 83 A4
Grafenschlag A . 97 C3
Grafenstein A . 110 C1
Gräfenthal D . . . 82 B3
Grafentonna D . . 82 A2
Grafenwöhr D . . 95 B3
Grafing D 108 A2
Grafling D 95 C4
Gräfsnäs S 54 B3
Gragnano I 170 C2
Grahovo SLO . . 122 A2
Graiguenamanagh IRL 30 B2
Grain UK 45 B4
Grainau D 108 B2
Graja de Iniesta E 158 B2
Grajera E 151 A4
Gram DK 59 C2
Gramais A 108 B1
Gramat F 129 B4
Gramatneusiedl A 111 A3
Grambow D 74 A3
Grammichele I 177 B3
Gramsh AL 182 C2
Gramzow D 74 A3
Gran N 48 B2
Granada E 163 A4
Granard IRL 27 C3
Grañas E 140 A3
Granátula de Calatrava E . . 157 B4
Grancey-le-Château F 105 B4
Grandas de Salime E 141 A4
Grandcamp-Maisy F 88 A2
Grand-Champ F 100 B3
Grand Couronne F 89 A5
Grand-Fougeray F 101 B4
Grândola P . . . 160 A1
Grandpré F 91 B4
Grandrieu F 117 C3
Grandson CH . . 106 C1
Grandvillars F . . 106 B1
Grandvilliers F . . 90 B1
Grañén E 145 C3
Grängärde S . . 50 B1
Grange IRL 26 B2
Grangemouth UK 35 B4
Grange-over-Sands UK 37 B4
Grängesberg S . . 50 B1
Granges-de-Crouhens F . . 145 B4
Granges-sur-Vologne F 106 A1
Gräningen D . . . 73 B4
Granitola-Torretta I 176 B1
Granja Évora P 155 C3
Porto P 148 A1
Granja de Moreruela E . . 142 C1
Granja de Torrehermosa E 156 B2
Gränna S 55 B5
Grannäs Västerbotten S 195 E7

Grannäs continued Västerbotten S 195 E8
Granö S 200 B5
Granollers E . . . 147 C3
Granowiec PL . . 85 A5
Granowo PL 75 B5
Gransee D 74 A2
Gransherad N . . 53 A5
Grantham UK . . 40 C3
Grantown-on-Spey UK 32 D3
Grantshouse UK 35 C5
Granville F 88 B2
Granvin N 46 B3
Grærup Strand DK 59 C1
Gräsås S 60 C2
Grasbakken N 193 B12
Grasberg D 72 A2
Grasmere UK . . 36 B3
Gräsmyr S 200 C5
Gräsö S 51 B5
Grassano I 172 B2
Grassau D 109 B3
Grasse F 132 B2
Grassington UK 40 A2
Græsted DK . . . 61 C2
Grästen DK . . . 64 B2
Grästorp S 54 B3
Gratkorn A 110 B2
Gråträsk S . . . 196 D2
Gratwein A 110 B2
Graulhet F 129 C4
Graus E 145 B4
Grávalos E 144 B2
Gravberget N . . 49 B4
Grave NL 80 A1
Gravedona I . . . 120 A2
Gravelines F . . . 78 A2
Gravellona Toce I 119 B5
Gravendal S . . . 50 B1
Gravens DK . . . 59 C2
Gravesend UK . . 45 B4
Graveson F . . . 131 B3
Gravina in Púglia I 172 B2
Gray F 105 B4
Grayrigg UK . . . 37 B4
Grays UK 45 B4
Grayshott UK . . 44 B3
Graz A 110 B2
Grazalema E . . 162 B2
Grążawy PL 69 B4
Grazzano Visconti I 120 C2
Greåker N 54 A2
Great Dunmow UK 45 B4
Great Malvern UK 39 B4
Great Torrington UK 42 B2
Great Waltham UK 45 B4
Great Yarmouth UK 41 C5
Grebbestad S . . 54 B2
Grebenstein D . . 81 A5
Grębocice PL . . 85 A4
Grębocin PL . . . 76 A3
Greding D 95 B3
Gredstedbro DK 59 C1
Greencastle IRL . 27 A3
Greenhead UK . 37 B4
Greenisland UK . 27 B5
Greenlaw UK . . 35 C5
Greenock UK . . 34 C3
Greenway UK . . 39 C2
Greenwich UK . . 45 B4
Grefrath D 80 A2
Greffern D 93 C4
Greifenburg A . 109 C4
Greiffenberg D . 74 A2
Greifswald D . . 66 B2
Grein A 110 A1
Greipstad N . . . 53 B3
Greiz D 83 B4
Grenaa DK 58 B3
Grenade F 129 C4
Grenade-sur-l'Adour F 128 C2
Grenchen CH . . 106 B2
Grendi N 53 B3
Grenivík IS . . . 191 B7
Grenoble F . . . 118 B2
Gréoux-les-Bains F 132 B1
Gresenhorst D . . 66 B1

Gressoney-la-Trinité I 119 B4
Gressoney-St.-Jean I 119 B4
Gressthal D 82 B2
Gressvik N 54 A1
Gresten A 110 B2
Gretna UK 36 B3
Greussen D 82 A2
Greve in Chianti I 135 B4
Greven Mecklenburg-Vorpommern D 73 A4
Nordrhein-Westfalen D . . . 71 B4
Grevena GR . . . 182 C3
Grevenbroich D 80 A2
Grevenbrück D . . 81 A4
Grevenmacher L 92 B2
Grevesmühlen D 65 C4
Grevestrand DK 61 D2
Grevie S 61 C2
Greystoke UK . . 36 B4
Greystones IRL . 30 A2
Grez-Doiceau B 79 B4
Grèzec F 129 B4
Grez-en-Bouère F 102 B1
Grezzana I 121 B4
Grgar SLO 122 A2
Grgurevci SRB . 127 B1
Gries A 108 B2
Griesbach D . . . 96 C1
Grieskirchen A 109 A4
Griffen A 110 C1
Grignan F 131 A3
Grignano I 122 B2
Grigno I 121 A4
Grignols F 128 B2
Grignon F 118 B3
Grijota E 142 B2
Grijpskerk NL . . 71 A3
Grillby S 56 A3
Grimaud F 132 B2
Grimbergen B . . 79 B4
Grimma D 83 A4
Grimmen D 66 B2
Grimmialp CH 106 C2
Grimsås S 60 B3
Grimsby UK . . . 41 B3
Grimslöv S 62 B2
Grímsstaðir IS . 191 B9
Grimstad N 53 B4
Grimstorp S . . . 62 A2
Grindavík IS . . . 190 D3
Grindelwald CH 106 C3
Grindheim N . . . 52 B3
Grindsted DK . . 59 C1
Griñón E 151 B4
Gripenberg S . . 62 A2
Gripsholm S . . . 56 A3
Grisolles F 129 C4
Grisslehamn S . . 51 B5
Gritley UK 33 C4
Grizebeck UK . . 36 B3
Grndina BIH . . . 124 C2
Gröbming A . . . 109 B4
Gröbzig D 83 A3
Grocka SRB . . . 127 C2
Gröditz D 83 A5
Gródki PL 77 A5
Grodków PL . . . 85 B5
Grodziec PL . . . 76 B3
Grödig A 109 B3
Grodzisk Mazowiecki PL 77 B5
Grodzisk Wielkoposki PL 75 B5
Groenlo NL 71 B3
Groesbeek NL . . 80 A1
Grohote HR . . . 138 B2
Groitzsch D 83 A4
Groix F 100 B2
Grójec PL 77 C5
Grom PL 77 A5
Gromiljca BIH . 139 B4
Gromnik PL 99 B4
Gromo I 120 B2

Gronau Niedersachsen D 72 B2
Nordrhein-Westfalen D . . . 71 B4
Grønbjerg DK . . 59 B1
Grönenbach D 107 B5
Grong N 199 A9
Grönhögen S . . 63 B4
Groningen NL 71 A3
Grønnestrand DK 58 A2
Grono CH 120 A2
Grönskåra S . . . 62 A3
Gropello Cairoli I 120 B1
Grorud N 48 C2
Grósio I 120 A3
Grošnica SRB . . 127 D2
Grossalmerode D 82 A1
Grossari A 109 B4
Gross Beeren D . 74 B2
Gross Berkel D . 72 B2
Grossbodungen D 82 A2
Grossbothen D . 83 A4
Gross-botwar D 94 C1
Grossburgwedel D 72 B2
Grosschönau D 84 B2
Gross-Döbln D . 74 A2
Grossenbrode D 65 B4
Grossenehrich D 82 A2
Grossengottern D 82 A2
Grossenhain D . 83 A5
Grossenkneten D 71 B5
Grossenlüder D 81 B5
Grossensee D . . 72 A3
Grossenzersdorf A 111 A3
Grosseto I 135 C4
Gross-Gerau D . 93 B4
Grossgerungs A 96 C2
Grossglobnitz A 97 C3
Grosshabersdorf D 94 B2
Grossharras A . . 97 C4
Grosshartmansdorf D 83 B5
Grosshöchstetten CH 106 C2
Gross Kreutz D . 74 B1
Grosskrut A . . . 97 C4
Gross Lafferde D 72 B3
Gross Leuthen D 74 B3
Grosslohra D . . . 82 A2
Grossmehring D 95 C3
Gross Muckrow D 74 B3
Gross Oesingen D 72 B3
Grossostheim D 93 B5
Grosspertholz A 96 C2
Grosspetersdorf A 111 B3
Grossräschen D 84 A2
Gross Reken D . 80 A3
Grossrinderfeld D 94 B1
Grossröhrsdorf D 84 A2
Gross Särchen D 84 A2
Grossschirma D 83 B5
Gross Schönebeck D 74 B2
Grossschweinbarth A 97 C4

Grosssiegharts A 97 C3
Grosssölk A . . . 109 B4
Gross Umstadt D 93 B4
Grosswarasdorf A 111 B3
Gross Warnow D 73 A4
Gross-Weikersdorf A 97 C3
Gross-Welle D . 73 A5
Grosswilfersdorf A 110 B2
Grostenquin F . 92 C2
Grosuplje SLO . 123 B3
Grotli N 198 C4
Grötlingbo S . . . 57 C4
Grottáglie I . . . 173 B3
Grottaminarda I 170 B3
Grottammare I 136 C2
Grotte di Castro I 168 A1
Grottéria I 175 C2
Gróttole I 172 B2
Grouw NL 70 A2
Grov N 194 B8
Grova N 53 A4
Grove F 140 B2
Grua N 48 B2
Grube D 65 B4
Grubišno Polje HR 124 B3
Grude BIH 138 B3
Grudusk PL 77 A5
Grudziądz PL . . 69 B3
Grue N 49 B4
Gruissan F 130 B2
Grullos E 141 A4
Grumo Áppula I 171 B4
Grums S 55 A4
Grünau im Almtal A 109 B4
Grünberg D 81 B4
Grünburg A . . . 110 B1
Grundarfjörður IS 190 C2
Grundforsen S . 49 A4
Grundlsee A . . . 109 B4
Grundsund S . . 54 B2
Grunewald D . . 84 A1
Grungedal N . . 53 A3
Grunow D 74 B3
Grünstadt D . . . 93 B4
Gruvberget S . . 50 A3
Gruyères CH . . 106 C2
Gruža SRB 127 D2
Grybów PL 99 B4
Gryfice PL 67 C4
Gryfino PL 74 A3
Gryfów Śląski PL 84 A3
Gryllefjord N . . 194 A8
Grymyr N 48 B2
Gryt S 56 B2
Grytgöl S 56 B1
Grythyttan S . . 55 A5
Grytnäs S 57 A3
Grzmiąca PL . . . 68 B1
Grzybno PL 74 A3
Grzywna PL 76 A3
Gschnitz A 108 B2
Gschwend D . . 94 C1
Gstaad CH 106 C2
Gsteig CH 119 A4
Guadahortuna E 163 A4
Guadalajara E . 151 B4
Guadalaviar E . 152 B2
Guadalcanal E . 156 B2
Guadalcázar E 162 A3
Guadalix de la Sierra E 151 B4
Guadálmez E . . 156 B3
Guadalupe E . . 156 A2
Guadamur E . . . 151 C3
Guadarrama E . 151 B4
Guadiana del Caudillo E 155 C3
Guadix E 164 B1

Gualchos E 163 B4
Gualdo Tadino I 136 B1
Gualtieri I 121 C3
Guarcino I 169 B3
Guarda P 149 B2
Guardamar del Segura E 165 A4
Guardão P 148 B1
Guardavalle I . . 175 C2
Guardea I 168 A2
Guárdia I 172 B1
Guardiagrele I 169 A4
Guárdia Sanframondi I 170 B2
Guardias Viejas E 164 C2
Guardiola de Berguedà E . . 147 B2
Guardo E 142 B2
Guareña E 156 B1
Guaro E 163 B3
Guarromán E . . 157 B4
Guasila I 179 C3
Guastalla I 121 C3
Gubbhögen S 199 A12
Gúbbio I 136 B1
Guben D 74 C3
Gúbin PL 74 C3
Gudå N 199 B8
Gudavac BIH . . 124 C2
Guddal N 46 A2
Güderup DK . . . 64 B2
Gudhem S 55 B4
Gudhjem DK . . 67 A3
Gudovac HR . . 124 B2
Gudow D 73 A3
Güdül TR 187 B7
Gudvangen N . . 46 B3
Guebwiller F . . 106 B2
Guéjar-Sierra E 163 A4
Guémené-Penfao F 101 B4
Guémené-sur-Scorff F 100 A2
Güeñes E 143 A3
Guer F 101 B3
Guérande F . . . 101 B3
Guéret F 116 A1
Guérigny F 104 B2
Guesa E 144 B2
Gueugnon F . . . 104 C3
Guglionesi I . . . 170 B2
Gühlen Glienicke D 74 A1
Guia P 154 B2
Guichen F 101 B4
Guidizzolo I . . . 121 B3
Guidónia-Montecélio I . . 168 B2
Guíglia I 135 A4
Guignes F 90 C2
Guijo E 156 B3
Guijo de Coria E 149 B3
Guijo de Santa Bábara E 150 B2
Guijuelo E 150 B2
Guildford UK . . 44 B3
Guillaumes F . . 132 A2
Guillena E 161 B3
Guillestre F . . . 118 C3
Guillos F 128 B2
Guilsfield UK . . 38 B3
Guilvinec F 100 B1
Guimarães P . . 148 A1
Guincho P 154 C1
Guînes F 78 B1
Guingamp F . . . 100 A2
Guipavas F 100 A1
Guisborough UK 37 B5
Guiscard F 90 B3
Guiscriff F 100 A2
Guise F 91 B3
Guisona E 147 C2
Guitiriz E 140 A3
Guîtres F 128 A2
Gujan-Mestras F 128 B1
Gulbene LV 8 D5
Gülçayır TR . . . 187 C6
Guldborg DK . . 65 B4
Gullabo S 63 B3
Gullane UK 35 B5

Gullbrå N 46 B3
Gullbrandstorp
S 61 C2
Gulleråsen S 50 A2
Gullhaug N 53 A6
Gullringen S 62 A3
Gullspång S 55 B5
Gullstein N 198 B5
Güllük TR 188 B2
Gülnar TR 23 C7
Gülpınar TR . . . 186 C1
Gülşehir TR 23 B8
Gulsvik N 48 B1
Gumiel de Hizán
E 143 C3
Gummersbach
D 81 A3
Gümüldür TR . 188 A2
Gümüşhacıköy
TR 23 A8
Gümüşova
TR 187 B5
Gundelfingen
D 94 C2
Gundel-fingen
D 106 A2
Gundelsheim D 93 B5
Gunderschoffen
F 93 C3
Gundertshausen
A 109 A3
Gundinci HR . . 125 B4
Gündoğmuş
TR 189 C7
Güney
Burdur TR 189 B4
Denizli TR 188 A4
Gunja HR 125 C4
Günlüce TR . . . 188 C3
Gunnarn S 195 E8
Gunnarsbyn S 196 C4
Gunnarskog S . .49 C4
Gunnebo S 62 A4
Gunnislake UK . .42 B2
Günselsdorf A 111 B3
Guntersblum D .93 B4
Guntersdorf A . .97 C4
Guntin E 140 B3
Günyüzü TR . . 187 C6
Günzburg D 94 C2
Gunzenhausen
D 94 B2
Güre
Balıkesir TR . . 186 C1
Uşak TR 186 D4
Gurk A 110 C1
Gurrea de Gállego
E 144 B3
Gürsu TR 186 B4
Gušće HR 124 B2
Gusev RUS 12 A5
Gúspini I 179 C2
Gusselby S 56 A1
Güssing A 111 B3
Gusswerk A . . . 110 B2
Gustav Adolf S . .49 B5
Gustavsberg S . .57 A4
Gustavsfors S . . .54 A3
Güstrow D 65 C5
Gusum S 56 B2
Gutcher UK 33 A5
Gutenstein A . . 110 B2
Gütersloh D 81 A4
Guttannen CH 106 C3
Guttaring A . . . 110 C1
Guttau D 84 A2
Güttingen CH . 107 B4
Gützkow D 66 C2
Guzów PL 77 B5
Gvardeysk RUS .12 A4
Gvarv N 53 A5
Gvozd MNE . . . 139 C5
Gvozdansko
HR 124 B2
Gwda Wielka
PL 68 B1
Gwennap UK . . .42 B1
Gy F 105 B4
Gyál H 112 B3
Gyarmat H 111 B4
Gyékényes H . . 124 A3
Gyé-sur-Seine
F 104 A3
Gyljen S 196 C5
Gylling DK 59 C3
Gyoma H 113 C4
Gyömöre H . . . 111 B4
Gyömrö H 112 B3
Gyón H 112 B3
Gyöngyfa H . . . 125 B3

Gyöngyös H . . 113 B3
Gyöngyöspata
H 113 B3
Gyönk H 112 C2
Györ H 111 B4
Györszemere
H 111 B4
Gypsera CH . . 106 C2
Gysinge S 51 B3
Gyttorp S 55 A5
Gyula H 113 C5
Gyulafirátót
H 112 B1
Gyulaj H 112 C2

H

Haacht B 79 B4
Haag
Nieder Österreich
A 110 A1
Ober Österreich
A 109 A4
D 108 A3
Haaksbergen
NL 71 B3
Haamstede NL . .79 A3
Haan D 80 A3
Haapajärvi FIN . . 3 E9
Haapsalu EST . . .8 C3
Haarlem NL 70 B1
Habas F 128 C2
Habay B 92 B1
Habo S 62 A2
Håbol S 54 B3
Habry CZ 97 B3
Habsheim F . . . 106 B2
Hachenburg D . .81 B3
Hacıbektaş TR . .23 B8
Hacılar TR 23 B8
Hacinas E 143 C3
Hackås S 199 C11
Hacketstown
IRL 30 B2
Hackthorpe UK .37 B4
Hadamar D 81 B4
Hådanberg S . . 200 C4
Haddington UK .35 C5
Hadersdorf am
Kamp A 97 C3
Haderslev DK . .59 C2
Haderup DK 59 B1
Hadım TR 23 C7
Hadleigh
Essex UK 45 B4
Suffolk UK 45 A4
Hadlow UK 45 B4
Hadmersleben
D 72 A1
Hadsten DK 59 B3
Hadsund DK 58 B3
Hadžići BIH . . . 139 B4
Hafnarfjörður
IS 190 C3
Hafnir IS 190 D3
Hafslo N 47 A4
Haganj HR 124 B2
Hagby S 63 B4
Hage D 71 A4
Hægebostad N .52 B3
Hægeland N 53 B3
Hagen
Niedersachsen
D 72 A1
Nordrhein-
Westfalen D . . .80 A3
Hagenbach D . . .93 B4
Hagenow D 73 A4
Hagetmau F . . . 128 C2
Hagfors S 49 B5
Häggenås S . . 199 B11
Hagondange F . .92 B2
Hagsta S 51 B4
Haguenau F 93 C3
Hahnbach D 95 B3
Hahnslätten D . .81 B4
Hahót H 111 C3
Haiger D 81 B4
Haigerloch D . . .93 C4
Hailsham UK . . .45 C4
Hainburg A . . . 111 A3
Hainfeld A 110 A2
Hainichen D 83 B5
Hajdúböszörmény
H 113 B5
Hajdúčica SRB 126 B2
Hajdúdorog
H 113 B5
Hajdúnánás
H 113 B5
Hajdúszoboszló
H 113 B5

Hajnáčka SK . . 113 A3
Hajnówka PL 13 B5
Hajós H 112 C3
Håkafot S 199 A11
Hakkas S 196 C4
Håksberg S 50 B2
Halaszi H 111 B4
Halberstadt D . .82 A3
Halberton UK . . .43 B3
Hald Ege DK . . .58 B2
Haldem D 71 B5
Halden N 54 A2
Haldensleben
D 73 B4
Halenbeck D . . .73 A5
Halesowen UK . .40 C1
Halesworth UK . .45 A5
Halfing D 109 B3
Halhjem N 46 B2
Håliden S 49 B5
Halifax UK 40 B2
Häljelöt S 56 B2
Halkirk UK 32 C3
Hall S 57 C4
Hall S 200 C3
Hallabro S 63 B3
Hällabrottet S . .56 A1
Halland UK 45 C4
Hällaryd S 63 B2
Hällaryd S 61 C3
Hällberga S 56 A2
Hällbybrunn S . .56 A2
Halle
B 79 B4
Nordrhein-
Westfalen D . . .72 B1
Sachsen-Anhalt
D 83 A3
Hälleberga S . . .63 B3
Hällefors S 55 A5
Hälleforsnäs S . .56 A2
Hallein A 109 B4
Hällekis S 55 B4
Hallen S 199 B11
Hallenberg D . . .81 A4
Hallencourt F . . .90 B1
Hällevadsholm
S 54 B2
Hällevik S 63 B2
Hälleviksstrand
S 54 B2
Hallingby N 48 B2
Hallingeberg S .62 A4
Hall in Tirol A . 108 B2
Hällnäs S 195 D9
Hällnäs S 56 B1
Hällnäs S 200 B5
Hallormsstaður
IS 191 B11
Hallsberg S 56 A1
Hällsta S 56 A2
Hallstahammar
S 56 A2
Hallstatt A 109 B4
Hallstavik S 51 B5
Halltorp S 63 B4
Halluin F 78 B3
Hallviken S . . . 199 B12
Hallworthy UK . .42 B2
Hallstad S 61 C2
Hals DK 58 A3
Halsa N 198 B5
Halstead UK 45 B4
Haltdalen N . . . 199 C8
Haltern D 80 A3
Haltwhistle UK . .37 B4
Halvarsgårdarna
S 50 B2
Halver D 80 A3
Halvrimmen
DK 58 A2
Ham F 90 B3
Hamar N 48 B3
Hamarhaug N . .46 B2
Hamarøy N . . . 194 B6
Hambach F 93 B3
Hambergen D . .72 A1
Hambergsund
S 54 B2
Hambledon UK .44 C2
Hambuhren D . .72 B2
Hamburg D 72 A3
Hamdibey TR . 186 C2
Hamdorf D 64 B2
Hämeenlinna
FIN 8 B4
Hameln = Hamlin
D 72 B2
Hamersleben D 73 B4
Hamidiye TR . . 187 C5
Hamilton UK . . .36 A2

Hamina FIN 8 B5
Hamlagrø N 46 B3
Hamlin = Hameln
D 72 B2
Hamm D 81 A3
Hammar S 55 B5
Hammarland
FIN 51 B6
Hammarö S 55 A4
Hammarstrand
S 200 C2
Hamme B 79 A4
Hammel DK 59 B2
Hammelburg D .82 B1
Hammelspring
D 74 A2
Hammenhög S . .66 A3
Hammerdal
S 199 B12
Hammerfest
N 192 B7
Hammershøj
DK 58 B2
Hammerum DK . .59 B2
Hamminkeln D .80 A2
Hamnavoe UK . .33 A5
Hamneda S 60 C3
Hamningberg
N 193 B14
Hamoir B 80 B1
Hamont B 80 A1
Hámor H 113 A4
Hamra
Gävleborg
S 51 A4
Gotland S 57 C4
Hamrångefjärden
S 51 B4
Hamstreet UK . .45 B4
Hamsund N . . . 194 B6
Han TR 187 C5
Hanaskog S 61 C4
Hanau D 81 B4
Händelöp S 62 A4
Handlová SK . . .98 C2
Hanerau-
Hademarschen
D 64 B2
Hånger S 60 B3
Hanhimaa FIN . 197 B8
Hankensbüttel
D 73 B3
Hankasalmi FIN . .8 A4
Hanko FIN 124 B2
Hannover D 72 B2
Hannut B 79 B5
Han Pijesak
BIH 139 A4
Hansnes N . . . 192 C3
Hanstedt D 72 A3
Hanstholm DK . . .58 A1
Hantsavichy BY .13 B7
Hanušovce CZ . .98 B4
Haparanda S . . 196 D7
Haradok BY 13 A8
Harads S 196 C4
Haradsbäck S . . .63 B2
Häradsbygden
S 50 B2
Harbo S 51 B4
Harboør DK 58 B1
Harburg
Bayern D 94 C2
Hamburg D 72 A2
Hårby DK 59 C3
Harc H 112 C2
Hardegarijp NL .70 A2
Hardegsen D . . .82 A1
Hardelot Plage
F 78 B1
Hardenbeck D . .74 A2
Hardenberg NL . .71 B3
Harderwijk NL . .70 B2
Hardheim D 94 B1
Hardt D 106 A3
Hareid N 198 C3
Haren
D 71 B4
NL 71 B3
Harestua N 48 B2
Harfleur F 89 A4
Harg S 51 B5
Hargicourt F 90 B3
Hargnies F 91 A4
Hargshamn S . . .51 B5
Härja S 55 B4
Harkány H 125 B4
Härkeberga S . . .56 A3
Harkebrügge
D 71 A4
Harlech UK 38 B2

Harleston UK . . .45 A5
Hårlev DK 65 A5
Harlingen NL . . .70 A2
Harlösa S 61 D3
Harlow UK 45 B4
Harmancık
TR 186 C4
Harmånger S . 200 E3
Harmanli BG . . 183 B7
Härnevi S 56 A3
Härnösand S . . 200 D3
Haro E 143 B4
Haroldswick
UK 33 A6
Háromfa H . . . 124 A3
Haroué F 92 C2
Harpenden UK . .44 B3
Harplinge S 60 C2
Harpstedt D 72 B1
Harrogate UK . . .40 A2
Harrow UK 44 B3
Härryda S 60 B2
Harsefeld D 72 A2
Harsewinkel D . .71 C5
Hârşova RO 17 C7
Harstad N 194 B7
Harsum D 72 B2
Harsvik N 199 A7
Harta H 112 C3
Hartberg A 110 B2
Hartburn UK 37 A5
Hartennes F 90 B3
Hartest UK 45 A4
Hartha D 83 A4
Hartland UK 42 B2
Hartlepool UK . .37 B5
Hartmanice CZ . .96 B1
Hartmannsdorf
D 83 B4
Harvassdal N . 195 E5
Harwell UK 44 B2
Harwich UK 45 B5
Harzgerode D . .82 A3
Häselgehr A . . . 108 B1
Haselünne D . . .71 B4
Haskovo BG . . . 183 B7
Hasköy TR 186 A1
Haslach D 106 A3
Haslach an der
Mühl A 96 C2
Hasle DK 67 A3
Haslemere UK . .44 B3
Haslev DK 65 A4
Hasloch D 94 B1
Hasparren F . . . 144 A2
Hassela S 200 D2
Hasselfelde D . .82 A2
Hasselfors S 55 A5
Hasselt
B 79 B5
NL 70 B3
Hassfurt D 94 A2
Hassleben D 74 B2
Hassleholm S . . .61 C3
Hasslö S 63 B3
Hassloch D 93 B4
Hästbo S 51 B4
Hastersboda
FIN 51 B7
Hästholmen S . .55 B5
Hastière-Lavaux
B 79 B4
Hastigrow UK . . .32 C3
Hastings UK 45 C4
Hästveda S 61 C3
Hasvik N 192 B6
Hatfield
Hertfordshire
UK 44 B3
South Yorkshire
UK 40 B2
Hatherleigh UK .42 B2
Hathersage UK . .40 B2
Hatlestrand N . .46 B2
Hattem NL 70 B3
Hatten
D 71 A5
F 93 C3
Hattfjelldal N . 195 E4
Hatting DK 59 C2
Hattingen D 80 A3
Hattstadt F 106 A2
Hattstedt D 64 B2
Hatvan H 112 B3
Hatvik N 46 B2
Hau D 80 A2
Haudainville F . .92 B1
Hauge N 52 B2
Haugesund N . . .52 A1
Haughom N 52 B2
Haugsdal N 46 B2

Haugsdorf A 97 C4
Haukedal N 46 A3
Haukeligrend
N 52 A3
Haukeliseter N .52 A3
Haukipudas FIN . .3 D9
Haulerwijk NL . .71 A3
Haunersdorf D . .95 C4
Haus N 46 B2
Hausach D 106 A3
Hausham D . . . 108 B2
Hausmannstätten
A 110 C2
Hausvik N 52 B2
Hautajärvi
FIN 197 C12
Hautefort F . . . 129 A4
Hauterives F . . 117 B5
Hauteville-
Lompnès F . . 118 B2
Haut-Fays B 91 A5
Hautmont F 79 B3
Hautrage B 79 B3
Hauzenberg D . .96 C1
Havant UK 44 C3
Havdhem S 57 C4
Havdrup DK 61 D2
Havelange B 79 B5
Havelberg D 73 B5
Havelte NL 70 B3
Haverfordwest
UK 39 C2
Haverhill UK 45 A4
Havering UK 45 B4
Håverud S 54 B3
Havířov CZ 98 B2
Havixbeck D 71 C4
Havlíčkův Brod
CZ 97 B3
Havndal DK 58 B3
Havneby DK 64 A1
Havnebyen DK .61 D1
Havnso DK 61 D1
Havøysund N . 193 A8
Havran TR 186 C2
Havrebjerg DK . .61 D1
Havsa TR 186 A1
Havstenssund
S 54 B2
Havza TR 23 A8
Hawes UK 37 B4
Hawick UK 35 C5
Hawkhurst UK . .45 B4
Hawkinge UK . . .45 B5
Haxey UK 40 B3
Hayange F 92 B2
Haydarlı TR . . . 189 A5
Haydon Bridge
UK 37 B4
Hayle UK 42 B1
Haymana TR . . 187 C7
Hay-on-Wye UK 39 B3
Hayrabolu TR . 186 A2
Haysyn UA 13 D8
Hayvoron UA . . .13 D8
Haywards Heath
UK 44 C3
Hazebrouck F . .78 B2
Hazlov CZ 83 B4
Heacham UK . . .41 C4
Headcorn UK . . .45 B4
Headford IRL . . .28 A2
Heanor UK 40 B2
Héas F 145 B4
Heathfield UK . .45 C4
Hebden Bridge
UK 40 B1
Heberg S 60 C2
Heby S 51 C3
Hechingen D . . .93 C4
Hechlingen D . . .94 C2
Hecho E 145 B3
Hechtel B 79 A5
Hechthausen D .72 A2
Heckelberg D . . .74 B2
Heckington UK . .41 C3
Hecklingen D . . .82 A3
Hed S 56 A1
Hedalen N 48 B1
Hedared S 60 B2
Heddal N 53 A5
Hédé F 101 A4
Hede S 199 C10
Hedekas S 54 B2
Hedemora S 50 B2
Hedenäset S . . 196 C6
Hedensted DK . .59 C2
Hedersleben D . .82 A3
Hedesunda S . . .51 B4
Hedge End UK . .44 C2
Hedon UK 41 B3
Heede D 71 B4

Heek D 71 B4
Heemstede NL . .70 B1
Heerde NL 70 B3
Heerenveen NL .70 B2
Heerhugowaard
N 70 B1
Heerlen NL 80 B1
Heeze NL 80 A1
Heggenes N 47 A6
Hegra N 199 B8
Hegyeshalom
H 111 B4
Hegyközség
H 111 B3
Heia N 199 A9
Heide D 64 B2
Heidelberg D . . .93 B4
Heiden D 80 A2
Heidenau D 84 B1
Heidenheim D . .94 C2
Heidenreichstein
A 97 C3
Heikendorf D . . .64 B3
Heikkilä FIN . . 197 C12
Heilam UK 32 C2
Heiland N 53 B4
Heilbad
Heiligenstadt
D 82 A2
Heilbronn D 93 B5
Heiligenblut
A 109 B3
Heiligendamm
D 65 B4
Heiligendorf D .73 B3
Heiligengrabe
D 73 A5
Heiligenhafen
D 65 B3
Heiligenhaus D .80 A2
Heiligenkreuz
A 111 C3
Heiligenstadt
D 94 B3
Heiloo NL 70 B1
Heilsbronn D . . .94 B2
Heim N 198 B6
Heimburg D 82 A2
Heimdal N 199 B7
Heinerscheid L .92 A2
Heinersdorf D . .74 B3
Heining D 96 C1
Heiningen D 94 C1
Heinola FIN 8 B5
Heinsberg D 80 A2
Heist-op-den-Berg
B 79 A4
Hejde S 57 C4
Hejdeby S 57 C4
Hejls DK 59 C2
Hejnice CZ 84 B3
Hel PL 69 A3
Helchteren B . . .79 A5
Heldburg D 82 B2
Helechosa E . . . 156 A3
Helensburgh
UK 34 B3
Helfenberg A . . .96 C2
Helgen N 53 A5
Helgeroa N 53 B5
Hella
IS 190 D5
N 46 A3
Helland N 194 B7
Hellas S 55 B3
Helleland N 52 B2
Hellendoorn
NL 71 B3
Hellenthal D 80 B2
Hellesøy N 46 B1
Hellesylt N 198 C3
Hellevoetsluis
NL 79 A4
Helligskogen
N 192 C4
Hellín E 158 C2
Hellissandur
IS 190 C2
Hellnar IS 190 C2
Hellum DK 58 A3
Hellvi S 57 C4
Hellvik N 52 B1
Helm-brechts D 83 B3
Helmond NL 80 A1
Helmsdale UK . .32 C3
Helmsley UK . . .37 B5
Helmstedt D 73 B3
Hel'pa SK 99 C3
Helsa D 82 A1
Helsby UK 38 A4
Helsingborg S . .61 C2

Helsinge DK.....61 C2
Helsingør DK.....61 C2
Helsinki FIN......8 B4
Helston UK.....42 B1
Hemau D......95 B3
Hemavan S....195 E6
Hemel Hempstead UK..............44 B3
Hemer D......81 A3
Héming F......92 C2
Hemmet DK...59 C1
Hemmingstedt D..............64 B2
Hemmoor D....64 C2
Hemnes N......54 A2
Hemnesberget N............195 D4
Hemse S......57 C4
Hemsedal N....47 B5
Hemslingen D..72 A2
Hemsworth UK.40 B2
Hen N.......48 B2
Henån S.......54 B2
Hendaye F....144 A2
Hendek TR.....187 B5
Hendungen D..82 B2
Henfield UK.....44 C3
Hengelo
 Gelderland NL...........71 B3
 Overijssel NL....71 B3
Hengersberg D.95 C5
Hengoed UK....39 C3
Hénin-Beaumont F............78 B2
Henley-on-Thames UK.............44 B3
Hennan S.....200 D1
Henneberg D..82 B2
Hennebont F..100 B2
Henne Strand DK..........59 C1
Hennigsdorf D..74 B2
Hennset N....198 B5
Hennstedt
 Schleswig-Holstein D............64 B2
 Schleswig-Holstein D............64 B2
Henrichemont F............103 B4
Henryków PL...85 B5
Henrykowo PL..69 A5
Hensås N.....47 A5
Henstedt-Ulzburg D............64 C2
Heppenheim D.93 B4
Herad
 Buskerud N...47 B6
 Vest-Agder N...52 B2
Heradsbygd N..48 B3
Heraklion = Iraklio GR.........185 D6
Herálec D.....97 B4
Herand N.....46 B3
Herbault F....103 B3
Herbern D.....81 A3
Herbertstown IRL............29 B3
Herbeumont B..91 B5
Herbignac F....101 B3
Herbisse F.....91 C4
Herbitzheim F.92 B3
Herbolzheim D............106 A2
Herborn D.....81 B4
Herbrechtingen D............94 C2
Herby PL.....86 B2
Herceg-Novi MNE........16 D3
Hercegovać HR.........124 B3
Hercegszántó H...........125 B4
Herchen D.....80 B3
Heréd H......112 B3
Hereford UK....39 B4
Herefoss N....53 B4
Hereke TR.....187 B4
Herencia E....157 A4
Herend H......111 B4
Herent B......79 A4
Herentals B....79 A4
Hérépian F....130 B2
Herflige DK....61 D2
Herford D......72 B1
Herguijuela E............156 A2
Héric F.......101 B4
Héricourt F...106 B1
Héricourt-en-Caux F............89 A4

Hérimoncourt F............106 B1
Heringsdorf D..65 B4
Herisau CH....107 B4
Hérisson F....103 C4
Herk-de-Stad B.79 B5
Herlufmagle DK...........65 A4
Hermagor A..109 C4
Hermannsburg D............72 B3
Hermansverk N............46 A3
Heřmanův Městec CZ...........97 B3
Herment F....116 B2
Hermeskeil D..92 B2
Hermisende E.141 C4
Hermonville F..91 B3
Hermsdorf D...83 B3
Hernani E....144 A2
Hernansancho E............150 B3
Herne D......80 A3
Herne Bay UK...45 B5
Hernes N.....48 B3
Herning DK....59 B1
Herøya N.....53 A5
Herramelluri E............143 B3
Herräng S.....51 B5
Herre N.......53 A5
Herrenberg D..93 C4
Herrera E....162 A3
Herrera de Alcántara E...155 B3
Herrera del Duque E............156 A2
Herrera de los Navarros E...152 A2
Herrera de Pisuerga E............142 B2
Herreros del Suso E............150 B2
Herrestad S...54 B2
Herrhamra S...57 B3
Herritslev DK...65 B4
Herrlisheim F..93 C3
Herrljunga S...55 B4
Herrnhut D....84 A2
Herrsching D..108 A2
Hersbruck D...95 B3
Hersby S.......57 A4
Herscheid D...81 A3
Herselt B......79 A4
Herso GR.....182 B4
Herstal B.....80 B1
Herstmonceux UK............45 C4
Herten D......80 A3
Hertford UK....44 B3
Hervás E.....149 B4
Hervik N......52 A1
Herxheim D....93 B4
Herzberg
 Brandenburg D............74 B1
 Brandenburg D............83 A5
 Niedersachsen D............82 A2
Herzberg D.....81 A4
Herzfelde D....74 B3
Herzlake D....71 B4
Herzogenaurach D............94 B2
Herzogenbuchsee CH..........106 B2
Herzogenburg A............110 A2
Herzsprung D..73 A5
Hesby N......52 A1
Hesdin F......78 B2
Hesel D.......71 A4
Heskestad N...52 B2
Hessdalen N..199 C8
Hesselager DK..65 A3
Hesseng N....193 C13
Hessisch Lichtenau D............82 A1
Hessisch-Oldendorf D............72 B2
Hestra S......60 B3
Heswall UK....38 A3
Hetlevik N....46 B2
Hettange-Grande F............92 B2
Hetton-le-Hole UK............37 B5
Hettstedt D....82 A3
Heuchin F.....78 B2
Heudicourt-sous-les-Côtes F...92 C1

Heunezel F....105 A5
Heuqueville F..89 A4
Heves H.....113 B4
Héviz H......111 C4
Hexham UK....37 B4
Heysham UK...36 B4
Heytesbury UK..43 A4
Hidas H.....125 A4
Hieflau A.....110 B1
Hiendelaencina E............151 A5
Hiersac F....115 C4
High Bentham UK...........37 B4
Highclere UK...44 B2
High Hesket UK.37 B4
Highley UK....39 B4
High Wycombe UK............44 B3
Higuera de Arjona E............157 C4
Higuera de Calatrava E...163 A3
Higuera de la Serena E....156 B2
Higuera de la Sierra E............161 B3
Higuera de Vargas E............155 C4
Higuera la Real E............161 A3
Higuers de Llerena E............156 B1
Higueruela E..158 C2
Híjar E......153 A3
Hilchenbach D..81 A4
Hildburghausen D............82 B2
Hilden D......80 A2
Hilders D.....82 B1
Hildesheim D..72 B2
Hilgay UK.....41 C4
Hillared S.....60 B3
Hille D.......72 B1
Hillegom NL....70 B1
Hillerød DK....61 D2
Hillerstorp S...60 B3
Hillesheim D...80 B2
Hillestad N....53 A6
Hillmersdorf D..83 A5
Hillsborough UK............27 B4
Hillswick UK....33 A5
Hilpoltstein D..95 B3
Hiltpoltstein D.94 B3
Hilvarenbeek NL...........79 A5
Hilversum NL...70 B2
Himarë AL....182 C1
Himbergen D..73 A3
Himeshaza H..125 A4
Himmelberg A............109 C5
Himmelpforten D............72 A2
Himód H.....111 B4
Hinckley UK....40 C2
Hindås S......60 B2
Hindelang D..108 B1
Hindelbank CH..........106 B2
Hinderavåg N..52 A1
Hindhead UK...44 B3
Hinjosa del Valle E............156 B1
Hinnerup DK...59 B3
Hinneryd S....61 C3
Hinojal E....155 B4
Hinojales E...161 B3
Hinojos E.....161 B3
Hinojosa del Duque E............156 B2
Hinojosas de Calatrava E...157 B3
Hinterhornbach A............108 B1
Hinterriss A...108 B2
Hintersee
 A............109 B4
 D............74 A3
Hinterstoder A............110 B1
Hintertux A...108 B2
Hinterweidenthal D............93 B3
Hinwil CH....107 B3
Hios GR.....185 A7
Hippolytushoef NL...........70 B1
Hirschau D....95 B3
Hirschfeld D...83 A5
Hirschhorn D..93 B4

Hirsingue F...106 B2
Hirson F......91 B4
Hirtshals DK...58 A2
Hirvaskoski FIN.........197 D10
Hirzenhain D..81 B5
Hisarcik TR...186 C4
Hishult S.....61 C3
Hissjön S....200 C6
Hitchin UK....44 B3
Hitra N......198 B5
Hittarp S.....61 C2
Hittisau A....107 B4
Hittun N......46 A1
Hitzacker D...73 A4
Hjallerup DK...58 A3
Hjällstad S....49 B5
Hjältevad S...62 A3
Hjärnarp S....61 C2
Hjartdal N....53 A4
Hjellestad N...46 B2
Hjelmeland N..52 A2
Hjelset N....198 C4
Hjerkinn N...198 C6
Hjerm DK.....58 B1
Hjerpsted DK..64 A1
Hjerting DK...59 C1
Hjo S........55 B5
Hjordkær DK..64 A2
Hjørring DK...58 A2
Hjorted S.....62 A4
Hjortkvarn S..56 B1
Hjortnäs S....50 B1
Hjortsberga S..62 B2
Hjukse N.....53 A5
Hjuksebo N...53 A5
Hjulsjö S.....55 A5
Hlinik nad Hronom SK...........98 C2
Hlinsko CZ....97 B3
Hlío IS......191 A10
Hlohovec SK...98 C1
Hlubokáné Vltavou CZ...96 B2
Hlučín CZ.....98 B2
Hlyboka UA...17 A6
Hlybokaye BY..13 A7
Hniezdne SK...99 B4
Hnilec SK.....99 C4
Hnúšt'a SK....99 C3
Hobol H.....125 A3
Hobro DK.....58 B2
Hobscheid L...92 B1
Hocalar TR...189 A4
Hochdonn D...64 B2
Hochdorf CH..106 B3
Hochspeyer D..93 B3
Höchst im Odenwald D..93 B5
Höckendorf D..83 B5
Hockenheim D..93 B4
Hoddesdon UK.44 B3
Hodejov SK....99 C3
Hodkovice CZ..84 B3
Hódmezóvásárhely H...........113 C4
Hodnet UK....38 B4
Hodonín CZ...98 C1
Hodslavice CZ..98 B2
Hoedekenskerke NL...........79 A3
Hoegaarden B..79 B4
Hoek van Holland NL...........79 A4
Hoenderlo NL..70 B2
Hof
 D............83 B3
 N............53 A6
Hofbieber D...82 B1
Hoff UK......37 B4
Hofgeismar D..81 A5
Hofheim
 Bayern D.....82 B2
 Hessen D....93 A4
Hofkirchen im Mühlkreis A...96 C1
Höfn IS......191 C10
Hofors S.....50 B3
Hofsós IS....190 B6
Hofstad N....199 A7
Höganäs S....61 C2
Högbo S......50 B3
Högebru N....46 A4
Högfors S....50 C2
Högklint S....57 C4
Högsäter S....54 B3

Högsby S......62 A4
Högsjö S......56 A1
Hogstad S....55 B6
Högyész H...112 C2
Hohenau A....97 C4
Hohenberg A.110 B2
Hohenbucko D..83 A5
Hohenburg D..95 B3
Hohendorf D...66 B1
Hohenems A..107 B4
Hohenhameln D............72 B3
Hohenhausen D............72 B1
Hohenkirchen D............71 A4
Hohenlinden D............108 A2
Hohenlockstedt D............64 C2
Hohenmölsen D............83 A4
Hohennauen D.73 B5
Hohen Neuendorf D............74 B2
Hohenseeden D............73 B5
Hohentauern A............110 B1
Hohentengen D............106 B3
Hohenwepel D.81 A5
Hohenwestedt D............64 B2
Hohenwutzen D............74 B3
Hohenzieritz D.74 A2
Hohn D......64 B2
Hohne D......72 B3
Hohnstorf D...73 A3
Højer DK.....64 B1
Højslev Stby DK...........58 B2
Hok S........62 A2
Hökerum S...60 B3
Hökhuvud S..51 B5
Hokksund N...53 A5
Hökön S......63 B2
Hol N.......47 B5
Hólar IS.....190 B6
Holašovice CZ..96 C2
Holbæk
 Aarhus Amt. DK...........58 B3
 Vestsjællands Amt. DK...........61 D1
Holbeach UK...41 C4
Holdenstedt D..73 B3
Holdhus N....46 B2
Holdorf D.....71 B5
Holeby DK.....65 B4
Hølen N......54 A1
Hølervassetr N............47 B6
Holešov CZ....98 B1
Holguera E...155 B4
Holić SK......98 C1
Holice
 CZ...........97 A3
 SK.........111 B4
Höljes S.....49 B4
Hollabrunn A..97 C4
Hollandstoun UK............33 B4
Høllen N.....53 B3
Hollfeld D....95 B3
Hollók'o H...112 B3
Hollstadt D....82 B2
Hollum NL....70 A2
Höllviksnäs S..66 A1
Holm N......195 E3
Hólmavík IS..190 B4
Holmbukt N..192 B5
Holmedal S....54 A2
Holmegil N....54 A2
Holmen N....48 B2
Holme-on-Spalding-Moor UK....40 B3
Holmes Chapel UK............38 A4
Holmestrand N.54 A1
Holmfirth UK...40 B2
Holmfoss N...193 C14
Holmsbu N....54 A1
Holmsjö S....63 B3
Holmsund S..200 C6
Holmsveden S..50 A3
Holmudden S..57 C5
Hölö S.......57 A3
Holøydal N...199 C8
Holsbybrunn S.62 A3
Holseter N....48 A1
Holsljunga S...60 B2

Holstebro DK...59 B1
Holsted DK.....59 C1
Holsworthy UK..42 B2
Holt
 D............64 B2
 IS..........190 D6
 N............53 B4
 Norfolk UK....41 C5
 Wrexham UK...38 A4
Holten NL.....71 B3
Holtwick D....71 B4
Holum N......52 B3
Holwerd NL...70 A2
Holycross IRL...29 B4
Holyhead UK...38 A2
Holýšov CZ....95 B5
Holywell UK...38 A3
Holywood UK..27 B5
Holzdorf D....83 A5
Holzhausen D..72 B1
Holzheim D...94 C2
Holzkirchen D............108 B2
Holzminden D..81 A5
Holzthaleben D............82 A2
Horcajo de los Montes E....156 A3
Horcajo de Santiago E...151 C4
Horcajo-Medianero E............150 B2
Horche E.....151 B4
Horda S......62 A2
Hordabø N....46 B1
Hordalia N....52 A2
Hordvik N....46 B2
Hořesedly CZ..83 B5
Horezu RO....17 C6
Horgen CH....107 B3
Horgoš SRB...126 A1
Horia RO.....126 A3
Hořice CZ.....84 B3
Horjul SLO...123 A3
Horka D......84 A2
Hörken S.....50 B1
Horki BY.....13 A9
Hörle S......60 B4
Horn
 A............97 C3
 D............81 A4
 N............48 B2
 S............62 A3
Hornachos E..156 B1
Hornachuelos E............162 A2
Horná Mariková SK...........98 B2
Hornanes N...46 C2
Horná Streda SK...........98 C1
Horná Štrubňa SK...........98 C2
Horná Súča SK.98 C1
Hornbæk
 Aarhus Amt. DK...........58 B2
 Frederiksværk DK...........61 C2
Hornberg D..106 A3
Hornburg D....73 B3
Horncastle UK..41 B3
Horndal S.....50 B3
Horndean UK..44 C2
Horne
 Fyns Amt. DK..64 A3
 Ribe Amt. DK..59 C1
Hörnebo S....55 B5
Hornefors S..200 C5
Horní Benešov CZ...........98 B1
Horní Cerekev CZ...........97 B3
Horní Jiřetín CZ...........83 B5
Horní Lomná CZ...........98 B2
Horní Maršov CZ...........85 B3
Horní Slavkov CZ...........83 B4
Horní Vltavice CZ...........96 C1
Hornnes N....53 B3
Horno D......84 A2
Hornos E.....164 A2
Hornoy-le-Bourg F............90 B1
Hornsea UK...41 B3
Hornsjø N....48 A2
Hornslet DK...59 B3
Hornstein A..111 B3
Hörnum D....64 B1
Hornum DK...58 B2
Horný Tisovnik SK...........99 C3
Horodenka UA..13 D6
Horodnya UA..13 C9
Horodok
 Khmelnytskyy UA..........13 D7
 Lviv UA.....13 D5
Horokhiv UA...13 C6
Horovice CZ...96 B1
Horred S.....60 B2
Hörröd S.....61 D4
Hörsching A..110 A1
Horsens DK...59 C2

Horsham UK 44 B3
Hørsholm DK . . 61 D2
Horslunde DK. . .65 B4
Horšovský Týn CZ . . .95 B4
Horst NL 80 A2
Horstel D 71 B4
Horsten D 71 A4
Horstmar D 71 B4
Hort H 113 B3
Horta P 148 A2
Horten N. 54 A1
Hortezuela E . . 151 A5
Hortiguela E . . 143 B3
Hortobágy H . . 113 B5
Horton in Ribblesdale UK . . .37 B4
Hørve DK 61 D1
Hörvik S 63 B2
Horwich UK 38 A4
Hosanger N. 46 B2
Hösbach D 93 A5
Hosena D 84 A2
Hosenfeld D . . .81 B5
Hosingen L 92 A2
Hosio FIN . . . 197 D8
Hospental CH. 107 C3
Hospital IRL. . . .29 B3
Hossegor F . . 128 C1
Hosszuhetény H. . . 125 A4
Hostal de Ipiés E . . . 145 B3
Hoštálkova CZ . .98 B1
Hostalric E . . . 147 C3
Hostens F 128 B2
Hostěradice CZ . . .97 C4
Hostinné CZ . . .85 B3
Hostomice CZ . .96 B2
Hostouň CZ 95 B4
Hotagen S . . . 199 B11
Hoting S 200 B2
Hotolisht AL . . 182 B2
Hotton B. 79 B5
Houdain F 78 B2
Houdan F 90 C1
Houdelaincourt F. . .92 C1
Houeillès F. . . 128 B3
Houffalize B . . .92 A1
Houghton-le-Spring UK. . . .37 B5
Houlberg DK. . .59 B2
Houlgate F. 89 A3
Hounslow UK . . .44 B3
Hourtin F 128 A1
Hourtin-Plage F. . . 128 A1
Houthalen B . . .79 A5
Houyet B. 79 B4
Hov
DK 59 C3
N. 48 B2
Hova S 55 B5
Høvåg N 53 B4
Hovborg DK . . .59 C1
Hovda N 47 B6
Hovden N. 52 A3
Hove UK 44 C3
Hovedgård DK. .59 C2
Hovelhof D 81 A4
Hoven DK 59 C1
Hovet N. 47 B5
Hovingham UK .40 A3
Hovmantorp S . .62 B3
Hovsta S 56 A1
Howden UK 40 B3
Howe D. 72 A3
Höxter D 81 A5
Hoya D 72 B2
Hoya de Santa Maria E 161 B3
Hoya-Gonzalo E 158 C2
Hoyanger N. . . .46 A3
Hoyerswerda D .84 A2
Høyjord N. 53 A6
Hoylake UK 38 A3
Høylandet N. . 199 A9
Hoym D. 82 A3
Høymyr N. 47 C6
Hoyocasero E . 150 B3
Hoyo de Manzanares E . . . 151 B4
Hoyo de Pinares E . . . 150 B3
Hoyos E 149 B3

Hoyos del Espino E. . . . 150 B2
Hrabušice SK. . .99 C4
Hradec Králové CZ . . .85 B3
Hradec nad Moravicí CZ. . .98 B1
Hrádek CZ 97 C4
Hrádek nad Nisou CZ. . . .84 B2
Hradiště SK 98 C2
Hrafnagil IS . . 191 B7
Hrafnseyri IS . 190 B2
Hranice
Severomoravsky CZ . . .98 B1
Západočeský CZ. . . .83 B4
Hranovnica SK . .99 C4
Hrasnica BIH . . 139 B4
Hrastnik SLO . . 123 A4
Hřensko CZ 84 B2
Hriňová SK. 99 C3
Hrisoupoli GR. 183 C6
Hrochov CZ 97 B4
Hrochův Tynec CZ . . .97 B3
Hrodna BY 13 B5
Hrodzyanka BY .13 B8
Hronov CZ 85 B4
Hronský Beňadik SK. . . .98 C2
Hrotovice CZ . . .97 B4
Hrtkovci SRB. . 127 C1
Hrun IS. 190 A5
Hrušov SK. . . . 112 A3
Hrušovany nad Jevišovkou CZ . . .97 C4
Hrvaćani BIH . . 124 C3
Hrvace HR . . . 138 B2
Hrymayliv UA. . 13 D7
Huben A 109 C3
Hückel-hoven D . . .80 A2
Hückeswagen D . . .80 A3
Hucknall UK. . . .40 B2
Hucqueliers F . .78 B1
Huddersfield UK . . .40 B2
Huddinge S 57 A3
Huddunge S 51 B3
Hude D 72 A1
Hudiksvall S . . 200 E3
Huélago E . . . 163 A4
Huélamo E . . . 152 B2
Huelgoat F. . . . 100 A2
Huelma E 163 A4
Huelva E 161 B3
Huéneja E 164 B2
Huércal de Almeria E . . . 164 C2
Huércal-Overa E . . . 164 B3
Huerta de Abajo E . . . 143 B3
Huerta del Rey E . . . 143 C3
Huerta de Valdecarabanos E. . . 151 C4
Huertahernando E. . . 152 B1
Huesa E 164 B1
Huesca E 145 B3
Huéscar E 164 B2
Huete E 151 B5
Huétor Tájar E. . . 163 A3
Hüfingen D . . . 106 B3
Hufthamar N. . .46 B2
Hugh Town UK. .42 B1
Huglfing D . . . 108 B2
Huissen NL. 70 C2
Huittinen FIN . . .8 B3
Huizen NL. 70 B2
Hulín CZ 98 B1
Hüls D 80 A2
Hulsig DK 58 A3
Hulst NL 79 A4
Hult S 62 A3
Hulta S. 56 B2
Hulteby S 55 A5
Hultsfred S. 62 A3
Humanes E . . . 151 B4
Humberston UK . . .41 B3
Humble DK 65 B3
Humenné SK. . . 12 D4
Humilladero E 163 A3

Humlebæk DK . 61 D2
Humlum DK. 58 B1
Hummelsta S . . .56 A2
Humpolec CZ . . .97 B3
Humshaugh UK . . .37 A4
Hundåla N 195 E3
Hundested DK . 61 D1
Hundorp N. 48 A1
Hundvåg N 52 A1
Hunedoara RO. .17 C5
Hünfeld D. 82 B1
Hungen D. 81 B4
Hungerford UK .44 B2
Hunndalen N . . .48 B2
Hunnebostrand S . . .54 B2
Hunstanton UK . . .41 C4
Huntingdon UK . . .44 A3
Huntley UK 39 C4
Huntly UK 33 D4
Hünxe D 80 A2
Hurbanovo SK 112 B2
Hürbel D 107 A4
Hurdal N 48 B3
Hurezani RO . . .17 C5
Hurlford UK 36 A2
Hurstbourne Tarrant UK . . .44 B2
Hurstpierpoint UK . . .44 C3
Hürth D 80 B2
Hurum N. 47 A5
Hurup DK 58 B1
Húsafell IS . . . 190 C5
Húsavík IS 191 A8
Husbands Bosworth UK. .44 A2
Husby
D 64 B2
DK 59 B1
Husey IS 191 B11
Huşi RO 17 B8
Husina BIH . . . 139 A4
Husinec CZ 96 B1
Husinish UK 31 B1
Huskvarna S . . .62 A2
Husnes N 46 C2
Husøy N 194 A8
Hustad N. 198 C4
Hüsten D. 81 A3
Hustopeče CZ . .97 C4
Hustopeče nad Bečvou CZ . . .98 B1
Husum
D 64 B2
S 200 C5
Husvika N. . . . 195 E3
Huta PL 75 B5
Hutovo BIH . . . 139 C3
Hüttenberg A. 110 C1
Hüttlingen D. . .94 C2
Huttoft UK 41 B4
Hutton Cranswick UK . . .40 B3
Hüttschlag A. . 109 B4
Huttwil CH. . . . 106 B2
Huy B 79 B5
Hüyük TR 189 B6
Hvåle N 47 B6
Hvaler N 54 A2
Hvalpsund DK . .58 B2
Hvammstangi IS . . . 190 B5
Hvammur IS . . 190 C4
Hvanneyri IS . . 190 C4
Hvar HR 138 B2
Hvarnes N. 53 A5
Hveragerði IS . 190 D4
Hvidbjerg DK . .58 B1
Hvide Sande DK . . .59 C1
Hvittingfoss N . .53 A6
Hvolsvøllur IS . 190 D5
Hybe SK. 99 B3
Hycklinge S 62 A3
Hyen N. 198 D2
Hyères F 132 B2
Hyères Plage F. . . 132 B2
Hylestad N. 52 A3
Hylke DK 59 C2
Hyllestad N 46 A1
Hyllstofta S 61 C3
Hyltebruk S. . . .60 B3
Hynnekleiv N. . .53 B4
Hythe
Hampshire UK . 44 C2

Hythe continued
Kent UK 45 B5
Hyvinkää FIN . . . 8 B4

I

Iam RO 127 B3
Iaşi RO. 17 B7
Iasmos GR . . . 183 B7
Ibahernando E . . . 156 A2
Ibarranguelua E . . . 143 A4
Ibbenbüren D . .71 B4
Ibeas de Juarros E . . . 143 B3
Ibestad N 194 B8
Ibi E. 159 C3
Ibiza = Eivissa E . . . 166 C1
İbradı TR 189 B6
İbriktepe TR . . 186 A1
Ibros E 157 B4
Ibstock UK. 40 C2
İçel TR. 23 C8
Ichenhausen D. .94 C2
Ichtegem B 78 A3
Ichtershausen D . . .82 B2
Idanha-a-Novo P . . . 155 B3
Idar-Oberstein D . . .93 B3
Idd N 54 A2
Idiazábal E . . . 144 B1
İdivuoma S . . . 196 A4
Idkerberget S . .50 B2
Idönn S 51 B5
Idre S 199 D9
İdrija SLO 123 A3
Idritsa RUS. 9 D6
Idstein D 81 B4
Idvor SRB 126 B2
Iecca Mare RO. 126 B2
Ielsi I 170 B2
Ieper = Ypres B .78 B2
Ierapetra GR . . 185 D6
Ierissos GR . . . 183 C5
Ifjord N 193 B11
Ig SLO 123 B3
Igal H 112 C1
Igea E 144 B1
Igea Marina I . . 136 A1
Igelfors S. 56 B1
Igersheim D. . . .94 B1
Igerøy N 195 E3
Iggesund S. . . . 200 E3
Iglesias E 143 B3
Iglésias I 179 C2
Igls A 108 B2
Igny-Comblizy F. . . .91 B3
Igorre E 143 A4
Igoumenitsa GR . . . 182 D2
Igries E 145 B3
Igualada E . . . 147 C2
Igüeña E 141 B4
Iguerande F . . 117 A4
Iharosberény H . . . 124 A3
İhlara TR 189 B6
Ihl'any SK 99 B4
Ihlienworth D . .64 C1
Ihringen D . . . 106 A2
İhsaniye TR . . . 187 C5
ii FIN 197 D8
Ijjärvi FIN . . . 193 C11
Ijsalmi FIN 3 E10
IJmuiden NL . . .70 B1
IJsselmuiden NL . . .70 B2
İkizdere TR 23 A9
İkast DK. 59 B2
İkervár H 111 B3
İlandža SRB . . 126 B2
İlanz CH 107 C4
İlava SK 98 C2
İlchester UK . . .43 B4
İlfeld D 82 A2
İlfracombe UK . .42 A2
İlgaz TR 23 A7
İlhavo P 148 B1
İlidža BIH. 139 B4
İlijaš BIH. 139 A4
İlirska Bistrica SLO . . . 123 B3
İlkeston UK 40 C2

Ilkley UK 40 B2
Illana E. 151 B5
Illano E. 141 A4
Illar E 164 C2
Illas E 141 A5
Illats F 128 B2
Illertissen D 94 C2
Illescas E 151 B4
Ille-sur-Têt F . . 146 B3
Illfurth F 106 B2
Illichivsk UA . . .17 B9
Illiers-Combray F . . .89 B5
Illkirch-Graffenstaden F . . .93 C3
Illmersdorf D . . .74 C2
Illmitz A 111 B3
Íllora E 163 A4
Illueca E 152 A2
Ilmajoki FIN. 8 A3
Ilmenau D 82 B2
Ilminster UK . . .43 B4
Ilok HR 126 B3
Ilomantsi FIN . . .9 A7
İlow PL 77 B5
İlowa PL 84 A3
İlowo-Osada PL . . .77 A5
Ilsenburg D 82 A2
Ilshofen D 94 B1
Ilz A 110 B2
İłża PL 87 A5
Imatra FIN 9 B6
Imielin PL. 86 B3
Imingen N 47 B5
Immeln S 63 B2
Immenhausen D . . .81 A5
Immenstadt D 107 B5
Immingham UK 41 B3
Imola I 135 A4
Imon E 151 A5
Imotski HR. . . . 138 B3
İmperia I 133 B4
Imphy F 104 C2
İmroz TR 183 C7
Imsland N. 52 A1
İmst A 108 B1
Inagh IRL. 28 B2
İnari FIN. 193 D10
Inca E 167 B2
Inchnadamph UK . . .32 C2
İncinillas E . . . 143 B3
İndal S. 200 D3
İndija SRB 127 B2
İndre Arna N . . .46 B2
İndre Billefjord N . . . 193 B9
İndre Brenna N . . . 193 B9
İğneada TR. . . 186 A2
İnebolu TR 23 A7
İnecik TR 186 B2
İnegöl TR 187 B4
İnerthal CH . . . 107 B3
İnfiesto E 142 A1
İngatorp S 62 A3
İngedal N 54 A2
İngelheim D 93 B4
İngelmunster B .78 B3
İngelstad S. 63 B2
İngleton UK 37 B4
İngolfsland N . .47 C5
İngolstadt D . . .95 C3
İngrandes
Maine-et-Loire F . . . 101 B5
Vienne F 102 C2
İngwiller F 93 C3
İnhisar TR 187 B5
İniesta E 158 B2
İnishannon IRL. .29 C3
İnishcrone IRL. .26 B1
İnke H 124 A3
İnke N. 124 A3
İnndyr N. 195 C5
İnnellan UK 34 C3
İnnerleithen UK . . .35 C4
İnnermessan UK . . .36 B2
İnnertkirchen CH . . . 106 C3
İnnervillgraten A . . . 109 C3
İnnsbruck A . . 108 B2
İnnset N 194 B9
İnnvik N 198 D3
İnönü TR 187 C5
İnowłódz PL . . .87 A4
İnowrocław PL. .76 B3
Ins CH. 106 B2

Insch UK 33 D4
Insjön S 50 B2
İnsko PL. 75 A4
İnstow UK 42 A2
İntepe TR 186 B1
İnterlaken CH. 106 C2
İntragna CH. . . 120 A1
İntrobio I 120 B2
İnverallochy UK . . .33 D5
İnveran
IRL 28 A2
UK 32 D2
İnveraray UK. . .34 B2
İnverbervie UK. 35 B5
İnvergarry UK. .32 D2
İnvergordon UK . . .32 D2
İnvergowrie UK . . .35 B4
İnverkeilor UK .35 B5
İnverkeithing UK . . .35 B4
İnvermoriston UK . . .32 D2
İnverness UK . . .32 D2
İnveruno I. . . . 120 B1
İnverurie UK . . .33 D4
İoannina GR . . 182 D2
İolanda di Savoia I . . . 121 C4
İon Corvin RO . .17 C7
İóppolo I 175 C1
İos GR. 185 C6
İpati GR 182 E4
İpsala TR 186 B1
İpswich UK 45 A5
İraklia GR 183 B5
İraklio = Heraklion GR . . . 185 D6
İrdning A 110 B1
İregszemcse H . . . 112 C2
İrgoli I 178 B3
İrig SRB 127 B1
İronbridge UK . .39 B4
İrpin UA 13 C9
İrrel D 92 B2
İrsina I 172 B2
İrsta S 56 A2
İrthlingborough UK . . .44 A3
İruela E 141 B4
İrún E 144 A2
İrurita E 144 A2
İrurzun E 144 B2
İrvine UK 36 A2
İrvinestown UK .27 B3
İsaba E 144 B3
İsabela E 157 B4
İsafjörður IS . . 190 A2
İsane N. 198 D2
İsaszeg H 112 B3
İsbister UK 33 A5
İscar E. 150 A3
İscehisar TR . . 187 D5
İschgl A 107 B5
İschia I 170 C1
İschia di Castro I . . . 168 A1
İschitella I . . . 171 B3
İsdes F 103 B4
İse N 54 A2
İselle I 119 A5
İseltwald CH . . 106 C2
İsen D 108 A3
İsenbüttel D . . .73 B3
İseo I 120 B3
İserlohn D 81 A3
İsérnia I 170 B2
İsfjorden N. . . 198 C4
İshëm AL 182 B1
İsigny-sur-Mer F . . .88 A2
İşıklı TR 189 A4
İsili I 179 C3
İskilip TR 23 A8
İsla Canela E . . 161 B2
İsla Cristina E . 161 B2
İslares E 143 A3
İsleham UK. 45 A4
İsle of Whithorn UK . . .36 B2
İsmaning D . . . 108 A2
İsna P 154 B3
İsnestoften N . 192 B7
İsny D 107 B5
İsoba E 142 A1
İsokylä
FIN 197 C10
S 196 B5

Isola del Gran Sasso d'Itália I . . . 169 A3
Isola della Scala I . . . 121 B4
Isola delle Fémmine I . . . 176 A2
Isola dei Liri I . 169 B3
Isola di Capo Rizzuto I . . . 175 C3
Isona E 147 B2
Ispagnac F . . . 130 A2
Isparta TR 189 B5
Isperih BG. 17 D7
Íspica I 177 C3
Isselburg D 80 A2
Issigeac F 129 B3
Issogne I 119 B4
Issoire F 116 B3
Issoncourt F . . .91 C5
Issoudun F . . . 103 C4
Is-sur-Tille F . . 105 B4
Issy-l'Evêque F . . . 104 C2
İstán E 162 B3
İstanbul TR . . . 186 A3
İstebna PL 98 B2
Ístia d'Ombrone I . . . 135 C4
Istiea GR 183 E5
Istres F 131 B3
Istvándi H. . . . 125 A3
Itea GR 184 A3
Ithaki GR 184 A1
Itoiz E 144 B2
Itrabo E 163 B4
Itri I 169 B3
Ittireddu I . . . 178 B2
Íttiri I. 178 B2
Itzehoe D 64 C2
Ivalo FIN . . . 193 D11
Iván H 111 B3
Ivanava BY 13 B6
Ivančice CZ 97 B4
Ivančna Gorica SLO . . . 123 B3
Iváncsa H 112 B2
Ivanec HR 124 A2
Ivanić Grad HR . . . 124 B2
Ivanjska BIH . . 124 C3
Ivanka SK 98 C2
Ivankovo UK . . 125 B4
Ivano-Frankivsk UA . . . 13 D6
Ivanovice na Hané CZ . . .98 B1
Ivanska HR. . . . 124 B2
Ivatsevichy BY .13 B6
Ivaylovgrad BG . . . 183 B8
Iveland N 53 B3
Ivoz Ramet B . . .79 B5
Ivrea I 119 B4
İvrindi TR 186 C2
Ivry-en-Montagne F . . . 104 B3
Ivry-la-Bataille F . . .90 C1
Ivybridge UK. . .42 B3
Iwaniska PL. . . .87 B5
Iwiny PL. 85 A3
Iwuy F 78 B3
Ixworth UK 45 A4
Izarra E 143 B4
Izbica Kujawska PL. . . .76 B3
Izbište SRB . . . 127 B3
Izeda P 149 A3
Izegem B 78 B3
Iznajar E 163 A3
Iznalloz E 163 A4
İznik TR 187 B4
Izola SLO 122 B2
Izsák H. 112 C3
Izsófalva H. 99 C4
İzyaslav UA 13 C7

J

Jabalquinto E . . . 157 B4
Jablanac HR . . 123 C3
Jablanica BIH . 139 B3
Jablonec nad Jizerou CZ . . .84 B3

Jablonec nad Nisou CZ 84 B3
Jablonica SK 98 C1
Jablonka PL....99 B3
Jabłonna PL....77 B5
Jablonnénad Orlicí CZ 97 A4
Jablonne Podještědí CZ 84 B2
Jablonov nad Turňou SK....99 C4
Jabłonowo Pomorskie PL .69 B4
Jablúnka CZ 98 B1
Jablunkov CZ ...98 B2
Jabučje SRB 127 C2
Jabugo E....161 B3
Jabuka SRB 127 C2
Jabukovac HR .124 B2
Jaca E............145 B3
Jáchymov CZ ...83 B4
Jacobidrebber D 72 B1
Jade D............71 A5
Jäderfors S......50 B3
Jädraås S.......50 B3
Jadraque E....151 B5
Jaén E............163 A4
Jagare BIH 124 C3
Jagel D............64 B2
Jagenbach A....96 C3
Jægerspris DK .61 D1
Jagodina SRB .127 D3
Jagodnjak HR .125 B4
Jagodzin PL....84 A3
Jagstheim D 94 B2
Jagstzell D....94 B2
Jahodna SK 111 A4
Jajce BIH 138 A3
Ják H............111 B3
Jakabszálbs H...............112 C3
Jäkkvik S......195 D8
Jakobsnes N .193 C14
Jakovlje HR 124 B1
Jakšić HR......125 B3
Jakubany SK 99 B4
Jalance E.......159 B2
Jalasjärvi FIN 8 A3
Jalhay B........80 B1
Jaligny-sur-Besbre F 117 A3
Jallais F........102 B1
Jalón E........159 C3
Jálons F......91 C4
Jamena SRB ...125 C5
Jamilena E....163 A4
Jämjö S.........63 B3
Jamnička Kiselica HR 124 B1
Jamno PL.......67 B5
Jamoigne B....92 B1
Jämsä FIN....8 A4
Jämshög S....63 B2
Jamu Mare RO 126 B3
Janakkala FIN 8 B4
Jandelsbrunn D 96 C1
Jänickendorf D .74 B2
Janikowo PL....76 B3
Janja BIH 125 C5
Janjina HR 138 C3
Janki
Łódzkie PL... 86 A3
Mazowieckie PL.............77 B5
Jankov CZ 96 B2
Jankowo Dolne PL.............76 B2
Jánoshalma H..............126 A1
Jánosháza H ...111 B4
Jánoshida H ...113 B4
Jánossomorja H..............111 B4
Janovice nad Uhlavou CZ ..96 B1
Janów PL......86 B3
Janowiec Wielkopolski PL.............76 B2
Janowo PL....77 A5
Jänsmässholmen S..............199 B10
Janville F 103 A3
Janzé F........101 B4
Jarabá SK......99 C3
Jaraczewo PL ..76 C2
Jarafuel E......159 B2
Jaraicejo E 156 A2
Jaraíz de la Vera E 150 B2

Jarak SRB 127 C1
Jarandilla de la Vera E.........150 B2
Jaray E........152 A1
Järbo S..........50 B3
Jard-sur-Mer F 114 B2
Jaren N 48 B2
Jargeau F 103 B4
Jarkovac SRB. 126 B2
Järlåsa S.......51 C4
Jarmen D 66 C2
Järna S..........57 A3
Jarnac F......115 C3
Järnäs S.......200 C5
Järnforsen S ...62 A3
Jarny F........92 B1
Jarocin PL.....76 C2
Jaroměř CZ ...85 B3
Jaroměřice nad Rokytnou CZ...97 B3
Jaroslav CZ ...97 A4
Jaroslavice CZ .97 C4
Jarosław PL....12 C5
Jarosławiec PL ..68 A1
Jarošov nad Nežárkou CZ ..96 B3
Järpås S.......55 B3
Järpen S 199 B10
Jarrow UK......37 B5
Järso FIN......51 B6
Järvenpää FIN ...8 B4
Jarvornik CZ ...85 B4
Järvsö S......200 E2
Jarzé F........102 B1
Jaša Tomic SRB 126 B2
Jasenak HR 123 B4
Jasenica BIH ..124 C2
Jasenice HR ...137 A4
Jasenovac HR ..124 B2
Jasenovo SRB .127 C3
Jasień PL......84 A3
Jasienica PL....84 A2
Jasło PL........112 B4
Jásova SK 112 B2
Jasseron F 118 A2
Jastarnia PL....69 A3
Jastrebarsko HR 123 B4
Jastrowie PL....68 B1
Jastrzębia-Góra PL.............77 A4
Jastrzębie Zdrój PL..............98 B2
Jászals-Lószentgyörgy H..............113 B4
Jászapáti H ...113 B4
Jászárokszállás H..............113 B4
Jászberény H ..113 B3
Jászdózsa H ...113 B4
Jászfényszaru H..............113 B3
Jászjakóhalma H..............113 B4
Jászkarajenő H..............113 B4
Jászkisér H....113 B4
Jászladány H ..113 B4
Jászszentlászló H..............113 C3
Jásztelek H ...113 B4
Játar E........163 B4
Jättendal S....200 E3
Jatznick D 74 A2
Jaun CH......106 C2
Jausiers F 132 A2
Jávea E........159 C4
Jävenitz D 73 B4
Javerlhac F ...115 C4
Javier E........145 B5
Javorani BIH ..124 C3
Javorina SK 99 B4
Javron F........89 B3
Jawor PL......85 A4
Jaworzno PL...86 B3
Jaworzyna Śl. PL.............85 B4
Jayena E......163 B4
Jazente P......148 A2
Jebel RO 126 B3
Jebjerg DK....58 B2
Jedburgh UK...35 C5
Jedlinsk PL....87 A5
Jedlnia PL......87 A5
Jedlnia Letnisko PL.............87 A5
Jednorożec PL ..77 A6
Jedovnice CZ ..97 B4
Jędrychów PL...69 B4
Jędrzejów PL...87 B4

Jedwabno PL ...77 A5
Jeesiö FIN.....197 B9
Jegłownik PL ...69 A4
Jegun F......129 C3
Jēkabpils LV 8 D4
Jektevik N......46 C2
Jektvik N.....195 D4
Jelcz-Laskowice PL.............85 A5
Jelenec SK 98 C2
Jelenia Góra PL .85 B3
Jelgava LV 8 D3
Jelka SK......111 A4
Jelling DK.....59 C2
Jels DK........59 C2
Jelsa
HR 138 B2
N.............. 52 A2
Jelšava SK......99 C4
Jemgum D 71 A4
Jemnice CZ ...97 B3
Jena D........82 B3
Jenaz CH......107 C4
Jenbach A 108 B2
Jenikow PL....75 A4
Jennersdorf A 111 C3
Jenny S........62 A4
Jerchel D......73 B4
Jeres del Marquesado E 164 B1
Jerez de la Frontera E 162 B1
Jerez de los Caballeros E . 155 C4
Jerica E........159 B3
Jerichow D...73 B5
Jerka PL......75 B5
Jermenovci SRB 126 B3
Jerslev DK....58 A3
Jerte E........150 B2
Jerup DK......58 A3
Jerxheim D ...73 B3
Jerzmanowice PL.............87 B3
Jerzu I 179 C3
Jerzwałd PL....69 B4
Jesberg D.....81 B5
Jesenice
Středočeský CZ 83 B5
Jesenice
Středočeský CZ 96 B2
Jeseník CZ ...85 B5
Jeseník SK.....99 C4
Jesi I 136 B2
Jésolo I 122 B1
Jessen D......83 A4
Jessenitz D....73 A4
Jessheim N 48 B3
Jessnitz D.....83 A4
Jesteburg D....72 A2
Jeumont F 79 B4
Jeven-stedt D...64 B2
Jever D........71 A4
Jevičko CZ....97 B4
Jevišovice CZ ..97 B3
Jevnaker N....48 B2
Jezerane HR ..123 B4
Jezero
BIH 138 A3
HR 123 B4
Jezów PL.....87 A3
Jičín CZ......84 B3
Jičíněves CZ ...84 B3
Jihlava CZ....97 B3
Jijona E......159 C3
Jilemnice CZ ...84 B3
Jílové CZ....84 B2
Jilovéu Prahy CZ 96 B2
Jimbolia RO...126 B2
Jimena E....163 A4
Jimena de la Frontera E . 162 B2
Jimera de Libar E 162 B2
Jimramov CZ ..97 B4
Jince CZ......96 B1
Jindřichovice CZ 83 B4
Jindřichův Hradec CZ 96 B3
Jirkov CZ......83 B5
Jistebnice CZ ..96 B2
Joachimsthal D .74 B2
João da Loura P 154 C2
Jobbágyi H ...112 B3
Jochberg A 109 B3
Jockfall S 196 C5

Jódar E........163 A4
Jodoigne B....79 B4
Joensuu FIN....9 A6
Joesjö S.....195 E5
Joeuf F........92 B1
Jõgeva EST.....8 C5
Johanngeorgenstadt D 83 B4
Johannishus S .63 B3
Johanniskirchen D 95 C4
Johansfors S...63 B3
John o'Groats UK 32 C3
Johnshaven UK .35 B5
Johnstone UK ..34 C3
Johnstown IRL .30 B1
Jõhvi EST......8 C5
Joigny F......104 B2
Joinville F......91 C5
Jokkmokk S...196 C2
Jöllenbeck D...72 B1
Jomala FIN.....51 B6
Jönåker S......56 B2
Jonava LT.....13 A6
Jonchery-sur-Vesle F 91 B3
Jondal N......46 B3
Jondalen N....53 A5
Joniškis LT......8 D3
Jönköping S ...62 A2
Jonkowo PL....69 B5
Jønnbu N......53 A5
Jonsberg S....56 B2
Jonsered S....60 B2
Jonstorp S....61 C2
Jonzac F 114 C3
Jorba E........147 C2
Jordanów PL...99 B3
Jordanowo PL ..75 B4
Jordanów Śląski PL.............85 B4
Jordbro S......57 A4
Jordbrua N ...195 D5
Jördenstorf D...66 C1
Jordet N........49 A4
Jordøse DK....59 C3
Jork D........72 A2
Jörlanda S....60 B1
Jormlien S ...199 A10
Jormvattnet S..............199 A11
Jörn S........200 A6
Jørpeland N....52 A2
Jorquera E....158 B2
Jošan HR.....123 C4
Jošavska BIH ..124 C3
Josipdol HR ...123 B4
Josipovac HR ..125 B4
Josselin F......101 B3
Jøssund N 199 A7
Jostedal N 47 A4
Jósvafő H 99 C4
Jou P..........148 A2
Jouarre F......90 C3
Joué-lès-Tours F 102 B2
Joué-sur-Erdre F 101 B4
Joue-sur-Loire Joughe F 131 A3
Joure NL......70 B2
Joutseno FIN ...9 B6
Joutsijärvi FIN 197 C10
Joux-la-Ville F. 104 B2
Jouy F........90 C1
Jouy-le-Châtel F 90 C3
Jouy-le-Potier F 103 B3
Joyeuse F 131 A3
Joze F........116 B3
Juankoski FIN ...8 A6
Juan-les-Pins F 132 B3
Jübek D........64 B2
Jubera E......144 B1
Jubrique E....162 B2
Jüchsen D.....82 B2
Judaberg N....54 A1
Judenburg A ..110 B1
Juelsminde DK .59 C3
Jugon-les-Lacs F 101 A3
Juillac F......129 A4
Juillan F......145 A4
Juist D........71 A4
Jukkasjärvi S .196 B3
Jule S.........199 A10
Julianadorp NL .70 B1
Julianstown

Jullouville F.....88 B2
Jumeaux F 117 B3
Jumièges F....89 A4
Jumilhac-le-Grand F 115 C5
Jumilla E......159 C2
Jumisko FIN. .197 C11
Juncosa E 153 A4
Juneda E......147 C1
Jung S........55 B4
Jungingen D...93 C5
Junglingster L ..92 B2
Juniville F......91 B4
Junosuando S .196 B5
Junqueira P ..149 A2
Junsele S......200 C2
Juoksengi S...196 C6
Juoksenki S....196 C6
Juprelle B......80 B1
Jura D.........69 A3
Jurbarkas LT ...12 A5
Jurjevo HR 123 C3
Jūrmala LV 8 D3
Jurmu FIN. ...197 D10
Juromenha P .155 C3
Jursla S........56 B2
Jussac F 116 C2
Jussey F......105 B4
Jussy F........90 B3
Juta H........125 A3
Jüterbog D....74 C2
Juuka FIN 3 E11
Juuma FIN ...197 C12
Juvigny-le-Terte F 88 B2
Juvigny-sous-Andaine F 88 B3
Juzennecourt F 105 A3
Jyderup DK....61 D1
Jyrkänkoski FIN. 197 C12
Jyväskylä FIN ...8 A4

K

Kaamanen FIN. 193 C10
Kaamasmukka FIN. 192 D6
Kaaresuvanto FIN. 192 D6
Kaarssen D 73 A4
Kaatscheuvel NL 79 A5
Kaba H........113 B5
Kåbdalis S 196 C3
Kačarevo SRB .127 C2
Kács H........113 B4
Kadan CZ 83 B5
Kadarkút H ...125 A3
Kadınhanı TR. 189 A7
Kaduy RUS 9 C10
Käfjälla S......56 A1
Kåfjord N 192 C7
Kåfjordbotn N. 192 C4
Kahla D.......82 B3
Kainach bei Voitsberg A ..110 B2
Kaindorf A 110 B2
Kainulasjärvi S..............196 C5
Kairala FIN 197 B10
Kaisepakte S .192 D3
Kaisersbach D...80 B1
Kaisersesch D .80 B3
Kaiserslautern

Kale
Antalya TR....189 C4
Denizli TR....188 B3
Kalecik TR......23 A7
Kalefeld D 82 A2
Kalesija BIH ...139 A4
Kalety PL......86 B2
Kalevala RUS...3 D12
Kalhovd N 47 B5
Kali HR........137 A4
Kalimnos GR ..188 C2
Kaliningrad RUS 69 A5
Kalinkavichy BY. 13 B8
Kalinovac HR . 124 A3
Kalinovik BIH .139 B4
Kalinovo SK ...99 C3
Kalirachi GR ..183 C6
Kaliska
Pomorskie PL ...68 A3
Pomorskie PL . 68 B3
Kalisko PL.....86 A3
Kalisz PL......86 A2
Kalisz Pomorski PL.............75 A4
Kaljord N 194 B6
Kalkan TR 189 C4
Kalkar D........80 A2
Kalkım TR 186 C2
Kall
D.............80 B2
S.............199 B10
Kållby S.......55 B4
Kållered S.....60 B2
Kållerstad S...60 B3
Kallinge S 63 B3
Kallmünz D ...95 B3
Kalló FIN......196 B7
Kallsedet S...199 B9
Källvik S......56 B3
Kalmar S......63 B4
Kalmthout B ..79 A4
Kalná S.......112 A2
Kalocsa H 112 C2
Kalokhorio CY 181 B2
Kalo Nero GR .184 B2
Kaloni GR 186 C1
Káloz H 112 C2
Kals A........109 B3
Kalsdorf A 110 C2
Kaltbrunn CH .107 B4
Kaltenbach A .108 B2
Kaltenkirchen D 64 C2
Kaltennordheim D 82 B2
Kaluđerovo SRB 127 B3
Kalundborg DK 61 D1
Kalush UA.....13 D6
Kalv S........60 B3
Kalvåg N......198 D1
Kalvehave DK...65 A5
Kalwang A 110 B1
Kalwaria-Zebrzydowska PL.............99 B3
Kalyazin RUS...9 D10
Kam H........111 B3
Kaman TR.....23 B7
Kamares GR ..185 C5
Kambos CY ...181 A1
Kamen D......81 A3
Kamenice nad Lipou CZ 96 B3
Kamen/AL. ...110 B2
Kameničná SK. 112 B2
Kamenný Most SK. 112 B2
Kamensko HR .138 B2
Kamenz D.....84 A2
Kamičak BIH ..124 C2
Kamień
Kamienec Zabk PL.............85 B4
Kamiena SK....99 B4
Kamień Krajeński PL.............76 A2
Kamienica Góra PL.............85 B4
Kamień Pomorski PL.............67 C3
Kamieńsk PL ..86 A3
Kamiros Skala GR 188 C2
Kamnik SLO...123 A3
Kampen NL....70 B2
Kampinos PL...77 B5
Kamp-Lintfort

Kampor HR ...123 C3
Kamyanets-Podil's'kyy UA 13 D7
Kamyanka-Buz'ka UA 13 C6
Kamýk nad Vltavou CZ 96 B2
Kanal SLO 122 A2
Kanalia GR ...182 D4
Kandalaksha RUS 3 C13
Kandanos GR .185 D4
Kandel D......93 B4
Kandern D ...106 B2
Kandersteg CH 106 C2
Kandila GR ...184 B3
Kandıra TR....187 A5
Kandyty PL....69 A5
Kanfanar HR ..122 B2
Kangasala FIN ..8 B4
Kangos S 196 B5
Kangosjärvi FIN 196 B6
Kaniów PL.....75 C3
Kanjiža SRB ...126 A2
Kankaanpää FIN .8 B3
Kannus FIN 3 E8
Kanturk IRL ...29 B3
Kapakli TR 186 A2
Kapellen
A. 110 B2
B. 79 A4
Kapellskär S ...57 A5
Kapfenberg A .110 B2
Kapfenstein A 110 C2
Kaplice CZ 96 C2
Kapljuh BIH ..124 C2
Kápolna H 113 B4
Kápolnásnyék H. 112 B2
Kaposfö H 125 A3
Kaposfüred H .125 A3
Kaposszekcsö H. 125 A4
Kaposvár H ...125 A3
Kapp N........48 B2
Kappel D 93 C3
Kappeln D.....64 B2
Kappelshamn S. 57 C4
Kappl A 107 B5
Kappstad S...55 A4
Kaprun A 109 B3
Kaptol HR.....125 B3
Kapuvár H 111 B4
Karaadilli TR . 189 A5
Karabiğa TR ..186 B2
Karabük TR....187 A7
Karaburun TR .186 D1
Karacabey TR .186 B3
Karacaköy TR .186 A3
Karacaören TR. 189 A5
Karacasu TR...188 B3
Karácsond H ..113 B4
Karád H.......112 C1
Karahallı TR ..189 A4
Karaisalı TR ...23 C8
Karaman
Balıkesir TR ..186 C3
Karaman TR ...23 C7
Karamanlı TR .189 B4
Karamürsel TR. 187 B4
Karan SRB 127 D1
Karancslapujto H. 113 A3
Karaova TR ...188 B2
Karapınar TR...23 C7
Karasjok N ...193 C9
Karasu TR 187 A5
Karataş
Adana TR 23 C8
Manisa TR ...188 A3
Karatoprak TR 188 B2
Karavostasi CY. 181 A1
Karben D......81 B4
Karbenning S ..50 B3
Kårböle S 199 D12
Karby
D.............64 B2
DK 58 B1
Kårby S 62 A4
Kårböle S 57 A4
Karcag H.....113 B4
Karczów PL....86 B1
Karczowiska PL .85 A4

Kardamena GR 188 C2
Kardamila GR . 185 A7
Kardamili GR . 184 C3
Kardašova Řečice CZ 96 B2
Kardis S 196 C6
Karditsa GR . 182 D3
Kärdla EST 8 C3
Kardoskút H . 113 C4
Kardzhali BG.. 183 B7
Karesuando S. 192 D6
Kargı TR......23 A8
Kargopol RUS...9 B11
Kargowa PL....75 B4
Karigasniemi FIN....193 C9
Karise DK 65 A5
Karistos GR ... 185 A5
Karkkila FIN.....8 B4
Karlholmsbruk S.............51 B4
Karlino PL......67 B4
Karlobag HR . 137 A4
Karlovac HR.. 123 B4
Karlovasi GR . 188 B1
Karlovčic SRB . 127 C2
Karlovice CZ....85 B5
Karlovo BG.... 17 D6
Karlovy Vary CZ............83 B4
Karłowice PL...86 B1
Karlsborg S....55 B5
Karlshamn S...63 B2
Karlshöfen D...72 A2
Karlshus N......54 A1
Karlskoga S....55 A5
Karlskrona S...63 B3
Karlsrud N......47 B5
Karlsruhe D....93 B4
Karlstad S......55 A4
Karlstadt D.....94 B1
Karlstetten A . 110 A2
Karlstift A......96 C2
Karlstorp S.....62 A3
Karmacs H ... 111 C4
Karmin PL......85 A5
Kärna S........60 B1
Karnobat BG... 17 D7
Karojba HR.... 122 B2
Karow D 73 A5
Karpacz PL....85 B3
Karpathos GR . 188 D2
Karpenisi GR . 182 E3
Karpuzlu TR... 188 B2
Kärrbo S 56 A2
Karrebaeksminde DK..............65 A4
Karshult S....60 B3
Karsin PL......68 B2
Kårsta S.......57 A4
Karstädt D 73 A4
Kartal TR..... 186 B4
Kartitsch A... 109 C3
Kartuzy PL....68 A3
Karungi S..... 196 C6
Karunki FIN ... 196 C7
Karup DK......59 B2
Karviná CZ.....98 B2
Kås DK.......58 A2
Kaş TR....... 189 C4
Kasaba TR.... 189 C4
Kašava CZ.....98 B1
Käseberga S ...66 A3
Kasejovice CZ...96 B1
Kasfjord N.... 194 B7
Kashin RUS....9 D10
Kašina HR.... 124 B2
Kasina-Wielka PL............99 B4
Kaskinen FIN....8 A2
Kašperské Hory CZ............96 B1
Kassandrino GR 183 C5
Kassel D.......81 A5
Kassiopi GR... 182 D1
Kastamonu TR .23 A7
Kastav HR.... 123 B3
Kasteli GR.... 185 D4
Kastellaun D...93 A3
Kastelli GR... 185 D6
Kaštel-Stari HR ... 138 B2
Kaštel Zegarski HR ... 138 A1
Kasterlee B 79 A4
Kastl D.........95 B3
Kastlösa S.....63 B4
Kastorf D 65 C3

Kastoria GR ... 182 C3
Kastorio GR ... 184 B3
Kastraki GR... 185 C6
Kastrosikia GR 182 D2
Kastsyukovichy BY............13 B10
Kaszaper H ... 113 C4
Katakolo GR . 184 B2
Katapola GR . 185 C6
Katastari GR . 184 B1
Katerbow D....74 B1
Katerini GR... 182 C4
Kathikas CY... 181 B1
Kätkesuando S............ 196 A6
Katlenburg-Lindau D............82 A2
Kato Achaia GR 184 A2
Káto Pyrgos CY 181 A1
Katouna GR... 182 E3
Katovice CZ....96 B1
Katowice PL....86 B3
Katrineberg S...50 A3
Katrineholm S . 56 B2
Kattarp S.....61 C2
Kattavia GR... 188 D2
Katthammarsvik S...........57 C4
Kattilstorp S ...55 B4
Katwijk NL.....70 B1
Katymár H ... 125 A5
Kąty Wrocławskie PL............85 A4
Katzenelnbogen D............81 B3
Katzhütte D....82 B3
Kaub D.........93 A3
Kaufbeuren D. 108 B1
Kauhajoki FIN....8 A3
Kauhava FIN ...8 A3
Kaukonen FIN . 196 B7
Kauliranta FIN 196 C6
Kaulsdorf D....82 B3
Kaunas LT......13 A5
Kaunisvaara S 196 B6
Kaupanger N ...47 A4
Kautokeino N . 192 C7
Kautzen A......97 C3
Kavadarci NMK 182 B4
Kavajë AL..... 182 B1
Kavaklıköy TR . 186 B1
Kavaklı TR ... 186 A2
Kavaklıdere TR 188 B3
Kavala GR.... 183 C6
Kavarna BG.... 17 D8
Kävlinge S.....61 D3
Kawakawköy TR . 188 A3
Kawcz-e PL....68 A1
Kaxås S 199 B10
Kaxholmen S ...62 A2
Käylä FIN..... 197 C12
Kaymakçı TR . 188 A3
Kaymaz TR... 187 C6
Kaynarca TR . 187 A5
Kayseri TR ... 23 B8
Kaysersberg F 106 A2
Kazanlak BG... 17 D6
Kazár H 113 A3
Kazimierza Wielka PL............87 B4
Kazincbarcika H............ 113 A4
Kaźmierz PL....75 B5
Kcynia PL......76 A2
Kdyně CZ......96 B1
Kea GR....... 185 B5
Keadew IRL....26 B2
Keady UK......27 B4
Kecel H....... 112 C3
Keçiborlu TR . 189 B5
Kecskemét H . 113 C3
Kėdainiai LT... 13 A5
Kędzierzyn-Koźle PL............86 B2
Keel IRL.......28 A1
Keenagh IRL...28 A1
Keerbergen B...79 A4
Kefalos GR... 188 C1
Kefken TR.... 187 A5
Kegworth UK ...40 C2
Kehl D.........93 C3
Kehrigk D......74 B2
Keighley UK....40 B2
Keila EST.......8 C4
Keillmore UK...34 C2
Keiss UK.......32 C3
Keith UK.......33 D4

Kelankylä FIN..........197 D10
Kelberg D......80 B2
Kelbra D.......82 A3
Kelč CZ........98 B1
Kelchsau A... 108 B3
Kelčyrë AL... 182 C2
Keld UK........37 B4
Kelebia H 126 A1
Kelekçi TR... 188 B4
Kelemér H.....99 C4
Keles TR...... 186 C4
Kelheim D.....95 C3
Kell D.........92 B2
Kellas UK..... 33 D4
Kellinghusen D .64 C2
Kelloselkä FIN...........197 C11
Kells IRL......27 C4
Kelmis B......80 B2
Kelokedhara CY 181 B1
Kelottijärvi FIN...........192 D6
Kelsall UK.....38 A4
Kelso UK......35 C5
Kelsterbach D..93 A4
Keltneyburn UK 35 B3
Kelujärvi FIN. 197 B10
Kemaliye TR . 188 A3
Kemalpaşa TR . 188 A2
Kematen A... 108 B2
Kemberg D.....83 A4
Kemer Antalya TR... 189 C5
Kemer Burdur TR. 189 B5
Kemer Muğla TR . 189 C4
Kemerkaya TR 187 D6
Kemeten A... 111 B3
Kemi FIN..... 196 D7
Kemijärvi FIN........197 C10
Keminmaa FIN...........196 D7
Kemnath D....95 B3
Kemnay UK.... 33 D4
Kemnitz Brandenburg D............74 B1
Kemnitz Mecklenburg-Vorpommern D............66 B2
Kempen D......80 A2
Kempsey UK...39 B4
Kempten D... 107 B5
Kemptthal CH. 107 B3
Kendal UK.....37 B4
Kenderes H ... 113 B4
Kengyel H.... 113 B4
Kenilworth UK .44 A2
Kenmare IRL...29 C2
Kenmore UK...35 B4
Kennacraig UK .34 C2
Kenyeri H 111 B4
Kenzingen D . 106 A2
Kepez TR..... 186 B1
Kępice PL.....68 A1
Kępno PL......86 A2
Kepsut TR.... 186 C3
Keramoti GR . 183 C6
Keräntöjärvi S............ 196 B6
Keratea GR... 185 B4
Kerava FIN 8 B4
Kerecsend H . 113 B4
Kerekegyhaza H 112 C3
Kerepestarcsa H 112 B3
Keri GR...... 184 B1
Kérien F...... 100 A2
Kerkafalva H . 111 C3
Kerken D.......80 A2
Kerkrade NL....80 B2
Kerkyra GR... 182 D1
Kerlouan F.... 100 A1
Kernascléden F 100 A2
Kernhof A.... 110 B2
Kerns CH..... 106 C3
Kerpen D......80 B2
Kerrysdale UK .31 B3
Kerteminde DK .59 C3
Kerzers CH... 106 C2
Keşan TR..... 186 B1
Kesgrave UK...45 A5
Kesh UK.......26 B3

Keskin TR......23 B7
Kesselfall A ... 109 B3
Kestenga RUS...3 D12
Keswick UK....36 B3
Keszthely H... 111 C4
Kétegyháza H. 113 C5
Kéthely H..... 111 C4
Kętrzyn PL.....12 A4
Kettering UK...44 A3
Kettlewell UK...40 A1
Kęty PL........99 B3
Ketzin D.......74 B1
Keula D........82 A2
Keuruu FIN.....8 A4
Kevelaer D.....80 A2
Kevermes H... 113 C5
Kevi SRB 126 B1
Keyingham UK .41 B3
Keynsham UK...43 A4
Kežmarok SK...99 B4
Khimki RUS....9 E10
Chişinău MD ...17 B8
Khmelnik UA... 13 D7
Khmelnytskyy UA 13 D7
Khodoriv UA . 13 D6
Kholm RUS.....9 D7
Khotyn UA.... 13 D7
Khoyniki BY... 13 C8
Khust UA...... 17 A5
Khvoynaya RUS...9 C9
Kiato GR..... 184 A3
Kibæk DK......59 B1
Kiberg N..... 193 B14
Kicasalih TR . 186 A1
Kičevo NMK.. 182 B3
Kidderminster UK 39 B4
Kidlington UK..44 B2
Kidsgrove UK..40 B1
Kidwelly UK...39 C2
Kiefersfelden D 108 B3
Kiel D.........64 B3
Kielce PL......87 B4
Kiełczygłów PL...........86 A3
Kielder UK.....37 A4
Kiełpino PL....68 A3
Kielpiny PL....77 A4
Kierinki FIN.. 197 B8
Kiernozia PL...77 B4
Kierspe D......81 A3
Kietrz PL......86 B2
Kietz D........74 B3
Kiev = Kyyiv UA 13 C9
Kiezmark PL...69 A3
Kiffisia GR... 185 A4
Kifino Selo BIH.......... 139 B4
Kihlanki FIN........ 196 B6
Kiistala FIN.. 197 B8
Kije PL........87 B4
Kijevo HR.... 138 B2
Kikallen N.....46 B2
Kikinda SRB.. 126 B2
Kil Örebro S ...55 A6
Värmland S 55 A4
Kila S.........55 A3
Kilafors S.....50 A3
Kilbaha IRL....29 B2
Kilbeggan IRL .30 A1
Kilberry UK....34 C2
Kilbirnie UK...34 C3
Kilboghamn N............ 195 D4
Kilbotn N.... 194 B7
Kilb Rabenstein A 110 A2
Kilchattan UK .34 C2
Kilchoan UK...34 B1
Kilcock IRL....30 A2
Kilconnell IRL .28 A3
Kilcormac IRL .28 A4
Kilcreggan UK .34 C3
Kilcullen IRL...30 A2
Kilcurry IRL....27 B4
Kildare IRL....30 A2
Kildinstroy RUS 3 B13
Kildonan UK...32 C3
Kildorrery IRL .29 B3
Kilegrend N....53 A4
Kilen N........53 A4
Kilgarvan IRL .29 C2
Kiliya UA......17 C8
Kilkee IRL.....29 B2
Kilkeel UK.....27 B4

Kilkelly IRL......26 C2
Kilkenny IRL....30 B1
Kilkieran IRL...28 A2
Kilkinlea IRL...29 B2
Kilkis GR..... 182 B4
Killadysert IRL .29 B2
Killala IRL.....26 B1
Killaloe IRL....28 B3
Killarney IRL...29 C2
Killashandra IRL 27 B3
Killashee IRL...28 A4
Killearn UK....34 B3
Killeberg S....61 C4
Killeigh IRL....28 A4
Killenaule IRL .29 B4
Killimor IRL....28 A3
Killin UK...... 34 B3
Killinaboy IRL .28 B2
Killinick IRL.... 30 B2
Killorglin IRL...29 B2
Killucan IRL....30 A1
Killybegs IRL...26 B2
Killyleagh UK ..27 B5
Kilmacrenan IRL 26 A3
Kilmacthomas IRL 30 B1
Kilmaine IRL...28 A2
Kilmallock IRL .29 B3
Kilmarnock UK .36 A2
Kilmartin UK...34 B2
Kilmaurs UK...36 A2
Kilmeadan IRL .30 B1
Kilmeedy IRL...29 B3
Kilmelford UK..34 B2
Kilmore Quay IRL 30 B2
Kilmuir UK.... 32 D2
Kilnaleck IRL...27 C3
Kilninver UK...34 B2
Kilpisjärvi FIN. 192 C4
Kilrea UK......27 B4
Kilrush IRL.....29 B2
Kilsmo S......56 A1
Kilsyth UK.....35 C3
Kiltoom IRL....28 A3
Kilwinning UK .36 A2
Kimasozero RUS 3 D12
Kimi GR...... 185 A5
Kimolos GR... 185 C5
Kimovsk RUS...9 E10
Kimratshofen D 107 B5
Kimry RUS.....9 D10
Kimstad S.....56 B1
Kinbrace UK...32 C3
Kincardine UK .35 B4
Kincraig UK... 32 D3
Kindberg A... 110 B2
Kindelbruck D .82 A3
Kingarrow IRL .26 B2
Kingisepp RUS...9 C6
Kingsbridge UK 43 B3
Kingsclere UK .44 B2
Kingscourt IRL .27 C4
King's Lynn UK .41 C4
Kingsteignton UK 43 B3
Kingston Greater London UK 44 B3
Kingston Moray UK.... 32 D3
Kingston Bagpuize UK 44 B2
Kingston upon Hull UK 40 B3
Kingswear UK .43 B3
Kingswood UK .43 A4
Kington UK.... 39 B3
Kingussie UK.. 32 D2
Kınık Antalya TR. 188 C4
İzmir TR . 186 C2
Kinloch Highland UK.. 31 B2
Highland UK. 32 C2
Kinlochbervie UK 32 C1
Kinlochewe UK .31 B3
Kinlochleven UK 34 B3
Kinloch Moidart UK 34 B2
Kinloch Rannoch UK 35 B3
Kinloss UK.... 32 D3
Kinlough IRL...26 B2
Kinn N........48 B2
Kinna S....... 60 B2
Kinnared S 60 C3

Kinnarp S 55 B4
Kinnegad IRL...30 A1
Kinne-Kleva S... 55 B4
Kinnitty IRL....28 A4
Kinrooi B......80 A1
Kinross UK.... 35 B4
Kinsale IRL.....29 C3
Kinsarvik N ...46 B3
Kintarvie UK...31 A2
Kintore UK.... 33 D4
Kinvarra IRL...28 A3
Kioni GR..... 184 A1
Kiparissia GR . 184 B2
Kipfenberg D...95 C3
Kippen UK.... 35 B3
Kiraz TR..... 188 A3
Kirazlı TR.... 186 B1
Kirberg D......81 B4
Kirchbach in Steiermark A............ 110 C2
Kirchberg CH 106 B2
Kirchberg Baden-Württemberg D............94 B1
Kirchberg Rheinland-Pfalz D............93 B3
Kirchberg am Wechsel A... 110 B2
Kirchberg an der Pielach A... 110 A2
Kirchberg in Tirol A............ 109 B3
Kirchbichl A.. 108 B3
Kirchdorf Bayern D ...96 C1
Kirchdorf Mecklenburg-Vorpommern D............65 C4
Kirchdorf Niedersachsen D............72 B1
Kirchdorf an der Krems A... 109 B5
Kirchdorf in Tirol A............ 109 B3
Kirchenlamitz D............83 B3
Kirchenthumbach D............95 B3
Kirchhain D....81 B4
Kirchheim Baden-Württemberg D............94 C1
Bayern D . 108 A1
Hessen D....81 B5
Kirchheimbolanden D............93 B4
Kirchhundem D............81 A4
Kirchlintein D .72 B2
Kirchschlag A 111 B3
Kirchweidach D............109 A3
Kirchzarten D 106 B2
Kircubbin UK...27 B5
Kireç TR..... 186 C3
Kırıkkale TR ...23 B7
Kirillov RUS....9 C11
Kirishi RUS.....9 C8
Kırka TR..... 187 C5
Kırkağaç TR... 186 C2
Kirkbean UK...36 B3
Kirkbride UK...36 B3
Kirkby UK.....38 A4
Kirkby Lonsdale UK 37 B4
Kirkby Malzeard UK 40 A2
Kirkbymoorside UK 37 B6
Kirkby Stephen UK 37 B4
Kirkcaldy UK...35 B4
Kirkcolm UK...36 B1
Kirkconnel UK .36 A2
Kirkcowan UK .36 B2
Kirkcudbright UK 36 B2
Kirkehamn N...52 B2
Kirke Hyllinge DK 61 D1
Kirkenær N....48 B3
Kirkenes N... 193 C14
Kirkham UK....38 A4
Kirkintilloch UK 35 C3
Kirkjubøur FO .4 A3
Kirkkonummi FIN 8 B4
Kırklareli TR . 186 A2

Kirkmichael UK .35 B4
Kirk Michael UK 36 B2
Kirkoswald UK .36 A2
Kirkpatrick Fleming UK 36 A3
Kirkton of Glenisla UK 35 B4
Kirkwall UK.... 33 C4
Kirkwhelpington UK 37 A5
Kirn D.........93 B3
Kirovsk RUS... 3 C13
Kirriemuir UK . 35 B5
Kırşehir TR 23 B8
Kirton UK......41 C3
Kirton in Lindsey UK 40 B3
Kirtorf D.......81 B5
Kiruna S..... 196 B3
Kisa S.........62 A3
Kisać SRB.... 126 B1
Kisbér H...... 112 B2
Kiseljak BIH... 139 B4
Kisielice PL.....69 B4
Kiskőre H.... 113 B4
Kiskőrös H.... 112 C3
Kiskunfélegyháza H 113 C3
Kiskunhalas H 112 C3
Kiskunlacháza H 112 B2
Kiskunmajsa H 113 C3
Kisláng H.... 112 C2
Kisslegg D... 107 B4
Kissolt H..... 112 C3
Kissónerga CY 181 B1
Kist D.........94 B1
Kistanje HR.. 138 B1
Kistelek H.... 113 C3
Kisterenye H . 113 A3
Kisújszállás H 113 B4
Kisvárda H..... 16 A5
Kisvejke H.... 112 C2
Kiszkowo PL...76 B2
Kiszombor H . 126 A2
Kitee FIN.......9 A7
Kithnos GR... 185 B5
Kiti CY...... 181 B2
Kitkiöjärvi S . 196 B6
Kitkiöjoki S . 196 B6
Kittelfjäll S... 195 E6
Kittendorf D...74 A1
Kittilä FIN... 196 B7
Kittlitz D......84 A2
Kittsee A..... 111 A4
Kitzbühel A... 109 B3
Kitzingen D....94 B2
Kiuruvesi FIN...3 E10
Kivertsi UA.... 13 C6
Kividhes CY... 181 B1
Kivik S........63 C2
Kivotos GR... 182 C3
Kıyıköy TR ... 186 A3
Kızılcabölük TR 188 B4
Kızılcadağ TR 189 B4
Kızılcahamam TR 23 A7
Kızılırmak TR ...23 A7
Kızılkaya TR . 189 B5
Kızılkuyu TR . 187 D6
Kızılören Afyon TR. 189 A5
Konya TR . 189 B7
Kjeldebotn N . 194 B7
Kjellerup DK...59 B2
Kjellmyra N....49 B4
Kjøllefjord N. 193 B11
Kjopmannskjaer N.............54 A1
Kjøpsvik N... 194 B7
Kľačno SK.....98 C2
Kladanj BIH... 139 A4
Kladnice HR.. 138 B2
Kladno CZ.....84 B2
Kladruby CZ....95 B4
Klagenfurt A . 110 C1
Klågerup S.....66 A2
Klagstorp S....66 A2
Klaipėda LT.....8 E2
Klaistow D.....74 B1
Klaksvík FO.....4 A3
Klana HR..... 123 B3
Klanac HR.... 123 C4
Klanjec HR... 123 A4

Klardorf D 95 B4
Klarup DK......58 A3
Klašnice BIH... 124 C3
Klässbol S......55 A3
Klášterec nad Ohří
CZ 83 B5
Kláštor pod
Znievom SK...98 C2
Klatovy CZ....96 B1
Klaus an der
Pyhrnbahn
A............. 110 B1
Klazienaveen
NL 71 B3
Klecko PL......76 B2
Kleczew PL.....76 B3
Klein Plasten D..74 A1
Klein Sankt Paul
A............ 110 C1
Kleinsölk A ... 109 C4
Kleinzell A 110 B2
Klejtrup DK....58 B2
Klek SRB 126 B2
Klenak SRB... 127 C1
Klenci pod
Cerchovem
CZ 95 B4
Klenica PL.....75 C4
Klenje SRB 127 C1
Klenoec NMK . 182 B2
Klenovec SK....99 C3
Klenovica HR . 123 B3
Klenovnik HR . 124 A2
Kleppe N.......52 B1
Kleppestø N ...46 B2
Kleptow D 74 A2
Kleszewo PL ...77 B6
Kleve D 80 A2
Klevshult S.....60 B4
Klewki PL 77 A5
Kličevac SRB .. 127 C3
Kliening A 110 C1
Klietz D 73 B5
Klikuszowa PL ..99 B3
Klimkovice CZ ..98 B2
Klimontów PL...87 B5
Klimovichi BY .. 13 B9
Klimpfjäll S ... 195 E5
Klin RUS.......9 D10
Klinča Sela
HR 123 B4
Klingenbach
A............ 111 B3
Klingenberg D .93 B5
Klingenmunster
D 93 B4
Klingenthal D..83 B4
Klinken D......73 A4
Klintehamn S .. 57 C4
Kliny PL.......48 A3
Kliplev DK.....64 B2
Klippan S......61 C3
Klis HR 138 B2
Klitmøller DK .. 58 A1
Klitten S 49 A6
Klixbüll D......64 B1
Kljajićevo SRB. 126 B1
Ključ BIH 138 A2
Klobouky CZ....97 C4
Klobuck PL.....86 B2
Klockestrand
S............ 200 D3
Kłodawa
Lubuskie PL...75 B4
Wielkopolskie
PL...........76 B3
Kłodzko PL.....85 B4
Kløfta N.......48 B3
Klokkarvik N...46 B2
Klokkerholm
DK 58 A3
Klokočov SK....98 B2
Kłomnice PL....86 B3
Klonowa PL.....86 A2
Kloosterzande
NL 79 A4
Kłopot PL......74 B3
Klos AL....... 182 B2
Klošter Ivanić
HR 124 B2
Kloster
D 66 B2
D 59 B1
Klösterle A 107 B5
Klostermansfeld
D 82 A3
Klosterneuburg
A............97 C4
Klosters CH ... 107 C4
Kloten CH..... 107 B3
Klötze D.......73 B4
Klöverträsk S . 196 D4

Klövsjö S..... 199 C11
Kluczbork PL...86 B2
Kluczewo PL ...54 A2
Kluisbergen B...79 B3
Klundert NL....79 A4
Klutz D........65 C4
Klwów PL......87 A4
Klyetsk BY 13 B7
Knaben N......52 B2
Knaften S..... 200 B4
Knapstad N....54 A2
Knäred S.......61 C3
Knaresborough
UK 40 A2
Knarvik N......46 B2
Knebel DK.....59 B3
Knebworth UK..44 B3
Knesebeck D....73 B3
Knesselare B...78 A3
Knežak SLO ... 123 B3
Kneževi Vinogradi
HR 125 B4
Kneževo HR ... 125 B4
Knić SRB 127 D2
Knighton UK ...39 B3
Knin HR 138 A2
Knislinge S.....61 C4
Knittelfeld A . 110 B1
Knivsta S......37 C4
Knock IRL......28 A3
Knocktopher
IRL 30 B1
Knokke-Heist
B.............78 A3
Knowle UK.....44 A2
Knurów PL.....86 B2
Knutby S.......51 C5
Knutsford UK ..38 A4
Kobarid SLO .. 122 A2
København =
Copenhagen
DK 61 D2
Kobenz A 110 B1
Kobersdorf A . 111 B3
Kobiernice PL...99 B3
Kobierzyce PL..85 B4
Kobilje SLO ... 111 C3
Kobiór PL......86 B2
Koblenz
CH 106 B3
D 81 B3
Kobryn BY 13 B6
Kobylanka PL...75 A3
Kobylin PL.....85 A5
Kobylniki PL....77 B5
Kocaali TR.... 187 A5
Kocaalilar TR . 189 B5
Kocaeli = İzmit
D 93 B4
Kočani NMK... 182 B4
Koçarlı TR.... 188 B2
Kočevje SLO .. 123 B3
Kočevska Reka
SLO 123 B3
Kochel am see
D 108 B2
Kocs H 112 B2
Kocsér H 113 B3
Koczala PL.... 112 C2
Kodal N.......54 A1
Kode S.........60 B1
Kodrab PL......86 A3
Koekelare B....78 A2
Kofçaz TR 186 A2
Köflach A 110 B2
Køge DK 61 D2
Kohlberg D 95 B4
Kohila EST.....8 C4
Kohtla-Järve
EST...........8 C5
Köinge S.......60 B2
Kojetín CZ.....98 B1
Kökar FIN......51 C7
Kokava SK.....99 C3
Kokkinotrimithia
CY 181 A2
Kokkola FIN... 3 E8
Kokori BIH.... 124 C3
Kokoski PL.....69 A3
Kola
BIH......... 124 C3
RUS...........3 B13
Köla S.........54 A3
Kolačin PL.....87 A4
Kolari FIN 196 B6
Kolárovo SK... 112 B1
Kolašin MNE .. 16 D3
Kolbäck S......56 A2
Kolbacz PL.....75 A3

Kolbeinsstaðir
IS 190 C3
Kolbermoor D 108 B3
Kolbnitz A 109 C4
Kolbotn N......54 A1
Kolbu N........48 B2
Kolby Kås DK...59 C3
Kolczewo PL....67 C3
Kolczyglowy
PL............68 A2
Kolding DK 59 C2
Kölesd H...... 112 C2
Kolgrov N......46 A1
Kolín CZ 97 A3
Kolind DK......59 B3
Kolinec CZ.....96 B1
Koljane HR.... 138 B2
Kølkær DK.....59 B2
Kölleda D......82 A3
Kollum NL.....70 A3
Köln = Cologne
D 80 B2
Kolo PL........76 B3
Kołobrzeg PL...67 B4
Kolochau D....83 A5
Kolomyya UA .. 13 D6
Kolonowskie
PL............86 B2
Koločev CZ.....95 B5
Kolpino RUS....9 C7
Kolrep D.......73 A5
Kölsillre S.... 199 C12
Kolsko PL......75 C4
Kolsva S.......56 A1
Kolta SK...... 112 A2
Kolunić BIH... 138 A2
Koluszki PL....87 A3
Kolut SRB 125 B4
Kolvereid N... 199 A8
Kølvrå DK......59 B2
Komadi H..... 113 B5
Komagvær N. 193 B14
Komarica BIH . 125 C3
Komárno SK... 112 B2
Komárom H... 112 B2
Komatou Yialou
CY 181 A3
Kombotí GR... 182 D3
Komen SLO ... 122 B2
Komin HR..... 138 B3
Komiža HR.... 138 B2
Komját H......99 C4
Komjatice SK.. 112 A2
Komletinci HR 125 B4
Komló H 125 A4
Kömlo H 113 B4
Komoča SK.... 112 B2
Komorniki PL...75 B5
Komorzno PL...86 A2
Komotini GR.. 183 B7
Konak SRB ... 126 B2
Konakovo RUS...9 D10
Konarzyny PL...68 B2
Kondias GR... 183 D7
Kondopaga RUS .9 A9
Kondorfa H... 111 C3
Kondoros H.... 113 C4
Konevo RUS...9 A11
Konga S.......63 B3
Köngäs FIN... 196 B7
Kongerslev DK. 58 B3
Kongsberg N...53 A5
Kongshamn N..53 B4
Kongsmark DK..64 A1
Kongsmoen N 199 A9
Kongsvik N....194 B7
Kongsvinger N..48 B3
Konice CZ......97 B4
Konie PL.......77 C5
Koniecpol PL...86 B3
Königsberg D...82 B2
Königsbronn D .94 C2
Königsbrück D .84 A1
Königsbrunn D .94 C2
Königsdorf D . 108 B2
Königsee D.....82 B2
Königshorst D..74 B1
Königslutter D .73 B3
Königssee D... 109 B3
Königstein
Hessen D.....81 B4
Sachsen D.....84 B2
Königstetten A .97 C4
Königswartha
D 84 A2
Königswiesen
A............96 C2
Königswinter
D 80 B3
Königs
Wusterhausen
D 74 B2

Konin PL.......76 B3
Konispol AL... 182 D2
Konitsa GR... 182 C2
Köniz CH...... 106 C2
Konjevići BIH . 139 A5
Konjevrate HR 138 B2
Konjic BIH.... 139 B3
Konjščina HR.. 124 A2
Könnern D.....83 A3
Konnerud N....53 A6
Konopiska PL...86 B2
Konotop PL....75 C4
Końskie PL.....87 A4
Konsmo N 52 B3
Konstancin-
Jeziorna PL...77 B6
Konstantynów
Łódźki PL.....86 A3
Konstanz D....107 B4
Kontich B......79 A4
Kontiolahti FIN . 9 A6
Konya TR..... 189 B7
Konz D........92 B2
Kópasker IS... 191 A9
Kópavogur IS . 190 C4
Kopčany SK....98 C1
Koper SLO 122 B2
Kopervik N 52 A1
Kópháza H.... 111 B3
Kopice PL......85 B5
Kopidlno CZ...84 B3
Köping S.......56 A1
Köpingebro S ..66 A2
Köpingsvik S...62 B4
Köpmanholmen
S............ 200 C4
Koppang N 48 A3
Koppangen N . 192 C4
Kopparberg S...50 C1
Koppelo FIN . 193 D11
Koppom S.....54 A3
Koprivlen BG . 183 B5
Koprivna BIH . 125 C4
Koprivnica
HR 124 A2
Köprübaşı
TR.......... 186 D3
Koprzywnica
PL............87 B5
Kopstal L......92 B2
Kopychyntsi
UA 13 D6
Kopytkowo PL .69 B3
Korbach D.....81 A4
Körbecke D....81 A4
Korçë AL..... 182 C2
Korčula HR.... 138 C3
Korczyców PL...75 B3
Korenica HR... 123 C4
Korenita SRB.. 127 C1
Korets UA......13 C7
Korfantów PL...85 B5
Körfez TR..... 187 B4
Korgen N..... 195 D4
Korinth D......59 C3
Korinthos = Corinth
GR 184 B3
Korita
BIH......... 138 A2
MNE......... 139 C5
Korithi GR.... 184 B1
Korkuteli TR . 189 B5
Körmend H... 111 B3
Korneuburg A . 97 C4
Kornevo RUS...69 A5
Kórnik PL......76 B2
Kornsjø N......54 B2
Környe H...... 112 B2
Koromačno
HR 123 B3
Koroni GR.... 184 C2
Koronos GR... 185 B6
Koronowo PL...76 A2
Körösladány
H............ 113 C5
Köröstarcsa
H............ 113 C5
Korosten UA... 13 C8
Korostyshev
UA 13 C8
Korpikå S..... 196 D6
Korpikylä FIN . 196 C6
Korpilombolo
S............ 196 C6
Korsberga
Jönköping S .. 62 A3
Skaraborg S .. 55 B5
Korskrogen S . 200 E1
Korsør DK.....65 A4

Korsun
Shevchenkovskiy
UA 13 D9
Kortemark B... 78 A3
Kortrijk B......78 B3
Korucu TR.... 186 C2
Koryčany CZ...98 B1
Korzeńsko PL...85 A4
Kos GR 188 C2
Kosakowo PL...69 A3
Kosanica MNE. 139 B5
Kösching D.....95 C3
Kościan PL.....75 B5
Kościelec PL....76 B3
Kościerzyna PL .68 A2
Koserow D.....66 B2
Košice SK..... 12 D4
Kosjerić SRB... 127 D1
Koška HR..... 125 B4
Koskullskulle
S............ 196 B3
Kosovska Mitrovica
KOS 16 D4
Kosta S........62 B3
Kostajnica
BIH......... 124 B2
Kostanjevica
SLO 123 B4
Kostelec nad
Černými Lesy
CZ 96 B2
Kostelec na Hané
CZ 97 B5
Kostice CZ.....84 B1
Kostkowo PL...68 A3
Kostojevići SRB 127 C1
Kostolac SRB.. 127 C3
Kostomłoty PL .85 A4
Kostopil UA... 13 C7
Kostów PL.....86 A2
Kostrzyn
Lubuskie PL...74 B3
Wielkopolskie
PL............76 B2
Koszalin PL....67 B5
Koszęcin PL....86 B2
Köszeg H 111 B3
Koszwaly PL....69 A3
Koszyce PL.....87 B4
Kotala FIN.... 197 B11
Kötelek H..... 113 B4
Köthen D......83 A3
Kotka FIN......8 B5
Kotomierz PL...76 A3
Kotor MNE.... 16 D3
Kotoriba HR... 124 A2
Kotorsko BIH.. 125 C4
Kotor Varoš
BIH......... 124 C3
Kotovsk UA.... 17 B8
Kotronas GR.. 184 C3
Kötschach D.. 109 C3
Kötzting D.....95 B4
Koudum NL....70 B2
Kouřim CZ.....96 A2
Kout na Šumave
CZ 95 B5
Kouvola FIN.....8 B5
Kovačevac
SRB 127 C2
Kovačica SRB.. 126 B2
Kovdor RUS... 197 B13
Kovel' UA..... 13 C6
Kovilj SRB.... 126 B2
Kovin SRB 127 C2
Kowal PL......77 B4
Kowalewo
Pomorskie PL .69 B3
Kowary PL.....85 B3
Köyceğiz TR.. 188 C3
Kozani GR.... 182 C3
Kozarac
BIH......... 124 C2
HR 124 B3
Kozárovce SK . 98 C2
Kozelets UA... 13 C9
Kozica HR..... 138 B3
Kozie Głowy PL 86 B3
Kozienice PL...87 A5
Kozina SLO ... 122 B2
Kozje SLO 123 A4
Kozluk BIH.... 139 A5
Koźmin PL.....86 A1

Koźminek PL...86 A2
Kozolupy CZ....96 B1
Kożuchów PL...84 A3
Kožuhe BIH ... 125 C4
Kozyatyn UA... 13 D8
Kozyürük TR . 186 A1
Kräckelbräken
S............ 49 A6
Kracow D......74 A3
Kraddsele S... 195 E7
Krag PL........68 A1
Kragenæs DK ..65 B4
Kragerø N 53 B5
Kragi PL.......68 B1
Kragujevac
SRB 127 C2
Kraiburg D ... 109 A3
Krajenka PL....68 B1
Krajišnik SRB.. 126 B2
Krajková CZ....83 B4
Krajné SK......98 C1
Krajnik Dolny
PL............74 A3
Krakača BIH... 124 B1
Kräklingbo S...57 C4
Kraków = Cracow
PL............99 A3
Krakow am See
D 73 A5
Králíky CZ.....85 B4
Kraljevica HR . 123 B3
Kraljevo SRB.. 16 D4
Kral'ovany SK..99 B3
Kráľov Brod
SK.......... 111 A4
Kralovice CZ...96 B1
Kralupy nad
Vltavou CZ....84 B2
Králův Dvůr CZ. 96 B2
Kramfors S.... 200 D3
Kramsach A... 108 B2
Kramsk PL.....76 B3
Krångede S... 200 C2
Kråmvik N.....53 A4
Kranenburg D .80 A2
Krania GR.... 182 D3
Krania Elasonas
GR 182 D4
Kranichfeld D..82 B3
Kranidi GR.... 184 B4
Kranj SLO 123 A3
Kranjska Gora
SLO 109 C4
Krapanj HR... 138 B1
Krapina HR... 124 A1
Krapje HR.... 124 B1
Krapkowice PL .86 B1
Kraselov CZ....96 B1
Krašić HR..... 123 B4
Kraslava LV 8 E5
Kraslice CZ.....83 B4
Krásná Hora nad
Vltavou CZ....96 B2
Krasna Lipa CZ .84 B2
Krásno SK.....98 B2
Krásno nad
Kysucou SK...98 B2
Krasnozavodsk
RUS..........9 D11
Krasnystaw PL. 13 C5
Krasnyy RUS...13 A9
Krasnyy Kholm
RUS..........9 C10
Krasocin PL....87 B4
Kraszewice PL .86 A2
Kraszkowice PL 86 A2
Kratigos GR... 186 C1
Kratovo NMK. 182 B4
Kraubath A ... 110 B1
Krausnick D....74 B2
Krautheim D...94 B1
Kravaře CZ.....85 B4
Kravarsko HR . 124 B2
Kraznějov CZ...96 B1
Krčedin SRB .. 126 B2
Kŭrdzhali BG.. 183 B7
Krefeld D......80 A2
Kregme DK 61 D2
Krembz D......73 A4
Kremenets UA . 13 C6
Kremmen D....74 B2
Kremna SRB... 127 D1
Kremnica SK...98 C2
Krempe D......64 C2
Krems
A............ 97 C3
Kremsbrücke A 109 C4
Kremsmünster
A............ 110 A1

Křemže CZ.....96 C2
Křenov CZ.....97 B4
Krepa PL.......76 C3
Krępa Krajeńska
PL............75 A5
Kreßberg D....94 B2
Kressbronn D. 107 B4
Krestena GR.. 184 B2
Kretinga LT ... 8 E2
Krettsy RUS....9 C8
Kreuth D..... 108 B2
Kreuzau D.....80 B2
Kreuzlingen
CH 107 B4
Kreuztal D.....81 B3
Krewelin D....74 B2
Krezluk BIH... 138 A3
Krichem BG .. 183 A6
Krieglach A... 110 B2
Kriegsfeld D ...93 B3
Kriens CH..... 106 B3
Krimml A 108 B3
Krimpen aan de
IJssel NL 79 A4
Křinec CZ......84 B3
Kristdala S.....62 A4
Kristiansand N. 53 B4
Kristianstad S..61 C4
Kristiansund
N............ 198 B4
Kristiinankaupunki
FIN...........8 A2
Kristinehamn S 55 A5
Kristinestad =
Kristiinankaupunki
FIN...........8 A2
Kriva Palanka
NMK 182 A4
Křivoklát CZ...96 A1
Kriz HR....... 124 B2
Křižanov CZ...97 B4
Križevci HR... 124 A2
Krk HR....... 123 B3
Krka SLO 123 B3
Krnjača SRB .. 127 C2
Krnjak HR.... 123 B4
Krnjeuša BIH . 124 C2
Krnjevo SRB.. 127 C3
Krnov CZ......98 A1
Krobia PL......85 A4
Kroczyce PL....86 B3
Krøderen N....48 B6
Krokees GR... 184 C3
Krokek S.......56 B2
Krokom S..... 199 B11
Krokowa PL....68 A3
Krokstad-elva
N............ 53 A5
Kroksund N....54 A2
Kroměříž CZ... 98 B1
Krommenie NL. 70 B1
Krompachy SK. 99 C4
Kronach D.....82 B3
Kronshagen D. 64 B2
Kronstadt RUS.. 9 C6
Kröpelin D.....65 B4
Kropp D.......64 B2
Kroppenstedt
D 73 B4
Kropstädt D....74 C1
Krościenko nad
Dunajcem PL..99 B4
Kröslin D......66 B2
Krośnice PL....85 A5
Krośniewice PL 77 B4
Krosno PL..... 12 D4
Krosno Odrzańskie
PL............75 B4
Krostitz D.....83 A4
Krotoszyn PL...85 A5
Krottendorf A. 110 B2
Krouna CZ.....97 B4
Krowiarki PL...86 B2
Krrabë AL..... 182 B1
Kršan HR..... 123 B3
Krško SLO 123 B4
Krstac MNE... 139 B4
Krstur SRB ... 126 A2
Křtiny CZ......97 B4
Kruft D........80 B3
Kruishoutem B. 79 B3
Krujë AL...... 182 B1
Krumbach
A............ 111 B3
D 94 C2
Krumovgrad
BG 183 B7
Krün D........ 108 B2

Krupá CZ 84 B1
Krupa na Vrbasu BIH 124 C3
Krupanj SRB . . 127 C1
Krupina SK 99 C3
Krupka CZ 84 B1
Krupki BY 13 A8
Kruså DK 64 B2
Kruščica BIH . . 139 A3
Kruševac SRB . . 16 D4
Kruševo NMK . 182 B3
Kruszwica PL . . 76 B3
Kruszyn PL 77 B4
Krychaw BY 13 B9
Krynica PL 99 B4
Krynica Morska PL 69 A4
Krzęcin PL 75 A4
Krzelów PL 85 A4
Krzepice PL 86 B2
Krzepielów PL . . 85 A4
Krzeszowice PL . 86 B3
Krzeszyce PL . . . 75 B4
Krzynowlaga Mała PL 77 A5
Krzywiń PL 75 C5
Krzyżanowice PL 98 B2
Krzyżowa PL 99 B3
Krzyż Wielkopolski PL 75 B5
Ksiaz Wielkopolski PL 87 B4
Książ Wielkopolski PL 76 B2
Ktębowiec PL . . 75 A5
Kübekháza H . 126 A2
Küblis CH 107 C4
Kuchary PL 86 A1
Kuchl A 109 B4
Kucice PL 77 B5
Kuciste HR 138 C3
Kuçovë AL 182 C1
Küçükbahçe TR 188 A1
Küçükköy TR . 186 C1
Küçükkuyu TR 186 C1
Kucura SRB 126 B1
Kuczbork-Osada PL 77 A5
Kuddby S 56 B2
Kudowa-Zdrój PL 85 B4
Kufstein A 108 B3
Kuggeboda S . . 63 B3
Kuggörana S . . 200 E3
Kühbach D 95 C3
Kuhmo FIN 3 D11
Kuhmoinen FIN . . 8 B4
Kuhnsdorf A . . 110 C1
Kuhstedt D 72 A1
Kuinre NL 70 B2
Kuivaniemi FIN 197 D8
Kuivastu EST 8 C3
Kukës AL 182 A2
Kuklin PL 77 A5
Kukljica HR . . . 137 A4
Kukujevci SRB. 127 B1
Kula
  Srbija SRB . . . 127 C3
  Vojvodina SRB 126 B1
  TR 188 A3
Kuldiga LV 8 D2
Kulen Vakuf BIH 124 C2
Kulina BIH 125 C4
Kullstedt D 82 A2
Kulmain D 95 B3
Kulmbach D . . . 82 B3
Kuloharju FIN 197 D11
Kulu TR 23 B7
Kumachevo RUS 69 A5
Kumafşarı TR . 189 B4
Kumane SRB . . . 126 B2
Kumanovo NMK 182 A3
Kumbağ TR . . . 186 B2
Kumdanlı TR . 189 A5
Kumkale TR . . 186 C1
Kumla S 55 A6
Kumlakyrkby S . 50 C3
Kumlinge FIN . . 51 B7
Kumluca TR . . 189 C5
Kumrovec HR . 123 A4
Kunadacs H . . . 112 C3

Kunágota H . . . 113 C5
Kunbaja H 126 A1
Kunda EST 8 C5
Kundl A 108 B2
Kunes N 193 B10
Kunfehértó H . 126 A1
Kungälv S 60 B1
Kungsäter S 60 B2
Kungsbacka S . . 60 B2
Kungsgården S . 50 B3
Kungshamn S . . 54 B2
Kungs-Husby S . 56 A3
Kungsör S 56 A2
Kunhegyes H . 113 B4
Kunmadaras H 113 B4
Kunovice CZ . . . 98 B1
Kunów PL 87 B5
Kunowo
  Wielkopolskie PL 76 C2
  Zachodnio-Pomorskie PL . 74 A3
Kunštát CZ 97 B4
Kunszállás H . . 113 C3
Kunszentmárton H 113 C4
Kunszentmiklós H 112 B3
Kunžak CZ 97 B3
Künzelsau D . . . 94 B1
Kuolayarvi RUS 197 C12
Kuolio FIN 197 D11
Kuopio FIN 8 A5
Kuosku FIN . . 197 B11
Kup
  H 111 B4
  PL 86 B1
Kupferzell D . . . 94 B1
Kupinec HR . . . 123 B4
Kupinečki Kraljevac HR . 124 B1
Kupinovo SRB. 127 C2
Kupirovo HR . 138 A2
Kupjak HR . . . 123 B3
Kuppenheim D 93 C4
Kupres BIH . . . 138 B3
Küps D 82 B3
Kurd H 112 C2
Küre TR 23 A7
Kuressaare EST . . 8 C3
Kurikka FIN 8 A3
Kuřim CZ 97 B4
Kuřivody CZ . . . 84 B2
Kurki PL 77 A5
Kurort Oberwiesenthal D 83 B4
Kurort Schmalkalden D 82 B2
Kurort Stolberg D 82 A2
Kurort Wippra D 82 A3
Kurów PL 12 C5
Kurowice PL . . . 86 A3
Kurravaara S . . 196 B3
Kursu FIN 197 C11
Kurşunlu
  Bursa TR 187 B4
  Çankırı TR 23 A7
Kurtakko FIN . . 196 B7
Kürten D 80 A3
Kurucaşile TR . 187 A7
Kurvinen FIN 197 D12
Kurzelów PL . . . 87 B3
Kusadak SRB . . 127 C2
Kuşadası TR . . 188 B2
Kusel D 93 B3
Kusey D 73 B4
Küsnacht CH . . 106 B3
Kütahya TR . . 187 C4
Kutenholz D . . . 72 A2
Kutina HR 124 B2
Kutjevo HR 125 B3
Kutná Hora CZ . 97 B3
Kutno PL 77 B4
Kuttara FIN . . 193 D10
Küttingen CH . 106 B3
Kúty SK 98 C1
Kuusamo FIN 197 D12
Kuusankoski FIN 8 B5
Kuvshinovo RUS . 9 D9
Kuzmin SRB . . . 127 B1
Kuźnia Raciborska PL 86 B2

Kuźnica Czarnkowska PL 75 B5
Kuźnica Żelichowska PL 75 B5
Kvaløysletta N 192 C2
Kvalsund N 192 B7
Kvam
  Nord-Trøndelag N 199 A8
  Oppland N . . . 198 D6
Kvamsøy N 46 A3
Kvænangsbotn N 192 C6
Kvanndal N 46 B3
Kvänum S 55 B4
Kværndrup DK . 59 C3
Kvås N 52 B3
Kvasice CZ 98 B1
Kvelde N 53 A5
Kvenna N 198 C5
Kvernaland N . . 52 B1
Kvibille S 60 C2
Kvicksund S 56 A2
Kvidinge S 61 C3
Kvikkjokk S . . 195 D8
Kvikne
  Hedmark N . . . 199 C7
  Oppland N . . 47 A6
Kvilda CZ 96 B1
Kville S 54 B2
Kvillsfors S 62 A3
Kvinesdal N 52 B2
Kvinlog N 52 B2
Kvinnherad N . . 46 C3
Kvissel N 58 A3
Kvissleby S . . . 200 D3
Kviteseid N 53 A4
Kvitsøy N 52 A1
Kwakowo PL . . . 68 A2
Kwidzyn PL 69 B3
Kwilcz PL 75 B5
Kyjov CZ 98 C1
Kyleakin UK 31 B3
Kyle of Lochalsh UK 31 B3
Kylerhea UK 31 B3
Kylestrome UK. 32 C1
Kyllburg D 92 A2
Kyllini GR 184 B2
Kynšperk nad Ohří CZ 83 B4
Kyperounda CY 181 B1
Kyrenia CY . . . 181 A2
Kyritz D 73 B5
Kyrkesund S 60 A1
Kyrkhult S 63 B2
Kyrksæterøra N 198 B6
Kysucké Nové Mesto SK 98 B2
Kythira GR . . . 184 C3
Kythréa CY . . . 181 A2
Kyustendil BG . 16 D5
Kyyiv = Kiev UA 13 C9
Kyyjärvi FIN 8 A4

L

Laa an der Thaya A 97 C4
La Adrada E . . . 150 B3
Laage D 65 C5
La Alameda E . 157 B4
La Alberca de Záncara E . . . 158 B1
La Albergueria de Argañán E . . 149 B3
La Albuera E . . 155 C4
La Aldea del Portillo del Busto E 143 B3
La Algaba E . . . 162 A1
La Aliseda de Tormes E . . . 150 B2
La Almarcha E. 158 B1
La Almolda E . 153 A3
La Almunia de Doña Godina E 152 A2
Laanila FIN . . 193 D11
La Arena E . . . 141 A4
La Aulaga E . . . 161 B3
La Balme-de-Sillingy F 118 B3
La Bañeza E . . 141 B5

La Barca de la Florida E 162 B2
La Barre-de-Monts F 114 B1
La Barre-en-Ouche F 89 B4
La Barrosa E . . . 162 B1
La Barthe-de-Neste F 145 A4
La Bassée F 78 B2
La Bassée F . . . 146 A2
La Bastide-de-Sèrou F 146 A2
La Bastide-des-Jourdans F . . . 132 B1
Labastide-Murat F 129 B4
La Bastide-Puylaurent F. 117 C3
Labastide-Rouairoux F . . 130 B1
Labastide-St Pierre F 129 C4
La Bathie F 118 B3
Lábatlan H 112 B2
La Baule-Escoublac F 101 B3
La Bazoche-Gouet F 102 A2
La Bégude-de-Mazenc F 131 A3
Labenne F 128 C1
La Bernerie-en-Retz F 114 A1
Labin HR 123 B3
La Bisbal d'Empordà F 147 C4
Lablachère F . . 131 A3
Lábod H 124 A3
Laboe D 64 B3
La Boissière F . . 89 A4
Labouheyre F. 128 B2
La Bourboule F 116 B2
La Bóveda de Toro E 150 A2
Łabowa PL 99 B4
La Brède F 128 B2
La Bresse F . . . 106 A1
La Bridoire F . . 118 B2
La Brillanne F . 132 B1
Labrit F 128 B2
Labros E 152 A2
La Bruffière F . . 114 B2
Labruguière F . 130 B1
Labrujo P 148 A1
L'Absie F 114 B3
La Bussière F . . 103 B4
Laç AL 182 B1
La Cabrera E . . . 151 B4
Lacanche F 104 B3
La Canourgue F 130 A2
La Capelle F 91 B3
Lacapelle-Marival F 129 B4
Láčarak SRB . . . 127 B1
La Cardanchosa E 156 B2
La Caridad E . . 141 A4
La Carlota E . . 162 A3
La Carolina E . . 157 B4
Lacaune F 130 B1
La Cava E 153 B4
La Cavalerie F . 130 A2
Laceby UK 41 B3
Lacedónia I . . . 172 A1
La Celle-en-Moravan F 104 B3
La Celle-St Avant F 102 B2
La Cerca E . . . 143 B3
Láces I 108 C1
La Chaise-Dieu F 117 B3
La Chaize-Giraud F 114 B2
La Chaize-le-Vicomte F 114 B2
La Chambre F . 118 B3

Lachania GR . . 188 D2
La Chapelaude F 116 A2
La Chapelle-d'Angillon F . . 103 B4
La Chapelle-en-Aalgaudémar F 118 C3
La Chapelle-en-Vercors F 118 C2
La Chapelle-Glain F 101 B4
La Chapelle-la-Reine F 90 C2
La Chapelle-Laurent F . . . 116 B3
La Chapelle-St Luc F 91 C4
La Chapelle-sur-Erdre F 101 B4
La Chapelle-Vicomtesse F 103 B3
La Charce F . . . 132 A1
La Charité-sur-Loire F 104 B2
La Chartre-sur-le-Loir F 102 B2
La Châtaigneraie F 114 B3
La Châtre F . . . 103 C3
La Chaussée-sur-Marne F 91 C4
La Chaux-de-Fonds CH 106 B1
Lachen CH . . . 107 B3
Lachendorf D . . 72 B3
La Cheppe F 91 B4
La Chèze F . . . 101 A3
Lachowice PL . . 99 B3
La Ciotat F . . . 132 B1
Láčko SK 99 B4
La Clayette F . . 117 A4
La Clusaz F . . . 118 B3
Lacock UK 43 A4
La Codosera E. 155 B3
La Concha E . . 143 A3
La Condamine-Châtelard F . 132 A2
Láconi I 179 C3
La Contienda E 161 A3
La Coquille F . . 115 C4
La Coronada E 156 B2
La Côte-St André F 118 B2
La Cotinière F . 114 C2
La Courtine F . 116 B2
Lacq F 145 A3
La Crau F 132 B2
La Crèche F . . . 115 B3
La Croix F 102 B2
Lacroix-Barrez F 116 C2
Lacroix-St Ouen F 90 B2
Lacroix-sur-Meuse F 92 C1
La Croix-Valmer F 132 B2
La Cumbre E . . 156 A2
Lácubegi E . . . 144 B2
Lad H 125 A3
Ladbergen D . . 71 B4
Ładek-Zdrój PL . 85 B4
Ladelund D . . . 64 B2
Ladendorf A . . . 97 C4
Ladignac-le-Long F 115 C5
Ladíspoli I 168 B2
Ladoeiro P 155 B3
Ladon F 103 B4
La Douze F . . . 129 A3
Ladushkin RUS. 69 A5
Ladybank UK . . . 35 B4
Laer D 71 B4
La Espina E . . . 141 A4
La Estrella E . . 156 A2
La Farga de Moles E 146 B2
La Fatarella E . 153 A4
La Felipa E . . . 158 B2
La Ferrière
  Indre-et-Loire F 102 B2
  Vendée F 114 B2
La Ferrière-en-Parthenay F. 115 B3
La Ferté-Alais F 90 C2

La Ferté-Bernard F 102 A2
La Ferté-Frênel F 89 B4
La Ferté-Gaucher F 90 C3
La Ferté-Imbault F 103 B3
La Ferté-Macé F 89 B3
La Ferté-Milon F 90 B3
La Ferté-sous-Jouarre F 90 C3
La Ferté-St-Aubin F 103 B3
La Ferté-St-Cyr F 103 B3
La Ferté-Vidame F 89 B4
La Ferté Villeneuil F 103 B3
Lafkos GR . . . 183 D5
La Flèche F . . . 102 B1
La Flotte F . . . 114 B2
Lafnitz A 111 B3
La Font de la Figuera E . . 159 C3
La Fouillade F . 130 A1
La Fregeneda E 149 B3
La Fresneda E 153 B4
La Fuencubierta E 162 A3
La Fuente de San Esteban E . 149 B3
La Fulioala E . . 147 C2
La Gacilly F . . 101 B3
La Galera E . . . 153 B4
Lagan S 60 C3
Loganadil I . . . 175 C1
Lagarde F 146 A2
La Garde-Freinet F 132 B2
Lagares
  Coimbra P . . . 148 B2
  Porto P 148 A1
La Garnache F . 114 B2
Lagaro I 135 A4
La Garriga E . . 147 C3
La Garrovilla E . 155 C4
Lagartera E . . . 150 C2
La Gaubretière F 114 B2
Lågbol S 51 B5
Lage D 72 C1
Lägerdorf D . . . 64 C2
Laggan UK 32 D2
Laggartorp S . . . 55 A5
Łagiewniki PL . . 85 B4
La Gineta E . . . 158 B1
Láglio I 120 B2
Lagnieu F . . . 118 B2
Lagny-sur-Marne F 90 C2
Lago
  Calabria I . . . 175 B2
  Veneto I . . . 121 B5
Lagôa P 160 B1
Lagoaça P 149 A3
Lagonegro I . . . 174 A1
Lagos
  GR 183 B7
  P 160 B1
Lagosanto I . . . 121 C5
Łagów
  Lubuskie PL . . 75 B4
  Świętokrzyskie PL 87 B5
La Granadella
  Alicante E . . 159 C4
  Lleida E 153 A4
La Grand-Combe F 131 A3
La Grande-Croix F 117 B4
La Grande-Motte F 131 B3
La Granja d'Escarp E 153 A4
La Granjuela E 156 B2
Lagrasse F . . . 146 A3
La Grave F . . . 118 B3
Laguardia E . . . 143 B4
La Guardia E . . 151 C4
La Guardia de Jaén E 163 A4

Laguenne F . . . 116 B1
Laguépie F . . . 129 B4
La Guerche-de-Bretagne F . . 101 B4
La Guerche-sur-l'Aubois F . . . 104 C1
La Guérinière F 114 B1
Laguiole F . . . 116 C2
Laguna de Duera E 150 A3
Laguna del Marquesado E 152 B2
Laguna de Negrillos E 142 B1
Lagundo I 108 C2
Lagunilla E . . . 149 B3
La Haba E 156 B2
Laharie F 128 B1
La Haye-du-Puits F 88 A2
La Haye-Pesnel F 88 B2
Lahden D 71 B4
La Herlière F . . . 78 B2
La Hermida E . 142 A2
La Herrera E . . 158 C1
Laheycourt F . . . 91 C5
La Higuera E . 158 C2
La Hiniesta E . 149 A4
Lahnstein D . . . 81 B3
Laholm S 61 C3
La Horcajada E 150 B2
La Horra E . . . 143 C3
Lahr D 93 C3
Lahti FIN 8 B4
La Hulpe B 79 B4
La Hutte F 89 B4
Laichingen D . . 94 C1
L'Aigle F 89 B4
La Iglesuela E. 150 B3
La Iglesuela del Cid E 153 B3
Laignes F 104 B3
Laimbach am Ostrong A . . . 97 C3
Laina E 152 A1
Lainio S 196 B5
Lairg UK 32 C2
La Iruela E . . . 164 B2
Laissac F 130 A1
Laisvall S 195 D8
Láives I 121 A4
La Javie F 132 A2
Lajkovac SRB . . 127 C2
La Jonchère-St Maurice F 116 A1
Lajoskomárom H 112 C2
Lajosmizse H . 112 B3
Lak H 112 C2
Lakenheath UK . 45 A4
Laki BG 183 B6
Lakitelek H . . . 113 C4
Lakki GR 185 D4
Lakolk DK 64 A1
Łąkorz PL 69 B4
Lakšárska Nová Ves SK 98 C1
Lakselv N 193 B8
Laksfors N 195 E4
Laktaši BIH . . . 124 C3
La Lantejuela E 162 A2
Lalapaşa TR . . 186 A1
L'Albagès E . . . 153 A4
Lalbenque F . . 129 B4
L'Alcúdia E . . . 159 B3
L'Aldea E 153 B4
Lalín E 140 B2
Lalinde F 129 B3
La Línea de la Concepción E 162 B2
Lalizolle F . . . 116 A3
La Llacuna E . 147 C2
Lalley F 118 C2
Lalm N 198 D6
La Loupe F 89 B5
La Louvière B . . 79 B4
L'Alpe-d'Huez F 118 B3
La Luisiana E . 162 A2
Laluque F 128 C1

Lam D...........95 B5
La Machine F.. 104 C2
la Maddalena
  I............... 178 A3
Lama dei Peligni
  I............ 169 A4
Lamadrid E.... 142 A2
Lamagistére F 129 B3
La Mailleraye-sur-
  Seine F.........89 A4
La Malène F... 130 A2
Lama Mocogno
  I............ 135 A3
La Mamola E.. 163 B4
La Manresana dels
  Prats E...... 147 C2
Lamarche F... 105 A4
Lamarche-sur-
  Saône F...... 105 B4
Lamargelle F.. 105 B3
Lamarosa P.... 154 B2
Lamarque F... 128 A2
Lamas P....... 148 B1
La Masadera
  E............ 145 C3
Lamas de Moaro
  P............ 140 B2
Lamastre F... 117 C4
La Mata E.... 150 C3
La Mata de
  Ledesma E.. 149 A4
La Mata de
  Monteagudo
  E............ 142 B1
Lambach A.... 109 A4
Lamballe F.... 101 A3
Lamberhurst
  UK 45 B4
Lambesc F 131 B4
Lambia GR.... 184 B2
Lambley UK....37 B4
Lambourn UK...44 B2
Lamego P..... 148 A2
La Meilleraye-de-
  Bretagne F.. 101 B4
La Ménitré F .. 102 B1
L'Ametlla de Mar
  E............ 153 B4
Lamia GR....182 E4
Lammhult S...62 A2
La Mojonera
  E............ 164 C2
La Mole F ... 132 B2
La Molina E ... 147 C3
La Monnerie-le-
  Montel F 117 B3
La Morera E.. 155 C4
La Mothe-Achard
  F............ 114 B2
Lamothe-Cassel
  F............ 129 B4
Lamothe-
  Montravel F.. 128 B3
La Mothe-St Héray
  F............ 115 B3
Lamotte-Beuvron
  F............ 103 B4
La Motte-
  Chalançon F. 131 A4
La Motte-du-Caire
  F............ 132 A2
La Motte-Servolex
  F............ 118 B2
Lampertheim D 93 B4
Lampeter UK...39 B2
L'Ampolla E .. 153 B4
Lamprechtshausen
  A............ 109 B3
Lamsfeld D ...74 C3
Lamspringe D..72 C3
Lamstedt D...72 A2
La Mudarra E.. 142 C2
La Muela E... 152 A2
La Mure F.... 118 C2
Lamure-sur-
  Azergues F... 117 A4
Lana I........ 108 C2
Lanaja E..... 145 C3
Lanarce F.... 117 C3
Lanark UK.....36 A3
La Nava E.... 161 B3
La Nava de
  Ricomalillo E. 156 A3
La Nava de
  Santiago E... 155 B4
Lancaster UK...37 B4
Lanchester UK..37 B5
Lanciano I.... 169 A4
Lancing UK 44 C3
Lançon-Provence
  F............ 131 B4
Lancova Vas
  SLO 124 A1

Landau
  Bayern D 95 C4
  Rheinland-Pfalz
  D...............93 B4
Landeck A 108 B1
Landen B 79 B5
Landerneau F. 100 A1
Landeryd S 60 B3
Landesbergen
  D..............72 B2
Landete E.... 158 B2
Landévant F .. 100 B2
Landévennec
  .... 100 A1
Landeyjahöfn
  .... 190 D5
Landivisiau F . 100 A1
Landivy F 88 B2
Landl A 108 B3
Landön S 199 B11
Landos F..... 117 C3
Landouzy-le-Ville
  .... 91 B4
Landquart CH. 107 C4
Landrecies F ...91 A3
Landreville F.. 104 A3
Landriano I... 120 B2
Landsberg D.. 108 A1
Lands-berg D ..83 A4
Landsbro S....62 A2
Landscheid D ..92 B2
Landshut D... 95 C4
Landskrona S . 61 D2
Landstuhl D ...93 B3
Lanesborough
  IRL 28 A4
Lanester F ... 100 B2
Lanestosa E.. 143 A3
La Neuve-Lyre
  F..............89 B4
La Neuveville
  CH 106 B2
Langå DK 59 B2
Langada GR.. 185 A7
Langadas GR. 183 C5
Langa de Duero
  E............ 151 A4
Langadia GR. 184 B3
Langangen N ...53 A5
Langared S 60 A2
Långaröd S ...61 D3
Langaryd S 60 B3
Långås S......60 C2
Långasjö S 63 B3
Langau A 97 C3
Langeac F.... 117 B3
Langeais F ... 102 B2
Langedijk NL ...70 B1
Langeln D 73 C3
Langelsheim D..72 C3
Langemark-
  Poelkapelle B .78 B2
Langen
  Hessen D 93 B4
  Niedersachsen
  D............. 72 A1
Langenau D...94 C2
Langenbruck
  CH 106 B2
Langenberg D .81 A4
Langenburg D .94 B1
Langenfeld A. 108 B1
Langenfeld D..80 A2
Langenhorn D..64 B1
Langenlois A...97 C3
Langenlonsheim
  D..............93 B3
Langennaudorf
  D..............83 A5
Langenneufnach
  D..............94 C2
Langenthal
  CH 106 B2
Langenzenn D .94 B2
Langeoog D ...71 A4
Langesund N ...53 A5
Langewiesen D.82 B2
Långflon S 49 A4
Langförden D..71 B5
Langhagen D ..73 A5
Langhirano I.. 120 C3
Langholm UK ..36 A4
Langholt IS .. 191 D7
Långlöt S 62 B4
Langnau CH .. 106 C2
Langø DK 65 B4
Langogne F ... 117 C3
Langon F..... 128 B2
Langquaid D...95 C3
Långrådna S ..56 B2
Langreo E 142 A1

Langres F 105 B4
Långsele S ... 200 C3
Långserud S ...54 A3
Langset N......48 B3
Langshyttan S .50 B3
Långträsk S.. 196 D3
Langstrand N . 192 B7
Långvik S......57 A4
Langwarden D .71 A5
Langwathby
  UK 37 B4
Langwedel D ..72 B2
Langwies CH.. 107 C4
Lanheses P... 148 A1
Lanildut F.... 100 A1
Lanjarón E... 163 B4
Lanmeur F ... 100 A2
Lanna
  Jönköping S 60 B3
  Örebro S 55 A5
Lännahult S...54 C1
Lannavaara S . 196 A4
Lannéanou F.. 100 A2
Lannemezan
  F............ 145 A4
Lanneuville-sur-
  Meuse F.......91 B5
Lannilis F 100 A1
Lannion F 100 A2
La Nocle-Maulaix
  F............ 104 C2
Lanouaille F .. 115 C5
Lansjärv S ... 196 C5
Lanškroun CZ...97 B4
Lanslebourg-Mont-
  Cenis F..... 119 B3
Lanta F...... 129 C4
Lantadilla E.. 142 B2
Lanton F..... 128 B1
Lantosque F .. 133 B3
La Nuez de Arriba
  E............ 143 B3
Lanusei I..... 179 C3
Lanúvio I.... 168 B2
Lanvollon F... 100 A3
Lánycsók H ... 125 A4
Lanz D........73 A4
Lanza E...... 140 A2
Lanzada I.... 120 A2
Lanzahita E... 150 B3
Lanžhot CZ ...97 C4
Lanzo Torinese
  I............. 119 B4
Laole SRB 127 C3
Laon F........91 B3
Laons F.......89 B5
La Paca E.... 164 B3
La Pacaudière
  F............ 117 A3
Lapalisse F ... 117 A3
La Palma d'Ebre
  E............ 153 A4
La Palma del
  Condado E... 161 B3
La Palme F ... 146 B4
La Palmyre F .. 114 C2
La Parra E ... 155 C4
Łapczyna Wola
  PL............87 B3
La Pedraja de
  Portillo E... 150 A3
La Peraleja E . 152 B1
La Petit-Pierre
  F............93 C3
Lapeyrade F .. 128 B2
Lapeyrouse F .. 116 A2
Lapford UK 42 B3
La Pinilla E... 165 B3
Lapithos CY... 181 A2
La Plagne F ... 118 B3
La Plaza E.... 141 A4
Laplume F.... 129 B3
La Pobla de Lillet
  E............ 147 B2
La Pobla de
  Vallbona E .. 159 B3
La Pobla Llarga
  E............ 159 B3
La Pola de Gordón
  E............ 142 B1
la Porta F 180 A2
Lapoutroie F .. 106 A2
La Póveda de Soria
  E............ 143 B4
Lapovo SRB .. 127 C3
Läppe S.......56 A1
Lappeenranta
  FIN........... 8 B6

Lappoluobbal
  N............. 192 C7
Lappträsk S... 196 C6
La Preste F ... 146 B3
La Primaube F 130 A1
Lapseki TR ... 186 B1
Lapua FIN......8 A3
La Puebla de
  Almoradie E . 157 A4
La Puebla de
  Cazalla E.... 162 A2
La Puebla de los
  Infantes E... 162 A2
La Puebla del Río
  E............ 162 A1
La Puebla de
  Montalbán
  E............ 150 C3
La Puebla de Roda
  E............ 145 B4
La Puebla de
  Valdavia E ... 142 B2
La Puebla de
  Valverde E ... 152 B3
La Pueblanueva
  E............ 150 C3
La Puerta de
  Segura E.... 164 A2
La Punt CH ... 107 C4
L'Áquila I.... 169 A3
La Quintana E . 162 A2
La Quintera E . 162 A2
La Rábita
  Granada E.. 164 C1
  Jaén E 163 A3
Laracha E.... 140 A2
Laragh IRL....30 A2
Laragne-Montéglin
  F............ 132 A1
La Rambla E.. 163 A3
L'Arboç E.... 147 C2
L'Arbresle F .. 117 B4
Lárbro S......57 C4
Larceveau F .. 144 A2
Larche
  Alpes-de-Haute-
  Provence F.. 132 A2
  Corrèze F ... 129 A4
Lárdal N......53 A4
Lærdalsøyri N ..47 A4
Lardosa P.... 155 B3
La Reale I.... 178 A2
Laredo E..... 143 A3
La Redondela
  E............ 161 B2
La Réole F ... 128 B2
Largentière F . 131 A3
L'Argentière-la-
  Bessée F.... 118 C3
Largs UK......34 C3
Larí I........ 134 B3
La Riera E.... 141 A4
La Riera de Gaià
  E............ 147 C2
La Rinconada
  E............ 162 A1
Lariño E...... 140 B1
Larino I...... 170 B2
Larisa GR.... 182 D4
La Rivière-
  Thibouville F..89 A4
Larkhall UK ...36 A3
Larkollen N....54 A1
Larmor-Plage
  F............ 100 B2
Larnaca CY... 181 B2
Larne UK......27 B5
La Robla E.... 142 B1
La Roca de la Sierra
  E............ 155 B4
La Roche CH .. 106 C2
La Rochebeaucourt-
  Argentine F . 115 C4
La Roche-Bernard
  F............ 101 B3
La Roche-Canillac
  F............ 116 B1
La Roche-Chalais
  F............ 128 A3
La Roche Derrien
  F............ 100 A2
La Roche-des-
  Arnauds F... 132 A1
La Roche-en-
  Ardenne B... 80 B1
La Roche-en-Brénil
  F............ 104 B3
La Rochefoucauld
  F............ 115 C4
La Roche-Guyon
  F............90 B1
La Rochelle F . 114 B2

La Roche-Posay
  F............ 115 B4
La Roche-sur-Foron
  F............ 118 A3
La Roche-sur-Yon
  F............ 114 B2
Larochette L...92 B2
La Rochette F . 131 A4
La Roda
  Albacete E ... 158 B1
  Oviedo E..... 141 A4
La Roda de
  Andalucía E.. 162 A3
Laroquebrou
  F............ 116 C2
La Roquebrussane
  F............ 132 B1
Laroque d'Olmes
  F............ 146 B2
La Roque-Gageac
  F............ 129 B4
La Roque-Ste
  Marguerite
  F............ 130 A2
Laroque-Timbaut
  F............ 129 B3
Larouco E.... 141 B3
Larraga E.... 144 B2
Larrau F...... 144 A3
Larrazet F ... 129 C4
Larsnes N.... 198 C2
La Rubia E.... 143 C4
Laruns F...... 145 A3
Larva E...... 164 B1
Larvik N......53 A6
La Sagrada E . 149 B3
La Salceda E . 151 A4
Lasalle F..... 131 A2
La Salle F.... 118 B3
La Salute di Livenza
  I............. 122 B1
La Salvetat-
  Peyralès F... 130 A1
La Salvetat-sur-
  Agout F..... 130 B1
Las Arenas E . 142 A2
La Sarraz CH . 105 C5
Lasarte E..... 144 A1
Låsby DK......59 B2
Las Cabezadas
  E............ 151 A4
Las Cabezas de San
  Juan E...... 162 B2
Las Correderas
  E............ 157 B4
Las Cuevas de
  Cañart E.... 153 B3
La Seca E.... 150 A3
La Selva del Camp
  E............ 147 C2
La Senia E.... 153 B4
La Serna E.... 142 B2
La Seu d'Urgell
  E............ 146 B2
La Seyne-sur-Mer
  F............ 132 B1
Las Gabias E . 163 A4
Las Herencias
  E............ 150 C3
Las Herrerías
  E............ 161 B2
Łasin PL......69 B4
Lask PL.......86 A3
Laska PL......68 B2
Łąsko SLO ... 124 A4
Laskowice PL...76 A3
Las Labores E . 157 A4
Las Mesas E.. 158 B1
Las Minas E.. 164 A3
Las Navas E.. 163 A3
Las Navas de la
  Concepción
  E............ 156 C2
Las Navas del
  Marqués E .. 150 B3
Las Navillas E . 157 A3
Las Negras E . 164 C3
La Solana E... 157 B4
La Souterraine
  F............ 116 A1
Las Pajanosas
  E............ 161 B3
Laspaules E .. 145 B4
Las Pedroñas
  E............ 158 B1
La Spézia I... 134 A2
Las Planes
  d'Hostoles E . 147 B3
Laspuña E.... 145 B4
Las Rozas
  Cantabria E . 142 B2
  Madrid E..... 151 B4

Lassan D.......66 C2
Lassay-les-
  Châteaux F....89 B3
Lasseube F... 145 A3
Lassigny F.....90 B2
La Storta I.... 168 B2
Lastovo HR ... 138 C2
Lastras de Cuéllar
  E............ 151 A3
Lästringe S....56 B3
Lastrup D......71 B4
Las Uces E.... 149 A3
La Suze-sur-Sarthe
  F............ 102 B2
Las Veguillas
  E............ 149 B4
Las Ventas con
  Peña Aguilera
  E............ 157 A3
Las Ventas de San
  Julián E 150 B2
Las Villes E... 153 B4
Latasa E...... 144 B2
Látky SK......99 C3
La Toba E 152 B2
La Toledana E . 157 A3
La Torre de
  Cabdella E... 146 B2
La Torre de Esteban
  Hambrán E.. 151 B3
La Torre del
  l'Espanyol E . 153 A4
La Torresaviñán
  E............ 152 B1
La Tour d'Aigues
  F............ 132 B1
La Tour de Peilz
  CH 106 C1
La Tour-du-Pin
  F............ 118 B2
La Tranche-sur-Mer
  F............ 114 B2
La Tremblade
  F............ 114 C2
La Trimouille
  F............ 115 B4
La Trinité F... 100 B2
La Trinité-Porhoët
  F............ 101 A3
Latrónico I... 174 A2
Latronquière
  F............ 116 C2
Latterbach CH 106 C2
La Turballe F . 101 B3
Laubach D.....81 B4
Laubert F..... 117 C3
Laucha D......83 A3
Lauchhammer
  D............84 A1
Lauchheim D..94 C2
Lauda-
  Königshofen
  D............94 B1
Laudal N......52 B3
Lauenau D....72 B2
Lauenburg D..73 A3
Lauf D........95 B3
Laufach D.....94 A1
Laufen
  CH 106 B2
  D............ 109 B3
Lauffen D.....93 B5
Laugar IS.... 191 B8
Laugarás IS .. 190 C5
Laugarbakki
  IS 190 B5
Laugarvatn IS. 190 C5
Laugharne UK .39 C2
Lauingen D...94 C2
Laujar de Andarax
  E............ 164 C2
Laukaa FIN.....8 A4
Lauker S 196 D2
Laukvik N.... 194 B5
La Uña E 142 A1
Launceston UK..42 B2
La Unión E ... 165 B4
Laupheim D...94 C1

Laurencekirk
  UK 35 B5
Laurencetown
  IRL 28 A3
Laurenzana I.. 172 B1
Lauria I...... 174 A1
Laurière F.... 116 A1
Laurieston UK..36 B2
Laurino I..... 172 B1
Lausanne CH.. 106 C1
Laussonne F.. 117 C4
Lauta D.......84 A2
Lautenthal D...82 A2
Lauterach A... 107 B4
Lauterbach D..81 B5
Lauterbrunnen
  CH 106 C2
Lauterecken D.93 B3
Lauterhofen D..95 B3
Lauvsnes N... 199 A7
Lauvvik N.....52 B2
Lauzerte F ... 129 B4
Lauzès F 129 B4
Lauzun F..... 129 B3
Lavagna I.... 134 A2
Laval F....... 102 A1
La Vall d'Uixó
  E............ 159 B3
Lavamünd A.. 110 C1
Lavara GR.... 186 A1
Lavardac F... 129 B3
Lavaris P..... 148 B1
Lavarone I... 121 B4
Lavau F...... 104 B1
Lavaur F..... 129 C4
La Vecilla de
  Curueño E... 142 B1
La Vega
  Asturias E.... 141 A5
  Asturias E.... 142 A1
  Cantabria E .. 142 A2
Lavelanet F .. 146 B2
La Velilla E... 151 A4
La Velles E... 150 A2
Lavello I...... 172 A1
Lavelsloh D...72 B1
Lavenham UK ..45 A4
Laveno I...... 120 B1
La Ventosa E . 152 B1
Lavezzola I... 135 A4
Laviano I..... 172 B1
La Victoria E.. 162 A3
Le Vid E 151 A4
Lavik N........46 A2
La Vilavella E. 159 B3
La Vilella Baixa
  E............ 147 C1
La Villa de Don
  Fadrique E... 157 A4
Lavilledieu F . 131 A3
La Villedieu F . 115 B3
La Ville Dieu-du-
  Temple F.... 129 B4
Lavino-Lido di
  Enea I....... 168 B2
Lavis I....... 121 A4
Lavit F....... 129 C3
Lavoncourt F . 105 B4
Lavos P...... 148 B1
La Voulte-sur-
  Rhône F 117 C4
Lavoûte-Chilhac
  F............ 117 B3
Lavradio P... 154 C1
Lavre P...... 154 C2
Lavrio GR.... 185 B5
La Wantzenau
  F............93 C3
Lawers UK.....35 B3
Ławy PL.......75 B3
Laxå S........55 B5
Laxamýri IS .. 191 B8
Laxe E....... 140 A2
Laxey UK......36 B2
Laxford Bridge
  UK 32 C1
Laxhall S.....55 B4
Laxsjö S..... 199 B11
Laxtjarn S.....49 B6
Laxvik S......61 C2
Laxviken S... 199 B11
La Yesa E.... 159 B3
Laza E....... 141 B3
Lazarevac
  SRB 127 C2
Lazarevo SRB . 126 B2
Lazise I...... 121 B3
Łaziska Grn. PL.86 B2
Lazkao E..... 144 A1

230 Láz – Lic

Lázně Bělohrad
CZ 84 B3
Lázně Bohdaneč
CZ 97 A3
Lázně Kynžvart
CZ 95 A4
Lazonby UK....37 B4
La Zubia E......163 A4
Łazy PL.......67 B5
Lazzaro I......175 C1
Lea UK.......40 B3
Leadburn UK...35 C4
Leadhills UK ...36 A3
Leap IRL.......29 C2
Leatherhead
UK.......44 B3
Łeba PL.......68 A2
Lebach D.......92 B2
Le Barcarès F..146 B4
Le Barp F......132 B2
Lebbeke B......79 A4
Lébény H 111 B4
Le Bessat F....117 B4
Le Blanc F.....115 B5
Le Bleymard F..130 A2
Łebno PL.......68 A3
Leboreiro E....140 B3
Lębork PL......68 A2
Le Boullay-Mivoye
F.......89 B5
Le Boulou F....146 B3
Le Bourg F.....129 B4
Le Bourg-d'Oisans
F.......118 B3
Le Bourget-du-Lac
F.......118 B2
Le Bourgneuf-la-
Forêt F.......101 A5
Le Bousquet d'Orb
F.......130 B2
Le Brassus CH.105 C5
Le Breuil F 117 A3
Le Breuil-en-Auge
F.......89 A4
Lebrija E......162 B1
Lebring A......110 C2
Le Brusquet F..132 A2
Le Bry CH 106 C2
Le Bugue F.....129 B3
Le Buisson F...129 B3
Lebus D.......74 B3
Lebusa D.......83 A5
Leca da Palmeira
P.......148 A1
Le Caloy F.....128 C2
Le Cap d'Agde
F.......130 B2
Le Cateau
Cambrésis F..91 A3
Le Caylar F....130 B2
Le Cayrol F....116 C2
Lecce I.......173 B4
Lecco I.......120 B2
Lécera E......153 A3
Lećevica HR....138 B2
Lech A.......107 B5
Le Chambon-
Feugerolles
F.......117 B4
Le Chambon-sur-
Lignon F 117 B4
Le Château
d'Oléron F ..114 C2
Le Châtelard
F.......118 B3
Le Châtelet F..103 C4
Le Chatelet-en-Brie
CZ.......90 C2
Lechbruck D...108 B1
Lechena GR....184 B2
Le Chesne F...91 B4
Le Cheylard F..117 C4
Lechlade UK ...44 B2
Lechovice CZ...97 C4
Leciñena E....145 C3
Leck D.......64 B1
Le Collet-de-Deze
F.......131 A2
Le Conquet F..100 A1
Le Creusot F...104 C3
Le Croisic F....101 B3
Le Crotoy F....78 B1
Lectoure F 129 C3
Łęczyca
Łódzkie PL.....77 B4

Łęczyca continued
Zachodnio-
Pomorskie PL . 75 A4
Ledaña E......158 B2
Ledbury UK....39 B4
Lede B.......79 B3
Ledečnad Sazavou
CZ.......97 B3
Ledenice CZ ...96 C2
Le Deschaux F 105 C4
Ledesma E.....149 A3
Lédignan F....131 B3
Lédigos E 142 B2
Ledmore UK ...32 C2
Lednice CZ.....97 C4
Lednicke-Rovné
SK.......98 B2
Le Donjon F...117 A3
Le Dorat F.....115 B5
Lędyczek PL...68 B1
Lędziny PL.....86 B3
Leeds UK.......40 B2
Leek
NL.......71 A3
UK.......40 B1
Leenaun IRL...28 A2
Leens NL.......71 A3
Leer D.......71 A4
Leerdam NL....79 A5
Leerhafe D....71 A4
Leese D.......72 B2
Leeuwarden
NL.......70 A2
Leezen D.......64 C3
Le Faou F......100 A1
Le Faoüet F ...100 A2
Lefka CY 181 A1
Lefkada GR....182 E1
Lefkimis GR...182 D2
Lefkoniko CY .181 A2
Le Folgoet F...100 A1
Le Fossat F....146 A2
Le Fousseret
F.......146 A2
Le Fugeret F ..132 A2
Leganés E.....151 B4
Legau D.......107 B5
Le Gault-Soigny
F.......91 C3
Legbąd PL.....68 B2
Legé F.......114 B2
Lège-Cap-Ferret
F.......128 B1
Legionowo PL ..77 B5
Léglise B......92 B1
Legnago I.....121 B4
Legnano I.....120 B1
Legnaro I......121 B4
Legnica PL.....85 A4
Łęgowo PL.....69 A3
Legrad HR 124 A2
Le Grand-Bornand
F.......118 B3
Le Grand-Bourg
F.......116 A1
Le Grand-Lucé
F.......102 B2
Le Grand-Pressigny
F.......102 C2
Le Grand-Quevilly
F.......89 A5
Le Grau-du-Roi
F.......131 B3
Léguevin F 129 C4
Legutiano E ...143 B4
Le Havre F.....89 A4
Lehesten D....82 B3
Lehnice SK.....111 A4
Lehnin D.......74 B1
Le Hohwald F...93 C3
Le Houga F....128 C2
Lehrberg D.....94 B2
Lehre D.......73 B3
Lehrte D.......72 B2
Lehsen D.......73 A4
Leibnitz A.....110 C2
Leicester UK ...40 C2
Leiden NL......70 B1
Leidschendam
NL.......70 B1
Leigh UK.......38 A4
Leighlinbridge
IRL.......30 B2
Leighton Buzzard
UK.......44 B3
Leikanger N...198 D3
Leimen D.......93 B4
Leinefelde D...82 A2
Leinesfjord N .194 C6
Leintwardine
UK.......39 B4
Leipojärvi S ..196 B4

Leipzig D.......83 A4
Leira
Nordland N...195 D4
Oppland N....47 B6
Leirämoen N..195 D5
Leiria P.......154 B2
Leirvassbu N...47 A5
Leirvik
Hordaland N... 52 A1
Sogn og Fjordane
N.......46 A2
Leisach A......109 C3
Leisnig D.......83 A4
Leiston UK.....45 A5
Leitholm UK ...35 C5
Leitrim IRL....26 C2
Leitza E.......144 A2
Leitzkau D.....73 B4
Lejkowo PL.....68 A1
Lekani GR.....183 B6
Łękawa PL.....86 A3
Łekawica PL ...99 B3
Lekeitio E.....143 A4
Lekenik HR....124 B2
Lekeryd S......62 A2
Leknes N.......194 B4
Łęknica PL.....84 A2
Leksand S......50 B1
Leksvik N 199 B7
Lekunberri E ..144 A2
Lekvattnet S ...49 B4
Le Lardin-St Lazare
F.......129 A4
Le Lauzet-Ubaye
F.......132 A2
Le Lavandou
F.......132 B2
Le Lion-d'Angers
F.......102 B1
Lelkowo PL.....69 A5
Le Locle CH ...106 B1
Le Loroux-
Bottereau F..101 B5
Le Louroux-
Béconnais F..101 B5
Lelów PL.......86 B3
Le Luc F.......132 B2
Le Lude F......102 B2
Lelystad NL....70 B2
Lem
Ringkøbing
DK.......59 B1
Viborg Amt.
DK.......58 B1
Le Malzieu-Ville
F.......116 C3
Le Mans F......102 A2
Le Mas-d'Azil
F.......146 A2
Le Massegros
F.......130 A2
Le Mayet-de-
Montagne F..117 A3
Le May-sur-Evre
F.......101 B5
Lembach F.....93 B3
Lemberg F.....93 B3
Lembeye F.....145 A3
Lemelerveld NL 71 B3
Le Mêle-sur-Sarthe
F.......89 B4
Le Ménil F.....105 A5
Le Merlerault F..89 B4
Le Mesnil-
sur-Oger F...91 C4
Lemförde D....71 B5
Lemgo D.......72 B1
Le Miroir F....105 C4
Lemland FIN...51 B7
Lemmer NL....70 B2
Le Molay-Littry
F.......88 A3
Le Monastier-sur-
Gazeille F ...117 C3
Le Monêtier-les-
Bains F.......118 C3
Le Mont-Dore
F.......116 B2
Le Montet F...116 A3
Le Mont-St Michel
F.......88 B2
Lempdes F.....116 B3
Le Muret F....128 B2
Le Muy F.......132 B2
Lemvig DK.....58 B1
Lemwerder D...72 A1
Lena
Norway N....48 B2
Lenart SLO....110 C2
Lenartovce SK ..99 C4
Lenauheim
RO.......126 B2
Lencloître F...102 C2
Lend A.......109 B4

Lendalfoot UK ..36 A2
Lendava SLO...111 C3
Lendery RUS 3 E12
Lendinara I....121 B4
Lendorf A......109 C4
Lendum DK.....58 A3
Le Neubourg F..89 A4
Lengefeld D....83 B5
Lengerich
Niedersachsen
D.......71 B4
Nordrhein-
Westfalen D...71 B4
Lenggries D...108 B2
Lengyeltóti H..111 C4
Lenhovda S....62 B3
Lenk CH.......106 C2
Lennartsfors S ..54 A2
Lennestadt D ..81 A4
Lennoxtown
UK.......35 C3
Leno I.......120 B3
Lénola I.......169 B3
Le Nouvion-en-
Thiérache F ...91 A3
Lens
B.......79 B3
F.......78 B2
Lensahn D.....65 B3
Lens Lestang
F.......117 B5
Lensvik N 198 B6
Lentellais E ...141 B3
Lentföhren D...64 C2
Lenti H.......111 C3
Lentini I......177 B3
Lenungshammar
S.......54 A3
Lenzburg CH..106 B3
Lenzen D.......73 A4
Lenzerheide
CH.......107 C4
Leoben A......110 B2
Leogang A.....109 B3
Leominster UK..39 B4
León E.......142 B1
Léon F.......128 C1
Leonberg D....93 C5
Léoncel F......118 C2
Leonding A....96 C2
Leonessa I....169 A2
Leonforte I....177 B3
Leonidio GR...184 B3
Leopoldsburg
B.......79 A5
Leopoldsdorf im
Marchfeld A..111 A3
Leopoldshagen
D.......74 A2
Leova MD......17 B8
Le Palais F.....100 B2
Le Parcq F.....78 B2
Lepe E.......161 B2
Le Péage-de-
Roussillon F..117 B4
Le Pellerin F...101 B4
Lepenou GR...182 E3
Le Perthus F...146 B3
Le Pertuis F...117 B4
Le Petit-Bornand
F.......118 B3
Lephin UK......31 B2
L'Épine F......132 A1
Lepoglava HR .124 A2
Le Poirè-sur-Vie
F.......114 B2
Le Pont-de-
Montvert F...130 A2
Le Porge F.....128 B1
Le Porge-Océan
F.......128 B1
Le Portel F.....78 B1
Le Pouldu F...100 B2
Le Pouliguen
F.......101 B3
Leppäjärvi
FIN.......192 D7
Leppävirta FIN...8 A5
Leppin D.......73 B4
Lepsény H 112 C2
Le Puy-en-Velay
F.......117 B3
Le Puy-Ste
Réparade F ..131 B4
Le Quesnoy F...79 B3
Léquile I.......173 B4
Le Rayol F.....132 B2

Leré F.......103 B4
Léricil I.......134 A2
Lerín E.......144 B2
Lerma E.......143 B3
Lerm-et-Musset
F.......128 B2
Lermoos A.....108 B1
Le Roeulx B....79 B4
Le Rouget F...116 C2
Lérouville F....92 C1
Le Rozier F....130 A2
Lerum S.......60 B2
Le Russey F...106 B1
Lervik N.......54 A1
Lerwick UK....33 A5
Lés E.......145 B4
Les Abrets F...118 B2
Les Aix-d'Angillon
F.......103 B4
Lesaka E.......144 A2
Les Ancizes-Comps
F.......116 B2
Les Arcs
Savoie F 119 B3
Var F 132 B2
Les-Aubiers F .102 C1
Les Baux-de-
Provence F...131 B3
Les Bézards F .103 B4
Les Bois CH ...106 B1
Les Bordes F ..103 B4
Les Borges
Blanques E ..147 C1
Les Borges del
Camp E.......147 C2
Les Brunettes
F.......104 C2
Lesbury UK 37 A5
Les Cabannes
F.......146 B2
L'Escala E.....147 B4
Lescar F.......145 A3
L'Escarène F ..133 B3
Lesce SLO.....123 A3
Lescheraines
F.......118 B3
Lesconil F......100 B1
Les Contamines-
Montjoié F ..118 B3
les Coves de
Vinroma E ...153 B4
Les Déserts F..118 B2
Les Deux-Alpes
F.......118 C3
Les Diablerets
CH.......119 A4
Lesdins F......90 B3
Les Echelles F .118 B2
Le Sel-de-Bretagne
F.......101 B4
Le Sentier CH .105 C5
Les Escaldes
AND.......146 B2
Les Essarts F ..114 B2
Les Estables
F.......117 C4
Les Eyzies-de-Tayac
F.......129 B4
Les Gets F.....118 A3
Les Grandes-Ventes
F.......89 A5
Les Haudères
CH.......119 A4
Les Herbiers F .114 B2
Les Hôpitaux-Neufs
F.......105 C5
Lesično SLO...123 A4
Lésina I.......171 B3
Lesjaskog N...198 C5
Lesjöfors S.....49 C6
Leskovac SRB ..16 D4
Leskova Dolina
SLO.......123 B3
Leskovec
CZ.......98 B1
SLO.......123 B4
Leskovice CZ...97 B3
Leskovik AL...182 C2
Leslie UK......35 B4
Les Lucs-sur-
Boulogne F ..114 B2
Les Mages F...131 A3
Lesmahagow
UK.......36 A3
Les Mazures F...91 B4
Les Mées F....132 A1
Lesmont F.....91 C4
Les Mureaux F..90 C1
Lésna PL.......84 A3
Lesneven F....100 A1
Leśnica PL.....86 B2
Lešnica SRB ..127 C1

Leśniów
Wielkopolski
PL.......75 C4
Lesnoye RUS ...9 C9
Les Omergues
F.......132 A1
Les Ormes-sur-
Voulzie F.....90 C3
Les Orres F ...132 A2
Le Souquet F..128 C1
Lesparre-Médoc
F.......128 A2
l'Espérance F ..91 B3
l'Esperou F....130 A2
Les Pieux F....88 A2
Lesponne F ...145 A4
Les Pons-de-Cé
F.......102 B1
Les Ponts-de-
Martel CH....106 C1
Le Praz F......119 B3
Les Riceys F...104 B3
Les Roches F ..117 B4
Les Rosaires F .101 A3
Les Rosiers F ..102 B1
Les Rousses F .105 C5
Les Sables-
d'Olonne E..114 B2
Lessach A......109 B4
Lessay F.......88 A2
Lessebo S......62 B3
Les Settons F ..104 B3
Lessines B.....79 B3
L'Estany E.....147 C3
Les Ternes F...116 B2
Lesterps F.....115 B4
Les Thilliers en-
Vexin F.......90 B1
Les Touches F .101 B4
Les Trois Moûtiers
F.......102 B2
Les Vans F.....131 A3
Les Verrières
CH.......105 C5
Les Vignes F ..130 A2
Leswalt UK....36 B1
Leszno
Mazowieckie
PL.......77 B5
Wielkopolski
PL.......85 A4
Leszno Górne
PL.......84 A3
Letchworth UK..44 B3
Le Teil F.......131 A3
Le Teilleul F...88 B3
Le Temple-de-
Bretagne F ..101 B4
Letenye H.....111 C3
Le Theil F......89 B4
Le Thillot F....106 B1
Letino I.......170 B2
Letohrad CZ...97 A4
Le Touquet-Paris-
Plage F.......78 B1
Le Touvet F...118 B2
Letovice CZ....97 B4
Le Translay F...90 B1
Le Tréport F...90 A1
Letschin D.....74 B3
Letterfrack IRL..28 A2
Letterkenny
IRL.......26 B3
Lettermacaward
IRL.......26 B2
Lettomanoppello...
Lettweiler D...93 B3
Letur E.......164 A2
Letux E.......153 A3
Letzlingen D...73 B4
Leucate F......146 B4
Leuchars UK ...35 B5
Leuglay F......105 B3
Leuk CH.......119 A4
Leukerbad CH .119 A4
Leumrabhagh
UK.......31 A2
Leuna D.......83 A4
Leusden NL....70 B2
Leutenberg D...82 B3
Leuterschach
D.......108 B1
Leutershausen
D.......94 B2
Leutkirch D....107 B5
Leuven B......79 B4
Leuze-en-Hainaut
B.......79 B3
Le Val F.......132 B2
Le Val-André
F.......101 A3
Le Val-d'Ajol
F.......105 B5

Levan AL.......182 C1
Levanger N ...199 B8
Levanjska Varoš
HR.......125 B4
Lévanto I......134 A2
Levaré F.......88 B3
Levata I.......120 B3
Leveld N.......47 B5
Leven
East Yorkshire
UK.......41 B3
Fife UK 35 B5
Leverano I....173 B3
Le Verdon-sur-Mer
F.......114 C2
Leverkusen D..80 A2
Levern D.......72 B1
Le Vernet F....132 A2
Levet F.......103 C4
Levice SK......112 A2
Lévico Terme
I.......121 A4
Levie F.......180 B2
Levier F.......105 C5
Le Vigan F....130 B2
Lévignen F.....90 B2
le Ville I.......135 B5
Levinovac HR .124 B3
Le Vivier-sur-Mer
F.......88 B2
Levoča SK.....99 B4
Levroux F......103 C3
Lewes UK......45 C4
Lewin Brzeski
PL.......85 B5
Lewisham UK ..44 B3
Leyburn UK....37 B5
Leyland UK....38 A4
Leysdown-on-Sea
UK.......45 B4
Leysin CH.....119 A4
Lezajsk PL.....12 C5
Lézardrieux F .100 A2
Lézat-sur-Léze
F.......146 A2
Lezay F.......115 B3
Lezhë AL......182 B1
Lézignan-Corbières
F.......130 B1
Lezignan-la-Cèbe
F.......130 B2
Lézinnes F 104 B3
Lezoux F.......117 B3
Lezuza E.......158 C1
Lhenice CZ....96 C2
Lherm F.......146 A2
Lhommaizé F .115 B4
L'Hospitalet de
l'Infant E 147 D1
L'Hospitalet de
Llobregat E ..147 C3
L'Hospitalet-du-
Larzac F......130 B2
Lhuître F......91 C4
Liancourt F....90 B2
Liart F.......91 B4
Liatorp S......63 B2
Liatrie UK.....32 C2
Libán CZ.......84 B3
Libceves CZ....84 B1
Liběchov CZ....84 B2
Liber E.......141 B3
Liberec CZ.....84 B3
Libiąż PL.......86 B3
Libina CZ.......98 B1
Libochovice CZ .84 B2
Libohovë AL...182 C2
Libourne F....128 B2
Libramont B....92 B1
Librazhd AL...182 B2
Librilla E.......165 B3
Libros E.......152 B2
Licata I.......176 B2
Licciana Nardi
I.......134 A3
Licenza I......169 A2
Liceros E......151 A4
Lich D.......81 B4
Lichères-près-
Aigremont F .104 B2
Lichfield UK ...40 C2
Lichtenau
A.......97 C3
D.......81 A4
Lichtenberg D .83 B3
Lichtenfels D...82 B3
Lichtensteig
CH.......107 B4
Lichtenstein D .83 B4
Lichtenvoorde
NL.......71 C3

Lichtervelde B ..78 A3
Lička Jesenica
  HR 123 B4
Lickershamn S ..57 C4
Lički Osik HR .. 123 C4
Ličko Lešce
  HR 123 C4
Licodía Eubéa
  I. 177 B3
Licques F......78 B1
Lida BY........13 B6
Lidar N........47 A6
Lidečko CZ....98 B2
Liden S....... 200 D2
Lidhult S......60 C3
Lidköping S...55 B4
Lido I 122 B1
Lido Azzurro I. 173 B3
Lido degli Estensi
  I. 122 C1
Lido degli Scacchi
  I. 122 C1
Lido della Nazioni
  I. 122 C1
Lido di Camaiore
  I. 134 B3
Lido di
  Casalbordino
  I. 169 A4
Lido di Castél
  Fusano I..... 168 B2
Lido di Cincinnato
  I. 168 B2
Lido di Classe
  I. 135 A5
Lido di Fermo
  I. 136 B2
Lido di Fondi I. 169 B3
Lido di Jésolo
  I. 122 B1
Lido di Lícola
  I. 170 C2
Lido di Metaponto
  I. 174 A2
Lido di Óstia I. 168 B2
Lido di Policoro
  I. 174 A2
Lido di Pomposa
  I. 122 C1
Lido di Savio I. 135 A5
Lido di Scanzano
  I. 174 A2
Lido di Siponto
  I. 171 B3
Lido di Squillace
  I. 175 C2
Lido di Volano
  I. 122 C1
Lido Riccio I.. 169 A4
Lidoríki GR.... 184 A3
Lido Silvana I . 173 B3
Lidsjöberg S .199 A12
Lidzbark PL....77 A4
Lidzbark
  Warmiński PL..69 A5
Liebenau
  A. 96 C2
  D 72 B2
Liebenwalde D..74 B2
Lieberose D....74 C3
Liebling RO .. 126 B3
Lieboch A...... 110 C2
Liège B........80 B1
Lieksa FIN..... 3 E12
Lienen D.......71 B4
Lienz A........ 109 C3
Liepāja LV......8 D2
Lier B.........79 A4
Lierbyen N....54 A1
Liernais F..... 104 B3
Liesing A...... 109 C3
Liestal CH..... 106 B2
Liétor E....... 158 C2
Lieurac F...... 146 B2
Lieurey F......89 A4
Liévin F........78 B2
Liezen A 110 B1
Liffol-le-Grand
  F............92 C1
Lifford IRL.....27 B3
Liffré F....... 101 A4
Ligardes F 129 B3
Lignano
  Sabbiadoro I.. 122 B2
Ligné F....... 101 B4
Lignières F... 103 C4
Ligny-en-Barrois
  F............92 C1
Ligny-le-Châtel
  F............ 104 B2
Ligoła Polska
  PL...........85 A5
Ligourio GR... 184 B4

Ligowo PL......77 B4
Ligueil F...... 102 B2
Likavka SK.....99 B3
Likenäs S......49 B5
Likhoslavl RUS...9 D9
Liknes N.......52 B2
Lild Strand DK ..58 A1
L'Île-Bouchard
  F............ 102 B2
I'Île-Rousse F . 180 A1
Lilienfeld A ... 110 A2
Lilienthal D....72 A1
Lilla Edet S....54 B3
Lilla Tjärby S...61 C3
Lille
  B.............79 A4
  F............78 B3
Lillebonne F....89 A4
Lillehammer N .48 A2
Lillerød DK.... 61 D2
Lillers F.......78 B2
Lillesand N....53 B4
Lillestrøm N...48 C3
Lillhärdal S .199 D11
Lillkyrka S.....56 A3
Lillo E........ 157 A4
Lillögda S..... 200 B3
Lillpite S..... 196 D4
Lima S.........49 B5
Limanowa PL ...99 B4
Limassol CY... 181 B2
Limavady UK...27 A4
Limbach-
  Oberfrohna D..83 B4
Limbaži LV......8 D4
Limbourg B....80 B1
Limburg D......81 B4
Lime DK........58 B3
Limedsforsen S .49 B5
Limenaria GR . 183 C6
Limenas
  Chersonisou
  GR 185 D6
Limerick IRL....29 B3
Limes I 121 B3
Limésy F.......89 A4
Limmared S....60 B3
Limni GR......183 E5
Limoges F.... 115 C5
Limogne-en-Quercy
  F............ 129 B4
Limoise F..... 104 C2
Limone Piemonte
  I. 133 A3
Limone sul Garda
  I. 121 B3
Limons F...... 117 B3
Limours F......90 C2
Limoux F...... 146 A3
Linares E..... 157 B4
Linares de Mora
  E 153 B3
Linares de Riofrío
  E 149 B4
Linaria GR.....183 E6
Linas de Broto
  E 145 B3
Lincoln UK.....40 B3
Lind DK........59 B1
Lindås N.......46 B2
Lindau D...... 107 B4
Lindberget N ..48 A3
Lindelse DK....65 B3
Lindenberg D ..74 B3
Lindenberg im
  Allgäu D 107 B4
Lindern D......71 B4
Linderöd S.... 61 D3
Lindesberg S...56 A1
Lindesnäs S....50 B1
Lindesnes N...52 C3
Lindholmen S..57 A4
Lindknud DK...59 C2
Lindlar D.......80 A3
Lindö S........56 B2
Lindome S......60 B2
Lindos GR.....188 C3
Lindoso P..... 148 A1
Lindow D.......74 B1
Lindsdal S.....62 B4
Lindshammar
  S 62 A3
Lindved DK....59 C2
Líně CZ........96 B1
Lingbo S.......50 A3
Lingen D.......71 B4
Lingfield UK...44 B3
Linghem S.....56 B1
Linguaglossa
  I. 177 B4
Linia PL........68 A2
Linie PL........74 A3

Liniewo PL.....68 A3
Linkenheim D ..93 B4
Linköping S....56 B1
Linksness UK...33 C3
Linlithgow UK .35 C4
Linneryd S.....63 B3
Linnes Hammarby
  S............51 C4
Linnich D......80 B2
Linsell S...... 199 C10
Linslade UK....44 B3
Linthal CH..... 107 C4
Linyola E..... 147 C1
Linz
  A.............. 96 C2
  D.............80 B3
Liomseter N.....47 A6
Lionárisso CY . 181 A3
Lioni I........ 172 B1
Lion-sur-Mer F ..89 A3
Lipany SK......99 B4
Lipar SRB..... 126 B1
Lípari I........ 177 A3
Lipcani MD.....17 A7
Lipen CZ.......98 B1
Liphook UK....44 B3
Lipiany PL......75 A3
Lipik HR....... 124 B3
Lipka PL........68 B2
Lipki Wielkie
  PL...........75 B4
Lipnica PL.....68 B2
Lipnica Murowana
  PL...........99 B4
Lipnik nad Bečvou
  CZ 98 B1
Lipno
  Kujawsko-
  Pomorskie PL ..77 B4
  Łódzkie PL.....86 A2
Liposthey F.... 128 B2
Lipovac HR.... 125 B5
Lipovec CZ......97 B4
Lipovets UA... 13 D8
Lipowiec PL....77 A6
Lipowina PL....69 A4
Lippborg D 81 A4
Lippó H....... 125 B4
Lippoldsberg
  D.............81 A5
Lippstadt D....81 A4
Lipsko PL......87 A5
Liptál CZ.......98 B1
Liptovská-Lúžna
  SK...........99 C3
Liptovská Osada
  SK...........99 C3
Liptovská-Teplička
  SK...........99 C4
Liptovský Hrádok
  SK...........99 B3
Liptovský Mikuláš
  SK...........99 B3
Lipusz PL......68 A2
Lipúvka CZ.....97 B4
Liré F......... 101 B4
Lisac BIH..... 139 A3
Lisbellaw UK...27 B3
Lisboa = Lisbon
  P........... 154 C1
Lisbon = Lisboa
  P........... 154 C1
Lisburn UK.....27 B4
Liscannor IRL ..28 B2
Lisdoonvarna
  IRL 28 A2
Lisewo PL......69 B3
Lisia Góra PL...87 B5
Lisięcice PL.....86 B1
Lisieux F......89 A4
Lisjö S........56 A2
Liskeard UK....42 B2
L'Isle CH..... 105 C5
L'Isle-Adam F ..90 B2
L'Isle-de-Noé
  F............ 145 A4
L'Isle-en-Dodon
  F............ 145 A4
L'Isle-Jourdain
  Gers F 129 C4
  Vienne F ... 115 B4
L'Isle-sur-la-Sorgue
  F............ 131 B4
L'Isle-sur-le-Doubs
  F............ 105 B5
L'Isle-sur-Serein
  F............ 104 B3
Lisle-sur-Tarn
  F............ 129 C4
Lismore IRL....29 B4
Lisnaskea UK ..27 B3

Lišov CZ........96 B2
Lisów
  Lubuskie PL....74 B3
  Śląskie PL......86 B2
Lisse NL........70 B1
Lissycasey IRL..28 B2
List D..........64 A1
Listerby S......63 B3
Listowel IRL....29 B2
Listrac-Médoc
  F............ 128 A2
Liszki PL.......99 A3
Liszkowo PL....76 A2
Lit S......... 199 B11
Litava SK.......99 C3
Litcham UK....41 C4
Lit-et-Mixe F .. 128 B1
Litija SLO..... 123 A3
Litke H....... 112 A3
Litlabø N.......52 A1
Litochoro GR.. 182 C4
Litoměřice CZ...84 B2
Litomyšl CZ.....97 B4
Litovel CZ......98 B1
Litschau A......96 C3
Littlehampton
  UK 44 C3
Littleport UK...45 A4
Littleton IRL....29 B4
Little Walsingham
  UK 41 C4
Litvínov CZ.....83 B5
Livadero GR... 182 C3
Livadhia CY... 181 B2
Livadi GR...... 182 C4
Livadia GR..... 184 A3
Livarot F.......89 B4
Liveras CY..... 181 A1
Livernon F.... 129 B4
Liverovici
  MNE 139 C5
Liverpool UK...38 A4
Livigno I...... 107 C5
Livingston UK..35 C4
Livno BIH..... 138 B2
Livold SLO.... 123 B3
Livorno I...... 134 B3
Livorno Ferraris
  I. 119 B5
Livron-sur-Drôme
  F............ 117 C4
Livry-Louvercy
  F............91 B4
Lixheim F...... 92 C3
Lixouri GR.... 184 A1
Lizard UK......42 C1
Lizy-sur-Ourcq
  F............90 B3
Lizzano I..... 173 B3
Lizzano in
  Belvedere I . 135 A3
Ljig SRB...... 127 C2
Ljørdalen N....49 A4
Ljosland N.....52 B3
Ljubija BIH.... 124 C2
Ljubinje BIH... 139 C4
Ljubljana SLO . 123 A3
Ljubno ob Savinji
  SLO 123 A3
Ljubovija SRB. 127 C1
Ljubuški BIH .. 138 B3
Ljugarn S......57 C4
Ljung S........60 B2
Ljunga S.......56 B2
Ljungaverk S .. 200 D2
Ljungby S......60 C3
Ljungbyhed S ..61 C3
Ljungbyholm S .63 B4
Ljungdalen S .. 199 C9
Ljungsarp S....60 B3
Ljungsbro S....56 B1
Ljungskile S....54 B2
Ljusdal S...... 200 E2
Ljusfallshammar
  S............56 B1
Ljusne S.......51 A4
Ljustero S.....57 A4
Ljutomer SLO . 111 C3
Lüki BG....... 183 B6
Lladurs E..... 147 B2
Llafranc F..... 147 C4
Llagostera E .. 147 C3
Llanaelhaiarn
  UK 38 B2
Llanarth UK....39 B2
Llanbedr UK...38 B2
Llanberis UK...38 A2
Llanbister UK ..39 B3
Llanbrynmair
  UK 39 B3
Llançà E...... 146 B4

Llandeilo UK....39 C3
Llandissilio UK ..39 C2
Llandovery UK ..39 C3
Llandrillo UK...38 B3
Llandrindod Wells
  UK 39 B3
Llandudec F ... 100 A1
Llandudno UK ..38 A3
Llandysul UK...39 B2
Llanelli UK.....39 C2
Llanerchymedd
  F............ 128 A2
Llanes E...... 142 A2
Llanfair Caereinion
  UK 38 B3
Llanfairfechan
  UK 38 A3
Llanfyllin UK...38 B3
Llangadog UK ..39 C3
Llangefni UK...38 A2
Llangollen UK..38 B3
Llangrannog
  UK 39 B2
Llangurig UK...39 B3
Llanidloes UK ..39 B3
Llanilar UK.....39 B2
Llanrhystud UK .39 B2
Llanrwst UK....38 A3
Llansannan UK..38 A3
Llansawel UK ..39 B2
Llanstephan
  UK 39 C2
Llanteno E 143 A3
Llanthony UK ..39 C3
Llantrisant UK ..39 C3
Llantwit-Major
  UK 39 C3
Llanuwchllyn
  UK 38 B3
Llanwddyn UK ..38 B3
Llanwrda UK...39 C3
Llanwrtyd Wells
  UK 39 B3
Llanybydder
  UK 39 B2
Llanymynech
  UK 38 B3
Llavorsí E..... 146 B2
Lleida E...... 153 A4
Llera E....... 156 B1
Llerena E..... 156 B1
Lles E........ 146 B2
Llessuí E..... 146 B2
Llinars E...... 147 B2
Lliria E....... 159 B3
Llívia E........41 B4
Llodio E...... 143 A4
Lloret de Mar
  F............ 147 C3
Llosa de Ranes
  I. 159 B3
Lloseta E..... 167 B2
Llucena del Cid
  E 153 B3
Llucmajor E... 167 B2
Llutxent E.... 159 C3
Llwyngwril UK .38 B2
Llyswen UK....39 B3
Lnáře CZ.......96 B1
Lniano PL......76 A3
Loanhead UK ..35 C4
Loano I....... 133 A4
Loarre E...... 145 B3
Löbau D........84 A2
Löbejün D......83 A3
Löberöd S......61 D3
Łobez PL.......75 A4
Löbnitz D......66 B1
Lobón E....... 155 C4
Loburg D.......73 B5
Łobżenica PL...76 A2
Locana I...... 119 B4
Locarno CH... 120 A1
Loccum D......72 B2
Loče SLO...... 123 A4
Lochailort UK ..34 B2
Lochaline UK ..34 B2
Lochans UK....36 B1
Locharbriggs
  UK 36 A3
Lochau A...... 107 B4
Lochcarron UK ..34 B2
Lochearnhead
  UK 34 B3
Lochem NL.....71 B3
Lochgelly UK...35 B4
Lochgilphead
  UK 34 B2
Lochgoilhead
  UK 34 B3

Lochinver UK ...32 C1
Loch nam Madadh
  UK 31 B1
Lochranza UK...34 C2
Ločika SRB ... 127 D3
Lockenhaus A. 111 B3
Lockerbie UK ..36 A3
Löcknitz D......74 A3
Locmaria F.... 100 B2
Locmariaquer
  F............ 100 B3
Locminé F..... 100 B3
Locorotondo I. 173 B3
Locquirec F.... 100 A2
Locri I........ 175 C2
Locronan F.... 100 A1
Loctudy F..... 100 B1
Lodares de Osma
  E 151 A5
Lodé I........ 178 B3
Lodeinoye Pole
  RUS 9 B8
Lodève F..... 130 B2
Lodi I........ 120 B2
Løding N...... 194 C5
Lödingen N .. 194 B6
Lodosa E...... 144 B1
Lödöse S.......54 B3
Łódź PL........86 A3
Loeches E..... 151 B4
Løfallstrand N ..46 B3
Lofer A....... 109 B3
Lofsdalen S .. 199 C10
Loftahammar S .62 A4
Lofthus N......46 B3
Loftus UK......37 B6
Loga N.........52 B2
Logatec SLO . 123 B3
Lögdeå S..... 200 C5
Lograto I...... 120 B3
Logroño E..... 143 B4
Logrosán E.... 156 A2
Løgstør DK.....58 B2
Løgten DK.....59 B3
Løgumgårde
  DK 64 A1
Løgumkloster
  DK 64 A1
Lohals DK......65 A3
Lohiniva FIN .. 197 B8
Lohja FIN......8 B4
Löhlbach D.....81 A4
Lohmen
  Mecklenburg-
  Vorpommern
  D.............65 C5
  Sachsen D....84 B2
Löhnberg D....81 B4
Lohne D........71 B5
Löhne D.......72 B1
Lohr D.........94 B1
Lohra D........81 B4
Lohsa D........84 A2
Loiano I...... 135 A4
Loimaa FIN......8 B3
Lóiri I........ 178 B3
Loitz D........66 C2
Loivos P...... 148 A2
Loivos do Monte
  P............ 148 A2
Loja E....... 163 A3
Lojanice SRB . 127 C1
Lojsta S.......57 C4
Løjt Kirkeby
  DK 64 A2
Lok SK........ 112 A2
Lokca SK.......99 B3
Løken N........54 A2
Lokeren B......79 A3
Loket CZ.......83 B4
Lokka FIN.... 197 B10
Løkken
  NL............79 A5
  DK 58 A2
Loknya RUS.....9 D7
Lökösháza H.. 113 C5
Lokve SRB.... 126 B3
Lollar D........81 B4
L'Olleria E.... 159 C3
Lölling-Graben
  A............ 110 C1
Lom
  BG 17 D5
  N............ 198 D5
  SK 99 C3
Lombez F..... 146 A1
Lomello I..... 120 B1
Łomianki PL....77 B5
Lomma S.......61 D2
Lommaryd S....62 A2
Lommatzsch D .83 A5
Lommel B......79 A5
Lommersum D..80 B2
Lomnice CZ....97 B4

Lomnice nad
  Lužnicí CZ....96 B2
Lomnice-nad
  Popelkou CZ..84 B3
Lompolo FIN . 196 A7
Łomża PL 12 B5
Lönashult S....63 B2
Lønborg DK....59 C1
Londerzeel B...79 A4
Londinières F ..89 A5
London UK.....44 B3
Lonevåg N.....46 B2
Longa GR..... 184 C2
Longare I..... 121 B4
Longares E.... 152 A2
Longarone I... 122 A1
Longastrino I . 135 A5
Long Bennington
  UK 40 C3
Longbenton
  UK 37 A5
Longchamp-sur-
  Aujon F 105 A3
Longchaumois
  F............ 118 A2
Long Eaton UK ..40 C2
Longeau F..... 105 B4
Longecourt-en-
  Plaine F 105 B4
Longeville-les-St
  Avold F 92 B2
Longeville-sur-Mer
  F............ 114 B2
Longford IRL...28 A4
Longframlington
  UK 37 A5
Longhope UK ..33 C3
Longhorsley
  UK 37 A5
Longhoughton
  UK 37 A5
Long Melford
  UK 45 A4
Longny-au-Perche
  F............89 B4
Longobucco I . 174 B2
Long Preston
  UK 40 A1
Longré F...... 115 B3
Longridge UK ..38 A4
Longroiva P... 149 B2
Long Sutton
  UK 41 C4
Longtown
  Cumbria UK . 36 A4
  Herefordshire
  UK 39 C4
Longué-Jumelles
  F............ 102 B1
Longuyon F....92 B1
Longvic F..... 105 B4
Longvilly B.....92 A1
Longwy F......92 B1
Lonigo I...... 121 B4
Löningen D....71 B4
Lonja HR...... 124 B2
Lønsdal N......95 A5
Lønset N...... 198 C6

Loreo I 122 B1
Loreto I 136 B2
Lorgues F 132 B2
Lorica I 174 B2
Lorient F 100 B2
Lorignac F 114 C3
Lörinci H 112 B3
Loriol-sur-Drôme
F 117 C4
Lormes F 104 B2
Loro Ciuffenna
I. 135 B4
Lorqui E 165 A3
Lörrach D 106 B2
Lorrez-le-Bocage
F 103 A4
Lorris F 103 B4
Lorup D 71 B4
Łoś PL 77 C5
Los S 199 D12
Losacino E 149 A3
Los Alcázares
E 165 B4
Los Arcos E 144 B1
Losar de la Vera
E 150 B2
Los Barios de Luna
E 141 B5
Los Barrios E . . . 162 B2
Los Caños de Meca
E 162 B1
Los Cerricos E . . 164 B2
Los Corrales E . . 162 A3
Los Corrales de
Buelna E 142 A2
Los Dolores E . . 165 B3
Losenstein A . . . 110 B1
Los Gallardos
E 164 B3
Losheim
Nordrhein-
Westfalen D . . 80 B2
Saarland D 92 B2
Los Hinojosos
E 158 B1
Los Isidros E . . . 159 B2
Los Molinos E . . 151 B3
Los Morales E . . 162 A2
Los Navalmorales
E 156 A3
Los Navalucillos
E 156 A3
Losne F 105 B4
Los Nietos E . . . 165 B4
Løsning DK 59 C2
Los Palacios y
Villafranca E . 162 A2
Los Pozuelos de
Calatrava E . . 157 B3
Los Rábanos
E 143 C4
Los Santos E . . . 149 B4
Los Santos de la
Humosa E . . . 151 B4
Los Santos de
Maimona E . . 155 C4
Lossburg D 93 C4
Losse F 128 B2
Losser NL 71 B4
Lossiemouth
UK 32 D3
Lössnitz D 83 B4
Loštice CZ 97 B4
Los Tijos E 142 A2
Lostwithiel UK . . 42 B2
Los Villares E . . 163 A4
Los Yébenes E . . 157 A4
Løten N 48 B3
Lotorp S 56 B1
Lottefors S 50 A3
Löttorp S 62 A5
Lotyń PL 68 B1
Lotzorai I 179 C3
Louargat F 100 A2
Loudéac F 101 A3
Loudun F 102 B2
Loué F 102 B2
Loughborough
UK 40 C2
Loughbrickland
UK 27 B4
Loughrea IRL . . 28 A3
Louhans F 105 C4
Louisburgh IRL . 28 A2
Loukhi RUS 3 C13
Loulay F 114 B3
Loulé P 160 B1
Louny CZ 84 B1
Lourdes F 145 A3
Lourenzá E 141 A3

Loures P 154 C1
Loures-Barousse
F 145 A4
Louriçal P 154 A2
Lourinhã P 154 B1
Lourmarin F . . . 131 B4
Loury F 103 B4
Lousa
Bragança P . 149 A2
Castelo Branco
P 155 B3
Lousã P 148 B1
Lousa P 154 C1
Lousada
E 140 B3
P 148 A1
Louth UK 41 B3
Loutra Edipsou
GR 183 E5
Loutraki GR . . . 184 B3
Loutropoli Thermis
GR 186 C1
Louverné F 102 A1
Louvie-Juzon
F 145 A3
Louviers F 89 A5
Louvigné-du-
Désert F 88 B2
Louvois F 91 B4
Lova I 121 B5
Lovasberény
H 112 B2
Lövåsen S 49 C5
Lovászpatona
H 111 B4
Lövberga S 200 C1
Lovech BG 17 D6
Lövenich D 80 A2
Lóvere I 120 B3
Lövestad S 61 D3
Loviisa FIN 8 B5
Lovikka S 196 B5
Lovinobaňa SK . . 99 C3
Loviste HR 138 B3
Lovke HR 123 B3
Lovnäs S 49 A5
Lövö H 111 B3
Lovosice CZ 84 B2
Lovozero RUS . . 3 C14
Lovran HR 123 B3
Lovreć HR 138 B2
Lovrenc na Pohorju
SLO 110 C2
Lovrin RO 126 B2
Lövstabruk S . . . 51 B4
Löwenberg D . . . 74 B2
Löwenstein D . . . 94 B1
Lowestoft UK . . . 41 C5
Lowick UK 37 A5
Łowicz PL 77 B4
Loxstedt D 72 A1
Loyew BY 13 C9
Lož SLO 123 B3
Loza CZ 96 B1
Łozina PL 85 A5
Loznica SRB . . . 127 C1
Lozničko Polje
SRB 127 C1
Lozorno SK 111 A4
Lozovik SRB . . . 127 C3
Lozoya E 151 B4
Lozoyuela E . . . 151 B4
Lozzo di Cadore
I 109 C3
Luanco E 141 A5
Luarca E 141 A4
Lubaczów PL . . . 13 C5
Lubań PL 84 A3
Lubanów PL 86 A3
Lubars D 73 B5
Lubasz PL 75 B5
Lubawa PL 69 B4
Lubawka PL 85 B4
Lübbecke D 72 B1
Lübben D 74 C3
Lübbenau D 84 A1
Lubczyna PL 74 A3
Lübeck D 65 C3
Lubenec CZ 83 B5
Lubersac F 115 C5
Lübesse D 73 A4
Lubia E 152 A1
Lubián E 141 B4
Lubiatowo PL . . 75 A4
Lubichowo PL . . 69 B3
Lubicz Dolny
PL 76 A3
Lubień PL 99 B3
Lubień Kujawski
PL 77 B4
Lubieszewo PL . 75 A4

Lubin
Dolnośląskie
PL 85 A4
Zachodnio-
Pomorskie PL . 67 C3
Lublin PL 12 C5
Lubliniec PL 86 B2
Lubmin D 66 B2
Lubniewice PL . . 75 B4
Lubochnia PL . . . 87 A4
Lubomierz
Dolnośląskie
PL 84 A3
Małopolskie
PL 99 B4
Lubomino PL . . . 69 A5
Luboń PL 76 B1
L'ubotín SK 99 B4
Lubowidz PL . . . 77 A4
Łubowo
Wielkopolskie
PL 76 B2
Zachodnio-
Pomorskie PL . 68 B1
Lubraniec PL . . . 76 B3
Lubrín E 164 B2
Lubrza PL 85 B5
Lubsko PL 84 A2
Lübtheen D 73 A4
Lubuczewo PL . . 68 A2
Luby CZ 83 B4
Lübz D 73 A5
Luc F 117 C3
Lucainena de las
Torres E 164 B2
Lucan IRL 30 A2
Lučani SRB 127 D2
Lúcar E 164 B2
Luçay-le-Mâle
F 103 B3
Lucca I 134 B3
Lucciana F 180 A2
Lucé F 90 C1
Luče SLO 123 A3
Lucena
Córdoba E . . . 163 A3
Huelva E 161 B3
Lucenay-les-Aix
F 104 C2
Lucenay-l'Evéque
F 104 B3
Luc-en-Diois F . . 118 C2
Lučenec SK 99 C3
Luceni E 144 C2
Lucens CH 106 C1
Lucera I 171 B3
Luceram F 133 B3
Lüchow D 73 B4
Luciana E 157 B3
Lucignano I 135 B4
Lucija SLO 122 B2
Lucka D 83 A4
Luckau D 84 A1
Luckenwalde D . 74 B2
Lückstedt D 73 B4
Luco dei Marsi
I 169 B3
Luc-sur-Mer F . . 89 A3
Ludanice SK 98 C2
Ludbreg HR 124 A2
Lüdenscheid D . . 81 A3
Lüderitz D 73 B4
Lüdersdorf D . . . 65 C3
Ludgershall UK . 44 B2
Ludgo S 56 B3
Lüdinghausen
D 80 A3
Ludlow UK 39 B4
Ludomy PL 75 B5
Ludvika S 50 B2
Ludweiler Warndt
D 92 B2
Ludwigsburg D . 94 C1
Ludwigsfelde D . 74 B2
Ludwigshafen
D 93 B4
Ludwigslust D . . 73 A4
Ludwigsstadt
D 82 B3
Ludza LV 8 D5
Luesia E 144 B2
Luftkurort
Arendsee D . . 73 B4
Lug
BIH 139 C4
HR 125 B4
Luga RUS 9 C6
Lugagnano Val
d'Arda I 120 C2
Lugano CH 120 A1
Lugau D 83 B4
Lugnas S 55 B4

Lúgnola I 168 A2
Lugny F 105 C3
Lugo
E 140 A3
I 135 A4
Lugoj RO 16 C4
Lugones E 141 A5
Lugros E 163 A4
Luhačovice CZ . . 98 B1
Luhe D 95 B4
Luino I 120 B1
Luintra E 140 B3
Lújar E 163 B4
Luka nad Jihlavou
CZ 97 B3
Lukavac BIH . . . 125 C4
Lukavika BIH . . . 125 C4
Lukovë AL 182 D1
Lukovica SLO . . 123 A3
Lukovit BG 17 D6
Lukovo HR 123 C3
Lukovo Šugorje
HR 137 A4
Łuków PL 12 C5
Lukowiec PL 86 A3
Łukowice Brzeskie
PL 85 B5
Luksefjell N 53 A5
Łukta PL 69 B5
Lula I 178 B3
Luleå S 196 D5
Lüleburgaz
TR 186 A2
Lumbarda HR . . 138 C3
Lumbier E 144 B2
Lumbrales E . . . 149 B3
Lumbreras E . . . 143 B4
Lumbres F 78 B2
Lumezzane I . . . 120 B3
Lumijoki FIN . . . 197 D8
Lumio F 180 A1
Lummelunda S . 57 C4
Lummen B 79 B5
Lumparland
FIN 51 B7
Lumpiaque E . . 152 A2
Lumsås DK 61 D1
Lumsden UK . . . 33 D4
Lumsheden S . . . 50 B3
Lun HR 123 C3
Luna E 144 B3
Lunamatrona
I 179 C2
Lunano I 136 B1
Lunas F 130 B2
Lund
N 199 A8
Skåne S 61 D3
Västra Götaland
S 54 A3
Lundamo N 199 B7
Lunde
DK 59 C1
Sogn og Fjordane
N 46 A3
Sogn og Fjordane
N 46 A3
Telemark N . . . 53 A5
S 200 D3
Lundebyvollen
N 49 B4
Lunden D 64 B2
Lunderseter N . . 49 B4
Lunderskov DK . 59 C2
Lundsberg S 55 A5
Lüneburg D 72 A3
Lunel F 131 B3
Lünen D 81 A3
Lunéville F 92 C2
Lungern CH 106 C3
Lungro I 174 B2
Luninyets BY . . . 13 B7
Lünne D 71 B4
Lunner N 48 B2
Lunteren NL 70 B2
Lunz am See
A 110 B2
Luogosanto I . . 178 A3
Łupawa PL 68 A2
Lupión E 157 B4
Lupoglav HR . . . 123 B3
Luppa D 83 A4
Luque E 163 A3
Lurago d'Erba
I 120 B2
Lúras I 178 B3
Lurcy-Lévis F . . . 104 C1
Lure F 105 B5
Lurgan UK 27 B4
Luri F 180 A2
Lury-sur-Arnon
F 103 B4

Lusigny-sur-Barse
F 104 A3
Lusnić BIH 138 B2
Luso P 148 B1
Lusówko PL 75 B5
Luspebryggan
S 196 B2
Luss UK 34 B3
Lussac F 128 B2
Lussac-les-
Châteaux F . . 115 B4
Lussac-les-Eglises
F 115 B5
Lussan F 131 A3
Lüssow D 65 C5
Lustenau A 107 B4
Luštěnice CZ . . . 84 B2
Luster N 47 A4
Lutago I 108 C2
Lutherstadt
Wittenberg D . 83 A4
Lütjenburg D . . . 65 B3
Lutnes N 49 A4
Lutocin PL 77 B4
Lutomiersk PL . . 86 A3
Luton UK 44 B3
Lutry CH 106 C1
Lutsk UA 13 C6
Lutter am
Barenberge D . 72 C3
Lutterworth UK . 40 C2
Lututów PL 86 A2
Lützen D 83 A4
Lutzow D 73 A4
Luusua FIN 197 C10
Luvos S 196 C1
Luxembourg L . . 92 B2
Luxeuil-les-Bains
F 105 B5
Luxey F 128 B2
Luz
Évora P 155 C3
Faro P 160 B1
Faro P 160 B2
Luzarches F 90 B2
Luže CZ 97 B4
Luzech F 129 B4
Luzern CH 106 B3
Luzino PL 68 A3
Luz-St Sauveur
F 145 B3
Luzy F 104 C2
Luzzi I 174 B2
L'viv UA 13 D6
Lwówek PL 75 B5
Lwówek Śląski
PL 84 A3
Lyakhavichy BY . 13 B7
Lybster UK 32 C3
Lychen D 74 A2
Lychkova RUS . . 9 D8
Lyckeby S 63 B3
Lycksele S 200 B4
Lydd UK 45 C4
Lydford UK 42 B2
Lydney UK 39 C4
Lyepyel' BY 13 A8
Lygna N 48 B2
Lykkja N 47 B5
Lykling N 52 A1
Lyme Regis UK . 43 B4
Lymington UK . . 44 C2
Lympne UK 45 B5
Lyndhurst UK . . . 44 C2
Lyneham UK . . . 43 A5
Lyness UK 33 C3
Lyngdal
Buskerud N . . 47 C6
Vest-Agder N . . 52 B3
Lyngør N 53 B5
Lyngsa DK 58 A3
Lyngseidet N . 192 C4
Lyngsnes N 199 A8
Lynmouth UK . . 42 A3
Lynton UK 42 A3
Lyntupy BY 13 A7
Lyon F 117 B4
Lyons-la-Forêt
F 90 B1
Lyozna BY 13 A9
Lyrestad S 55 B5
Lysánad Labem
CZ 84 B2
Lýsápod Makytou
SK 98 B2
Lysebotn N 52 A2
Lysekil S 54 B2
Lysice CZ 97 B4
Lysomice PL 76 A3
Lysøysund N . . . 198 B6
Lysvik S 49 B5

Łyszkowice PL . . 77 C4
Lytham St Anne's
UK 38 A3
Lyuban RUS 9 C7
Lyubertsy RUS . . 9 E10
Lyubimets BG . 183 B8
Lyuboml' UA . . . 13 C6
Lyubytino RUS . . 9 C8

M

Maaninkavaara
FIN 197 C11
Maarheeze NL . . 80 A1
Maaseik B 80 A1
Maastricht NL . . 80 B1
Mablethorpe
UK 41 B4
Mably F 117 A4
Macael E 164 B2
Maçanet de
Cabrenys E . . 146 B3
Mação P 154 B2
Macau F 128 A2
Maccagno-Agra
I 120 A1
Maccarese I . . . 168 B2
Macchiagódena
I 170 B2
Macclesfield
UK 40 B1
Macduff UK 33 D4
Maceda E 140 B3
Macedo de
Cavaleiros P . 149 A3
Maceira
Guarda P 148 B2
Leiria P 154 B2
Macelj HR 124 A1
Macerata I 136 B2
Macerata Féltria
I 136 B1
Machault F 91 B4
Machecoul F . . . 114 B2
Machrihanish
UK 34 C2
Machynlleth
UK 39 B3
Macieira E 148 A1
Maciejowice PL . 87 A5
Macinaggio F . . 180 A2
Mackenrode D . 82 A2
Mačkovci SLO . . 111 C3
Macomer I 178 B2
Macon B 91 A4
Mâcon F 117 A4
Macotera E 150 B2
Macroom IRL . . . 29 C3
Macugnaga I . . 119 B4
Madan BG 183 B6
Madängsholm
S 55 B4
Madaras H 126 A1
Maddaloni I . . . 170 B2
Made NL 79 A4
Madeley UK 38 B4
Maderuelo E . . . 151 A4
Madetkoski
FIN 197 B9
Madley UK 39 B4
Madocsa H 112 C2
Madona LV 8 D5
Madonna di
Campiglio I . . 121 A3
Madrid E 151 B4
Madridejos E . . 157 A4
Madrigal de las
Altas Torres
E 150 A2
Madrigal de la Vera
E 150 B2
Madrigalejo E . . 156 A2
Madrigalejo de
Monte E 143 B3
Madriguera E . . 151 A4
Madrigueras
E 158 B2
Madroñera E . . . 156 A2
Mael-Carhaix
F 100 A2
Maella E 153 A4
Maello E 150 B3
Maesteg UK 39 C3
Mafra P 154 C1
Magacela E 156 B2
Magallón E 144 C2
Magaña E 144 C2
Magasa I 121 B3
Magaz E 142 C2
Magdeburg D . . 73 B4

Magenta I 120 B1
Magescq F 128 C1
Maghera UK 27 B4
Magherafelt UK 27 B4
Maghull UK 38 A4
Magilligan UK . 27 A4
Magione I 135 B5
Magiotto P 154 C1
Maglaj BIH 125 C4
Maglehem S 63 C2
Magliano de'Marsi
I 169 A3
Magliano in
Toscana I 168 A1
Magliano Sabina
I 168 A2
Maglić SRB 126 B1
Maglie I 173 B4
Maglöd H 112 B3
Magnac-Bourg
F 115 C5
Magnac-Laval
F 115 B5
Magnieres F . . . 92 C2
Magnor N 49 C4
Magnuszew PL . 87 A5
Magny-Cours
F 104 C2
Magny-en-Vexin
F 90 B1
Mágocs H 125 A4
Maguilla I 156 B2
Maguiresbridge
UK 27 B3
Magyarbóly
H 125 B4
Magyarkeszi
H 112 C2
Magyarszék H . 125 A4
Mahide E 141 C4
Mahilyow BY . . 13 B9
Mahmudiye
TR 187 C5
Mahora E 158 B2
Mahovo HR . . . 124 B2
Mähring D 95 B4
Maia
E 144 A2
P 148 A1
Maials E 153 A4
Maîche F 106 B1
Máida I 175 C2
Maiden Bradley
UK 43 A4
Maidenhead
UK 44 B3
Maiden Newton
UK 43 B4
Maidstone UK . . 45 B4
Maienfeld CH . . 107 B4
Maignelay
Montigny F . . 90 B2
Maijanen FIN . 197 B8
Maillezais F . . . 114 B3
Mailly-le-Camp
F 91 C4
Mailly-le-Château
F 104 B2
Mainar E 152 A2
Mainbernheim
D 94 B2
Mainburg D 95 C3
Mainhardt D . . . 94 B1
Maintal D 81 B4
Maintenon F . . . 90 C1
Mainvilliers F . . 90 C1
Mainz D 93 A4
Maiorca P 148 B1
Mairena de Aljarafe
E 162 A1
Mairena del Alcor
E 162 A2
Maisach D 108 A2
Maishofen A . . . 109 B3
Maison-Rouge
F 90 C3
Maissau A 97 C3
Maisse F 90 C2
Maizières-lès-Vic
F 92 C2
Maja HR 124 B2
Majadahonda
E 151 B4
Majadas E 150 C2
Majavatn N . . . 195 E4
Majs H 125 B4
Majšperk SLO . . 123 A4
Makarska HR . . 138 B3
Makkum NL 70 A2
Maklár H 113 B4
Makó H 126 A2
Makoszyce PL . . 85 B5

Makov SK 98 B2
Mąkowarsko
 PL. 76 A2
Maków Mazowiecki
 PL. 77 B6
Maków
 Podhalański
 PL. 99 B3
Makrakomi
 GR 182 E4
Maksniemi
 FIN. 196 D7
Malå S 195 E9
Mala Bosna
 SRB 126 A1
Malacky SK 97 C5
Maladzyechna
 BY. 13 A7
Málaga E. 163 B3
Malagón E 157 A4
Malaguilla E 151 B4
Malahide IRL. 30 A2
Mala Kladuša
 BIH. 124 B1
Mala Krsna
 SRB 127 C3
Malalbergo I 121 C4
Malá Lehota SK . 98 C2
Malanów PL. 76 C3
Mala Pijace
 SRB 126 A1
Mala Subotica
 HR 124 A2
Malaucène F . . . 131 A4
Malaunay F 89 A5
Malaya Vishera
 RUS 9 C8
Malborghetto
 I. 109 C4
Malbork PL. 69 A4
Malborn D 92 B2
Malbuisson F . . 105 C5
Malcésine I. 121 B3
Malchin D. 74 A1
Malching D 96 C1
Malchow D. 73 A5
Malcocinado
 E. 156 B2
Malczyce PL. 85 A4
Maldegem B 79 A3
Maldon UK. 45 B4
Małdyty PL. 69 B4
Malè I 121 A3
Malemort F 129 A4
Malente D 65 B3
Målerås S 62 B3
Males GR. 185 D6
Malesherbes F . . 90 C2
Malesina GR . . . 183 E5
Malestroit F 101 B3
Maletto I. 177 B3
Malexander S . . . 56 B1
Malgrat de Mar
 E. 147 C3
Malhadas P . . . 149 A3
Malia
 CY 181 B1
 GR 185 D6
Malicorne-sur-
 Sarthe F. 102 B1
Malijai F 132 A2
Målilldjös SRB . 126 B1
Malilla S 62 A3
Mali Lošinj
 HR 137 A3
Malin IRL. 28 A3
Malinec SK 99 C3
Malingsbo S 50 C2
Maliniec PL 76 B3
Malinska HR . . . 123 B3
Maliq AL 182 C2
Maljevac HR . . . 123 B4
Malkara TR. 186 B1
Małki PL. 69 B4
Malko Tarnovo
 BG 17 D7
Mallaig UK 34 A2
Mallaranny IRL. . . 28 A2
Mallemort F . . . 131 B4
Mallén E 144 C2
Malléon F 146 A2
Mallersdorf-
 Pfaffenberg D . 95 C4
Málles Venosta
 I. 108 C1
Malling DK. 59 B3
Mallnitz A 109 C4
Mallow IRL. 29 B3
Mallwyd UK. 38 B3
Malm N 199 A8
Malmbäck S 62 A2
Malmberget S . 196 B3
Malmby S. 56 A3

Malmédy B. 80 B2
Malmesbury
 UK 43 A4
Malmköping S . . 56 A2
Malmö S 61 D3
Malmon S 54 B2
Malmslätt S 56 B1
Malnate I 120 B1
Malo I 121 B4
Małogoszcz PL. . 87 B4
Malogo JCH. . . . 120 A2
Małomice PL. . . . 84 A3
Måløy N. 198 D2
Malpartida E. . . 155 B4
Malpartida de la
 Serena E 156 B2
Malpartida de
 Plasencia E. . . 150 C1
Malpas
 E. 145 B4
 UK 38 A4
Malpica P 155 B3
Malpica de
 Bergantiños
 E. 140 A2
Malpica de Tajo
 E. 150 C3
Malsch D 93 C4
Malšice CZ 96 B2
Malta A 109 C4
Maltat F. 104 C2
Maltby UK 40 B2
Malung S 49 B5
Malungsfors S . . 49 B5
Maluszów PL. . . . 75 B4
Maluszyn PL. . . . 87 B3
Malva E 142 B1
Malvaglia CH . . 120 A1
Malveira P 154 C1
Malvik N. 199 B7
Malyn UA 13 C8
Mamarrosa P . . 148 B1
Mamer L. 92 B2
Mamers F 89 B4
Mamirolle F . . . 105 B5
Mammendorf
 D 108 A2
Mámmola I 175 C2
Mamoiada I. . . . 178 B3
Mamonovo
 RUS 69 A4
Mamuras AL . . 182 B1
Maña SK 112 A2
Manacor E 167 B3
Manavgat TR. . 189 C6
Mancera de Abajo
 E. 150 B2
Mancha Real
 E. 163 A4
Manchester UK . 40 B1
Manching D. . . . 95 C3
Manchita E. . . . 156 B1
Manciano I. . . . 168 A1
Manciet F 128 C3
Mandal N 52 B3
Mandanici I . . . 177 A4
Mándas I. 179 C3
Mandatoriccio
 I. 174 B2
Mandayona E . 151 B5
Mandelieu-la-
 Napoule F . . . 132 B2
Mandello del Lário
 I. 120 B2
Mandelsloh D. . 72 B2
Manderfeld B . . 80 B2
Manderscheid
 D 80 B2
Mandino Selo
 BIH. 138 B3
Mandoudi GR. . 183 E5
Mandra GR. . . . 185 A4
Mandraki GR. . . 188 C2
Mandúria I. . . . 173 B3
Mane
 Alpes-de-Haute-
 Provence F . . 132 B1
 Haute-Garonne
 F 145 A4
Manérbio I. . . . 120 B3
Mañeru E 144 B2
Manetin CZ 96 B1
Manfredónia
 I. 171 B3
Mangalia RO. . . 17 D8
Manganeses de la
 Lampreana
 E. 149 A4
Manganeses de la
 Polvorosa E. . 141 B5
Manger N 46 B2
Mangiennes F . 92 B1

Mangotsfield
 UK 43 A4
Mångsbodarna
 S. 49 A5
Manguálde P . . 148 B2
Maniago I. 122 A1
Manilva E 162 B2
Manisa TR. 186 D2
Manises E. 159 B3
Mank A 110 A2
Månkarbo S. . . . 51 B4
Manlleu E 147 C3
Manna DK. 58 A2
Männedorf
 CH 107 B3
Mannersdorf am
 Leithagebirge
 A. 111 B3
Mannheim D. . . 93 B4
Manningtree
 UK 45 B5
Manoppello I. 169 A4
Manorbier UK. . 39 C2
Manorhamilton
 IRL 26 B2
Manosque F . . 132 B1
Manowo PL. . . . 67 B5
Manresa E 147 C2
Månsarp S 62 A2
Månsåsen S . . 199 B11
Manschnow D . 74 B3
Mansfeld D 82 A3
Mansfield UK . . 40 B2
Mansilla de Burgos
 E. 143 B3
Mansilla de las
 Mulas E 142 B1
Manskog S. 55 A3
Manso F 180 A1
Manteigas P . . 148 B2
Mantel D. 95 B4
Mantes-la-Jolie
 F. 90 C1
Mantes-la-Ville
 F. 90 C1
Manthelan F . . 102 B2
Mantorp S. 56 B1
Mántova I. 121 B3
Mänttä FIN. 8 A4
Mäntyjärvi
 FIN. 197 C10
Manuel E. 159 B3
Manyas TR. . . . 186 B2
Manzanal de Arriba
 E. 141 B4
Manzanares
 E. 157 A4
Manzanares el Real
 E. 151 B4
Manzaneda
 León E 141 B4
 Orense E. 141 B3
Manzanedo E . 143 B3
Manzaneque
 E. 157 A4
Manzanilla E . . 161 B3
Manzat F 116 B2
Manziana I. . . . 168 A2
Manziat F 117 A4
Maó E 167 B4
Maoča BIH . . . 125 C4
Maqueda E. . . . 150 B3
Mara E 152 A2
Maramaereğlisi
 TR. 186 B2
Maranchón E . . 152 A1
Maranello I. . . . 135 A3
Marano I 170 C2
Marano Lagunare
 I. 122 B2
MaransF 114 B2
Maratea I 174 C2
Marateca P. . . . 154 C2
Marathokambos
 GR 188 B1
Marathónas
 GR 185 A4
Marathóvouno
 CY 181 A2
Marazion UK. . . 42 B1
Marbach
 Baden-Württemberg
 D. 94 C1
 Hessen D. 82 B1
 F 92 C2
Marbäck S 60 B3
Marboz F 118 A2
Marburg D. 81 B4

Marcali H 111 C4
Marčana HR. . . 122 C2
Marcaria I. 121 B3
Marcelová SK . 112 B2
Marcenat F. . . . 116 B2
March UK 41 C4
Marchamalo E 151 B4
Marchaux F . . . 105 B5
Marche-en-
 Famenne B. . . . 79 B5
Marchegg A . . . 111 A3
Marchena E . . . 162 A2
Marchenoir F . 103 B3
Marcheprime
 F. 128 B2
Marciac F 128 C3
Marciana Marina
 I. 134 C3
Marcianise I. . . 170 B2
Marcigny F 117 A4
Marcilla E 144 B2
Marcillac-la-
 Croisille F . . . 116 B2
Marcillac-Vallon
 F. 130 A1
Marcillat-en-
 Combraille F . 116 A2
Marcille-sur-Seine
 F. 91 C3
Marcilloles F . . 118 B2
Marcilly-le-Hayer
 F. 91 C3
Marcinkowice
 PL. 75 A5
Marciszów PL. . 85 B4
Marck F 78 B1
Marckolsheim
 F. 106 A2
Marco de
 Canevezes P . 148 A1
Mårdsele S. . . . 200 B5
Mårdsjö S. 200 C1
Mareham le Fen
 UK 41 B3
Marek S. 62 A3
Marennes F . . . 114 C2
Maresquel F . . . 78 B1
Mareuil F 115 C4
Mareuil-en-Brie
 F. 91 C3
Mareuil-sur-Arnon
 F. 103 C4
Mareuil-sur-Lay
 F. 114 B2
Mareuil-sur-Ourcq
 F. 90 B3
Margam UK. . . . 39 C3
Margariti GR. . 182 D2
Margate UK. . . . 45 B5
Margaux F 128 A2
Margerie-Hancourt
 F. 91 C4
Margès F. 117 B5
Margherita di
 Savóia I. 171 B4
Margita SRB. . . 126 B3
Margone I. 119 B4
Margonin PL. . . 76 B2
Marguerittes
 F. 131 B3
Margut F. 91 B5
María E 164 B2
Mariager DK. . . 58 B2
Mariana E 152 B1
Maria Neustift
 A. 110 B1
Mariannelund
 S. 62 A3
Marianópoli I . 176 B2
Mariánské Lázně
 CZ 95 B4
Mariapfarr A . . 109 B4
Maria Saal A . . 110 C1
Mariazell A . . . 110 B2
Maribo DK. 65 B4
Maribor SLO . . 110 C2
Marieberg S . . . 56 A1
Mariefred S . . . 56 A3
Mariehamn FIN . 51 B6
Marienbaum D. 80 A2
Marienberg D. . 83 B5
Marienheide D. . 81 A3
Mariental D . . . 73 B3
Mariestad S . . . 55 B4
Marieux F 90 A2
Marigliano I. . . 170 C2
Marignane F . . 131 B4
Marigny
 Jura F 105 C4
 Manche F 88 A2

Marigny-le-Châtel
 F. 91 C3
Marija Bistrica
 HR 124 A2
Marijampolė
 LT 13 A5
Marín E 140 B2
Marina HR 138 B2
Marina del Cantone
 I. 170 C2
Marina di
 Acquappesa
 I. 174 B1
Marina di Alberese
 I. 168 A1
Marina di
 Amendolara
 I. 174 B2
Marina di Árbus
 I. 179 C2
Marina di Campo
 I. 134 C3
Marina di Carrara
 I. 134 A3
Marina di
 Castagneto-
 Donorático I . 134 B3
Marina di Cécina
 I. 134 B3
Marina di Gáiro
 I. 179 C3
Marina di Ginosa
 I. 173 B2
Marina di Gioiosa
 Iónica I 175 C2
Marina di Grosseto
 I. 135 C3
Marina di Léuca
 I. 173 C4
Marina di Massa
 I. 134 A3
Marina di Nováglie
 I. 173 C4
Marina di Pisa
 I. 134 B3
Marina di Ragusa
 I. 177 C3
Marina di Ravenna
 I. 135 A5
Marina di Torre
 Grande I 179 C2
Marinaleda E . 162 A3
Marina Romea
 I. 135 A5
Marine de Sisco
 F. 180 A2
Marinella I. . . . 176 B1
Marinella di
 Sarzana I. . . . 134 A3
Marineo I. 176 B2
Marines F 90 B1
Maringues F . . 116 B3
Marinha das Ondas
 P. 154 A2
Marinha Grande
 P. 154 B2
Marinhas P. . . . 148 A1
Marino I. 168 B2
Marjaliza E. . . . 157 A4
Markabygd N. . 199 B8
Markaryd S 61 C3
Markdorf D. . . . 107 B4
Markelo NL. . . . 71 B3
Market
 Harborough
 UK 40 C3
Markethill UK. . 27 B4
Market Rasen
 UK 40 B3
Market Warsop
 UK 40 B2
Market Weighton
 UK 40 B3
Markgröningen
 D 93 C5
Markhausen D. . 71 B4
Marki PL. 77 B6
Markina-Xemein
 E. 143 A4
Markinch UK. . . 35 B4
Märkische
 Buchholz D. . . 74 B2
Markitta S 196 B4
Markkleeberg
 D 83 A4
Marknesse NL. . 70 B2
Markneukirchen
 D 83 B4

Markopoulo
 GR 185 B4
Markovac
 Srbija SRB . . . 127 C3
 Vojvodina
 SRB 126 B3
Markowice PL. . 86 B2
Markranstädt
 D 83 A4
Marksuhl D 82 B2
Markt Allhau
 A. 111 B3
Markt Bibart D. . 94 B2
Marktbreit D. . . 94 B2
Markt Erlbach
 D 94 B2
Markt-heidenfeld
 D 94 B1
Markt Indersdorf
 D 95 C3
Marktl D. 95 C4
Marktleuthen
 D 83 B3
Marktoberdorf
 D 108 B1
Marktredwitz
 D 95 A4
Markt Rettenbach
 D 108 B1
Markt Schwaben
 D 108 A2
Markt-Übelbach
 A. 110 B2
Markusica HR . 125 B4
Markušovce SK . 99 C4
Marl D. 80 A3
Marlborough
 Devon UK. 42 B3
 Wiltshire UK . . 44 B2
Marle F 91 B3
Marlieux F 117 A5
Marlow
 D 66 B1
 UK 44 B3
Marma S 51 B4
Marmagne F . . 104 C3
Marmande F . . 128 B3
Marmara TR. . . 186 B2
Marmaris TR. . . 188 C3
Marmelete P. . . 160 B1
Marmolejo E. . . 157 B3
Marmoutier F. . 93 C3
Marnay F 105 B4
Marne D 64 C2
Marnheim D . . . 93 B4
Marnitz D 73 A4
Maroldsweisach
 D 82 B2
Marolles-les-
 Braults F 89 B4
Maromme F . . . 89 A5
Marone I. 120 B3
Maronia GR. . . 183 C7
Maroslele H. . . 126 A2
Maróstica I. . . . 121 B4
Marotta I. 136 B2
Marpisa GR . . . 185 B6
Marquion F 78 B3
Marquise F 78 B1
Marradi I. 135 A4
Marrasjärvi
 FIN. 197 C8
Marraskoski
 FIN. 197 C8
Marratxi E. . . . 166 B2
Marrúbiu I 179 C2
Marrum NL. 70 A2
Marrupe E 150 B3
Marsac F 129 C5
Marsac-en-
 Livradois F. . . 117 B3
Marság lia I. . . . 120 C2
Marsala I. 176 B1
Marsberg D. . . . 81 A4
Marsciano I . . . 135 C5
Marseillan F . . 130 B2
Marseille =
 Marseilles F. . 131 B4
Marseille-en-
 Beauvaisis F . 90 B1
Marseilles =
 Marseille F . . 131 B4
Mársico Nuovo
 I. 172 B1
Marske-by-the-Sea
 UK 37 B5
Mars-la-Tours F 92 B1
Marsliden S. . . 195 E6
Marson F 91 C4
Märsta S 57 A3
Marstal DK. . . . 65 B3
Marstrand S. . . 60 B1

Martano I. 173 B4
Martel F. 129 B4
Martelange B . . 92 B1
Martfeld D 72 B2
Martfü H 113 B4
Martham UK . . . 41 C5
Marthon F 115 C4
Martiago E. . . . 149 B3
Martigné-Briand
 F. 102 B1
Martigné-Ferchaud
 F. 101 B4
Martigne-sur-
 Mayenne F . . . 102 A1
Martigny CH . . 119 A4
Martigny-les-Bains
 F. 105 A4
Martigues F. . . 131 B4
Martim-Longo
 P. 160 B2
Martin SK 98 B2
Martina CH . . . 108 C1
Martina Franca
 I. 173 B3
Martinamor E. . 150 B2
Martin de la Jara
 E. 162 A3
Martinengo I. . 120 B2
Martin Muñoz de
 las Posadas
 E. 150 A3
Martinsberg A . 97 C3
Martinšćica
 HR 123 C3
Martinshöhe D . 93 B3
Martinsicuro I. 136 C2
Martinszell D . 107 B5
Mártis I 178 B2
Martofte DK . . . 59 C3
Martonvásár
 H 112 B2
Martorell E. . . . 147 C2
Martos E 163 A4
Martres Tolosane
 F. 146 A1
Martti FIN. . . . 197 B11
Marugán E 150 B3
Maróggio I. . . . 173 B3
Marvão P 155 B3
Marvejols F . . . 130 A2
Marville F 92 B1
Marwald PL. . . . 77 A4
Marykirk UK . . . 35 B5
Marypark UK . . 32 D3
Maryport UK . . 36 B3
Marytavy UK. . . 42 B2
Marzabotto I. . 135 A4
Marzahne D. . . 73 B5
Marzamemi I. . 177 C4
Marzocca I. . . . 136 B2
Mas-Cabardès
 F. 146 A3
Máscali I 177 B4
Mascaraque E. 157 A4
Mascarenhas
 P. 149 A2
Mascioni I 169 A3
Mas de Barberáns
 E. 153 B4
Mas de las Matas
 E. 153 B3
Masegoso E . . 158 C1
Masegoso de
 Tajuña E 151 B5
Masera I 119 A5
Masevaux F. . . 106 B1
Masfjorden N. . 46 B2
Masham UK . . . 37 B5
Masi N 192 C7
Maside E 140 B2
Maslacq F. . . . 144 A3
Maslinica HR. . 138 B2
Maslovare
 BIH. 138 A3
Masone I. 133 A4
Massa I. 134 A3
Massa Fiscáglia
 I. 121 C5
Massafra I. . . . 173 B3
Massa Lombarda
 I. 135 A4
Massa Lubrense
 I. 170 C2
Massamagrell
 E. 159 B3
Massa Maríttima
 I. 135 B3

Massa Martana
I 136 C1
Massanassa E . 159 B3
Massarosa I . . . 134 B3
Massat F 146 B2
Massay F 103 B3
Massbach D 82 B2
Masseret F 116 B1
Masseube F . . . 145 A4
Massiac F 116 B3
Massignac F . . 115 C4
Massing D 95 C4
Massmechelen
B 80 B1
Masterud N 49 B4
Mästocka S 61 C3
Masty BY 13 B6
Masúa I 179 C2
Masueco E 149 A3
Masugnsbyn
S 196 B5
Mašun SLO 123 B3
Maszewo
Lubuskie PL 75 B3
Zachodnio-
Pomorskie PL . 75 A4
Mata de Alcántara
E 155 B4
Matala GR 185 E5
Matalascañas
E 161 B3
Matalebreras
E 144 C1
Matallana de Torio
E 142 B1
Matamala E . . . 151 A5
Mataporquera
E 142 B2
Matapozuelos
E 150 A3
Mataró E 147 C3
Matarocco I . . . 176 B1
Matélica I 136 B2
Matera I 172 B2
Mátészalka H . . 16 B5
Matet E 159 B3
Matfors S 200 D3
Matha F 115 C3
Mathay F 106 B1
Matignon F . . . 101 A3
Matilla de los
Caños del Rio
E 149 B4
Matlock UK 40 B2
Matosinhos P . 148 A1
Matour F 117 A4
Mátrafüred H . 113 B3
Mátraterenye
H 113 A3
Matre
Hordaland N . . . 46 B2
Hordaland N . . . 52 A1
Matrei am Brenner
A 108 B2
Matrei in Osttirol
A 109 B3
Matrice I 170 B2
Matsdal S 195 E6
Mattarello I . . . 121 A4
Mattersburg
A 111 B3
Mattighofen
A 109 A4
Mattinata I . . . 171 B4
Mattos P 154 B2
Mattsee A 109 B3
Mattsmyra S . . . 50 A2
Måttsund S . . . 196 D5
Matulji HR 123 B3
Maubert-Fontaine
F 91 B4
Maubeuge F . . . 79 B3
Maubourguet
F 145 A4
Mauchline UK . . 36 A2
Maud UK 33 D4
Mauer-kirchen
A 109 A4
Mauern D 95 C3
Mauguio F 131 B3
Maulbronn D . . . 93 C4
Maule F 90 C1
Mauléon F 114 B3
Mauléon-Barousse
F 145 B4
Mauléon-Licharre
F 144 A3
Maulévrier F . . 114 A3
Maum IRL 28 A2
Maurach A 108 B2

Maure-de-Bretagne
F 101 B4
Maureilhan F . 130 B2
Mäureni RO 126 B3
Mauriac F 116 B2
Mauron F 101 A3
Maurs F 116 C2
Maury F 146 B3
Maussane-les-
Alpilles F 131 B3
Mautern A 97 C3
Mauterndorf
A 109 B4
Mautern im
Steiermark
A 110 B1
Mauthausen
A 110 A1
Mauthen A 109 C3
Mauvezin F . . . 129 C3
Mauzé-sur-le-
Mignon F 114 B3
Maxent F 101 B3
Maxey-sur-Vaise
F 92 C1
Maxial P 154 B1
Maxieira P 154 B2
Maxwellheugh
UK 35 C5
Mayalde E 149 A4
Maybole UK 36 A2
Mayen D 80 B3
Mayenne F 88 B3
Mayet F 102 B2
Mayorga E 142 B1
Mayres F 117 C4
Mayrhofen A . . 108 B2
Mazagón E 161 B3
Mazaleón E . . . 153 A4
Mazamet F 130 B1
Mazan F 131 A4
Mazara del Vallo
I 176 B1
Mazarambroz
E 157 A3
Mazarete E 152 B1
Mazaricos E . . . 140 B2
Mazarrón E . . . 165 B3
Mažeikiai LT 8 D3
Mazères F 146 A2
Mazères-sur-Salat
F 145 A4
Mazières-en-Gâtine
F 115 B3
Mazin HR 138 A1
Mazuelo E 143 B3
Mazyr BY 13 B8
Mazzarino I . . . 177 B3
Mazzarrà
Sant'Andrea
I 177 A4
Mazzo di Valtellina
I 120 A3
Mchowo PL 77 A5
Mdzewo PL 77 B5
Mealabost UK . . 31 A2
Mealhada P . . . 148 B1
Méan B 79 B5
Meana Sardo
I 179 C3
Meaulne F 103 C4
Meaux F 90 C2
Mebonden N . . 199 B8
Mecerreyes E . 143 B3
Mechelen B 79 A4
Mechernich D . . 80 B2
Mechnica PL . . . 86 B2
Mechowo PL . . . 67 C4
Mechterstädt
D 82 B2
Mecidiye TR . . 186 B1
Mecikal PL 68 B2
Mecina-Bombarón
E 164 C1
Mecitözü TR . . . 23 A8
Meckenbeuren
D 107 B4
Meckenheim
Rheinland-Pfalz
D 80 B3
Meckenheim
Rheinland-Pfalz
D 93 B4
Meckesheim D . 93 B4
Mecseknádasd
H 125 A4
Meda
I 120 B2
P 149 B2
Medak HR 137 A4
Medborg PL . . . 86 B2
Medebach D . . . 81 A4
Medelim P 155 A3
Medemblik NL . 70 B2

Medena Selista
BIH 138 A2
Medesano I . . . 120 C3
Medevi S 55 B5
Medgidia RO . . . 17 C8
Medgyesháza
H 113 C5
Medhamn S 55 A4
Mediaş RO 17 B6
Medicina I 135 A4
Medinaceli E . . 152 A1
Medina de las
Torres E 155 C4
Medina del Campo
E 150 A3
Medina de Pomar
E 143 B3
Medina de Ríoseco
E 142 C1
Medina Sidonia
E 162 B2
Medinilla E . . . 150 B2
Medja SRB . . . 126 B2
Medjedja BIH . 139 B5
Medulin HR . . . 122 C2
Meduno I 122 A1
Medveda SRB . 127 C3
Medvedov SK . 111 B4
Medvezhyegorsk
RUS 9 A9
Medvide HR . . . 137 A4
Medvode SLO . 123 A3
Medzev SK 99 C4
Medžitlija
NMK 182 C3
Meerane D 83 B4
Meerle B 79 A4
Meersburg D . 107 B4
Meeuwen B 79 A5
Megalo Horio
GR 188 C2
Megalopoli
GR 184 B3
Megara E 185 A4
Megève F 118 B3
Meggenhofen
A 109 A4
Megra RUS 9 B10
Megyaszó H . . 113 A5
Mehamn N . . . 193 A11
Mehedeby S . . . 51 B4
Méhkerék H . . 113 C5
Mehun-sur-Yèvre
F 103 B4
Meigle UK 35 B4
Meijel NL 80 A1
Meilen CH 107 B3
Meilhan F 128 C2
Meimôa P 149 B2
Meina I 119 B5
Meine D 73 B3
Meinersen D . . . 72 B3
Meinerzhagen
D 81 A3
Meiningen D . . . 82 B2
Meira E 141 A3
Meiringen CH . 106 C3
Meisenheim D . 93 B3
Meissen D 83 A5
Meitingen D . . . 94 C2
Meix-devant-Virton
B 92 B1
Meka PL 86 A2
Meka Gruda
BIH 139 B4
Mel I 121 A5
Melbu N 194 B5
Melč CZ 98 B1
Meldal N 198 B6
Méldola I 135 A5
Meldorf D 64 B2
Melegnano I . . . 120 B2
Melenci SRB . . 126 B2
Melendugno I . 173 B4
Melfi I 172 B1
Melfjordbotn
N 195 D4
Melgaço P 140 B2
Melgar de Arriba
E 142 B1
Melgar de
Fernamental
E 142 B2
Melgar de Yuso
E 142 B2
Melhus N 199 B7
Meliana E 159 B3
Melide
CH 120 B1
E 140 B2
Melides P 160 A1
Meligales GR . . 184 B2
Melilli I 177 B4

Melinovac HR . 124 C1
Melisenda I . . . 179 C3
Melisey F 105 B5
Mélito di Porto
Salvo I 175 D1
Melk A 110 A2
Melksham UK . . 43 A4
Mellakoski
FIN 196 C7
Mellanström
S 195 E9
Mellbystrand S . 61 C2
Melle
B 79 A3
D 71 B5
F 115 B3
Mellendorf D . . 72 B2
Mellerud S 54 B3
Mellieħa M . . . 175 C3
Mellösa S 56 A2
Mellrichstadt D . 82 B2
Mělnické Vtelno
CZ 84 B2
Melnik BG 183 B5
Mělník CZ 84 B2
Melón E 140 B2
Melrose UK 35 C5
Mels CH 107 B4
Melsungen D . . . 82 A1
Meltaus FIN . . 197 C8
Meltham UK 40 B2
Melton Mowbray
UK 40 C3
Meltosjärvi
FIN 196 C7
Melun F 90 C2
Melvaig UK 31 B3
Melvich UK 32 C3
Mélykút H . . . 126 A1
Melzo I 120 B2
Memaliaj AL . . 182 C1
Membrilla E . . . 157 B4
Membrio E 155 B3
Memer F 129 B4
Memmelsdorf
D 94 B2
Memmingen
D 107 B5
Memoria P . . . 154 B2
Menággio I . . . 120 A2
Menai Bridge
UK 38 A2
Menasalbas E . 157 A3
Menat F 116 A2
Mendavia E . . . 144 B1
Mendaza E 144 B1
Mende F 130 A2
Menden D 81 A3
Menderes TR . 188 A2
Mendig D 80 B3
Mendiga P 154 B2
Mendrisio CH . 120 B1
Ménéac F 101 A3
Menemen TR . 188 A2
Menen B 78 B3
Menesjärvi
FIN 193 D10
Menetou-Salon
F 103 B4
Menfi I 176 B1
Ménföcsanak
H 111 B4
Mengamuñoz
E 150 B3
Mengen
D 107 A4
TR 187 B7
Mengeš SLO . . . 123 A3
Mengibar E . . . 157 C4
Mengkofen D . . 95 C4
Menou F 104 B2
Mens F 118 C2
Menslage D 71 B4
Menstrask S . . 200 A5
Mentana I 168 A2
Menton F 133 B3
Méntrida E 151 B3
Méobecq F . . . 115 B5
Méounes-les-
Montrieux F . 132 B1
Meppel NL 70 B3
Meppen D 71 B4
Mequinenza E 153 A4
Mer F 103 B3
Mera
Coruña E 140 A2
Coruña E 140 A3
Meråker N . . . 199 B8
Merano I 108 C2
Merate I 120 B2
Mercatale I . . . 135 B5
Mercatino Conca
I 136 B1

Mercato San
Severino I 170 C2
Mercato Saraceno
I 135 B5
Merching D . . . 108 A1
Merchtem B 79 B4
Merdrignac F . 101 A3
Merdžanići
BIH 139 B3
Meré E 142 A2
Mere UK 43 A4
Meréville F 90 C2
Merfeld D 80 A3
Méribel F 118 B3
Méribel Motraret
F 118 B3
Meriç TR 186 A1
Mérida E 155 C4
Mérignac F . . . 128 B2
Měřín CZ 97 B3
Mering D 94 C2
Merkendorf D . 94 B2
Merklín CZ 96 B1
Merksplas B . . . 79 A4
Merlânna S 56 A2
Merlimont Plage
F 78 B1
Mern DK 65 A5
Merne H 111 C4
Mersch L 92 B2
Merseburg D . . . 83 A3
Mers-les-Bains
F 90 A1
Merthyr Tydfil
UK 39 C3
Mertingen D . . . 94 C2
Mértola P 160 B2
Méru F 90 B2
Merufe P 140 B2
Mervans F 105 C4
Merville F 78 B2
Méry-sur-Seine
F 91 C3
Merzen D 71 B4
Merzifon TR . . . 23 A8
Merzig D 92 B2
Mesagne I 173 B3
Mesão Frio P . 148 A2
Mesas de Ibor
E 156 A2
Meschede D . . . 81 A4
Meschers-sur-
Gironde F . . . 114 C3
Meslay-du-Maine
F 102 B1
Mesna N 48 A2
Mesnalien N . . . 48 A2
Mesocco CH . . 120 A2
Mésola I 122 C1
Mesologi GR . . 184 A2
Mesopotamo
GR 182 D2
Mesoraca I . . . 175 B2
Messac F 101 B4
Messancy B 92 B1
Messdorf D 73 B4
Messei F 88 B3
Messejana P . . 160 B1
Messelt N 48 A3
Messina I 177 A4
Messincourt F . 91 B5
Messingen D . . . 71 B4
Messini GR . . . 184 B3
Messkirch D . . 107 B4
Messlingen S . 199 C9
Messtetten D . 107 A4
Mesta E 185 A6
Mestanza E . . . 157 B3
Městec Králové
CZ 84 B3
Mestlin D 73 A4
Město Albrechtice
CZ 85 B5
Město Libavá
CZ 98 B1
Město Touškov
CZ 96 B1
Mestre I 122 B1
Mesvres F 104 C3
Mesztegnyő
H 111 C4
Meta I 170 C2
Metajna HR . . . 137 A4
Metelen D 71 B4
Methana GR . . 185 B4
Methlick UK 33 D4
Methven UK 35 B4
Methwold UK . . 41 C4
Metković HR . . 139 B3
Metlika SLO . . 123 B4
Metnitz A 110 C1
Metsäkylä
FIN 197 D11
Metslawier
NL 70 A3

Metsovo GR . . . 182 D3
Metten D 95 C4
Mettendorf D . . 92 B2
Mettet B 79 B4
Mettingen D . . . 71 B4
Mettlach D 92 B2
Mettlen CH . . . 106 C2
Mettmann D . . . 80 A2
Metz F 92 B2
Metzervisse F . 92 B2
Metzingen D . . . 94 C1
Meulan F 90 B1
Meung-sur-Loire
F 103 B3
Meuselwitz D . . 83 A4
Meuzac F 115 C5
Mevagissey
UK 42 B2
Mexborough
UK 40 B2
Meximieux F . 118 B2
Mey UK 32 C3
Meyenburg D . 73 A5
Meyerhöfen D . 71 B5
Meylan F 118 B2
Meymac F 116 B2
Meyrargues F 132 B1
Meyrueis F . . . 130 A2
Meyssac F 129 A4
Meysse F 117 C4
Meyzieu F 117 B4
Mèze F 130 B2
Mézériat F 117 A5
Mežica SLO . . . 110 C1
Mézidon-Canon
F 89 A3
Mézières-en-
Brenne F 115 B5
Mézières-sur-
Issoire F 115 B4
Mézilhac F 117 C4
Mézilles F 104 B2
Mézin F 128 B3
Mezőberény
H 113 C5
Mezőcsát H . . 113 B4
Mezőfalva H . . 112 C2
Mezőhegyes
H 126 A2
Mezőkeresztes
H 113 B4
Mezőkomárom
H 112 C2
Mezőkovácsháza
H 113 C4
Mezőkövesd
H 113 B4
Mezőörs H 111 B4
Mézos F 128 B1
Mezőszilas H . 112 C2
Mezőtúr H . . . 113 B4
Mezquita de Jarque
E 153 B3
Mezzano
Emilia Romagna
I 135 A5
Trentino Alto Adige
I 121 A4
Mezzojuso I . . 176 B2
Mezzoldo I . . . 120 A2
Mezzolombardo
I 121 A4
Mgarr M 175 C3
Miajadas E . . . 156 A2
Miały PL 75 B5
Mianowice PL . 68 A2
Miasteczko
Krajeńskie PL . 76 A2
Miastko PL 68 A1
Miava SK 12 D4
Michałowice
PL 87 A3
Michelau D 94 A2
Michelbach D . 94 B1
Micheldorf A . 110 B1
Michelhausen
A 110 A2
Michelsneukirchen
D 95 B4
Michelstadt D . 93 B5
Michendorf D . 74 B2
Mickleover UK . 40 B1
Middelburg NL . 79 A3
Middelfart DK . 59 C2
Middelharnis
NL 79 A4
Middelstum NL . 71 A3
Middlesbrough
UK 37 B5

Middleton Cheney
UK 44 A2
Middleton-in-
Teesdale UK . . 37 B4
Middletown UK 27 B4
Middlewich UK . 38 A4
Middlezoy UK . . 43 A4
Midhurst UK . . . 44 C3
Midleton IRL . . . 29 C3
Midlum D 64 C1
Midsomer Norton
UK 43 A4
Midtgulen N . 198 D2
Midtskogberget
N 49 A4
Midwolda NL . . 71 A4
Mid Yell UK 33 A5
Miechów PL . . . 87 B4
Miedes de Aragón
E 152 A2
Miedes de Atienza
E 151 A4
Międzybodzie
Bielskie PL 99 B3
Międzybórz PL . 85 A1
Międzychód PL . 75 B4
Międzylesie PL . 85 B4
Międzyrzec
Podlaski PL . . . 12 C5
Międzyrzecz PL . 75 B4
Międzywodzie
PL 67 B3
Międzyzdroje
PL 67 B3
Miejska Górka
PL 85 A4
Mielan F 145 A4
Mielec PL 87 B5
Mielęcin PL 75 A3
Mielno
Warmińsko-
Mazurskie PL . 77 A5
Zachodnio-
Pomorskie PL . 67 B5
Miengo E 143 A3
Mieraslompolo
FIN 193 C11
Miercurea Ciuc
RO 17 B6
Mieres
Asturias E . . . 141 A5
Girona E 147 B3
Mierzyn PL 86 A3
Miesau D 93 B3
Miesbach D . . . 108 B2
Mieścisko PL . . 76 B2
Mieste D 73 B4
Miesterhorst D . 73 B4
Mieszków PL . . 76 B2
Mieszkowice
PL 74 B3
Mietków PL 85 B4
Migennes F . . . 104 B2
Miggiano I . . . 173 C4
Migliánico I . . . 169 A4
Migliarino I . . . 121 C4
Miglionico I . . . 172 B2
Mignano Monte
Lungo I 169 B3
Migné F 115 B5
Miguel Esteban
E 157 A4
Miguelturra E . 157 B4
Mihajlovac
SRB 127 C2
Miháld H 111 C4
Mihalgazi TR . 187 B5
Mihaliçcık TR . 187 C6
Mihályi H 111 B4
Mihla D 82 A2
Mihohnić HR . . 123 B3
Miholjsko HR . 123 B4
Mihovljan HR . 124 A1
Mijares E 150 B3
Mijas E 163 B3
Mike H 124 A3
Mikines GR . . . 184 B3
Mikkeli FIN 8 B5
Mikkelvik N . . . 192 B3
Mikleuš HR 125 B3
Mikołajki
Pomorskie PL . 69 B4
Mikolów PL 86 B2
Mikonos GR . . . 185 B6
Mikorzyn PL . . . 86 A2
Mikro Derio
GR 183 B8
Mikstat PL 86 A1
Mikulášovice
CZ 84 B2
Mikulov CZ 97 C4
Mikulovice CZ . 85 B5

Milagro E 144 B2
Miłakowo PL....69 A5
Milan = Milano
I............... 120 B2
Miland N.......47 C5
Milano = Milan
I............... 120 B2
Milano Marittima
I............... 135 A5
Milas TR....... 188 B2
Milazzo I....... 177 A4
Mildenhall UK...45 A4
Milejewo PL....69 A4
Milelín CZ......85 B3
Miletić SRB.... 125 B5
Miletićevo
SRB 126 B3
Mileto I....... 175 C2
Milevsko CZ....96 B2
Milford IRL....26 A3
Milford Haven
UK 39 C1
Milford on Sea
UK 44 C2
Milhão P..... 149 A3
Milići BIH..... 139 A5
Miličín CZ......96 B2
Milicz PL......85 A5
Milín CZ........96 B2
Militello in Val di
Catánia I.... 177 B3
Miljevina BIH . 139 B4
Milkowice PL...85 A4
Millançay F.... 103 B3
Millares E..... 159 B3
Millas F....... 146 B3
Millau F...... 130 A2
Millesimo I.... 133 A4
Millevaches F.. 116 B2
Millom UK......36 B3
Millport UK....34 C3
Millstatt A 109 C4
Millstreet
Cork IRL......29 B2
Waterford IRL..29 B4
Milltown
Galway IRL... 28 A3
Kerry IRL......29 B1
Milltown Malbay
IRL...........28 B2
Milly-la-Forêt
F..............90 C2
Milmarcos E... 152 A2
Milmersdorf D..74 A2
Milna HR...... 138 B2
Milnthorpe UK..37 B4
Milogórze PL...69 A5
Miłomłyn PL....69 B4
Milos GR..... 185 C5
Milošovo SRB . 127 C3
Miłosław PL....76 B2
Milot AL...... 182 B1
Miłówka PL....99 B3
Miltach D......95 B4
Miltenberg D...94 B1
Milton Keynes
UK 44 A3
Miltzow D......66 B2
Milverton UK...43 A3
Milzyn PL......76 B3
Mimice HR 138 B2
Mimizan F..... 128 B1
Mimizan-Plage
F............. 128 B1
Mimoň CZ......84 B2
Mina de Juliana
P............. 160 B1
Mina de São
Domingos P.. 160 B2
Minas de Riotinto
E............. 161 B3
Minateda E ... 158 C2
Minaya E...... 158 B1
Minde P...... 154 B2
Mindelheim D 108 A1
Mindelstetten
D..............95 C3
Minden D.......72 B1
Mindszent H.. 113 C4
Minehead UK...43 A3
Mineo I....... 177 B3
Minerbe I..... 121 B4
Minérbio I.... 121 C4
Minervino Murge
I............. 171 B4
Minglanilla E.. 158 B2
Mingorria E... 150 B3
Minnesund N...48 B3
Miño E....... 140 A2
Miño de San
Esteban E.. 151 A4
Minsen D......71 A4
Minsk BY......13 B7

Mińsk Mazowiecki
PL..............12 B4
Minsterley UK...39 B4
Mintlaw UK 33 D4
Minturno I.... 169 B3
Mionica
BIH......... 125 C4
SRB 127 C2
Mios F....... 128 B2
Mira
E............. 158 B2
I............. 121 B5
P............. 148 B1
Mirabel E 155 B4
Mirabel-aux-
Baronnies F . 131 A4
Mirabella Eclano
I............. 170 B3
Mirabella
Imbàccari I ... 177 B3
Mirabello I.... 121 C4
Miradoux F ... 129 B3
Miraflores de la
Sierra E 151 B4
Miralrio E.... 151 B5
Miramar P 148 A1
Miramare I... 136 A1
Miramas F ... 131 B3
Mirambeau F . 114 C3
Miramont-de-
Guyenne F ... 129 B3
Miranda de Arga
E............. 144 B2
Miranda de Ebro
E............. 143 B4
Miranda do Corvo
P............. 148 B1
Miranda do Douro
P............. 149 A3
Mirande F.... 129 C3
Mirandela P... 149 A2
Mirandilla E... 155 C4
Mirándola I... 121 C4
Miranje HR.... 137 A4
Mirano I..... 121 B5
Miras AL..... 182 C2
Miravet E.... 153 A4
Miré F....... 102 B1
Mirebeau F ... 102 C2
Mirebeau-sur-Bèze
F............. 105 B4
Mirecourt F ... 105 A5
Mirepoix F.... 146 A2
Mires GR..... 185 D5
Miribel F..... 117 B4
Miričina BIH.. 125 C4
Mirina GR.... 183 D7
Mirna SLO...... 123 B4
Miroslav CZ....97 C4
Mirosławice PL..85 A4
Mirosławiec
PL..............75 A5
Mirošov CZ....96 B1
Mirotice CZ....96 B2
Mirovice CZ....96 B2
Mirow D........74 A1
Mirsk PL........84 B3
Mirzec PL......87 A5
Misi FIN...... 197 C9
Misilmeri I ... 176 A2
Miske H....... 112 C3
Miskolc H 113 A4
Mislinja SLO .. 110 C2
Missanello I ... 174 A2
Missillac F.... 101 B3
Mistelbach
A............. 97 C4
D..............95 B3
Misten N..... 194 B6
Misterbianco I 177 B4
Misterhult S ...62 A4
Mistretta I ... 177 B3
Misurina I.... 109 C3
Mitchelstown
IRL...........29 B3
Mithimna GR. 186 C1
Mithoni GR... 184 C2
Mitilini GR.... 186 C1
Mitilini GR... 188 B1
Mittelberg
Tirol A....... 108 B1
Vorarlberg A . 107 B5
Mittenwald D. 108 B2
Mittenwalde D..74 B2
Mitterback A.. 110 B2
Mitterdorf im
Mürztal A .. 110 B2
Mitter-Kleinarl
A............. 109 B4
Mittersill A... 109 B3
Mitterskirchen
D..............95 C4

Mitterteich D ...95 B4
Mitton F 128 B2
Mittweida D ...83 B4
Mitwitz D......82 B3
Mizhhir'ya UA . 13 D5
Mjällby S........63 B2
Mjåvatn N 53 B4
Mjöbäck S.....60 B2
Mjölby S......56 B1
Mjölfjell N 46 B3
Mjøndalen N...53 A6
Mjørlund N 48 B2
Mladá Boleslav
CZ............84 B2
Mladá Vožice
CZ............96 B2
Mladé Buky CZ..85 B3
Mladenovac
SRB 127 C2
Mladenovo
SRB 126 B1
Mladikovine
BIH......... 139 A3
Mława PL......77 A5
Mlinište BIH... 138 A2
Młodzieszyn
PL..............77 B5
Młogoszyn PL..77 B4
Młynary PL.....69 A4
Mnichóvice CZ..96 B2
Mnichovo Hradiště
CZ............84 B2
Mníšek nad
Hnilcom SK ...99 C4
Mniszek PL.....87 A4
Mniszków PL...87 A4
Mo
Hedmark N....48 B3
Hordaland N...46 B2
Møre og Romsdal
N........... 198 C5
Telemark N .. 53 A3
Gävleborg S . 51 A3
Västra Götaland
S..............54 B2
Moaña E..... 140 B2
Moate IRL.....28 A4
Mocejón E... 151 C4
Močenok SK .. 111 A4
Mochales E... 152 A1
Mochowo PL...77 B4
Mochy PL......75 B5
Mockern D.... 73 B4
Mockfjärd S...50 B1
Möckmühl D...94 B1
Mockrehna D ..83 A4
Moclín E..... 163 A4
Mócsa H..... 112 B2
Mócsény H.... 125 A4
Modane F..... 118 B3
Modbury UK ...42 B3
Módena I.... 121 C3
Módica I..... 177 C3
Modigliana I... 135 A4
Mödling A 111 A3
Modliszewice
PL..............87 A4
Modliszewko
PL..............76 B2
Modogno I... 171 B4
Modolo I......178 B2
Modra SK......98 C1
Modran BIH... 125 C3
Modriča BIH... 125 C4
Mööruðalur
IS.......... 191 B10
Modrý Kamen
SK............99 C3
Moëlan-sur-Mer
F............. 100 B2
Moelfre UK.....38 A2
Moelv N........48 B2
Moen N...... 194 A9
Moena I...... 121 A4
Moerbeke B...79 A3
Moers D.......80 A2
Móes P...... 148 B2
Moffat UK......36 A3
Mogadouro P. 149 A3
Mogata S......56 B2
Móggio Udinese
I............. 122 A2
Mogielnica PL..87 A4
Mogilany PL...99 B3
Mogilno PL.... 76 B2
Mogliano I... 136 B2
Mogliano Véneto
I............. 122 B1
Mogor E...... 140 B2
Mógoro I..... 179 C2

Moguer E 161 B3
Mohács H 125 B4
Moheda S......62 A2
Mohedas E... 149 B3
Mohedas de la Jara
E............. 156 A2
Mohelnice CZ...97 B4
Mohill IRL.....26 C3
Möhlin CH 106 B2
Moholm S......55 B5
Mohorn D......83 A5
Mohyliv-Podil's'kyy
UA 13 D7
Moi N..........52 B2
Moià E...... 147 C3
Móie I....... 136 B2
Moimenta da Beira
P............. 148 B2
Moi Rana N... 195 D5
Moirans F.... 118 B2
Moirans-en-
Montagne F.. 118 A2
Moisaküla EST .. 8 C4
Moissac F.... 129 B4
Moita
Coimbra P .. 148 B1
Guarda P ... 149 B2
Santarém P .. 154 B2
Setúbal P ... 154 C1
Moita dos Ferreiros
P............. 154 B1
Moixent E.... 159 C3
Mojacar E.... 164 B3
Mojados E... 150 A3
Mojmírovce
SK........... 112 A2
Mojtin SK......98 C2
Möklinta S.....50 B3
Mokošica HR... 139 C4
Mokronog
SLO.......... 123 B4
Mokro Polje
HR.......... 138 A2
Mokrzyska PL...99 A4
Møkster N.....46 B2
Mol
B............. 79 A5
SRB 126 B2
Mola di Bari I . 173 A3
Molai GR..... 184 C3
Molare I..... 133 A4
Molaretto I... 119 B4
Molas F...... 145 A4
Molassano I... 134 A1
Mölbergen D ...71 B4
Mold UK.......38 A3
Molde N..... 198 C4
Møldrup DK....58 B2
Moledo do Minho
P............. 148 A1
Molfetta I.... 171 B4
Molfsee D......64 B3
Molières F.... 129 B4
Molina de Aragón
E............. 152 B2
Molina de Segura
E............. 165 A3
Molinar E.... 143 A3
Molinaseca E.. 141 B4
Molinella I.... 121 C4
Molinet F.... 104 C2
Molinicos E... 158 C1
Molini di Tures
I........... 108 C2
Molinos de Duero
E............. 143 C4
Molins de Rei
E............. 147 C3
Moliterno I... 174 A1
Molkom S......55 A4
Möllbrücke A . 109 C4
Mölle S........61 C2
Molledo E.... 142 A2
Möllenbeck D ...74 A2
Mollerussa E .. 147 C1
Mollet de Perelada
E............. 146 B3
Mollina E.... 163 A3
Mölln D........73 A3
Mollösund S...54 B2
Möllorp S.....55 B5
Mölnbo S......56 A3
Mölndal S.....60 B2
Mölnlycke S...60 B2
Molompize F.. 116 B3
Moloy F...... 105 B3
Molsheim F....93 C3
Moltzow D.....73 A5
Molve HR..... 124 A3

Molveno I.... 121 A3
Molvizar E 163 B4
Molzbichl A... 109 C4
Mombaróccio
I............. 136 B1
Mombeltrán
E............. 150 B2
Mombris D......93 A5
Mombuey E... 141 B4
Momchilgrad
BG 183 B7
Mommark DK...64 B3
Mommenheim
F.............. 93 C3
Monaghan IRL ..27 B4
Monar Lodge
UK 32 D2
Monasterace
Marina I.... 175 C2
Monasterevin
IRL............30 A1
Monasterio de
Rodilla E.... 143 B3
Monastir I.... 179 C3
Monbahus F.. 129 B3
Monbazillac F.. 129 B3
Moncada E.... 159 B3
Moncalieri I... 119 B4
Moncalvo I.... 119 B5
Monção P..... 140 B2
Moncarapacho
P............. 160 B2
Moncel-sur-Seille
F............. 92 C2
Monchegorsk
RUS 3 C13
Mönchengladbach
= Munchen-
Gladbach D...80 A2
Mónchio della Corti
I............. 134 A3
Monchique P. 160 B1
Monclar-de-Quercy
F............. 129 C4
Moncofa E.... 159 B3
Moncontour F 101 A3
Moncoutant F. 114 B3
Monda E..... 162 B3
Mondariz E... 140 B2
Mondavio I... 136 B1
Mondéjar E... 151 B4
Mondello I.... 176 A2
Mondim de Basto
P............. 148 A2
Mondolfo I... 136 B2
Mondoñedo
E............. 141 A3
Mondorf-les-Bains
L.............92 B2
Mondoubleau
F............. 102 B2
Mondovì I ... 133 A3
Mondragon F . 131 A3
Mondragone I 170 B1
Mondsee A.... 109 B4
Monéglia I... 134 A2
Monegrillo E.. 153 A3
Monein F.... 145 A3
Monemvasia
GR 184 C4
Mónesi I..... 133 A3
Monesiglio I.. 133 A4
Monesterio E . 161 A3
Monestier-de-
Clermont F.. 118 C2
Monestiés F... 130 A1
Monéteau F... 104 B2
Moneygall IRL..28 B4
Moneymore
UK 27 B4
Monfalcone I.. 122 B2
Monfero E.... 140 A2
Monflanquin
F............. 129 B3
Monfort
Moyuela E .. 152 A2
Monghidoro I. 135 A4
Monguelfo I .. 108 C3
Monheim D....94 C2
Moniaive UK...36 A3
Monifieth UK...35 B5

Monikie UK ...35 B5
Monistrol-d'Allier
F............. 117 C3
Monistrol de
Montserrat E. 147 C2
Monistrol-sur-Loire
F............. 117 B4
Mönkebude D ..74 A2
Monken UK 36 A2
Monmouth UK .39 C4
Monnaie F 102 B2
Monnerville F...90 C2
Monnickendam
NL 70 B2
Monolithos
GR 188 C2
Monópoli I... 173 B3
Monor H...... 112 B3
Monóvar E.... 159 C3
Monpazier F .. 129 B3
Monreal
E............... 144 B2
Monreal del Campo
E............. 152 B2
Monreale I... 176 A2
Monroy E.... 156 A1
Monroyo E ... 153 B3
Mons B.......79 B3
Monsaraz P... 155 C3
Monschau D...80 B2
Monségur F... 128 B3
Monsélice I... 121 B4
Mønshaug N...46 B3
Monster NL....70 B1
Mönsterås S ...62 A4
Monsummano
Terme I..... 135 B3
Montabaur D ...81 B3
Montagnac F.. 130 B2
Montagnana I.. 121 B4
Montaigu F ... 114 B2
Montaigu-de-
Quercy F ... 129 B4
Montaiguët-en-
Forez F 117 A3
Montaigut F .. 116 A2
Montaigut-sur-
Save F...... 129 C4
Montainville F..90 C1
Montalbán de
Córdoba E .. 163 A3
Montalbano
Elicona I.... 177 A4
Montalbano Iónico
I............. 174 A2
Montalbo E... 158 B1
Montalcino I... 135 B4
Montaldo di Cósola
I............. 120 C2
Montalegre P. 148 A2
Montalieu-Vercieu
F............. 118 B2
Montalivet-les-
Bains F..... 114 C2
Montallegro I.. 176 B2
Montalto delle
Marche I.... 136 C2
Montalto di Castro
I............. 168 A1
Montalto Pavese
I............. 120 C2
Montalto Uffugo
I............. 174 B2
Montalvão P .. 155 B3
Montamarta E 149 A4
Montana BG ... 17 D5
Montana-Vermala
CH 119 A4
Montánchez
E............. 156 A1
Montanejos
E............. 153 B3
Montano Antilia
I............. 172 B1
Montans F.... 129 C4
Montargil P... 154 B2
Montargis F... 103 B4
Montastruc-la-
Conseillère F. 129 C4
Montauban F. 129 B4
Montauban-de-
Bretagne F .. 101 A3
Montbard F... 104 B3
Montbarrey F. 105 B4
Montbazens F. 130 A1
Montbazon F. 102 B2
Montbéliard F 106 B1
Montbenoit F. 105 C5
Montbeugny
F............. 104 C2
Montblanc E. 147 C2
Montbozon F. 105 B5

Montbrison F . 117 B4
Montbron F.. 115 C4
Montbrun-les-Bains
F............. 131 A4
Montceau-les-
Mines F 104 C3
Montcenis F .. 104 C3
Montchanin F. 104 C3
Montcornet F...91 B4
Montcuq F.... 129 B4
Montdardier
F............. 130 B2
Mont-de-Marsan
F............. 128 C2
Montdidier F...90 B2
Monteagudo
E............. 165 A3
Monteagudo de las
Vicarias E ... 152 A1
Montealegre
E............. 142 C2
Montealegre del
Castillo E.... 159 C2
Montebello Iónico
I............. 175 D1
Montebello
Vicentino I... 121 B4
Montebelluna
I............. 121 B5
Montebourg F . 88 A2
Montebruno I. 134 A2
Monte-Carlo
MC.......... 133 B3
Montecarotto
I............. 136 B2
Montecassiano
I............. 136 B2
Montecastrilli
I............. 168 A2
Montecatini Terme
I............. 135 B3
Montécchio
Maggiore I... 121 B4
Montech F.... 129 C4
Montechiaro d'Asti
I............. 119 B5
Monte Clara P. 155 B3
Monte Clérigo
P............. 160 B1
Montecórice I. 170 C2
Montecorvino
Rovella I.... 170 C2
Monte da Pedra
P............. 155 B3
Monte de Goula
P............. 155 B3
Montederramo
E............. 141 B3
Montedoro I .. 176 B2
Monte do Trigo
P............. 155 C3
Montefalco I . 136 C1
Montefalcone di
Val Fortore I . 170 B3
Montefalcone nel
Sánnio I.... 170 B2
Montefano I.. 136 B2
Montefiascone
I............. 168 A2
Montefiorino
I............. 134 A3
Montefortino
I............. 136 C2
Montefranco
I............. 168 A2
Montefrío E... 163 A4
Montegiordano
Marina I.... 174 A2
Montegiórgio
I............. 136 B2
Monte Gordo
P............. 160 B2
Montegranaro
I............. 136 B2
Montehermoso
E............. 149 B3
Montejicar E.. 163 A4
Montejo de la
Sierra E 151 A4
Montejo de Tiermes
E............. 151 A4
Monte Juntos
P............. 155 C3
Montel-de-Gelat
F............. 116 B2
Monteleone di
Púglia I..... 171 B3

Monteleone di
Spoleto I..... 169 A2
Monteleone
d'Orvieto I... 135 C5
Montelepre I.. 176 A2
Montelibretti
I.............. 168 A2
Montelier F ... 117 C5
Montélimar F . 131 A3
Montella
E.............. 146 B2
I.............. 170 C3
Montellano I . 162 A2
Montelupo
Fiorentino I.. 135 B4
Montemaggiore
Belsito I...... 176 B2
Montemagno
I.............. 119 C5
Montemayor
E.............. 163 A3
Montemayor de
Pinilla E...... 150 A3
Montemésola
I.............. 173 B3
Montemilleto
I.............. 170 B2
Montemilone
I.............. 172 A1
Montemolin E 161 A3
Montemónaco
I.............. 136 C2
Montemor-o-Novo
P............. 148 B1
Montemor-o-Velho
P............. 148 B1
Montemurro
I.............. 174 A1
Montendre F . 128 A2
Montenegro de
Cameros E ... 143 B4
Montenero di
Bisáccia I.... 170 B2
Monteneuf F . 101 B3
Monteparano
I.............. 173 B3
Montepescali
I.............. 135 C4
Montepiano I . 135 A4
Monte Porzio
I.............. 136 B2
Montepulciano
I.............. 135 B4
Monte Real P.. 154 B2
Montereale I.. 169 A3
Montereale
Valcellina I.. 122 A1
Montereau-Faut-
Yonne F......90 C2
Monte Redondo
P............. 154 B2
Monterénzio I. 135 A4
Monte Romano
I.............. 168 A1
Monteroni d'Arbia
I.............. 135 C4
Monteroni di Lecce
I.............. 173 B3
Monterosso al Mare
I.............. 134 A2
Monterosso Almo
I.............. 177 B3
Monterosso Grana
I.............. 133 A3
Monterotondo
I.............. 168 A2
Monterotondo
Maríttimo I... 135 B3
Monterrey E .. 141 C3
Monterroso E . 140 B3
Monterrubio de la
Serena E 156 B2
Monterubbiano
I.............. 136 B2
Montesa E 159 C3
Montesalgueiro
E............. 140 A2
Monte San
Giovanni
Campano I ... 169 B3
Montesano sulla
Marcellana I . 174 A1
Monte San Savino
I.............. 135 B4
Monte Sant'Ángelo
I.............. 171 B3
Montesárchio
I.............. 170 B2
Montescaglioso
I.............. 171 C4

Montesclaros
E............. 150 B3
Montesilvano
I.............. 169 A4
Montespértoli
I.............. 135 B4
Montesquieu-
Volvestre F .. 146 A2
Montesquiou
F............. 129 C3
Montestruc-sur-
Gers F........ 129 C3
Montes Velhos
P............. 160 B1
Montevarchi I. 135 B4
Montéveglio I. 135 A4
Monte Vilar P . 154 B1
Montfaucon F. 101 B4
Montfaucon-
d'Argonne F ..91 B5
Montfaucon-en-
Velay F....... 117 B4
Montferrat
Isère F 118 B2
Var F 132 B2
Montfort-en-
Chalosse F ... 128 C2
Montfort-l'Amaury
F.............90 C1
Montfort-le-
Gesnois F 102 A2
Montfort-sur-Meu
F............. 101 A4
Montfort-sur-Risle
F.............89 A4
Montgai E..... 147 C1
Montgaillard
F............. 145 A4
Montgenèvre
F............. 118 C3
Montgiscard
F............. 146 A2
Montgomery
UK............39 B3
Montguyon F . 128 A2
Monthermé F ..91 B4
Monthey CH .. 119 A3
Monthois F 91 B4
Monthureux-sur-
Saône F...... 105 A4
Monti I........ 178 B3
Monticelli d'Ongina
I.............. 120 B2
Montichiari I.. 120 B3
Monticiano I.. 135 B4
Montiel E 158 C1
Montier-en-Der
F.............91 C4
Montieri I..... 135 B4
Montignac F .. 129 A4
Montigny-le-Roi
F............. 105 B3
Montigny-lès-Metz
F.............92 B2
Montigny-sur-Aube
F............. 105 B3
Montijo
E............. 155 C4
P............. 154 C2
Montilla E.... 163 A3
Montillana E .. 163 A4
Montilly F..... 104 C2
Montivilliers F ..89 A4
Montjaux F ... 130 A1
Montjean-sur-Loire
F............. 102 B1
Montjhéry F ...90 C2
Montlieu-la-Garde
F............. 128 A2
Mont-Louis F . 146 B3
Montlouis-sur-Loire
F............. 102 B2
Montluçon F .. 116 A2
Montluel F 117 B5
Montmarault
F............. 116 A2
Montmartin-sur-
Mer F.........88 B2
Montmédy F ...92 B1
Montmélian F. 118 B3
Montmeyan F. 132 B2
Montmeyran
F............. 117 C4
Montmirail
Marne F 91 C3
Sarthe F 102 A2
Montmiral F . 117 B5
Montmirat F . 131 B3
Montmirey-le-
Château F ... 105 B4
Montmoreau-St
Cybard F..... 115 C4

Montmorency
F.............90 C2
Montmorillon
F............. 115 B4
Montmort-Lucy
F.............91 C3
Montoir-de-
Bretagne F .. 101 B3
Montoire-sur-le-
Loir F........ 102 B2
Montoito P.... 155 C3
Montolieu F .. 146 A3
Montório al
Vomano I 169 A3
Montoro E 157 B3
Montpellier F . 131 B2
Montpezat-de-
Quercy F..... 129 B4
Montpezat-sous-
Bouzon F.... 117 C4
Montpon-
Ménestérol
F............. 128 A3
Montpont-en-
Bresse F..... 105 C4
Montréal
Aude F 146 A3
Gers F 128 C2
Montredon-
Labessonnié
F............. 130 B1
Montréjeau F . 145 A4
Montrésor F .. 103 B3
Montresta I ... 178 B2
Montret F..... 105 C4
Montreuil
Pas de Calais
F.............78 B1
Seine St Denis
F.........90 C2
Montreuil-aux-
Lions F.......90 B3
Montreuil-Bellay
F............. 102 B1
Montreux CH . 106 C1
Montrevault
F............. 101 B4
Montrevel-en-
Bresse F..... 118 A2
Montrichard F 103 B3
Montricoux F . 129 B4
Mont-roig del
Camp E 147 C1
Montrond-les-Bains
F............. 117 B4
Montroy E 159 B3
Montsalvy F .. 116 C2
Montsauche-les-
Settons F 104 B3
Montseny E .. 147 C3
Montsoreau F . 102 B2
Mont-sous-Vaudrey
F............. 105 C4
Monts-sur-Guesnes
F............. 102 C2
Mont-St Aignan
F.............89 A5
Mont-St Vincent
F............. 104 C3
Montsùrs F .. 102 A1
Montuenga E . 150 A3
Montuïri E.... 167 B3
Monturque E . 163 A3
Monza I....... 120 B2
Monzón E 145 C4
Monzón de
Campos E ... 142 B2
Moorbad
Lobenstein D ..83 B3
Moordorf D....71 A4
Moorslede B ...78 B3
Moos D....... 107 B3
Moosburg D ...95 C3
Moosburg im
Kärnten A ... 110 C1
Mór H........ 112 B2
Mora E....... 157 A4
Móra P....... 154 C2
Mora S........50 A1
Moraby S......50 B2
Mòra d'Ebre
E............. 153 A4
Mora de Rubielos
E............. 153 B3
Moradillo de Roa
E............. 151 A4
Morag PL......69 B4
Mórahalom H. 126 A1
Moraime E.... 140 A1
Morais P...... 149 A3
Mòra la Nova
E............. 153 A4

Moral de Calatrava
E............. 157 B4
Moraleda de
Zafayona E... 163 A4
Moraleja E.... 149 B3
Moraleja del Vino
E............. 150 A2
Morales del Vino
E............. 150 A2
Morales de Toro
E............. 150 A2
Morales de
Valverde E ... 141 C5
Moralina E 149 A3
Morano Cálabro
I.............. 174 B2
Mörarp S.......61 C2
Morasverdes
E............. 149 B3
Morata de Jalón
E............. 152 A2
Morata de Jiloca
E............. 152 A2
Morata de Tajuña
E............. 151 B4
Moratalla E ... 164 A3
Moravče SLO.. 123 A3
Moravec CZ....97 B4
Moravita RO .. 126 B3
Morávka CZ....98 B2
Moravská Třebová
CZ.............97 B4
Moravské
Budějovice
CZ.............97 B3
Moravské Lieskové
SK.............98 C1
Moravske Toplice
SLO.......... 111 C3
Moravský-Beroun
CZ.............98 B1
Moravsky Krumlov
CZ.............97 B4
Moravský Svätý
Ján SK........98 C1
Morawica PL...87 B4
Morawin PL....86 A2
Morbach D.....92 B3
Morbegno I... 120 A2
Morbier F..... 105 C5
Mörbisch am See
A............. 111 B3
Mörbylånga S...63 B4
Morcenx F 128 B2
Morciano di
Romagna I... 136 B1
Morcone I..... 170 B2
Morcuera E ... 151 A4
Mordelles F... 101 A4
Mordoğan TR . 188 A1
Moréac F...... 100 B3
Morebattle UK . 35 C5
Morecambe UK . 36 B4
Moreda
Granada E.... 163 A4
Oviedo E 142 A1
Moreruela de
Tábara E 149 A4
Morés E....... 152 A2
Móres I....... 178 B2
Morestel F.... 118 B2
Moretonhampstead
UK............43 B3
Moreton-in-Marsh
UK............44 B2
Moret-sur-Loing
F.............90 C2
Moretta I..... 119 C4
Moreuil F......90 B2
Morez F....... 105 C5
Mörfelden D ...93 B4
Morgat F..... 100 A1
Morges CH ... 105 C5
Morgex I..... 119 B4
Morgongåva S..51 C3
Morhange F....92 C2
Morhet B......92 B1
Mori I........ 121 B3
Morialmé B 79 B4
Morianes P.... 160 B2
Moriani Plage
F............. 180 A2
Mórichida H .. 111 B4
Moriles E..... 163 A3
Morille F...... 150 B2
Moringen D....82 A1
Morjärv S..... 196 C5
Morkarla S.....51 B4
Mørke DK......59 B3

Mørkøv DK..... 61 D1
Morkovice-Slížany
CZ.............98 B1
Morlaàs F 145 A3
Morlaix F 100 A2
Morley F.......91 C5
Mörlunda S 62 A3
Mormanno I .. 174 B1
Mormant F.....90 C2
Mornant F 117 B4
Mornay-Berry
F............. 103 B4
Morón de Almazán
E............. 152 A1
Morón de la
Frontera E ... 162 A2
Morović SRB . 125 B5
Morozzo I.... 133 A3
Morpeth UK...37 A5
Morphou CY .. 181 A1
Mörrum S.......63 B2
Morsbach D....81 B3
Mörsch D......93 C4
Mörsil S...... 199 B10
Morsum D.....64 B1
Mørsvikbotn
N............. 194 C6
Mortagne-au-
Perche F 89 B4
Mortagne-sur-
Gironde F ... 114 C3
Mortagne-sur-
Sèvre F...... 114 B3
Mortágua P .. 148 B1
Mortain F.....88 B3
Mortara I..... 120 B1
Morteau F 105 B5
Mortegliano
I.............. 122 B2
Mortelle I 177 A4
Mortemart F.. 115 B4
Mortimer's Cross
UK............39 B4
Mortrée F......89 B4
Mörtschach A. 109 C3
Mortsel B......79 A4
Morud DK......59 C3
Morwenstow
UK............42 B2
Moryń PL......74 B3
Morzeszczyn
PL.............69 B3
Morzewo PL....69 B4
Morzine F 118 A3
Mosbaḥ D.....93 B5
Mosbjerg DK... 58 A3
Mosby N.......53 B3
Mosca P...... 149 A3
Moscavide P . 154 C1
Moščenica
HR........... 124 B2
Moščenice
HR........... 123 B3
Moščenicka Draga
HR........... 123 B3
Mosciano
Sant'Ángelo
I.............. 136 C2
Mościsko PL....85 B4
Moscow = Moskva
RUS............9 E10
Mosina PL.....75 B5
Mosjøen N... 195 E4
Moskog N......46 A3
Moskorzew PL..87 B3
Moskosel S... 196 D2
Moskuvarra
FIN.......... 197 B9
Moskva = Moscow
RUS............9 E10
Moslavina
Podravska
HR........... 125 B3
Moşniţa Nouă
RO........... 126 B3
Moso in Passíria
I............. 108 C2
Mosonmagyaróvár
H............ 111 B4
Mošorin SRB . 126 B2
Mósovce SK....98 C2
Mosqueruela
E............. 153 B3
Moss N.........54 A1
Mossfellsbær
IS........... 190 C4
Mössingen D...93 C5
Møsstrand N...47 C5
Mosta M..... 175 C3
Mostar BIH... 139 B3
Mosterhamn N..52 A1
Mostki PL......75 B4

Most na Soči
SLO.......... 122 A2
Móstoles E ... 151 B4
Mostová SK... 111 A4
Mostowo PL....68 A1
Mostuéjouls F 130 A2
Mosty PL.......75 A3
Mostys'ka UA .. 13 D5
Mosvik N..... 199 B7
Mota del Cuervo
E............. 158 B1
Mota del Marqués
E............. 150 A2
Motala S.......55 B6
Motherwell UK .35 C4
Möthlow D.....74 B1
Motilla del Palancar
E............. 158 B2
Motnik SLO ... 123 A3
Motovun HR .. 122 B2
Motril E...... 163 B4
Motta I....... 121 B4
Motta di Livenza
I.............. 122 B1
Motta
Montecorvino
I.............. 170 B3
Motta Visconti
I.............. 120 B1
Mottisfont UK...44 B2
Móttola I..... 173 B3
Mou DK.......58 B3
Mouchard F .. 105 C4
Moudon CH .. 106 C1
Moudros GR .. 183 D7
Mougins F.... 132 B2
Mouilleron-en-
Pareds F 114 B3
Mouliherne F . 102 B2
Moulinet F ... 133 B3
Moulins F 104 C2
Moulins-Engilbert
F............. 104 C2
Moulins-la-Marche
F.............89 B4
Moulismes F . 115 B4
Moult F.......89 A3
Mountain Ash
UK............39 C3
Mountbellew
IRL............28 A3
Mountfield UK .27 B3
Mountmellick
IRL............30 A1
Mountrath IRL .30 A1
Mountsorrel
UK............40 C2
Moura P...... 160 A2
Mourão P 155 C3
Mourenx F ... 145 A3
Mouriés F 131 B3
Mourmelon-le-
Grand F......91 B4
Mouronho P . 148 B1
Mourujärvi
FIN.......... 197 C11
Mouscron B ...78 B3
Mousehole UK..42 B1
Moussac F.... 131 B3
Moussey F.....92 C2
Mousteru F .. 100 A2
Moustey F.....90 B2
Moustiers-Ste
Marie F 132 B2
Mouthe F 105 C5
Mouthier-Haute-
Pierre F 105 B5
Mouthoumet
F............. 146 B3
Moutier CH .. 106 B2
Moûtiers F ... 118 B3
Moutiers-les-
Mauxfaits F . 114 B2
Mouy F........90 B2
Mouzaki GR .. 182 D3
Mouzon F......91 B5
Møvik N.......46 B2
Moville IRL....27 A3
Moy
Highland UK . 32 D2
Tyrone UK 27 B4
Moycullen IRL .28 A2
Moyenmoutier
F.............92 C2
Moyenvic F....92 C2
Moylough IRL..28 A3
Mózar E...... 141 C5
Mozhaysk RUS ..9 E10
Mozirje SLO .. 123 A3
Mözs H....... 112 C2
Mozzanica I .. 120 B2

Mrčajevci
SRB.......... 127 D2
Mrkonjić Grad
BIH........... 138 A3
Mrkopalj HR . 123 B3
Mrocza PL......76 A2
Mroczeń PL....86 A1
Mroczno PL....69 B4
Mrzezyno PL...67 B4
Mšec CZ.......84 B1
Mšeno CZ......84 B2
Mstów PL......86 B3
Mstislaw BY ...13 A9
Mszana Dolna
PL............99 B4
Mszczonów PL..77 C5
Muć HR....... 138 B2
Múccia I...... 136 B2
Much D........80 B3
Mücheln D.....83 A3
Much Marcle
UK............39 C4
Muchów PL....85 A4
Much Wenlock
UK............39 B4
Mucientes E .. 142 C2
Muckross IRL ..29 B2
Mucur TR.......23 B8
Muda P....... 160 B1
Mudanya TR . 186 B3
Mudau D.......93 B5
Müden D.......72 B3
Mudersbach D .81 B3
Mudurnu TR . 187 B6
Muel E....... 152 A2
Muelas del Pan
E............. 149 A4
Muess D.......73 A4
Muff IRL.......27 A3
Mugardos E .. 140 A2
Muge P....... 154 B2
Mügeln
Sachsen D 83 A5
Sachsen-Anhalt
D.............83 A5
Múggia I..... 122 B2
Mugnano I... 135 B5
Mugron F 128 C2
Mugueimes E. 140 C3
Muhi H....... 113 B4
Mühlacker D ..93 C4
Mühlbach am
Hochkönig
A............. 109 B4
Mühlberg
Brandenburg
D.............83 A5
Thüringen D ..82 B2
Mühldorf
D............ 109 A3
A.............95 C4
Muhleberg
CH........... 106 C2
Mühleim D ... 107 A3
Muhlen-Eichsen
D.............65 C4
Mühlhausen
Bayern D 94 B2
Thüringen D ..82 A2
Mühltroff D....83 B3
Muhos FIN ... 3 D10
Muhr A....... 109 B4
Muine Bheag
IRL............30 B2
Muirkirk UK ...36 A2
Muir of Ord UK .32 D2
Muirteira P .. 154 B1
Mukacheve UA. 12 D5
Muker UK......37 B4
Mula E....... 165 A3
Mugla TR..... 188 B3
Mulben UK 32 D3
Mulegns CH .. 107 C4
Mules I....... 108 C2
Mülheim D....80 A2
Mulhouse F .. 106 B2
Mljava SLO .. 123 B3
Mullanys Cross
IRL............26 B2
Müllheim D .. 106 B2
Mullinavat IRL .30 B1
Mullingar IRL .30 A1
Mullion UK....42 B1
Müllrose D.....74 B3
Muljši S.......60 B3
Mulseryd S....60 B3
Munaðarnes
IS........... 190 A4
Munana E.... 150 B2
Muñás E..... 141 A4
Münchberg D ..83 B3
Müncheberg D. 74 B3

München = Munich D ... 108 A2
Munchen-Gladbach = Mönchengladbach D ... 80 C2
Münchhausen D ... 81 B4
Mundaka E ... 143 A4
Münden D ... 82 A1
Munderfing A. 109 A4
Munderkingen D ... 107 A4
Mundesley UK ... 41 C5
Munera E ... 158 B1
Mungia E ... 143 A4
Munich = München D ... 108 A2
Muñico E ... 150 B2
Muniesa E ... 153 A3
Munka-Ljungby S ... 61 C2
Munkebo DK ... 59 C3
Munkedal S ... 54 B2
Munkflohögen S ... 199 B11
Munkfors S ... 49 C5
Munktorp S ... 56 A2
Münnerstadt D ... 82 B2
Muñopepe E. 150 B3
Muñotello E... 150 B2
Münsingen CH ... 106 C2
Münsingen D ... 94 C1
Munsö S ... 57 A3
Münster CH ... 106 C3
Münster Hessen D ... 93 B4
Münster D ... 72 B3
Münster F ... 71 C4
Munster F.... 106 A2
Münster E ... 143 A4
Münzkirchen A .96 C1
Muodoslompolo S ... 196 B6
Muonio FIN ... 196 B6
Muotathal CH. 107 C3
Muradiye TR . 186 D2
Murakeresztúr H... 124 A2
Murán SK ... 99 C4
Murano I ... 122 B1
Muras E ... 140 A3
Murat F ... 116 B2
Muratlı TR.. 186 A2
Murato F ... 180 A2
Murat-sur-Vèbre F ... 130 B1
Murau A ... 109 B5
Muravera I ... 179 C3
Murazzano I .. 133 A4
Murça P ... 148 A2
Murchante E .. 144 B2
Murchin D ... 66 C2
Murcia E ... 165 B3
Murczyn PL ... 76 B2
Mur-de-Barrez F ... 116 C2
Mur-de-Bretagne F ... 100 A2
Mur-de-Sologne F ... 103 B3
Mureck A ... 110 C2
Mürefte TR.. 186 B2
Muret F ... 146 A2
Murg CH ... 107 B4
Murguia E .. 143 B4
Muri CH ... 106 B3
Murias de Paredes E ... 141 B4
Muriedas E .. 143 A3
Muriel Viejo E . 143 C4
Murillo de Rio Leza E ... 143 B4
Murillo el Fruto E ... 144 B2
Murjek S ... 196 C3
Murlaggan UK ... 34 B2
Murmansk RUS ... 3 B13
Murmashi RUS ... 3 B13
Murnau D ... 108 B2
Muro E ... 167 B3
Muro F ... 180 A1
Muro de Alcoy E ... 159 C3
Murol F ... 116 B2
Muro Lucano I 172 B1
Muron F ... 114 B3
Muros E ... 140 B1
Muros de Nalón E ... 141 A4

Murowana Goślina PL ... 76 B2
Mürren CH ... 106 C2
Murrhardt D ... 94 C1
Murska Sobota SLO ... 111 C3
Mursko Središce HR ... 111 C3
Murtas E ... 164 C1
Murten CH.... 106 C2
Murter HR ... 137 B4
Murtiçi TR... 189 C6
Murtosa P.... 148 B1
Murtovaara FIN... 197 D12
Murvica HR ... 137 A4
Murviel-lès-Béziers F ... 130 B2
Mürzsteg A ... 110 B2
Murzynowo PL.. 75 B4
Mürzzuschlag A... 110 B2
Musculdy F ... 144 A3
Muskö S ... 57 A4
Mušov CZ... 97 C4
Musselburgh UK ... 35 C4
Musselkanaal NL ... 71 B4
Mussidan F .. 129 A3
Mussomeli I... 176 B2
Musson B ... 92 B1
Mussy-sur-Seine F ... 104 B3
Mustafakemalpaşa TR... 186 B3
Muszaki PL... 77 A5
Muszyna PL... 99 B4
Mut TR... 23 C7
Muta SLO ... 110 C2
Muthill UK ... 35 B4
Mutné SK ... 99 B3
Mutriku E ... 143 A4
Muttalip TR .. 187 C5
Mutterbergalm A... 108 B2
Muurola FIN .. 197 C8
Muxía E ... 140 A1
Muxika-Ugarte E ... 143 A4
Muzillac F.... 101 B3
Mužla SK... 112 B2
Muzzano del Turgnano I ... 122 B2
Mybster UK ... 32 C3
Myckelgensjö S ... 200 C3
Myennes F ... 104 B1
Myjava SK... 98 C1
Myking N... 46 B2
Mykland N.... 53 B4
Myra N... 53 B5
Myrdal N... 46 B4
Myre Nordland N .. 194 A6
Myre Nordland N .. 194 B6
Myresjö S ... 62 A2
Mýri IS ... 191 B8
Myrtou CY ... 181 A2
Mysen N... 54 A2
Mysłakowice PL... 85 B3
Myślenice PL... 99 B3
Myślibórz PL... 75 B3
Mysłowice PL.. 86 B3
Myszków PL... 86 B3
Mytishchi RUS ... 9 E10
Mýtna SK... 99 C3
Mýtne Ludany SK... 112 A2
Mýto CZ... 96 B1

N

Nafplio GR ... 184 B3
Nagel D... 95 B3
Nagele NL... 70 B2
Naggen S ... 200 D2
Nagłowice PL.. 87 B4
Nagold D... 93 C4
Nagore E ... 144 B2
Nagyatád H... 124 A3
Nagybajom H . 124 A3
Nagybaracska H... 125 A4
Nagybátony H... 113 B3
Nagyberény H... 112 C2
Nagybörzsöny H... 112 C2
Nagycenk H... 111 B3
Nagycserkesz H... 113 B5
Nagydorog H . 112 C2
Nagyfüged H . 113 B4
Nagyhersány H... 125 B4
Nagyigmánd H... 112 B2
Nagyiván H... 113 B4
Nagykanizsa H... 111 C3
Nagykáta H... 113 B3
Nagykonyi H.. 112 C2
Nagykörös H.. 113 B3
Nagykörü H... 113 B4
Nagylóc H.... 112 A3
Nagymágocs H... 113 C4
Nagymányok H... 125 A4
Nagymaros H . 112 B3
Nagyoroszi H . 112 A3
Nagyrábé H... 113 B5
Nagyréde H... 113 B3
Nagyszékely H... 112 C2
Nagyszénás H. 113 C4
Nagyszokoly H... 112 C2
Nagytőke H... 113 C4
Nagyvázsony H... 111 C4
Nagyvenyim H... 112 C2
Naharros E... 152 B1
Naila D... 83 B3
Nailloux F.... 146 A2
Nailsworth UK . 43 A4
Naintré F.... 115 B4
Nairn UK... 32 D3
Najac F... 129 B4
Nájera E ... 143 B4
Nak H... 112 C2
Nakksjø N... 53 A5
Nakło nad Notecią PL... 76 A2
Nakskov DK... 65 B4
Nalda E ... 143 B4
Nälden S... 199 B11
Nálepkovo SK.. 99 C4
Nalliers F.... 114 B2
Nallıhan TR .. 187 B6
Nalzen F ... 146 B2
Nalžouské Hory CZ... 96 B1
Namdalseid N 199 A8
Náměšt'nad Oslavou CZ ... 97 B4
Námestovo SK . 99 B3
Namná N... 49 B4
Namsos N ... 199 A8
Namsskogan N... 199 A10
Namur B... 79 B4
Namysłów PL.. 86 A1
Nançay F.... 103 B4
Nanclares de la Oca E ... 143 B4
Nancy F... 92 C2
Nangis F... 90 C3
Nannestad N.. 48 B3
Nant F... 130 A2
Nanterre F.... 90 C2
Nantes F.... 101 B4
Nanteuil-le-Haudouin F... 90 B2
Nantiat F.... 115 B5
Nantua F.... 118 A2
Nantwich UK .. 38 A4
Naoussa Cyclades GR .. 185 B6
Naoussa Imathia GR .. 182 C4
Napajedla CZ.. 98 B1
Napiwoda PL .. 77 A5

Naples = Nápoli I ... 170 C2
Nápoli = Naples I ... 170 C2
Nar S ... 57 C4
Nara N ... 46 A1
Naraval E ... 141 A4
Narberth UK ... 39 C2
Nærbø N... 52 B1
Narbonne F .. 130 B1
Narbonne-Plage F ... 130 B2
Narbuvollen N... 199 C8
Narcao I... 179 C2
Nardò I... 173 B4
Narkaus FIN... 197 C9
Narken S.... 196 C5
Narmo N... 48 B3
Narni I... 168 A2
Naro I... 176 B2
Naro Fominsk RUS ... 9 E10
Narón E ... 140 A2
Narros del Castillo E ... 150 B2
Narta HR.... 124 B2
Naruszewo PL.. 77 B5
Narva EST... 8 C6
Narvik N.... 194 B8
Narzole I.... 133 A3
Näs FIN... 51 B7
Näs S... 50 B1
Näs S... 57 C4
Näsåker S ... 200 C2
Năsăud RO.... 17 B6
Nasavrky CZ .. 97 B3
Nasbinals F .. 116 C3
Næsbjerg DK... 59 C1
Näshull S... 62 A3
Našice HR.... 125 B4
Nasielsk PL... 77 B5
Naso I... 177 A3
Nassau D... 81 B3
Nassenfels D... 95 C3
Nassenheide D .74 B2
Nassereith A . 108 B1
Nässjö S... 62 A2
Nastätten D... 81 B3
Næstved DK ... 65 A4
Näsum S... 63 B2
Näsviken S .. 199 B12
Natalinci SRB . 127 C2
Naters CH.... 119 A5
Nattavaara S . 196 C3
Natters A.... 108 B2
Nattheim D.... 94 C2
Nättraby S.... 63 B3
Naturno I.... 108 C1
Naucelle F ... 130 A1
Nauders A.... 108 C1
Nauen D... 74 B1
Naul IRL... 30 A2
Naumburg D... 83 A3
Naundorf D.... 83 A5
Naunhof D.... 83 A4
Naustdal N ... 46 A2
Nautijaur S .. 196 C2
Nautsi RUS... 193 D13
Nava E ... 142 A1
Navacerrada E ... 151 B3
Navaconcejo E ... 149 B4
Nava de Arévalo E ... 150 B3
Nava de la Asunción E... 150 A3
Nava del Rey E ... 150 A2
Navafría E.... 151 A4
Navahermosa E ... 157 A3
Navahrudak BY .13 B6
Naval E ... 145 B4
Navalcán E... 150 B2
Navalcarnero E ... 151 B3
Navaleno E... 143 C4
Navalmanzano E ... 150 A3
Navalmoral E . 150 B3
Navalmoral de la Mata E ... 150 C2
Navalón E... 159 C3
Navalonguilla E ... 150 B2
Navalperal de Pinares E ... 150 B3
Navalpino E... 157 A3

Navaltalgordo E ... 150 B3
Navaltoril E... 156 A3
Navaluenga E. 150 B3
Navalvillar de Pela E ... 156 A2
Navan IRL... 30 A2
Navaperal de Tormes E.... 150 B3
Navapolatsk BY... 13 A8
Navarclés E .. 147 C2
Navarredonda de Gredos E.... 150 B2
Navarrenx F .. 144 A3
Navarrés E... 159 B3
Navarrete E... 143 B4
Navarrevisca E ... 150 B3
Navás E ... 147 C2
Navasfrias E . 149 B3
Navata E ... 147 B3
Nave I... 120 B3
Nave de Haver P ... 149 B3
Nävekvarn S... 56 B2
Navelli I... 169 A3
Navenby UK ... 40 B3
Näverkärret S.. 56 A1
Naverstad S... 54 B2
Navés E ... 147 C2
Navezuelas E . 156 A2
Navia E ... 141 A4
Navia de Suarna E ... 141 B4
Navilly F.... 105 C4
Năvodari RO... 17 C8
Naxos GR.... 185 B6
Nay F... 145 A3
Nazaré P.... 154 B1
Nazarje SLO... 123 A3
Nazilli TR.... 188 B3
Nazza D... 82 A2
Nea Anchialos GR ... 182 D4
Nea Epidavros GR ... 184 B4
Nea Flippias GR ... 182 D2
Nea Kalikratia GR ... 183 C5
Nea Makri GR . 185 A4
Nea Moudania GR ... 183 C5
Neap UK... 33 A5
Nea Peramos GR ... 183 C6
Neapoli Kozani GR ... 182 C3
Neapoli Kriti GR.... 185 D6
Neapoli Lakonia GR .. 184 C4
Nea Stira GR . 185 A5
Neath UK... 39 C3
Nea Visa GR .. 186 A1
Nea Zichni GR. 183 B5
Nebljusi HR... 124 C1
Neblo SLO.... 122 A2
Nebolchy RUS ... 9 C8
Nebra D... 82 A3
Nebreda E.... 143 C3
Nechanice CZ .. 84 B3
Neckargemünd D ... 93 B4
Neckarsulm D.. 94 B1
Neda E ... 140 A2
Nedelišće HR . 124 A2
Nederweert NL .80 A1
Nedreberg N... 48 B3
Nedre Gärdsjö S... 50 B2
Nedre Soppero S... 196 A4
Nedstrand N... 52 A1
Nedvědice CZ.. 97 B4
Nędza PL... 86 B2
Neede NL... 71 B3
Needham Market UK ... 45 A5
Needingworth UK ... 44 A3
Neermoor D... 71 A4
Neeroeteren B .80 A1

Neerpelt B ... 79 A5
Neesen D... 72 B1
Neetze D... 73 A3
Nefyn UK... 38 B2
Negotin SRB .. 16 C5
Negotino NMK ... 182 B4
Negrar I.... 121 B3
Negredo E... 151 A5
Negreira E... 140 B2
Nègrepelisse F ... 129 B4
Negru Vodă RO ... 17 D8
Negueira de Muñiz E ... 141 A4
Neheim D... 81 A3
Neila E ... 143 B4
Néive I... 119 C5
Nejdek CZ.... 83 B4
Nekla PL... 76 B2
Neksø DK... 67 A4
Nelas P.... 148 B2
Nelaug N... 53 B4
Nelidovo RUS ... 9 D8
Nelim FIN... 193 D12
Nellingen D.... 94 C1
Nelson UK... 40 B1
Neman RUS ... 12 A5
Nemea GR.... 184 B3
Nemesgörzsöny H... 111 B4
Nemeskér H... 111 B3
Nemesnádudvar H... 125 A5
Nemesszalók H... 111 B4
Nemesvámos H. 111 B4
Németkér H... 112 C2
Nemours F ... 103 A4
Nemška Loka SLO ... 123 B4
Nemšová SK... 98 C2
Nenagh IRL ... 28 B3
Nenince SK... 112 A3
Nenita GR.... 185 A7
Nenzing A ... 107 B4
Neochori GR . 182 D3
Neo Chori GR . 184 A2
Neon Petritsi GR ... 183 B5
Nepi I... 168 A2
Nepomuk CZ... 96 B1
Nérac F... 129 B3
Neratovice CZ .. 84 B2
Nerchau D.... 83 A4
Néré F... 115 C3
Neresheim D... 94 C2
Nereto I.... 136 C2
Nerezine HR . 123 C3
Nerežišća HR . 138 B2
Neringa LT.... 12 A4
Néris-les-Bains F ... 116 A2
Nerito I.... 169 A3
Nerja E ... 163 B4
Néronde F ... 117 B4
Nérondes F... 103 C4
Nerpio E ... 164 A2
Nersingen D... 94 C2
Nerva E ... 161 B3
Nervesa della Battáglia I... 121 B5
Nervieux F... 117 B4
Nes Buskerud N... 48 B1
Nes Hedmark N... 48 B2
Nes Nordland N... 194 C5
Nes N... 46 A3
Nes N... 198 B6
Nes NL ... 70 A2

Nes Akershus N .48 B3
Nes Sør-Trøndelag N... 198 B6
Nesbyen N.... 47 B6
Neset N... 199 D7
Nesflaten N... 52 A2
Nesjahverri IS ... 191 C10
Neskaupstaður IS ... 191 B12
Nesland N.... 53 A3
Neslandsvatn N... 53 B5
Nesle F... 90 B2
Nesna N.... 195 D4
Nesoddtangen N... 48 C2
Nesovice CZ... 98 B1
Nesselwang D 108 B1
Nesslau CH... 107 B4
Nessmersiel D .71 A4
Nesso I.... 120 B2
Nesterov RUS .13 C5
Nestorio GR . 182 C3
Nesttun N.... 46 B2
Nesvady SK... 112 B2
Nesvatnstemmen N... 53 B4
Nether Stowey UK ... 43 A3
Netland N.... 52 B2
Netolice CZ ... 96 B2
Netphen D.... 81 B4
Netstal CH ... 107 B4
Nettancourt F .. 91 C4
Nettetal D... 80 A2
Nettlingen D... 72 B3
Nettuno I.... 168 B2
Neualbenreuth D ... 95 B4
Neubeckum D .81 A4
Neubrandenburg D ... 74 A2
Neubruchhausen D ... 72 B1
Neubukow D... 65 B4
Neuburg D.... 94 C3
Neuchâtel CH. 106 C1
Neu Darchau D .73 A3
Neudau A.... 111 B3
Neudietendorf D ... 82 B2
Neudorf D.... 93 B4
Neuenbürg D... 93 C4
Neuenburg D.. 71 A4
Neuendorf D... 66 B2
Neuenhagen D ... 74 B2
Neuenhaus D.. 71 B3
Neuenkirchen Niedersachsen D... 71 B5
Neuenkirchen Niedersachsen D ... 72 A2
Neuenkirchen Nordrhein-Westfalen D ... 71 B4
Neuenkirchen Nordrhein-Westfalen D ... 81 B3
Neuenrade D... 81 A3
Neuenwalde D .64 C1
Neuerburg D... 92 A2
Neufahrn Bayern D ... 95 C3
Neufahrn Bayern D ... 95 C4
Neuf-Brisach F ... 106 A2
Neufchâteau B... 92 B1
Neufchâteau F ... 92 C1
Neufchâtel-en-Bray F ... 90 B1
Neufchâtel-sur-Aisne F... 91 B4
Neuflize F.... 91 B4
Neugersdorf D .84 B2
Neuharlingersiel D ... 71 A4
Neuhaus Bayern D ... 95 B3
Neuhaus Bayern D ... 96 C1
Neuhaus Niedersachsen D... 64 C2
Neuhaus Niedersachsen D ... 73 A3
Neuhaus Niedersachsen D ... 81 A5
Neuhaus a Rennweg D .82 B3
Neuhausen CH ... 107 B3
Neuhausen D... 83 B5
Neuhausen ob Eck D ... 107 B3
Neuhof Bayern D ... 94 B2
Neuhof Hessen D ... 81 B5
Neuhofen an der Krems A ... 110 A1
Neuillé-Pont-Pierre F ... 102 B2
Neuilly-en-Thelle F ... 90 B2
Neuilly-le-Réal F ... 104 C2
Neuilly-l'Évêque F ... 105 B4
Neuilly-St Front F ... 90 B3
Neu-Isenburg D ... 93 A4
Neukalen D ... 66 C1
Neu Kaliss D ... 73 A4
Neukirch D ... 84 A2

Neukirchen
A.............. 109 A4
Hessen B 81 B5
Schleswig-Holstein
D.................64 B1
Neukirchen am Grossvenediger
A.............. 109 B3
Neukirchen bei Heiligen Blut
D 95 B4
Neukloster *D* ...65 C4
Neulengbach
A.............. 110 A2
Neulise *F*...... 117 B4
Neu Lübbenau
D..................74 B2
Neum *BIH* 139 C3
Neumagen *D* ...92 B2
Neumarkt *D* 95 B3
Neumarkt am Wallersee *A*.. 109 B4
Neumarkt im Hausruckkreis
A.............. 109 A4
Neumarkt im Mühlkreis *A*....96 C2
Neumarkt im Steiermark
A.............. 110 B1
Neumarkt Sankt Veit *D*..........95 C4
Neumünster
D..................64 B2
Neunburg vorm Wald *D*.........95 B4
Neung-sur-Beuvron
F.............. 103 B3
Neunkirch
Luzern CH 106 B3
Schaffhausen
CH 107 B3
Neunkirchen
A.............. 111 B3
Nordrhein-Westfalen D....80 B3
Saarland D 92 B3
Neunkirchen am Brand *D*........94 B3
Neuötting *D* ...95 C4
Neupetershain
D..................84 A2
Neuravensburg
D.............. 107 B4
Neureut *D* 93 B4
Neuruppin *D* ...74 B1
Neusäss *D*......94 C2
Neusiedl *A* 111 B3
Neuss *D*........80 A2
Neussargues-Moissac *F* 116 B2
Neustadt
Bayern D......94 B2
Bayern B 95 B4
Bayern D 95 C3
Brandenburg
D................73 B5
Hessen D 81 B5
Niedersachsen
D.................72 B2
Rheinland-Pfalz
D.................93 B4
Sachsen D 84 A2
Schleswig-Holstein
D.................65 B3
Thüringen D ..82 B3
Thüringen D ..83 B3
Neustadt-Glewe
D..................73 A4
Neustift im Stubaital *A*.. 108 B2
Neustrelitz *D* ...74 A2
Neutal *A*...... 111 B3
Neutrebbin *D* ..74 B3
Neu-Ulm *D*.....94 C2
Neuves-Maisons
F.................92 C2
Neuvic
Corrèze F 116 B2
Dordogne F .. 129 A3
Neuville-aux-Bois
F.............. 103 A4
Neuville-de-Poitou
F.............. 115 B4
Neuville-les-Dames
F.............. 117 A5
Neuville-sur-Saône
F.............. 117 B4
Neuvy-le-Roi
F.............. 102 B2

Neuvy-Santour
F.............. 104 A2
Neuvy-St Sépulchre
F.............. 103 C3
Neuvy-sur-Barangeon *F*. 103 B4
Neuwied *D*.....80 B3
Neuzelle *D* 74 B3
Névache *F* 118 B3
Neveklov *CZ* ...96 B2
Nevel *RUS*...... 9 D6
Neverfjord *N*. 192 B7
Nevers *F* 104 C2
Nevesinje *BIH*. 139 B4
Névez *F* 100 B2
Nevlunghavn *N* 53 B5
Nevşehir *TR* 23 B8
New Abbey *UK*..36 B3
New Aberdour
UK 33 D4
New Alresford
UK 44 B2
Newark-on-Trent
UK 40 B3
Newbiggin-by-the-Sea *UK* 37 A5
Newbliss *IRL* ...27 B3
Newborough
UK 38 A2
Newbridge *IRL* ..30 A2
Newbridge on Wye
UK 39 B3
Newburgh
Aberdeenshire
UK 33 D4
Fife UK 35 B4
Newbury *UK* ...44 B2
Newby Bridge
UK 36 B4
Newcastle *UK* ..27 B5
Newcastle Emlyn
UK 39 B2
Newcastleton
UK 37 A4
Newcastle-under-Lyme *UK* 40 B1
Newcastle upon Tyne *UK* 37 B5
Newcastle West
IRL 29 B2
New Costessey
UK 41 C5
New Cumnock
UK 36 A2
Newent *UK*.....39 C4
New Galloway
UK 36 A2
Newham *UK*...45 B4
Newhaven *UK*..45 C4
Newington *UK*..45 B5
Newinn *IRL*.....29 B4
Newlyn *UK*.....42 B1
Newmachar *UK* 33 D4
Newmarket
IRL 29 B3
Suffolk UK ... 45 A4
Western Isles
UK 31 A2
Newmarket-on-Fergus *IRL*......28 B3
New Mills *UK*...40 B2
New Milton *UK*..44 C2
New Pitsligo
UK 33 D4
Newport
Mayo IRL 28 A2
Tipperary IRL...29 B3
Isle of Wight
UK 44 C2
Pembrokeshire
UK 39 B2
Telford & Wrekin
UK 38 B4
Newport-on-Tay
UK 35 B5
Newport Pagnell
UK 44 A3
Newquay *UK*...42 B1
New Quay *UK* ..39 B2
New Radnor *UK* 39 B3
New Romney
UK 45 C4
New Ross *IRL*...30 B2
New Scone *UK* .35 B4
Newton Abbot
UK 43 B3
Newton Arlosh
UK 36 B3
Newton Aycliffe
UK 37 B5

Newton Ferrers
UK 42 B2
Newtonhill *UK* . 33 D4
Newtonmore
UK 32 D2
Newton Stewart
UK 36 B2
Newtown
Herefordshire
UK 39 B4
Powys UK......39 B3
Newtownabbey
UK 27 B5
Newtownards
UK 27 B5
Newtownbutler
UK 27 B3
Newtown Cunningham
IRL 27 B3
Newtownhamilton
UK 27 B4
Newtownmount-kennedy *IRL*
.................30 A2
Newtown St Boswells *UK*...35 C5
Newtown Sands
IRL 29 B2
Newtownstewart
UK 27 B3
Nexon *F*...... 115 C5
Neyland *UK* 39 C2
Nibbiano *I* 120 C2
Nibe *DK*.......58 B2
Nicastro *I* 175 C2
Niccone *I*..... 135 B5
Nice *F* 133 B3
Nickelsdorf *A* . 111 B4
Nicolosi *I*..... 177 B4
Nicosia
CY 181 A2
I 177 B3
Nicótera *I* 175 C1
Nidda *D*........81 B5
Niğde *TR*......23 C8
Nidzica *PL* 77 B5
Niebla *E*...... 161 B3
Nieborów *PL*....77 B5
Niebüll *D*.......64 B1
Niechanowo *PL* .76 B2
Niechorze *PL*...67 B4
Niedalino *PL*....67 B5
Niederaula *D* ...82 B1
Niederbipp
CH 106 B2
Niederbronn-les-Bains *F* 93 C3
Niederfischbach
D................81 B3
Niedergörsdorf
D..................74 C1
Niederkrüchten
D..................80 A2
Niederndorf *A* 108 B3
Nieder-Olm *D* ..93 B4
Niedersachswerfen
D..................82 A2
Niederstetten
D..................94 B1
Niederurnen
CH 107 B4
Niederwölz *A* . 110 B1
Niedoradz *PL* ...85 A3
Niedzica *PL*.....99 B4
Niegosławice
PL..............85 A3
Nieheim *D*......81 A5
Niemcza *PL*.....85 B4
Niemegk *D*......74 B1
Niemisel *S* 196 C5
Niemodlin *PL* ...85 B5
Nienburg
Niedersachsen
D..................72 B2
Sachsen-Anhalt
D 83 A3
Niepołomice
PL..............99 A4
Nierstein *D* 93 B4
Niesky *D*........84 A2
Niestronno *PL* ..76 B2
Nieśwień *PL*.....87 A4
Nieszawa *PL*....76 B3
Nieul-le-Dolent
F.............. 114 B2
Nieul-sur-Mer
F.............. 114 B2
Nieuw-Amsterdam
NL 71 B3
Nieuw-Buinen
NL 71 B3
Nieuwegein *NL* .70 B2

Nieuwe Niedorp
NL 70 B1
Nieuwe-Pekela
NL 71 A3
Nieuwerkerken
B..................79 B5
Nieuwe-schans
NL 71 A4
Nieuwolda *NL*...71 A3
Nieuwpoort *B*...78 A2
Nieuw-Weerdinge
NL 71 B3
Nigrita *GR*.... 183 C5
Nigüelas *E* 163 B4
Níjar *E*........ 164 C2
Nijemci *HR*.... 125 B5
Nijkerk *NL* 70 B2
Nijlen *B*........79 A4
Nijmegen *NL* ...80 A1
Nijverdal *NL* ...71 B3
Nikel *RUS* 193 C14
Nikinci *SRB*.... 127 C1
Nikiti *GR* 183 C5
Nikitsch *A*..... 111 B3
Nikkaluokta
S............. 196 B2
Nikla *H*....... 111 C4
Niklasdorf *A* .. 110 B2
Nikšić *MNE* ... 139 C4
Nilivaara *S* ... 196 B4
Nîmes *F* 131 B3
Nimis *I* 122 A2
Nimtofte *DK* ...58 B3
Nin *HR*....... 137 A4
Nindorf *D*......64 B2
Ninemilehouse
IRL 30 B1
Ninove *B*.......79 B4
Niort *F* 114 B3
Niš *SRB*....... 16 D4
Nisa *P* 155 B3
Niscemi *I*..... 177 B3
Niskala *FIN* .. 197 D10
Nissafors *S*.....60 B3
Nissan-lez-Ensérune *F* .. 130 B2
Nissedal *N*.... 53 A4
Nissoøger *DK* .. 58 B2
Nissumby *DK* ..58 B1
Nisterud *N*.....53 A5
Niton *UK*.......44 C2
Nitra *SK*....... 98 C2
Nitrianske-Pravno
SK.............. 98 C2
Nitrianske Rudno
SK.............. 98 C2
Nitry *F* 104 B2
Nittedal *N*......48 B2
Nittenau *D* 95 B4
Nittendorf *D*...95 B3
Nivala *FIN*..... 3 E26
Nivelles *B*......79 B4
Nivnice *CZ* 98 C1
Nižná *SK*.......99 B3
Nižná Boca *SK*..99 C3
Nižne Repaše
SK.............. 99 B4
Nizza Monferrato
I.............. 119 C5
Njarðvík *IS* ... 190 D3
Njegoševo
SRB 126 B1
Njivice *HR*.... 123 B3
Njurundabommen
S............. 200 D3
Njutånger *S* ... 200 E3
Noailles *F*......90 B2
Noain *E*....... 144 B2
Noale *I*....... 121 B5
Noalejo *E*..... 163 A4
Nobljeza *E*.... 151 C4
Noceda *E*..... 141 B4
Nocera Inferiore
I.............. 170 C2
Nocera Terinese
I.............. 175 B2
Nocera Umbra
I.............. 136 B1
Noceto *I*...... 120 C3
Noci *I*........ 173 B3
Nociglia *I*..... 173 B4
Nodeland *N*....53 B3
Nödinge *S*......60 B2
Nods *F*....... 105 B5
Nœux-les-Mines
F................78 B2
Noez *F*....... 157 A3
Nogales *E*..... 155 C4
Nogara *I*...... 121 B4
Nogarejas *E*... 141 B4
Nogaro *F* 128 C2
Nogent *F* 105 A4

Nogent l'Artaud
F..................90 C3
Nogent-le-Roi
F..................90 C1
Nogent-le-Rotrou
F..................89 B4
Nogent-sur-Seine
F..................91 C3
Nogent-sur-Vernisson *F* .. 103 B4
Nogersund *S*....63 B2
Noguera *E* 152 B2
Noguerones *E*. 163 A3
Nohfelden *D* ...92 B3
Nohn *D*........80 B2
Noia *E*........ 140 B2
Noicàttaro *I* .. 173 A2
Noirétable *F* .. 117 B3
Noirmoutier-en-l'Île *F* 114 A1
Noja *E*........ 143 A3
Nojewo *PL* 75 B5
Nokia *FIN* 8 B3
Nol *S*...........60 B2
Nola *I*........ 170 C2
Nolay *F*....... 104 C3
Noli *I*......... 133 A4
Nolnyra *S*......51 B4
Nombela *E*.... 150 B3
Nomeny *F*......92 C2
Nomexy *F*......92 C2
Nonancourt *F* ..89 B5
Nonant-le-Pin
F..................89 B4
Nonántola *I*... 121 C4
Nonaspe *E*.... 153 A4
None *I*........ 119 C4
Nontron *F*..... 115 C4
Nonza *F*...... 180 A2
Noordhorn *NL* .71 A3
Noordwijk *NL* ..70 B1
Noordwijkerhout
NL 70 B1
Noordwolde *NL* 70 B3
Noppikoski *S* ...50 A1
Nora *S* 56 A6
Nøragersdal *DK* .58 B2
Norberg *S*......50 B2
Norboda *S*.... 51 B5
Nórcia *I*....... 136 C2
Nordagutu *N* ..53 A5
Nordanás *S* ... 200 B4
Nordausques
F..................78 B2
Nordborg *DK* ..64 A2
Nordby
Aarhus Amt.
DK 59 C3
Ribe Amt. DK... 59 C1
Norddeich *D* ...71 A4
Norddorf *D* 64 B1
Norden *D*......71 A4
Nordenham *D* .72 A1
Norderhov *N*...48 B2
Norderney *D* ...71 A4
Norderstapel *D* .64 B2
Norderstedt *D* .64 C3
Nordfjord *N*. 193 B14
Nordfjordeid
N............. 198 D3
Nordfold *N*.... 194 C6
Nordhalben *D* ..82 B3
Nordhausen *D* .82 A2
Nordheim vor der Rhön *D*........82 B2
Nordholz *D*.....64 C1
Nordhorn *D*....71 B4
Nordingrå *S*... 200 D4
Nordkjosbotn
N............. 192 C3
Nordli *N*...... 199 A10
Nordmaling *S*. 200 C5
Nordmark *S*....50 B4
Nordmela *N*... 194 A6
Nord-Odal *N* ...48 B3
Nordre Osen *N*. 48 A3
Nordstemmen
D..................72 B2
Nordstrand *D* ..64 B1
Nordvågen
N............. 193 B10
Nordwalde *D* ...71 B4
Noreña *E*...... 141 A5
Noresund *N*....48 B1
Norheimsund
N............. 46 B2
Norie *S*........63 B2
Norma *I*...... 169 B2
Nornäs *S*...... 49 A5

Norrahammar
S...............62 A2
Norråker *S* 200 B1
Norrala *S*......51 A3
Norra Vi *S*......62 A3
Nørre Aaby *DK* .59 C2
Nørre Alslev
DK 65 B4
Nørre Lyndelse
DK 59 C3
Nørre Nebel
DK 59 C1
Nørre Snede
DK 59 C2
Nørresundby
DK 58 A2
Nørre Vorupør
DK 58 B1
Norrfjärden *S* . 196 D4
Norrhed *S* 196 C3
Norrhult Klavreström
S...............62 A3
Norrköping *S* . 56 B2
Norrskedika *S* . 51 B5
Norrsundet *S* ..51 B4
Norrtälje *S*.....57 A4
Nors *DK*.......58 A1
Norsbron *S* 55 A4
Norsholm *S*....56 B1
Norsjö *S*...... 200 B5
Nörten-Hardenberg
D................82 A1
Northallerton
UK 37 B5
Northampton
UK 44 A3
North Berwick
UK 35 B5
North Charlton
UK 37 A5
North Frodingham
UK 40 B3
North Kessock
UK 32 D2
North Molton
UK 42 A3
North Petherton
UK 43 A4
Northpunds *UK* 33 B5
North Somercotes
UK 41 B4
North Tawton
UK 42 B3
North Thoresby
UK 41 B3
North Walsham
UK 41 C5
Northwich *UK*...38 A4
Norton *UK*......40 A3
Nortorf *D*......64 B2
Nort-sur-Erdre
F.............. 101 B4
Nörvenich *D*....80 B2
Norwich *UK*....41 C5
Nossa Senhora do Cabo *P*....... 154 C1
Nossebro *S*.....55 B3
Nössemark *S*...54 A2
Nossen *D*.......83 A5
Notaresco *I*... 169 A3
Noto *I*........ 177 C4
Notodden *N*....53 A5
Nottingham
UK 40 C2
Nottuln *D*......71 C4
Nouan-le-Fuzelier
F.............. 103 B4
Nouans-les-Fontaines *F* .. 103 B3
Nougaroulet
F.............. 129 C3
Nouvion *F*......78 B1
Nouzonville *F* ...91 B4
Nova *H*....... 111 C3
Nová Bystrica
SK.............. 99 C3
Nová Bystřice
CZ 97 B3
Nova Crnja
SRB 126 B2
Novaféltria *I* .. 135 B5
Nova Gorica
SLO 122 B2

Nova Gradiška
HR 124 B3
Nováky *SK* 98 C2
Novalesa *F* ... 118 B2
Novales *E*..... 145 B3
Nova Levante
I.............. 108 C2
Novalja *HR*.... 137 A3
Nová Paka *CZ* ..84 B3
Nova Pazova
SRB 127 C2
Nová Pec *CZ* ...96 C1
Novara *I*...... 120 B1
Novara di Sicilia
I.............. 177 A4
Nova Siri *I*.... 174 A2
Novate Mezzola
I.............. 120 A2
Nova Topola
BIH 124 B3
Novaya Ladoga
RUS 9 B8
Nova Zagora
BG 17 D6
Nové Hrady
CZ 96 C2
Novelda *E*..... 165 A4
Novellara *I*.... 121 C3
Nové Město *S*..98 C1
Nové Město nad Metují *CZ*.....85 B4
Nové Město na Moravě *CZ*....97 B4
Nové Město pod Smrkem *CZ*....84 B3
Nové Mitrovice
CZ 96 B1
Noventa di Piave
I.............. 122 B1
Noventa Vicentina
I.............. 121 B4
Novés *E*...... 151 B3
Noves *F* 131 B3
Nové Sady *SK*..98 C1
Novés de Segre
E.............. 147 B2
Nové Strašeci
CZ 84 B1
Nové Zámky
SK............ 112 B2
Novgorod *RUS* ...9 C7
Novi Bečej
SRB 126 B2
Novi di Módena
I.............. 121 C3
Novigrad
Istarska HR . 122 B2
Zadarsko-Kninska
HR 137 A4
Novi Grad *BIH*. 124 B2
Novigrad
Podravski HR 124 A2
Novi Kneževac
SRB 126 B2
Novi Ligure *I* .. 120 C1
Noville *B*.......92 A1
Novi Marof
HR 123 B3
Novi Pazar
BG 17 D7
SRB 16 D4
Novi Sad *SRB*.. 126 B1
Novi Slankamen
SRB 126 B2
Novi Travnik
BIH 139 A3
Novi Vinodolski
HR 123 B3
Novohrad-Volynskyy *UA* ..13 C7
Novo Mesto
SLO 123 B4
Novo Miloševo
SRB 126 B2
Novorzhev *RUS* ..9 D6
Novo Selo
BIH 125 B3
Novoselytsya
UA 17 A7
Novosokolniki
RUS 9 D6
Novoveská Huta
SK............ 99 C4
Novovolynsk
UA 13 C6
Novska *HR* 124 B2
Nový Bor *CZ* ...84 B2
Nový Bydžov
CZ 84 B3
Novy-Chevrières
F..................91 B4

Novy Dwór Mazowiecki PL...........77 B5
Nový-Hrozenkov CZ 98 B2
Nový Jičín CZ ...98 B2
Nový Knín CZ ...96 B2
Nowa Cerekwia PL..............86 B1
Nowa Dęba PL ..87 B5
Nowa Karczma PL..............68 A3
Nowa Kościół PL..............85 A3
Nowa Ruda PL ..85 B4
Nowa Słupia PL..............87 B5
Nowa Sól PL.....85 A3
Nowa Wieś PL...69 B4
Nowa-Wieś Wielka PL..............76 B3
Nowe PL 69 B3
Nowe Brzesko PL..............87 B4
Nowe Grudze PL..............77 B4
Nowe Kiejkuty PL..............77 A6
Nowe Miasteczko PL..............85 A3
Nowe Miasto Mazowieckie PL..............77 B5
Mazowieckie PL..............87 A4
Nowe Miasto Lubawskie PL ..69 B4
Nowe Miasto nad Wartą PL.......76 B2
Nowe Skalmierzyce PL..............86 A2
Nowe Warpno PL..............74 A3
Nowica PL........69 A4
Nowogard PL ...75 A4
Nowogród Bobrzanski PL .84 A3
Nowogrodziec PL..............84 A3
Nowosolna PL ..86 A3
Nowy Dwór Gdański PL.....69 A4
Nowy Korczyn PL..............87 B4
Nowy Sącz PL ...99 B4
Nowy Staw PL ...69 A4
Nowy Targ PL ...99 B4
Nowy Tomyśl PL..............75 B5
Nowy Wiśnicz PL..............99 B4
Noyalo F 101 B3
Noyal-Pontivy F 100 A3
Noyant F 102 B2
Noyelles-sur-Mer F 78 B1
Noyen-sur-Sarthe F 102 B1
Noyers F 104 B2
Noyers-sur-Cher F 103 B3
Noyers-sur-Jabron F 132 A1
Noyon F 90 B2
Nozay F 101 B4
Nuaillé F 102 B1
Nuaillé-d'Aunis F 114 B3
Nuars F 104 B2
Nubledo E 141 A5
Nuéno E 145 B3
Nuestra Señora Sa Verge des Pilar E 166 C1
Nueva E 142 A2
Nueva Carteya E 163 A3
Nuevalos E 152 A2
Nuits F 104 B3
Nuits-St Georges F 105 B3
Nule I 178 B3
Nules E 159 B3
Nulvi I 178 B2
Numana I 136 B2
Numansdorp NL 79 A4
Nümbrecht D ...81 B3
Nunchritz D.....83 A5
Nuneaton UK ...40 C2
Nunnanen FIN 196 A7
N Unnaryd S 60 B3

Nuñomoral E.. 149 B3
Nunspeet NL.....70 B2
Nuorgam FIN 193 B11
Núoro I 178 B3
Nurallao I 179 C3
Nuremberg = Nürnberg D 94 B3
Nurmes FIN 3 E11
Nürnberg = Nuremberg D..94 B3
Nurri I..........179 C3
Nürtingen D 94 C1
Nus I...........119 B4
Nusnäs S........50 B1
Nusplingen D. 107 A3
Nuštar HR.......125 B4
Nuupas FIN 197 C9
Nyåker S.......200 C5
Nyáregyháza H..............112 B3
Nyarlörinc H ...113 C3
Nyasvizh BY.....13 B7
Nybble S........55 A5
Nybergsund N .49 A4
Nybøl DK.......64 B2
Nyborg DK 59 C3
S..............196 D6
Nybro S........62 B3
Nybster UK 32 C3
Nyby DK........65 B5
Nye S...........62 A3
Nyékládháza H..............113 B4
Nyergesujfalu H..............112 B2
Nyhammar S....50 B1
Nyhyttan S......55 A5
Nyirád H........111 B4
Nyírbátor H....16 B5
Nyiregyháza H..16 B4
Nyker DK........67 A3
Nykil S..........56 B1
Nykirke N.......48 B2
Nykøbing Falster DK 65 B4
Vestsjællands Amt. DK 61 D1
Nykøbing Mors DK 58 B1
Nyköping S......56 B3
Nykroppa S.....55 A5
Nykvarn S......56 A3
Nykyrke S.......55 B5
Nyland S.......200 C3
Nylars DK.......67 A3
Nymburk CZ 84 B3
Nynäshamn S...57 B3
Nyon CH 118 A3
Nyons F 131 A4
Nýřany CZ......96 B1
Nýřsko CZ.......95 B5
Nyrud N........193 C13
Nysa PL 85 B5
Nysäter S.......55 A3
Nyseter N......198 C5
Nyskoga S......49 B4
Nysted DK......65 B4
Nystrand N.....53 A5
Nyúl H..........111 B4
Nyvoll N........192 B7

Oberhausen D ..80 A2
Oberhof D.......82 B2
Oberkirch D.....93 C4
Oberkirchen D..81 A4
Oberkochen D..94 C2
Obermassfeld-Grimmenthal D 82 B2
Ober-Morlen D .81 B4
Obermünchen D 95 C3
Obernai F 93 C3
Obernberg A....96 C1
Obernburg D ...93 B5
Oberndorf D....93 C4
Oberndorf bei Salzburg A ...109 B3
Obernkirchen D 72 B2
Oberort A......110 B2
Oberpullendorf A..............111 B3
Oberriet CH....107 B4
Oberröblingen D 82 A3
Oberrot D.......94 B1
Oberstaufen D 107 B5
Oberstdorf D ..107 B5
Obertauern A .109 B4
Obertilliach A .109 C3
Obertraubling D 95 C4
Obertraun A ..109 B4
Obertrubach D .95 B3
Obertrum A....109 B4
Oberursel D.....81 B4
Obervellach A 109 C4
Oberviechtach D 95 B4
Oberwart A ...111 B3
Oberwesel D ...93 A3
Oberwinter D...80 B3
Oberwölzstadt A..............110 B1
Oberzell D......96 C1
Öblarn A........109 B4
Obidos P 154 B1
Obing D 109 B3
Objat F 129 A4
Objazda PL......68 A2
Öblarn A.......109 B5
Obninsk RUS 9 E10
O Bolo E 141 B3
Oborniki PL.....75 B5
Oborniki Śląskie PL..............85 A4
Obornjača SRB 126 B1
Obrenovac SRB 127 C2
Obrež SRB......127 C1
Obrigheim D....93 B5
Obrov SLO 123 B3
Obrovac HR 137 A4
SRB 126 B1
Obrovac Sinjski HR 138 B2
Obruk TR........23 B7
Obrzycko PL....75 B5
Obudovac BIH 125 C4
Ocaña E 151 C4
O Carballiño E 140 B2
Occhiobello I.. 121 C4
Occimiano I 119 B5
Očevlja BIH 139 A4
Ochagavia E 144 B2
Ochiltree UK ...36 A2
Ochla PL........84 A3
Ochotnica-Dolna PL..............99 B4
Ochotnica-Górna PL..............99 B4
Ochsenfurt D ..94 B2
Ochsenhausen D 107 A4
Ochtendung D..80 B3
Ochtrup D.......71 B4
Ocieka PL.......87 B5
Ockelbo S.......51 B3
Öckerö S........60 B1
Ocnița MD 17 A7
O Corgo E 141 B3
Očová SK.......99 C3
Ócsa H 112 B3
Ócseny H 125 A4
Ócsöd H........113 C4
Octeville F......88 A2
Ocypel PL.......69 B3
Ödåkra S........61 C2
Odby DK........58 B1

Odda N 46 B3
Odder DK 59 C3
Ödeborg S 54 B2
Odeceixe P.....160 B1
Odechów PL....87 A5
Odeleite P 160 B2
Odemira P 160 B1
Ödemiş TR 188 A2
Odensbacken S .56 A1
Odense DK......59 C3
Odensjö Jönköping S ...62 A2
Kronoberg S ...60 C3
Oderberg D 74 B3
Oderzo I 122 B1
Odesa = Odessa UA 17 B9
Ödeshög S 55 B5
Odessa = Odesa UA 17 B9
Odiáxere P.....160 B1
Odie UK 33 B4
Odiham UK 44 B3
Odintsovo RUS..9 E10
Odivelas P 160 A1
Odolanów PL...85 A5
Odón E 152 B2
Odorheiu Secuiesc RO 17 B6
Odrowaz PL.....87 A4
Odry CZ.........98 B1
Odrzywół PL....87 A4
Ødsted DK......59 C2
Odžaci SRB.....126 B1
Odžak BIH......125 B4
Oebisfelde D....73 B3
Oederan D......83 B5
Oeding D........71 C3
Oegstgeest NL..70 B1
Oelde D.........81 A4
Oelsnitz D......83 B4
Oer-Erkenschwick D 80 A3
Oerlinghausen D 72 C1
Oettingen D 94 C2
Oetz A 108 B1
Oeventrop D....81 A4
Offanengo I....120 B2
Offenbach D....81 B4
Offenburg D....93 C3
Offida I 136 C2
Offingen D......94 C2
Offranville F....89 A5
Ofte N 53 A4
Ofterschwang D 107 B5
Oggiono I......120 B2
Ogihares E.....163 A4
Ogliastro Cilento I..............132 A1
Ogliastro Marina I..............170 C2
Ogmore-by-Sea UK 39 C3
Ogna N 52 B1
Ogre LV 8 D4
Ogrodzieniec PL..............86 B3
Ogulin HR......123 B4
Ögur IS.........190 A3
Ohanes E 164 B2
Ohey B..........79 B5
Ohlstadt D.....108 B2
Ohrdorf D.......73 B3
Ohrdruf D.......82 B2
Ohrid NMK.....182 B2
Öhringen D.....94 B1
Oia E 140 B2
Oião P..........148 B1
Oiartzun E.....144 A2
Oijärvi FIN 197 D8
Oilgate IRL......30 B2
Oimbra E 148 A2
Oiselay-et-Grachoux F ...105 B4
Oisemont F.....90 B1
Oisterwijk NL ..79 A5
Öja S...........57 C4
Öje S 49 B5
Ojén E..........162 B3
Ojrzeń PL.......77 B5
Ojuelos Altos E 156 B2
Okalewo PL.....77 A4
Okány H........113 C5
Okehampton UK 42 B2
Oklaj HR........138 B2
Øksneshamn N 194 B6
Okoč SK........111 B4
Okoličné SK....99 B3
Okonek PL......68 B1

Okonin PL.......69 B3
Okřisky CZ......97 B3
Oksa PL.........87 B4
Oksbøl DK 59 C1
Oksby DK.......59 C1
Øksfjord N 192 B6
Øksna N 48 B3
Okučani HR 124 B3
Okulovka RUS ...9 C8
Ólafsfjörður IS 191 A7
Ólafsvík IS.....190 C2
ÖLagnö S........57 A4
Olagüe E.......144 B2
Oland N.........53 B4
Olargues F 130 B1
Oława PL........85 B5
Olazagutia E...144 B1
Olbernhau D....83 B5
Ólbia I 178 B3
Olching D.......108 A2
Oldbury UK.....43 A4
Oldcastle IRL....27 C3
Old Deer UK....33 D4
Oldeberkoop NL 70 B3
Oldeboorn NL..70 A2
Olden N 198 D3
Oldenbrok D....71 A5
Oldenburg Niedersachsen D 71 A5
Schleswig-Holstein D 65 B3
Oldenzaal NL...71 B3
Olderdalen N .192 C4
Olderfjord N ..193 B9
Oldersum D.....71 A4
Oldervik N 192 C2
Oldham UK 40 B1
Oldisleben D....82 A3
Oldmeldrum UK 33 D4
Olea E 142 B2
Oleby S.........49 B5
Olechów PL.....87 A5
Oledo P.........155 B3
Oléggio I.......120 B1
Oleiros Coruña E.....140 A2
Coruña E.....140 B1
P 154 B3
Oleksandriya UA 13 C7
Olen B 79 A4
Ølen N..........52 A1
Olenegorsk RUS 3 B13
Olenino RUS.....9 C8
Olesa de Montserrat E. 147 C2
Oleśnica PL.....85 A5
Oleśnice CZ....97 B4
Olešno PL.......86 B2
Olesno PL.......86 B2
Oletta F........180 A2
Olette F........146 B3
Olevsk UA.......13 C7
Olfen D..........80 A3
Ølgod DK........59 C1
Olginate I......120 B2
Ølgod DK........59 C1
Olgrinmore UK 32 C3
Olhão P.........160 B2
Olhava FIN 197 D8
Olhavo P 154 B1
Oliana E 147 B2
Olias del Rey E 151 C4
Oliena I 178 B3
Oliete E 153 B3
Olimbos I......188 D2
Olite E 144 B2
Oliva E 159 C3
Oliva de la Frontera E 155 C4
Oliva de Mérida E 156 B1
Oliva de Plasencia E 149 B3
Olivadi I 175 C2
Olival P.........154 B2
Olivar E 163 B4
Olivares E 161 B3
Olivares de Duero E 142 C2
Olivares de Júcar E 158 B1
Oliveira de Azeméis P 148 B1
Oliveira de Frades P 148 B1

Oliveira do Conde P 148 B2
Oliveira do Douro P 148 A1
Oliveira do Hospital P 148 B2
Olivenza E 155 C3
Olivet F 103 B3
Olivone CH 107 C3
Öljehult S.......63 B3
Olkusz PL.......86 B3
Ollerton UK 40 B2
Ollerup DK......65 A3
Olliergues F ...117 B3
Ölmbrotorp S..56 A1
Ölme S..........55 A4
Olmedilla de Alarcón E....158 B1
Olmedillo de Roa E 143 C3
Olmedo E 150 A3
I..............178 B2
Olmeto F.......180 B1
Opeinde NL.....70 A3
Olmillos de Castro E 149 A3
Olmos de Ojeda E 142 B2
Olney UK........44 A3
Ólobok PL......86 A2
Olocau del Rey E 153 B3
Olofström S....63 B2
Olomouc CZ....98 B1
Olonets RUS 9 B8
Olonne-sur-Mer F 114 B2
Olonzac F......130 B1
Oloron-Ste Marie F 145 A3
Olost E 147 C3
Olot E 147 B3
Olovo BIH......139 A4
Olpe D..........81 A3
Olsberg D......81 A4
Olserud S.......55 A4
Olshammar S ..55 B5
Olshanka UA ...13 D9
Olszanica PL....85 A3
Olsztyn Śląskie PL.....86 B3
Warmińsko-Mazurskie PL..69 B5
Olsztynek PL....77 A5
Olszyna PL......84 A3
Olszyny PL......77 A6
Oltedal N.......52 B2
Olten CH.......106 B2
Olteniţa RO.....17 C7
Olula del Rio E 164 B2
Ølve N..........46 B2
Olvega E 144 C2
Olvera E 162 B2
Olzai I..........178 B3
Omagh UK 27 B3
Omalos GR 185 D4
Omegna I.......119 B5
Omiš HR 138 B2
Omišalj HR.....123 B3
Ommen NL......71 B3
Omodhos CY...181 B1
Omoljica SRB ..127 C2
On B 79 B5
Oña E 143 B3
Onano I 168 A1
O Näsberg S....49 B5
Oñati E 143 A4
Onda E 159 B3
Ondara E 159 C4
Ondarroa E 143 A4
Onesse-et-Laharie F 128 B1
Oneşti RO......17 B7
Onhaye B.......79 B4
Onich UK........34 B2
Onil E 159 C3
Onis E 142 A2
Önnestad S.....61 C4
Onsala S........60 B2
Ontinyent E....159 C3
Ontur E 158 C2
Onzain F........103 B3
Onzonilla E 142 B1
Oostburg NL....79 A3
Oostende B 78 A2
Oosterend NL..70 A2
Oosterhout NL..79 A4
Oosterwolde NL 71 B3
Oosterzele B ...79 B3
Oosthuizen NL..70 B2

Oostkamp B 78 A3
Oostmalle B....79 A4
Oost-Vlieland NL 70 A2
Oostvoorne NL.79 A4
Ootmarsum NL.71 B3
Opalenica PL...75 B5
O Páramo E ...140 B3
Oparany CZ.....96 B2
Opatija HR 123 B3
Opatów Śląskie PL.....86 B2
Świętokrzyskie PL..............87 B5
Wielkopolskie PL..............86 A2
Opatówek PL...86 A2
Opatowiec PL...87 B4
Opava CZ 98 B1
O Pedrouzo E .140 B2
Opeinde NL.....70 A3
Oper Thalkirchdorf D 107 B5
Opglabbeerk B .80 A1
Opicina I 122 B2
O Pino E.......140 B2
Oplotnica SLO 123 A4
Opmeer NL.....70 B1
Opochka RUS ...9 D6
Opočno CZ.....85 B4
Opoczno PL....87 A4
Opole PL........86 B1
Oporów PL.....77 B4
O Porriño E....140 B2
Opovo SRB.....127 B2
Oppach D 84 A2
Oppdal N......198 C6
Oppeby Östergötland S 56 B1
Södermanland S 56 B2
Oppedal N......46 A2
Oppegård N 54 A1
Oppenau D 93 C4
Oppenberg A ..110 B1
Oppenheim D...93 B4
Óppido Lucano I..............172 B1
Óppido Mamertina I..............175 C1
Opponitz A 110 B1
Oppstad N......48 B3
Oprtalj HR 122 B2
Opsaheden S ..49 B5
Opuzen HR 138 B3
Ora CY 181 B2
I..............121 A4
Orada P 155 C3
Oradea RO......16 B4
Oradour-sur-Glane F 115 C5
Oradour-sur-Vayres F 115 C4
Oragonja SLO. 122 B2
Orah BIH 139 C4
Orahova BIH ..138 A3
Orahovica HR .125 B3
Orahovo BIH ..125 C3
Oraison F 132 B1
Orajärvi FIN ..196 C7
Orange F 131 A3
Orani I 178 B3
Oranienbaum D 83 A4
Oranienburg D.74 B2
Oranmore IRL...28 A3
Orašac SRB....127 C2
Orašje BIH 125 B4
Oravská Lesná SK 99 B3
Oravská Polhora SK 99 B3
Oravské Veselé SK 99 B3
Oravsky-Podzámok SK 99 B3
Orba E 159 C3
Ørbæk DK.......59 C3
Orbassano I ...119 B4
Orbe CH 105 C5
Orbec F..........89 A4
Orbetello I.....168 A1
Orbetello Scalo I..............168 A1

Orbigny F..... 103 B3
Ørby DK........59 B3
Örbyhus S.....51 B4
Orce E........ 164 B2
Orcera E..... 164 A2
Orchamps-Vennes
F............. 105 B5
Orches F...... 102 C2
Orchete E..... 159 C3
Orchies F.....78 B3
Orchowo PL....76 B3
Orcières F.... 118 C3
Ordes E....... 140 A2
Ordhead UK... 33 D4
Ordino AND... 146 B2
Ordizia E..... 144 A1
Orduña E..... 143 B4
Ore S.........50 A2
Orea E........ 152 B2
Orebić HR.... 138 C3
Örebro S......56 A1
Öregcsertő H . 112 C3
Öregrund S....51 B5
Orehoved DK ...65 B4
Orellana E.... 156 A2
Orellana de la
Sierra E..... 156 A2
Ören TR...... 188 B2
Örencik TR... 187 C4
Orestiada GR . 186 A1
Organyà E.... 147 B2
Orgaz E....... 157 A4
Orgelet F..... 105 C4
Ørgenvika N...48 B1
Orgères-en-Beauce
F............. 103 A3
Orgibet F..... 145 B4
Orgnac-l'Aven
F............. 131 A3
Orgon F...... 131 B4
Orgósolo I.... 178 B3
Orhaneli TR... 186 C3
Orhangazi TR . 187 B4
Orhei MD 17 B8
Orhomenos
GR.......... 184 A3
Oria E........ 164 B2
Ória I......... 173 B3
Origny-Ste Benoite
F.............91 B3
Orihuela E.... 165 A4
Orihuela del
Tremedal E .. 152 B2
Orikum AL.... 182 C1
Oriola P...... 154 C3
Oriolo I....... 174 A2
Oriovac HR.... 125 B3
Orissaare EST 8 C3
Oristano I.... 179 C2
Őriszentpéter
H............ 111 C3
Ørje N........54 A2
Orjiva E...... 163 B4
Orkanger N .. 198 B6
Örkelljunga S...61 C3
Örkény H..... 112 B3
Orlamünde D...82 B3
Orléans F..... 103 B3
Orlová CZ.....98 B2
Orlovat SRB... 126 B2
Ormea I...... 133 A3
Ormelet N.....54 A1
Ormemyr N...53 A5
Ormilia GR... 183 C5
Ormos GR.... 185 B5
Ormož SLO... 124 A2
Ormskirk UK...38 A4
Ornans F..... 105 B5
Ornäs S.......50 B2
Ørnes N...... 195 D4
Orneta PL.....69 A5
Ørnhøj DK....59 B1
Ornö S........57 A4
Örnsköldsvik
S........... 200 C4
Orolik HR.... 125 B4
Orom SRB.... 126 B1
Oron-la-Ville
CH.......... 106 C1
Oronsko PL....87 A4
Oropa I....... 119 B4
Oropesa
Castellón de la
Plana E 153 B4
Toledo E.... 150 C2
O Rosal E.... 140 C2
Orosei I...... 178 B3
Oroshaza H... 113 C4
Oroslavje HR.. 124 B1
Oroszlány H .. 112 B2

Oroszlo H..... 125 A4
Orotelli I..... 178 B3
Orozko E..... 143 A4
Orphir UK.....33 C3
Orpington UK...45 B4
Orreaga-
Roncesvalles
E............. 144 A2
Orrefors S.....62 B3
Orrviken S... 199 B11
Orsa S.........50 A1
Orsara di Púglia
I............. 171 B3
Orsay F........90 C2
Orscholz D.....92 B2
Orsennes F.... 103 C3
Orserum S.....55 B5
Orsha BY..... 13 A9
Orsières CH... 119 A4
Örsjö S........63 B3
Örslev DK.....65 A4
Örslösa S......55 B3
Orsogna I..... 169 A4
Orsomarso I... 174 B1
Orșova RO 16 C5
Ørsta N....... 198 C3
Ørsted DK.....58 B3
Ørsundsbro S...56 A3
Ortaca TR.... 188 C3
Ortakent TR... 188 B2
Ortaklar TR... 188 B2
Ortaköy TR....23 B8
Orta Nova I... 171 B3
Ortel 168 A2
Ortenburg D...96 C1
Orth A....... 111 A3
Orthez F..... 128 C2
Ortigueira E... 140 A3
Ortilla E...... 145 B3
Ortisei I...... 108 C2
Ortişoara RO.. 126 B3
Ortnevik N.....46 A3
Orton UK......37 B4
Ortona I...... 169 A4
Ortrand D.....84 A1
Orubica HR ... 124 B3
Ørum DK......58 B2
Orune I....... 178 B3
Orusco E 151 B4
Orvalho P.... 155 A3
Orvault F..... 101 B4
Ørvella N.....53 A5
Orvieto I..... 168 A2
Orvínio I..... 169 A2
Oryahovo BG ..17 D5
Orzesze PL....86 B2
Orzinuovi I.... 120 B2
Orzivécchi I... 120 B2
Orzyny PL.....77 A6
Os
Hedmark N ...48 B3
Hedmark N . 199 C8
Osann-Monzel
D............92 B2
Osbruk S......62 A2
Øsby DK......59 C2
Osby S........61 C3
Ošćadnica SK ..98 B2
Oschatz D.....83 A5
Oschersleben
D............73 B4
Ošćhiri I...... 178 B3
Osciłowo PL....77 B5
Osdorf D......64 B3
Osečina SRB... 127 C1
Osečná CZ.....84 B2
Oseja de Sajambre
E............. 142 A1
Osek CZ......84 B1
Osen N....... 199 A7
Osera de Ebro
E............. 153 A3
Osidda I...... 178 B3
Osie PL........69 B3
Osieczna
Pomorskie PL ..68 B3
Wielkopolskie
PL........... 75 C5
Osieczno PL...75 A4
Osiek
Kujawsko-
Pomorskie PL .76 B3
Kujawsko-
Pomorskie PL . 77 A4
Pomorskie PL ..69 B3
Świętokrzyskie
PL............87 B5
Osiek nad Notecią
PL............76 A2
Osielsko PL....76 A3
Osijek HR..... 125 B4
Osilnica SLO . 123 B3
Ósilo I........ 178 B2

Ósimo I....... 136 B2
Osinja BIH.... 125 C3
Osintorf BY....13 A9
Osipaonica
SRB......... 127 C3
Osjaków PL....86 A2
Oskamull UK...34 B1
Oskarshamn S .62 A4
Oskarström S...60 C2
Oslany SK.....98 C2
Oslavany CZ....97 B4
Ošlje HR...... 139 C3
Oslo N........48 C2
Øslos DK......58 A1
Osmancık TR....23 A8
Osmaneli TR .. 187 B4
Ósmo S.......57 B3
Osnabrück D ...71 B5
Ośno Lubuskie
PL............75 B3
Osoblaha CZ...85 B5
Osor HR...... 123 C3
Osorno E..... 142 B2
Øsøyra N......46 A2
Øsøyro N......46 B2
Óspakseyri IS . 190 B4
Os Peares E... 140 B3
Ospedaletti I.. 133 B3
Ospitaletto I.. 120 B3
Oss NL........80 A1
Ossa de Montiel
E............. 158 C1
Ossi I......... 178 B2
Ossjøen N.....47 B5
Óssun F...... 145 A3
Ostanå S......61 C4
Ostanvik S.....50 A2
Ostashkov RUS ..9 D8
Østavall S.... 200 D1
Ostbevern D ...71 B4
Østborg N... 199 A10
Østby N.......49 A4
Osted DK......61 D1
Ostenfeld D....64 B2
Oster UA......13 C9
Osterburg D...73 B4
Osterburken D..94 B1
Osterbybruk S .51 B4
Osterbyhavn
DK...........58 A4
Österbymo S...62 A3
Ostercappeln D 71 B5
Österfärnebo S .51 B3
Osterfeld D....83 A3
Österforse S .. 200 C3
Osterhever D...64 B1
Osterhofen D ..95 C5
Osterholz-
Scharmbeck
D............72 A1
Øster Hornum
DK...........58 B2
Øster Hurup DK 58 B3
Østerild DK....58 A1
Øster Jølby DK .58 B1
Österlövsta S...51 B4
Øster-marie DK .67 A4
Ostermiething
A........... 109 A3
Osterode am Harz
D............82 A2
Ostersiel D....64 B1
Östersund S . 199 B11
Øster Tørslev
DK...........58 B3
Östervåla S....51 B4
Östervallskog
S............54 A2
Ostervrå S.....58 A3
Osterwieck D ..73 C3
Osterzell D... 108 B1
Ostffyasszonyfa
H........... 111 B4
Östfora S.....51 C4
Östhammar S...51 B5
Ostheim F.... 106 A2
Ostheim vor der
Rhön D.......82 B2
Osthofen D....93 B4
Ostiano I..... 120 B3
Ostíglia I..... 121 B4
Ostiz E........ 144 B2
Östmark S.....49 B4
Östnor S......50 A1
Ostojićevo
SRB......... 126 B2
Ostra I........ 136 B2
Östra Amtervik
S............55 A4
Ostrach D.... 107 B4

Östra Husby S...56 B2
Östra Ljungby
S............61 C2
Östra Ryd S....56 B2
Ostrau D......83 A5
Ostrava CZ.....98 B2
Øster Halsen N..53 A6
Østrhauderfehn
D............71 A4
Ostritz D......84 A2
Ostróda PL....69 B4
Ostroh UA.....13 C7
Ostrołęka PL...12 B4
Ostropole PL...68 B1
Ostrorog PL....75 B5
Ostrošovac
BIH......... 124 C1
Ostrov
CZ...........83 B4
RUS...........8 D6
Ostrov nad Oslavou
CZ...........97 B3
Ostrówek PL...86 A2
Ostrowiec PL...68 A1
Ostrowiec-
Świętokrzyski
PL............87 B5
Ostrowite PL...77 A4
Ostrów
Mazowiecka
PL............12 B4
Ostrowo PL... 76 B3
Ostrów
Wielkopolski
PL............86 A1
Ostróżac BIH.. 139 B3
Ostrzeszów PL..86 A1
Ostseebad
Kühlungsborn
D............65 B4
Ostuni I...... 173 B3
Osuna E...... 162 A2
Osvětimany
CZ...........98 B1
Oswestry UK...38 B3
Oświęcim PL...86 B3
Osztopán H... 111 C4
Oteiza E...... 144 B2
Otelec RO..... 126 B2
Oteo E........ 143 A3
Oterbekk N....54 A1
Otero de Herreros
E............. 151 B3
Otero de O Bodas
E............. 141 C4
Othem S......57 C4
Otley UK......40 B2
Otmuchów PL..85 B5
Otočac HR.... 123 C4
Otok
Splitsko-Dalmatinska
HR......... 138 B2
Vukovarsko-Srijemska
HR......... 125 B4
Otoka BIH.... 124 C2
Otranto I..... 173 B4
Otrić HR...... 138 A2
Otricoli I..... 168 A2
Otrokovice CZ .98 B1
Otta N........ 198 D6
Ottana I...... 178 B3
Ottaviano I... 170 C2
Ottenby S.....63 B4
Ottendorf-Okrilla
D............84 A1
Ottenhöfen D ..93 C4
Ottenschlag A .97 C3
Ottensheim A .96 C2
Ottenbach D...93 B3
Otterbäcken S .55 B5
Otterberg D....93 B3
Otterburn UK ..37 A4
Otter Ferry UK .34 B2
Otterndorf D...64 C1
Ottersberg D ...72 A2
Ottersweier D .93 C4
Otterup DK....59 C3
Ottery St Mary
UK...........43 B3
Ottignies B....79 B4
Ottmarsheim
F............ 106 B2
Ottobeuren D . 107 B5
Ottobrunn D ..95 C3
Öttömös H.... 126 A1
Ottone I...... 120 C2
Ottsjö S...... 199 B10
Ottweiler D....92 B3
Otúr E........ 141 A4
Otveşti RO.... 126 B3
Ötvöskónyi H . 124 A3
Otwock PL.....12 B4
Ouanne F.... 104 B2
Ouarville F....90 C1

Oucques F.... 103 B3
Oud-Beijerland
NL...........79 A4
Ouddorp NL...79 A3
Oudemirdum
NL...........70 B2
Oudenaarde B .79 B3
Oudenbosch
NL...........79 A4
Oudenburg B ..78 A3
Oude-Pekela
NL...........71 A4
Oude-Tonge
NL...........79 A4
Oudewater NL .70 B1
Oud Gastel NL .79 A4
Oudon F...... 101 B4
Oue DK........58 B2
Oughterard IRL .28 A2
Ouguela P.... 155 B3
Ouistreham F ..89 A3
Oulainen FIN....3 D9
Oulchy-le-Château
F............91 B3
Oullins F..... 117 B4
Oulmes F..... 114 B3
Oulton UK.....41 C5
Oulton Broad
UK...........41 C5
Oulu FIN.......3 D9
Oulx I........ 119 B3
Oundle UK....40 C3
Ouranopoli
GR.......... 183 C6
Ourém P..... 154 B2
Ourense E.... 140 B3
Ourique P.... 160 B1
Ourol E....... 140 A3
Ouroux-en-Morvan
F............ 104 B2
Ousdale UK ...32 C3
Oust F....... 146 B2
Outakoski
FIN.......... 193 C10
Outeiro P.... 148 B1
Outeiro de Rei
E............. 140 A3
Outes E...... 140 B2
Outokumpu FIN..9 A6
Outreau F.....78 B1
Ouzouer-le-Marché
F............ 103 B3
Ouzouer-sur-Loire
F............ 103 B4
Ouzouer-sur-Trézée
F............ 104 B1
Ovada I...... 133 A4
Ovar P....... 148 B1
Ovelgönne D ..72 A1
Overath D.....80 B3
Overbister UK ..33 B4
Øverbygd N... 194 B9
Overdinkel NL .71 B4
Överhörnäs S ..56 A3
Overhalla N... 199 A8
Over-jerstal DK .59 C2
Overlade DK...58 B2
Överlida S.....60 B2
Overloon NL...80 A1
Overmark FIN...3 E9
Overpelt B....79 A5
Overton UK....38 B4
Øvre Årdal N...47 A4
Övre Rendal
N........... 199 D8
Övre Sirdal N...52 B2
Övre Soppero
S............ 196 A4
Ovruch UA....13 C8
Ovtrup DK.....59 C1
Owińska PL....76 B1
Oxabäck S.....60 B2
Oxberg S......49 A6
Oxelösund S...56 B3
Oxford UK.....44 B2
Oxie S........61 D3
Oxilithos GR... 185 A5
Oxted UK......45 B4
Oyaca TR..... 187 C7
Øye N........47 A5
Øyenkilen N...54 A1
Øyer N........48 A2
Øyeren N......49 B4
Oyfiell N......53 A4

Øygärdslia N...53 B4
Oykel Bridge
UK...........32 D2
Øymark N.....54 A2
Oyonnax F.... 118 A2
Øyslebo N.....52 B3
Øystese N.....46 B3
Oyten D.......72 A2
Øyuvsbu N....52 A3
Ozaeta E...... 143 B4
Ozalj HR...... 123 B4
Ożarów PL.....87 B5
Ożarów Maz
PL............77 B5
Ożbalt SLO ... 110 C2
Ozd H........ 113 A4
Ożd'any SK.....99 C3
Ozieri I....... 178 B3
Ozimek PL.....86 B2
Ozimica BIH... 139 A4
Ozora H...... 112 C2
Ozorków PL....77 C4
Ozzano Monferrato
I............. 119 B5

P

Paakkola FIN. 196 D7
Paal B.........79 A5
Pabianice PL...86 A3
Pacanów PL....87 B5
Paceco I...... 176 B1
Pachino I..... 177 C4
Pačir SRB..... 126 B1
Pack A........ 110 B2
Paços de Ferreira
P............. 148 A1
Pacov CZ......96 B3
Pacsa H...... 111 C4
Pacy-sur-Eure
F............89 A5
Paczków PL....85 B5
Padany RUS....3 E13
Padborg DK....64 B2
Padej SRB.... 126 B2
Paderborn D ...81 A4
Paderne P.... 160 B1
Padiham UK....40 B1
Padina SRB... 126 B2
Padinska Skela
SRB......... 127 C2
Padornelo P.. 148 A1
Pádova I...... 121 B4
Padragkút I... 111 B4
Padrón E...... 140 B2
Padru I....... 178 B3
Padstow UK....42 B2
Padul E....... 163 A4
Padula I...... 172 B1
Paesana I..... 119 C4
Paese I....... 121 B5
Pag HR....... 137 A4
Paganico I.... 135 C4
Pagánica I.... 169 A3
Pagani I...... 170 C2
Paglieta I..... 169 A4
Pagny-sur-Moselle
F............92 C2
Páhi H....... 112 C3
Pahkakumpu
FIN.......... 197 C11
Pahl D....... 108 B2
Paide EST......8 C4
Paignton UK...43 B3
Pailhès F..... 146 A2
Paimboeuf F .. 101 B3
Paimpol F.... 100 A2
Paimpont F... 101 A3
Painswick UK ..43 A4
Painten D.....95 C3
Paisley UK.....34 C3
Pajala S...... 196 B6
Pajares E..... 141 A5
Pajares de los
Oteros E..... 142 B1
Pająreczno PL .75 A5
Paka H....... 111 C4
Pakość PL.....76 B3
Pakoštane HR. 137 B4
Pakrac HR.... 124 B3
Paks H....... 112 C2
Palacios de la Sierra
E............. 143 C3
Palacios de la
Valduerna E.. 141 B5
Palacios del Sil
E............. 141 B4

Palacios de
Sanabria E ... 141 B4
Palaciosrubios
E............. 150 A2
Palafrugell E .. 147 C4
Palagiano I.... 173 B3
Palagonía I... 177 B3
Paláia I....... 135 B3
Palaiokastritsa
GR.......... 182 D1
Palaiseau F 90 C2
Palamas GR .. 182 D4
Palamòs E.... 147 C4
Palanga LT 8 E2
Palanzano I... 134 A3
Palárikovo SK. 112 A2
Palas de Rei E . 140 B3
Palata I....... 170 B2
Palau I....... 178 A3
Palavas-les-Flots
F............. 131 B2
Palazuelos de la
Sierra E..... 143 B3
Palazzo Adriano
I............. 176 B2
Palazzo del Pero
I............. 135 B4
Palazzolo Acréide
I............. 177 B3
Palazzolo sull Oglio
I............. 120 B2
Palazzo San
Gervásio I... 172 B1
Palazzuolo sul
Senio I...... 135 A4
Paldiski EST....8 C4
Pale BIH...... 139 B4
Palekastro
GR.......... 185 D7
Palena I...... 169 B4
Palencia E.... 142 B2
Palenciana E . 163 A3
Paleochora
GR.......... 185 D4
Paléometokho
CY.......... 181 A2
Palermo I..... 176 A2
Paleros GR.... 182 E2
Palestrina I... 169 B2
Pálfa H...... 112 C2
Palfau A...... 110 B1
Palhaça P.... 148 B1
Palheiros da Tocha
P............. 148 B1
Palheiros de
Quiaios P ... 148 B1
Paliaopoli GR . 185 B5
Palić SRB..... 126 A1
Palidoro I..... 168 B2
Palinuro I.... 172 B1
Paliouri GR... 183 D5
Paliseul B.....91 B5
Pallanza I..... 119 B5
Pallares E..... 161 A3
Pallaruelo de
Monegros E . 153 A3
Pallas Green
IRL...........29 B3
Pallerols E.... 146 B2
Palling D...... 109 A3
Palluau F..... 114 B2
Palma P..... 154 C2
Palma Campánia
I............. 170 C2
Palma del Río
E............. 162 A2
Palma de Mallorca
E............. 166 B2
Palma di
Montechiaro
I............. 176 B2
Palmanova I.. 122 B2
Palma Nova E . 166 B2
Palmela P.... 154 C2
Palmerola E.. 147 B3
Palmi I....... 175 C1
Pälmonostora
H........... 113 C3
Palo del Colle
I............. 171 B4
Palojärvi FIN . 192 D7
Palojoensuu
FIN.......... 196 A6
Palomares del
Campo E.... 158 B1
Palomas E.... 156 B1
Palombara Sabina
I............. 168 A2
Palos de la Frontera
E............. 161 B3

Palotaboszok
H............. 125 A4
Palotás H 112 B3
Pals E 147 C4
Pålsboda S..... 56 A1
Paluzza I 109 C4
Pamhagen A . 111 B3
Pamiers F 146 A2
Pamiętowo PL .76 A2
Pampaneira E. 163 B4
Pamparato I . . 133 A3
Pampilhosa
  Aveiro P ... 148 B1
  Coimbra P .. 148 B2
Pampliega E . . 143 B3
Pamplona E... 144 B2
Pampow D.....73 A4
Pamukçu TR . . 186 C2
Pamukkale TR 188 B4
Pamukova TR . 187 B5
Panagyurishte
  BG 17 D6
Pancalieri I.... 119 C4
Pančevo SRB . 127 C2
Pancey F 91 C5
Pancorvo E. . . 143 B3
Pancrudo E . . 152 B2
Pandino I 120 B2
Pandrup DK....58 A2
Panenský-Týnec
  CZ 84 B1
Panes E 142 A2
Panevėžys LT ... 8 E4
Pangbourne
  UK 44 B2
Panissières F . 117 B4
Panki PL 86 B2
Pannes F 103 A4
Panningen NL...80 A1
Pannonhalma
  H........... 111 B4
Pano Lefkara
  CY 181 B2
Pano Panayia
  CY 181 B1
Panormos GR . 185 B6
Panschwitz-Kuckau
  D 84 A2
Pansdorf D.....65 C3
Pantano de Cijara
  E 156 A3
Panticosa E.. 145 B3
Pantín E 140 A2
Pantoja E 151 B4
Pantón E 140 B3
Panxon E..... 140 B2
Páola I 174 B2
Paola M 175 C3
Pápa H 111 B4
Papasídero I .. 174 B1
Pápateszér H . 111 B4
Papenburg D ...71 A4
Paphos CY 181 B1
Pappenheim D .94 C2
Paprotnia PL....77 B5
Parábita I 173 B4
Paracin SRB . . 127 D3
Parád H 113 B4
Parada
  Bragança P . 149 A3
  Viseu P 148 B1
Paradas E 162 A2
Paradela E ... 140 B3
Parades de
  Rubiales E ... 150 A2
Paradinas de San
  Juan E 150 B2
Paradiso di
  Cevadale I ... 108 C1
Paradyż PL......87 A4
Parainen FIN 8 B3
Parakhino
  Paddubye RUS . 9 C8
Parakka S 196 B4
Paralimni CY . 181 A2
Parallo Astros
  GR 184 B3
Paramé F......88 B2
Paramithia
  GR 182 D2
Páramo E 141 A4
Páramo del Sil
  E 141 B4
Parandaça P . 148 A2
Paravadella E . 141 A3
Paray-le-Monial
  F 104 C2
Parceiros P... 154 B2
Parcey F 105 B4
Parchim D 73 A4
Parciaki PL.....77 A6
Parcoul F......86 A2
Pardilla E 151 A4

Pardubice CZ ...97 A3
Paredes
  E 151 B5
  P 148 A1
Paredes de Coura
  P 140 C2
Paredes de Nava
  E 142 B2
Paredes de
  Siguenza E... 151 A5
Pareja E...... 151 B5
Parennes F.... 102 A1
Parenti I 175 B2
Parentis-en-Born
  F 128 B1
Parey D 73 B4
Parfino RUS 9 D7
Parga GR..... 182 D2
Pargny-sur-Saulx
  F 91 C4
Pari-Gagné F.. 117 A4
Parigné-l'Évêque
  F 102 B2
Parikkala FIN ... 9 B6
Paris F 90 C2
Parisot F 129 B4
Parkalompolo
  S 196 B5
Parkano FIN.....8 A3
Parknasilla IRL . 29 C2
Parla E 151 B4
Parlavá E 147 B4
Parma I 120 C3
Parndorf A ... 111 B3
Párnica SK 99 B3
Parnu EST 8 C4
Parolis E 164 A2
Paros GR 185 B6
Parrillas E ... 150 B2
Parsberg D 95 B3
Parstein D 74 B3
Partakko FIN. 193 C11
Partanna I ... 176 B1
Parthenay F .. 102 C1
Partinico I ... 176 B2
Partizani SRB . 127 C2
Partizánske SK ..98 C2
Partney UK.....41 B4
Páryd S........63 B3
Parzymiechy
  PL..........86 A2
Pașcani RO....17 B7
Pasewalk D 74 A2
Pašina Voda
  MNE 139 B5
Påskallavik S . . 62 A4
Paslęk PL......69 A4
Pašman HR. . . 137 B4
Passage East
  IRL 30 B2
Passail A 110 B2
Passais F 88 B3
Passau D 96 C1
Passeguero P. 148 B1
Passignano sul
  Trasimeno I . 135 B5
Passo di Tréia
  I 136 B2
Passopisciaro
  I 177 B4
Passow D......74 A3
Passy F 118 B3
Pastavy BY 13 A7
Pástena I 170 B2
Pastrana E ... 151 B5
Pastrengo I .. 121 B3
Pásztó H 113 B3
Pata SK........98 C1
Patay F 103 A3
Pateley Bridge
  UK 40 A2
Paterek PL.....76 A2
Paterna E 159 B3
Paterna del Campo
  E 161 B3
Paterna del Madera
  E 158 C1
Paterna de Rivera
  E 162 B2
Paternion A .. 109 C4
Paternò I 177 B3
Paternópoli I . 170 C3
Patersdorf D ...95 B4
Paterswolde
  NL 71 A3
Patitiri GR.... 183 D5
Patmos GR... 188 B1
Patna UK......36 A2
Patnow PL.....76 B3
Patovina FIN. 193 C11
Patopirtti
  FIN 197 B12

Patos AL 182 C1
Patra = Patras
  GR 184 A2
Patras = Patra
  GR 184 A2
Patreksfjörður
  IS 190 B2
Patrickswell IRL 29 B3
Patrimonio F.. 180 A2
Patrington UK . .41 B3
Pattada I 178 B3
Pattensen
  Niedersachsen
  D........... 72 A3
Pattensen
  Niedersachsen
  D...........72 B2
Patterdale UK ..36 B4
Patti I 177 A3
Páty H 112 B2
Pau F....... 145 A3
Pauillac F 128 A2
Paularo I 109 C4
Paulhaguet F . 117 B3
Paulhan F 130 B2
Paulilátino I . . 178 B2
Paulström S...62 A3
Paullo I 120 B2
Paulstown IRL . . 30 B1
Pausa D 83 B3
Pauträsk S ... 200 B3
Pavia
  I 120 B2
  P 154 C2
Pavias E 159 B3
Pavilly F 89 A4
Pavilosta LV....8 D2
Pavullo nel
  Frignano I... 135 A3
Pawlowice PL...86 A1
Pawlowice PL....98 B2
Paxi GR 182 D2
Payallar TR ... 189 C6
Payerne CH ... 106 C1
Paymogo E ... 161 B2
Payrac F 129 B4
Pazardzhik
  BG 183 A6
Pazaryeri TR . 187 B4
Pazin HR 122 B2
Pazlcs F 146 B3
Pčelić HR 85 C4
Peal de Becerro
  E 164 B1
Peasmarsh UK . .45 C4
Peć RUS 16 D4
Péccioli I 135 B3
Pécel H 112 B3
Pechao P 160 B2
Pechenga RUS .3 B12
Pechenizhyn
  UA 13 D6
Pecica RO.... 126 A3
Pecincı SRB ... 127 C1
Pecka SRB.... 127 C1
Peckelsheim D . .81 A5
Pečory RUS.....8 D5
Pécs H 125 A4
Pécsvárad H . 125 A4
Peczniew PL.....86 A2
Pedaso I 136 B2
Pedavena I ... 121 A4
Pedérobba I .. 121 B4
Pedersker DK...67 A3
Pedescala I ... 121 B4
Pedrafita E ... 141 B3
Pedrajas de San
  Esteban E . . 150 A3
Pedralba E ... 159 B3
Pedralba de la
  Praderia E ... 141 B4
Pedraza E 151 A4
Pedreguer E . 159 C4
Pedrera E 162 A3
Pedro Bernardo
  E 150 B3
Pedroche E ... 156 B3
Pedrógão P ... 160 A2
Pedrogao P ... 149 B2
Pedrógão Grande
  P 154 B2
Pedrola E 144 C2
Pedro-Martínez
  E 164 B1
Pedro Muñoz
  E 158 B1
Pedrosa del Rey
  E 150 A2
Pedrosa del Río
  Urbel E 143 B3
Pedrosa de
  Tobalina E ... 143 B3

Pedrosillo de los
  Aires E 150 B2
Pedrosillo el Ralo
  E 150 A2
Pędzewo PL....76 A3
Peebles UK.....35 C4
Peel UK 36 B2
Peenemünde D .66 B2
Peer B 79 A5
Pega P 149 B2
Pegalajar E ... 163 A4
Pegau D 83 A4
Peggau A 110 B2
Pegli I 133 A4
Pegnitz D 95 B3
Pego E 159 C3
Pegões-Estação
  P 154 C2
Pegões Velhos
  P 154 C2
Pegów PL......85 A4
Pegswood UK. . .37 A5
Peguera I 166 B2
Pehlivanköy
  TR. 186 A1
Peine D 72 B3
Peisey-Nancroix
  F 118 B3
Peissenberg D 108 B2
Peiting D..... 108 B1
Peitz D 84 A2
Péjo I 121 A3
Pelagićevo
  BIH. 125 C4
Pelahustán E . 150 B3
Pełczyce PL....75 A4
Pelhřimov CZ ..97 B3
Pélissanne F . 131 B4
Pelkosenniemi
  FIN. 197 B10
Pellegrino
  Parmense I . . 120 C2
Pellegrue F ... 128 B3
Pellérd H..... 125 A4
Pellestrina I .. 122 B1
Pellevoisin F . 103 C3
Pellizzano I ... 121 A3
Pello
  FIN. 196 C7
  S 196 C6
Peloche E 156 A2
Pelplin PL 69 B3
Pelussin F 117 B4
Pély H 113 B4
Pembroke UK . .39 C2
Pembroke Dock
  UK 39 C2
Peñacerrada
  E 143 B4
Penacova P . 148 B1
Peña de Cabra
  E 149 B4
Peñafiel E 151 A3
Penafiel P 148 A1
Peñaflor E 162 A2
Peñalba de
  Santiago E . . 141 B4
Peñalsordo E . 156 B2
Penalva do Castelo
  P 148 B2
Penamacôr P . 149 B2
Peñaranda de
  Bracamonte
  E 150 B2
Peñaranda de
  Duero E 143 C3
Peñarroya de
  Tastavins E . 153 B4
Peñarroya-
  Pueblonuevo
  E 156 B2
Peñarrubia E . 141 B3
Penarth UK 39 C3
Peñascosa E . 158 C1
Peñas de San Pedro
  E 158 C2
Peñausende
  E 149 A4
Penc H 112 B3
Pencoed UK....39 C3
Pendalofos
  GR 182 C3
Pendeen UK....42 B1
Pendine UK....39 C2
Pendueles E . 142 A2
Penedono P . 148 B2
Penela P 154 A2
Pénestin F ... 101 B3
Penhas Juntas
  P 149 A2
Peniche P 154 B1
Penicuik UK....35 C4

Penig D 83 B4
Penilhos P ... 160 B2
Peñíscola E .. 153 B4
Penistone UK ...40 B2
Penkridge UK .40 C1
Penkun D......74 A3
Penmarch F .. 100 B1
Pennabilli I .. 135 B5
Penne I 169 A3
Penne-d'Agenais
  F 129 B3
Pennes I 108 C2
Pennyghael UK .34 B1
Peno RUS 9 D8
Penpont UK....36 A3
Penrhyndeudraeth
  UK 38 A3
Penrith UK.....37 B4
Penryn UK.....42 B1
Pentraeth UK . .38 A2
Penybontfawr
  UK 38 B3
Penygroes
  Carmarthenshire
  UK 39 C2
  Gwynedd UK. . 38 A2
Penzance UK...42 B1
Penzberg D .. 108 B2
Penzlin D 74 A2
Pepinster B 80 B1
Peqin AL 182 B1
Pér H 111 B4
Pera Boa P ... 148 B2
Perachora GR . 184 A3
Perafita P 148 A1
Peraleda de la Mata
  E 150 C2
Peraleda del
  Zaucejo E ... 156 B2
Peraleda de San
  Román E 156 A2
Perales de
  Alfambra E . . 152 B2
Perales del Puerto
  E 149 B3
Perales de Tajuña
  E 151 B4
Peralta E 144 B2
Peralta de la Sal
  E 145 C4
Peralva P 160 B2
Peralveche E . 152 B1
Perama GR .. 185 D5
Peranka FIN . 197 D12
Perbál H 112 B2
Perchtoldsdorf
  A 111 A3
Percy F 88 B2
Perdasdefogu
  I 179 C3
Perdiguera E . 145 C3
Peredo P 149 A3
Peregu Mare
  RO 126 A2
Pereiro
  Faro P 160 B2
  Guarda P .. 149 B2
  Santarém P . 154 B2
Pereiro de Aguiar
  E 140 B3
Perelada E ... 147 B4
Perelejos de las
  Truchas E ... 152 B2
Pereña E 149 A3
Pererruela E . 149 A4
Perfugas I 178 B2
Perg A 110 A1
Pérgine Valsugana
  I 121 A4
Pérgola I 136 B1
Pergusa I 177 B3
Periam RO ... 126 A2
Periana E 163 B3
Périers F 88 A2
Périgueux F . 129 A3
Perino I 120 C2
Perjasica HR . 123 B4
Perković HR. . 138 B2
Perlberg D.....73 A4
Perlez SRB.... 126 B2
Përmet AL.... 182 C2
Pernarec CZ....95 B5
Pernek SK......98 C1
Pernes P 154 B2
Pernes-les-
  Fontaines F . 131 A4
Pernik BG 17 D5
Pernink CZ.....83 B4
Pernitz A..... 110 B2
Pernu FIN . 197 C10
Pérols F 131 B2

Péronne F......90 B2
Péronnes B 79 B4
Pero Pinheiro
  P 154 C1
Perorrubio E . 151 A4
Perosa Argentina
  I 119 C4
Perozinho P .. 148 A1
Perpignan F . 146 B3
Perranporth UK 42 B1
Perranzabuloe
  E 42 B1
Perrecy-les-Forges
  F 104 C3
Perrero I 119 C4
Perros-Guirec
  F 100 A2
Persan F 90 B2
Persberg S....55 A5
Persenbeug A. 110 A2
Pershore UK . .44 A1
Persön S 196 D5
Perstorp S....61 C3
Perth UK 35 B4
Pertisau A ... 108 B2
Pertoča SLO. . 111 C3
Pertuis F 131 B4
Peručac SRB. . 127 D1
Perúgia I 136 B1
Perušić HR ... 123 C4
Péruwelz B....79 B3
Pervomaysk
  UA 13 D9
Perwez B 79 B4
Pesadas de Burgos
  E 143 B3
Pesaguero E . 142 A2
Pésaro I 136 B1
Pescantina I . 121 B3
Pescara I 169 A4
Pescasséroli I . 169 B3
Peschici I 171 B4
Peschiera del Garda
  I 121 B3
Péscia I 135 B3
Pescina I 169 A3
Pescocostanzo
  I 169 B4
Pescopagano
  I 172 B1
Pesco Sannita
  I 170 B2
Peshkopi AL . 182 B2
Peshtera BG. . 183 A6
Pesmes F 105 B4
Pesnica SLO. . 110 C2
Peso da Régua
  P 93 C3
Pesquera de Duero
  E 142 C2
Pessac F 128 B2
Pessoux B.....79 B5
Pestovo RUS....9 C9
Petäjäskoski
  FIN. 197 C8
Petalidi GR.. 184 C2
Pétange L ... 92 B1
Petas GR 182 D3
Peteranec HR 124 A2
Peterborough
  UK 41 C3
Peterculter UK 33 D4
Peterhead UK. 33 D5
Peterlee UK . ..37 B5
Petersfield UK .44 B3
Petershagen
  Brandenburg
  D...........74 B2
Petershausen
  D...........95 C3
Peterswell IRL . . 28 A3
Pétervására
  H.......... 113 A4
Petília Policastro
  I 175 B2
Petín E 141 B3
Pětipsy CZ.....83 B5
Petkus D 74 C2
Petlovac HR. . 125 B4
Petlovača SRB 127 C1
Petöfiszállás
  H.......... 113 C3
Petra E 167 B3
Petralia Sottana
  I 177 B3
Petrčane HR . 137 B4
Petrella Tifernina
  I 170 B2
Petrer E 159 C3

Petreto-Bicchisano
  F 180 B1
Petrich BG ... 183 B5
Petritoli I 136 B2
Petrijevci HR . 125 B4
Petrinja HR . . 124 B2
Petrodvorets
  RUS 9 C6
Pétrola E 158 C2
Petronà I 175 B2
Petronell A ... 111 A3
Petroşani RO .. 17 C5
Petrovac SRB . 127 C3
Petrovaradin
  SRB 126 B1
Petrovice
  BIH. 139 A4
  CZ 84 B1
Petrovo RUS . . 69 A5
Petrozavodsk
  RUS 9 B9
Pettenbach A . 109 B5
Pettigo IRL ... 26 B3
Petworth UK . .44 C3
Peuerbach A . . 96 C1
Peuntenansa
  E 142 A2
Peurasuvanto
  FIN. 197 B9
Pevensey Bay
  UK 45 C4
Peveragno I .. 133 A3
Pewsey UK ... 44 B2
Pewsum D.....71 A4
Peyrat-le-Château
  F 116 B1
Peyrehorade
  F 128 C1
Peyriac-Minervois
  F 146 A3
Peyrins F 117 B5
Peyrissac F ... 116 B1
Peyrolles-en-
  Provence F . 132 B1
Peyruis F 132 A1
Pézarches F....90 C2
Pézenas F ... 130 B2
Pezinok SK ... 111 A4
Pezuls F 129 B3
Pfaffenhausen
  D 108 A1
Pfaffenhofen
  Bayern D ... 94 C2
  Bayern D ... 95 C3
Pfaffenhoffen
  F 93 C3
Pfäffikon CH . 107 B3
Pfarrkirchen D .95 C4
Pfeffenhausen
  D 95 C3
Pfetterhouse
  F 106 B2
Pforzheim D ...93 C4
Pfreimd D 95 B4
Pfronten D ... 108 B1
Pfullendorf D . 107 B4
Pfullingen D ...94 C1
Pfunds A 108 C1
Pfungstadt D . .93 B4
Pfyn CH 107 B3
Phalsbourg F ..92 C3
Philippeville B .79 B4
Philippsreut D .96 C1
Philippsthal D .82 B1
Piacenza I 120 B2
Piacenza d'Adige
  I 121 B4
Piádena I 120 B3
Piana F 180 A1
Piana Crixia I . 133 A4
Piana degli
  Albanesi I ... 176 B2
Piana di Monte
  Verna I 170 B2
Piancastagnáio
  I 135 C4
Piandelagotti
  I 134 A3
Pianella
  Abruzzi I . . . 169 A4
  Toscana I ... 135 B4
Pianello Val Tidone
  I 120 C2
Pianoro I 135 A4
Pians A 108 B1
Pias P 160 A2
Piaseczno PL...77 B6
Piasek PL......74 B3
Piaski PL......77 B5
Piastów PL.....77 B5

Piaszczyna PL....68 A2
Piątek PL.......77 B4
Piatra Neamţ
RO.............17 B7
Piazza al Sérchio
I.............134 A3
Piazza Armerina
I.............177 B3
Piazza Brembana
I.............120 B2
Piazze I.......135 C4
Piazzola sul Brenta
I.............121 B4
Picassent E....159 B3
Piccione I.....136 B1
Picerno I......172 B1
Picher D.......73 A4
Pickering UK...40 A3
Pico I.........169 B3
Picón E........157 A3
Picquigny F....90 B2
Piechowice PL..84 B1
Piecnik PL.....75 A5
Piedicavallo I.119 B4
Piedicroce F...180 A2
Piedimonte Etneo
I.............177 B4
Piedimonte Matese
I.............170 B2
Piedimulera I..119 A5
Piedipaterno I.136 C1
Piedrabuena
E.............157 A3
Piedraescrita
E.............156 A3
Piedrafita E...142 A1
Piedrahita E...150 B2
Piedralaves E..150 B3
Piedras Albas
E.............155 B4
Piedras Blancas
E.............141 A5
Piegaro I......135 C5
Piekary Śl. PL..86 B2
Piekoszów PL...87 B4
Pieksämäki FIN..8 A5
Pielenhofen D..95 B3
Pielgrzymka PL.85 A3
Pieniężno PL...69 A5
Pieńsk PL......84 A3
Pienza I.......135 B4
Piera E........147 C2
Pieranie PL....76 B3
Pierowall UK...33 B4
Pierre-Buffière
F.............115 C5
Pierrecourt F..105 B4
Pierre-de-Bresse
F.............105 C4
Pierrefeu-du-Var
F.............132 B2
Pierrefitte-Nestalas
F.............145 B3
Pierrefitte-sur-Aire
F.............92 C1
Pierrefonds F..90 B2
Pierrefontaine-les-
Varans F......105 B5
Pierrefort F...116 C2
Pierrelatte F..131 A3
Pierrepont
Aisne F.......91 B3
Meurthe-et-Moselle
F.............92 B1
Piesendorf A..109 B3
Pieštany SK....98 C1
Pieszkowo PL...69 A5
Pieszyce PL....85 B4
Pietarsaari FIN.3 E8
Pietragalla I..172 B1
Pietra Ligure I.133 A4
Pietralunga I..136 B1
Pietramelara I.170 B2
Pietraperzia I.177 B3
Pietrasanta I..134 B3
Pietravairano
I.............170 B2
Pieve del Cáiro
I.............120 B1
Pieve di Bono
I.............121 B3
Pieve di Cadore
I.............122 A1
Pieve di Cento
I.............121 C4
Pieve di Soligo
I.............121 B5
Pieve di Teco
I.............133 A3
Pievepélago I..134 A3

Pieve Santo
Stefano I.....135 B5
Pieve Torina I..136 B2
Piges GR.......182 D3
Píglio I........169 B3
Pigna I........133 B3
Pignan F.......130 B2
Pignataro
Maggiore I...170 B2
Piittisjärvi FIN 197 C9
Pijnacker NL...70 B1
Pikalevo RUS...9 C9
Piła PL........75 A5
Pilar de la
Horadada E..165 B4
Pilas E........161 B3
Pilastri I......121 C4
Piława Górna
PL...........85 B4
Piławki PL.....69 B4
Pilchowice PL..86 B2
Pilea GR.......183 C5
Pilgrimstad
S............199 C12
Pili
Dodekanisa
GR..........188 C2
Trikala GR...182 D3
Pilica PL......86 B3
Pilis H........112 B3
Piliscaba H....112 B2
Pilisszántó H..112 B2
Pilisvörösvár
H............112 B2
Pilos GR.......184 C2
Pilsting D.....95 C4
Pilszcz PL.....98 A1
Pilterud N.....48 C2
Pilu RO........113 C5
Pina de Ebro
E............153 A3
Piñar E........163 A4
Pınarbaşı TR...186 C1
Pınarhisar TR..186 A2
Pinas F........145 A4
Pincehely H....112 C2
Pineda de la Sierra
E............143 B3
Pineda de Mar
E............147 C3
Pinerella I....135 A5
Pinerolo I.....119 C4
Pineta Grande
I............170 C1
Pineto I.......169 A4
Piney F........91 C4
Pinggau A.....111 B3
Pinhal Novo P.154 C2
Pinhão P.......148 A2
Pinheiro
Aveiro P.....148 A1
Aveiro P.....148 B1
Pinheiro Grande
P............154 B2
Pinhel P.......149 B2
Pinhoe UK.....43 B3
Pinilla E......158 C2
Pinilla de Toro
E............150 A2
Pinkafeld A....111 B3
Pinneberg D...72 A2
Pinnow D.......74 C3
Pino F.........180 A2
Pino del Rio E.142 B2
Pino de Val E..140 B2
Pinofranqueado
E............149 B3
Pinols F.......117 B3
Piñor E........140 B2
Pinoso E.......159 C2
Pinos del Valle
E............163 B4
Pinoso E.......159 C2
Pinos Puente
E............163 A4
Pinsk BY......13 B7
Pintamo FIN...197 D10
Pinto E........151 B4
Pinzano al
Tagliamento
I............122 A1
Pinzio P.......149 B2
Pinzolo I......121 A3
Pióbbico I.....136 B1
Piombino I.....134 C3
Pionki PL......87 A5
Pionsat F......116 A2
Pióraco I......136 B1
Piornal E......150 B2
Piotrkowice PL..87 B4
Piotrków-Kujawski
PL...........76 B3

Piotrków
Trybunalski
PL...........86 A3
Piotrowo PL....75 B5
Piove di Sacco
I............121 B5
Piovene I......121 B4
Piperskärr S...62 A4
Pipriac F......101 B4
Piraeus = Piraeus
Piran SLO......122 B2
Pireas = Piraeus
GR..........185 B4
Piré-sur-Seiche
F............101 A4
Pirgi GR.......185 A6
Pirgos
Ilia GR......184 B2
Kriti GR.....185 D6
Piriac-sur-Mer
F............101 B3
Piringsdorf A..111 B3
Pirmasens D...93 B3
Pirna D........84 B1
Pirnmill UK....34 C2
Pirot SRB......16 D5
Pirovac HR.....137 B4
Pirttikoski FIN.197 D9
Pirttivuopio S.196 B2
Pisa I.........134 B3
Pisany F.......114 C3
Pisarovina HR.124 B1
Pischelsdorf in der
Steiermark
A............110 B2
Pişchia RO.....126 B3
Pisciotta I....172 B1
Písek CZ.......96 B2
Pisogne I......120 B3
Pissos F.......128 B2
Pissouri CY....181 B1
Pisticci I......174 A2
Pistóia I......135 B3
Piteå S........196 D4
Piteşti RO.....17 C6
Pithiviers F...103 A4
Pitigliano I...168 A1
Pitkyaranta RUS.9 B7
Pitlochry UK...35 B4
Pitomača HR....124 B3
Pitres E.......163 B4
Pittentrail UK.32 D2
Pitvaros H.....126 A2
Pivka SLO......123 B3
Pivnice SRB....126 B1
Piwniczna PL...99 B4
Pizarra E......163 B3
Pizzano I......121 A3
Pizzighettone
I............120 B2
Pizzo I........175 C2
Pízzoli I......169 A3
Pizzolungo I...176 A1
Pjätteryd S....61 C4
Plabennec F....100 A1
Placencia E....143 A4
Plaffeien CH...106 C2
Plaisance
Gers F.......128 C3
Haute-Garonne
F............129 C4
Plaka GR.......183 D7
Plan E.........145 B4
Planá CZ.......95 B4
Planánad Lužnicí
CZ...........96 B2
Plaňany CZ.....96 A3
Planchez F.....104 B3
Plancoët F.....101 A3
Plancy-l'Abbaye
F............91 C3
Plan-de-Baix
F............118 C2
Plandište SRB.126 B3
Plan-d'Orgon
F............131 B3
Plánice CZ.....96 B1
Planina
SLO.........123 A4
SLO.........123 B3
Plankenfels D..95 B3
Plasencia E....149 B4
Plasenzuela E.156 A1
Plaški HR......123 B4
Plassen
Buskerud N..47 B4
Hedmark N...49 A4
Plášt'ovce SK..112 A3
Plasy CZ.......96 B1
Platamona Lido
I............178 B2
Platania I.....175 B2

Platanos GR....185 D4
Platí I.........175 C2
Platičevo SRB..127 C1
Platja d'Aro E.147 C4
Plattling D....95 C4
Plau D.........73 A5
Plaue
Brandenburg
D...........73 B5
Thüringen D..82 B2
Plauen D.......83 B4
Plavecký Mikuláš
SK...........98 C1
Plavinas LV....8 D4
Plavna SRB.....125 B5
Plavnica SK....99 B4
Plavno HR......138 A2
Pléaux F.......116 B2
Pleine-Fougères
F............88 B2
Pleinfeld D....94 B2
Pleinting D....95 C5
Plélan-le-Grand
F............101 B3
Plémet F.......101 A3
Pléneuf-Val-André
F............101 A3
Plentzia E.....143 A4
Plérin F.......101 A3
Plešivec SK....99 C4
Plessa D.......83 A5
Plessé F.......101 B4
Plestin-les-Grèves
F............100 A2
Pleszew PL.....76 C2
Pleternica HR.125 B3
Plettenberg D.81 A3
Pleubian F.....100 A2
Pleumartin F..115 B4
Pleumeur-Bodou
F............100 A2
Pleurs F.......91 C3
Pleven BG......17 D6
Plevnik-Drienové
SK...........98 B2
Pleyben F......100 A2
Pleyber-Christ
F............100 A2
Pliego E.......165 B3
Pliešovce SK...99 C3
Plitvička Jezera
HR...........123 C4
Plitvički Ljeskovac
HR...........123 C4
Ploaghe I......178 B2
Ploče HR.......138 B3
Plochingen D..94 C1
Płock PL.......77 B4
Ploemeur F....100 B2
Ploërmel F....101 B3
Ploeuc-sur-Lie
F............101 A3
Plogastel St
Germain F...100 B1
Plogoff F......100 A1
Ploiești RO....17 C7
Plomari GR.....186 D1
Plombières-les-
Bains F......105 B5
Plomin HR......123 B3
Plön D.........65 B3
Plonéour-Lanvern
F............100 B1
Płonia PL......74 A3
Płoniawy PL....77 B6
Płońsk PL......77 B5
Płoskinia PL...69 A4
Plössberg D....95 B4
Płoty PL.......75 A4
Plouagat F....100 A2
Plouaret F....100 A2
Plouarzel F....100 A1
Plouay F.......100 B2
Ploubalay F...101 A3
Ploubazlanec
F............100 A2
Ploudalmézeau
F............100 A1
Ploudiry F.....100 A1
Plouescat F....100 A1
Plouézec F.....100 A2
Plougasnou F..100 A2
Plougastel-Daoulas
F............100 A1
Plougonven F..100 A2
Plougonver F..100 A2
Plougrescant
F............100 A2
Plouguenast
F............101 A3
Plouguerneau
F............100 A1
Plouha F.......100 A3

Plouhinec F....100 A1
Plouigneau F..100 A2
Ploumanac'h F.100 A2
Plounévez-Quintin
F............100 A2
Plouray F......100 A2
Plouzévédé F..100 A1
Plovdiv BG.....183 A6
Plozévet F.....100 B1
Plumbridge UK.27 B3
Pluméliau F...100 B3
Plumlov CZ.....97 B5
Plungė LT......8 E2
Pluty PL.......69 A5
Pluvigner F...100 B3
Plužine
BIH..........139 B4
MNE.........139 B4
Pluznica PL....76 A3
Plymouth UK...42 B2
Plymstock UK..42 B2
Płytnica PL....68 B1
Plyusa RUS.....9 C6
Plzeň CZ.......96 B1
Pniewy PL......75 B5
Pobes E........143 B4
Pobiedziska PL.76 B2
Pobierowo PL..67 B3
Pobla de Segur
E............145 B4
Pobla-Tornesa
E............153 B4
Pobra de Trives
E............141 B3
Pobra do Brollón
E............141 B3
Pobra do
Caramiñal E.140 B2
Pobudje BIH...139 A5
Počátky CZ.....97 B3
Poceirão P.....154 C2
Pöchlarn A.....110 A2
Pociecha PL....87 A4
Pockau D.......83 B5
Pocking D......96 C1
Pocklington UK.40 B3
Poćkuny PL....69 A5
Pocola RO......16 B4
Poćmo-Gradec
SLO.........123 A4
Podbořany CZ..83 B5
Podbrdo SLO...122 A2
Podčetrtek
SLO.........123 A4
Poddębice PL..76 C3
Poděbrady CZ..84 B3
Podence P......148 A2
Podensac F....128 B2
Podenzano I...120 C2
Podersdorf am See
A............111 B3
Podgaje PL.....68 B1
Podgora HR.....138 B3
Podgóra PL.....87 A5
Podgorač HR...125 B4
Podgorica MNE.16 D3
Podgorje SLO..123 B3
Podgrad SLO...123 B3
Podhájska SK..112 A2
Podkova BG....183 B7
Podlapača HR..123 C4
Podlejki PL....69 B5
Podlužany SK..98 C2
Podnovlje BIH.125 C4
Podolie SK.....98 C1
Podolínec SK..99 B4
Podolsk RUS...9 E10
Podporozhy RUS.9 B9
Podromanija
BIH..........139 B4
Podturen HR...111 C3
Podvin CZ......97 C4
Podwilk PL.....99 B3
Poetto I.......179 C3
Poffabro I.....122 A1
Pöggstall A....97 C3
Pogny F........91 C4
Pogorzela PL..85 A5
Pogorzelice PL.68 A2

Pogradec AL...182 C2
Pogrodzie PL..69 A4
Pohorelá SK....99 C4
Pohořelice CZ..97 C4
Pohronská Polhora
SK...........99 C3
Poiares P......148 B1
Poio E.........140 B2
Poirino I......119 C4
Poisson F......117 A4
Poissons F.....91 C5
Poissy F.......90 C2
Poitiers F.....115 B4
Poix-de-Picardie
F............90 B1
Poix-Terron F..91 B4
Pokka FIN.....197 A8
Pokój PL.......86 B1
Pokupsko HR...124 B1
Pol E..........141 A3
Pola RUS.......9 D7
Pol a Charra UK.31 B1
Pola de Allande
E............141 A4
Pola de Laviana
E............142 A1
Pola de Lena
E............141 A5
Pola de Siero
E............142 A1
Pola de Somiedo
E............141 A4
Polaincourt-et-
Clairefontaine
F............105 B5
Połajewo PL....75 B5
Polán E........151 C3
Polanica-Zdrój
PL...........85 B4
Połaniec PL....87 B5
Polanów PL.....68 A1
Polatı TR......187 C7
Polatsk BY.....13 A8
Polch D........80 B3
Polcirckeln S..196 C4
Pólczno PL.....68 A2
Połczyn-Zdrój
PL...........67 C5
Polegate UK...45 C4
Poleñino E.....145 C3
Polesella I....121 C4
Polessk RUS...12 A4
Polgár H.......113 B5
Polgárdi H.....112 B2
Polhov Gradec
SLO.........123 A3
Police F.......74 A3
Police nad Metují
CZ...........85 B4
Polichnitos
GR..........186 C1
Polička CZ.....97 B4
Poličnik HR...137 A4
Policoro I.....174 A2
Policzna PL....87 A5
Poligiros GR..183 C5
Polignano a Mare
I............173 B3
Poligny F.....105 C4
Polis CY.......181 A1
Polistena I....175 C2
Polizzi Generosa
I............176 B3
Poljana SRB...127 C3
Poljanak HR...123 C4
Poljčane SLO..123 A4
Polje BIH......125 C3
Polkowice PL..85 A4
Pöllau A.......110 B2
Pollença E.....167 B3
Pollenfeld D...95 C3
Pollfoss N.....198 D4
Póllica I......170 C3
Polminhac F...116 C2
Polná CZ.......97 B3
Polná RUS......9 C6
Polne PL.......75 A5
Polomka SK....99 C3
Polonne UA....13 C7
Polperro UK...42 B2
Polruan UK.....42 B2
Pöls A.........110 B1
Polska Cerekiew
PL...........86 B2

Polyarnyye Zori
RUS..........3 C13
Polzela SLO....123 A4
Pomarance I...135 B3
Pomarez F.....128 C2
Pomárico I....172 B2
Pomáz H........112 B3
Pombal P.......154 B2
Pomeroy UK....27 B4
Pomézia I......168 B2
Pommard F.....105 B3
Pommelsbrunn
D............95 B3
Pomonte I.....134 C3
Pomorie BG....17 D7
Pomos CY......181 A1
Pompei I.......170 C2
Pompey F.......92 C2
Pomposa I.....122 C1
Poncin F.......118 A2
Pondorf D......95 C3
Ponferrada E..141 B4
Poniec PL......85 A4
Ponikva SLO...123 A4
Poniky SK......99 C3
Pons F.........114 C3
Ponsacco I....134 B3
Pont I.........119 B4
Pont-a-Celles
B............79 B4
Pontacq F.....145 A3
Pontailler-sur-
Saône F......105 B4
Pont-a-Marcq F.78 B3
Pont-à-Mousson
F............92 C2
Pontão P.......154 B2
Pontardawe UK 39 C3
Pontarddulais
UK...........39 C2
Pontarion F...116 B1
Pontarlier F..105 C5
Pontassieve I.135 B4
Pontaubault F.88 B2
Pont-Audemer
F............89 A4
Pontaumur F...116 B2
Pont-Authou F.100 B3
Pont-Aven F...100 B2
Pont Canavese
I............119 B4
Pontcharra F..118 B3
Pontcharra-sur-
Turdine F....117 B4
Pontchâteau
F............101 B3
Pont-Croix F..100 A1
Pont-d'Ain F..118 A2
Pont-de-Beauvoisin
F............118 B2
Pont-de-Buis-lès-
Quimerch F..100 A1
Pont-de-Chéruy
F............118 B2
Pont de Dore
F............117 C4
Pont-de-Labeaume
F............117 C4
Pont-de-l'Arche
F............89 A5
Pont de Molins
E............147 B3
Pont-de-Roide
F............106 B1
Pont-de-Salars
F............130 A1
Pont-d'Espagne
F............145 B3
Pont de Suert
E............145 B4
Ponte a Moriano
I............134 B3
Ponte Arche I.121 A3
Pontearenas E.140 B2
Pontebba I....109 C4
Ponte Cáffaro
I............121 B3
Pontecagnano
I............170 C2
Ponte-Caldelas
E............140 B2
Pontecesures
E............140 B2
Pontecorvo I..169 B3

Ponte da Barca
P. 148 A1
Pontedássio I. . 133 B4
Pontedécimo
I. 131 B4
Ponte de Lima
P. 148 A1
Ponte dell'Ólio
I. 120 C2
Pontedera I. . . 134 B3
Ponte de Sor
P. 154 B2
Pontedeume
E. 140 A2
Ponte di Barbarano
I. 121 B4
Ponte di Legno
I. 121 A3
Ponte di Nava
I. 133 A3
Ponte di Piave
I. 122 B1
Ponte Felcino
I. 136 B1
Pontefract UK. . . 40 B2
Ponte Gardena
I. 108 C2
Ponteginori I. . 135 B3
Pontelagoscuro
I. 121 C4
Ponteland UK. . 37 A5
Pontelandolfo
I. 170 B2
Ponte-Leccia
F. 180 A2
Pontelongo I. . 121 B5
Ponte nelle Alpi
I. 122 A1
Pont-en-Royans
F. 118 B2
Pontenure I. . . 120 C2
Pontenx-les-Forges
F. 128 B2
Ponterwyd UK . 39 B3
Ponte San Giovanni
I. 136 B1
Ponte San Pietro
I. 120 B2
Pontevedra E . 140 B2
Pontevico I. . . 120 B3
Pont Farcy F. . . 88 B2
Pontfaverger-
Moronvillers
F. 91 B4
Pontgibaud F . 116 B2
Ponticino I. . . 135 B4
Pontigny F. . . . 104 B2
Pontijou F 103 B3
Pontínia I. . . . 169 B3
Pontinvrea I. . 133 A4
Pontivy F 100 A3
Pont-l'Abbé F . 100 B1
Pont-l'Évêque
F. 89 A4
Pontlevoy F. . . 103 B3
Pontoise F 90 B2
Pontones E . . . 164 A2
Pontonx-sur-
l'Abour F. . . . 128 C2
Pontoon IRL . . . 26 C1
Pontorson F. . . 88 B2
Pontrémoli I. . 134 A2
Pont-Remy F. . . 90 A1
Pontresina CH 107 C4
Pontrhydfendigaid
UK 39 B3
Pontrieux F . . . 100 A2
Ponts E 147 C2
Ponts-aux-Dames
F. 90 C2
Pont Scorff F. . . 100 B2
Pöntsö FIN . . . 196 B7
Ponza I. 169 C2
Poo E 142 A2
Poole UK. 43 B5
Poolewe UK. . . 31 B3
Poperinge B . . 78 B2

Pópoli I 169 A3
Popovac SRB. . 127 D3
Popovača HR . . 124 B2
Popow PL. 77 B4
Poppel B. 79 A5
Poppenhausen
Bayern D 82 B2
Hessen D 82 B1
Poppi I. 135 B4
Poprad SK. 99 B4
Popučke SRB. . 127 C1
Pópulo P. 148 A2
Populónia I. . . 134 C3
Pörböly H. . . . 125 A4
Porcuna E. . . . 163 A3
Pordenone I. . 122 B1
Pordic F. 100 A3
Poręba PL. 86 B3
Poreč HR. 122 B2
Pori FIN 8 B2
Porjus S. 196 C2
Porkhov RUS. . . . 9 D6
Porlezza I. . . . 120 B2
Porlock UK. 43 A3
Pörnbach D . . . 95 C3
Pornic F. 101 B3
Pornichet F . . . 101 B3
Porodin SRB . . 127 C3
Poronin PL. . . . 99 B3
Poros
Attiki GR. 185 B4
Kefalonia GR. . 184 A1
Poroszló H . . . 113 B4
Porozina HR . . 123 B3
Porquerolles
F. 132 C2
Porrentruy CH 106 B2
Porreres E. . . . 167 B3
Porretta Terme
I. 135 A3
Porsgrunn N. . . 53 A5
Porspoder F . . 100 A1
Port-a-Binson
F. 91 B3
Portacloy IRL. . . 26 B1
Portadown UK. 27 B4
Portaferry UK. . 27 B5
Portaje E. 155 B4
Portalegre P . . 155 B3
Portarlington
IRL 30 A1
Port Askaig UK. 34 C1
Portavadie UK. 34 C2
Portavogie UK. 27 B5
Portbail F. 88 A2
Port Bannatyne
UK 34 C2
Portbou E. . . . 146 B4
Port-Camargue
F. 131 B3
Port Charlotte
UK 34 C1
Port d'Andratx
E. 166 B2
Port-de-Bouc
F. 131 B3
Port-de-Lanne
F. 128 C1
Port de Pollença
E. 167 B3
Port-des-Barques
F. 114 C2
Port de Sóller
E. 166 B2
Portegrandi I . 122 B1
Portel P. 155 C3
Portela P. 148 B1
Port Ellen UK. . 34 C1
Portelo P. 141 C4
Portemouro E . 140 B2
Port-en-Bessin
F. 88 A3
Port'Ercole I . . 168 A1
Port Erin UK. . . 36 B2
Portes-lès-Valence
F. 117 C4
Portets F. 128 B2
Port Eynon UK . 39 C2
Portezuelo E . . 155 B4
Port Glasgow
UK 34 C3
Portglenone
UK 27 B4
Porthcawl UK . . 39 C3
Port Henderson
UK 31 B3
Porthleven UK . 42 B1
Porthmadog
UK 38 B2
Porticcio F . . . 180 B1
Portici I. 170 C2
Portico di Romagna
I. 135 A4

Portilla de la Reina
E. 142 A2
Portillo E. 150 A3
Portimao P. . . 160 B1
Portinatx E. . . 166 B1
Portinho da
Arrabida P . . 154 C1
Port Isaac UK. . . 42 B2
Portishead UK . 43 A4
Port-Joinville
F. 114 B1
Portknockie
UK 33 D4
Port-la-Nouvelle
F. 130 B2
Portlaoise IRL. . 30 A1
Portlethen UK . 33 D4
Port Logan UK . 36 B2
Port Louis F. . . 100 B2
Portmagne IRL. 29 C1
Portmahomack
UK 32 D3
Portman E. . . . 165 B4
Port Manech F 100 B2
Portnacroish
UK 34 B2
Portnahaven
UK 34 C1
Port Nan Giuran
UK 31 A2
Port-Navalo F. . 100 B3
Port Nis UK. . . . 31 A2
Porto
F. 180 A1
P. 148 A1
Porto-Alto P . . 154 C2
Porto Azzurro
I. 134 C3
Portocannone
I. 170 B3
Porto Cerésio
I. 120 B1
Porto Cervo I. . 178 A3
Porto Cesáreo
I. 173 B3
Porto Colom E 167 B3
Porto Covo P. . 160 B1
Porto Cristo E . 167 B3
Porto d'Áscoli
I. 136 C2
Porto de Lagos
P. 160 B1
Porto de Mos
P. 154 B2
Porto de Rei P. 154 C2
Porto do Son
E. 140 B2
Porto Empédocle
I. 176 B2
Portoferráio I. . 134 C3
Portofino I. . . . 134 A2
Porto Garibaldi
I. 122 C1
Portogruaro I. 122 B1
Portokhelion
GR 184 B4
Portomaggiore
I. 121 C4
Portomarin E . 140 B3
Porton UK. 44 B2
Portonovo E . . 140 B2
Portopalo di Capo
Passero I 177 C4
Porto Petro E . 167 B3
Porto Pino I . . 179 D2
Porto Potenza
Picena I 136 B2
Portør N 53 B5
Porto Recanati
I. 136 B2
Porto San Giórgio
I. 136 B2
Porto Sant'Elpídio
I. 136 B2
Porto Santo
Stéfano I. . . . 168 A1
Portoscuso I . . 179 C2
Porto Tolle I. . . 122 C1
Porto Tórres I . 178 B2
Porto-Vecchio
F. 180 B2
Portovénere I . 134 A2
Portpatrick UK . 36 B1
Portreath UK. . . 42 B1
Portree UK. 31 B2
Portroe IRL. . . . 28 B3
Portrush UK. . . . 27 A4
Port St Mary UK 36 B2
Portsall F. 100 A1
Portsmouth UK 44 C2
Portsoy UK. . . . 33 D4
Port-Ste Marie
F. 129 B3

Portstewart UK .27 A4
Port-St-Louis-du-
Rhône F. 131 B3
Port-sur-Saône
F. 105 B5
Port Talbot UK . .39 C3
Portugalete E. 143 A4
Portumna IRL . . 28 A3
Port-Vendres
F. 146 B4
Port William
UK 36 B2
Porvoo FIN. 8 B4
Porzuna E. . . . 157 A3
Posada
Oviedo E. . . . 141 A5
Oviedo E. . . . 142 A2
I. 178 B3
Posada de Valdeón
E. 142 A2
Posadas E. . . . 162 A2
Poschiavo CH . 120 A3
Posedarje HR . 137 A4
Posio FIN. 197 C11
Positano I. . . . 170 C2
Possagno I. . . . 121 B4
Posseck D. 83 B4
Possesse F 91 C4
Pössneck D . . . 83 B3
Posta I. 169 A3
Postal I. 108 C2
Posta Piana I. . 172 A1
Postbauer-Heng
D. 95 B3
Posterholt NL. . 80 A2
Postioma I. . . . 121 B5
Postira HR 138 B2
Postojna SLO . 123 B3
Postoloprty CZ .84 B1
Postomino PL. . 68 A1
Posušje BIH. . . 138 B3
Potamos
Attiki GR. 184 C3
Attiki GR. 184 D4
Potegowo PL. . .68 A2
Potenza I. 172 B1
Potenza Picena
I. 136 B2
Potes E. 142 A2
Potigny F. 89 B3
Potočari BIH . . 127 C1
Potoci
BIH. 138 A2
BIH. 139 B3
Potony H. 125 B3
Potries E. 159 C3
Potsdam D. 74 B2
Potštát CZ. 98 B1
Pottenbrunn
A. 110 A2
Pottendorf A. . 111 B3
Pottenstein
A. 111 B3
D. 95 B3
Potters Bar UK . 44 B3
Pöttmes D 94 C3
Pöttsching A . . 111 B3
Potworów PL . . 87 A4
Pouancé F . . . 101 B4
Pougues-les-Eaux
F. 104 B2
Pouilly-en-Auxois
F. 104 B3
Pouilly-sous
Charlieu F. . . 117 A4
Pouilly-sur-Loire
F. 104 B1
Poujol-sur-Orb
F. 130 B2
Poullaouen F . 100 A2
Poulton-le-Fylde
UK 38 A4
Poundstock UK .42 B2
Pourcy F 91 B3
Pourrain F . . . 104 B2
Poussu FIN . . 197 D12
Pouyastruc F . 145 A4
Pouy-de-Touges
F. 146 A2
Pouzauges F . . 114 B3
Pova de Santa Iria
P. 154 C1
Póvoa
Beja P. 161 A2
Santarém P . . 154 B2
Póvoa de Lanhoso
P. 148 A1

Póvoa de Varzim
P. 148 A1
Póvoa e Meadas
P. 155 B3
Powidz PL. 76 B2
Poyales del Hoyo
E. 150 B2
Poynton UK. . . . 40 B1
Poyntz Pass
UK 27 B4
Poysdorf A. 97 C4
Poza de la Sal
E. 143 B3
Pozaldez E. . . . 150 A3
Pozán de Vero
E. 145 B4
Pozanti TR 23 C8
Požarevac
SRB 127 C3
Požega
HR 125 B3
SRB 127 D2
Poznań PL. 76 B1
Pozo Alcón E. . 164 B2
Pozoantiguo
E. 150 A2
Pozoblanco E . 156 B3
Pozo Cañada
E. 158 C2
Pozo de
Guadalajara
E. 151 B4
Pozo de la Serna
E. 157 B4
Pozohondo E . 158 C2
Pozondón E. . . 152 B2
Pózrzadło Wielkie
PL. 75 A4
Pozuel del Campo
E. 152 B2
Pozuelo de Alarcón
E. 151 B4
Pozuelo de
Calatrava E . 157 B4
Pozuelo del
Páramo E . . . 142 B1
Pozuelo de Zarzón
E. 149 B3
Pozzallo I. 177 C3
Pozzomaggiore
I. 178 B2
Pozzo San Nicola
I. 178 B2
Pozzuoli I. 170 C2
Pozzuolo I. . . . 135 B4
Prača BIH. 139 B4
Prachatice CZ. . 96 B1
Prada E. 141 B3
Pradelle F. 118 C2
Pradelles F. . . . 117 C3
Prades
E. 147 C1
F. 146 B3
Pradła PL. 86 B3
Prado
E. 142 A1
P. 148 A1
Prado del Rey
E. 162 B2
Pradoluengo
E. 143 B3
Pragelato I. . . . 119 B3
Pragersko
SLO 123 A4
Prägraten A. . . 109 B3
Prague = Praha
CZ. 84 B2
Praha = Prague
CZ. 84 B2
Prahecq F 115 B3
Praia E. 154 B1
Práia a Mare I . 174 B1
Praia da Rocha
P. 160 B1
Praia da Viera
P. 154 B2
Praia de Mira
P. 148 B1
Praiano I. 170 C2
Pralboino I. . . 120 B3
Pralognan-la-
Vanoise F . . . 118 B3
Pramanda GR . 182 D3
Pranjani SRB . . 127 C2
Prapatnica HR 138 B2
Præstø DK. 65 A5
Pratau D 83 A4

Prat de Compte
E. 153 B3
Pratdip E. 147 C1
Pratella I 170 B2
Prato I. 135 B4
Prátola Peligna
I. 169 A3
Pratola Serra I. 170 C2
Prats-de-Mollo-la-
Preste F 146 B3
Prauthoy F. . . . 105 B4
Pravia E. 141 A4
Praxmar A 108 B2
Prayssac F 129 B4
Prazzo I. 132 A3
Prebold SLO . . 123 A4
Préchac F 128 B2
Précy-sur-Thil
F. 104 B3
Predáppio I . . . 135 A4
Predazzo I 121 A4
Předin CZ. 97 B3
Preding A. 110 C2
Predjame SLO. 123 B3
Preditz A 109 B4
Predmeja SLO. 122 B2
Predoi I. 108 B3
Pré-en-Pail F. . . 89 B3
Prees UK. 38 B4
Preetz D 64 B3
Préfailles F . . . 101 B3
Pregarten A . . . 96 C2
Pregrada HR . . 123 A4
Preignan F . . . 129 C3
Preiļi LV. 8 D5
Preitenegg A . 110 C1
Prekaja BIH . . . 138 A2
Preko HR. 137 A4
Preljina SRB. . . 127 D2
Prelog HR 124 A2
Prelošćica HR . 124 B2
Přelouč CZ. 97 A3
Prem SLO 123 B3
Premantura
HR 122 C2
Prémery F 104 B2
Prémia I. 119 A5
Premià de Mar
E. 147 C3
Premnitz D 73 B5
Prémont F. 91 A3
Prenzlau D. 74 A2
Preodac BIH. . . 138 A2
Přerov CZ. 98 B1
Prerow D 66 B1
Presencio E . . . 143 B3
Presicce I. 173 C4
Presly F. 103 B4
Prešov SK. 12 D4
Pressac F. 115 B4
Pressath D. 95 B3
Pressbaum A. . 111 A3
Prestatyn UK. . . 38 A3
Prestebakke N . 54 B2
Presteigne UK . 39 B3
Přeštice CZ. . . . 96 B1
Preston
Lancashire
UK 38 A4
Scottish Borders
UK 35 C5
Prestonpans
UK 35 C5
Prestwich UK. . 40 B1
Prestwick UK. . 36 A2
Prettin D. 83 A4
Pretoro I. 169 A4
Pretzchendorf
D. 83 B5
Pretzier D. 73 B4
Pretzsch D 83 A4
Preuilly-sur-Claise
F. 115 B4
Prevalje SLO . . 110 C1
Prevenchères
F. 131 A2
Préveranges
F. 116 A2
Preveza GR. . . . 182 E2
Prevršac HR . . . 124 B2
Prezid HR 123 B3
Priaranza del
Bierzo E. . . . 141 B4
Priay F 118 A2
Pribeta SK 112 B2
Priboj
BIH. 125 C4
SRB 16 D3
Přibor CZ. 98 B2
Příbram CZ. . . . 96 B2
Pribylina SK . . . 99 B3
Přibyslav CZ. . . 97 B3
Pridjel BIH. . . . 125 C4

Priego E. 152 B1
Priego de Córdoba
E. 163 A3
Priekule LV. 8 D2
Prien D. 109 B3
Prienai LT. 13 A5
Prievidza SK. . . 98 C2
Prigradica HR . 138 C2
Prigrevica SRB 125 B5
Prijeboj HR . . . 123 C4
Prijedor BIH. . . 124 C2
Prijepolje SRB. 16 D3
Prilep NMK. . . . 182 B3
Priluka BIH. . . . 138 B2
Primda CZ. 95 B4
Primel-Trégastel
F. 100 A2
Primišje HR . . . 123 B4
Primorsk
Kaliningrad
RUS 69 A5
Severo-Zapadnyy
RUS 9 B6
Primošten HR . 138 B1
Primstal D 92 B2
Princes Risborough
UK 44 B3
Princetown UK. 42 B2
Principina a Mare
I. 135 C4
Priolo Gargallo
I. 177 B4
Prioro E 142 B2
Priozersk RUS . . 9 B7
Pirerchnyy
RUS 193 C14
Prisoje BIH. . . . 138 B3
Priština KOS . . . 16 D4
Pritzerbe D 73 B5
Pritzier D. 73 A4
Pritzwalk D 73 A5
Privas F 117 C4
Priverno I. 169 B3
Privlaka
Vukovarsko-
Srijemska
HR 125 B4
Zadarska HR . . 137 A4
Prizna HR 123 C3
Prizren KOS . . . 16 D4
Prizzi I 176 B2
Prnjavor
BIH. 125 C3
HR 124 B1
SRB 127 C1
Proaza E 141 A4
Probištadia D . . 82 B3
Probus UK. 42 B2
Próchnio I. . . . 134 C3
Prochowice PL. 85 A4
Prócida I. 170 C2
Prodhromos
CY 181 B1
Prodo I. 135 C5
Proença-a-Nova
P. 154 B3
Proença-a-Velha
P. 155 A3
Profondeville
B. 79 B4
Prokuplje SRB. . 16 D4
Propriano F. . . 180 B1
Prosec CZ. 97 B4
Prösen D. 83 A5
Prosenjakovci
SLO 111 C3
Prosotsani GR. 183 B5
Prostějov CZ. . . 98 B1
Prószków PL. . . 86 B1
Proszowice PL . 87 B4
Protić BIH 138 A2
Protivanov CZ. . 97 B4
Protivín CZ. . . . 96 B2
Prötzel D. 74 B2
Provins F. 90 C3
Prozor BIH 139 B3
Prudhoe UK . . . 37 B5
Prudnik PL. . . . 85 B5
Pruggern A . . . 109 B4
Prügy H 113 A5
Prüm D. 80 B2
Pruna E. 162 B2
Prunelli-di-
Fiumorbo F . 180 A2
Prunetta I 135 A3
Pruniers F 103 C4
Prusice PL. 85 A4
Pruské SK 98 B2
Pruszcze PL. . . . 76 A3

Pruszcz Gdański
PL. 69 A3
Pruszków PL 77 B5
Prutz A. 108 B1
Prüzen D. 65 C5
Pružina SK 13 B6
Pürvomay BG. 183 A7
Pryzlęg PL. 75 B4
Przasnysz PL. . . .77 A5
Przechlewo PL. .68 B2
Przecław PL. 87 B5
Przedbórz PL. . . .87 A3
Przedecz PL. 76 B3
Przejeslav PL. . . .84 A3
Przemków PL. . . .85 A3
Przemocze PL. . .75 A3
Przemyśl PL. . . . 12 D5
Przerąb PL. 87 A3
Przewodnik PL. .69 B3
Przewodowo
Parcele PL. 77 B5
Przewóz PL. 84 A2
Przezmark PL. . . .69 B4
Przodkowo PL. . .68 A3
Przybiernów
PL. 75 A3
Przyborowice
PL. 77 B5
Przybyszew PL. .87 A4
Przybyszów PL. .86 A3
Przyłęg PL. 75 B4
Przysucha PL. . . .87 A4
Przytoczna PL. . .75 B4
Przytyk PL. 87 A4
Przywidz PL. 68 A3
Psachna GR 185 A4
Psara GR 185 A6
Psary PL. 76 C3
Pskov RUS 8 D6
Pszczew PL. 75 B4
Pszczółki PL. 69 A3
Pszczyna PL. 98 B2
Pszów PL. 86 B2
Pteleos GR 182 D4
Ptolemaida
GR 182 C3
Ptuj SLO. 124 A1
Ptusza PL. 68 B1
Puch A. 109 B4
Puchberg am
Schneeberg
A. 110 B2
Puchevillers F. . . .90 A2
Puchheim D. . . .108 A2
Púchov SK 98 B2
Pučišća HR 138 B2
Puck PL. 69 A3
Pucoł E. 159 B3
Puconci SLO. . . .111 C3
Pudasjärvi
FIN. 197 D10
Puderbach D. . . .81 B3
Pudozh RUS. . . .9 B10
Puebla de Albortón
E. 153 A4
Puebla de Alcocer
E. 156 B2
Puebla de Beleña
E. 151 B4
Puebla de Don
Fadrique E . . 164 B2
Puebla de Don
Rodrigo E . 156 A3
Puebla de Guzmán
E. 161 B2
Puebla de la
Calzada E . . .155 C4
Puebla de la Reina
E. 156 B1
Puebla de Lillo
E. 142 A1
Puebla del Maestre
E. 161 A3
Puebla del Principe
E. 158 C1
Puebla de Obando
E. 155 B4
Puebla de Sanabria
E. 141 B4
Puebla de Sancho
Pérez E. 155 C4
Puente Almuhey
E. 142 B2
Puente de Domingo
Flórez E 141 B4
Puente de Génave
E. 164 A2
Puente del
Congosto E . .150 B2

Puente de
Montañana
E. 145 B4
Puente Duero
E. 150 A3
Puente-Genil
E. 162 A3
Puente la Reina
E. 144 B2
Puente la Reina de
Jaca E 144 B3
Puentelarra E . . 143 B3
Puente Mayorga
E. 162 B2
Puente Viesgo
E. 143 A3
Puertas
Asturias E . . .142 A2
Salamanca E . .149 A3
Puerto de
Mazarrón E . .165 B3
Puerto de Santa
Cruz E 156 A2
Puerto de San
Vicente E 156 A2
Puerto-Lápice
E. 157 A4
Puertollano E . 157 B3
Puerto Lumbreras
E. 164 B3
Puerto Moral
E. 161 B3
Puerto Real E . . 162 B1
Puerto Rey E . . . 156 B2
Puerto Seguro
E. 149 B3
Puerto Serrano
E. 162 B2
Puget-Sur-Argens
F. 132 B2
Puget-Théniers
F. 132 B2
Puget-ville F . . . 132 B2
Pugnochiuso I 171 B4
Puigcerdà E 146 B2
Puigpunyent
E. 166 B2
Puig Reig E. 147 C2
Puillon F 128 C2
Puimichel F 132 B2
Puimoisson F . . 132 B2
Puiseaux F. 103 A4
Puisieux F. 90 A2
Puisserguier F . 130 B2
Puivert F. 146 B3
Pujols F 128 B2
Pukanec SK 98 C2
Pukavik S 63 B2
Pukë AL. 182 A1
Pula
HR 122 C2
I. 179 C2
Puławy PL. 12 C4
Pulborough UK .44 C3
Pulfero I 122 A2
Pulgar E. 157 A3
Pulheim D 80 A2
Pulkau A 97 C3
Pulpí E 164 B3
Pulsano I. 173 B3
Pulsnitz D. 84 A2
Pułtusk PL. 77 B6
Pumpsaint UK . .39 B3
Punat HR. 123 B3
Punta Marina
I. 135 A5
Punta Prima E . 167 B4
Punta Sabbioni
I. 122 B1
Puntas de Calnegre
E. 165 B3
Punta Umbria
E. 161 B3
Puolanka FIN . .3 D10
Puoltikasvaara
S. 196 B4
Puoltsa S. 196 B2
Puračić BIH. . . . 125 C4
Purbach am
Neusiedler See
A. 111 B3
Purchena E. 164 B2
Purfleet UK 45 B4
Purgstall A. 110 A2
Purkersdorf A. 111 A3
Purmerend NL . .70 B1
Purullena E 164 B1
Pushkin RUS 9 C7
Pushkino RUS. .9 D10
Püspökladány
H. 113 B5
Pusté Ulany
SK. 111 A4

Pustoshka RUS . . .9 D6
Puszcza Mariańska
PL. 77 C5
Puszczykowo
PL. 75 B5
Pusztamagyaród
H. 111 C3
Pusztamonostor
H. 113 B3
Pusztaszabolcs
H. 112 B2
Pusztavám H. . . 112 B2
Putanges-Pont-
Ecrepin F. 89 B3
Putbus D. 66 B2
Putignano I 173 B3
Putlitz D. 73 A5
Putnok H 99 C4
Putte B. 79 A4
Puttelange-aux-
Lacs F 92 B2
Puttelingen D. . .92 B2
Putten NL. 70 B2
Puttgarden D. . .65 A4
Püttlingen D 92 B2
Putzu Idu I 179 B2
Puy-Guillaume
F. 117 B3
Puylaroque F . . 129 B4
Puylaurens F. . .146 A3
Puy-l'Évêque
F. 129 B3
Puymirol F 129 B3
Puyôo F 128 C2
Puyrolland F. . . 114 B3
Pwllheli UK 38 B2
Pyetrikaw BY . . .13 B8
Pyhäjärvi FIN . . . 3 E9
Pyhäkylä
FIN. 197 D11
Pyla CY. 181 B2
Pyla-sur-Mer
F. 128 B1
Pyrzyce PL 75 A3
Pysely CZ 96 B2
Pyskowice PL. . .86 B2
Pytalovo RUS . . .8 D5
Pyzdry PL 76 B2

Quakenbrück
D. 71 B4
Quarré-les-Tombes
F. 104 B2
Quarteira P 160 B1
Quartu Sant'Élena
I. 179 C3
Quatre-Champs
F. 91 B4
Quedlinburg D. .82 A3
Queensferry
Edinburgh
UK 35 C4
Flintshire UK . 38 A3
Queige F 118 B3
Queipo E. 161 B3
Queixans E. 146 B2
Quel E. 144 B1
Quelaines-St-Gault
F 102 B1
Queljada P 148 A1
Quemada E 143 C3
Quercalbs E 147 B3
Quercianella I. 134 B3
Querfurt D. 82 A3
Quérigut F 146 B3
Quero
E. 157 A4
I. 121 B4
Querqueville F . .88 A2
Quesada E 164 B1
Questembert
F. 101 B3
Quettehou F 88 A2
Queuvauvillers F 90 B2
Quiaois P 148 B1
Quiberon F 100 B2
Quiberville F. . . .89 A4
Quickborn D. . . .64 C2
Quiévrain B 79 B3
Quillan F. 146 B3
Quillebeuf F 89 A4
Quimper F 100 A1
Quimperlé F . . .100 B2
Râda
Skaraborg S. . .55 B4
Värmland S . . .49 B5
Radalj SRB. 127 C1
Rădăuți RO. 17 B6
Radda in Chianti
I. 135 B4

Quinson F. 132 B2
Quinssaines F. 116 A2
Quinta-Grande
P. 154 C2
Quintana de la
Serena E 156 B2
Quintana del
Castillo E. . . .141 B4
Quintana del Marco
E. 141 B5
Quintana del
Puenta E 142 B2
Quintana-Martin
Galindez E . . 143 B3
Quintanaortuño
E. 143 B3
Quintanapalla
E. 143 B3
Quintanar de la
Orden E 157 A4
Quintanar de la
Sierra E. 143 C3
Quintanar del Rey
E. 158 B2
Quintanilla de la
Mata E. 143 C3
Quintanilla del
Coco E. 143 C3
Quintanilla de
Onésimo E . . .150 A3
Quintanilla de
Somoza E. . . .141 B4
Quintas de
Valdelucio E . 142 B2
Quintela P 148 B2
Quintin F 100 A3
Quinto E 153 A3
Quinzano d'Oglio
I. 120 B3
Quiroga E. 141 B3
Quismondo E . .150 B3
Quissac F 131 B2
Quistello I. 121 B3

Raab A. 96 C1
Raabs an der Thaya
A. 97 C3
Raahe FIN 3 D9
Raajärvi FIN . . .197 C9
Raalte NL 71 B3
Raamsdonksveer
NL 79 A4
Raanujarvi
FIN. 196 C7
Raattama FIN . 196 A7
Rab HR 123 C3
Rabac HR 123 B3
Rábade E. 140 A3
Rábafüzes H . . .111 C3
Rábahidvég H 111 B3
Rabanales E . . . 149 A3
Rábapatona
H. 111 B4
Rabapordány
H. 111 B4
Rabastens F . . . 129 C4
Rabastens-de-
Bigorre F 145 A4
Rabat M. 175 C3
Rabat = Victoria
M. 175 C3
Rabča SK. 99 B3
Rabe SRB. 126 A2
Rácalmás H 112 B2
Racalmuto I. . . .176 B2
Racconigi I. 119 C4
Rače SLO. 123 A4
Rachecourt-sur-
Marne F. 91 C4
Raciąż PL. 77 B5
Racibórz PL. 86 B2
Račinovci HR. . 125 C4
Ráckeve H 112 B2
Racławice PL. . . .87 B4
Racławice Śląskie
PL. 86 B1
Racot PL. 75 B5

Raddusa I 177 B3
Radeberg D. 84 A1
Radebeul D 84 A1
Radeburg D 84 A1
Radeče SLO 123 A4
Radekhiv UA 13 C6
Radenci SLO . . .111 C3
Radenthein A . 109 C4
Radevormwald
D. 80 A3
Radičófani I 135 C4
Radicóndoli I . .135 B4
Radišiči BIH . . . 138 B3
Radizel SLO 110 C2
Radków PL. 85 B4
Radlje ob Dravi
SLO 110 C2
Radlów PL. 87 B4
Radmer an der
Stube A 110 B1
Radnejaur S. . . .195 E9
Radnice CZ. 96 B1
Radohova BIH. 138 A3
Radojevo SRB. 126 B2
Radolfzell D . . .107 B3
Radom PL. 87 A5
Radomice PL. . . .77 A4
Radomin PL. 77 A4
Radomsko PL. . .86 A3
Radomyshl UA . .13 C8
Radomyśl Wielki
PL. 87 B5
Radošina SK 98 C1
Radošovce SK. . .98 C1
Radoszewice
PL. 86 A2
Radoszyce PL. . .87 A4
Radotin CZ. 96 B2
Radovets BG. . 186 A1
Radoviš NMK. . 182 B4
Radovljica
SLO 123 A3
Radowo Wielkie
PL. 75 A4
Radstadt A. 109 B3
Radstock UK 43 A4
Raduc HR 137 A4
Raduša NMK. . . 182 A3
Radviliškis LT . . .8 E3
Radzanów
Mazowieckie
PL. 77 B5
Mazowieckie
PL. 87 A4
Radziejów PL. . .76 B3
Radziejowice
PL. 77 B5
Radzyń Chełmiński
PL. 69 B3

Raeren B. 80 B2
Raesfeld D. 80 A2
Raffadali I. 176 B2
Rafina GR 185 A4
Rafsbotn N. 192 B7
Ragachow BY . . .13 B9
Ragály H. 99 C4
Rägelehe DK. . . .61 C2
Raglan UK 39 C4
Ragnitz A 110 C2
Ragusa I 177 C3
Rahden D. 72 B1
Råholt N 48 B3
Raiano I. 169 A3
Raigada E 141 B3
Rain D 94 C2
Rainbach im
Mühlkreis A . . .96 C2
Rainham UK 45 B4
Rairiz de Veiga
E. 140 B3
Raisdorf D 64 B3
Raisio FIN. 8 B3
Raiskio FIN. . .197 D9
Raiva
Aveiro P 148 A1
Coimbra P . . .148 B1
Raja-Jooseppi
FIN. 193 D12
Rajec SK. 98 B2
Rajecké Teplice
SK. 98 B2
Rajevo Selo
HR 125 C4
Rajhrad CZ. 97 B4
Rajić HR. 124 B3
Rajka H 111 B4
Rakaca H. 99 C4
Rakamaz H. . . . 113 A5

Rakek SLO 123 B3
Rakhiv UA. 17 A6
Rakitna SLO. . . .123 B3
Rakitovo BG . . .183 B6
Rakkestad N 54 A2
Rákóczifalva
H. 113 B4
Rakoniewice PL 75 B5
Rakoszyce PL. . .85 A4
Raková SK 98 B2
Rakovac BIH . . .125 B3
Rakovica HR . . .123 C4
Rakovník CZ 96 A1
Rakow D. 66 B2
Raków PL. 87 B5
Rakvere EST. 8 C5
Ralja SRB. 127 C2
Rälla S 62 B4
Ramacca I. 177 B3
Ramacastañas
E. 150 B2
Ramacca I 177 B3
Ramales de la
Victoria E 143 A3
Ramberg N 194 B4
Rambervillers
F. 92 C2
Rambouillet F. . .90 C1
Rambucourt F . .92 C1
Ramdala S. 63 B3
Ramerupt F 91 C4
Ramingstein
A. 109 B4
Ramirás E 140 B2
Ramiswil CH . . .106 B2
Ramkvilla S 62 A2
Ramme D. 58 B1
Rämmen S 49 B6
Ramnäs S. 56 A2
Ramnes N. 54 A1
Râmnicu Vâlcea
RO 17 C6
Ramonville-St Agne
F. 129 C4
Rampside UK . . .36 B3
Ramsau D 109 B3
Ramsbeck D 81 A4
Ramsberg S. 56 A1
Ramsele S 200 C2
Ramsey
Cambridgeshire
UK 44 A3
Isle of Man UK .36 B2
Ramsgate UK . . .45 B5
Ramsjö S. 200 D1
Ramstein-
Meisenbach D .93 B3
Ramsund N 194 B7
Ramundberget
S 199 C9
Ramvik S 200 D3
Ranalt A 108 B2
Rånäs S. 51 C5
Rånåsfoss N 48 B3
Rance B 79 B4
Ránchio I. 135 B5
Randaberg N . . .52 A1
Randalstown
UK 27 B4
Randan F 117 A3
Randazzo I. 177 B3
Rânddalen S . . .199 C10
Randegg A. 110 A1
Randers DK. 58 B3
Randijaur S 196 C2
Randin E 140 C3
Randsverk N . . .198 D6
Råneå S 196 D5
Rånes F 89 B3
Rângedala S 60 B3
Ranis D 82 B3
Rankweil A 107 B4
Rånnaväg S. 60 B3
Rännelanda S . . .54 B2
Ränneslöv S 61 C3
Rannoch Station
UK 34 B3
Ranovac SRB . . .127 C3
Ransäter S. 55 A4
Ransbach-
Baumbach D. .81 B3
Ransta S. 56 A2
Ranttila FIN . . .193 C9
Ranua FIN. 197 D9
Ranum DK. 58 B2
Ranvalhal P 154 B1
Raon-l'Étape F . .92 C2
Ráossi I 121 B4
Rapallo I 134 A2
Rapla EST 8 C4
Rapness N. 33 B4
Rapolano Terme
I. 135 B4

Rapolla I 172 B1
Raposa P. 154 B2
Rapperswil
CH 107 B3
Raša HR 123 B3
Rasal E 145 B3
Rascafría E 151 B4
Rasdorf D. 82 B1
Raseiniai LT. 13 A5
Rašica SLO 123 B3
Rasines E 143 A3
Rasquera E 153 A4
Rássina I 135 B4
Rastatt D. 93 C4
Rastede D. 71 A5
Rastenberg D . .82 A3
Rastošnica
BIH. 125 C4
Rastovac MNE. 139 C4
Rasueros E 150 A2
Rasy PL. 86 A3
Raszków PL. 86 A1
Rätan S 199 C11
Rateče SLO. 109 C4
Ratekau D 65 C3
Ratež SLO 123 B4
Rathangan IRL . .30 A2
Rathcoole IRL . . .30 A2
Rathcormack
IRL 29 B3
Rathdrum IRL . . .30 B2
Rathebur D 74 A2
Rathenow D 73 B5
Rathfriland UK . .27 B4
Rathkeale IRL . . .29 B3
Rathmelton IRL .27 A3
Rathmolyon
IRL 30 A2
Rathmore IRL . . .29 B2
Rathmullan IRL .27 A3
Rathnew IRL 30 B2
Rathvilly IRL 30 B2
Ratibořské Hory
CZ 96 B2
Ratingen D 80 A2
Ratková SK 99 C4
Ratkovo SRB . . 126 B1
Ratne UA. 13 C6
Rattelsdorf D . . .94 A2
Ratten A 110 B2
Rattosjärvi
FIN. 196 C7
Rattray UK 35 B4
Rättvik S. 50 B2
Ratvika N 199 B7
Ratzeburg D 65 C3
Rätzlingen D . . .73 B4
Raucourt-et-Flaba
F. 91 B4
Raudeberg N . . 198 D2
Raufarhöfn
IS 191 A10
Raufoss N. 48 B2
Rauhala FIN . . .196 B7
Rauland N. 53 A4
Raulhac F 116 C2
Raulia N. 195 E5
Rauma FIN 8 B2
Raundal N. 46 B3
Rauris A 109 B4
Rautas S. 196 B2
Rautavaara FIN . 3 E11
Rauville-la-Bigot
F. 88 A2
Rauzan F 128 B2
Ravanusa I 176 B2
Rava-Rus'ka
UA 13 C5
Ravča HR. 138 B3
Ravels B. 79 A4
Rävemåla S 63 B3
Ravenglass UK . .36 B3
Ravenna I. 135 A5
Ravensburg D 107 B4
Rävlanda S. 60 B2
Ravna Gora
SLO 110 C1
Ravnje SRB. 127 C1
Ravno BIH. 139 C3
Ravno Selo
SRB 126 B1
Rawa Mazowiecka
PL. 87 A4
Rawicz PL. 85 A4
Rawtenstall UK .40 B1
Rayleigh UK. 45 B4
Ražana SRB 127 C1
Ražanac HR 137 A4
Razboj BIH. 124 B3

Razes F 115 B5
Razgrad BG 17 D7
Razkrižie SLO 111 C3
Razlog BG 183 B5
Razo E 140 A2
Reading UK 44 B3
Réalmont F 130 B1
Rebais F 90 C3
Reboly RUS 3 E12
Rebordelo P 149 A2
Recanati I 136 B2
Recas E 151 B4
Recco I 134 A2
Recess IRL 28 A2
Recey-sur-Ource F 105 B3
Recezinhos P 148 A1
Rechnitz A 111 B3
Rechytsa BY 13 B9
Recke D 71 B4
Recklinghausen D 80 A3
Recoaro Terme I 121 B4
Recogne B 92 B1
Recoules-Prévinquières F 130 A1
Recsk H 113 B4
Recz PL 75 A4
Reda PL 69 A3
Redalen N 48 B2
Redange L 92 B1
Redcar UK 37 B5
Redditch UK 44 A2
Redefin D 73 A4
Redhill UK 44 B3
Redics H 111 C3
Redkino RUS 9 D10
Redland UK 33 B3
Redlin D 73 A5
Redon F 101 B3
Redondela E 140 B2
Redondo P 155 C3
Red Point UK 31 B3
Redruth UK 42 B1
Redzikowo PL 68 A2
Reepham UK 41 C5
Rees D 80 A2
Reeth UK 37 B5
Reetz D 73 A4
Reftele S 60 B3
Regalbuto I 177 B3
Regen D 95 C5
Regensburg D 95 B4
Regenstauf D 95 B4
Reggello I 135 B4
Réggio di Calábria I 175 C1
Reggiolo I 121 C3
Réggio nell'Emília I 121 C3
Reghin RO 17 B6
Régil E 144 A1
Regna S 56 B1
Regniéville F 92 C1
Regny F 117 B4
Rego da Leirosa P 154 A2
Regöly H 112 C2
Regueiro E 140 B2
Reguengo
Portalegre P 155 B3
Santarém P 154 B2
Reguengos de Monsaraz P 155 C3
Rehau D 83 B4
Rehburg D 72 B2
Rehden D 72 B1
Rehna D 65 C4
Reichelsheim D 93 B4
Reichelshofen D 94 B2
Reichenau A 110 B2
Reichenbach
Sachsen D 83 B4
Sachsen D 84 A2
Reichenfels A 110 B1
Reichensachsen D 82 A2
Reichertshofen D 95 C3
Reichshoffen F 93 C3
Reiden CH 106 B2
Reigada
E 141 A4
P 149 B3
Reigate UK 44 B3
Reillanne F 132 B1
Reillo E 158 B2
Reims F 91 B4
Reinach CH 106 B3
Reinbek D 72 A3
Reinberg D 66 B2
Reine N 194 C4
Reinfeld D 65 C3
Reinheim D 93 B4
Reinli N 47 B6
Reinosa E 142 A2
Reinstorf D 65 C4
Reinsvoll N 48 B2
Reisach A 109 C4
Reiss UK 32 C3
Reitan N 199 C8
Reit im Winkl D 109 B3
Rejmyre S 56 B1
Rekavice BIH 124 C3
Rekovac SRB 127 D3
Relleu E 159 C3
Rém H 125 A5
Remagen D 80 B3
Rémalard F 89 B4
Rembercourt-aux-Pots F 91 C5
Remedios P 154 B1
Remels D 71 A4
Remetea Mare RO 126 B3
Remich L 92 B2
Rémilly F 92 B2
Remiremont F 105 A5
Remolinos E 144 C2
Remoulins F 131 B3
Remscheid D 80 A3
Rémuzat F 131 A4
Rena N 48 A3
Renaison F 117 A3
Renazé F 101 B4
Renchen D 93 C4
Rencurel F 118 B2
Rende I 174 B2
Rendina GR 182 D3
Rendsburg D 64 B2
Renedo E 150 A3
Renens CH 105 C5
Renfrew UK 34 C3
Rengsjö S 50 A3
Reni UA 17 C8
Rennebu N 198 C6
Rennerod D 81 B4
Rennertshofen D 94 C3
Rennes F 101 A4
Rennes-les-Bains F 146 B3
Rennweg A 109 B4
Rens DK 64 B2
Rensjön S 196 A2
Rentería E 144 A2
Rentjärn S 200 A4
Répcelak H 111 B4
Repojoki FIN 193 D9
Repvåg N 193 B9
Requena E 159 B2
Réquista F 130 A1
Rerik D 65 B4
Resana I 121 B4
Resarö S 57 A4
Reschen = Résia I 108 C1
Resen NMK 182 B3
Resende P 148 A2
Résia = Reschen I 108 C1
Reşiţa
RO 16 C4
RO 126 B3
Resko PL 67 C4
Resnik SRB 127 C2
Ressons-sur-Matz F 90 B2
Restábal E 163 B4
Resuttano I 177 B3
Retamal E 155 C4
Retford UK 40 B3
Rethel F 91 B4
Rethem D 72 B2
Rethimno GR 185 D5
Retie B 79 A5
Retiers F 101 B4
Retortillo E 149 B3
Retortillo de Soria E 151 A4
Retournac F 117 B4
Rétság H 112 B3
Rettenegg A 110 B2
Retuerta del Bullaque E 157 A3
Retz A 97 C3
Retzbach D 94 B1
Reuden D 73 B5
Reuilly F 103 B4
Reus E 147 C2
Reusel NL 79 A5
Reuterstadt Stavenhagen D 74 A1
Reuth D 95 B4
Reutlingen D 94 C1
Reutte A 108 B1
Reuver NL 80 A2
Revel F 146 A2
Revello I 119 C4
Revenga E 151 B3
Revest-du-Bion F 132 A1
Révfülöp H 111 C4
Revigny-sur-Ornain F 91 C4
Revin F 91 B4
Řevnice CZ 96 B2
Řevničov CZ 84 B1
Revo I 121 A4
Revsnes N 47 A4
Revúca SK 99 C4
Rewa PL 69 A3
Rewal PL 67 B4
Rexbo S 50 B2
Reyðarfjörður IS 191 B11
Reyero E 142 B1
Reykhólar IS 190 B3
Reykholt
Árnessýsla IS 190 C5
Borgarfjarðarsýsla IS 190 C4
Reykjahlið IS 191 B9
Reykjavík IS 190 C4
Rezé F 101 B4
Rēzekne LV 8 D5
Rezovo BG 17 E8
Rezzato I 120 B3
Rezzoáglio I 134 A2
Rhade D 72 A2
Rhaunen D 93 B3
Rhayader UK 39 B3
Rheda-Wiedenbrück D 81 A4
Rhede
Niedersachsen D 71 A4
Nordrhein-Westfalen D 80 A2
Rheinau D 93 C3
Rheinbach D 80 B2
Rheinberg D 80 A2
Rheine D 71 B4
Rheinfelden D 106 B2
Rheinsberg D 74 A1
Rhêmes-Notre-Dame I 119 B4
Rhenen NL 70 C2
Rhens D 81 B3
Rheydt D 80 A2
Rhiconich UK 32 C2
Rhinow D 73 B5
Rhiw UK 38 B2
Rho I 120 B2
Rhodes GR 188 C3
Rhondda UK 39 C3
Rhosllanerchrugog UK 38 A3
Rhosneigr UK 38 A2
Rhossili UK 39 C2
Rhubodach UK 34 C2
Rhuddlan UK 38 A3
Rhyl UK 38 A3
Rhynie UK 33 D4
Riala S 57 A4
Riallé F 101 B4
Riaño E 142 B1
Riano I 168 A2
Rians F 132 B1
Rianxo E 140 B2
Riaza E 151 A4
Riba E 143 A3
Ribadavia E 140 B2
Ribadeo E 141 A3
Riba de Saelices E 152 B1
Ribadesella E 142 A1
Ribaflecha E 143 B4
Ribaforada E 144 C2
Ribare SRB 127 C3
Riba-roja d'Ebre E 153 A4
Riba-Roja de Turia E 159 B3
Ribe DK 59 C1
Ribeauvillé F 106 A2
Ribécourt-Dreslincourt F 90 B2
Ribeira da Pena P 148 A2
Ribeira de Piquín E 141 A3
Ribemont F 91 B3
Ribera I 176 B2
Ribérac F 129 A3
Ribera de Cardós E 146 B2
Ribera del Fresno E 156 B1
Ribesalbes E 159 A3
Ribes de Freser E 147 B3
Ribiers F 132 A1
Ribnica
BIH 139 A4
SLO 123 B3
Ribnica na Potorju SLO 110 C2
Ribnik HR 123 B4
Rîbniţa MD 17 B8
Ribnitz-Damgarten D 66 B1
Ribolla I 135 C4
Říčany CZ 97 B4
Říčany CZ 96 B2
Ríccia I 170 B2
Riccione I 136 A1
Ricco Del Golfo I 134 A2
Richebourg F 105 A4
Richelieu F 102 B2
Richisau CH 107 B3
Richmond
Greater London UK 44 B3
North Yorkshire UK 37 B5
Richtenberg D 66 B1
Richterswil CH 107 B3
Rickling D 64 B3
Rickmansworth UK 44 B3
Ricla E 152 A2
Riddarhyttan S 50 C2
Ridderkerk NL 79 A4
Riddes CH 119 A4
Ridjica SRB 125 B5
Riec-sur-Bélon F 100 B2
Ried A 109 A4
Riedenburg D 95 C3
Ried im Oberinntal A 108 B1
Riedlingen D 107 A4
Riedstadt D 93 B4
Riegersburg A 110 C2
Riego de la Vega E 141 B5
Riego del Camino E 149 A4
Riello E 141 B5
Riemst B 80 B1
Rienne B 91 B4
Riénsena E 142 A2
Riesa D 83 A5
Riese Pio X I 121 B4
Riesi I 177 B3
Riestedt D 82 A3
Rietberg D 81 A4
Rieti I 169 A2
Rietschen D 84 A2
Rieumes F 146 A2
Rieupeyroux F 130 A1
Rieux-Volvestre F 146 A2
Riez F 132 B2
Rīga LV 8 D4
Riggisberg CH 106 C2
Rignac F 130 A1
Rignano Gargánico I 171 B3
Rigolato I 109 C3
Rigside UK 36 A3
Rigutino I 135 B4
Riihimäki FIN 8 B4
Rijeka HR 123 B3
Rijen NL 79 A4
Rijkevorsel B 79 A4
Rijssen NL 71 B3
Rila BG 183 A5
Rilić BIH 138 B3
Rilievo I 176 B1
Rillé F 102 B2
Rillo de Gallo E 152 B2
Rimavská Baňa SK 99 C3
Rimavská Seč SK 99 C4
Rimavská Sobota SK 99 C4
Rimbo S 57 A4
Rimforsa S 56 B1
Rímini I 136 A1
Rîmnicu Sărat RO 17 C7
Rimogne F 91 B4
Rimpar D 94 B1
Rimske Toplice SLO 123 A4
Rincón de la Victoria E 163 B3
Rincón de Soto E 144 B2
Rindal N 198 B6
Rinde N 46 A3
Ringarum S 56 B2
Ringaskiddy IRL 29 C3
Ringe DK 59 C3
Ringebu N 48 A2
Ringkøbing DK 59 B1
Ringsaker N 48 B2
Ringsted DK 61 D1
Ringwood UK 44 C2
Rinkaby S 63 C2
Rinkabyholm S 63 B4
Rinlo E 141 A3
Rinn A 108 B2
Rinteln D 72 B2
Rio E 140 B3
Riobo E 140 B2
Riodeva E 152 B2
Rio do Coures P 154 B2
Rio Douro P 148 A2
Riofrio E 150 B3
Rio Frio P 154 C2
Riofrio de Aliste E 149 A3
Rio frio de Riaza E 151 A4
Riogordo E 163 B3
Rioja E 164 C2
Riola I 135 A4
Riola Sardo I 179 C2
Riolobos E 155 B4
Riom F 116 B3
Riomaggiore I 134 A2
Rio Maior P 154 B2
Rio Marina I 134 C3
Riom-ès-Montagnes F 116 B2
Rion-des-Landes F 128 C2
Rionegro del Puente E 141 B4
Rionero in Vúlture I 172 B1
Riopar E 158 C1
Riós E 141 C3
Rioseco E 142 A1
Rioseco de Tapia E 141 B5
Rio Tinto P 148 A1
Riotord F 117 B4
Riotorto E 141 A3
Rioz F 105 B5
Ripač BIH 124 C1
Ripacándida I 172 B1
Ripanj SRB 127 C2
Ripatransone I 136 C2
Ripley UK 40 B2
Ripoll E 147 B3
Ripon UK 40 A2
Riposto I 177 B4
Ripsa S 56 B2
Risan MNE 16 D3
Risbäck S 200 B1
Risca UK 39 C3
Rischenau D 81 A5
Riscle F 128 C2
Risebo S 56 B2
Risnes N 46 A2
Rišňovce SK 98 C1
Risør N 53 B5
Risøyhamn N 194 B6
Rissna S 199 B12
Ritsem S 194 C8
Ritterhude D 72 A1
Riutula FIN 193 D10
Riva del Garda I 121 B3
Riva Lígure I 133 B3
Rivanazzano I 120 C2
Rivarolo Canavese I 119 B4
Rivarolo Mantovano I 121 B3
Rive-de-Gier F 117 B4
Rivedoux-Plage F 114 B2
Rivello I 174 A1
Rivergaro I 120 C2
Rives F 118 B2
Rivesaltes F 146 B3
Rivignano I 122 B2
Rivne UA 13 C7
Rívoli I 119 B4
Rivolta d'Adda I 120 B2
Rixheim F 106 B2
Rixo S 54 B2
Riza GR 183 C5
Rizokarpaso CY 181 A3
Rjukan N 47 C5
Rø DK 67 A3
Rö S 57 A4
Roa
E 143 C3
N 48 B2
Roade UK 44 A3
Roager DK 59 C1
Roaldkvam N 52 A2
Roanne F 117 A4
Röbäck S 200 C6
Robakowo PL 69 B3
Róbbio I 120 B1
Röbel D 73 A5
Roberton UK 35 C5
Robertsfors S 200 B6
Robertville B 80 B2
Robin Hood's Bay UK 37 B6
Robleda E 149 B3
Robledillo de Trujillo E 156 A2
Robledo
Albacete E 158 C1
Orense E 141 B4
Robledo de Chavela E 151 B3
Robledo del Buey E 156 A3
Robledo del Mazo E 156 A3
Robledollano E 156 A2
Robles de la Valcueva E 142 B1
Robliza de Cojos E 149 B4
Robres E 145 C3
Robres del Castillo E 144 B1
Rocafort de Queralt E 147 C2
Rocamadour F 129 B4
Roccabernarda I 175 B2
Roccabianca I 120 B3
Roccadáspide I 172 B1
Rocca di Mezzo I 169 A3
Rocca di Papa I 168 B2
Roccagorga I 169 B3
Rocca Imperiale I 174 A2
Roccalbegna I 135 C4
Roccalumera I 177 B4
Roccamena I 176 B2
Roccamonfina I 170 B1
Roccanova I 174 A2
Roccapalumba I 176 B2
Roccapassa I 169 A3
Rocca Priora I 136 B2
Roccaraso I 169 B4
Rocca San Casciano I 135 A4
Roccasecca I 169 B3
Rocca Sinibalda I 169 A2
Roccastrada I 135 B4
Roccatederighi I 135 B4
Roccella Iónica I 175 C2
Rocchetta Sant'António I 172 A1
Rocester UK 40 C2
Rochdale UK 40 B1
Rochechouart F 115 C4
Rochefort
B 79 B5
F 114 C3
Rochefort-en-Terre F 101 B3
Rochefort-Montagne F 116 B2
Rochefort-sur-Nenon F 105 B4
Roche-lez-Beaupré F 105 B5
Rochemaure F 131 A3
Rocheservière F 114 B2
Rochester
Medway UK 45 B4
Northumberland UK 37 A4
Rochlitz D 83 A4
Rociana del Condado E 161 B3
Rockenhausen D 93 B3
Rockhammar S 56 A1
Rockneby S 62 B4
Ročko Polje HR 123 B3
Ročov CZ 84 B1
Rocroi F 91 B4
Rodach D 82 B2
Roda de Bara E 147 C2
Roda de Ter E 147 C3
Rodalben D 93 B3
Rødberg N 47 B5
Rødby DK 65 B4
Rødbyhavn DK 65 B4
Rødding
Sonderjyllands Amt. DK 59 C2
Viborg Amt. DK 58 B1
Rödeby S 63 B3
Rodeiro E 140 B3
Rødekro DK 64 A2
Roden NL 71 A3
Ródenas E 152 B2
Rodenkirchen D 72 A1
Rödental D 82 B3
Rödermark D 93 B4
Rodewisch D 83 B4
Rodez F 130 A1
Rodi Gargánico I 171 B3
Roding D 95 B4
Rödjebro S 51 B4
Rødkærsbro DK 59 B2
Rodolivas GR 183 C5
Rodoñá E 147 C2
Rødvig DK 65 A5
Roermond NL 80 A1
Roesbrugge B 78 B2
Roeschwoog F 93 C4
Roeselare B 78 B3
Roetgen D 80 B2
Roffiac F 116 B3
Röfors S 55 B5
Rofrano I 172 B1
Rogač HR 138 B2
Rogačica SRB 127 C1
Rogalinek PL 76 B1
Rogaška Slatina SLO 123 A4
Rogatec SLO 123 A4
Rogatica BIH 139 B5
Rogatyn UA 13 D6
Rogätz D 73 B4
Roggendorf D 65 C4
Roggiano Gravina I 174 B2
Roghadal UK 31 B2
Rogliano
F 180 A2
I 175 B2
Rognan N 195 C6
Rogne N 47 A6
Rognes F 131 B4
Rogny-les-7-Ecluses F 103 B4
Rogowo PL 76 B2
Rogoznica HR 138 B1
Rogoźnica PL 85 A4
Rogoźno PL 76 B1
Rohan F 101 A3
Röhlingen D 94 C2
Rohožnik SK 98 C1
Rohr D 82 B2
Rohrbach A 96 C1
Rohrbach-lès-Bitche F 92 B3
Rohrberg D 73 B4
Rohr im Gebirge A 110 B2

Röhrnbach D 96 C1
Roisel F 90 B3
Roja LV 8 D3
Rojales E 165 A4
Röjeråsen S 50 B1
Rojewo PL 76 B3
Rokiciny PL 87 A3
Rokietnica PL 75 B5
Rokiškis LT 8 E4
Rokitki PL 85 A3
Rokycany CZ 96 B1
Rolampont F 105 B4
Rold DK 58 B2
Røldal N 52 A2
Rolde NL 71 B3
Rolfs S 196 D6
Rollag N 47 B6
Rollán E 149 B4
Rolle CH 105 C5
Roma S 57 C4
Roma = Rome I 168 B2
Romagnano Sésia I 119 B5
Romagné F 88 B2
Romakloster S 57 C4
Roman RO 17 B7
Romana I 178 B2
Romanèche-Thorins F 117 A4
Romano di Lombardia I 120 B2
Romanshorn CH 107 B4
Romans-sur-Isère F 118 B2
Rombas F 92 B2
Rome = Roma I 168 B2
Romeán E 141 B3
Romenay F 105 C4
Romeral E 157 A4
Römerstein D 94 C1
Rometta I 177 A4
Romford UK 45 B4
Romhány H 112 B3
Römhild D 82 B2
Romilly-sur-Seine F 91 C3
Romont CH 106 C1
Romorantin-Lanthenay F 103 B3
Romrod D 81 B5
Romsey UK 44 C2
Rømskog N 54 A2
Rønbjerg DK 58 B1
Roncal E 144 B3
Ronce-les-Bains F 114 C2
Ronchamp F 106 B1
Ronchi dei Legionari I 122 B2
Ronciglione I 168 A2
Ronco Canavese I 119 B4
Ronco Scrivia I 120 C1
Ronda E 162 B2
Rønde DK 59 B3
Rone S 57 C4
Ronehamn S 57 C4
Rong N 46 B1
Rönnäng S 60 B1
Rønne DK 67 A3
Ronneburg D 83 B4
Ronneby S 63 B3
Rönneshytta S 55 B6
Rönninge S 57 A3
Rönnöfors S 199 B10
Rönö S 56 B2
Ronov nad Doubravou CZ 97 B3
Ronse B 79 B3
Roosendaal NL 79 A4
Roosky IRL 26 C3
Ropczyce PL 87 B5
Ropeid N 52 A2
Ropinsalmi FIN 192 D5
Ropuerelos del Páramo E 141 B5
Roquebilière F 133 A3
Roquebrun F 130 B2
Roquecourbe F 130 B1
Roquefort F 128 B2
Roquemaure F 131 A3
Roquesteron F 132 B3
Roquetas de Mar E 164 C2
Roquetes E 153 B4
Roquevaire F 132 B1
Røra N 199 B8
Rörbäcksnäs S 49 A4
Rørbæk DK 58 B2
Rore BIH 138 A2
Röro S 60 B1
Røros N 199 C8
Rorschach CH 107 B4
Rørvig DK 61 D1
Rørvik N 199 A8
Rörvik S 62 A2
Rosà I 121 B4
Rosal de la Frontera E 161 B2
Rosalina Mare I 122 B1
Rosa Marina I 173 B3
Rosans F 132 A1
Rosário P 160 B1
Rosarno I 175 C1
Rosbach D 81 B3
Rosche D 73 B3
Rościszewo PL 77 B4
Roscoff F 100 A2
Roscommon IRL 28 A3
Roscrea IRL 28 B4
Rosdorf D 82 A1
Rose I 174 B2
Rosegg A 109 C5
Rosehall UK 32 D2
Rosehearty UK 33 D4
Rosel UK 88 A1
Rosell E 153 B4
Roselló E 153 A4
Rosendal N 46 C3
Rosenfeld D 93 C4
Rosenfors S 62 A3
Rosenheim D 108 B3
Rosenow D 74 A2
Rosenthal D 81 A4
Rosersberg S 57 A3
Roses E 147 B4
Roseto degli Abruzzi I 169 A4
Roseto Valfortore I 170 B3
Rosheim F 93 C3
Rosia I 135 B4
Rosice CZ 97 B4
Rosières-en-Santerre F 90 B2
Rosignano Maríttimo I 134 B3
Rosignano Solvay I 134 B3
Roşiori-de-Vede RO 17 C6
Roskhill UK 31 B2
Roskilde DK 61 D2
Roskovec AL 182 C1
Röslau D 83 B3
Roslev DK 58 B1
Rosmaninhal P 155 B3
Rosnowo PL 67 B5
Rosolini I 177 C3
Rosova MNE 139 B5
Rosoy F 104 A2
Rosporden F 100 B2
Rosquete P 154 B2
Rosrath D 80 B3
Rossa CH 120 A2
Rossano I 174 B2
Rossas
Aveiro P 148 B1
Braga P 148 A1
Rossdorf D 82 B2
Rossett UK 38 A4
Rosshaupten D 108 B1
Rossiglione I 133 A4
Rossignol B 92 B1
Rossla D 82 A3
Rosslare IRL 30 B2
Rosslare Harbour IRL 30 B2
Rosslau D 83 A4
Rosslea UK 27 B3
Rossleben D 82 A3
Rossön S 200 C2
Ross-on-Wye UK 39 C4
Rossoszyca PL 86 A2
Rosswein D 83 A5
Röstånga S 61 C3
Roštár SK 99 C4
Rostock D 65 B5
Rostrenen F 100 A2
Røsvik N 194 C6
Rosvik S 196 D4
Rosyth UK 35 B4
Röszke H 126 A2
Rot S 49 A6
Rota E 161 C3
Rota Greca I 174 B2
Rot am See D 94 B2
Rotberget N 49 B4
Rotella I 136 C2
Rotenburg
Hessen D 82 B1
Niedersachsen D 72 A2
Roth
Bayern D 94 B3
Rheinland-Pfalz D 81 B3
Rothbury UK 37 A5
Rothemühl D 74 A2
Röthenbach D 95 B3
Rothenburg D 84 A2
Rothenburg ob der Tauber D 94 B2
Rothéneuf F 88 B2
Rothenklempenow D 74 A3
Rothenstein D 94 C3
Rotherham UK 40 B2
Rothes UK 32 D3
Rothesay UK 34 C2
Rothwell UK 44 A3
Rotnes N 48 B2
Rotonda I 174 B2
Rotondella I 174 A2
Rotova E 159 C3
Rott
Bayern D 108 B1
Bayern D 108 B3
Rottach-Egern D 108 B2
Röttenbach D 94 B3
Rottenbuch D 108 B1
Rottenburg
Baden-Württemberg D 93 C4
Bayern D 95 C4
Rottenmann A 110 B1
Rotterdam NL 79 A4
Rotthalmünster D 96 C1
Rottingdean UK 44 C3
Röttingen D 94 B1
Rottleberode D 82 A2
Rottne S 62 A2
Rottneros S 55 A4
Rottofreno I 120 B2
Rottweil D 107 A3
Rötz D 95 B4
Roubaix F 78 B3
Roudnice nad Labem CZ 84 B2
Roudouallec F 100 A2
Rouen F 89 A5
Rouffach F 106 B2
Rougé F 101 B4
Rougemont F 105 B5
Rougemont-le-Château F 106 B1
Rouillac F 115 C3
Rouillé F 115 B4
Roujan F 130 B2
Roulans F 105 B5
Roundwood IRL 30 A2
Rousínov CZ 97 B4
Roussac F 115 B5
Roussennac F 130 A1
Rousses F 130 A2
Roussillon F 117 B4
Rouvroy-sur-Audry F 91 B4
Rouy F 104 B2
Rovanieman maalaiskunta FIN 197 C8
Rovaniemi FIN 197 C8
Rovato I 120 B2
Rovensko pod Troskami CZ 84 B3
Roverbella I 121 B3
Rovereto I 121 B4
Rövershagen D 65 B5
Roverud N 49 B4
Rovigo I 121 B4
Rovinj HR 122 B2
Rovišce HR 124 B2
Rów PL 74 B3
Rowy PL 68 A2
Royal Leamington Spa UK 44 A2
Royal Tunbridge Wells UK 45 B4
Royan F 114 C2
Royat F 116 B3
Roybon F 118 B2
Roybridge UK 34 B3
Roye F 90 B2
Royère-de-Vassivière F 116 B1
Røykenvik N 48 B2
Royos E 164 B2
Røyrvik N 199 A10
Royston UK 44 A3
Rozadas E 141 A4
Rozalén del Monte E 151 C5
Różańsko PL 75 B3
Rozay-en-Brie F 90 C2
Roždalovice CZ 84 B3
Rozdilna UA 17 B9
Rozental PL 69 B4
Rozhyshche UA 13 C6
Rožmitál pod Třemšínem CZ 96 B1
Rožňava SK 99 C4
Rožnov pod Radhoštěm CZ 98 B2
Rozoy-sur-Serre F 91 B4
Rozprza PL 86 A3
Roztoky CZ 84 B2
Rozvadov CZ 95 B4
Rozzano I 120 B2
Rrëshen AL 182 B1
Rrogozhine AL 182 B1
Ruanes E 156 A2
Rubbestadneset N 46 C2
Rubi E 147 C3
Rubiá E 141 B4
Rubiacedo de Abajo E 143 B3
Rubielos Bajos E 158 B1
Rubielos de Mora E 153 B3
Rubiera I 121 C3
Rubik AL 182 B1
Rucandio E 143 B3
Rud
Akershus N 48 B3
Buskerud N 48 B2
Ruda
PL 86 A2
S 62 A4
Rudabánya H 99 C4
Ruda Maleniecka PL 87 A4
Ruda Pilczycka PL 87 A4
Ruda Śl. PL 86 B2
Ruddervorde B 78 A3
Ruden A 110 C1
Rudersberg D 94 C1
Rudersdorf A 111 B3
Rüdersdorf D 74 B2
Ruderting D 96 C1
Rüdesheim D 93 B3
Rudkøbing DK 65 B3
Rudmanns A 97 C3
Rudna
CZ 96 A2
PL 85 A4
Rudnik SRB 127 C2
Rudniki
Opolskie PL 86 A2
Śląskie PL 86 B3
Rudno
Dolnośląskie PL 85 A4
Pomorskie PL 69 B3
Rudnya RUS 13 A9
Rudolstadt D 82 B3
Rudowica PL 84 A3
Rudozem BG 183 B6
Rudskoga S 55 A5
Rudston UK 40 A3
Ruds Vedby DK 61 D1
Rudy PL 86 B2
Rue F 78 B1
Rueda E 150 A3
Rueda de Jalón E 152 A2
Ruelle-sur-Touvre F 115 C4
Ruerrero E 143 B3
Ruffano I 173 C4
Ruffec F 115 B4
Rufina I 135 B4
Rugby UK 44 A2
Rugeley UK 40 C2
Ruggstrop S 62 B4
Rugles F 89 B4
Rugozero RUS 3 D13
Rühen D 73 B3
Ruhla D 82 B2
Ruhland D 84 A1
Ruhle D 71 B4
Ruhpolding D 109 B3
Ruhstorf D 96 C1
Ruidera E 158 C1
Ruillé-sur-le-Loir F 102 B2
Ruinen NL 71 B3
Ruiselede B 78 A3
Ruka FIN 197 C12
Rulles B 92 B1
Rülzheim D 93 B4
Rum H 111 B3
Ruma SRB 127 B1
Rumboci BIH 138 B3
Rumburk CZ 84 B2
Rumenka SRB 126 B1
Rumia PL 69 A3
Rumigny F 91 B4
Rumilly F 118 B2
Rumma S 56 B2
Rumney UK 39 C3
Rumont F 91 C5
Runa P 154 B1
Runcorn UK 38 A4
Rundmoen N 195 D5
Rungsted DK 61 D2
Runhällen S 51 B3
Runowo PL 69 A5
Runtuna S 56 B3
Ruokojärvi FIN 196 B7
Ruokolahti FIN 9 B6
Ruokto S 196 B2
Ruoms F 131 A3
Ruoti I 172 B1
Rupa HR 123 B3
Ruppichteroth D 80 B3
Rupt-sur-Moselle F 106 B1
Rus E 157 B4
Ruse BG 17 D7
Ruše SLO 110 C2
Rusele S 200 B4
Ruševo HR 125 B4
Rush IRL 30 A2
Rushden UK 44 A3
Rusiec PL 86 A2
Rusinowo
Zachodnio-Pomorskie PL 67 C4
Zachodnio-Pomorskie PL 75 A5
Ruskele S 200 B4
Ruski Krstur SRB 126 B1
Ruskington UK 40 B3
Rusovce SK 111 A4
Rüsselsheim D 93 B4
Russelv N 192 C4
Russi I 135 A5
Rust A 111 B3
Rustefjelbma N 193 B12
Rustrel F 131 B4
Ruszki PL 77 B5
Ruszów PL 84 A3
Rute E 163 A3
Rüthen D 81 A4
Rutherglen UK 35 C3
Ruthin UK 38 A3
Ruthven UK 32 D2
Ruthwell UK 36 B3
Rüti CH 107 B3
Rutigliano I 173 A3
Rutledal N 46 A2
Rutvik S 196 D5
Ruurlo NL 71 B3
Ruuvaoja FIN 197 B11
Ruvo del Monte I 172 B1
Ruvo di Púglia I 171 B4
Ruynes-en-Margeride F 116 C3
Ružic HR 138 B2
Ružomberok SK 99 B3
Ruzsa H 126 A1
Ry DK 59 B2
Rybany SK 98 C2
Rybina PL 69 A4
Rybnik PL 86 B2
Rychliki PL 69 B4
Rychlocice PL 86 A2
Rychnov nad Kněžnou CZ 85 B4
Rychnowo PL 77 A5
Rychtal PL 86 A1
Rychwał PL 76 B3
Ryczywół PL 87 A5
Ryczywól PL 75 B5
Ryd S 63 B2
Rydaholm S 62 B2
Rydal S 60 B2
Rydbo S 57 A4
Rydboholm S 60 B2
Ryde UK 44 C2
Rydöbruk S 60 C3
Rydsgård S 66 A2
Rydsnäs S 62 A3
Rydultowy PL 86 B2
Rydzyna PL 85 A4
Rye UK 45 C4
Rygge N 54 A1
Ryjewo PL 69 B3
Rykene N 53 B4
Rymań PL 67 C4
Rýmařov CZ 98 B1
Rynarzewo PL 76 A2
Ryomgård DK 59 B3
Rypefjord N 192 B7
Rypin PL 77 A4
Rysjedalsvika N 46 A2
Ryssby S 60 C4
Rytel PL 68 B2
Rytinki FIN 197 D10
Rytro PL 99 B4
Rywociny PL 77 A5
Rzeczenica PL 68 B2
Rzeczniów PL 87 A5
Rzeczyca PL 87 A4
Rzęgnowo PL 77 A5
Rzejowice PL 87 A3
Rzemień PL 87 B5
Rzepin PL 75 B3
Rzesznikowo PL 67 C4
Rzeszów PL 12 C4
Rzgów PL 86 A3
Rzhev RUS 9 D9

S

Saal
Bayern D 82 B2
Bayern D 95 C3
Saalbach A 109 B3
Saalburg D 83 B3
Saales F 92 C3
Saalfeld D 82 B3
Saalfelden am Steinernen Meer A 109 B3
Saanen CH 106 C2
Saarbrücken D 92 B2
Saarburg D 92 B2
Saarijärvi FIN 8 A4
Saari-Kämä FIN 197 C9
Saarlouis D 92 B2
Saas-Fee CH 119 A4
Šabac SRB 127 C1
Sabadell E 147 C3
Sabáudia I 169 B3
Sabbioneta I 121 C3
Sabero E 142 B1
Sabiñánigo E 145 B3
Sabiote E 157 B4
Sables-d'Or-les-Pins F 101 A3
Sablé-sur-Sarthe F 102 B1
Sabóia P 160 B1
Saborsko HR 123 B4
Sæbøvik N 52 A1
Sabres F 128 B2
Sabrosa P 148 A2
Sabugal P 149 B2
Sabuncu TR 187 C5
Sæby DK 58 A3
Săcălaz RO 126 B3
Sacecorbo E 152 B1
Saceda del Rio E 151 B5
Sacedón E 151 B5
Săcele RO 17 C6
Saceruela E 156 B3
Sachsenburg A 109 C4
Sachsenhagen D 72 B2
Sacile I 122 B1
Sacramenia E 151 A4
Sada E 140 A2
Sádaba E 144 B2
Saddell UK 34 C2
Sadernes E 147 B3
Sadki PL 76 A2
Sadkowice PL 87 A4
Sadlinki PL 69 B3
Sadów PL 75 B3
Sadská CZ 84 B2
Saelices E 151 C5
Saelices de Mayorga E 142 B1
Saerbeck D 71 B4
Saeul L 92 B1
Safaalan TR 186 A3
Safara P 161 A2
Säffle S 55 A3
Saffron Walden UK 45 A4
Safranbolu TR 187 A7
Säfsnäs S 50 B1
Şag RO 126 B3
Sagard D 66 B2
S'Agaro E 147 C4
Sågmyra S 50 B2
Sagone F 180 A1
Sagres P 160 C1
Ságújfalu H 113 A3
Sagunt E 159 B3
Sagvåg N 52 A1
Ságvár H 112 C2
Sagy F 105 C4
Sahagún E 142 B1
Šahy SK 112 A2
Saignelégier CH 106 B1
Saignes F 116 B2
Saija FIN 197 B11
Saillagouse F 146 B3
Saillans F 118 C2
Sains Richaumont F 91 B3
St Abb's UK 35 C5
St Affrique F 130 B1
St Agnan F 104 C2
St Agnant F 114 C3
St Agnes UK 42 B1
St Agrève F 117 B4
St Aignan F 103 B3
St Aignan-sur-Roë F 101 B4
St Albans UK 44 B3
St Alban-sur-Limagnole F 117 C3
St Amand-en-Puisaye F 104 B2
St Amand-les-Eaux F 79 B3
St Amand-Longpré F 103 B3
St Amand-Montrond F 103 C4
St Amans F 117 C3
St Amans-Soult F 130 B1
St Amant-Roche-Savine F 117 B3
St Amarin F 106 B1
St Ambroix F 131 A3
St Amé F 106 A1
St Amour F 118 A2
St André-de-Corcy F 117 B4
St André-de-Cubzac F 128 B2
St André-de-l'Eure F 89 B5
St André-de-Roquepertuis F 131 A3
St André-de-Sangonis F 130 B2
St Andre-de-Valborgne F 130 A2
St André-les-Alpes F 132 B2
St Andrews UK 35 B5
St Angel F 116 B2
St Anthème F 117 B3
St Antoine F 180 A2
St Antoine-de-Ficalba F 129 B3
St Antönien CH 107 C4
St Antonin-Noble-Val F 129 B4
St Août F 103 C3
St Armant-Tallende F 116 B3
St Arnoult F 90 C1
St Asaph UK 38 A3
St Astier F 129 A3

St Athan UK 39 C3
St Auban F 132 B2
St Aubin
CH 106 C1
F 105 B4
UK 88 A1
St Aubin-d'Aubigne F 101 A4
St Aubin-du-Cormier F 101 A4
St Aubin-sur-Aire F 92 C1
St Aubin-sur-Mer F 89 A3
St Aulaye F 128 A3
St Austell UK 42 B2
St Avit F 116 B2
St Avold F 92 B2
St Aygulf F 132 B2
St Bauzille-de-Putois F 130 B2
St Béat F 145 B4
St Beauzély F 130 A1
St Bees UK 36 B3
St Benim-d'Azy F 104 C2
St Benoît-du-Sault F 115 B5
St Benoit-en-Woëvre F 92 C1
St Berthevin F 102 A1
St Blaise-la-Roche F 92 C3
St Blazey UK 42 B2
St Blin F 105 A4
St Bonnet F 118 C3
St Bonnet Briance F 115 C5
St Bonnet-de-Joux F 104 C3
St Bonnet-le-Château F 117 B4
St Bonnet-le-Froid F 117 B4
St Brévin-les-Pins F 101 B3
St Briac-sur-Mer F 101 A3
St Brice-en-Coglès F 88 B2
St Brieuc F 101 A3
St Bris-le-Vineux F 104 B2
St Broladre F 88 B2
St Calais F 102 B2
St Cannat F 131 B4
St Cast-le-Guildo F 101 A3
St Céré F 129 B4
St Cergue CH 118 A3
St Cergues F 118 A3
St Cernin F 116 B2
St Chamant F 116 B1
St Chamas F 131 B4
St Chamond F 117 B4
St Chély-d'Apcher F 116 C3
St Chély-d'Aubrac F 116 C2
St Chinian F 130 B1
St Christol F 131 A4
St Christol-lès-Alès F 131 A3
St Christoly-Médoc F 114 C3
St Christophe-du-Ligneron F 114 B2
St Christophe-en-Brionnais F 117 A4
St Ciers-sur-Gironde F 128 A2
St Clair-sur-Epte F 90 B1
St Clar F 129 C3
St Claud F 115 C4
St Claude F 118 A2
St Clears UK 39 C2
St Columb Major UK 42 B2
St Come-d'Olt F 130 A1
St Cosme-en-Vairais F 89 B4
St Cyprien
Dordogne F 129 B4
Pyrenées-Orientales F 146 B4
St Cyr-sur-Loire F 102 B2
St Cyr-sur-Mer F 132 B1
St Cyr-sur-Methon F 117 A4
St David's UK 39 C1
St Denis F 90 C2
St Denis-d'Oléron F 114 B2
St Denis d'Orques F 102 A1
St Didier F 117 A4
St Didier-en-Velay F 117 B4
St Dié F 92 C2
St Dier-d'Auvergne F 117 B3
St Dizier F 91 C4
St Dizier-Leyrenne F 116 A1
St Dogmaels UK 39 B2
Ste Adresse F 89 A4
Ste Anne F 89 B4
Ste Anne-d'Auray F 100 B3
Ste Croix CH 105 C5
Ste Croix-Volvestre F 146 A2
Ste Engrâce F 144 A3
Ste Enimie F 130 A2
St Efflam F 100 A2
Ste Foy-de-Peyrolières F 146 A2
Ste Foy-la-Grande F 128 B3
Ste Foy l'Argentiere F 117 B4
Ste Gauburge-Ste Colombe F 89 B4
Ste Gemme la Plaine F 114 B2
Ste Geneviève F 90 B2
St Égrève F 118 B2
Ste Hélène F 128 B2
Ste Hélène-sur-Isère F 118 B3
Ste Hermine F 114 B2
Ste Jalle F 131 A4
Ste Livrade-sur-Lot F 129 B3
St Eloy-les-Mines F 116 A2
Ste Marie-aux-Mines F 106 A2
Ste Marie-du-Mont F 88 A2
Ste Maure-de-Touraine F 102 B2
Ste Maxime F 132 B2
Ste Ménéhould F 91 B4
Ste Mère-Église F 88 A2
St Emiland F 104 C3
St Émilion F 128 B2
St Enoder UK 42 B2
Sainteny F 88 A2
Ste Ode B 92 A1
Saintes F 114 C3
Ste Savine F 91 C4
Ste Sévère-sur-Indre F 103 C4
Ste Sigolène F 117 B4
St Esteben F 144 A2
St Estèphe F 128 A2
Ste Suzanne F 102 A1
St Étienne F 117 B4
St Etienne-de-Baigorry F 144 A2
St Étienne-de-Cuines F 118 B3
St Etienne-de-Fursac F 116 A1
St Etienne-de-Montluc F 101 B4
St Etienne-de-St Geoirs F 118 B2
St Étienne-de-Tinée F 132 A2
St Étienne-du-Bois F 118 A2
St Étienne-du-Rouvray F 89 A5
St Etienne-les-Orgues F 132 A1
Ste Tulle F 132 B1
St Fargeau F 104 B2
St Félicien F 117 B4
St Felix-de-Sorgues F 130 B1
St Félix-Lauragais F 146 A2
Saintfield UK 27 B5
St Fillans UK 35 B3
St Firmin F 118 C3
St Florent F 180 A2
St Florentin F 104 B2
St Florent-le-Vieil F 101 B4
St Florent-sur-Cher F 103 C4
St Flour F 116 B3
St Flovier F 103 C3
St Fort-sur-le-Né F 115 C3
St Fulgent F 114 B2
St Galmier F 117 B4
St Gaudens F 145 A4
St Gaultier F 115 B5
St Gély-du-Fesc F 130 B2
St Genest-Malifaux F 117 B4
St Gengoux-le-National F 104 C3
St Geniez F 132 A2
St Geniez-d'Olt F 130 A1
St Genis-de-Saintonge F 114 C3
St Genis-Pouilly F 118 A3
St Genix-sur-Guiers F 118 B2
St Georges Buttavent F 88 B3
St Georges-d'Aurac F 117 B3
St Georges-de-Commiers F 118 B2
St Georges-de-Didonne F 114 C3
St Georges-de-Luzençon F 130 A1
St Georges-de Mons F 116 B2
St Georges-de-Reneins F 117 A4
St Georges d'Oléron F 114 C2
St Georges-en-Couzan F 117 B3
St Georges-lès-Baillargeaux F 115 B4
St Georges-sur-Loire F 102 B1
St Georges-sur-Meuse B 79 B5
St Geours-de-Maremne F 128 C1
St Gérand-de-Vaux F 117 A3
St Gérand-le-Puy F 117 A3
St Germain F 105 B5
St Germain-Chassenay F 104 C2
St Germain-de-Calberte F 130 A2
St Germain-de-Confolens F 115 B4
St Germain-de-Joux F 118 A2
St Germain-des-Fossés F 117 A3
St Germain-du-Bois F 105 C4
St Germain-du-Plain F 105 C3
St Germain-du Puy F 103 B4
St Germain-en-Laye F 90 C2
St Germain-Laval F 117 B4
St Germain-Lembron F 116 B3
St Germain-les-Belles F 116 B1
St Germain-Lespinasse F 117 A3
St Germain-l'Herm F 117 B3
St Gervais-d'Auvergne F 116 A2
St Gervais-les-Bains F 118 B3
St Gervais-sur-Mare F 130 B2
St Gildas-de-Rhuys F 100 B3
St Gildas-des-Bois F 101 B3
St Gilles
Gard F 131 B3
St Gilles *continued*
Ille-et-Vilaine F 101 A4
St Gilles-Croix-de-Vie F 114 B2
St Gingolph F 119 A3
St Girons
Ariège F 146 B2
Landes F 128 C1
St Girons-Plage F 128 C1
St Gobain F 91 B3
St Gorgon-Main F 105 B5
St Guénolé F 100 B1
St Harmon UK 39 B3
St Helens UK 38 A4
St Helier UK 88 A1
St Herblain F 101 B4
St Hilaire
Allier F 104 C2
Aude F 146 A3
St Hilaire-de-Riez F 114 B2
St Hilaire-des-Loges F 114 B3
St Hilaire-de-Villefranche F 114 C3
St Hilaire-du-Harcouët F 88 B2
St Hilaire-du-Rosier F 118 B2
St Hippolyte
Aveyron F 116 C2
Doubs F 106 B1
St Hippolyte-du-Fort F 130 B2
St Honoré-les-Bains F 104 C2
St Hubert B 92 A1
St Imier CH 106 B2
St Issey UK 42 B2
St Ives
Cambridgeshire UK 44 A3
Cornwall UK 42 B1
St Izaire F 130 B1
St Jacques-de-la-Lande F 101 A4
St Jacut-de-la-Mer F 101 A3
St James F 88 B2
St Jaume d'Enveja E 153 B4
St Jean-Brévelay F 101 B3
St Jean-d'Angély F 114 C3
St Jean-de-Belleville F 118 B3
St Jean-de-Bournay F 118 B2
St Jean-de-Braye F 103 B3
St Jean-de-Côle F 115 C4
St Jean-de-Daye F 88 A2
St Jean de Losne F 105 B4
St Jean-de-Luz F 144 A2
St Jean-de-Maurienne F 118 B3
St Jean-de-Monts F 114 B1
St Jean-d'Illac F 128 B2
St Jean-du-Bruel F 130 A2
St Jean-du-Gard F 131 A2
St Jean-en-Royans F 118 B2
St Jean-la-Riviere F 133 B3
St Jean-Pied-de-Port F 144 A2
St Jean-Poutge F 129 C3
St Jeoire F 118 A3
St Joachim F 101 B3
St Johnstown IRL 27 B3
St Jorioz F 118 B3
St Joris Winge B 79 B4
St Jouin-de-Marnes F 102 C1
St Juéry F 130 B1
St Julien F 118 A2
St Julien-Chapteuil F 117 B4
St Julien-de-Vouvantes F 101 B4
St Julien-du-Sault F 104 A2
St Julien-du-Verdon F 132 B2
St Julien-en-Born F 128 B1
St Julien-en-Genevois F 118 A3
St Julien-l'Ars F 115 B4
St Julien la-Vêtre F 117 B3
St Julien-Mont-Denis F 118 B3
St Julien-sur-Reyssouze F 118 A2
St Junien F 115 C4
St Just
F 131 A3
UK 42 B1
St Just-en-Chaussée F 90 B2
St Just-en-Chevalet F 117 B3
St Justin F 128 C2
St Just-St Rambert F 117 B4
St Keverne UK 42 B1
St Lary-Soulan F 145 B4
St Laurent-d'Aigouze F 131 B3
St Laurent-de-Chamousset F 117 B4
St Laurent-de-Condel F 89 A3
St Laurent-de-la-Cabrerisse F 146 A3
St Laurent-de-la-Salanque F 146 B3
St Laurent-des-Autels F 101 B4
St Laurent-du-Pont F 118 B2
St Laurent-en-Caux F 89 A4
St Laurent-en-Grandvaux F 105 C4
St Laurent-Médoc F 128 A2
St Laurent-sur-Gorre F 115 C4
St Laurent-sur-Mer F 88 A3
St Laurent-sur-Sèvre F 114 B3
St Leger B 92 B1
St Léger-de-Vignes F 104 C2
St Léger-sous-Beuvray F 104 C3
St Léger-sur-Dheune F 104 C3
St Léonard-de-Noblat F 116 B1
St Leonards UK 45 C4
St Lô F 88 A2
St Lon-les-Mines F 128 C1
St Louis F 106 B2
St Loup F 117 A3
St Loup-de-la-Salle F 105 C3
St Loup-sur-Semouse F 105 B5
St Lunaire F 101 A3
St Lupicin F 118 A2
St Lyphard F 101 B3
St Lys F 146 A2
St Macaire F 128 B2
St Maclou F 89 A4
St Maixent-l'École F 115 B3
St Malo F 88 B1
St Mamet-la-Salvetat F 116 C2
St Mandrier-sur-Mer F 132 B1
St Marcel
Drôme F 117 C4
Saône-et-Loire F 105 C3
St Marcellin F 118 B2
St Marcellin sur Loire F 117 B4
St Marcet F 145 A4
St Mards-en-Othe F 104 A2
St Margaret's-at-Cliffe UK 45 B5
St Margaret's Hope UK 33 C4
St Mars-la-Jaille F 101 B4
St Martin-d'Ablois F 91 C3
St Martin-d'Auxigny F 103 B4
St Martin-de-Belleville F 118 B3
St Martin-de-Bossenay F 91 C3
St Martin-de-Crau F 131 B3
St Martin-de-Londres F 130 B2
St Martin-d'Entraunes F 132 A2
St Martin-de-Queyrières F 118 C3
St Martin-de-Ré F 114 B2
St Martin des Besaces F 88 A3
St Martin-d'Estreaux F 117 A3
St Martin-de-Valamas F 117 C4
St Martin-d'Hères F 118 B2
St Martin-du-Frêne F 118 A2
St Martin-en-Bresse F 105 C4
St Martin-en-Haut F 117 B4
St Martin-la-Méanne F 116 B1
St Martin-Osmonville F 90 B1
St Martin-sur-Ouanne F 104 B2
St Martin-Valmeroux F 116 B2
St Martin-Vésubie F 133 A3
St Martory F 145 A4
St Mary's UK 33 C4
St Mathieu F 115 C4
St Mathieu-de-Tréviers F 131 B2
St Maurice CH 119 A3
St Maurice-Navacelles F 130 B2
St Maurice-sur-Moselle F 106 B1
St Mawes UK 42 B1
St Maximin-la-Ste Baume F 132 B1
St Méard-de-Gurçon F 128 B3
St Médard-de-Guizières F 128 A2
St Médard-en-Jalles F 128 B2
St Méen-le-Grand F 101 A3
St Menges F 91 B4
St Merløse DK 61 D1
St Město CZ 85 B4
St M'Hervé F 101 A4
St Michel
Aisne F 91 B4
Gers F 145 A4
St Michel-Chef-Chef F 101 B3
St Michel-de-Castelnau F 128 B2
St Michel-de-Maurienne F 118 B3
St Michel-en-Grève F 100 A2
St Michel-enl'Herm F 114 B2
St Michel-Mont-Mercure F 114 B3
St Mihiel F 92 C1
St Monance UK 35 B5
St Montant F 131 A3
St Moritz CH 107 C4
St Nazaire F 101 B3
St Nazaire-en-Royans F 118 B2
St Nazaire-le-Désert F 131 A4
St Nectaire F 116 B2
St Neots UK 44 A3
St Nicolas-de-Port F 92 C2
St Nicolas-de-Redon F 101 B3
St Nicolas-du-Pélem F 100 A2
St Niklaas B 79 A4
St Omer F 78 B2
St Pair-sur-Mer F 88 B2
St Palais F 144 A2
St Palais-sur-Mer F 114 C2
St Pardoux-la-Rivière F 115 C4
St Paul-Cap-de-Joux F 129 C4
St Paul-de-Fenouillet F 146 B3
St Paul-de-Varax F 118 A2
St Paulien F 117 B3
St Paul-le-Jeune F 131 A3
St Paul-lès-Dax F 128 C1
St Paul-Trois-Châteaux F 131 A3
St Pé-de-Bigorre F 145 A3
St Pée-sur-Nivelle F 144 A2
St Péravy-la-Colombe F 103 B3
St Péray F 117 C4
St Père-en-Retz F 101 B3
St Peter Port UK 88 A1
St Petersburg = Sankt-Peterburg RUS 9 C7
St Philbert-de-Grand-Lieu F 114 A2
St Pierre F 130 B1
St Pierre-d'Albigny F 118 B3
St Pierre-d'Allevard F 118 B3
St Pierre-de-Chartreuse F 118 B2
St Pierre-de-Chignac F 129 A3
St Pierre-de-la-Fage F 130 B2
St Pierre-d'Entremont F 118 B2
St Pierre-d'Oléron F 114 C2
St Pierre-Eglise F 88 A2
St Pierre-en-Port F 89 A4
St Pierre-le-Moûtier F 104 C2
St Pierre Montlimart F 101 B4
St Pierre-Quiberon F 100 B2
St Pierre-sur-Dives F 89 A3
St Pierreville F 117 C4
St Pieters-Leeuw B 79 B4
St Plancard F 145 A4
St Poix F 101 B4
St Pol-de-Léon F 100 A2
St Polgues F 117 B3
St Pol-sur-Ternoise F 78 B2
St Pons-de-Thomières F 130 B1
St Porchaire F 114 C3
St Pourçain-sur-Sioule F 116 A3
St Priest F 117 B4
St Privat F 116 B2
St Quay-Portrieux F 100 A3
St Quentin F 90 B3
St Quentin-la-Poterie F 131 A3
St Quentin-les-Anges F 102 B1
St Rambert-d'Albon F 117 B4

St Rambert-en-
Bugey F...... 118 B2
St Raphaël F .. 132 B2
St Rémy-de-
Provence F... 131 B3
St Rémy-du-Val
F.............89 B4
St Remy-en-
Bouzemont F ..91 C4
St Renan F 100 A1
St Révérien F .. 104 B2
St Riquier F 90 A1
St Romain-de-
Colbosc F 89 A4
St Rome-de-Cernon
F............. 130 A1
St Rome-de-Tarn
F............. 130 A1
St Sadurní d'Anoia
E............. 147 C2
St Saëns F 89 A5
St Sampson UK..88 A1
St Samson-la-
Poterie F 90 B1
St Saturnin-de-
Lenne F 130 A2
St Saturnin-lès-Apt
F............. 131 B4
St Saulieu F 90 B2
St Saulge F 104 B2
St Sauveur
Finistère F 100 A2
Haute-Saône
F............. 105 B5
St Sauveur-de-
Montagut F .. 117 C4
St Sauveur-en-
Puisaye F 104 B2
St Sauveur-en-Rue
F............. 117 B4
St Sauveur-
Lendelin F 88 A2
St Sauveur-le-
Vicomte F 88 A2
St Sauveur-sur-
Tinée F 132 A3
St Savin
Gironde F 128 A2
Vienne F 115 B4
St Savinien F ... 114 C3
St Savournin
F............. 131 B4
St Seine-l'Abbaye
F............. 105 B3
St Sernin-sur-Rance
F............. 130 B1
St Sevan-sur-Mer
F.............88 B1
St Sever F 128 C2
St Sever-Calvados
F.............88 B2
St Sorlin-d'Arves
F............. 118 B3
St Soupplets F ..90 B2
St Sulpice F ... 129 C4
St Sulpice-Laurière
F............. 116 A1
St Sulpice-les-
Feuilles F 115 B5
St Symphorien
F............. 128 B2
St Symphoriende-
Lay F 117 B4
St Symphorien
d'Ozon F 117 B4
St Symphoriensur-
Coise F 117 B4
St Teath UK 42 B2
St Thégonnec
F............. 100 A2
St Thiébault F .. 105 A4
St Trivier-de-
Courtes F 118 A2
St Trivier-sur-
Moignans F .. 117 A4
St Trojan-les-Bains
F............. 114 C2
St Tropez F 132 B2
St Truiden B 79 B5
St Vaast-la-Hougue
F.............88 A2
St Valérien F ... 104 A2
St Valery-en-Caux
F.............89 A4
St Valéry-sur-
Somme F 78 B1
St Vallier
Drôme F 117 B4
Saône-et-Loire
F............. 104 C3

St Vallier-de-Thiey
F............. 132 B2
St Varent F 102 C1
St Vaury F 116 A1
St Venant F 78 B2
St Véran F 119 C3
St Vincent I.... 119 B4
St Vincent-de-
Tyrosse F 128 C1
St Vit F 105 B4
St Vith B.......80 B2
St Vivien-de-Médoc
F............. 114 C2
St Yan F 117 A4
St Ybars F 146 A2
St Yorre F 117 A3
St Yrieix-la-Perche
F............. 115 C5
Saissac F 146 A3
Saja E 142 A2
Sajan SRB 126 B2
Šajkaš SRB 126 B2
Sajókaza H 99 C4
Sajószentpéter
H............. 113 A4
Sajóvámos H .. 113 A4
Sakarya TR 187 B5
Šakiai LT 13 A5
Sakskøbing DK .65 B4
Sakule SRB 126 B2
Sala S 50 C3
Šaľa SK 111 A4
Sala Baganza
I............. 120 C3
Sala Consilina
I............. 172 B1
Salakovac SRB 127 C3
Salamanca E .. 150 B2
Salamina GR .. 185 B4
Salandra I..... 172 B2
Salaparuta I... 176 B1
Salar E 163 A3
Salardú E 145 B4
Salas E 141 A4
Salas de los
Infantes E 143 B3
Salau F 146 B2
Salavaux CH .. 106 C2
Salbertrand I . 119 B3
Salbohed S 50 C3
Salbris F 103 B4
Salbu N 46 A2
Salce E 141 B4
Salching D 95 C4
Salcombe UK ..43 B3
Saldaña E 142 B2
Saldus LV 8 D7
Sale I 120 C1
Saleby S 55 B4
Salem D 107 B4
Salemi I 176 B1
Salen N 199 A8
Sälen S 49 A5
Salen
Argyll & Bute
UK
Highland UK ...34 B2
Salernes F 132 B2
Salerno I 170 C2
Salers F 116 B2
Salford UK 40 B1
Salgótarján
H............. 113 A3
Salgueiro P ... 155 B3
Salhus N 46 B2
Sali HR 137 B4
Sálice Salentino
I............. 173 B3
Salientes E ... 141 B4
Salies-de-Béarn
F............. 144 A3
Salies-du-Salat
F............. 145 A4
Salignac-Eyvigues
F............. 129 B4
Saligney-sur-
Roudon F 104 C2
Salihli TR 188 A3
Salihorsk BY ...13 B7
Salinas
Alicante E 159 C3
Huesca E 145 B4
Salinas de
Medinaceli E . 152 A1
Salinas de Pisuerga
E............. 142 B2
Salindres F ... 131 A3
Saline di Volterra
I............. 135 B3
Salins-les-Bains
F............. 105 C4
Salir P 160 B1
Salisbury UK ...44 B2

Salla
A............. 110 B1
FIN........... 197 C11
Sallachy UK 32 C2
Sallanches F .. 118 B3
Sallent E 147 C2
Sallent de Gállego
E............. 145 B3
Salles F 128 B2
Salles-Curan
F............. 130 A1
Salles-sur-l'Hers
F............. 146 A2
Sallins IRL 30 A2
Sällsjö S 199 B10
Salmerón E ... 152 B1
Salmiech F ... 130 A1
Salmivaara
FIN........... 197 C11
Salmoral E ... 150 B2
Salo FIN........8 B3
Salò I 121 B3
Salobreña E .. 163 B4
Salon-de-Provence
F............. 131 B4
Salonica =
Thessaloniki
GR........... 182 C4
Salonta RO.....16 B4
Salorino E 155 B3
Salornay-sur-Guye
F............. 104 C3
Salorno I 121 A4
Salou E 147 C2
Šalovci SLO ... 111 C3
Salsbruket N . 199 A8
Salses-le-Chateau
F............. 146 B3
Salsomaggiore
Terme I 120 C2
Salt E 147 C3
Saltaire UK 40 B2
Saltara I 136 B1
Saltash UK 42 B2
Saltburn-by-the-
Sea UK 37 B6
Saltcoats UK ...34 C3
Saltfleet UK ...41 B4
Salto P 148 A2
Saltrød N 53 B4
Saltsjöbaden S .57 A4
Saltvik
FIN............51 B7
S 62 A4
Saludécio I ... 136 B1
Salussola I ... 119 B5
Saluzzo I 119 C4
Salvacañete E . 152 B2
Salvada P 160 B2
Salvagnac F ... 129 C4
Salvaterra E .. 155 C4
Salvaterra de
Magos P 154 B2
Salvaterra do
Extremo P ... 155 B4
Salvatierra
Avila E 143 B4
Badajoz E 155 C4
Salvatierra de
Santiago E ... 156 A1
Salviac F 129 B4
Salzburg A ... 109 B4
Salzgitter D....72 B3
Salzgitter Bad
D 72 B3
Salzhausen D ..72 A3
Salzhemmendorf
D 72 B2
Salzkotten D ...81 A4
Salzmünde D ...83 A3
Salzwedel D 73 B4
Šamac BIH 125 B4
Samadet F 128 C2
Samandıra
TR........... 186 B4
Samassi I 179 C2
Samatan F 146 A1
Sambiase I 175 C2
Sambir UA 13 D5
Samborowo PL .69 B4
Sambuca di Sicilia
I............. 176 B2
Samedan CH.. 107 C4
Samer F 78 B1
Sami GR 184 A1
Şamlı TR 186 C2
Sammichele di Bari
I............. 173 B2
Samnaun CH .. 107 C5
Samobor HR .. 123 B4
Samoëns F ... 118 A3
Samogneux F ...91 B5
Samokov BG ...17 D5

Samora Correia
P............. 154 C2
Šamorín SK ... 111 A4
Samos
E............. 141 B3
GR........... 188 B1
Samos SRB 126 B2
Samothraki
GR........... 183 C7
Samper de Calanda
E............. 153 A3
Sampéyre I ... 133 A3
Sampieri I..... 177 C3
Sampigny F 92 C1
Samplawa PL ..69 B4
Samproniano
I............. 168 A1
Sámsø DK 65 B4
Samsun TR 23 A8
Samtens D......66 B2
Samugheo I... 179 C2
San Adrián E .. 144 B2
San Agustín E . 164 C2
San Agustín de
Guadalix E ... 151 B4
San Alberto I.. 135 A5
San Amaro E .. 140 B2
Sânandrei RO. 126 B3
San Andrès de
Rabanedo E .. 142 B1
San Antanio di
Santadi I..... 179 C2
San Antólin de Ibias
E............. 141 A4
San Arcángelo
I............. 174 A2
San Asensio E . 143 B4
San Bartolomé de
las Abiertas
E............. 150 C3
San Bartolomé de
la Torre E 161 B2
San Bartolomé
Pinares E 150 B3
San Bartolomeo in
Galdo I 170 B3
San Benedetto del
Tronto I 136 C2
San Benedetto in
Alpe I 135 B4
San Benedetto Po
I............. 121 B3
San Benito E . 156 B3
San Benito de la
Contienda E . 155 C3
San Biágio Plátani
I............. 176 B2
San Biágio
Saracinisco I . 169 B3
San Bonifacio
I............. 121 B4
San Calixto E . 156 C2
San Cándido I . 109 C3
San Carlo
CH........... 119 A5
E............. 157 B4
San Carlos del Valle
E............. 157 B4
San Casciano dei
Bagni I 135 C4
San Casciano in Val
di Pesa I 135 B4
San Cataldo
Puglia I 173 B4
Sicilia I 176 B2
San Cebrián de
Castro E 149 A4
Sancergues F . 104 B1
Sancerre F 103 B4
San Cesário di
Lecce I 173 B4
Sancey-le-Long
F............. 105 B5
Sanchiorian E . 150 B3
San Chírico Raparo
I............. 174 A2
Sanchonuño
E............. 151 A3
San Cibrao das
Viñas E 140 B3
San Cipirello I . 176 B2
San Ciprián E . 141 A3
San Clemente
E............. 158 B1
San Clodio E . 141 B3
Sancoins F 104 C1
San Colombano al
Lambro I 120 B2
San Costanzo
I............. 136 B2
San Crisóbal de
Entreviñas E . 142 B1

San Cristóbal de la
Polantera E . 141 B5
San Cristóbal de la
Vega E 150 A3
San Cristovo E 141 C3
Sancti-Petri E . 162 B1
Sancti-Spiritus
E............. 149 B3
Sand
Hedmark N ...48 B3
Rogaland N... 52 A2
San Fele I 172 B1
San Felice Circeo
I............. 169 B3
San Felices E .. 143 B3
San Felices de los
Gallégos E ... 149 B3
San Felice sul
Panaro I 121 C4
San Ferdinando di
Púglia I 171 B4
San Fernando
E............. 162 B1
San Fernando de
Henares E ... 151 B4
San Fili I 174 B2
San Foca I 173 B4
San Fratello
I............. 177 B3
Sangatte F 78 B1
San Gavino
Monreale I ... 179 C2
San Gémini Fonte
I............. 168 A2
Sangerhausen
D 82 A3
San Germano
Vercellese I .. 119 B5
San Giácomo
Trentino Alto
Adige I 108 C2
Umbria I 136 C1
San Gimignano
I............. 135 B4
San Ginésio I . 136 B2
Sangineto Lido
I............. 174 B1
San Giórgio a Liri
I............. 169 B3
San Giorgio della
Richinvelda
I............. 122 A1
San Giórgio del
Sánnio I 170 B2
San Giórgio di
Lomellina I .. 120 B1
San Giorgio di
Nogaro I 122 B2
San Giorgio di
Piano I 121 C4
San Giórgio Iónico
I............. 173 B3
San Giovanni a Piro
I............. 172 B1
San Giovanni
Bianco I 120 B2
San Giovanni di
Sinis I 179 C2
San Giovanni in
Croce I 120 B3
San Giovanni in
Fiore I 174 B2
San Giovanni in
Persiceto I ... 121 C4
San Giovanni
Reatino I 169 A2
San Giovanni
Rotondo I ... 171 B3
San Giovanni
Suérgiu I 179 C2
San Giovanni
Valdarno I ... 135 B4
San Giuliano Terme
I............. 134 B3
San Giustino I . 135 B5
San Godenzo I . 135 B4
Sangonera la Verde
E............. 165 B3
San Gregorio
Magno I 172 B1
Sangüesa E ... 144 B2
Sanguinet F .. 128 B1
San Giuseppe Jato
I............. 176 B2
Sanica BIH 124 C2
Sanitz D 65 B5
San Javier E .. 165 B4
San Jorge E ... 154 B2
San José E 164 C2
San Juan E ... 143 B3
San Juan de
Alicante E ... 165 A4
San Juan de la Nava
E............. 150 B3
San Justo de la
Vega E 141 B4
Sankt Aegyd am
Neuwalde A . 110 B2
Sankt Andrä
A............. 110 C1
Sankt Andreasberg
D 82 A2
Sankt Anna S ..56 B2

Sankt Anna am
Aigen A 110 C2
Sankt Anton am
Arlberg A 107 B5
Sankt Anton an der
Jessnitz A 110 B2
Sankt Augustin
D 80 B3
Sankt Blasien
D 106 B3
Sankt Englmar
D 95 B4
Sankt Gallen
A............. 110 B1
CH........... 107 B4
Sankt Gallenkirch
A............. 107 B4
Sankt Georgen
A 96 C2
D 106 A3
Sankt Georgen am
Reith A 110 B1
Sankt Georgen ob
Judenburg A. 110 B1
Sankt Georgen ob
Murau A 109 B5
Sankt Gilgen
A............. 109 B4
Sankt Goar D...81 B3
Sankt Goarshausen
D 81 B3
Sankt Ingbert
D 92 B3
Sankt Jacob A. 109 C5
Sankt Jakob in
Defereggen
A............. 109 C3
Sankt Johann am
Tauern A 110 B1
Sankt Johann am
Wesen A 109 A4
Sankt Johann im
Pongau A 109 B4
Sankt Johann in
Tirol A 109 B3
Sankt Katharein an
der Laming
A............. 110 B2
Sankt Kathrein am
Hauenstein
A............. 110 B2
Sankt Lambrecht
A............. 110 B1
Sankt Leonhard am
Forst A 110 A2
Sankt Leonhard in
Pitztal A 108 B1
Sankt Lorenzen
A............. 109 C3
Sankt Marein
Steiermark
A............. 110 B2
Steiermark A . 110 B2
Sankt Margarethen
im Lavanttal
A............. 110 C1
Sankt Margrethen
CH........... 107 B4
Sankt Michael
A............. 110 B2
Sankt Michael im
Burgenland
A............. 111 B3
Sankt Michael in
Lungau A 109 B4
Sankt
Michaelisdonn
D 64 C2
Sankt Niklaus
CH........... 119 A4
Sankt Nikolai im
Sölktal A 109 B5
Sankt Olof S ...63 C2
Sankt Oswald
D 96 C1
Sankt Paul
A............. 112 C1
D 132 A2
Sankt Peter D . 106 A3
Sankt Peter am
Kammersberg
A............. 110 B1
Sankt-Peterburg =
St Petersburg
RUS...........9 C7
Sankt Peter-Ording
D 64 B1
Sankt Pölten
A............. 110 A2
Sankt Radegund
A............. 110 C1
Sankt Ruprecht an
der Raab A . 110 B2

Sankt Salvador A.............110 C1
Sankt Stefan A.............110 C1
Sankt Stefan an der Gail A......109 C4
Sankt Stefan im Rosental A....110 C2
Sankt Valentin A.............110 A1
Sankt Veit an der Glan A......110 C1
Sankt Veit an der Gölsen A....110 A2
Sankt Veit in Defereggen A.............109 C3
Sankt Wendel D.............92 B3
Sankt Wolfgang A.............109 B4
D.............108 A3
San Lazzaro di Sávena I.....135 A4
San Leo I.....135 B5
San Leonardo de Yagüe E.....143 C3
San Leonardo in Passiria I.....108 C2
San Lorenzo al Mare I.....133 B3
San Lorenzo a Merse I.....135 B4
San Lorenzo Bellizzi I.....174 B2
San Lorenzo de Calatrava E...157 B4
San Lorenzo de El Escorial E....151 B3
San Lorenzo de la Parrilla E....158 B1
San Lorenzo di Sebato I.....108 C2
San Lorenzo in Campo I.....136 B1
San Lorenzo Nuovo I.....168 A1
San Lourenco P.....160 A1
San Luca I.....175 C2
Sanlúcar de Barrameda E.161 C3
Sanlúcar de Guadiana E...160 B2
Sanlúcar la Mayor E.....161 B3
San Lúcido I...174 B2
Sanluri I...179 C2
San Marcello I.....136 B2
San Marcello Pistoiese I.....135 A3
San Marcial E.149 A4
San Marco I...170 C2
San Marco Argentano I..174 B2
San Marco dei Cavoti I....170 B2
San Marco in Lámis I.............171 B3
San Marino RSM.....136 B1
San Martín de Castañeda E.141 B4
San Martín de la Vega E.....151 B4
San Martín de la Vega del Alberche E.............150 B2
San Martín del Tesorillo E...162 B2
San Martín de Luiña E.....141 A4
San Martín de Montalbán E.....157 A3
San Martín de Oscos E.....141 A4
San Martín de Pusa E...150 C3
San Martín de Unx E.....144 B2
San Martín de Valdeiglesias E.....150 B3
San Martino di Campagna I..122 A1
San Martino di Castrozza I..121 A4
San-Martino-di-Lota F.....180 A2
San Martino in Pénsilis I.....170 B3

San Mateo de Gallego E....144 C3
San Máuro Forte I.............172 B2
San Michele all'Adige I.....121 A4
San Michele di Ganzaria I.....177 B3
San Michele Mondovi I....133 A3
San Miguel de Aguayo E.....142 A2
San Miguel de Bernuy E.....151 A4
San Miguel del Arroyo E.....150 A3
San Miguel de Salinas E.....165 B4
Sànmihaiu Roman RO.............126 B3
San Millán de la Cogolla E.....143 B4
San Miniato I...135 B3
San Muñoz E...149 B3
Sànna S........55 B5
Sannazzaro de'Burgondi I.............120 B1
Sanne D.........73 B4
Sannicandro di Bari I.............171 B4
Sannicandro Gargánico I..171 B3
San Nicola del'Alto I.............174 B2
San Nicolás del Puerto E....156 C2
Sânnicolau Mare RO.............126 A2
San Nicolò Gerrei I.............179 C3
San Nicolò I.....174 B2
Sannidal I.....53 B5
Sanniki PL......77 B4
Sanok PL.......12 D5
San Pablo de los Montes E....157 A3
San Pancrázio Salentino I...173 B3
San Pantaleo I.............178 A3
San Páolo di Civitate I.....171 B3
San Pawl il-Bahar M.....175 C3
San Pedro Albacete E....158 C1
Oviedo E....141 A4
San Pedro de Alcántara E..162 B3
San Pedro de Ceque E.....141 B4
San Pedro del Arroyo E....150 B3
San Pedro del Pinatar E.....165 B4
San Pedro del Romeral E....143 A3
San Pedro de Merida E....156 B1
San Pedro de Valderaduey E.............142 B2
San Pedro Manrique E..144 B1
San Pellegrino Terme I.....120 B2
San Piero a Sieve I.............135 B4
San Piero in Bagno I.............135 B4
San Piero Patti I.............177 A3
San Pietro I...177 B3
San Pietro in Casale I.............121 C4
San Pietro in Gu I.............121 B4
San Pietro in Palazzi I.....135 B3
San Pietro in Volta I.............122 B1
San Pietro Vara I.............134 A2
San Pietro Vernótico I...173 B3
San Polo d'Enza I.............135 B4
Sanquhar UK...36 A3
San Quírico d'Órcia I.............135 B4

San Rafael del Rio E.............153 B4
San Remo I....133 B3
San Román de Cameros E....143 B4
San Roman de Hernija E.....150 A2
San Román de la Cuba E.......142 B2
San Roman de los Montes E....150 B3
San Romao P...155 C3
San Roque E...162 B2
San Roque de Riomera E....143 A3
San Rufo I....172 B1
San Sabastián de los Ballesteros E.............162 A3
San Salvador de Cantamuda E.............142 B2
San Salvo I...170 A2
San Salvo Marina I.............170 A2
San Sebastián de los Reyes E...151 B4
San Sebastiano Curone I....120 C2
San Secondo Parmense I...120 C3
Sansepolcro I..135 B5
San Serverino Marche I....135 B4
San Severino Lucano I....174 A2
San Severo I...171 B3
San Silvestre de Guzmán E...161 B2
Sanski Most BIH.......124 C2
San Sosti I....174 B2
San Stéfano di Cadore I....109 C3
San Stino di Livenza I....122 B1
Santa Agnès E 166 B1
Santa Amalia E.............156 A1
Santa Ana Cáceres E....156 A2
Jaén E.....163 A4
Santa Ana de Pusa E.............150 C3
Santa Barbara E.............153 B4
Santa Bárbara P.............160 B1
Santa Barbara de Casa E.....161 B2
Santa Bárbara de Padrões P...160 B2
Santacara E...144 B2
Santa Catarina P.............160 B2
Santa Caterina di Pittinuri I...178 B2
Santa Caterina Villarmosa I...177 B3
Santa Cesárea Terme I....173 B4
Santa Clara-a-Nova P.............160 B1
Santa Clara-a-Velha P.............160 B1
Santa Cruz da Louredo P....160 B2
Santa Coloma de Farners E...147 C3
Santa Coloma de Gramenet E...147 C3
Santa Coloma de Queralt E....147 C2
Santa Colomba de Curueño E...142 B1
Santa Colomba de Somoza E...141 B4
Santa Comba E.............140 A2
Santa Comba Dáo P.............148 B1
Santa Comba de Rossas P....149 A3
Santa Cristina I.............120 B2
Santa Cristina de la Polvorosa E..141 B5
Santa Croce Camerina I...177 C3
Santa Croce di Magliano I...170 B2
Santa Cruz E.............140 A2

Santa Cruz continued P.............154 B1
Santa Cruz de Alhama E...163 A4
Santa Cruz de Campezo E...143 B4
Santa Cruz de Grio E.............152 A2
Santa Cruz de la Salceda E...151 A4
Santa Cruz de la Sierra E.....156 A2
Santa Cruz de la Zarza E.......151 C4
Santa Cruz del Retamar E...151 B3
Santa Cruz del Valle E.............150 B2
Santa Cruz de Moya E.............159 B2
Santa Cruz de Mudela E....157 B4
Santa Cruz de Paniagua E...149 B3
Santa Doménica Talao I....171 B3
Santa Doménica Vittória I....177 B3
Santa Elena E..157 B4
Santa Elena de Jamuz E....141 B5
Santa Eufemia Santaella E....162 A3
Santa Eufémia d'Aspromonte I.............175 C1
Santa Eulalia E.............152 B2
Santa Eulália P.............155 C3
Santa Eulalia de Oscos E....141 A3
Santa Eulàlia des Riu E....166 C1
Santa Fe E....163 A4
Santa Fiora I....135 C4
Sant'Àgata dei Goti I.............170 B2
Sant'Àgata d'Ésaro I.............174 B1
Sant'Àgata di Puglia I....171 B3
Sant'Agata Feltria I.............135 B5
Sant'Àgata Militello I.............177 A3
Santa Gertrude I.............121 A5
Santa Giustina I.............121 A5
Sant Agustí de Lluçanès E...147 B3
Santa Iria P....160 B2
Santa Leocadia P.............148 A1
Santa Lucia del Mela I....177 A4
Santa Lucia-di-Porto-Vecchio F.............180 B2
Santa Luzia P .160 B1
Santa Maddalena Vallalta I...108 C3
Santa Magdalena de Polpis E..153 B4
Santa Margalida E.............167 B3
Santa Margarida P.............154 B2
Santa Margarida do Sado P....160 A1
Santa Margaridao de Montbuí E.............147 C2
Santa Margherita I.............134 A2
Santa Margherita di Belice I....176 B2
Santa Margherita Ligure I....134 A2
Santa Maria CH.....108 C1
E.............144 B3
Santa Maria al Bagno I....173 B3
Santa Maria Cápua Vétere I....170 B2
Santa Maria da Feira P.....148 B1

Santa Maria de Cayón E......143 A3
Santa Maria de Corcó E......147 B3
Santa Maria de Huerta E.....152 A1
Santa Maria de la Alameda E...151 B3
Santa Maria de las Hoyas E.....143 C3
Santa Maria de la Camí E......167 B2
Santa Maria del Campo E.....143 B3
Santa Maria del Campo Rus E.158 B1
Santa Maria della Versa I.....120 C2
Santa Maria de Moya E.............120 B2
Santa Maria de Taro I.....134 A2
Santa Maria de Mercadillo E.143 C3
Santa Maria de Nieva E.....164 B3
Santa Maria de Trassierra E..156 C3
Santa Maria di Licodia I.....177 B3
Santa Maria-di-Réspéscia I...168 A1
Santa Maria la Palma I.....178 B2
Santa María la Real de Nieva E.....150 A3
Santa María Maggiore I.....119 A5
Santa Marina del Rey E.....141 B5
Santa Marinella I.............168 A1
Santa Marta Albacete E....158 B1
Badajoz E.....155 C4
Santa Marta de Magasca E...156 A1
Santa Marta de Penaguião P..148 A2
Santa Marta de Tormes E.....150 B2
Santana Évora P.....154 C2
Setúbal P.....154 C1
Sântana RO.....126 A3
Santana da Serra P.............160 B1
Sant'Ana de Cambas P.....160 B2
Santana do Mato P.............154 C2
Sant'Anastasia I.............170 C2
Sant'Andrea Frius I.............179 C3
Sant'Ángelo dei Lombardi I...172 B1
Sant'Ángelo in Vado I.....136 B1
Sant'Ángelo Lodigiano I...120 B2
Santa Ninfa I...176 B1
Sant'Antíoco I.179 C2
Sant Antoni de Calonge E....147 C4
Sant Antoni de Portmany E..166 C1
Sant'Antonio-di-Gallura I.....178 B3
Santanyí E.....167 B3
Santa Olalla Huelva E.....161 B3
Toledo E.....150 B3
Santa Pau E....147 B3
Santa Pola E...165 A4
Santa Ponça E..166 B2
Santarcángelo di Romagna I...136 A1
Santarém P...154 B2
Santa Severa F.............180 A2
I.............168 A1
Santa Severina I.............175 B2
Santas Martas E.............142 B1
Santa Sofía I.135 B4
Santa Susana E.............154 C2

Santa Suzana P.............155 C2
Santa Teresa di Riva I.............177 B4
Santa Teresa Gallura I.....178 A3
Santa Uxía E..140 B2
Santa Valburga I.............108 C1
Santa Vittória in Matenano I...136 B2
Sant Boi de Llobregat E...147 C3
Sant Carles de la Ràpita E...153 B4
Sant Carlos E..166 B1
Santa Caterina I.............135 C4
Sant Celoni E...147 C3
Sant Climent E.............167 B4
Santed E.....152 A2
Sant'Egídio alla Vibrata I...136 C2
Sant'Elia a Pianisi I.............170 B2
Sant'Elia Fiumerapido I.............169 B3
Santélices E...143 A3
San Telmo E...161 B3
Sant'Elpídio a Mare I.............136 B2
Santéramo in Colle I.............171 C4
Santervas de la Vega E.....142 B2
Sant'Eufemia Lamezia I.....175 C2
Sant Feliu E...147 C3
Sant Feliu de Codines E....147 C3
Sant Feliu de Guixols E.....147 C4
Sant Feliu Sasserra E.............147 C3
Sant Ferran E.............166 C1
Sant Francesc de Formentera E.............166 C1
Sant Francesc de ses Salines E..166 C1
Santhià I.....119 B5
Sant Hilari Sacalm E.............147 C3
Sant Hipólit de Voltregà E...147 B3
Santiago de Alcántara E....155 B3
Santiago de Calatrava E...163 A3
Santiago de Compostela E.............140 B2
Santiago de la Espada E....164 A2
Santiago de la Puebla E....150 B2
Santiago de la Ribera E.....165 B4
Santiago del Campo E.....155 B4
Santiago de Litem P.............154 B2
Santiago do Cácem P.............160 B1
Santiago do Escoural P....154 C2
Santiago Maior P.............155 C3
Santibáñez de Béjar E....150 B2
Santibáñez de la Peña E.....142 B2
Santibáñez de la Sierra E....149 B3
Santibáñez del Alto E.....149 B3
Santibáñez el Bajo E.....149 B3
Santillana E.142 A2
Santiponce E.161 A3
San Tirso de Abres E.............141 A3
Santisteban del Puerto E....157 B4
Santiuste de San Juan Bautiste E.............150 A3
Santiz E.....149 A4

Sant Jaume dels Domenys E...147 C2
Sant Joan Baptista E.............166 B1
Sant Joan de les Abadesses E..147 B3
Sant Jordi E.....153 B4
Sant Josep de sa Talaia E.....166 C1
Sant Juliáde Loria AND.............146 B2
Sant'Ilario d'Enza I.............121 C3
Sant Llorenç Morunys E....147 B2
Sant Llorençdes Carctassar E..167 B3
Sant Llorenç Savall E.............147 C3
Sant Luis E....167 B4
Sant Mart ide Llemaná E....147 B3
Sant Marti de Maldá E.....147 C2
Sant Marti Sarroca E.............147 C2
Sant Mateu E...153 B4
Sant Miquel E..166 B1
Santo Aleixo P.............161 A2
Santo Amado P.............161 A2
Santo Amaro P.............155 C3
Santo André E.............160 A1
Santo Domingo E.............155 C3
Santo Domingo de la Calzada E.143 B4
Santo Domingo de Silos E.....143 C3
Santo Estêvão Faro P.....160 B2
Santarém P....154 C2
Santok PL.......75 B4
Santomera E...165 A3
Santoña E.....143 A3
Santo-Pietro-di-Tenda F....180 A2
Sant'Oreste I..168 A2
Santo Spírito I 171 B4
Santo Stefano d'Aveto I....134 A2
Santo Stéfano di Camastra I...177 A3
Santo Stefano di Magra I.....134 A2
Santo Stéfano Quisquina I..176 B2
Santo Tirso P...148 A1
Santotis E.....142 A2
Santo Tomé E..164 A1
Santovenia Burgos E.....143 B3
Zamora E.....142 C1
Sant Pau de Seguries E....147 B3
Santpedor E...147 C2
Sant Pere de Riudebitles E.............147 C2
Sant Pere Pescador E.............147 B4
Sant Pere Sallavinera E...147 C2
Sant Quirze de Besora E.....147 B3
Sant Rafel E...166 C1
Sant Ramon E..147 C2
Santu Lussurgiu I.............178 B2
Santutzi I.....143 A3
San Valentino alla Muta I.....108 C1
San Venanzo I..135 C5
San Vicente de Alcántara E...155 B3
San Vicente de la Arana E.....144 B1
San Vicente de la Barquera E..142 A2
San Vicente de la Sonsierra E..143 B4
San Vicente de Toranzo E....143 A3
San Vietro E...149 A3
San Vigilio I...108 C2

San Vincente del Raspeig E 165 A4
San Vincenzo I 134 B3
San Vito I 179 C3
San Vito al Tagliamento I 122 B1
San Vito Chietino I 169 A4
San Vito dei Normanni I ... 173 B3
San Vito di Cadore I 108 C3
San Vito lo Capo I 176 A1
San Vito Romano I 169 B2
Sanxenxo E 140 B2
Sanza I 172 B1
São Aleixo P ... 155 C3
São Barnabé P 160 B1
São Bartoloméda Serra P 160 A1
São Bartolomeu de Messines P ... 160 B1
São Bento P ... 140 C2
São Brás P 160 B2
São Brás de Alportel P 160 B2
São Braz do Reguedoura P 154 C2
São Cristóvão P 154 C2
São Domingos P 160 B1
São Geraldo P . 154 C2
São Jacinto P . 148 B1
São João da Madeira P ... 148 B1
São João da Pesqueira P .. 148 A2
São João da Ribeira P 154 B2
São João da Serra P 148 B1
São João da Venda P 160 B2
São Jóao dos Caldeireiros P 160 B2
São Julião P ... 155 B3
São Leonardo P 155 C3
São Luís P 160 B1
São Manços P . 155 C3
São Marcos da Ataboeira P .. 160 B2
Saõ Marcos da Serra P 160 B1
São Marcos de Campo P 155 C3
São Martinho da Cortiça P 148 B1
São Martinho das Amoreiras P .. 160 B1
São Martinho do Porto P 154 B1
São Matias
Beja P 160 A2
Évora P 154 C2
São Miguel d'Acha P 155 A3
São Miguel de Machede P ... 155 C3
São Pedro da Torre P 140 C2
São Pedro de Cadeira P ... 154 B1
São Pedro de Moel P 154 B1
São Pedro de Solis P 160 B2
São Pedro do Sul P 148 B1
Saorge F 133 B3
São Romão P . 154 C2
São Sebastião dos Carros P 160 B2
São Teotónio P 160 B1
São Torcato P . 148 A1
Sapataria P ... 154 B1
Sapes GR 183 B7
Sapiãos P 148 A2
Sa Pobla E 167 B3
Sappada I 109 C3
Sappen N 192 C5

Sapri I 174 A1
Sarajärvi FIN 197 D10
Sarajevo BIH .. 139 B4
Saramon F 129 C3
Sarandë AL 182 D2
Saranovo SRB . 127 C2
Saraorci SRB .. 127 C3
Sa Rapita E 167 B3
Saray TR 186 A2
Saraycik TR ... 187 C4
Sarayköy TR .. 188 B3
Saraylar TR ... 186 B2
Sarayönü TR .. 189 A7
Sarbia PL 75 B5
Sarbinowo
Zachodnio-Pomorskie PL .. 67 B4
Zachodnio-Pomorskie PL .. 74 B3
Sárbogárd H .. 112 C2
Sarcelles F 90 B2
Sarche I 121 A3
Sardara I 179 C2
Sardoal P 154 B2
Sardón de Duero E 150 A3
Sare F 144 A2
S'Arenal E 166 B2
Šarengrad HR . 125 B5
Sarentino I 108 C2
Sarezzo I 120 B3
Sargans CH ... 107 B4
Sári H 112 B3
Saribeyler TR . 186 C2
Sarıcakaya TR 187 B5
Sari-d'Orcino F 180 A1
Sarıgöl TR 188 A3
Sarıkaya TR ... 23 B8
Sarıköy TR 186 B2
Sarilhos Grandes P 154 C2
Sariñena E 145 C3
Sarıoba TR 187 C7
Sárisáp H 112 B2
Sariyer TR 186 A4
Sarkad H 113 C5
Sárkeresztes H 112 B2
Sárkeresztúr H 112 B2
Särkijärvi FIN . 196 B6
Şarkikaraağaç TR 189 A6
Şarköy TR 186 B2
Sarlat-la-Canéda F 129 B4
Sarliac-sur-l'Isle F 129 A3
Sármellék H ... 111 C4
Särna S 199 D10
Sarnadas P ... 155 B3
Sarnano I 136 B2
Sarnen CH 106 C3
Sarnesfield UK . 39 B4
Sárnico I 120 B2
Sarno I 170 C2
Sarnonico I ... 121 A4
Sarnow D 74 A2
Sarny UA 13 C7
Särö S 60 B1
Saronno I 120 B2
Sárosd H 112 B2
Sárovce SK 112 A2
Sarpoil F 117 B3
Sarpsborg N ... 54 A2
Sarracín E 143 B3
Sarral E 147 C2
Sarralbe F 92 B3
Sarrancolin F .. 145 B4
Sarras F 117 B4
Sarre-Union F .. 92 C2
Sarreaus E 140 B3
Sarrebourg F .. 92 C2
Sarreguemines F 92 B3
Sárrétudvari H 112 C2

Sárszentmihaly H 112 B2
Sárszentmiklós H 112 C2
Sarteano I 135 C4
Sartène F 180 B1
Sartilly F 88 B2
Sartirana Lomellina I 120 B1
Saruhanlı TR .. 186 D2
Sárvár H 111 B3
Sarvisvaara S . 196 C4
Sarzana I 134 A2
Sarzeau F 101 B3
Sarzedas P 155 B3
Sasalli TR 188 A1
Sasamón E 142 B2
Sa Savina E 166 C1
Sásd H 125 A4
Sasino PL 68 A2
Sássari I 178 B2
Sassello I 133 A4
Sassenberg D . 71 C5
Sassetta I 134 B3
Sassnitz D 66 B2
Sassocorvaro I 136 B1
Sasso d'Ombrone I 135 C4
Sassoferrato I . 136 B1
Sassoleone I .. 135 A4
Sasso Marconi I 135 A4
Sassuolo I 135 A3
Sástago E 153 A3
Šaštinske Stráže SK 98 C1
Sas van Gent NL 79 A3
Såtåhaugen N 199 C7
Satão P 148 B2
Sâtenäs S 55 B3
Sáter S 50 B2
Sätila S 60 B2
Satillieu F 117 B4
Satnica Đakovačka HR 125 B4
Sátoraljaújhely FIN 16 A4
Satow D 65 C4
Sätra-brunn S .. 50 C3
Sætre N 54 A1
Satrup D 64 B2
Satteins A 107 B4
Satu Mare RO ... 17 B5
Saturnia I 168 A1
Saucats F 128 B2
Saucelle E 149 A3
Sauda N 52 A2
Sauðárkrókur IS 191 B6
Saudasjøen N .. 52 A2
Sauerlach D ... 108 B2
Saugues F 117 C3
Sauherad N ... 53 A5
Saujon F 114 C3
Sauland N 53 A4
Saulces Monclin F 91 B4
Saulgau D 107 A4
Saulgub D 107 B3
Saulieu F 104 B3
Saulnot F 106 B1
Sault F 131 A4
Sault-Brénaz F 118 B2
Sault-de-Navailles F 128 C2
Saulx F 105 B5
Saulxures-sur-Moselotte F .. 106 B1
Saulzais-le-Potier F 103 C4
Saumos F 128 B1
Saumur F 102 B1
Saunavaara FIN 197 B10
Saundersfoot UK 39 C2
Saurat F 146 B2
Saurbær
Borgarfjarðarsýsla IS 190 C4
Dalasýsla IS .. 190 B4
Eyjafjarðarsýsla IS 191 B7
Sáuris I 109 C3
Sausset-les-Pins F 131 B4
Sauteyrargues F 131 B2
Sauvagnat F .. 116 B2

Sauve F 131 B2
Sauveterre-de-Béarn F 144 A3
Sauveterre-de-Guyenne F ... 128 B2
Sauviat-sur-Vige F 116 B1
Sauxillanges F 117 B3
Sauzet
Drôme F 117 C4
Lot F 129 B4
Sauzé-Vaussais F 115 B4
Sauzon F 100 B2
Sava I 173 B3
Sävar S 200 C6
Sævareid N ... 46 B2
Savarsin RO 16 B5
Sävast S 196 D4
Savastepe TR . 186 C2
Savci SLO 111 C3
Säve S 60 B1
Savelletri I 173 B3
Savelli I 174 B2
Savenay F 101 B4
Saverdun F ... 146 A2
Saverne F 93 C3
Savières F 91 C3
Savigliano I ... 119 C4
Savignac-les-Eglises F 129 A3
Savignano Irpino I 171 B3
Savignano sul Rubicone I .. 136 A1
Savigny-sur-Braye F 102 B2
Saviñán E 152 A2
Savines-le-lac F 132 A2
Savino Selo SRB 126 B1
Saviore I 135 A5
Sävja S 51 C4
Šavnik MNE ... 139 C5
Savognin CH .. 107 C4
Savona I 133 A4
Savonlinna FIN 9 B6
Savournon F . 132 A1
Sævråsvåg N .. 46 B2
Sävsjö S 62 A2
Savsjön S 50 C1
Sävsjöström S . 62 A3
Savudrija HR .. 122 B2
Savukoski FIN 197 B11
Sawbridgeworth UK 44 B4
Sawtry UK 44 A3
Sax E 159 C3
Saxdalen S 50 B1
Saxilby UK 40 B3
Saxmundham UK 45 A5
Saxnäs S 195 F6
Saxthorpe UK . 41 C5
Sayalonga E .. 163 B3
Sayatón E 151 B5
Sayda D 83 B5
Säytsjärvi FIN 193 C11
Sazava CZ 97 B3
Sázava CZ 96 B2
Scaër F 100 A2
Scafa I 169 A4
Scalasaig UK .. 34 B1
Scalby UK 40 A3
Scalea I 174 B1
Scaletta Zanclea I 177 B4
Scalloway UK . 33 A5
Scandale I 175 B2
Scandiano I ... 121 C3
Scandicci I 135 B4
Scandolara Ravara I 120 B3
Scanno I 169 B3
Scansano I 168 A1
Scanzano Jónico I 174 A2
Scarborough UK 40 A3
Scardovari I ... 122 C1
Scardoy UK ... 32 D2
Scarperia I 135 B4
Scarriff IRL 28 B3
Scey-sur-Saône et St Albin F 105 B4
Schachendorf A 111 B3

Schaffhausen CH 107 B3
Schafstädt D ... 83 A3
Schafstedt D 64 B2
Schäftlarn D .. 108 B2
Schagen NL 70 B1
Schaikau D 82 B3
Schangnau CH 106 C2
Schapbach D .. 93 C4
Scharbeutz D .. 65 B3
Schärding A ... 96 C1
Scharnitz A ... 108 B2
Scharrel D 71 A4
Schattendorf A 111 B3
Scheemda NL ... 71 A3
Scheessel D 72 A2
Schéggia I 136 B1
Scheibbs A 110 A2
Scheibenberg D 83 B4
Scheidegg D .. 107 B4
Scheifling A ... 110 B1
Scheinfeld D ... 94 B2
Schelklingen D . 94 C1
Schenefeld
Schleswig-Holstein D 64 B2
Schleswig-Holstein D 72 A2
Schenkenzell D 82 B1
Scherfede D 81 A5
Schermbeck D .. 80 A2
Scherpenzeel NL 70 B2
Schesslitz D 94 B3
Scheveningen NL 70 B1
Schiedam NL ... 79 A4
Schieder-Schwalenberg D 72 C2
Schierling D ... 95 C4
Schiers CH 107 C4
Schildau D 83 A4
Schillingen D .. 92 B2
Schillingsfürst D 94 B2
Schilpário I ... 120 A3
Schiltach D 93 C4
Schiltigheim F . 93 C3
Schio I 121 B4
Schirmeck F ... 92 C3
Schirnding D .. 83 B4
Schkeuditz D .. 83 A4
Schkölen D 83 A4
Schlabendorf D 84 A1
Schladming A . 109 B4
Schladen D 73 B3
Schlangen D ... 81 A4
Schleiden D 80 B2
Schleiz D 83 B3
Schleswig D 64 B2
Schleusingen D . 82 B2
Schliengen D . 106 B2
Schliersee D .. 108 B3
Schlitz D 81 B5
Schloss Neuhans D 81 A4
Schlossvippach D 82 A3
Schlotheim D .. 82 A2
Schluchsee D . 106 B3
Schlüchtern D .. 82 B1
Schmallenberg D 81 A4
Schmelz D 92 B2
Schmidmühlen D 95 B3
Schmölln
Brandenburg D 74 A3
Sachsen D ... 83 B4
Schnaittach D . 95 B3
Schneeberg D . 83 B4
Schneizlreuth D 109 B3
Schöder A 109 B5
Schoenberg D . 80 B2
Schollene D 73 B5
Schöllkrippen A 111 B3

Schomberg D . 107 A3
Schönach D 95 C4
Schönau
Baden-Württemberg D 106 B2
Bayern D 95 C4
Schönbeck D ... 74 A2
Schönberg
Bayern D 96 C1
Mecklenburg-Vorpommern D 65 C3
Schleswig-Holstein D 65 C3
Schönberg im Stubaital A ... 108 B2
Schönebeck D . 73 B4
Schöneck D 83 B4
Schönecken-D. . 80 B2
Schönermark D 74 A2
Schönewalde D 83 A5
Schongau D... 108 B1
Schöngrabern A 97 C4
Schönhagen D . 81 A5
Schönhausen D 73 B5
Schöningen D . 73 B3
Schönkirchen D 64 B3
Schönsee D 95 B4
Schöntal D 94 B1
Schönthal D ... 95 B4
Schönwald D... 93 C4
Schönwalde D . 65 B3
Schoondijke NL 79 A3
Schoonebeek NL 71 B3
Schoonhoven NL 79 A4
Schopfheim D 106 B2
Schöppenstedt D 73 B3
Schörfling A .. 109 B4
Schorndorf D .. 94 C1
Schortens D ... 71 A4
Schotten D 81 B5
Schramberg D 106 A3
Schraplau D ... 83 A3
Schrattenberg A 97 C4
Schrecksbach D 81 B5
Schrems A 96 C3
Schrobenhausen D 95 C3
Schröcken A .. 107 B5
Schrozberg D .. 94 B1
Schruns A 107 B4
Schüpfheim CH 106 C3
Schüttorf D 71 B4
Schwaan D 65 C5
Schwabach D .. 95 B3
Schwäbisch Gmünd D 94 C1
Schwäbisch Hall D 94 B1
Schwabmünchen D 108 A1
Schwaförden D . 72 B1
Schwaigern D . 93 B5
Schwalmstadt D 81 B5
Schwanberg A 110 C2
Schwanden CH 107 C4
Schwandorf D . 95 B4
Schwanebeck D 73 C4
Schwanenstadt A 109 A4
Schwanewede D 72 A1
Schwanfeld D .. 94 B2
Schwangau D 108 B1
Schwarmstedt D 72 B2
Schwarza D 82 B2
Schwarzach am Main D 94 B2

Schwarzenbek D 72 A3
Schwarzenberg D 83 B4
Schwarzenburg CH 106 C2
Schwarzenfeld D 95 B4
Schwarz-heide D 84 A1
Schwaz A 108 B2
Schwechat A . 111 A3
Schwedt D 74 A3
Schwei D 71 A5
Schweich D 92 B2
Schweighausen D 106 A2
Schweinfurt D . 94 A2
Schweinitz D ... 83 A5
Schweinrich D . 74 A1
Schwelm D 80 A3
Schwemsal D .. 83 A4
Schwendt A ... 109 B3
Schwenningen D 107 A3
Schwepnitz D . 84 A1
Schwerin D 73 A4
Schwerte D 81 A3
Schweskau D .. 73 B4
Schwetzingen D 93 B4
Schwyz CH 107 B3
Sciacca I 176 B2
Scicli I 177 C3
Sciechów PL ... 75 B3
Scigliano I 175 B2
Scilla I 175 C1
Šcinawa PL 85 A4
Scionzier F 118 A3
Scoglitti I 177 C3
Scole UK 45 A5
Sconser UK 31 B2
Scopello
Piemonte I ... 119 B5
Sicilia I 176 A1
Scordia I 177 B3
Scorzè I 121 B5
Scotch Corner UK 37 B5
Scotter UK 40 B3
Scourie UK 32 C1
Scousburgh UK . 33 B5
Scrabster UK .. 32 C3
Screeb IRL 28 A2
Scremerston UK 37 A5
Scritto I 136 B1
Scunthorpe UK . 40 B3
Scuol UK 107 C5
Scúrcola Marsicana I 169 A3
Seaford UK 45 C4
Seaham UK ... 37 B5
Seahouses UK . 37 A5
Seascale UK ... 36 B3
Seaton UK 43 B3
Sebazac-Concourès F 130 A1
Seben TR 187 B6
Sebersdorf A . 110 B2
Sebezh RUS 8 D6
Sebnitz D 84 B2
Seborga I 133 B3
Seby S 63 B4
Seč
Vychodočeský CZ 97 B3
Západočeský CZ 96 B1
Sečanj SRB ... 126 B2
Secemin PL 87 B3
Séchault F 91 B4
Seckau A 110 B1
Seclin F 78 B3
Secondigny F . 114 B3
Seda P 155 B3
Sedan F 91 B4
Sedano E 143 B3
Sedbergh UK .. 37 B4
Sedella E 163 B3
Séderon F 131 A4
Sedgefield UK . 37 B5
Sedico I 121 A5
Sédières F 116 B1
Sedlarica HR .. 124 B3
Sedlčany CZ 96 B2
Sedlec-Prčice CZ 96 B2
Sedlice CZ 96 B1
Sędziejowice PL 86 A3
Sędziszów PL .. 87 B4

Sędziszów
Małopolski
PL..............87 B5
Seebach F.........93 C3
Seeboden A..... 109 C4
Seefeld
Brandenburg
D..............74 B2
Niedersachsen
D............. 71 A5
Seefeld in Tirol
A............ 108 B1
Seeg D........ 108 B1
Seehausen
Sachsen-Anhalt
D..............73 B4
Sachsen-Anhalt
D..............73 B4
Seeheim-
Jugenheim D ..93 B4
Seelbach D......93 C3
Seelow D........74 B3
Seelze D 72 B2
Seerhausen D...83 A5
Sées F..........89 B4
Seesen D........82 A2
Seeshaupt D.. 108 B2
Seewalchen A. 109 B4
Seferihisar TR. 188 A1
Sefkerin SRB .. 127 B2
Segård N......48 B2
Segerstad S.....55 A4
Segesd H..... 124 A3
Seglinge FIN ...51 B7
Segmon S.......55 A4
Segonzac F ... 115 C3
Segorbe E....... 159 B3
Segovia E 151 B3
Segré F....... 101 B5
Segura
E........ 144 B1
P........ 155 B3
Segura de León
E....... 161 A3
Segura de los
Baños E...... 152 B3
Ségur-les-Villas
F....... 116 B2
Segurilla E... 150 B3
Sehnde D 72 B2
Seia P 148 B2
Seiches-sur-le-Loir
F......... 102 B1
Seifhennersdorf
D..............84 B2
Seignelay F... 104 B2
Seijo E 140 C2
Seilhac F... 116 B1
Seilles B.........79 B5
Seim N.........46 B2
Seinäjoki FIN....8 A3
Seissan F.... 145 A4
Seitenstetten Markt
A........... 110 A1
Seixal P...... 154 C1
Seiz A........ 110 B1
Seizthal A..... 110 B1
Sejerslev DK ...58 B1
Seksna RUS ...9 C11
Selárdalur IS.. 190 B1
Selárgius I... 179 C3
Selb D..........83 B4
Selby UK.......40 B2
Selca HR 138 B2
Selce HR 123 B3
Selçuk TR 188 B2
Selde DK.......58 B2
Selenča SRB... 126 B1
Selendi
Manisa TR .. 186 D2
Manisa TR .. 186 D3
Selenicë AL... 182 C1
Sélestat F..... 106 A2
Seleuš SRB ... 126 B2
Selevac SRB.. 127 C2
Selfoss IS...... 190 D5
Selgua E 145 C4
Selice SK...... 112 A1
Seligenstadt D..93 A4
Seligenthal D..82 B2
Selimiye TR ... 188 B2
Selizharovo RUS .9 D8
Selja S 50 A1
Seljänö S..... 198 C2
Seljelvnes N .. 192 C3
Seljord N.......53 A4
Selkirk UK.....35 C5
Sellano I...... 136 C1
Selles-St Denis
F......... 103 B3
Selles-sur-Cher
F......... 103 B3
Sellières F..... 105 C4

Sellin D 66 B2
Sellye H........ 125 B3
Selm D..........80 A3
Selnica ob Dravi
SLO 110 C2
Selongey F.... 105 B4
Selonnet F ... 132 A2
Selow D..........65 C4
Selsey UK 44 C3
Selsingen D....72 A2
Selters D.......81 B3
Seltz F...........93 C4
Selva E........ 167 B2
Selva di Cadore
I............. 108 C3
Selva di Val
Gardena I... 108 C2
Selvik
Sogn og Fjordane
N........... 46 A2
Vestfold N 54 A1
Selvino I...... 120 B2
Selyatyn UA... 17 B6
Sem N..........54 A1
Semeljci HR ... 125 B4
Semič SLO..... 123 B4
Semide
F...........91 B4
P........... 148 B1
Semily CZ.......84 B3
Seminara I... 175 C1
Semlac RO ... 126 A2
Semlacu Mare
RO 126 B3
Semmen-
stedt
D............73 B3
Šempeter SLO. 123 A4
Semriach A ... 110 B2
Semur-en-Auxois
F......... 104 B3
Sena E 145 C3
Sena de Luna
E........ 141 B5
Senarpont F ...90 B1
Sénas F...... 131 B4
Senčanski
Trešnjevac
SRB 126 B1
Sencelles E... 167 B2
Senčur SLO... 123 A3
Senden
Bayern D 94 C2
Nordrhein-
Westfalen D.. 80 A3
Sendenhorst D..81 A3
Sendim P 149 A3
Senec SK 111 A4
Senefe B 79 B4
Séneghe I 178 B2
Senés E...... 164 B2
Senez F 132 B2
Senftenberg D..84 A1
Sengouagnet
F......... 145 B4
Sengwarden D..71 A5
Senica SK......98 C1
Senice na Hané
CZ............98 B1
Senigállia I ... 136 B2
Senirkent TR .. 189 A5
Sénis I........ 179 C2
Senise I...... 174 A2
Senj HR....... 123 C3
Senjehopen N 194 A8
Senftenberg D..84 A1
Senjski Rudnik
SRB 127 D3
Senlis F........90 B2
Sennan S.......60 C2
Sennecey-le-Grand
F......... 105 C3
Sennen UK......42 B1
Senno BY 13 A8
Sénnori I..... 178 B2
Sennwald CH . 107 B4
Sennybridge
UK............39 C3
Senohrad SK ...99 C3
Senonches F...90 B2
Senones F......92 C2
Senorbì I..... 179 C3
Senovo SLO... 123 A4
Senožeče
SLO 123 B3
Senožeti SLO.. 123 A3
Sens F........ 104 A2
Sens-de-Bretagne
F......... 101 A4
Senta SRB.... 126 B2
Senterada E... 145 B4
Sentilj SLO... 110 C2
Šentjernej
SLO 123 B4

Šentjur SLO ... 123 A4
Senumstad N ...53 B4
Seoane E...... 141 B3
Seon CH 106 B3
Sépeaux F 104 B2
Sépey CH 119 A4
Sepino I....... 170 B2
Sępólno Krajeńskie
PL............76 A2
Seppenrade D ..80 A3
Seppois F 106 B2
Septemvri BG . 183 A6
Septeuil F......90 C1
Sepúlveda E .. 151 A4
Sequals I..... 122 A1
Sequeros E.... 149 B3
Seraincourt F ..91 B4
Seraing B.......80 B1
Seravezza I ... 134 B3
Sered' SK......98 C1
Seredka RUS ...8 C6
Şereflikoçhisar
TR............23 B7
Seregélyes H .. 112 B2
Seregno I 120 B2
Sérent F...... 101 B3
Serfaus A 108 B1
Sergiyev Posad
RUS 9 D11
Seriate I...... 120 B2
Sérifontaine F ..90 B1
Serifos GR..... 185 B5
Sérignan F 130 B2
Serik TR...... 189 C6
Serina I 120 B2
Serinhisar TR.. 188 B4
Sermaises F....90 C2
Sermaize-les-Bains
F...........91 C4
Sérmide I 121 C4
Sermoneta I .. 169 B2
Sernache de
Bonjardim P . 154 B2
Sernancelhe P 148 B2
Serock PL......77 B6
Serón E 164 B2
Serón de Najima
E......... 152 A1
Serooskerke
NL 79 A3
Seròs E...... 153 A4
Serpa P...... 160 B2
Serracapriola
I............ 171 B3
Serrada E 150 A3
Serra de Outes
E........ 140 B2
Serradifalco I . 176 B2
Serradilla E .. 155 B4
Serradilla del
Arroyo E ... 149 B3
Serradilla del Llano
E......... 149 B3
Serramanna I . 179 C2
Serramazzoni
I............ 135 A3
Serranillos E .. 150 B3
Serrapetrona
I............ 136 B2
Serra San Bruno
I............ 175 C2
Serra San Quírico
I............ 136 B2
Serrastretta I . 175 B2
Serravalle
Piemonte I ... 119 B5
Umbria I 136 C2
Serravalle di
Chienti I... 136 B1
Serravalle Scrívia
I............ 120 C1
Serres F...... 172 B1
Serrejón E ... 150 C2
Serres
F........ 132 A1
GR 183 B5
Serrières F ... 117 B4
Serrières-de-Briord
F........ 118 B2
Sersale I..... 175 B2
Sertã P 154 B2
Sertig Dörfli
CH 107 C4
Servance F.... 106 B1
Serverette F .. 117 C3
Servia GR 182 C4
Servian F 130 B2
Serviers I..... 131 A3
Servigliano I . 136 B2
Sésklo GR..... 182 D4
Sesena Nuevo
E......... 151 B4
Sesimbra E.... 154 C1

Seskarö S 196 D6
Seskinore UK ...27 B3
Sesma E...... 144 B1
Sessa Aurunca
I............ 170 B1
Ses Salines E .. 167 B3
Sesta Godano
I........... 134 A2
Šestanovac
HR 138 B2
Sestao E 143 A4
Sestino I..... 135 B5
Sesto I........ 109 C3
Sesto Calende
I............ 120 B1
Sesto Fiorentino
I............ 135 B4
Séstola I..... 135 A3
Sesto San Giovanni
I............ 120 B2
Sestriere I.... 119 C3
Sestri Levante
I........... 134 A2
Sestroretsk RUS . 9 B7
Sestu I....... 179 C3
Sesvete HR.... 124 B2
Setcases E 146 B3
Sète F........ 130 B2
Setenil E..... 162 B2
Setermoen N . 194 B9
Šetonje SRB... 127 C3
Setskog N......54 A2
Settalsjølia N . 199 C7
Séttimo Torinese
I............ 119 B4
Settimo Vittone
I............ 119 B4
Settle UK........40 A1
Setúbal P 154 C2
Seubersdorf D ..95 B3
Seui I........ 179 C3
Seúlo I....... 179 C3
Seurre F...... 105 C4
Sevel DK 58 B1
Sevenoaks UK ..45 B4
Sévérac-le-Château
F......... 130 A2
Sever do Vouga
P......... 148 B1
Severin HR.... 123 B4
Severomorsk
RUS 3 B13
Séveso I..... 120 B2
Ševětín CZ......96 B2
Sevettijärvi
FIN 193 C12
Sévigny F......91 B4
Sevilla = Seville
E......... 162 A2
Sevilla la Nueva
E......... 151 B3
Sevilleja de la Jara
E......... 156 A3
Sevlievo BG... 17 D6
Sevnica SLO... 123 A4
Sevojno SRB .. 127 D1
Sevrier F..... 118 B3
Sexdrega S.....60 B2
Seyches F..... 129 B3
Seyda D........83 A4
Seydişehir TR . 189 B6
Seyðisfjörður
IS 191 B12
Seyitgazi TR ... 187 C5
Seyitömer TR . 187 C4
Seymen TR.... 186 A2
Seyne F...... 132 A2
Seynes F..... 131 A3
Seyssel F..... 118 B2
Seyssel F..... 118 B2
Sežana SLO ... 122 B2
Sézanne F......91 C3
Sezulfe P..... 149 A2
Sezze I....... 169 B3
Sfântu Gheorghe
RO 17 C6
Sforzacosta I . 136 B2
Sgarasta Mhor
UK 31 B1
's-Gravendeel
NL 79 A4
's-Gravenhage =
The Hague NL..70 B1
's-Gravenzande
NL 79 A4
Shaftesbury UK 43 A4
Shaldon UK.....43 B3
Shalskiy RUS...9 B9
Shanagolden
IRL 29 B2
Shanklin UK....44 C2
Shap UK........37 B4

Sharpness UK ..43 A4
Shawbury UK ..38 B4
's-Heerenberg
NL 80 A2
Sheerness UK ..45 B4
Sheffield UK ...40 B2
Shefford UK....44 A3
Shëmri AL..... 182 A2
Shenfield UK...45 B4
Shëngjergj AL 182 B2
Shepetivka UA ..13 C7
Shepshed UK ...40 C2
Shepton Mallet
UK 43 A4
Sherborne UK...43 B4
Shercock IRL ...27 C4
Sheringham UK 41 C5
's-Hertogenbosch
NL 79 A5
Shiel Bridge
UK 32 D1
Shieldaig UK...31 B3
Shijak AL..... 182 B1
Shillelagh IRL ..30 B2
Shimsk RUS....9 C7
Shipston-on-Stour
UK 44 A2
Shklow BY 13 A9
Shkodër AL... 182 A1
Shoeburyness
UK 45 B4
Shoreham-by-Sea
UK 44 C3
Shotley Gate
UK 45 B5
Shrewsbury UK .38 B4
Shugozero RUS ..9 C9
Shumen BG ... 17 D7
Siabost UK.....31 A2
Siamanna I... 179 C2
Sianów PL......67 B5
Šiauliai LT..... 13 A5
Siátista GR... 182 C3
Siauges-St Romain
F......... 117 B3
Šiaulai LT...... 8 E3
Sibari I....... 174 B2
Sibbhult S......63 B2
Šibenik HR... 138 B1
Siberstedt D....64 B2
Sibiu RO...... 17 C6
Sibnica SRB .. 127 C2
Sibsey UK......41 B4
Siculiana I.... 176 B2
Šid SRB...... 125 B5
Sidari GR..... 182 D1
Siddeburen D ..71 A3
Sidensjö S 200 C4
Siderno I..... 175 C2
Sidirokastro
GR 183 B5
Sidmouth UK ..43 B3
Sidzina PL......99 B3
Siebe N...... 192 D7
Siebenlehn D ..83 A5
Siedlce PL..... 12 B5
Siedlce PL......75 A4
Siedlinghausen
D............81 A4
Siedlisko PL....75 B5
Siegburg D.....80 B3
Siegen D........81 B4
Siegenburg D ..95 C3
Sieghartskirchen
A........... 111 A3
Siegsdorf D... 109 B3
Siekierki PL....74 B3
Sielpia PL......87 A4
Siemiany PL....69 B4
Siena I....... 135 B4
Sieniawka PL ..84 A2
Sienno PL......87 A5
Sieppijärvi
FIN 196 B7
Sieradz PL......86 A2
Sieraków
Śląskie PL...86 B2
Wielkopolskie
PL............75 B5
Sierakowice PL.68 A2
Sierck-les-Bains
F...........92 B2
Sierentz F.... 106 B2
Sierning A.... 110 A1
Sierpc PL......77 B4
Sierra de Fuentes
E......... 155 B4
Sierra de Luna
E......... 144 B3
Sierra de Yeguas
E......... 162 A3
Sierre CH..... 119 A4
Siestrzeń PL....77 B5

Sietamo E..... 145 B3
Siewierz PL.....86 B3
Sigdal N........48 B1
Sigean F...... 130 B1
Sigerfjord N .. 194 B6
Sighetu-Marmatiei
RO 17 B5
Sighişoara RO.. 17 B6
Sigillo I...... 136 B1
Siglufjörður
IS 191 A7
Sigmaringen
D........... 107 A4
Signa I....... 135 B4
Signes F...... 132 B1
Signy-l'Abbaye
F...........91 B4
Signy-le-Petit F 91 B4
Sigogne F..... 115 C3
Sigri GR...... 183 D7
Sigtuna S......57 A3
Sigueiro E.... 140 B2
Sigüenza E ... 151 A5
Sigües E...... 144 B2
Sigulda LV 8 D4
Siilinjärvi FIN . 8 A5
Sikenäs S......52 B2
Sikfors S..... 196 D4
Sikia GR...... 183 C5
Sikinos GR ... 185 C6
Sikkilsdalseter
N............47 A6
Siklós H...... 125 B4
Sikórz PL......77 B4
Sikselet S 195 D8
Silandro I.... 108 C1
Silánus I..... 178 B2
Silbaš SRB.... 126 B1
Şile TR....... 187 A4
Siles E....... 164 A2
Silgueiros P .. 148 B2
Silivri TR...... 23 C7
Siliqua I..... 179 C2
Silistra BG...... 17 C7
Silivri TR..... 186 A3
Siljan N.........53 A5
Siljansnäs S....50 B1
Silkeborg DK...59 B2
Silla E....... 159 B3
Sillamäe EST ...8 C5
Silleda E..... 140 B2
Sillé-le-Guillaume
F......... 102 A1
Sillenstede D ...71 A4
Sillerud S......54 A3
Sillian A...... 109 C3
Silloth UK......36 B3
Silno PL........68 B2
Silnowo PL.....68 B1
Silo HR...... 123 B3
Sils E........ 147 C3
Silsand N..... 194 A8
Silte S.........57 C4
Silute LT....... 12 A4
Silvalen N.... 195 E3
Silvaplana CH. 107 C4
Silvares P.... 148 B2
Silvberg S......50 B2
Silverdalen S ..62 A3
Silvermines IRL .28 B3
Silverstone UK .44 A2
Silverton UK ...43 B3
Silves P...... 160 B1
Silvi Marina I . 169 A4
Simandre F... 105 C3
Šimanovci
SRB 127 C2
Simard F..... 105 C4
Simat de Valldigna
E......... 159 B3
Simav TR..... 186 C3
Simbach
Bayern D 95 C4
Bayern D 95 C5
Simbário I.... 175 C2
Simeonovgrad
BG 183 A7
Simeria RO.... 17 C5
Simi GR...... 188 C2
Simićevo SRB . 127 C3
Simitli BG..... 183 B5
Simlångsdalen
S............ 60 C3
Simmerath D ..80 B2
Simmern D 93 B3
Simo FIN..... 197 D8
Simonovce SK ..99 C4
Simonsbath UK .43 A3
Simonstorp S ..56 B2
Simontornya
H........... 112 C2

Simplon CH... 119 A5
Simrishamn S ...63 C2
Sinaia RO 17 C6
Sinalunga I... 135 B4
Sinarcas E.... 159 B2
Sincan TR..... 187 C7
Sincanlı TR.... 187 D5
Sindal DK......58 A3
Sindelfingen D..93 C5
Sindia I...... 178 B2
Sındırgı TR... 186 C3
Sinekli TR..... 186 A3
Sines P....... 160 B1
Sinetta FIN.... 197 C8
Sineu E....... 167 B3
Singen D...... 107 B3
Singleton UK...44 C3
Singsås N..... 199 C7
Siniscóla I.... 178 B3
Sinj HR....... 138 B2
Sinlabajos E.. 150 A3
Sinn D.........81 B4
Sínnai I...... 179 C3
Sinnes N......52 B2
Sinop TR.......23 A8
Sins CH...... 106 B3
Sinsheim D 93 B4
Sint Annaland
N............79 A4
Sint Annaparochie
NL 70 A2
Sint Athonis NL .80 A1
Sint Nicolaasga
NL 70 B2
Sint Oedenrode
NL 79 A5
Sintra P...... 154 C1
Sinzheim D 93 C4
Sinzig D........80 B3
Siófok H...... 112 C2
Sion CH...... 119 A4
Sion Mills UK ...27 B3
Siorac-en-Périgord
F......... 129 B3
Šipanska Luka
HR 139 C3
Šipovo BIH.... 138 A3
Sira N.........52 B2
Siracusa I.... 177 B4
Siret RO....... 17 B7
Sirevåg N......52 B1
Sirig SRB..... 126 B1
Sirkka FIN.... 196 B7
Sirmione I.... 121 B3
Sírnio FIN.... 197 D11
Sirok H...... 113 B4
Široké SK......99 C4
Široki Brijeg
BIH 139 B3
Sirolo I...... 136 B2
Siruela E..... 156 B2
Sisak HR..... 124 B2
Sisante E..... 158 B1
Šišljavić HR ... 123 B4
Sissach CH ... 106 B2
Sissonne F......91 B3
Sistelo P..... 140 C2
Sisteron F..... 132 A1
Sistiana I..... 122 B2
Sistranda N .. 198 B5
Sitasjaurestugorna
S............ 194 C8
Sitges E..... 147 C2
Sitia GR...... 185 D7
Sittard NL......80 A1
Sittensen D 72 A2
Sittingbourne
UK 45 B4
Sitzenroda D ...83 A4
Sivac SRB.... 126 B1
Sivaslı TR.... 189 A4
Siverić HR.... 138 B2
Sivrihisar TR . 187 C6
Sixt-Fer-á-Cheval
F......... 119 A3
Siziano I..... 120 B2
Sizun F....... 100 A1
Sjenica SRB .. 16 D3
Sjoa N....... 198 D6
Sjøåsen N.... 199 A8
Sjöbo S....... 61 D3
Sjøenden
Hedmark N ... 48 A3
Hedmark N ... 48 B3
Sjøholt N.... 198 C3
Sjøli N........48 A3
Sjølund DK.....59 C2
Sjørring DK....58 B1

Sjötofta S.....60 B3
Sjötorp S.......55 B4
Sjoutnäset S. 199 A11
Sjøvegan N ... 194 B8
Sjuntorp S 54 B3
Skåbu N........47 A6
Skafså N 53 A4
Skaftafell ÍS .. 191 D9
Skagaströnd
ÍS 190 B5
Skagen DK.....58 A3
Skagersvik S...55 B5
Skaiå N 53 B3
Skaidi N....... 193 B8
Skala GR 184 A1
Skała PL.......87 B3
Skaland N..... 194 A8
Skala Oropou
GR 185 A4
Skala-Podilska
UA 13 D7
Skalat UA 13 D6
Skalbmierz PL ..87 B4
Skålevik N 53 B4
Skalica SK.....98 C1
Skalité SK.....98 B2
Skällinge S.....60 B2
Skalná CZ......83 B4
Skals DK 58 B2
Skælskør DK ...65 A4
Skalstugan S.. 199 B9
Skanderborg
DK 59 B2
Skånes-Fagerhult
S 61 C3
Skåne-Tranås
S 61 D3
Skånevik N 52 A1
Skänninge S...55 B6
Skanör med
Falsterbo S.....66 A1
Skåpafors S....54 A3
Skąpe PL.......75 B4
Skara S........55 B4
Skærbæk DK ...64 A1
Skarberget N . 194 B7
Skärblacka S...56 B1
Skarð ÍS...... 190 B3
Skarda S...... 200 B4
Skare N 46 C3
Skåre S........55 A4
Skärhamn S...60 B1
Skarnes N......48 B3
Skärplinge S...51 B4
Skarpnatö FIN ..51 B6
Skarp Salling
DK 58 B2
Skarrild DK 59 C1
Skarstad N... 194 B7
Skärstad S.....62 A2
Skarsvåg N ... 193 A9
Skarszewy PL ..69 A3
Skårup DK 65 A3
Skärvången
S 199 B11
Skarvsjöby S...195 F8
Skaryszew PL ...87 A5
Skarżysko-
Kamienna PL...87 A4
Skarzyso Ksiazece
PL............87 A4
Skatoy N.......53 B5
Skattkärr S....55 A4
Skattungbyn S..50 A1
Skatval N 199 B7
Skaulo S...... 196 B4
Skave DK 59 B1
Skawina PL 99 B3
Skebobruk S...51 C5
Skebokvarn S..56 A2
Skedala S......61 C2
Skedevi S......56 B1
Skedsmokorset
N.............48 B3
Skee S 60 B2
Skegness UK...41 B4
Skei N.........46 A3
Skela SRB 127 C2
Skelani BIH....127 D1
Skellefteå S.. 2 D7
Skelleftehamn S. 2 D7
Skelmersdale
UK 38 A4
Skelmorlie UK . 34 C3
Skelund DK 58 B3
Skender Vakuf
BIH.......... 138 A3
Skene S.......60 B2
Skępe PL.......77 B4
Skepplanda S..60 B2

Skeppshult S...60 B3
Skerries IRL 30 A2
Ski N 54 A1
Skiathos GR... 183 D5
Skibbereen IRL..29 C2
Skibotn N..... 192 C4
Skidra GR..... 182 C4
Skien N........53 A5
Skierniewice
PL............77 C5
Skillingaryd S..60 B4
Skillinge S 63 C2
Skillingmark S . 49 C4
Skilloura CY...181 A2
Skinnardai S...57 A4
Skinnskatteberg
S 50 C2
Skipmannvik
N............ 195 C6
Skipness UK ...34 C2
Skipsea UK.....41 B3
Skipton UK.....40 B1
Skiptvet N.....54 A2
Skiros GR.....183 E6
Skivarp S 66 A2
Skive DK 58 B2
Skjånes N 193 B12
Skjærhalden N..54 A2
Skjeberg N.....54 A2
Skjeggedal N ..46 B3
Skjeljanger N ..46 B1
Skjeljavik N ...46 C2
Skjern DK 59 C1
Skjervøy N... 192 B4
Skjold
Rogaland N.... 52 A1
Troms N 192 C3
Skjoldastraumen
N.............52 A1
Skjolden N......47 A4
Skjønhaug N...54 A2
Skjøtningsberg
N........... 193 A11
Škocjan SLO ... 123 B4
Skoczów PL.....98 B2
Skodborg DK ...59 C2
Škofja Loka
SLO 123 A3
Škofljica SLO.. 123 B3
Skog S 51 A3
Skoganvarre
N............ 193 C9
Skogen S......54 A3
Skogfoss N... 193 C13
Skoghall S 55 A4
Skogly N..... 193 C13
Skogn N 199 B8
Skognes N ... 192 C3
Skogstorp
Halland S 60 C2
Södermanland
S 56 A2
Skoki PL 76 B2
Skokloster S ...57 A3
Sköldinge S....56 A2
Skole UA 13 D5
Skollenborg N..53 A5
Sköllersta S ...56 A1
Skomlin PL.....86 A2
Skonseng N... 195 D5
Skopelos GR .. 183 D5
Skopje NMK.. 182 A3
Skoppum N....54 A1
Skórcz PL 69 B3
Skorogoszcz PL 86 B1
Skoroszów PL...85 A5
Skorovatn N . 199 A10
Skorped S..... 200 C3
Skørping DK ...58 B2
Skotfoss N.....53 A5
Skotniki PL 87 A3
Skotselv N.....48 C1
Skotterud N ...49 C4
Skottorp S.....61 C2
Skovby DK 64 B2
Skövde S......55 B4
Skovsgård DK.. 58 A2
Skrad HR...... 123 B3
Skradin HR.... 138 B1
Skradnik HR... 123 B4
Skråmestø N...46 B1
Škrdlovice CZ...97 B3
Skrea S........60 C2
Skreia N.......48 B2
Skrolsvik N... 194 A7
Skruv S........63 B3
Skrwilno PL....77 A4
Skrydstrup DK..59 C2
Skucani BIH... 138 B2
Skudeneshavn
N............ 52 A1
Skui N.........48 C2
Skulsk PL 76 B3

Skultorp S 55 B4
Skultuna S 56 A2
Skuodas LT......8 D2
Skurup S.......66 A2
Skute N........48 B2
Skuteč CZ......97 B3
Skutskär S 51 B4
Skutvik N 194 B6
Skvyra UA..... 13 D8
Skwierzyna PL ..75 B4
Skýcov SK......98 C2
Skyllberg S....55 B5
Skyttmon S... 200 C1
Skyttorp S.....51 B4
Sládkovičovo
SK........... 111 A4
Slagelse DK 61 D1
Slaghøren NL ...71 B3
Slagnäs S..... 195 E9
Slaidburn UK ...40 B1
Slane IRL.......30 A2
Slangerup DK .. 61 D2
Slano HR...... 139 C3
Slantsy RUS 8 C6
Slaný CZ.......84 B2
Slap SLO 122 A2
Šlapanice CZ...97 B4
Slåstad N 48 B3
Slatina
BIH.......... 139 B3
HR 125 B3
RO 17 C6
Slatiňany CZ...97 B3
Slatinice CZ....98 B1
Slättberg S....50 A1
Slattum N......48 C2
Slavičín CZ.....98 B1
Slavkov CZ.....98 C1
Slavkovica
SRB 127 C2
Slavkov u Brna
CZ 97 B4
Slavonice CZ...97 C3
Slavonski Brod
HR 125 B4
Slavošovce SK .99 C4
Slavskoye RUS..69 A5
Slavuta UA 13 C7
Sława
Lubuskie PL.... 85 A4
Zachodnio-
Pomorskie PL. 67 C4
Slawharad BY ..13 B9
Sławków PL....86 B3
Sławno
Wielkopolskie
PL............76 B2
Zachodnio-
Pomorskie PL. 68 A1
Sławoborze PL..67 C4
Sl'ažany SK 98 C2
Sleaford UK....40 C3
Sleðbrjótur
ÍS 191 B11
Sledmere UK...40 A3
Sleights UK 37 B6
Slemmestad N .54 A1
Šlesín PL.......76 B3
Sliač SK........99 C3
Sliema M..... 175 C3
Sligo IRL.......26 B2
Slite S.........57 C4
Slitu N.........54 A2
Sliven BG 17 D7
Śliwice PL......68 B3
Slobozia RO.... 17 C7
Slochteren NL ..71 A3
Slöinge S......60 C2
Słomniki PL....87 B4
Slonim BY......13 B6
Słońsk PL......75 B3
Slootdorp NL ..70 B1
Slottsbron S...54 A4
Slough UK 44 B3
Slövag N.......46 B2
Slovenj Gradec
SLO 110 C2
Slovenska Bistrica
SLO 123 A4
Slovenská L'upča
SK............99 C3
Slovenske Konjice
SLO 123 A4
Štúbice PL.....74 B3
Sluderno I.... 108 C1
Sluis NL 78 A3
Šluknov CZ.....84 A2

Slunj HR 123 B4
Słupca PL 76 B2
Słupia PL.......87 A3
Słupiec PL......85 B4
Słupsk PL......68 A2
Slutsk BY...... 13 B7
Smålandsstenar
S.............60 B3
Smalåsen N ...195 E4
Smardzewo PL..75 B4
Smarhon BY... 13 A7
Smarje SLO ... 123 A4
Šmarjeta SLO . 123 B4
Šmartno SLO.. 123 A3
Smečno CZ.....84 B2
Smedby S......63 B4
Smède CZ......96 C2
Smederevo
SRB 127 C2
Smederevska
Palanka SRB . 127 C2
Smedjebacken
S.............50 B2
Smęgorzów PL..87 B5
Smeland N.....53 B4
Smidary CZ.....84 B3
Šmigiel PL 75 B5
Smilde NL......71 B3
Smiřice CZ.....85 B3
Smithfield UK .36 B4
Šmitovo PL.....75 A5
Smögen S......54 B2
Smogulec PL...76 A2
Smołdzino PL...68 A2
Smolenice SK ..98 C1
Smolensk RUS 13 A10
Smolník SK.....99 C4
Smolyan BG.. 183 B6
Smygehamn S ..66 A2
Smykow PL.....87 A4
Snainton UK ...40 A3
Snaith UK......40 B2
Snaptun DK....59 C3
Snarby N..... 192 C3
Snarum N......48 B1
Snåsa N 199 A9
Snedsted DK...58 B1
Sneek NL.......70 A2
Sneem IRL......29 C2
Snejbjerg DK...59 B1
Snillfjord N... 198 B6
Šnjegotina
BIH.......... 125 C3
Snøde DK 65 A3
Snøfjord N.... 193 B8
Snogebæk DK..67 A4
Snyatyn UA ... 13 D6
Soave I....... 121 B4
Sober E....... 140 B3
Sobernheim D .93 B3
Soběslav CZ....96 B2
Sobota
Dolnośląskie
PL............ 85 A3
Łódzkie PL....77 B4
Sobotište SK...98 C1
Sobotka CZ.....84 B3
Sobótka
Dolnośląskie
PL............85 B4
Wielkopolskie
PL............86 A1
Sobra HR..... 139 C3
Sobrado
Coruña E 140 A2
Lugo E 141 B3
Sobral da Adica
P 161 A2
Sobral de Monte
Agraço P 154 C1
Sobreira Formosa
P 154 B3
Søby DK 64 B3
Soca SLO 122 A2
Sochaczew PL...77 B5
Sochos GR 183 C5
Socodor RO ... 113 C5
Socol RO...... 127 C3
Socovos E 164 A3
Socuéllamos E 158 B1
Sodankylä
FIN.......... 197 B9
Soderåkra S ...63 B4
Söderala S.....51 A3
Söderås S......50 B2
Söderbärke S..50 B2
Söderby-Karl S .51 C5
Söderfors S.....51 B4
Söderhamn S...51 A4
Söderköping S..56 B2
Söderö S.......51 B6
Södertälje S....57 A3

Södingberg A. 110 B2
Södra Finnö S...56 B2
Södra Ny S.....55 A4
Södra Råda S...55 A5
Södra Sandby
S 61 D3
Södra Vi S......62 A3
Sodražica SLO. 123 B3
Sodupe E 143 A3
Soengas P 148 A1
Soest
D 81 A4
NL 70 B2
Sofades GR... 182 D4
Sofia BG....... 17 D5
Sofikon GR.... 184 B4
Şofronea RO .. 126 A3
Sögel D........71 B4
Sogliano al
Rubicone I ... 135 A5
Sogndalsfjøra
N.............46 A4
Søgne N 53 B3
Söğütköy TR .. 188 C3
Soham UK......45 A4
Sohland D 84 A2
Sohren D.......93 B3
Soignies B 79 B4
Soissons F 90 B3
Söjtör H...... 111 C3
Sokal' UA 13 C6
Sökmen D 82 A3
Söke TR...... 188 B2
Sokna N........48 B1
Sokndal N 52 B2
Soknedal N... 199 C7
Soko BIH..... 125 C4
Sokolac BIH .. 139 B4
Sokółka PL.... 13 B5
Sokolov CZ.....83 B4
Sokołów Podlaski
PL............ 12 B5
Sola N.........52 B1
Solana de los
Barros E 155 C4
Solana del Pino
E 157 B3
Solánas I..... 179 C3
Solares E 143 A3
Solarino I.... 177 B4
Solarussa I... 179 C2
Solas UK 31 B1
Solberg S..... 200 C3
Solberga S.....62 A2
Solber-gelva
N.............53 A6
Solbjørg N 46 B2
Solbra I....... 166 C2
Solčany SK 98 C2
Solčava SLO.. 123 A3
Solda I....... 108 C1
Sölden A..... 108 C2
Solec Kujawski
PL............76 A3
Soleils F...... 132 B2
Solenzara F... 180 B2
Solera E...... 163 A4
Solesmes F 79 B3
Soleto I...... 173 B4
Solgne F.......92 C2
Solheim N......46 B2
Solheimsvik N..52 A2
Solignac F 115 C5
Solihull UK 44 A2
Solin HR...... 138 B2
Solingen D.....80 A3
Sölle E....... 168 B2
Solivella E 147 C2
Solkan SLO... 122 B2
Söll A........ 108 B3
Sollana E..... 159 B3
Sollebrunn S...54 B3
Sollefteå S.... 200 C3
Sollenau A.... 111 B3
Sollen-tuna S ..57 A3
Sóller E 166 B2
Sollerön S.....50 B1
Søllested DK ...65 B4
Solliès-Pont F . 132 B2
Sollihøgda N...48 C2
Solnechnogorsk
RUS 9 D10
Solnice CZ.....85 B4
Solofra I...... 170 C2
Solomiac F ... 129 C3
Solopaca I.... 170 B2
Solórzano E... 143 A3
Solothurn CH . 106 B2
Solre-le-Château

Soltszentimre
H 112 C3
Soltvadkert H. 112 C3
Solumsmoen N .48 C1
Solund N.......46 A1
Solva UK 39 C1
Sölvesborg S...63 B2
Solymár H 112 B2
Somain F 78 B3
Somberk H ... 125 A4
Sombernon F . 104 B3
Sombor SRB.. 125 B5
Sombreffe B ...79 B4
Sör SRB 127 C1
Sora I........ 169 B3
Soragna I.... 120 C3
Söräker S 200 D3
Sorano I...... 168 A1
Sorbara I.... 121 C4
Sorbas E...... 164 B2
Sórbolo I..... 121 C3
Sörbygden S.. 200 D2
Sordal N...... 52 B3
Sordale UK.....32 C3
Sore F........ 128 B2
Sörenberg CH. 106 C3
Soresina I.... 120 B2
Sorèze F 146 A3
Sörforsa S.... 200 E3
Sorges F 115 C4
Sórgono I.... 179 B3
Sorgues F 131 A3
Sorgun TR......23 B8
Soria I........ 144 A3
Soriano Cálabro
I........... 175 C2
Soriano nel Cimino
I........... 168 A2
Sorihuela del
Guadalimar
E 164 A1
Sørkjosen N... 192 C4
Sørli N 199 A10
Sörmark S.....49 B4
Sörmjöle S ... 200 C6
Sörmo N 194 B9
Sornac F...... 116 B2
SørO DK....... 61 D1
Soroca MD.... 17 A8
Sørreisa N ... 194 A9
Sorrento I.... 170 C2
Sorsele S..... 195 E8
Sörsjön N......49 A5
Sorso I....... 178 B2
Sort E 146 B2
Sortavala RUS...9 B7
Sortino I...... 177 B4
Sortland N... 194 B6
Sørum N.......48 B2
Sørumsand N..48 C3
Sorunda S.....57 A3
Sörup D.......64 B2
Sørvågen N... 194 C4
Sørværr N ... 192 B6
Sorvik S........50 B2
Sörvika N 199 C8
Sos F......... 128 B3
Sösdala S......61 C3
Sos del Rey
Católico E ... 144 B2
Sošice HR 123 B4
Sośnica PL.....75 A5
Sośnicowice PL .86 B2
Sośno PL.......76 A2
Sosnovyy Bor
RUS 9 C6
Sosnowiec PL...86 B3
Sospel F...... 133 B3
Šoštanj SLO ... 123 A4
Sotaseter N.. 198 D4
Sotillo de Adrada
E 150 B3
Sotillo de la Ribera
E 143 C3
Sotin HR...... 125 B5
Sotkamo FIN.. 3 D11
Sotobañado y
Priorato E ... 142 B2
Soto de la Marina
E 143 A3
Soto del Barco
E 141 A4
Soto de los Infantes
E 141 A4
Soto de Real E 151 B4
Soto de Ribera
E 141 A5
Sotoserrano E 149 B3
Soto y Amío E . 141 B5
Sotresgude E . 142 B2
Sotrondio E... 142 A1
Sotta F....... 180 B2

Sottomarina I . . 122 B1
Sottrum D 72 A2
Sottunga FIN. . . 51 B7
Sotuelamos E . 158 B1
Souain F 91 B4
Soual F 146 A3
Soucy F 104 A2
Souda GR 185 D5
Soudron F 91 C4
Souesmes F . . 103 B4
Soufflenheim F .93 C3
Soufli GR 186 A1
Souillac F 129 B4
Souilly F 91 B5
Soulac-sur-Mer
  F 114 C2
Soulaines-Dhuys
  F 91 C4
Soulatgé F . . . 146 B3
Soultz-Haut-Rhin
  F 93 C3
Soultz-sous-Forêts
  F 93 C3
Soumagne B . . .80 B1
Soumoulou F . 145 A3
Souppes-sur-Loing
  F 103 A4
Souprosse F . . 128 C2
Sourdeval F 88 B3
Soure P 154 A2
Sournia F 146 B3
Souro Pires P . . 149 B2
Sourpi GR 182 D4
Sours F 90 C1
Sousceyrac F . . 116 C2
Sousel P 155 C3
Soustons F 128 C1
Söğüt
  Bilecik TR 187 B5
  Burdur TR 189 B6
Soutelo de Montes
  E 140 B2
Southam UK 44 A2
Southampton
  UK 44 C2
Southborough
  UK 45 B4
South Brent UK .42 B3
South Cave UK . .40 B3
Southend UK . . .34 C2
Southend-on-Sea
  UK 45 B4
South Hayling
  UK 44 C3
South Molton
  UK 42 A3
South Ockendon
  UK 45 B4
South Petherton
  UK 43 B4
Southport UK . . .38 A3
South Shields
  UK 37 B5
South Tawton
  UK 42 B3
Southwell UK . . .40 B3
Southwold UK . .45 A5
South Woodham
  Ferrers UK 45 B4
Söğütlü TR 187 B5
Souto P 148 B2
Soutochao E . . 141 C3
Souto da
  Carpalhosa
  P 154 B2
Souvigny F . . . 104 C2
Souzay-Champigny
  F 102 B1
Soverato I 175 C2
Soveria Mannelli
  I 175 B2
Sövestad S 66 A2
Sovetsk RUS . . . 12 A4
Soviči BIH 138 B3
Sovicille I 135 B4
Søvik N 198 C3
Sowerby UK 37 B5
Soyaux F 115 C4
Sozopol BG 17 D7
Spa B 80 B1
Spadafora I . . . 177 A4
Spaichingen
  D 107 A3
Spakenburg NL 70 B2
Spalding UK 41 C3
Spálené Poříčí
  CZ 96 B1
Spalt D 94 B2
Spangenberg
  D 82 A1
Spangereid N . . .52 B3
Spantekow D . . .74 A2
Sparanise I 170 B2

Sparbu N 199 B8
Sparkær DK 58 B2
Sparkford UK . . .43 A4
Sparreholm S . . .56 A2
Spartà I 177 A4
Sparta = Sparti
Sparti = Sparta
  GR 184 B3
Spean Bridge
  UK 34 B3
Speicher D 92 B2
Speichersdorf
  D 95 B3
Spello I 136 C1
Spenge D 72 B1
Spennymoor
  UK 37 B5
Spentrup DK . . .58 B3
Sperenberg D . .74 B2
Sperlinga I 177 B3
Sperlonga I . . . 169 B3
Spetalen N 54 A1
Spetses GR . . . 184 B4
Speyer D 93 B4
Spézet F 100 A2
Spezzano Albanese
  I 174 B2
Spezzano della Sila
  I 174 B2
Spiddle IRL 28 A2
Spiegelau D 96 C1
Spiekeroog D . . .71 A4
Spiez CH 106 C2
Spigno Monferrato
  I 133 A4
Spijk NL 71 A3
Spijkenisse NL . .79 A4
Spili GR 185 D5
Spilimbergo I . . 122 A1
Spilsby UK 41 B4
Spinazzola I . . . 172 B2
Spincourt F 92 B1
Spind N 52 B2
Spindleruv-Mlyn
  CZ 84 B3
Spinoso I 174 A1
Špišić Bukovica
  HR 124 B3
Spišská Belá
  SK 99 B4
Spišská Nová Ves
  SK 99 C4
Spisská Stará Ves
  SK 99 B4
Spišské-
  Hanušovce
  SK 99 B4
Spišské Podhradie
  SK 99 C4
Spišský Vlachy
  SK 99 C4
Spišský-Štvrtok
  SK 99 C4
Spital A 110 B1
Spital am
  Semmering
  A 110 B2
Spittal an der Drau
  A 109 C4
Spittle of Glenshee
  UK 35 B4
Spitz A 97 C3
Spjald DK 59 B1
Spjærøy N 54 A1
Spjelkavik N . . 198 C3
Spjutsbygd S . . .63 B3
Split HR 138 B2
Splügen CH . . . 107 C4
Spodsbjerg DK .65 B3
Spofforth UK . . .40 B2
Spohle D 71 A5
Spoleto I 136 C1
Spoltore I 169 A4
Spondigna I . . . 108 C1
Sponvika N 54 A2
Spornitz D 73 A4
Spotorno I 133 A4
Spraitbach D . . .94 C1
Sprakensehl D . .72 B3
Spremberg D . . .84 A2
Spresiano I 122 B1
Sprimont B 80 B1
Springe D 72 B2
Sproatley UK . . .41 B3
Spydeberg N . . .54 A2
Spytkowice PL . .99 B3
Squillace I 175 C2
Squinzano I . . . 173 B4
Sračinec HR . . . 124 A2

Srbac BIH 124 B3
Srbobran SRB . 126 B1
Srebrenica
  BIH 127 C1
Srebrenik BIH . 125 C4
Sredets BG 17 D7
Središče SLO . . 124 A2
Šrem PL 76 B2
Sremska Mitrovica
  SRB 127 C1
Sremski Karlovci
  SRB 126 B1
Srní CZ 96 B1
Srnice Gornje
  BIH 125 C4
Srock PL 86 A3
Środa Śląska
  PL 85 A4
Środa Wielkopolski
  PL 76 B2
Srpska Crnja
  SRB 126 B2
Srpski Itebej
  SRB 126 B2
Srpski Miletić
  SRB 125 B5
Staatz A 97 C4
Stabbursnes
  N 193 B8
Staberdorf D . . .65 B4
Stabroek B 79 A4
Stachy CZ 96 B1
Staðarfell IS . . . 190 B3
Stade D 72 A2
Staden B 78 B3
Stadl an der Mur
  A 109 B4
Stadskanaal NL 71 B3
Stadtallendorf
  D 81 B5
Stadthagen D . .72 B2
Stadtilm D 82 B3
Stadtkyll D 80 B2
Stadtlauringen
  D 82 B2
Stadtlengsfeld
  D 82 B2
Stadtlohn D 71 C3
Stadtoldendorf
  D 82 A1
Stadtroda D 83 B3
Stadtsteinach
  D 82 B3
Stäfa CH 107 B3
Staffanstorp S . 61 D3
Staffelstein D . .82 B2
Staffin UK 31 B2
Stafford UK 40 C1
Stainach A 110 B1
Staindrop UK . . .37 B5
Staines-upon-
  Thames UK . . .44 B3
Stainville F 91 C5
Stainz A 110 C2
Staithes UK 37 B6
Staiti I 175 D2
Stäket S 57 A3
Stakroge DK 59 C1
Štalcerji SLO . . 123 B3
Stalden CH 119 A4
Stalham UK 41 C5
Stallarholmen
  S 56 A3
Ställberg S 50 C1
Ställdalen S 50 C1
Stallhofen A . . . 110 B2
Stalon S 195 F6
Stalowa Wola
  PL 12 C5
Stamford UK . . .40 C3
Stamford Bridge
  UK 40 B3
Stamnes N 46 B2
Stams A 108 B1
Stamsried D 95 B4
Stamsund N . . . 194 B4
Stanford le Hope
  UK 45 B4
Stånga S 57 C4
Stange N 48 B3
Stanghella I . . . 121 B4
Stanhope UK . . .37 B5
Stanjel SLO . . . 122 B2
Staňkov CZ 95 B5
Stankovci HR . . 137 B4
Stanley UK 37 B5
Stans CH 106 C3
Stansted
  Mountfitchet
  UK 45 B4
Stanzach A 108 B1
Stapar SRB 125 B5

Staphorst NL . . .70 B3
Staplehurst UK .45 B4
Stąporków PL . . .87 A4
Stara Baška
  HR 123 C3
Stara Fužina
  SLO 122 A2
Stara Kamienica
  PL 84 B3
Stara Kiszewa
  PL 68 B3
Stará Ľubovňa
  SK 99 B4
Stara Moravica
  SRB 126 B1
Stara Novalja
  HR 137 A3
Stara Pazova
  SRB 127 C2
Stará Turá SK . . .98 C1
Staraya Russa
  RUS 9 D7
Stara Zagora
  BG 17 D6
Stärbsnäs S 51 C6
Starčevo SRB . . 127 C2
Stare Dłutowo
  PL 77 A4
Staré Hamry
  CZ 98 B2
Stare Jablonki
  PL 69 B5
Staré Město CZ .98 B1
Stare Pole PL . . .69 A4
Stare Sedlo CZ .96 B2
Stare Strącze
  PL 85 A4
Stargard
  Szczeciński
  PL 75 A4
Stårheim N . . . 198 D2
Stari Banovci
  SRB 127 C2
Starigrad
  Ličko-Senjska
  HR 123 C3
  Splitsko-Dalmatinska
  HR 138 B2
Stari Gradac
  HR 124 B3
Starigrad-Paklenica
  HR 137 A4
Stari Jankovci
  HR 125 B4
Stari Majdan
  BIH 124 C2
Stari-Mikanovci
  HR 125 B4
Staritsa RUS 9 D9
Starkenbach
  A 108 B1
Starnberg D . . . 108 B2
Starogard D 75 A4
Starogard Gdański
  PL 69 B3
Starý Hrozenkov
  CZ 98 C1
Stary Jaroslaw
  PL 68 A1
Stary Plzenec
  CZ 96 B1
Stary Sącz PL . . .99 B4
Starý Smokovec
  SK 99 B4
Staryy Chartoriysk
  UA 13 C6
Staškov SK 98 B2
Stassfurt D 82 A3
Staszów PL 87 B5
Stathelle N 53 A5
Staufen D 106 B2
Staunton UK . . .39 C4
Stavang N 46 A1
Stavanger N 52 B1
Stavåsnäs S 49 B4
Stavby S 51 B5
Staveley UK 40 B2
Stavelot B 80 B1
Stavenisse NL . .79 A4
Stavern N 53 B6

Stavnäs S 55 A3
Stavoren NL 70 B2
Stavros
  CY 181 A1
  GR 183 C5
Stavroupoli
  GR 183 B6
Stavseng N 47 A6
Stavsjø N 48 B2
Stavsnäs S 57 A4
Stawiszyn PL . . .76 C3
Steane N 53 A4
Steblevë AL . . . 182 B2
Stechelberg
  CH 106 C2
Štěchovice CZ . .96 B2
Stechow D 73 B5
Steckborn CH . 107 B3
Stede Broek NL .70 B2
Steeg A 107 B5
Steenbergen
  NL 79 A4
Steenvoorde F . .78 B2
Steenwijk NL . . .70 B3
Stefanje HR . . . 124 B2
Steffisburg
  CH 106 C2
Stegaurach D . .94 B2
Stege DK 65 B5
Stegelitz D 74 A2
Stegersbach
  A 111 B3
Stegna PL 69 A4
Steimbke D 72 B2
Stein am Rhein
  CH 107 B3
Steinau
  Bayern D 81 B5
  Niedersachsen
  D 64 C1
Steinbeck D 74 B2
Steinberg am Rofan
  A 108 B2
Steindorf A . . . 109 C5
Steine N 46 B2
Steinen D 106 B2
Steinfeld
  A 109 C4
  D 71 B5
Steinfurt D 71 B4
Steingaden D . 108 B1
Steinhagen D . .72 B1
Steinheid D 82 B3
Steinheim
  Bayern D 107 A5
  Nordrhein-
  Westfalen D . . .81 A5
Steinhöfel D 74 B3
Steinhorst D 72 B3
Steinigtwolmsdorf
  D 84 A2
Steinkjer N . . . 199 A8
Steinsholt N 53 A5
Stekene B 79 A4
Stelle D 72 A3
Stellendam NL . .79 A4
Stenåsa S 63 B4
Stenay F 91 B5
Stenberga S 62 A3
Stendal D 73 B4
Stenhammar S . .55 B4
Stenhamra S . . .57 A3
Stenlose DK 61 D2
Stensätra S 50 B3
Stensele S 195 E8
Stenstorp S 55 B4
Stenstrup DK . . .65 A3
Stenudden S . . 195 D8
Stenungsund
  S 54 B2
Štěpánov CZ . . .98 B1
Stephanskirchen
  D 108 B3
Stepnica PL 74 A3
Stepojevac
  SRB 127 C2
Stepping DK 59 C2
Sterbfritz D 82 B1
Sterdyń-Osada
  PL 77 B6
Sternberg D 65 C4
Šternberk CZ . . .98 B1
Sterup D 64 B2
Stes Maries-de-la-
  Mer F 131 B3
Stęszew PL 75 B5

Štěti CZ 84 B2
Stevenage UK . .44 B3
Stewarton UK . . .36 A2
Steyerburg D . . .72 B2
Steyning UK 44 C3
Steyr A 110 A1
Stężyca PL 68 A2
Stezzano I 120 B2
Stia I 135 B4
Stibb Cross UK .42 B2
Sticciano Scalo
  I 135 C4
Stidsvig S 61 C3
Stiens NL 70 A2
Stige DK 59 C3
Stigen S 54 B3
Stigliano I 174 A2
Stigtomta S 56 B2
Stilida GR 182 E4
Stilla N 192 C7
Stillington UK . .40 A2
Stilo I 175 C2
Stintino I 178 B2
Štip NMK 182 B4
Stira GR 185 A5
Stirling UK 35 B4
Štitar HR 99 C4
Štíty CZ 97 B4
Štitnik SK 99 C4
Stjärnhov S 56 A3
Stjärnsund S . . .50 B3
Stjørdalshalsen
  N 199 B7
Stobnica PL 87 A3
Stobno PL 75 A5
Stobreč HR 138 B2
Stochov CZ 84 B1
Stockach D . . . 107 B4
Stöckalp CH . . . 106 C3
Stockaryd S 62 A2
Stockbridge
  UK 44 B2
Stockerau A 97 C4
Stockheim D . . .82 B3
Stockholm S 57 A4
Stockport UK . . .40 B1
Stocksbridge
  UK 40 B2
Stockton-on-Tees
  UK 37 B5
Stod CZ 96 B1
Stöde S 200 D2
Stødi N 195 D6
Stoer UK 32 C1
Stoholm DK 58 B2
Stoke Ferry UK .41 C4
Stoke Fleming
  UK 43 B3
Stoke Mandeville
  UK 44 B3
Stoke-on-Trent
  UK 40 B1
Stokesley UK . . .37 B5
Stokke N 54 A1
Stokkemarke
  DK 65 B4
Stokken N 53 B4
Stokksund N . . 199 A7
Stokkvågen
  N 195 D4
Stokmarknes
  N 194 B5
Štoky CZ 97 B3
Stolac BIH 139 B3
Stolberg D 80 B2
Stolin BY 13 C7
Stollberg D 83 B4
Stöllet S 49 B5
Stollhamm D . . .71 A5
Stolno PL 76 A3
Stolpen D 84 A2
Stolzenau D 72 B2
Stompetoren
  NL 70 B1
Ston HR 139 C3
Stonařov CZ 97 B3
Stone UK 40 C1
Stonehaven UK .35 B5
Stonehouse UK .36 A3
Stongfjorden N .46 A2
Stonndalen N . .47 B4
Stony Stratford
  UK 44 A3
Stopnica PL 87 B4
Storå S 56 A1
Storås N 198 B6
Storby FIN 51 B6
Stordal
  Møre og Romsdal
  N 198 C4

Stordal continued
  Nord-Trøndelag
  N 199 B8
Store UK 33 B4
Storebø N 46 B2
Storebro S 62 A3
Store Damme
  DK 65 B5
Store Heddinge
  DK 65 A5
Store Herrestad
  S 66 A2
Store Levene S . 55 B3
Storelv N 192 B6
Store Molvik
  N 193 B12
Støren N 199 B7
Store Skedvi S . .50 B2
Store Vika S 57 B3
Storfjellseter
  N 199 D7
Storfjord N 192 C3
Storfjorden N . 198 C3
Storfors S 55 A5
Storforshei N . 195 D5
Storhøliseter N .47 A6
Storjord N 195 D6
Storkow
  Brandenburg
  D 74 B2
  Mecklenburg-
  Vorpommern
  D 74 A3
Storli N 198 C6
Storlien S 199 B9
Stornara I 171 B3
Stornoway UK . .31 A2
Storo I 121 B3
Storozhynets
  UA 17 A6
Storrington UK .44 C3
Storseleby S . . 200 B2
Storsjön S 50 A3
Storslett N 192 C5
Storsteinnes
  N 192 C3
Storsund S 196 D3
Storuman S . . . 195 E8
Störvattnet S . . 199 C9
Storvik
  N 195 D4
  S 50 B3
Štos SK 99 C4
Stössen D 83 A3
Stotel D 72 A1
Stötten D 108 B1
Stotternheim
  D 82 A3
Stouby DK 59 C2
Stourbridge UK 40 C1
Stourport-on-
  Severn UK 39 B4
Støvring DK 58 B2
Stow UK 35 C5
Stowbtsy BY . . . 13 B7
Stowmarket
  UK 45 A5
Stow-on-the-Wold
  UK 44 B2
Straach D 73 C5
Strabane UK 27 B3
Strachan UK 33 D4
Strachur UK 34 B2
Stracin NMK . . 182 A4
Strackholt D 71 A4
Stradbally IRL . . .29 B1
Stradella I 120 B2
Straelen D 80 A2
Stragari SRB . . 127 C2
Stráháč CZ 96 B1
Strålsnäs S 55 B6
Stralsund D 66 B2
Strand N 48 A3
Stranda N 198 C3
Strandby DK 58 A3
Strandebarm N .46 B3
Strandhill IRL . . .26 B2
Strandlykkja N . .48 B3
Strandvik N 46 B2
Strangford UK . .27 B5
Strängnäs S 56 A3
Strångsjö S 56 B2
Strání CZ 98 C1
Stranice SLO . . 123 A4
Stranorlar IRL . . .26 B3
Stranraer UK . . .36 B1
Strasatti I 176 B1
Strasbourg F . . .93 C3
Strasburg D 74 A2

Strašice CZ....96 B1
Stråssa S.......56 A1
Strassburg A . 110 C1
Strass im
Steiermark
A............ 110 C2
Strasskirchen
D 95 C4
Strasswalchen
A............ 109 B4
Stratford-upon-
Avon UK 44 A2
Strathaven UK . .36 A2
Strathdon UK .. 32 D3
Strathkanaird
UK 32 D1
Strathpeffer
UK 32 D2
Strathy UK ...32 C3
Strathyre UK ...34 B3
Stratinska BIH 124 C2
Stratton UK ...42 B2
Straubing D....95 C4
Straulas I...... 178 B3
Straume N 53 A5
Straumen
Nordland N ... 194 C6
Nord-Trøndelag
N............. 199 B8
Straumsjøen
N............. 194 B5
Straumsnes N. 194 C6
Straupitz D ...74 C3
Strausberg D ..74 B2
Straussfurt D ..82 A3
Strawczyn PL ..87 B4
Straža
SLO 123 B4
SRB 127 C3
Stražnad Nezárkou
CZ 96 B2
Strážnice CZ ..98 C1
Strážný CZ 96 C1
Stráž Pod Ralskem
CZ 84 B2
Štrbské Pleso
SK............99 B4
Strečno SK 98 B2
Street UK 43 A4
Strehla D......83 A5
Strekov SK ... 112 B2
Strem A 111 B3
Stremska-Rača
SRB 127 C1
Strengberg A . 110 A1
Strengelvåg
N............. 194 B6
Stresa I...... 119 B5
Streufdorf D ...82 B2
Strib DK......59 C2
Striberg S......55 A5
Stříbro CZ......95 B4
Strichen UK ... 33 D4
Strigno I...... 121 A4
Štrigova HR ... 111 C3
Strijen NL......79 A4
Strizivojna HR 125 B4
Strmica HR ... 138 A2
Strmilov CZ....97 B3
Ströhen D......72 B1
Strokestown
IRL 28 A3
Stromberg
Nordrhein-
Westfalen D... 81 A4
Rheinland-Pfalz
D..............93 B3
Stromeferry UK 31 B3
Strömnäs S ... 200 B2
Stromness UK ..33 C3
Strömsberg S ..51 B4
Strömsbruk S . 200 E3
Strömsfors S ..56 B2
Strömsnäsbruk
S.............61 C3
Strömstad S ...54 B2
Strömsund
Jämtland
S............ 199 B12
Västerbotten
S............. 195 E7
Stronachlachar
UK 34 B3
Stróngoli I 174 B3
Stronie Śląskie
PL............85 B4
Strontian UK ...34 B2
Stroppiana I ... 119 B5
Stroud UK......43 A4
Stroumbi CY .. 181 B1

Stróża PL.......99 B3
Strücklingen D..71 A4
Struer DK 58 B1
Struga NMK... 182 B2
Strugi Krasnyye
RUS 9 C6
Strumica NMK 182 B4
Strumien PL....98 B2
Struy UK 32 D2
Stružec HR 124 B2
Stryków PL.....77 C4
Stryn N 198 D3
Stryy UA 13 D5
Strzałkowo PL ..76 B2
Strzegocin PL ..77 B5
Strzegom PL....85 B4
Strzegowo PL...77 B5
Strzelce PL.....77 B4
Strzelce Krajeńskie
PL............75 B4
Strzelce Kurowo
PL............75 B4
Strzelce Opolskie
PL............86 B2
Strzelin PL.....85 B5
Strzelno PL.....76 B3
Strzepcz PL 68 A3
Strzybnica PL ..86 B2
Strzygi PL......77 A4
Stubbeköbing
DK............65 B5
Stuben A...... 107 B5
Stubenberg A. 110 B2
Stubline SRB .. 127 C2
Studená CZ 97 B3
Studenci HR... 138 B3
Studenka CZ ...98 B2
Studenzen A .. 110 B2
Studienka SK ...98 C1
Studland UK ...43 B5
Studley UK 44 A2
Studzienice PL..68 A2
Stuer D 73 A5
Stugudal N ... 199 C8
Stugun S..... 200 C1
Stuhr D 72 A1
Stukenbrock D..81 A4
Stülpe D 74 B2
Stupava SK.... 111 A4
Stupnik HR... 124 B1
Stupsk PL......77 A5
Sturkö S 63 B3
Sturminster
Newton UK...43 B4
Štúrovo SK.... 112 B2
Sturton UK 40 B3
Stuttgart D 94 C1
Stvolny CZ.....96 A1
Stykkishólmur
IS 190 B3
Styri N 48 B3
StysÖ S 60 B1
Suances E 142 A2
Subbiano I 135 B4
Subiaco I..... 169 B3
Subotica SRB. 126 A1
Subotište SRB. 127 C1
Sučany SK......98 B2
Suceava RO 17 B7
Sucha-Beskidzka
PL............99 B3
Suchacz PL.....69 A4
Suchań PL......75 A4
Suchdol nad
Lužnicie CZ ...96 C2
Suchedniów
PL............87 A4
Suchorze PL ...68 A2
Suchteln D.....80 A2
Sucina E 165 B4
Suckow D 73 A4
Sućuraj HR ... 138 B3
Súðavík IS ... 190 A3
Sudbury UK ...45 A4
Suddesjaur S 195 E10
Suden D 64 B1
Süderbrarup D..64 B2
Süderlügum D ..64 B1
Sudomĕřice u
Bechyně CZ...96 B2
Sudovec HR ... 124 A2
Sueca E 159 B3
Suelli I 179 C3
Sugenheim D ..94 B2
Sugères I 117 B3
Sugny B 91 B4
Suhl D 82 B2
Suhlendorf D ..73 B3
Suhopolje HR . 124 B3
Suho Polje
BIH 125 C5
Suhut TR 189 A5

Šuica BIH..... 138 B3
Suippes F 91 B4
Sukošan HR... 137 A4
Sükösd H 125 A4
Sukόw PL......87 B4
Šul'a SK 99 C3
Suldalsosen N ..52 A2
Suldrup DK 58 B2
Sulechów PL ...75 B4
Sulęcin PL.....75 B4
Sulęczyno PL ..68 A2
Sulejów PL.....87 A3
Süleymanlı
TR. 186 D2
Sulgen CH 107 B4
Sulibórz PL....75 A4
Sulina RO 17 C8
Sulingen D.....72 B1
Suliszewo PL...75 A4
Sulitjelma N . 195 C7
Sułkowice PL... 99 B3
Süller TR 189 A4
Sully-sur-Loire
F 103 B4
Sulmierzyce
Łódzkie PL . 86 A3
Wielkopolskie
PL............ 85 A5
Sulmona I.... 169 A3
Süloğlu TR ... 186 A1
Sułoszowa PL...87 B3
Sulów PL......85 A5
Sulsdorf D.....65 B3
Sultandağı
TR. 189 A6
Sülüklü TR ... 187 D7
Suluova TR....23 A8
Sulvik S 54 A3
Sülysáp H 112 B3
Sülz D 93 C4
Sulzbach
Baden-Württemberg
D...........94 B1
Baden-Württemberg
D.... 94 C1
Bayern D 93 B5
Saarland D 92 B3
Sulzbach-
Rosenberg D...95 B3
Sülze D 72 B3
Sulzfeld D......93 B5
Sumartin HR . 138 B2
Sumburgh UK...33 B5
Sümeg H 111 C4
Sumiswald
CH 106 B2
Sundern D 81 A4
Sundhultsbrunn
S............62 A2
Sundsås S.... 195 D6
Sundom S..... 196 D5
Sunds DK 59 B2
Sundsfjord N . 195 D5
Sundsvall S ... 200 D3
Sungurlu TR ...23 A8
Suni I 178 B2
Sunja HR 124 B2
Sunnansjö S...50 B1
Sunnaryd S 60 B3
Sunndalsøra
N............ 198 C5
Sunne S 49 C5
Sunnemo S 49 C5
Sunnersberg S. 55 B4
Suolovuopmio
N............ 192 C7
Suomussalmi
FIN........... 3 D11
Suoyarvi RUS .. 9 A8
Super Sauze F . 132 A2
Supetar HR ... 138 B2
Supetarska Draga
HR 123 C3
Supino I...... 169 B3
Šuplja Stijena
MNE 139 B5
Surahammar S. 56 A2
Šurany SK ... 112 A2
Surazh TR 13 A9

Surbo I....... 173 B4
Surčin SRB ... 127 C2
Surgères F 114 B3
Surhuisterveen
NL 70 A3
Súria E 147 C2
Surin F 115 B4
Surka N 48 B2
Surnadalsøra
N........... 198 C5
Sursee CH.... 106 B3
Surte S.......60 B2
Surwold D 71 B4
Sury-le-Comtal
F 117 B4
Susa I 119 B4
Šušara SRB ... 127 C3
Susch CH..... 107 C5
Suseganal 122 B1
Süsel D 65 B3
Sušice CZ 96 B1
Sušnjevica
HR 123 B3
Sussen D......94 C1
Susurluk TR .. 186 C3
Susz PL........69 B4
Sütçüler TR .. 189 B5
Sutivan HR... 138 B2
Sutjeska SRB . 126 B2
Sutri I....... 168 A2
Sutton UK 44 B3
Sutton Coldfield
UK 40 C2
Sutton-in-Ashfield
UK 40 B2
Sutton-on-Sea
UK 41 B4
Sutton-on-Trent
UK 40 B3
Sutton Scotney
UK 44 B2
Sutton Valence
UK 45 B4
Suvaja BIH ... 124 C2
Suvereto I.... 135 B3
Suwałki PL....12 A5
Suze-la-Rousse
F 131 A3
Suzzara I..... 121 C3
Svabensverk S .50 A2
Svalbarð IS . 191 A10
Svalöv S 61 D3
Svanabyn S ... 200 B2
Svanberga S ...51 C5
Svaneke DK ...67 A4
Svanesund S ..54 B2
Svängsta S 63 B2
Svannäs S 195 D9
Svanskog S 54 A3
Svanstein S ... 196 C6
Svappavaara
S............ 196 B4
Svärdsjö S 50 B2
Svarstad N 53 A5
Svartå S.......55 A5
Svärta S.......56 B3
Svartå S.......55 A4
Svartbyn S ... 196 C5
Svärtinge S 56 B2
Svartlå S..... 196 D4
Svartnäs S.....50 B3
Svartnes N ... 195 C5
Svarttjärn S .. 195 E7
Svatsum N 48 A1
Svätý Jur SK... 111 A4
Svätý Peter
SK........... 112 B2
Svedala S 61 D3
Sveg S 199 C11
Sveindi N 52 B3
Sveio N 52 A1
Svejbæk DK ...59 B2
Švelgen N.... 198 D2
Svelvik N 54 A1
Svendborg DK .65 A3
Svene N 53 A5
Svenljunga S ..60 B3
Svennevad S ..56 A1
Svenstavik S . 199 C11
Svenstrup DK..58 B2
Švermov CZ....84 B2
Švermov CZ....84 B2
Sveti Ivan Zabno
HR 124 B2
Sveti Ivan Zelina
HR 124 B2
Sveti Nikole
NMK 182 B3
Sveti Rok HR . 137 A4
Světla nad Sázavou
CZ 97 B3
Svetlyy RUS ...69 A5
Svetvinčenat
HR 122 B2

Švica HR 123 C4
Svidnik SK 12 D4
Švihov CZ......96 B1
Svilajnac SRB . 127 C3
Svilengrad BG 183 B8
Svindal N 54 A2
Svinhult S.....62 A3
Svinna SK 98 C2
Svinninge
DK 61 D1
S............57 A4
Sviritsa RUS ...9 B8
Svishtov BG ...17 D6
Svislach BY....13 B6
Svit SK 99 B4
Svitavy CZ 97 B4
Svodín SK.... 112 B2
Svolvær N.... 194 B5
Svortemyr N ..46 A2
Svortland N....52 A1
Svratka CZ 97 B4
Svrčinovec SK..98 B2
Svullrya N.....49 B4
Svyetlahorsk
BY............13 B8
Swadlincote
UK 40 C2
Swaffham UK ..41 C4
Swanage UK ...43 B5
Swanley UK ...45 B4
Swanlinbar IRL .26 B3
Swansea UK ...39 C3
Swarzędz PL ...76 B2
Swatragh UK...27 B4
Świątki PL 69 B5
Świdnica
Dolnośląskie
PL...........85 B4
Lubuskie PL... 84 A3
Świdnik PL....12 C5
Świdwin PL....67 C4
Świebodzice PL 85 B4
Świebodzin PL .75 B4
Świecie PL 76 A3
Świedziebnia
PL............77 A4
Świeradów Zdrój
PL............84 B3
Świerki PL 85 B4
Świerzawa PL ..85 A3
Świerzno PL ...67 C3
Święta PL 74 A3
Święta Anna PL 86 B3
Świętno PL.....75 B5
Swifterbant NL .70 B2
Swindon UK ...44 B2
Swineshead UK .41 C3
Swinford IRL ..26 C2
Świnoujście PL .66 C3
Swinton UK ...35 C5
Swobnica PL...74 A3
Swords IRL 30 A2
Swornegacie
PL............68 B2
Sya S..........56 B1
Syasstroy RUS .. 9 B8
Sycewice PL ...68 A1
Sychevka RUS...9 E9
Syców PL......86 A1
Sycowice PL ...75 B4
Sydnes N......52 A1
Syfteland N....46 B2
Syke D 72 B1
Sykkylven N . 198 C3
Sylling N......48 C2
Sylte N 198 C4
Symbister UK ..33 A5
Symington UK .36 A3
Symonds Yat
UK 39 C4
Sypniewo
Kujawsko-
Pomorskie PL . 76 A2
Wielkopolskie
PL............68 B1
Syserum S 62 A4
Sysslebäck S ..49 B4
Syväjärvi FIN . 197 B8
Szabadbattyán
H........... 112 B2
Szabadegyháza
H........... 112 B2
Szabadszállás
H........... 112 C3
Szadek PL.....86 A2
Szajol H 113 B4
Szakály H 112 C2
Szakcs H 112 C2
Szakmár H ... 112 C3
Szalánta H ... 125 B4
Szałas PL......87 A4
Szalkszentmárton
H........... 112 C3

Szalonna H 99 C4
Szamocin PL ...76 A2
Szamotuły PL ..75 B5
Szany H 111 B4
Szarvas H 113 C4
Szarvaskö H .. 113 B4
Szászvár H ... 125 A4
Százhalombatta
H........... 112 B2
Szczawa PL 99 B4
Szczawnica PL ..99 B4
Szczecin PL....74 A3
Szczecinek PL..68 B1
Szczekociny
PL............87 B3
Szczerców PL ..86 A3
Szczucin PL....87 B5
Szczuczarz PL ..75 A5
Szczuki PL.....77 B5
Szczurowa PL ..87 B4
Szczytna PL ...85 B4
Szczytno PL....77 A5
Szczyty PL.....86 A2
Szécsény H ... 112 A3
Szederkény H. 125 B4
Szedres H 112 C2
Szeged H 126 A2
Szeghalom H . 113 B5
Szegvár H 113 C4
Székesfehérvár
H........... 112 B2
Székkutas H .. 113 C4
Szekszárd H .. 125 A4
Szemplino Czarne
PL............77 A5
Szemud PL.....68 A3
Szendehely H. 112 B3
Szendrő H 99 C4
Szentendre H . 112 B3
Szentes H 113 C4
Szentgotthárd
H........... 111 C3
Szentlászló H . 125 A3
Szentlörinc H . 125 A3
Szentmártonkáta
H........... 113 B3
Szenyér H 111 C4
Szeremle H ... 125 A4
Szerencs H ... 113 A5
Szerep H 113 B5
Szigetszentmiklós
H........... 112 B3
Szigetvár H .. 125 A3
Szikáncs H ... 126 A2
Szikszó H 113 A4
Szil H 111 B4
Szilvásvárad
H........... 113 A4
Szklarska Poreba
PL............84 B3
Szlichtyngowa
PL............85 A4
Szob H 112 B2
Szolnok H ... 113 B4
Szombathely
H........... 111 B3
Szorosad H ... 112 C2
Szpetal Graniczny
PL............77 B4
Szprotawa PL..84 A3
Szreńsk PL.....77 A5
Sztum PL......69 B4
Sztutowo PL...69 A4
Szubin PL......76 A2
Szücsi H 113 B3
Szulmierz PL...77 B5
Szulok H 124 A3
Szumanie PL ..77 B4
Szwecja PL 75 A5
Szydłów
Łódzkie PL . 86 A3
Świętokrzyskie
PL............87 B5
Szydłowiec PL .87 A4
Szydlowo PL...77 A5
Szydłowo PL...75 A5
Szymanów PL..77 B5
Szynkielów PL..86 A2

T

Taastrup DK...61 D2
Tab H 112 C2
Tabanera la Launga
E 151 A3
Tabaqueros E 158 B2
Tábara E 149 A4
Tabenca de
Cerrato E ... 142 B2
Tabernas E ... 164 B2

Tabiano Bagni
I............ 120 C3
Taboada E.... 140 B3
Taboadela E .. 140 B3
Tábor CZ 96 B2
Táborfalva H . 112 B3
Taboriste HR . 124 B2
Tábua P 148 B1
Tabuaco P... 148 A2
Tabuenca E .. 152 A2
Tabuyo del Monte
E 141 B4
Täby S 57 A4
Táč H........ 112 B2
Tachov CZ.....95 B4
Tadcaster UK ..40 B2
Tadley UK.....44 B2
Tafalla E 144 B2
Tafjord N.... 198 C4
Taganheira P . 160 B1
Tågarp S 61 D2
Tággia I...... 133 B3
Tagliacozzo I . 169 A3
Táglio di Po I . 121 B5
Tagnon F......91 B4
Tahal E...... 164 B2
Tahitótfalu H . 112 B3
Tahtaköprü
TR. 187 C4
Tailfingen D .. 107 A4
Taillis F...... 101 A4
Tain UK 32 D2
Tain-l'Hermitage
F 117 B4
Taipadas P .. 154 C2
Taivalkoski
FIN........ 197 D11
Takene S.......55 A4
Takovo SRB .. 127 C2
Taksony H ... 112 B3
Tal E 140 B2
Talachyn BY....13 A8
Talamello I ... 135 B5
Talamone I... 168 A1
Talant F 105 B3
Talarrubias E . 156 A2
Talaván E 155 B4
Talavera de la
Reina E 150 C3
Talavera la Real
E 155 C4
Talayuela E .. 150 C2
Talayuelas E . 159 B2
Talgarth UK ..39 C3
Talgje N...... 52 A1
Talhadas P... 148 B1
Táliga E 155 C3
Talizat F..... 116 B3
Talladale UK ..31 B3
Talla I 135 B4
Tallaght IRL ...30 A2
Tallard F 132 A2
Tällberg S 50 B1
Tallberg S ... 196 C5
Tallinn EST 8 C4
Talloires F.... 118 B3
Tallow IRL 29 B3
Tallsjö S..... 200 B4
Tallvik S 196 C5
Talmont-St Hilaire
E 141 B4
Talmont-sur-
Gironde F ... 114 C3
Talne UA 13 D9
Talsano I..... 173 B3
Talsi LV........8 D3
Talvik N 192 B6
Talybont UK ..39 B3
Tal-Y-Llyn UK. .38 B3
Tamajón E ... 151 B4
Tamame E.... 149 A4
Tamames E ... 149 B3
Tamarit de Mar
E 147 C2
Tamarite de Litera
E 145 C4
Tamási H 112 C2
Támara E 142 B2
Tamási H 112 C2
Tambach-Dietharz
D 82 B2
Tameza E 141 A4
Tammisaari FIN .. 8 B3
Tampere FIN ...8 B3
Tamsweg A ... 109 B4
Tamurejo E .. 156 B3
Tamworth UK ..40 C2
Tana bru N ... 193 B12
Tañabueyes E . 143 B3
Tanakajd H ... 111 B3
Tananger N ...52 B1

Tanaunella I 178 B3
Tancarville F 89 A4
Tandsjöborg S 199 D11
Tånga S 61 C2
Tangelic H 112 C2
Tangen N 48 B3
Tangerhütte D 73 B4
Tangermünde D 73 B4
Tanhua FIN 197 B10
Taninges F 118 A3
Tankavaara FIN 197 A10
Tann D 82 B2
Tanna D 83 B3
Tannadice UK 35 B5
Tannåker S 60 C3
Tännäs S 199 C9
Tannay
 Ardennes F 91 B4
 Nièvre F 104 B2
Tannenbergsthal D 83 B4
Tännesberg D 95 B4
Tannheim A 108 B1
Tannila FIN 197 D8
Tanowo PL 74 A3
Tanum S 54 B2
Tanumshede S 54 B2
Tanus F 130 A1
Tanvald CZ 84 B3
Taormina I 177 B4
Tapa EST 8 C4
Tapfheim D 94 C2
Tapia de Casariego E 141 A4
Tapio F 146 A2
Tápióbicske H 112 B3
Tápiógyörgye H 113 B3
Tápióság H 112 B3
Tápiószecső H 112 B3
Tápiószele H 113 B3
Tápiószentmárton H 113 B3
Tapolca H 111 C4
Tapolcafő H 111 B4
Tar HR 122 B2
Tarabo S 60 B2
Taradell E 147 C3
Tarakli TR 187 B5
Taramundi E 141 A3
Tarancón E 151 B4
Táranto I 173 B3
Tarare F 117 B4
Tarascon F 131 B3
Tarascon-sur-Ariège F 146 B2
Tarashcha UA 13 D9
Tarazona E 144 C2
Tarazona de la Mancha E 158 B2
Tarbena E 159 C3
Tarbert
 IRL 29 B2
 UK 34 C2
Tarbes F 145 A4
Tarbet UK 34 B3
Tarbolton UK 36 A2
Tarcento I 122 A2
Tarčin BIH 139 B4
Tarczyn PL 77 C5
Tardajos E 143 B3
Tardelcuende E 151 A5
Tardets-Sorholus F 144 A3
Tardienta E 145 C3
Tärendö S 196 B5
Targon F 128 B2
Targovishte BG 17 D7
Târgovişte RO 17 C6
Târgu-Jiu RO 17 C5
Târgu Mureş RO 17 B6
Târgu Ocna RO 17 B7
Târgu Secuiesc RO 17 C7
Tarifa E 162 B2
Tariquejas E 161 B2
Tarján H 112 B2
Tárkany H 112 B2
Tarland UK 33 D4
Tarłów PL 87 A5
Tarm DK 59 C1
Tarmstedt D 72 A2
Tärnaby S 195 E6
Tarnalelesz H 113 A4
Tarnaörs H 113 B4
Tárnăveni RO 17 B6

Tårnet N 193 C14
Tarnobrzeg PL 87 B5
Tarnos F 128 C1
Tarnów
 Lubuskie PL 75 B3
 Małopolskie PL 87 B4
Tarnowo Podgórne PL 75 B5
Tarnowskie Góry PL 86 B2
Tärnsjö S 51 B3
Tärnvik N 194 C6
Tarouca P 148 A2
Tarp D 64 B2
Tarquinia I 168 A1
Tarquinia Lido I 168 A1
Tarragona E 147 C2
Tàrrajaur S 196 C2
Tàrrega E 147 C2
Tarrenz A 108 B1
Tårs
 Nordjyllands DK 58 A3
 Storstrøms DK 65 B4
Tarsia I 174 B2
Tarsus TR 23 C8
Tartas F 128 C2
Tartu EST 8 C5
Tarves UK 33 D4
Tarvísio I 109 C4
Taşağıl TR 189 C6
Täsch CH 119 A4
Taşköprü TR 23 A8
Tasov CZ 97 B4
Tasovčići BIH 139 B3
Taşucu TR 23 C7
Tát H 112 B2
Tata H 112 B2
Tatabánya H 112 B2
Tataháza H 126 A1
Tatarbunary UA 17 C8
Tatárszentgyörgy H 112 B3
Tatranská-Lomnica SK 99 B4
Tau N 52 A1
Tauberbischofsheim D 94 B1
Taucha D 83 A4
Taufkirchen D 95 C4
Taufkirchen an der Pram A 96 C1
Taulé F 100 A2
Taulignan F 131 A3
Taulov DK 59 C2
Taunton UK 43 A4
Taunusstein D 81 B4
Tauragė LT 12 A5
Taurianova I 175 C2
Taurisano I 173 C4
Tauste E 144 C2
Tauves F 116 B2
Tavankut SRB 126 A1
Tavannes CH 106 B2
Tavarnelle val di Pesa I 135 B4
Tavas TR 188 B4
Tavaux F 105 B4
Tävelsås S 62 B2
Taverna I 175 B2
Taverne CH 120 A1
Tavernelle I 135 B5
Tavernes de la Valldigna E 159 B3
Tavérnola Bergamasca I 120 B3
Taverny F 90 B2
Tavescan E 146 B2
Taviano I 173 C4
Tavira P 160 B2
Tavistock UK 42 B2
Tavşanlı TR 187 C4
Tayinloan UK 34 C2
Taynuilt UK 34 B2
Tayport UK 35 B5
Tázlár H 112 C3
Tazones E 142 A1
Tczew PL 69 A3
Tczów PL 87 A5
Teangue UK 31 B3
Teano I 170 B2
Tebay UK 37 B4
Tébar E 158 B1
Techendorf A 109 C4
Tecklenburg D 71 B4
Tecko-matorp S 61 D3
Tecuci RO 17 C7
Tefenni TR 189 B4

Tegelsmora S 51 B4
Tegernsee D 108 B2
Teggiano I 172 B1
Tegoleto I 135 B4
Teichel D 82 B3
Teignmouth UK 43 B3
Teillay F 101 B4
Teillet F 130 B1
Teisendorf D 109 B3
Teistungen D 82 A2
Teixeiro E 140 A2
Tejada de Tiétar E 150 B2
Tejado E 152 A1
Tejares E 150 B2
Tejn DK 67 A3
Teke TR 187 A4
Tekirdağ TR 186 B2
Tekovské-Lužany SK 112 A2
Telavåg N 46 B1
Telč CZ 97 B3
Telese Terme I 170 B2
Telford UK 38 B4
Telfs A 108 B2
Telgárt SK 99 C4
Telgte D 71 C4
Telšiai LT 8 E3
Telti I 178 B3
Teltow D 74 B2
Tembleque E 157 A4
Temelín CZ 96 B2
Temerin SRB 126 B1
Temiño E 143 B3
Témpio Pausánia I 178 B3
Templederry IRL 28 B3
Templemore IRL 28 B4
Temple Sowerby UK 37 B4
Templin D 74 A2
Temse B 79 A4
Tenay F 118 B2
Ten Boer NL 71 A3
Tenbury Wells UK 39 B4
Tenby UK 39 C2
Tence F 117 B4
Tende F 133 A3
Tenhult S 62 A2
Tenja HR 125 B4
Tennevoll N 194 B8
Tensta S 51 B4
Tenterden UK 45 B4
Teo E 140 B2
Teora I 172 B1
Tepasto FIN 196 B7
Tepelenë AL 182 C2
Teplá CZ 95 B4
Teplice CZ 84 B1
Teplička nad Váhom SK 98 B2
Tepsa FIN 197 B8
Tera E 143 C4
Téramo I 169 A3
Ter Apel NL 71 B4
Terborg NL 71 C3
Terchová SK 99 B3
Terebovlya UA 13 D6
Teremia Mare RO 126 B2
Terena P 155 C3
Teresa de Cofrentes E 159 B2
Terešov CZ 96 B1
Terezín CZ 84 B2
Terezino Polje HR 124 B3
Tergnier F 90 B3
Teriberka RUS 3 B14
Terlizzi I 171 B4
Termas de Monfortinho P 155 A4
Terme di Súio I 169 B3
Terme di Valdieri I 133 A3
Termens E 145 C4
Termes F 116 C3
Términi Imerese I 176 B2
Terminillo I 169 A2
Térmoli I 170 B3
Termonfeckin IRL 27 C4
Ternberg A 110 B1
Terndrup DK 58 B3
Terneuzen NL 79 A3

Terni I 168 A2
Ternitz A 111 B3
Ternopil UA 13 D6
Terpni GR 183 C5
Terracina I 169 B3
Terråk N 195 E3
Terralba I 179 C2
Terranova di Pollino I 174 B2
Terranova di Sibari I 174 B2
Terras do Bouro P 148 A1
Terrasini I 176 A2
Terrassa E 147 C3
Terrasson-Lavilledieu F 129 A4
Terrazos E 143 B3
Terriente E 152 B2
Terrugem P 155 C3
Tertenía I 179 C3
Teruel E 152 B2
Tervola FIN 196 C7
Tervuren B 79 B4
Terzaga E 152 B2
Tešanj BIH 125 C3
Tesáske-Mlyňany SK 98 C2
Tesllć BIH 125 C3
Tessin D 66 B1
Tessy-sur-Vire F 88 B2
Tét H 111 B4
Tetbury UK 43 A4
Teterchen F 92 B2
Teterow D 65 C5
Teteven BG 17 D6
Tetiyev UA 13 D8
Tetovo NMK 182 A2
Tettau D 82 B3
Tettnang D 107 B4
Teublitz D 95 B4
Teuchern D 83 A4
Teulada
 E 159 C4
 I 179 D2
Teupitz D 74 B2
Teurajärvi S 196 C5
Teutschenthal D 83 A3
Tevel H 112 C2
Teviothead UK 36 A4
Tewkesbury UK 39 C4
Thale D 82 A3
Thalfang D 92 B2
Thalgau A 109 B4
Thalkirch CH 107 C4
Thalmässing D 95 B3
Thalwil CH 107 B3
Thame UK 44 B3
Thann F 106 B2
Thannhausen D 94 C2
Thaon-les-Vosges F 105 A5
Tharandt D 83 B5
Tharsis E 161 B2
Thasos GR 183 C6
Thatcham UK 44 B2
Thaxted UK 45 B4
Thayngen CH 107 B3
Theale UK 44 B2
The Barony UK 33 B3
Thebes = Thiva GR 185 A4
Theding-hausen D 72 B2
Theessen D 73 B5
The Hague = 's-Gravenhage NL 70 B1
Themar D 82 B2
The Mumbles UK 39 C3
Thénezay F 102 C1
Thenon F 129 A4
Therouanne F 78 B2
Thessaloniki = Salonica GR 182 C4
Thetford UK 45 A4
Theux B 80 B1
Thézar-les-Corbières F 146 A3
Thèze F 145 A3
Thiberville F 89 A4
Thibie F 91 C4
Thiéblemont-Farémont F 91 C4
Thiendorf D 84 A1
Thiene I 121 B4
Thierrens CH 106 C1
Thiers F 117 B3
Thiesi I 178 B2

Thiessow D 66 B2
Thiezac F 116 B2
þingeyri IS 190 B2
þingeyrri IS 190 B2
þingvellir IS 190 C4
Thionville F 92 B2
Thíra GR 185 C6
Thiron-Gardais F 89 B4
Thirsk UK 37 B5
Thisted DK 58 B1
Thiva = Thebes GR 185 A4
Thivars F 90 C1
Thiviers F 115 C4
Thizy F 117 A4
Tholen NL 79 A4
Tholey D 92 B3
Thomas Street IRL 28 A3
Thomastown IRL 30 B1
Thônes F 118 B3
Thonnance-les-Joinville F 91 C5
Thonon-les-Bains F 118 A3
Thorame-Basse F 132 A2
Thorame-Haute F 132 A2
Thorens-Glières F 118 A3
Thorigny-sur-Oreuse F 91 C3
Thörl A 110 B2
þorlákshöfn IS 190 D4
Thornaby on Tees UK 37 B5
Thornbury UK 43 A4
Thorne UK 40 B3
Thornhill
 Dumfries & Galloway UK 36 A3
 Stirling UK 35 B3
Thornthwaite UK 36 B3
Thornton-le-Dale UK 40 A3
þórshöfn IS 191 A10
Thouarcé F 102 B1
Thouars F 102 C1
Thrapston UK 44 A3
Threlkeld UK 36 B3
Thrumster UK 32 C3
Thueyts F 117 C4
Thuin B 79 B4
Thuir F 146 B3
Thurnau D 95 A3
Thun CH 106 C2
Thuret F 116 B3
Thurey F 105 C4
Thüringen A 107 B4
Thurins F 117 B4
Thürkow D 65 C5
Thurmaston UK 40 C2
Thursby UK 36 B3
Thurso UK 32 C3
Thury-Harcourt F 89 B3
Thusis CH 107 C4
Thyborøn DK 58 B1
Thyregod DK 59 C2
Tibi E 159 C3
Tibro S 55 B5
Tidaholm S 55 B4
Tidan S 55 B5
Tidersrum S 62 A3
Tiedra E 150 A2
Tiefenbach D 95 B4
Tiefencastel CH 107 C4
Tiefenort D 82 B2
Tiefensee D 74 B2
Tiel NL 79 A5
Tielmes E 151 B4
Tielt B 78 A3
Tienen B 79 B4
Tiengen D 106 B3
Tientega E 142 A1
Tierce F 102 B1
Tierga E 152 A2
Tiermas E 144 B2
Tierp S 51 B4
Tierrantona E 145 B4
Tighina MD 17 B8
Tighnabruaich UK 34 C2
Tignes F 119 B3
Tigy F 103 B4
Tihany H 112 C1

Tijnje NL 70 A2
Tijola E 164 B2
Tikhvin RUS 9 C8
Tilburg NL 79 A5
Til Châtel F 105 B4
Tilh F 128 C2
Tillac F 145 A4
Tillberga S 56 A2
Tille F 90 B2
Tillicoultry UK 35 B4
Tilloy Bellay F 91 B4
Tilly F 115 B5
Tilly-sur-Seulles F 88 A3
Tim DK 59 B1
Timau I 109 C4
Timbaki GR 185 D5
Timi CY 181 B1
Timişoara RO 126 B3
Timmele S 60 B3
Timmendorfer Strand D 65 C3
Timmernabben S 62 B4
Timoleague IRL 29 C3
Timolin IRL 30 B2
Timrå S 200 D3
Timsfors S 61 C3
Timsgearraidh UK 31 A1
Tinajas E 152 B1
Tinalhas P 155 B3
Tinchebray F 88 B3
Tincques F 78 B2
Tineo E 141 A4
Tinglev DK 64 B2
Tingsryd S 63 B2
Tingstäde S 57 C4
Tingvoll N 198 C5
Tinlot B 79 B5
Tinnoset N 53 A5
Tinos GR 185 B6
Tintagel UK 42 B2
Tinténiac F 101 A4
Tintern UK 39 C4
Tintigny B 92 B1
Tione di Trento I 121 A3
Tipperary IRL 29 B3
Tiptree UK 45 B4
Tirana = Tiranë AL 182 B1
Tiranë = Tirana AL 182 B1
Tirano I 120 A3
Tiraspol MD 17 B8
Tire TR 188 A2
Tires I 108 C2
Tiriez E 158 C1
Tirig E 153 B4
Tiriolo I 175 C2
Tirnavos GR 182 D4
Tirrénia I 134 B3
Tirschenreuth D 95 B4
Tirstrup DK 59 B3
Tirteafuera E 157 B3
Tisno HR 137 B4
Tišnov CZ 97 B4
Tisovec SK 99 C3
Tisselskog S 54 B3
Tistedal N 54 A2
Tisvildeleje DK 61 C2
Tiszaalpár H 113 C3
Tiszabög H 113 B5
Tiszacsege H 113 B5
Tiszadorogma H 113 B5
Tiszaföldvár H 113 C4
Tiszafüred H 113 B4
Tiszajenő H 113 B4
Tiszakécske H 113 C4
Tiszakürt H 113 C4
Tiszalök H 113 A5
Tiszalúc H 113 A5
Tiszanána H 113 B4
Tiszaörs H 113 B4
Tiszaroff H 113 B4
Tiszasüly H 113 B4
Tiszasziget H 126 A2
Tiszaszőlős H 113 B4
Tiszaújváros H 113 B5
Tiszavasvári H 113 B5
Titaguas E 159 B2
Titel SRB 126 B2
Titisee-Neustadt D 106 B3

Tito I 172 B1
Titran N 198 B5
Tittling D 96 C1
Tittmoning D 109 A3
Titz D 80 A2
Tiurajärvi FIN 196 B7
Tived S 55 B5
Tiverton UK 43 B3
Tivisa E 153 A4
Tívoli I 168 B2
Tjällmo S 56 B1
Tjåmotis S 195 D9
Tjæreborg DK 59 C1
Tjautjas S 196 B3
Tjøme N 54 A1
Tjong N 195 D4
Tjonnefoss N 53 B4
Tjörn IS 190 B5
Tjörnarp S 61 D3
Tjøtta N 195 E3
Tkon HR 137 B4
Tleń PL 68 B3
Tlmače SK 98 C2
Tłuchowo PL 77 B4
Tlumačov CZ 98 B1
Tóalmas H 112 B3
Toano I 134 A3
Toba D 82 A2
Tobarra E 158 C2
Tobermore UK 27 B4
Tobermory UK 34 B1
Toberonochy UK 34 B2
Tobha Mor UK 31 B1
Tobo S 51 B4
Tocane-St Apre F 129 A3
Tocha P 148 B1
Tocina E 162 A2
Töcksfors S 54 A2
Tocón E 163 A4
Todal N 198 C5
Todi I 136 C1
Todmorden UK 40 B1
Todorici BIH 138 A3
Todtmoos D 106 B3
Todtnau D 106 B2
Toén E 140 B3
Tofta
 Gotland S 57 C4
 Skaraborg S 55 B4
Toftbyn S 50 B2
Tofte N 54 A1
Töftedal S 54 B2
Tofterup DK 59 C1
Toftlund DK 59 C2
Tófü H 125 A4
Tohmo FIN 197 C10
Tokaj H 113 A5
Tokarnia P 87 B4
Tokary P 76 C3
Tokod H 112 B2
Tököl H 112 B2
Tolastadh bho Thuath UK 31 A2
Toledo E 151 C3
Tolentino I 136 B2
Tolfa I 168 A1
Tolg S 62 A2
Tolga N 199 C8
Tolkmicko PL 69 A4
Tollarp S 61 D3
Tollered S 60 B2
Tølløse DK 61 D1
Tolmachevo RUS 9 C6
Tolmezzo I 122 A2
Tolmin SLO 122 A2
Tolna H 112 C2
Tolnanémedi H 112 C2
Tolob UK 33 B5
Tolosa
 E 144 A1
 P 155 B3
Tolox E 162 B3
Tolpuddle UK 43 B4
Tolva
 E 145 B4
 FIN 197 C11
Tolve I 172 B2
Tomar P 154 B2
Tomaševac SRB 126 B2
Tomašica BIH 124 C2
Tomášikovo SK 111 A4
Tomášouka BY 13 C5
Tomášovce SK 99 C3

256 Tom – Trž

Tomaszów
Mazowiecki
PL.............87 A4
Tomatin UK.... 32 D3
Tombeboeuf
F............. 129 B3
Tomdoun UK... 32 D1
Tomelilla S......66 A2
Tomellosa E.. 151 B5
Tomelloso E . 157 A4
Tomiño E 140 C2
Tomintoul UK.. 32 D3
Tomislavgrad
BIH............. 138 B3
Tomisław PL ...84 A3
Tomisławice
PL...........76 B3
Tomnavoulin
UK 32 D3
Tompa H...... 126 A1
Tompaládony
H............. 111 B3
Tomra N 198 C3
Tomter N 54 A1
Tona E 147 C3
Tonara I...... 179 B3
Tonbridge UK...45 B4
Tondela P..... 148 B1
Tønder DK 64 B1
Tongeren B 79 B5
Tongue UK.... 32 C2
Tönisvorst D ...80 A2
Tønjum N 47 A4
Tonkopuro
FIN............197 C11
Tonnay-Boutonne
F............. 114 C3
Tonnay-Charente
F............. 114 C3
Tonneins F 129 B3
Tonnerre F 104 B2
Tonnes N 195 D4
Tönning D 64 B1
Tonsåsen N 47 B6
Tønsberg N 54 A1
Tonstad N 52 B2
Toomyvara IRL..28 B3
Toormore IRL ...29 C2
Topares E..... 164 B2
Topas E 150 A2
Topliţa RO 17 B6
Topola SRB... 127 C2
Topolčani
NMK 182 B3
Topol'čany SK..98 C2
Topol'čianky
SK............98 C2
Topolje HR.... 124 B2
Topólka PL..... 76 B3
Topol'niky SK. 111 B4
Topolovăţu Mare
RO 126 B3
Toponár H 125 A3
Toporów P.....75 B4
Topsham UK...43 B3
Topusko HR... 124 B1
Toques E...... 140 B3
Torà E........ 147 C2
Toral de los
Guzmanes E . 142 B1
Toral de los Vados
E............. 141 B4
Torbali TR..... 188 A2
Torbjörntorp S..55 B4
Torbole I..... 121 B3
Torchiarolo I . 173 B4
Torcross UK....43 B3
Torcy-le-Petit F.89 A5
Torda SRB..... 126 B2
Tørdal N 53 A4
Tordehumos
E............. 142 C1
Tordera E..... 147 C3
Tordesillas E . 150 A2
Tordesilos E.. 152 B2
Töre S...... 196 D5
Töreboda S.....55 B5
Toreby DK 65 B4
Torekov S......61 C2
Torella dei
Lombardi I .. 170 C3
Torelló E .. 147 B3
Toreno E..... 141 B4
Torfou F...... 114 A2
Torgau D......83 A5
Torgelow D ...74 A3
Torgueda P....84 B3
Torhamn S......63 B3
Torhop N 193 B11
Torhout B......78 A3

Torigni-sur-Vire
F.............88 A3
Torija E 151 B4
Toril E....... 152 B2
Torino = Turin
I.............. 119 B4
Toritto I....... 171 C4
Torkovichi RUS ..9 C7
Torla E....... 145 B3
Tormac RO.... 126 B3
Törmänen
FIN...........193 D11
Tormestorp S ...61 C3
Tórmini I..... 121 B3
Tornada P.... 154 B1
Tornal'a SK.....99 C4
Tornavacas E . 150 B2
Tornby DK 58 A2
Tornesch D....72 A2
Torness UK.... 32 D2
Torniella I.... 135 B4
Tornimparte I. 169 A3
Torning DK 59 B2
Tornio FIN 196 D7
Tornjoš SRB ... 126 B1
Tornos E...... 152 B2
Toro E........ 150 A2
Törökszentmiklós
H............. 113 B4
Toropets RUS ...9 D7
Torpa S.......61 C3
Torpè I....... 178 B3
Torphins UK ... 33 D4
Torpo N.......47 B5
Torpoint UK...42 B2
Torpsbruk S ...62 A2
Torquay UK....43 B3
Torquemada
E............. 142 B2
Torralba de Burgo
E............. 151 A5
Torralba de
Calatrava E . 157 A4
Torrão P 154 C2
Torre Annunziata
I............. 170 C2
Torreblacos E . 143 C4
Torreblanca E. 153 B4
Torreblascopedro
E............. 157 B4
Torrecaballeros
E............. 151 A3
Torrecampo E. 156 B3
Torre Canne I . 173 B3
Torre Cardela
E............. 163 A4
Torrecilla E .. 152 B1
Torrecilla de la Jara
E............. 156 A3
Torrecilla de la
Orden E..... 150 A2
Torrecilla del Pinar
E............. 151 A3
Torrecilla en
Cameros E . 143 B4
Torrecillas de la
Tiesa E 156 A2
Torre das Vargens
P............ 154 B3
Torre de Coelheiros
E............. 154 C3
Torre de Dom
Chama P.... 149 A2
Torre de Juan Abad
E............. 157 B4
Torre del Bierzo
E............. 141 B4
Torre del Burgo
E............. 151 B4
Torre del Campo
E............. 163 A4
Torre del Greco
I............. 170 C2
Torre del Lago
Puccini I.... 134 B3
Torre dell'Orso
I............. 173 B4
Torre del Mar
E............. 163 B3
Torredembarra
E............. 147 C2
Torre de Miguel
Sesmero E .. 155 C4
Torre de Moncorvo
P............ 149 A2
Torre de Santa
Maria E 156 A1
Torredonjimeno
E............. 163 A4
Torre do Terranho
P............ 148 B2
Torre Faro I... 177 A4
Torregrosa E . 147 C1

Torreira P..... 148 B1
Torrejoncillo
E............. 155 B4
Torrejón de Ardoz
E............. 151 B4
Torrejón de la
Calzada E ... 151 B4
Torrejón del Rey
E............. 151 B4
Torrejón el Rubio
E............. 156 A1
Torrelaguna E 151 B4
Torrelapaja E . 152 A2
Torre la Ribera
E............. 145 B4
Torrelavega E . 142 A2
Torrelobatón
E............. 150 A2
Torrelodones
E............. 151 B4
Torre los Negros
E............. 152 B2
Torremaggiore
I............. 171 B3
Torremanzanas
E............. 159 C3
Torremayor E . 155 C4
Torremezzo di
Falconara I... 174 B2
Torremocha E . 156 A1
Torremolinos
E............. 163 B3
Torrenieri I... 135 B4
Torrenostra E . 153 B4
Torrenova I... 168 B2
Torrent E..... 159 B3
Torrente de Cinca
E............. 153 A4
Torrenueva
Ciudad Real
E............. 157 B4
Granada E .. 163 B4
Torreorgaz E . 155 B4
Torre Orsáia I . 172 B1
Torre-Pacheco
E............. 165 B4
Torre Péllice I . 119 C4
Torreperogil E 157 B4
Torres E...... 163 A4
Torresandino
E............. 143 C3
Torre Santa
Susanna I.... 173 B3
Torres-Cabrera
E............. 163 A3
Torres de la
Alameda E . 151 B4
Torres Novas
P............ 154 B2
Torres Vedras
P............ 154 B1
Torrevieja E.. 165 B4
Torricella I... 173 B3
Torri del Benaco
I............. 121 B3
Torridon UK....31 B3
Torriglia I..... 134 A2
Torrijos E..... 151 C3
Tørring DK....59 C2
Torrita di Siena
I............. 135 B4
Torroal P..... 154 C2
Torroella de
Montgrí E... 147 B4
Torrox E...... 163 B4
Torsåker S..... 50 B3
Torsås S...... 63 B4
Torsby S...... 49 B4
Torshälla S.....56 A2
Tórshavn FO ...4 A3
Torslanda S....60 B1
Torsminde DK . 59 B1
Torsnes N.....46 B3
Törtel H...... 113 B3
Tórtola de
Esguevá E... 142 C2
Tórtoli I...... 179 C3
Tórtona I..... 120 C1
Tórtora I..... 174 B1
Tortoreto Lido
I............. 136 C2
Tórtorici I..... 177 A3
Tortosa E..... 153 B4
Tortosendo P . 148 B2
Tortuera E.... 152 B2
Tortuero E.... 151 B4
Toruń PL......76 A3
Torup S........60 C3
Tor Vaiánica I . 168 B2

Torver UK......36 B3
Tørvikbygde N..46 B3
Torviscón E ... 163 B4
Torzhok RUS 9 D9
Torzym PL..... 75 B4
Tosbotn N.... 195 E3
Toscolano-
Maderno I.... 121 B3
Tosno RUS 9 C7
Tossa de Mar
E............. 147 C3
Tossåsen S... 199 C10
Trängslet S.....49 A5
Tänhult S......60 B3
Tosse F....... 128 C1
Tösse S....... 54 B3
Tossicia I..... 169 A3
Tostedt D.....72 A2
Tosya TR.......23 A8
Tószeg H..... 113 B4
Toszek PL......86 B2
Totana E..... 165 B3
Totebo S......62 A4
Tôtes F....... 89 A5
Tótkomlós H.. 113 C4
Totland N.... 198 D2
Tøtlandsvik N...52 A2
Totnes UK......43 B3
Tótszerdahely
H............. 124 A2
Tøttdal N 199 A8
Totton UK......44 C2
Touça P...... 149 A2
Toucy F....... 104 B2
Toul F........ 92 C1
Toulon F..... 132 B1
Toulon-sur-Allier
F............. 104 C2
Toulon-sur-Arroux
F............. 104 C3
Toulouse F ... 129 C4
Tourcoing F.....78 B3
Tour de la Parata
F............. 180 B1
Tourlaville F ... 88 A2
Tournai B......78 B3
Tournan-en-Brie
F.............90 C2
Tournay F..... 145 A4
Tournon-d'Agenais
F............. 129 B3
Tournon-St Martin
F............. 115 B4
Tournon-sur-
Rhône F..... 117 B4
Tournus F..... 105 C3
Touro
E............. 140 B2
Tourriers F 115 C4
Tours F....... 102 B2
Tourteron F....91 B4
Tourves F..... 132 B1
Toury F....... 103 A3
Touvedo P.... 148 A1
Touvois F..... 114 B2
Toužim CZ.....83 B4
Tovačov CZ....98 B1
Tovariševo
SRB 126 B1
Tovarnik HR .. 125 B5
Tovdal N......53 B4
Towcester UK..44 A3
Town Yetholm
UK 35 C5
Tråastølen N...47 B4
Trabada E.... 141 A3
Trabadelo E.. 141 B4
Trabanca E.... 149 A3
Trabazos E... 149 A3
Traben-Trarbach
D.............92 B3
Trabia I...... 176 B2
Tradate I..... 120 B1
Trädet S......60 B3
Trafaria P 154 C1
Tragacete E.. 152 B2
Tragwein A....96 C2
Traiguera E.. 153 B4
Trainel F......91 C3
Traisen A..... 110 A2
Traismauer A ..97 C3
Traitsching D...95 B4
Trákhonas CY. 181 A2
Tralee IRL......29 B2
Tramacastilla de
Tena E 145 B3
Tramagal P... 154 B2
Tramariglio I . 178 B2
Tramatza I.... 179 B2
Tramelan CH...106 B2
Tramonti di Sopra
I............. 122 A1
Tramore IRL....30 B1

Trampot F 92 C1
Trana I...... 119 B4
Tranås S...... 55 B5
Tranbjerg DK ..59 B3
Tranby N......54 A1
Trancoso P... 148 B2
Tranebjerg DK..59 C3
Tranekær DK...65 B3
Tranemo S....60 B3
Tranent UK.....35 C5
Tranevåg N 52 B2
Trängslet S.....49 A5
Tränhult S.....60 B3
Trani I....... 171 B4
Trans-en-Provence
F............. 132 B2
Transtrand S...49 A5
Tranum DK 58 A2
Tranvik S......57 A4
Trápani I..... 176 A1
Trappes F......90 C2
Traryd S......61 C3
Trasacco I.... 169 B3
Trasierra E... 156 B1
Träslövsläge S..60 B2
Trasmiras E .. 140 B3
Traspinedo E. 150 A3
Trate SLO.... 110 C2
Trauchgau D.. 108 B1
Traun A...... 110 A1
Traunreut D .. 109 B3
Traunstein D.. 109 B3
Traunwalchen
D............. 109 B3
Tråvad S......55 B4
Travemünde D..65 C3
Traversétolo I. 120 C3
Travnik
BIH.......... 139 A3
SLO 123 B3
Travo
Romano I... 168 A2
Trawsfynydd
UK 38 B3
Trbovlje SLO . 123 A4
Trbušani SRB . 127 D2
Trbány F..... 116 A3
Třebařov CZ...97 B4
Trebatsch D....74 B3
Trebbin D.....74 B2
Trebechovice pod
Orebem CZ ..85 B3
Trebel D......73 B4
Třebenice CZ...84 B1
Trebeurden F . 100 A2
Trebić CZ......97 B3
Trebinje BIH .. 139 C4
Trebisacce I... 174 B2
Trebitz D......83 A4
Trebnje SLO... 123 B4
Třeboň CZ.....96 B2
Třebovice CZ...97 B4
Trebsen D.....83 A4
Trebujena E... 161 C3
Trecastagni I.. 177 B4
Trecate I..... 120 B1
Trecenta I.... 121 B4
Tredegar UK...39 C3
Tredózio I.... 135 A4
Treffen A..... 109 C4
Treffort F..... 118 A2
Treffurt D.....82 A2
Trefnant UK ...38 A3
Tregaron UK...39 B3
Trégastel-Plage
F............. 100 A2
Tregnago I.... 121 B4
Tregony UK....42 B2
Tréguier F..... 100 A2
Trehörningsjö
S......... 200 C4
Tréia I....... 136 B2
Treignac F.... 116 B1
Treignat F.... 116 A2
Treignes B.....79 B4
Treis-Karden D..80 B3
Trekanten S....63 B4
Trélazé F..... 102 B1
Trélissac F.... 129 A3
Trelleborg S....66 A2
Trélon F......91 A4
Tremblay-le-
Vicomte F.....89 B5
Tremés P..... 154 B2
Tremezzo I.... 120 B2
Trémp E...... 145 B4

Triptis D........83 B3
Triste E....... 144 B3
Trittau D...... 72 A3
Trivento I..... 170 B2
Trivero I..... 119 B5
Trivigno I..... 172 B1
Trnava
HR 125 B4
SK............98 C1
Trnovec SK.... 112 A1
Trnovo BIH.... 139 B4
Trnovska vas
SLO 110 C2
Troarn F......89 A3
Trochtelfingen
D............. 94 C1
Trödje S...... 51 B4
Troense DK....65 A3
Trofa P...... 148 A1
Trofaiach A... 110 B2
Trofors N..... 195 E4
Trogir HR..... 138 B2
Trøgstad N.....54 A2
Tróia I....... 171 B3
Troia I...... 154 C2
Troina I...... 177 B3
Troisdorf D....80 B3
Trois-Ponts B..80 B1
Troisvierges L..92 A2
Trojane SLO... 123 A3
Troldhede DK..59 C1
Trollhättan S...54 B3
Trolog BIH.... 138 B2
Tromello I..... 120 B1
Tromøy N.....53 B4
Tromsø N 192 C3
Trondheim N . 199 B7
Tronget F..... 116 A3
Trönninge S...61 C2
Trönningeby S..60 B2
Trönö S....... 51 A3
Tronzano-
Vercellese I... 119 B5
Trôo F....... 102 B2
Troon UK...... 36 A2
Tropea I...... 175 C1
Tropy Sztumskie
PL............ 69 B4
Trosa S....... 57 B3
Trösken S..... 50 B3
Trosly-Breuil F . 90 B3
Trossingen D . 107 A3
Trostberg D... 109 A3
Trouville-sur-Mer
F.............89 A4
Trowbridge UK .43 A4
Troyes F..... 104 A3
Trpanj HR.... 138 B3
Trpinja HR.... 125 B4
Tršće CZ......98 B1
Trstená SK.....99 B3
Trstenci BIH... 125 B3
Trsteno HR.... 139 C3
Trstice SK..... 111 A4
Trstin SK......98 C1
Trubia E...... 141 A5
Trubjela MNE . 139 C4
Truchas E.... 141 B4
Trujillanos E .. 155 C4
Trujillo E..... 156 A2
Trumieje PL....69 B4
Trun
CH 107 C3
F.............89 B4
Truro UK......42 B1
Trusetal D.....82 B2
Truskavets' UA. 13 D5
Trustrup DK ...59 B3
Trutnov CZ....85 B3
Tryserum S....56 B2
Trysil N....... 49 A4
Tryszczyn PL...76 A2
Trzcianka PL...75 A5
Trzciel PL..... 75 B4
Trzcińsko Zdrój
PL............ 74 B3
Trzebiatów PL..67 B4
Trzebiel PL....84 A2
Trzebielino PL..68 A2
Trzebień PL....84 A3
Trzebiez PL....74 A3
Trzebnica PL...85 A5
Trzebnice PL...85 A4
Trzeciewiec PL..76 A3
Trzemeszno PL..76 B2
Trzemeszno-
Lubuskie PL ..75 B4
Trzetrzewina
PL............ 99 B4
Tržič SLO..... 123 A3

Tsamandas
GR 182 D2
Tschagguns A. 107 B4
Tschernitz D ...84 A2
Tsebrykove
UA 17 B9
Tsyelyakhany
BY............13 B6
Tua P........ 148 A2
Tuam IRL.....28 A3
Tubbercurry
IRL 26 B2
Tubbergen NL .71 B3
Tubilla del Lago
E 143 C3
Tübingen D....93 C5
Tubize B 79 B4
Tučapy CZ 96 B2
Tučepi HR 138 B3
Tuchan F..... 146 B3
Tüchen D 73 A5
Tuchola PL....76 A2
Tuchomie PL...68 A2
Tuchów PL.....99 B5
Tuczno PL.....75 A5
Tuddal N......53 A4
Tudela E..... 144 B2
Tudela de Duero
E 150 A3
Tudweiliog UK ..38 B2
Tuejar E..... 159 B2
Tuffé F 102 A2
Tufsingdalen
N............ 199 C8
Tuhaň CZ 84 B2
Tui E 140 B2
Tukhkala
RUS 197 D13
Tukums LV 8 D3
Tula I........ 178 B2
Tulcea RO 17 C8
Tul'chyn UA 13 D8
Tulette F 131 A3
Tuliszków PL...76 B3
Tulla IRL......28 B3
Tullamore IRL ...30 A1
Tulle F 116 B1
Tullins F..... 118 B2
Tulln A........97 C4
Tullow IRL.....30 B2
Tułowice PL....85 B5
Tulppio FIN .. 197 B12
Tulsk IRL......28 A3
Tumba S.......57 A3
Tummel Bridge
UK 35 B3
Tun S..........55 B3
Tuna
Kalmar S 62 A4
Uppsala S.....51 B5
Tuna Hästberg
S............50 B2
Tunçbilek TR . 187 C4
Tunes P 160 B1
Tungelsta S ...57 A4
Tunnerstad S ...55 B5
Tunnhovd N ...47 B5
Tunstall UK 45 A5
Tuohikotti FIN ... 8 B5
Tuoro sul
Trasimeno I .. 135 B5
Tupadly PL....76 B3
Tupanari BIH .. 139 A4
Tupik RUS 9 E8
Tuplice PL....84 A2
Tura H 112 B3
Turanj HR 137 B4
Turany SK......99 B3
Turbe BIH 139 A3
Turbenthal
CH 107 B3
Turcia E..... 141 B5
Turčianske Teplice
SK...........98 C2
Turcifal P.... 154 B1
Turckheim F .. 106 A2
Turda RO......17 B5
Turégano E ... 151 A4
Turek PL......76 B3
Turgutlu TR.. 188 A2
Turgutreis TR . 188 B2
Turi I........ 173 B3
Turin = Torino
I............ 119 B4
Turis E 159 B3
Türje H 111 C4
Turka UA...... 12 D5
Türkheim D .. 108 A1
Türkmenli
TR.......... 186 C1
Turku FIN 8 B3
Turleque E ... 157 A4

Turňa nad Bodvou
SK............99 C4
Turnberry UK ..36 A2
Turnhout B....79 A4
Türnitz A..... 110 B2
Turnov CZ......84 B3
Turnu RO..... 126 A3
Turnu Măgurele
RO 17 D6
Turón E 164 C1
Turoszów PL....84 B2
Turowo PL 77 A5
Turquel P 154 B1
Turri I....... 179 C2
Turries F..... 132 A2
Turriff UK 33 D4
Tursi I....... 174 A2
Turtmann
CH 119 A4
Turtola FIN... 196 C6
Turze PL.......86 A1
Turzovka SK ...98 B2
Tusa I....... 177 B3
Tuscania I.... 168 A1
Tuse DK.......61 D1
Tušilovic HR... 123 B4
Tuszyn PL......86 A3
Tutow D.......66 C2
Tutrakan BG ...17 C7
Tuttlingen D . 107 B3
Tutzing D 108 B2
Tuzla
BIH.......... 125 C4
TR............ 23 C8
Tuzluçu TR.. 189 A6
Tvååker S 60 B2
Tvärålund S .. 200 B5
Tvärskog S 63 B4
Tvedestrand N .53 B4
Tveit
Hordaland N ...47 B4
Rogaland N.... 52 A2
Tver RUS 9 D9
Tverrelvmo N . 192 D3
Tversted DK....58 A3
Tving S.......63 B3
Tvrdošín SK ...99 B3
Tvrdošovce
SK.......... 112 A2
Twardogóra
PL...........85 A5
Twatt UK......33 B3
Twello NL......70 B3
Twimberg A . 110 C1
Twist D 71 B4
Twistringen D .72 B1
Tworóg PL......86 B2
Twyford
Hampshire
UK 44 B2
Wokingham
UK 44 B3
Tyachiv UA.....17 A5
Tychówko PL...67 C5
Tychowo PL....67 C5
Tychy PL......86 B2
Tydal N 199 B8
Týec nad Labem
CZ............97 A3
Tyfors S......50 B5
Tygelsjö S....61 D2
Tylldal N 199 C7
Tylstrup DK....58 A2
Tymbark PL....99 B4
Tymowa PL.....99 B4
Tyndrum UK ...34 B3
Týnec nad Sázavou
CZ............96 B2
Tynemouth
UK 37 A5
Tyngsjö S.....49 B5
Týniště Orlicí
CZ............85 B4
Týn nad Vltavou
CZ............96 B2
Tynset N 199 C7
Tyresö S......57 A4
Tyringe S.....61 C3
Tyrislöt S 56 B2
Tyristrand N ...48 B2
Tyrrellspass
IRL...........30 A1
Tysnes N......46 B2
Tysse N 46 B2
Tyssebotn N ...46 B2
Tyssedal N....46 B3
Tystberga S...56 B3
Tysvær N 52 A1
Tywyn UK......39 B2
Tzermiado
GR 185 D6
Tzummarum
NL...........70 A2

U

Ub SRB....... 127 C2
Ubby DK.......61 D1
Úbeda E..... 157 B4
Überlingen D . 107 B4
Ubidea E..... 143 A4
Ubli HR...... 138 C2
Ubrique E.... 162 B2
Ucero E 143 C3
Uchaud F 131 B3
Uchte D.......72 B1
Uckerath D....80 B3
Uckfield UK ...45 C4
Ucklum S......54 B2
Uclés E...... 151 C5
Ucria I....... 177 A3
Udbina HR ... 137 A4
Uddebo S......60 B3
Uddeholm S ...49 B5
Uddevalla S...54 B2
Uddheden S ...49 C4
Uden NL.......80 A1
Uder D........82 A2
Udica SK......98 B2
Údine I...... 122 A2
Udvar H...... 125 B4
Ueckermünde
D 74 A3
Uelsen D......71 B3
Uelzen D......73 B3
Uetendorf CH. 106 C2
Uetersen D....72 A2
Uetze D.......72 B3
Uffculme UK ...43 B3
Uffenheim D ...94 B2
Ugarana E.... 143 A4
Ugento I..... 173 C4
Ugerløse DK...61 D1
Uggerby DK....58 A3
Uggerslev DK ...59 C3
Uggiano la Chiesa
I............ 173 B4
Ugijar E..... 164 C1
Ugine F...... 118 B3
Uglejevik BIH. 125 C5
Uglenes S.....46 B2
Uglich RUS.....9 D11
Ugljane HR.... 138 B2
Ugod H 111 B4
Uherské Hradiště
CZ............98 B1
Uherský Brod
CZ............98 B1
Uherský Ostroh
CZ............98 C1
Uhingen D 94 C1
Uhlířské-Janovice
CZ............96 B3
Uhniv UA......13 C6
Uhřičeves CZ ..96 A2
Uhyst D.......84 A2
Uig UK........31 B2
Uitgeest NL ...70 B1
Uithoorn NL ...70 B1
Uithuizen NL...71 A3
Uithuizermeeden
NL...........71 A3
Úivar RO..... 126 B2
Ujazd
Łódzkie PL ... 87 A3
Opolskie PL...86 B2
Ujezd u Brna
CZ............97 B4
Ujhartyán H .. 112 B3
Újkigyós H.... 113 C5
Ujpetre H.... 125 B4
Ujsolt H......112 C3
Ujszász H.... 113 B4
Ujszentmargita
H............ 113 B5
Ujué E....... 144 B2
Ukanc SLO ... 122 A2
Ukmergé LT .. 13 A6
Ula TR....... 188 B3
Ul'anka SK.....99 C3
Ulaş TR...... 186 A2
Ulassai I..... 179 C3
Ulbjerg DK....58 B2
Ulbster UK....32 C3
Ulceby UK.....40 B3
Ulcinj MNE... 16 E3
Uldum DK......59 C2
Ulea E....... 165 A3
Uleila del Campo
E 164 B2
Ulez AL...... 182 B1
Ulfborg DK....59 B1
Ullånger S... 200 C4
Ullapool UK...32 D1

Ullared S......60 B2
Ullatti S..... 196 B4
Ullatun N.....52 A2
Ulldecona E .. 153 B4
Ulldemolins E. 147 C1
Ullerslev DK...59 C3
Ullervad S....55 B4
Ullès H...... 126 A1
Üllö H....... 112 B3
Ulm D.........94 C1
Ulme P...... 154 B2
Ulmen D.......80 B2
Ulnes N.......47 B6
Ulog BIH..... 139 B4
Uløybukta N ...192 B6
Ulricehamn S ...60 B3
Ulrichstein D...81 B5
Ulrika S......56 B1
Ulriksfors S .. 200 C1
Ulrum NL......71 A3
Ulsberg N.... 198 C6
Ulsta UK......33 A5
Ulsted DK.....58 A3
Ulsteinvik N . 198 C2
Ulstrup
Vestsjællands
Amt. DK 59 C3
Viborg Amt.
DK 59 B2
Ulsvåg N..... 194 B6
Ulubey TR.... 188 A4
Uluborlu TR .. 189 A5
Ulukışla TR....23 C8
Ulverston UK ...36 B3
Ulvik N.......46 B3
Umag HR..... 122 B2
Uman UA...... 13 D9
Umba RUS......3 C14
Umbértide I.. 135 B5
Umbriático I .. 174 B2
Umčari SRB .. 127 C2
Umeå S...... 200 C6
Umgransele S. 200 B4
Umhausen A.. 108 B1
Umka SRB.... 127 C2
Umljanovic
HR.......... 138 B2
Umnäs S..... 195 E7
Ümraniye TR.. 186 A4
Unaðsdalur IS. 190 A3
Unapool UK....32 C1
Unari FIN.... 197 B8
Unbyn S..... 196 D4
Uncastillo E.. 144 B2
Undenäs S....55 B5
Undersaker
S........... 199 B10
Undredal N ...46 B4
Unešić HR.... 138 B2
Úněšov CZ.....96 B1
Ungheni MD...17 B7
Unhais da Serra
P........... 148 B2
Unhošt CZ.....84 B2
Unichowo PL...68 A2
Uničov CZ.....98 B1
Uniejów PL....76 C3
Unisław PL....76 A3
Unkel D.......80 B3
Unken A...... 109 B3
Unna D........81 A3
Unnaryd S....60 C3
Unquera E.... 142 A2
Unterach A... 109 B4
Unterägeri
CH 107 B3
Unterammergau
D 108 B2
Unterhaching
D 108 A2
Unteriberg
CH 107 B3
Unterkochen D .94 C2
Unter
Langkampfen
A............ 108 B3
Unterlaussa A. 110 B1
Unterlüss D....72 B3
Untermünkheim
D 94 B1
Unterschächen
CH 107 C3
Unterschleissheim
D 95 C3
Unterschwaningen
D 94 B2
Untersiemau D .82 B2
Unter-steinbach
D 94 B2
Unterweissenbach
A............ 110 C1
Unterzell D....95 B4
Upavon UK....44 B2
Úpice CZ......85 B4

Upiłka PL.....68 B2
Upphärad S....54 B3
Uppingham UK .40 C3
Upplands-Väsby
S............57 A3
Uppsala S.....51 C4
Uppsjøhytta N. 48 A1
Upton-upon-
Severn UK....39 B4
Ur F 146 B2
Uras I....... 179 C2
Uraz PL.......85 A4
Urbánia I.... 136 B1
Urbino I..... 136 B1
Urçay F...... 103 C4
Urda E 157 A4
Urdax E...... 144 A2
Urdilde E.... 140 B2
Urdos F...... 145 B3
Urk NL........70 B2
Úrkút H...... 111 B4
Urla TR...... 188 A1
Urlingford IRL .30 B1
Urnäsch CH .. 107 B4
Urnes N.......47 A4
Uroševac KOS... 16 D4
Urracal E.... 164 B2
Urries E...... 144 B2
Urroz E...... 144 B2
Ursensollen D..95 B3
Urshult S......63 B2
Uršna Sela
SLO 123 B4
Urszulewo PL ..77 B4
Ury F.........90 C2
Urziceni RO....17 C7
Urzulei I..... 178 B3
Usagre E..... 156 B1
Uşak TR...... 187 D4
Usedom D......66 C2
Useldange L...92 B1
Usèllus I..... 179 C2
Ushakovo RUS .69 A5
Usingen D.....81 B4
Usini I....... 178 B2
Uskedal N.....46 C2
Üsküdar TR .. 186 A4
Uslar D.......82 A1
Úsov CZ.......97 B5
Usquert NL....71 A3
Ussassai I.... 179 C3
Ussé F....... 102 B2
Usséglio I.... 119 B4
Ussel
Cantal F 116 B2
Corrèze F 116 B2
Usson-du-Poitou
F........... 115 B4
Usson-en-Forez
F........... 117 B3
Usson-les-Bains
F........... 146 B3
Ustaoset N....47 B5
Ustaritz F.... 144 A2
Ústěk CZ......84 B2
Uster CH..... 107 B3
Ústí CZ.......98 B1
Ustikolina BIH. 139 B4
Ústí nad Labem
CZ............84 B2
Ústí nad Orlicí
CZ............97 B4
Ustiprača BIH . 139 B5
Ustka PL......68 A1
Ust Luga RUS... 8 C6
Ustroń PL.....98 B2
Ustronie Morskie
PL............67 B4
Ustyuzhna
RUS 9 C10
Uszód H...... 112 C2
Utåker N......52 A1
Utansjö S.... 200 D3
Utebo E...... 152 A3
Utena LT..... 13 A6
Utery CZ......95 B5
Uthaug N.... 198 B6
Utiel E...... 159 B2
Utne N........46 B3
Utö S.........57 B4
Utrecht NL....70 B2
Utrera E..... 162 A2
Utrillas E.... 153 B3
Utsjoki FIN.. 193 C11
Utstein kloster
N............52 A1
Uttendorf A .. 109 B3
Utterslev DK...65 B4
Uttoxeter UK ...40 C2
Utvälinge S....61 C2
Utvorda N.... 199 A7

Uusikaarlepyy
FIN............ 3 E8
Uusikaupunki
FIN............ 8 B2
Uvaly CZ......96 A2
Uvdal N.......47 B5
Uza F 128 B1
Uzdin SRB.... 126 B2
Uzdowo PL....77 A5
Uzein F...... 145 A3
Uzel F....... 100 A3
Uzerche F.... 116 B1
Uzès F....... 131 B3
Uzhhorod UA .. 12 D5
Uzhok UA..... 12 D5
Užice SRB.... 127 D1
Uznach CH.... 107 B3
Üzümlü
Konya TR 189 B6
Muğla TR 188 C4
Uzunköprü
TR.......... 186 A1

V

Vaalajärvi FIN. 197 B9
Vaas F....... 102 B2
Vaasa FIN 8 A2
Vaasen NL.....70 B2
Vabre F...... 130 B1
Vác H........ 112 B3
Vacha D.......82 B2
Váchartyán H . 112 B3
Väckelsäng S ...63 B2
Vacqueyras F . 131 A3
Vad S.........50 B2
Vada I....... 134 B3
Väddö S.......51 C5
Väderstad S...55 B5
Vadheim N.....46 A2
Vadillo de la Sierra
E 143 B3
Vadla N...... 135 A4
Vado I....... 135 A4
Vado Ligure I. 133 A4
Vadsø N..... 193 B13
Vadstena S....55 B5
Vaduz FL..... 107 B4
Våg N........ 195 E3
Vågåmo N.... 198 D6
Væggerløse DK .65 B4
Vaggeryd S....62 A2
Vaghia GR.... 184 A4
Vaglia I..... 135 B4
Váglio Basilicata
I............ 172 B1
Vagney F..... 106 A1
Vagnhärad S...57 B3
Vagnsunda S...57 A4
Vagos P...... 148 B1
Vai GR....... 185 D7
Vaiano I..... 135 B4
Vaiges F..... 102 A1
Vaihingen D ...93 C4
Vaillant F.... 105 B4
Vailly-sur-Aisne
F............91 B3
Vailly-sur-Sauldre
F........... 103 B4
Vairano Scalo
I............ 170 B2
Vaison-la-Romaine
F........... 131 A4
Vaite F...... 105 B4
Väjern S......54 B2
Vajszló H.... 125 B3
Vaksdal N.....46 B2
Valaam RUS....9 B7
Valada P..... 154 B2
Valadares P.. 148 A1
Valado P..... 154 B1
Valandovo
NMK........ 182 B4
Valašská SK ...99 C3
Valašská Belá
SK...........98 C2
Valašská Dubová
SK...........99 B3
Valašské Klobouky
CZ............98 B2
Valašské Meziříčí
CZ............98 B1
Valberg F.... 132 A2
Vålberg S.....55 A4
Valbo S.......51 B4

Valbom P 148 A1
Valbondione I. 120 A3
Valbonnais F.. 118 C2
Valbuena de Duero
E 142 C2
Vålcani RO ... 126 B2
Valdagno I... 121 B4
Valdahon F .. 105 B5
Valdaracete E. 151 B4
Valday RUS 9 D8
Valdealgorfa
E 153 B3
Valdecaballeros
E 156 A2
Valdecabras E. 152 B1
Valdecarros E. 150 B2
Valdeconcha
E 151 B5
Valdeflores E . 161 B3
Valdefresno E. 142 B1
Valdeganga E. 158 B2
Valdelacasa S. 150 B2
Valdelacasa de Tajo
E 156 A2
Valdelarco E . 161 B3
Valdelosa E .. 149 A4
Valdeltormo E 153 B4
Valdelugeros
E 142 B1
Valdemanco de
Esteras E .. 156 B3
Valdemarsvik S .56 B2
Valdemorillo
E 151 B3
Valdemoro E . 151 B4
Valdemoro Sierra
E 152 B2
Valdenoceda
E 143 B3
Valdeobispo E 149 B3
Valdeolivas E . 152 B1
Valdepeñas E. 157 B4
Valdepeñas de
Jaén E..... 163 A4
Valdepiélago
E 142 B1
Valderas E... 142 B1
Valdéricé I... 176 A1
Valderrobres
E 153 B4
Valdesalor E . 155 A4
Valde San Lorenzo
E 141 B4
Val de Santo
Domingo E .. 150 B3
Val d'Esquières
F........... 132 B2
Valdestillas E. 150 A3
Valdetorres E . 156 B1
Valdetorres de
Jarama E .. 151 B4
Valdeverde
E 150 C2
Valdevimbre
E 142 B1
Valdieri I.... 133 A3
Valdilecha E . 151 B4
Val-d'Isère F . 119 B3
Valdobbiádene
I............ 121 B4
Valdocondes
E 143 C3
Valdoviño E . 140 A2
Valea lui Mihai
RO 16 B5
Vale de Açor
Beja P 160 B2
Portalegre P. 154 B3
Vale de Agua
P........... 160 B1
Vale de Cambra
P........... 148 B1
Vale de Lobo
P........... 160 B1
Vale de Prazeres
P........... 148 B2
Vale de Reis P. 154 C2
Vale de Rosa
P........... 160 B2
Vale de Santarém
P........... 154 B2
Vale de Vargo
P........... 160 B2
Valéggio sul
Mincio I.... 121 B3
Valeiro P.... 154 C2

Valença P 140 B2
Valençay F 103 B3
Valence
Charente F .. 115 C4
Drôme F 117 C4
Valence d'Agen
F.............. 129 B3
Valence d'Albigeois
F.............. 130 A1
Valence-sur-Baise
F.............. 129 C3
Valencia E.... 159 B3
Valencia de
Alcántara E .. 155 B3
Valencia de Don
Juan E...... 142 B1
Valencia de las
Torres E.... 156 B1
Valencia del
Ventoso E.... 161 A3
Valencia de
Mombuey E.. 161 A2
Valenciennes F .79 B3
Valensole F... 132 B1
Valentano I.... 168 A1
Valentigney F. 106 B1
Valentine F ... 145 A4
Valenza I...... 120 B1
Valenzuela E .. 163 A3
Valenzuela de
Calatrava E .. 157 B4
Våler
Hedmark N 48 B3
Østfold N 54 A1
Valera de Abajo
E............ 158 B1
Valeria E.... 158 B1
Valestrand N.. 52 A1
Valestrandsfossen
N............46 B2
Valevåg N...... 52 A1
Valfabbrica I.. 136 B1
Valflaunes F . 131 B2
Valga EST 8 D5
Valgorge F ... 131 A3
Valgrisenche I 119 B4
Valguarnera
Caropepe I... 177 B3
Valhelhas P ... 148 B2
Valjevo SRB ... 127 C1
Valka LV........ 8 D4
Valkeakoski FIN.. 8 B4
Valkenburg NL.. 80 B1
Valkenswaard
NL............79 A5
Valkó H...... 112 B3
Valla S........ 56 A2
Vallada E...... 159 C3
Valladö E...... 141 A4
Valladolid E.... 150 A3
Vallåkra S ... 61 D2
Vallata I...... 172 A1
Vallberga S ... 61 C3
Vall d'Alba E .. 153 B3
Valldemossa
E............ 166 B2
Valle N........ 52 A3
Valle Castellana
I............ 136 C2
Valle de Abdalajís
E............ 163 B3
Valle de
Cabuérniga
E............ 142 A2
Valle de la Serena
E............ 156 B2
Valle de Matamoros
E............ 155 C4
Valle de Santa Ana
E............ 155 C4
Valledolmo I.... 176 B2
Valledoria I.... 178 B2
Vallelado E.... 150 A3
Vallelunga
Pratameno I.. 176 B2
Valle Mosso I.. 119 B5
Vallendar D.... 81 B3
Vallentuna S... 57 A4
Vallerås S...... 49 B5
Valleraugue F. 130 A2
Vallermosa I.. 179 C2
Vallet F...... 101 B4
Valletta M.... 175 C3
Valley UK...... 38 A2
Vallfogona de
Riucorb E ... 147 C2
Valli del Pasúbio
I............ 121 B4
Vallo della Lucánia
I............ 172 B1

Valloire F 118 B3
Vallombrosa I. 135 B4
Vallon-Pont-d'Arc
F............ 131 A3
Vallorbe CH.... 105 C5
Vallouise F 118 C3
Valls E........ 147 C2
Vallset N........ 48 B3
Vallsta S...... 50 A3
Vallstena S.... 57 C4
Valmadrid E... 153 A3
Valmiera LV.... 8 D4
Valmojado E... 151 B3
Valmont F...... 89 A4
Valmontone I.. 169 B2
Valö S........ 51 B5
Valognes F.... 88 A2
Valonga P.... 148 B1
Valongo P.... 148 A1
Válor E...... 164 C1
Valoria la Buena
E............ 142 C2
Valozhyn BY ...13 A7
Valpaços P.... 148 A2
Valpelline I.... 119 B4
Valpiana I.... 135 B3
Valpovo HR 125 B4
Valras-Plage F 130 B2
Valréas F...... 131 A3
Vals CH 107 C4
Valsavarenche
I............ 119 B4
Välse DK...... 65 B4
Valsequillo E.. 156 B2
Valsjöbyn S .. 199 A11
Vals-les-Bains
F............ 117 C4
Valsonne F 117 B4
Valstagna I.... 121 B4
Val-Suzon F... 105 B3
Valtablado del Rio
E............ 152 B1
Valþjofsstaður
IS 191 B11
Val Thorens F . 118 B3
Valtice CZ...... 97 C4
Valtiendas E .. 151 A4
Valtierra E 144 B2
Valtopina I.... 136 B1
Valtorta I.... 120 B2
Valtournenche
I............ 119 B4
Valverde E 158 B1
Valverde de
Burguillos E.. 155 C4
Valverde de Júcar
E............ 158 B1
Valverde de la Vera
E............ 150 B2
Valverde de la
Virgen E...... 142 B1
Valverde del
Camino E ... 161 B3
Valverde del Fresno
E............ 149 B3
Valverde de Llerena
E............ 156 B2
Valverde de Mérida
E............ 156 B1
Valvträsk S.... 196 C4
Vamberk CZ 85 B4
Vamdrup DK.... 59 C2
Våmhus S...... 50 A1
Vamlingbo S... 57 D4
Vammala FIN ...8 B3
Vamos GR.... 185 D5
Vámosmikola
H............ 112 B2
Vámosszabadi
H............ 111 B4
Vanault-les-Dames
F............ 91 C4
Vandel DK...... 59 C2
Vandenesse F. 104 C2
Vandenesse-en-
Auxois F 104 B3
Vandóies I.... 108 C2
Väne-Åsaka S.. 54 B3
Vänersborg S .. 54 B3
Vänersnäs S... 54 B3
Vang N...... 47 A5
Vänge S...... 51 C4
Vangsnes N... 46 A3
Vänjaurbäck
S 200 B4
Vännacka S... 54 A3
Vannareid N .. 192 B3
Vännäs S.... 200 C5
Vannes F...... 101 B3
Vannsätter S.. 51 A3
Vannvåg N... 192 B3
Vansbro S.... 50 B1

Vanse N........ 52 B2
Vantaa FIN 8 B4
Vanttauskoski
FIN.......... 197 C9
Vanviken N... 199 B7
Vanyarc H.... 112 B3
Vaour F...... 129 B4
Vapnyarka UA . 13 D8
Vaprio d'Adda
I............ 120 B2
Vaqueiros P... 160 B2
Vara S........ 55 B3
Varacieux F ... 118 B2
Varades F 101 B4
Varages F 132 B1
Varaldsøy N... 46 B2
Varallo I...... 119 B5
Varangerbotn
N............ 193 B12
Varano de'Melegari
I............ 120 C3
Varaždin HR .. 124 A2
Varaždinske
Toplice HR... 124 A2
Varazze I.... 133 A4
Varberg S...... 60 B2
Vardal N...... 48 B2
Varde DK...... 59 C1
Vårdö FIN...... 51 B7
Vardø N...... 193 B15
Vardomb H.... 125 A4
Varejoki FIN.. 196 C7
Varel D...... 71 A5
Varèna LT...... 13 A6
Varenna I.... 120 A2
Varennes-en-
Argonne F ... 91 B5
Varennes-le-Grand
F............ 105 C3
Varennes-St
Sauveur F... 105 C4
Varennes-sur-Allier
F............ 117 A3
Varennes-sur-
Amance F ... 105 B4
Vareš BIH 139 A4
Varese I...... 120 B1
Varese Ligure
I............ 134 A2
Värfurile RO ... 16 B5
Vårgårda S... 60 A2
Vargas
E............ 143 A3
P............ 154 B2
Vargön S...... 54 B3
Varhaug N... 52 B1
Variaş RO ... 126 A3
Variaşu Mic
RO 126 A3
Varilhes F.... 146 A2
Varin SK...... 98 B2
Väring S...... 55 B4
Váriz P...... 149 A3
Varkaus FIN ... 8 A5
Varmahlíð IS . 190 B6
Varmaland IS . 190 C4
Värmlands Bro
S............ 55 A4
Värmskog S... 55 A3
Varna
BG 17 D7
SRB........ 127 C1
Varnamo S.... 60 B4
Varnhem S.... 55 B4
Varnsdorf CZ .. 84 B2
Varös S........ 60 B2
Varoška Rijeka
BIH.......... 124 B2
Városlőd H... 111 B4
Várpalota H.. 112 B2
Varreddes F... 90 C2
Vars F...... 118 C3
Varsi I...... 120 C2
Varsseveld NL.71 C3
Vårsta S...... 57 A3
Vartdal N... 198 C3
Vartofta S.... 55 B4
Várvik S...... 54 A3
Várvölgy H... 111 C4
Varzi I...... 120 C2
Varzjelas P... 148 B1
Varzo I...... 119 A5
Varzy F...... 104 B2
Vasad H...... 112 B3
Väse S........ 55 A4
Vašica SRB ... 125 B5
Vasilevichy BY .13 B8
Väskinde S.... 57 C4
Vaskút H...... 125 A4
Vaslui RO ... 17 B7

Vassbotn N 53 B4
Vassenden N....47 A6
Vassieux-en-
Vercors F.... 118 C2
Vassmolösa S .. 63 B4
Vassy F........ 88 B3
Västansjö S ... 195 E6
Västanvik S... 50 B1
Västerås S.... 56 A2
Västerby S.... 50 B2
Västerfärnebo
S............ 50 C3
Västergarn S.. 57 C4
Västerhaninge
S............ 57 A4
Västervik S.... 62 A4
Vasto I...... 170 A2
Västra Ämtervik
S............ 55 A4
Västra-Bodarne
S............ 60 B2
Västra Karup S.61 C2
Vasvár H.... 111 B3
Vasylkiv UA ... 13 C9
Vát H........ 111 B3
Vatan F...... 103 B3
Väte S........ 57 C4
Vathia GR 184 C3
Vatican City =
Cittádel Vaticano
I............ 168 B2
Vatili CY...... 181 A2
Vatin SRB 126 B3
Vatland N...... 52 B3
Vatnar N...... 53 A5
Vatne N...... 48 C1
Vatne N...... 53 B3
Vatnestrøm N.. 53 B4
Vätö S........ 51 C5
Vatra-Dornei
RO 17 B6
Vatry F........ 91 C4
Vattholma S... 51 B4
Vättis CH.... 107 C4
Vauchamps F .. 91 C3
Vauchassis F .. 104 A2
Vaucouleurs F ..92 C1
Vaudoy-en-Brie
F............ 90 C3
Vaulen N...... 52 B1
Vaulruz CH... 106 C1
Vaulx Vraucourt
F............ 90 A2
Vaumas F 104 C2
Vausseroux F . 115 B3
Vauvenargues
F............ 132 B1
Vauvert F 131 B3
Vauvillers F .. 105 B5
Vaux-sur-Sure
B.......... 92 B1
Vawkavysk BY ..13 B6
Vaxholm S.... 57 A4
Växjö S...... 62 B2
Våxtorp S.... 61 C3
Vayrac F.... 129 B4
Važec SK...... 99 B3
Veberöd S 61 D3
Vechelde D.... 72 B3
Vechta D...... 71 B5
Vecinos E 149 B4
Vecsés H...... 112 B3
Vedavågen N .. 52 A1
Veddige S...... 60 B2
Vedersø DK.... 59 B1
Vedeseta I 120 B2
Vedevåg S.... 56 A1
Vedra E...... 140 B2
Vedum S...... 55 B3
Veendam NL.. 71 A3
Veenendaal NL .70 B2
Vega
Asturias E.... 142 A1
Asturias E.... 141 A4
Vega de Espinareda
E............ 141 B4
Vega de Infanzones
E............ 142 B1
Vegadeo E.... 141 A3
Vega de Pas E.. 143 A3
Vega de Valcarce
E............ 141 B4
Vega de
Valdetronco
E............ 150 A2
Vegårshei N... 53 B4
Vegas de Coria
E............ 149 B3
Vegas del Condado
E............ 142 B1

Veghel NL...... 80 A1
Veglast D...... 66 B1
Véglie I...... 173 B3
Veguillas E... 151 B4
Vegusdal N.... 53 B4
Veidholmen N 198 B4
Veidnes N... 193 B10
Veikåker N... 48 B1
Veinge S...... 61 C3
Vejbystrand S.. 61 C2
Vejen DK...... 59 C2
Vejer de la Frontera
E............ 162 B2
Vejle DK...... 59 C2
Vejprty CZ...... 83 B5
Velada E...... 150 B3
Vela Luka HR.. 138 C2
Velayos E.... 150 B3
Velbert D...... 80 A3
Velburg D...... 95 B3
Velde N...... 199 A8
Velden
Bayern D 95 B3
Bayern D .. 95 C4
Velden am Worther
See A...... 109 C5
Velefique E... 164 B2
Velen D...... 80 A2
Velenje SLO... 123 A4
Veles NMK.... 182 B3
Velesevec HR.. 124 B2
Velešín CZ...... 96 C2
Velestino GR.. 182 D4
Velez Blanco
E............ 164 B2
Vélez de
Benaudalla E. 163 B4
Vélez-Málaga
E............ 163 B3
Vélez Rubio E. 164 B2
Veliki Radinci
SRB........ 127 B1
Velika HR 125 B3
Velika Gorica
HR.......... 124 B2
Velika Grdevac
HR.......... 124 B3
Velika Greda
SRB........ 126 B3
Velika Ilova
BIH.......... 125 C3
Velika Kladuša
BIH.......... 124 B1
Velika Kopanica
HR.......... 125 B4
Velika Krsna
SRB........ 127 C2
Velika Obarska
BIH.......... 125 C5
Velika Pisanica
HR.......... 124 B3
Velika Plana
SRB........ 127 C3
Velika Zdenci
HR.......... 124 B3
Velike Lašče
SLO.......... 123 B3
Velike Središte
SRB........ 126 B3
Veliki Gaj SRB. 126 B3
Veliki Popović
SRB........ 127 C3
Velikiye Luki
RUS.......... 9 E7
Veliko Gradište
SRB........ 127 C3
Veliko Orašje
SRB........ 127 C3
Veliko Selo
SRB........ 127 C3
Veliko Tarnovo
BG 17 D6
Velilla del Río
Carrió E 142 B2
Velilla de San
Antonio E ... 151 B4
Velingrad BG .. 183 A6
Velizh RUS 9 E7
Veljun HR.... 123 B4
Velká Bíteš CZ .. 97 B4
Velká Hleďsbe
CZ............ 95 B4
Velká Lomnica
SK............ 99 B4
Velkánad Veličkou
CZ............ 98 C1
Velké Bystřice
CZ............ 98 B1
Velké Heraltice
CZ............ 98 B1
Velké Karlovice
CZ............ 98 B2

Vel'ke'Kostol'any
SK............ 98 C1
Vel'ké Leváre
SK............ 97 C5
Vel'ké Meziříčí
CZ............ 97 B4
Velké Pavlovice
CZ............ 97 C4
Vel'ké Rovné
SK............ 98 B2
Vel'ké Uherce
SK............ 98 C2
Vel'ké Zálužie
SK............ 98 C1
Vel'ký Blahovo
SK............ 99 C4
Velky Bor CZ.. 96 B1
Vel'ký Cetin
SK............ 112 A2
Vel'ký Krtíš
SK............ 112 A3
Vel'ký Meder
SK............ 111 B4
Velky Ujezd CZ .98 B1
Vellahn D...... 73 A3
Velles F...... 103 C3
Velletri I...... 168 B2
Vellinge S...... 66 A2
Vellisca E 151 B5
Velliza E 150 A3
Vellmar D...... 81 A5
Velp NL...... 70 B2
Velten D...... 74 B2
Velvary CZ...... 84 B2
Velvendos GR. 182 C4
Vemb DK...... 59 B1
Vemdalen S .. 199 C10
Veme N...... 48 B2
Véménd H.... 125 A4
Vemmedrup
DK............ 61 D2
Vena S...... 62 A3
Venaco F...... 180 A2
Venafro I...... 169 B4
Venarey-les-
Laumes F ... 104 B3
Venaria I...... 119 B4
Venasca I...... 133 A3
Vence F...... 132 B3
Venda Nova
Coimbra P ... 154 A2
Leiria P 154 B2
Vendas Novas
P............ 154 C2
Vendays-
Montalivet F. 114 C2
Vendel S...... 51 B4
Vendelso S...... 57 A4
Vendeuil F 91 B3
Vendeuvre-sur-
Barse F 104 A3
Vendoeuvres
F............ 115 B5
Vendôme F 103 B3
Venelles F 131 B4
Veness UK...... 33 B4
Venézia = Venice
I............ 122 B1
Venialbo E 150 A2
Venice = Venézia
I............ 122 B1
Vénissieux F .. 117 B4
Venjan S...... 49 B5
Venlo NL...... 80 A2
Vennesla N.... 53 B3
Vennesund N .195 E3
Vennezey F.... 92 C2
Venn Green UK..42 B2
Venosa I...... 172 B1
Venray NL...... 80 A1
Vent A...... 108 C1
Venta de Baños
E............ 142 C2
Venta del Moro
E............ 158 B2
Venta de los Santos
E............ 157 B4
Ventas de Huelma
E............ 163 A4
Ventas de
Zafarraya E . 163 B3
Ventavon F ... 132 A1
Ventimíglia I.. 133 B3
Ventnor UK.... 44 C2
Ventosa de la Sierra
E............ 143 C4

Ventosilla E ... 143 C4
Ventspils LV..... 8 D2
Venturina I.... 134 B3
Venzolasca F.. 180 A2
Venzone I..... 122 A2
Vép H........ 111 B3
Vera
E............ 164 B3
N............ 199 B9
Vera Cruz P ... 160 A2
Vera de Bidasoa
E............ 144 A2
Vera de Moncayo
E............ 144 C2
Verbánia I 119 B5
Verbería F...... 90 B2
Verbicaro I.... 174 B1
Verbier CH.... 119 A4
Vercelli I...... 119 B5
Vercel-Villedieu-le-
Camp F 105 B5
Verchen D...... 66 C1
Vercheny F.... 118 C2
Verclause F ... 131 A4
Verdalsøra N. 199 B8
Verden D...... 72 B2
Verdens Ende
N............ 54 A1
Verdikoussa
GR.......... 182 D3
Verdille F 115 C3
Verdú E...... 147 C2
Verdun F...... 92 B1
Verdun-sur-
Garonne F ... 129 C4
Verdun-sur-le-
Doubs F 105 C4
Veresegyház
H............ 112 B3
Verfeil F 129 C4
Vergato I.... 135 A4
Vergel E...... 159 C4
Vergeletto CH 120 A1
Verges E...... 147 B4
Vergiate I.... 120 B1
Vergt F...... 129 A3
Veria GR 182 C4
Verín E...... 141 C3
Veringenstadt
D............ 107 A4
Verl D........ 81 A4
Verma N...... 198 C5
Vermand F.... 90 B3
Vermelha P ... 154 B1
Vermenton F.. 104 B2
Vernago I...... 108 C1
Vernante I 133 A3
Vernantes F .. 102 B2
Venár SK...... 99 C4
Vernasca I 120 C2
Vernayaz CH .. 119 A4
Vernazza I 134 A2
Vern-d'Anjou
F............ 102 B1
Verneřice CZ... 84 B2
Vernet F 146 A2
Vernet-les-Bains
F............ 146 B3
Vernier CH.... 118 A3
Vernio I...... 135 A4
Vernole I...... 173 B4
Vernon F...... 90 B1
Vernoux-en-
Vivarais F ... 117 C4
Veróce H...... 112 B3
Verolanuova I. 120 B3
Véroli I...... 169 B3
Verona I...... 121 B4
Verpelét H.... 113 B4
Verrabotn N .. 199 B7
Verrès I...... 119 B4
Verrey-sous-
Salmaise F .. 104 B3
Verrières F .. 115 B4
Versailles F.... 90 C2
Versam CH.... 107 C4
Verseg H.... 112 B3
Versmold D.... 71 B5
Versoix CH.... 118 A3
Verteillac F ... 115 C4
Vértesacsa H.. 112 B2
Vertou F...... 101 B4
Vertus F...... 91 C3
Verviers B...... 80 B1
Vervins F...... 91 B3
Verwood UK.... 43 B5
Veryan UK...... 42 B2
Veržej SLO.... 111 C3
Verzuolo I.... 133 A3
Verzy F...... 91 B4

Vescovato F... 180 A2
Vése H........ 124 A3
Veselie BG..... 17 D7
Veselínad Lužnicí
CZ............96 B2
Veselínad Moravou
CZ............98 C1
Vésíme I..... 119 C5
Veskoniemi
FIN.........193 D11
Vesoul F..... 105 B5
Vespolate I... 120 B1
Vessigebro S...60 C2
Vestbygd N....52 B2
Vestenanova I 121 B4
Vester Husby S . 56 B2
Vester Nebel
DK............59 C2
Vesterøhavn
DK............58 A3
Vester Torup
DK............58 A2
Vester Vedsted
DK............59 C1
Vestervig DK...58 B1
Vestfossen N...53 A5
Vestmannaeyjar
IS...........190 D5
Vestmarka N...48 C3
Vestnes N..... 198 C4
Vestone I..... 120 B3
Vestre Gausdal
N............123 B3
Vestre Jakobselv
N............193 B13
Vestre Slidre N. . 47 A5
Vesyegonsk
RUS...........9 C10
Veszprém H.... 112 B1
Veszprémvarsány
H............112 B1
Vésztö H..... 113 C5
Vetlanda S.....62 A3
Vetovo HR 125 B3
Vetralla I.... 168 A2
Větrný Jeníkov
CZ............97 B3
Vétroz CH.... 119 A4
Vetschau D....84 A2
Vettasjärvi S.. 196 B4
Vetto I....... 134 A3
Vetulónia I... 135 C3
Veules-les-Roses
F.............89 A4
Veulettes-sur-Mer
F.............89 A4
Veum N........53 A4
Veurne B......78 A2
Veverská Bítýška
CZ............97 B4
Vevey CH..... 106 C1
Vevi GR..... 182 C3
Vevring N.....46 A2
Vex CH....... 119 A4
Veynes F..... 132 A1
Veyre-Monton
F............116 B3
Veyrier F.... 118 B3
Vézelay F.... 104 B2
Vézelise F.....92 C2
Vézenobres F . 131 A3
Vezins F..... 102 B1
Vézins-de-Lévézou
F............130 A1
Vezirhan TR... 187 B5
Vezirköprü TR . 23 A8
Vezza di Óglio
I............120 A3
Vezzani F.... 180 A2
Vezzano I.... 121 A4
Vezzano sul
Cróstolo I... 121 C3
Vi S......... 200 D3
Viadana I.... 121 C3
Via Gloria P... 160 B2
Viana F...... 143 B4
Viana do Alentejo
P............154 C2
Viana do Bolo
E............141 B3
Viana do Castelo
P............148 A1
Vianden L.....92 B2
Viannos GR... 185 D6
Viaréggio I... 134 B3
Viator E..... 164 C2
Vibble S......57 C4
Viborg DK....58 B2
Vibo Valéntia
I............175 C2
Vibraye F.... 102 A2
Vic E........ 147 C3
Vícar E...... 164 C2

Vicarello I.... 134 B3
Vicari I...... 176 B2
Vicchio I..... 135 B4
Vicdesses F... 146 B2
Vic-en-Bigorre
F............145 A4
Vicenza I.... 121 B4
Vic-Fézensac
F............129 C3
Vichy F...... 117 A3
Vickan S......60 B2
Vickerstown
UK............65 B4
Vic-le-Comte
F............116 B3
Vico F....... 180 A1
Vico del Gargano
I............171 B3
Vico Equense
I............170 C2
Vicopisano I . . 134 B3
Vicosoprano
CH........... 120 A2
Vicovaro I.... 169 A2
Vic-sur-Aisne F. . 90 B3
Vic-sur-Cère F. 116 C2
Victoria = Rabat
M........... 175 C3
Vidago P..... 148 A2
Vidauban F... 132 B2
Vide P....... 148 B2
Videbæk DK....59 B1
Videm SLO.... 123 B3
Videseter N... 198 D4
Vidigueira P.. 160 A2
Vidin BG...... 16 D5
Vidlin UK......33 A5
Vidsel S..... 196 D3
Vidzy BY......13 A7
Viechtach D....95 B4
Vieille-Brioude
F............117 B3
Vielha F..... 154 B2
Vieira do Minho
P............148 A1
Vieiros P..... 155 C3
Vielha E..... 145 B4
Vielle-Aure F. . 145 B4
Viellespesse F . 116 B3
Viellevigne F . . 114 B2
Vielmur-sur-Agout
F............130 B1
Vielsalm B 80 B1
Viels Maison F . 91 C3
Vienenburg D . . 73 C3
Vienna = Wien
A........... 111 A3
Vienne F..... 117 B4
Vieritz D......73 B5
Viernheim D....93 B4
Vierraden D....74 A3
Viersen D.....80 A2
Vierville-sur-Mer
F.............88 A3
Vierzon F.... 103 B4
Vieselbach D...82 B3
Vieste I..... 171 B4
Vietas S..... 194 C9
Vieteren B....78 B2
Vietri di Potenza
I............172 B1
Vietri sul Mare
I............170 C2
Vieux-Boucau-les-
Bains F..... 128 C1
Vif F........ 118 B2
Vig DK........ 61 D1
Vigásio I.... 121 B3
Vigáun A..... 109 B4
Vigeland N....52 B3
Vigeois F.... 116 B1
Vigévano I... 120 B1
Viggianello I . . 174 B2
Viggiano I.... 174 A1
Vigliano I.... 169 A3
Vigmostad N...52 B3
Vignale I.... 119 B5
Vignanello I . . 168 A2
Vigneulles-lès-
Hattonchâtel
F............92 C1
Vignevieille F . 146 B3
Vignola I.... 135 A4
Vignory F.... 105 A4
Vignoux-sur-
Barangeon F . 103 B4
Vigo E....... 140 B2
Vigo di Fassa I . 121 A4
Vigone I..... 119 C4
Vigrestad N....52 B1
Vihiers F.... 102 B1
Viitasaari FIN . . 8 A4
Vík IS....... 190 D6

Vik
Nordland N ... 195 E3
Rogaland N.....52 B1
Sogn og Fjordane
N............ 46 A3
S............ 63 C2
Vika S........50 B2
Vikajärvi FIN . . 197 C9
Vikane N......54 A1
Vikarbyn S....50 B2
Vike N........46 B2
Vikedal N.....52 A1
Vikeland N....53 B3
Viken
Jämtland
S...........199 A10
Skåne S... 61 C2
Viker N......48 B2
Vikersund N...48 C1
Vikesá N......52 B2
Vikevåg N.....52 A1
Vikingstad S...56 B1
Vikmanshyttan
S............50 B2
Vikna N..... 199 A7
Víkøy N......46 B3
Vikran
Troms N ... 192 C2
Troms N ... 194 B7
Viksjö S..... 200 D3
Viksøyri N.....46 A3
Viksta S......51 B4
Vila Boim P... 155 C3
Vila Châde Ourique
P............154 B2
Viladamat E.. 147 B4
Vila de Cruces
E............140 B2
Vila de Rei P... 154 B2
Vila do Bispo
P............148 A1
Vila do Conde
P............148 A1
Viladrau E... 147 C3
Vila Flor P... 149 A2
Vila Franca das
Navas P..... 149 B2
Vilafranca del
Maestrat E.. 153 B3
Vilafranca del
Penedès E... 147 C2
Vila Franca de Xira
P............154 C1
Vila Fresca P . 154 C1
Vilagarcía de
Arousa E... 140 B2
Vilajuiga E... 147 B4
Vilamarín E.. 140 B3
Vilamartín de
Valdeorras E . 141 B3
Vila Nogueira
P............154 C1
Vila Nova da
Baronia P.... 154 C2
Vilanova de
Castelló E... 159 B3
Vila Nova de
Cerveira P... 140 C2
Vila Nova de
Famalicão P . 148 A1
Vila Nova de Foz
Côa P....... 149 A2
Vila Nova de Gaia
P............148 A1
Vila Nova de
Milfontes P . 160 B1
Vila Nova de Paiva
P............148 B2
Vila Nova de São
Bento P..... 161 B2
Vilanova de Sau
E............147 C3
Vilanova i la Geltrú
E............147 C2
Vilapedre E.. 140 A3
Vila Pouca de
Aguiar P.... 148 A2
Vila Praja de
Ancora P.... 148 A1
Vilarandelo P . 148 A2
Vilar de Santos
E............140 B3
Vilardevós E . . 141 C3
Vila Real P... 148 A2
Vila-real de los
Infantes E... 159 B3
Vila Real de Santo
António P... 160 B2
Vilar Formoso
P............149 B3
Vila-Rodona E . 147 C2
Vila Ruiva P... 160 A2
Vilasantar E . 140 A2

Vilaseca E..... 147 C2
Vila Seca P.... 148 B1
Vilassar de Mar
E............147 C3
Vilasund S 195 D5
Vila Velha de
Ródão P..... 155 B3
Vila Verde
Braga P..... 148 A1
Lisboa P..... 154 B1
Vila Verde de
Filcalho P... 161 B2
Vila Viçosa P . . 155 C3
Vilches E.... 157 B4
Vildbjerg DK....59 B1
Vilémov CZ....97 B3
Vileyka BY....13 A7
Vilhelmina S . . 200 B2
Vília GR..... 184 A4
Viljandi EST....8 C4
Villabáñez E . . 150 A3
Villablanca E . 161 B2
Villablino E... 141 B4
Villabona E... 144 A1
Villabragima
E............142 C1
Villabuena del
Puente E.... 150 A2
Villacadima E . 151 A4
Villacañas E... 157 A4
Villacarriedo
E............143 A3
Villacarrillo E . 164 A1
Villa Castelli I . 173 B3
Villacastín E... 150 B3
Villach A..... 109 C4
Villacidro I... 179 C2
Villaconejos E. 151 B4
Villaconejos de
Trabaque E . 152 B1
Villa Cova de Lixa
P............148 A1
Villada E..... 142 B2
Villadangos del
Páramo E... 141 B5
Villadecanes
E............141 B4
Villa del Prado
E............150 B3
Villa del Rio E . 157 C3
Villadepera E . 149 A3
Villa de Peralonso
E............149 A3
Villa di Chiavenna
I............120 A2
Villadiego E . . 142 B2
Villadompardo
E............163 A3
Villadóssola I . 119 A5
Villaeles de
Valdavia E... 142 B2
Villaescusa de Haro
E............158 B1
Villafáfila E . . 142 C1
Villafeliche E . 152 A2
Villaflores E . . 150 A2
Villafrades de
Campos E... 142 B2
Villafranca
Avila E...... 150 B2
Navarra E... 144 B2
Villafranca de
Córdoba E... 157 C3
Villafranca del
Bierzo E..... 141 B4
Villafranca de los
Barros E..... 155 C4
Villafranca de los
Caballeros E . 157 A4
Villafranca di
Verona I.... 121 B3
Villafranca in
Lunigiana I... 134 A2
Villafranca-Montes
de Oca E.... 143 B3
Villafranca Tirrena
I............177 A4
Villafranco del
Campo E.... 152 B2
Villafranco del
Guadalquivir
E............161 B3
Villafrati I... 176 B2
Villafrechós E . 142 C1
Villafruela E . 143 C3
Villagarcía de las
Torres E..... 156 B1
Villagonzalo E . 156 B1
Villagotón E . . 141 B4
Villagrains F . 128 B2
Villaharta E . 156 B3

Villahermosa
E............158 C1
Villaherreros
E............142 B2
Villahoz E.... 143 B3
Villaines-la-Juhel
F.............89 B3
Villajoyosa E . 159 C3
Villalago I.... 169 B3
Villalba
E............140 A3
I............176 B2
Villalba de Calatrava E. 157 B4
Villalba de Guardo
E............142 B2
Villalba del Alcor
E............161 B3
Villalba del Rey
E............151 B5
Villalcampo E . 149 A3
Villalcázar de Sirga
E............142 B2
Villalengua E . 152 A2
Villalgordo del
Júcar E..... 158 B1
Villalgordo del
Marquesado
E............158 B1
Villalmóndar
E............143 B3
Villalón de Campos
E............142 B1
Villalonga E . . 159 C3
Villalonso E . . 150 A2
Villalpando E . 142 C1
Villaluenga E . 151 B4
Villalumbroso
E............142 B2
Villálvaro E . . 143 C3
Villamalea E . . 158 B2
Villamanán E . 142 B1
Villamanín E . . 142 B1
Villamanrique
E............158 C1
Villamanrique de la
Condesa E . . 161 B3
Villamanrique de
Tajo E...... 151 B4
Villamañtilla
E............151 B3
Villamar I.... 179 C2
Villamartín E . 162 B2
Villamartín de
Campos E... 142 B2
Villamartín de Don
Sancho E.... 142 B1
Villamassárgia
I............179 C2
Villamayor E . 142 A1
Villamayor de
Calatrava E . . 157 B3
Villamayor de
Campos E... 142 C1
Villamayor de
Santiago E... 157 A5
Villamblard F . 129 A3
Villamejil E... 141 B4
Villamesías E . 156 A2
Villaminaya
E............157 A4
Villa Minozzo
I............134 A3
Villamor de los
Escuderos E . 150 A2
Villamoronta
E............142 B2
Villamuelas E . 151 C4
Villamuriel de
Cerrato E.... 142 B2
Villandraut F . 128 B2
Villanova I... 173 B3
Villanova d'Asti
I............119 C4
Villanova del
Battista I.... 171 B3
Villanova
Monteleone
I............178 B2
Villante E.... 143 B3
Villantério I... 120 B2
Villanubla E . . 142 C2
Villanueva de
Alcardete E . 157 A4
Villanueva de
Alcorón E... 152 B1

Villanueva de
Algaidas E... 163 A3
Villanueva de
Argaña E.... 143 B3
Villanueva de
Bogas E..... 157 A4
Villanueva de
Córdoba E... 156 B3
Villanueva de
Gállego E... 144 C3
Villanueva del
Aceral E.... 150 A3
Villanueva de la
Concepción
E............163 B3
Villanueva de la
Fuente E..... 158 C1
Villanueva de la
Jara E...... 158 B2
Villanueva de la
Reina E..... 157 B4
Villanueva del
Arzobispo E . 164 A2
Villanueva del
Serena E.... 156 B2
Villanueva del
Sierra E..... 149 B3
Villanueva de las
Manzanas E . 142 B1
Villanueva de las
Peras E..... 141 C5
Villanueva de las
Torres E..... 164 B1
Villanueva de la
Vera E...... 150 B2
Villanueva del
Campo E.... 142 C1
Villanueva del Duque
E............156 B3
Villanueva del
Fresno E..... 155 C3
Villanueva del
Huerva E.... 152 A2
Villanueva de los
Castillejos E . 161 B2
Villanueva de los
Infantes E... 157 B5
Villanueva del Rey
E............156 B2
Villanueva del Rio
E............157 B5
Villanueva del Rio y
Minas E..... 162 B2
Villanueva del
Rosario E... 163 B3
Villanueva del
Trabuco E... 163 B3
Villanueva de Mesía
E............163 A4
Villanueva de Nía
E............142 B2
Villanueva de Oscos
E............141 A4
Villanueva de San
Carlos E..... 157 B4
Villanueva de San
Juan E...... 162 B2
Villanueva de Tapia
E............163 A3
Villanueva de
Valdegovia
E............143 B3
Villány H..... 125 B4
Villaputzu I... 179 C3
Villaquejida E . 142 B1
Villaquilambre
E............142 B1
Villaquiran de los
Infantes E... 142 B2
Villaralto E . . 156 B3
Villarcayo E . . 143 B3
Villard-de-Lans
F............118 B2
Villar de Barrio
E............140 B3
Villar de Cañas
E............158 B1
Villar de Chinchilla
E............158 C2
Villar de Ciervo
E............149 B3
Villardeciervos
E............141 C4
Villar de Domingo
García E.... 152 B1
Villardefrades
E............142 C1
Villar del Arzobispo
E............159 B3
Villar del Buey
E............149 A3
Villar del Cobo
E............152 B2

Villar del Humo
E............158 B2
Villar de los
Navarros E . . 152 A2
Villar del Pedroso
E............156 A2
Villar del Rey
E............155 B4
Villar del Rio E . 143 B4
Villar del Saz de
Navalón E... 152 B1
Villar de Rena
E............156 A2
Villarejo E.... 151 A4
Villarejo de Fuentes
E............158 B1
Villarejo de Orbigo
E............141 B5
Villarejo de
Salvanes E... 151 B4
Villarejo-
Periesteban
E............158 B1
Villares del Saz
E............158 B1
Villaretto I... 119 B4
Villargordo del
Cabiel E..... 158 B2
Villarino E... 149 A3
Villarino de Conso
E............141 B3
Villarluengo E . 153 B3
Villarobe E... 143 B3
Villarosa I.... 177 B3
Villar Perosa I . 119 C4
Villarramiel E . 142 B2
Villarrasa E... 161 B3
Villarreal de San
Carlos E..... 150 C1
Villarrín de Campos
E............142 C1
Villarrobledo
E............158 B1
Villarroya de la
Sierra E..... 152 A2
Villarroya de los
Pinares E.... 153 B3
Villarrubia de los
Ojos E...... 157 A4
Villarrubia de
Santiago E... 151 C4
Villarrubio E . . 151 C5
Villars-les-Dombes
F............117 A5
Villarta E.... 158 B2
Villarta de los
Montes E.... 156 A3
Villarta de San Juan
E............157 A4
Villasana de Mena
E............143 A3
Villasandino E . 142 B2
Villa San Giovanni
I............175 C1
Villa Santa Maria
I............169 B4
Villasante E . . 143 A3
Villa Santina I . 122 A1
Villasarracino
E............142 B2
Villasayas E . . 151 A5
Villasdardo E . 149 A3
Villaseca de
Henares E... 151 B5
Villaseca de Laciana
E............141 B4
Villaseca de la
Sagra E..... 151 C4
Villaseco de los
Gamitos E... 149 A3
Villaseco de los
Reyes E..... 149 A3
Villasequilla de
Yepes E..... 151 C4
Villasimíus I... 179 C3
Villasmundo I . 177 B4
Villasor I..... 179 C2
Villastar E.... 152 B2
Villastellone I . 119 C4
Villatobas E... 151 C4
Villatorp E.... 150 B2
Villatoya E.... 158 B2
Villavaliente E . 158 B2
Villavelayo E . 143 B4
Villavella E... 141 B3
Villaver de de
Gualimar
E............158 C1
Villaverde del Rio
E............162 A2

Villaviciosa E.. 142 A1
Villaviciosa de Córdoba E 156 B3
Villaviciosa de Odón E........ 151 B4
Villavieja de Yeltes E............. 149 B3
Villayón E.... 141 A4
Villé F........93 C3
Villebois-Lavalette F............. 115 C4
Villecerf F......90 C2
Villecomtal F. 130 A1
Villedieu-les-Poêles F.............88 B2
Villedieu-sur-Indre F............. 103 C3
Ville-di-Pietrabugno F............ 180 A2
Villedômain F. 103 B3
Villefagnan F . 115 B4
Villefontaine F............ 118 B2
Villefort F..... 131 A2
Villefranche-d'Albigeois F............ 130 B1
Villefranche-d'Allier F 116 A2
Villefranche-de-Lauragais F.. 146 A2
Villefranche-de-Lonchat F.... 128 B3
Villefranche-de-Panat F...... 130 A1
Villefranche-de-Rouergue F.. 130 A1
Villefranche-du-Périgord F ... 129 B4
Villefranche-sur-Cher F....... 103 B3
Villefranche-sur-Mer F........ 133 B3
Villefranche-sur-Saône F...... 117 A4
Villegenon F.. 103 B4
Villel E....... 152 B2
Villemaur-sur-Vanne F...... 104 A2
Villemontais F 117 B3
Villemur-sur-Tarn F............ 129 C4
Villena E..... 159 C3
Villenauxe-la-Grande F.....91 C3
Villenave-d'Ornon F............ 128 B2
Villeneuve CH 119 A3
F............ 129 B5
Villeneuve-d'Ascq F.............78 B3
Villeneuve-de-Berg F............ 131 A3
Villeneuve-de-Marsan F.... 128 C2
Villeneuve-de-Rivière F 145 A4
Villeneuve-la-Guyard F......90 C3
Villeneuve-l'Archevêque F............ 104 A2
Villeneuve-le-Comte F.......90 C2
Villeneuve-lès-Avignon F... 131 B3
Villeneuve-les-Corbières F . 146 B3
Villeneuve-St Georges F.....90 C2
Villeneuve-sur-Allier F...... 104 C2
Villeneuve-sur-Lot F............ 129 B3
Villeneuve-sur-Yonne F...... 104 A2
Villeréal F ... 129 B3
Villerias E ... 142 C2
Villeromain F . 103 B3
Villers-Bocage Calvados F... 88 A3
Somme F 90 B2
Villers-Bretonneux F.............90 B2
Villers-Carbonnel F.............90 B2
Villers-Cotterêts F.............90 B3

Villersexel F... 105 B5
Villers-Farlay F............ 105 C4
Villers-le-Gambon B.............79 B4
Villers-le-Lac F............ 106 B1
Villers-sur-Mer F.............89 A3
Villerupt F.....92 B1
Villerville F....89 A4
Villeseneux F ..91 C4
Ville-sous-la-Ferté F............ 105 A3
Ville-sur-Illon F............ 105 A5
Ville-sur-Tourbe F.............91 B4
Villetrun F ... 103 B3
Villetta Barrea I............ 169 B3
Villeurbanne F............ 117 B4
Villeveyrac F . 130 B2
Villevocance F 117 B4
Villiers-St-Benoit F............ 104 B2
Villiers-St-Georges F.............91 C3
Villingen D... 106 A3
Villmar D......81 B4
Villoldo E 142 B2
Villon F 104 B3
Villoria E 150 B2
Vilnes N.......46 A1
Vilnius LT 13 A6
Vils A............ 108 B1
DK...........58 B1
Vilsbiburg D...95 C4
Vilseck D......95 B3
Vilshofen D...96 C1
Vilshult S......63 B2
Vilusi MNE ... 139 C4
Vilvestre E ... 149 A3
Vilvoorde B ...79 B4
Vimeiro P 154 B1
Vimercate I ... 120 B2
Vimianzo E... 140 A1
Vimieiro P ... 154 C3
Vimioso P.... 149 A3
Vimmerby S...62 A3
Vimoutiers F...89 B4
Vimperk CZ ...96 B1
Vimy F........78 B2
Vinadi CH 108 C1
Vinadio I..... 133 A3
Vinaixa E..... 147 C1
Vinarós E 153 B4
Vinäs S........50 B1
Vinay F...... 118 B2
Vinberg S.....60 C2
Vinca F....... 146 B3
Vinča SRB ... 127 C2
Vinchiaturo I.. 170 B2
Vinci I....... 135 B3
Vindeby DK....65 A3
Vindelgransele S............ 195 E9
Vindeln S 200 B5
Vinderup DK... 58 B1
Vindsvik N.....52 A2
Vinets F.......91 C4
Vineuil F..... 103 B3
Vinga RO.... 126 A3
Vingåker S.....56 A1
Vingrau F 146 B3
Vingrom N.....48 A2
Vinhais P.... 149 A3
Vinica HR 124 A2
NMK 182 B4
SK.......... 112 A3
SLO 123 B4
Viniegra de Arriba E............ 143 B4
Vinje Hordaland N... 46 B3
Sør-Trøndelag Telemark N ... 53 A3
Vinkovci HR... 125 B4
Vinliden S.... 200 B3
Vinninga S.... 55 B4
Vinnytsya UA .. 13 D8
Vinon F...... 103 B4
Vinon-sur-Verdon F............ 132 B1
Vinslöv S......61 C3
Vinstra N......48 A1
Vintjärn S.....50 B3
Vintrosa S.....55 A5

Viñuela E 163 B3
Viñuela de Sayago E............ 149 A4
Viñuelas E ... 151 B4
Vinuesa E 143 C4
Vinzelberg D...73 B4
Viöl D.........64 B2
Viola I....... 133 A3
Violay F...... 117 B4
Vipava SLO.... 122 B2
Vipiteno I 108 C2
Vipperow D....74 A1
Vir BIH......... 138 B3
HR 137 A4
Vira CH....... 120 A1
Vire F.........88 B3
Vireda S.......62 A2
Vireux F...... 91 A4
Virgen A 109 B3
Virgen de la Cabeza E............ 157 B3
Virginia IRL ...27 C3
Virieu F...... 118 B2
Virieu-le-Grand F............ 118 B2
Virje HR...... 124 A2
Virkkunen FIN......... 197 D10
Virklund DK....59 B2
Virovitica HR.. 124 B3
Virsbo S.......50 C3
Virserum S.....62 A3
Virtaniemi FIN......... 193 D12
Virton B........92 B1
Virtsu EST......8 C3
Viry F........ 118 A3
Vis HR........ 138 B2
Visbek D.......71 B5
Visby DK 64 A1
S 57 C4
Visé B.........80 B1
Višegrad BIH .. 139 B5
Viserba I..... 136 A1
Viseu P...... 148 B2
Visiedo E..... 152 B2
Viskafors S....60 B2
Visland N..... 52 B2
Vislanda S.....62 B2
Visnes N.......52 A1
Višnja Gora SLO 123 B3
Višnjan HR.... 122 B2
Višnové CZ....97 C4
Visnums-Kil S.. 55 A5
Viso del Marqués E............ 157 B4
Visoko BIH......... 139 B4
SLO 123 A3
Visone I...... 119 C5
Visp CH...... 119 A4
Vissefjärda S.. 63 B3
Visselhövede D............72 B2
Vissenbjerg DK .59 C3
Visso I....... 136 C2
Vistabella del Maestrat E ... 153 B3
Vistheden S .. 196 D3
Vita I........ 176 B1
Vitanje SLO .. 123 A4
Vitebsk = Vitsyebsk BY...........13 A9
Viterbo I..... 168 A2
Vitez BIH 139 A3
Vithkuq AL ... 182 C2
Vitigudino E .. 149 A3
Vitina BIH......... 138 B3
GR 184 B3
Vitis A........97 C3
Vítkov CZ......98 B1
Vitoria-Gasteiz E............ 143 B4
Vitré F....... 101 A4
Vitrey-sur-Mance F............ 105 B4
Vitry-en-Artois F.............78 B2
Vitry-le-François F.............91 C4
Vitry-sur-Seine F.............90 C2
Vitsand S......49 B4
Vitsyebsk = Vitebsk BY...........13 A9
Vittangi S.... 196 B4
Vittaryd S.....60 C3
Vitteaux F.... 104 B3
Vittel F...... 105 A4

Vittinge S......51 C4
Vittória I..... 177 C3
Vittório Véneto I............ 122 B1
Vittsjö S.......61 C3
Viù I......... 119 B4
Viul N.........48 B2
Vivario F..... 180 A2
Viveiro E..... 140 A3
Vivel del Rio Martin E............ 152 B3
Viver E....... 159 B3
Viverols F.... 117 B3
Viveros E..... 158 C1
Viviers F..... 131 A3
Vivonne F.... 115 B4
Vivy F........ 102 B1
Vize TR....... 186 A2
Vizille F...... 118 B2
Viziñada HR... 122 B2
Viziru RO......17 C7
Vizovice CZ....98 B1
Vizvár H 124 A3
Vizzavona F... 180 A2
Vizzini I...... 177 B3
Vlachiotis GR . 184 C3
Vlachovo CZ...98 B2
Vlachovo SK ...99 C4
Vláchovo Březi CZ...........96 B1
Vladimirci SRB 127 C1
Vladimirovac SRB 127 B2
Vladislav CZ ...97 B3
Vlagtwedde NL .71 A4
Vlajkovac SRB . 127 B3
Vlasenica BIH . 139 A4
Vlašim CZ......96 B2
Vlatković BIH . 138 A3
Vledder NL.....70 B3
Vlissingen NL...79 A3
Vlkolínec SK ...99 B3
Vlorë AL 182 C1
Vlotho D.......72 B1
Vnanje Gorice SLO 123 B3
Vobarno I 121 B3
Vočin HR..... 124 B3
Vöcklabruck A............ 109 A4
Vöcklamarkt A............ 109 B4
Vodanj SRB .. 127 C2
Voderady SK...98 C1
Vodice Istarska HR ... 123 B3
Šibenska HR . 137 B4
SLO 123 A3
Vodňany CZ....96 B2
Vodnjan HR... 122 C2
Vodskov DK....58 A3
Voe UK........33 A5
Voerså DK.....58 A3
Voghera I 120 C2
Vogogna I 119 A5
Vogošća BIH .. 139 B4
Vogué F...... 131 A3
Vohburg D.....95 C3
Vohenstrauss D............95 B4
Vöhl D........81 A4
Vöhrenbach D............ 106 A3
Vöhringen D...94 C2
Void-Vacon F...92 C1
Voiron F..... 118 B2
Voise F........90 C1
Voisey F...... 105 B4
Voiteg RO.... 126 B3
Voiteur F..... 105 C4
Voitsberg A .. 110 B2
Vojakkala FIN. 196 D7
Vojens DK.....59 C2
Vojka SRB ... 127 C2
Vojlovica SRB . 127 C2
Vojnić HR 123 B4
Vojnik SLO ... 123 A4
Vojník SRB ... 126 B3
Vojvoda Stepa SRB 126 B2
Volada GR ... 188 D2
Volargne I.....121 B3
Volary CZ......96 C1
Volče SLO 122 A2
Volda N...... 198 C3
Volendam NL...70 B2
Volimes GR ... 184 B1
Volissos GR .. 185 A6
Volkach D.....94 B2
Völkermarkt

Volkhov RUS.....9 C8
Völklingen D....92 B2
Volkmarsen D .81 A5
Voll N........ 198 C4
Vollenhove NL .70 B2
Vollore-Montagne F............ 117 B3
Vollsjö S 61 D3
Volodymyr-Volyns'kyy UA 13 C6
Volokolamsk RUS 9 D9
Volos GR..... 182 D4
Volosovo RUS...9 C6
Volovets UA ... 13 D5
Voltággio I.... 120 C1
Volta Mantovana I............ 121 B3
Volterra I 135 B3
Voltri I....... 133 A4
Volturara Áppula I............ 170 B3
Volturara Irpina I............ 170 C2
Volvic F...... 116 B3
Volx F........ 132 B1
Volyně CZ......96 B1
Vonitsa GR ... 182 E2
Vönöck H 111 B4
Vonsild DK.....59 C2
Voorschoten NL...........70 B1
Vopnafjörður IS 191 B11
Vorau A 110 B2
Vorbasse DK...59 C2
Vorchdorf A .. 109 B4
Vorden D 71 B5
NL 70 B3
Vordernberg A............ 110 B2
Vordingborg DK 65 A4
Vorë AL 182 B1
Voreppe F 118 B2
Vorey F...... 117 B3
Vorgod DK.....59 B1
Vormsund N...48 B3
Võru EST.......8 D5
Voskopojë AL . 182 C2
Voss N........50 A2
Votice CZ......96 B2
Voué F........91 C4
Vouillé F..... 115 B4
Voulx F........90 C2
Voussac F.... 116 A3
Vouvray F.... 102 B2
Vouvry CH ... 119 A3
Vouzela P.... 148 B1
Vouziers F....91 B4
Voves F...... 103 A3
Voxna S.......50 A2
Voy UK........33 B3
Voynitsa RUS ..3 D12
Voznesenye RUS 9 B9
Vrå DK 58 A2
S 60 C3
Vráble SK......98 C2
Vračovici MNE 139 C4
Vračev Gaj SRB 127 C3
Vraćevsnica SRB 127 C2
Vrådal N...... 53 A4
Vrakneika GR . 184 A2
Vrana HR..... 123 C3
Vranduk BIH .. 139 A3
Vrångö S......60 B1
Vrani RO..... 127 B3
Vranić SRB ... 127 C2
Vraniči BIH... 139 B4
Vranja HR 123 B3
Vranjak BIH .. 125 C4
Vranje SRB ... 16 D4
Vranovice CZ...97 C4
Vranov nad Dyjí CZ...........97 C3
Vransko SLO .. 123 A3
Vrapčići BIH.. 139 B3
Vratimov CZ...98 B2
Vratsa BG ... 17 D5
Vrbanja HR .. 125 C4
Vrbanjci BIH .. 124 C3
Vrbas SRB ... 126 B1
Vrbaška BIH .. 124 B3
Vrbnik Primorsko-Goranska HR 123 B3

Vrbnik continued Zadarsko-Kninska HR 138 A2
Vrbno pod Pradědem CZ ..85 B5
Vrboska HR... 138 B2
Vrbov SK......99 B4
Vrbovce SK....98 C1
Vrbové SK.....98 C1
Vrbovec HR... 124 B2
Vrbovski SRB. 127 C2
Vrbovsko HR.. 123 B4
Vrchlabí CZ....84 B3
Vrčin SRB 127 C2
Vrdy CZ.......97 B3
Vrebac HR ... 137 A4
Vreden D 71 B3
Vreoci SRB ... 127 C2
Vretstorp S 55 A5
Vrginmost HR. 124 B1
Vrgorac HR .. 138 B3
Vrhnika SLO .. 123 B3
Vrhovine HR .. 123 B4
Vrhpolje SRB.. 127 C1
Vriezenveen NL...........71 B3
Vrigne-aux-Bois F.............91 B4
Vrigstad S.....62 A2
Vrlika HR..... 138 B2
Vrnograč BIH.. 124 B1
Vron F.........78 B1
Vroomshoop NL...........71 B3
Vroutek CZ....83 B5
Vrpolje HR ... 125 B4
Vršac SRB ... 126 B3
Vrsar HR..... 122 B2
Vrsi HR....... 137 A4
Vrtoče BIH ... 124 C2
Vrútky SK......98 B2
Všeruby CZ....95 B4
Všestary CZ....85 B3
Vsetín CZ......98 B1
Vučkovica SRB 127 D2
Vught NL......79 A5
Vuillafans F... 105 B5
Vukovar HR... 125 B5
Vuku N....... 199 B8
Vulcan RO.....17 C5
Vulcăneşti MD ..17 C8
Vuoggatjálme S........... 195 D7
Vuojärvi FIN.. 197 C9
Vuolijoki FIN...3 D10
Vuollerim S... 196 C3
Vuotso FIN... 197 A10
Vuzenica SLO .110 C2
Vyartsilya RUS ..9 A7
Vyborg RUS....9 B6
Vyčapy CZ.....97 B3
Vyčapy-Opatovce SK 98 C2
Východna SK...99 C3
Vydrany SK ... 111 A4
Vydrino RUS ..9 B10
Vyerkhnyadzvinsk BY...........13 A7
Vyhne SK......98 C2
Vy-lès Lure F .. 105 B5
Vylkove UA ...17 C8
Vynohradiv UA .17 A5
Vyshniy Volochek RUS 9 D9
Vyškov CZ..... 97 B5
Vysoká nad Kysucou SK ...98 B2
Vysoké Mýto CZ...........97 B4
Vysokovsk RUS 9 D10
Vyšší Brod CZ ..96 C2
Vytegra RUS ..9 B10

W

Waabs D.......64 B2
Waalwijk NL...79 A5
Waarschoot B .79 A3
Wabern D.....81 A5
Wąbrzeźno PL .69 B3
Wąchock PL...87 A5
Wachow D.....74 B1
Wachów PL....86 B2
Wächtersbach D............81 B5
Wackersdorf D .95 B4
Waddington UK...........40 B3
Wadebridge UK...........42 B2
Wadelsdorf D ..84 A2

Wädenswil CH 107 B3
Wadern D......92 B2
Wadersloh D...81 A4
Wadlew PL.....86 A3
Wadowice PL ...99 B3
Wagenfeld D...72 B1
Wageningen NL...........70 C2
Waghäusel D ..93 B4
Waging D..... 109 B3
Wagrain A ... 109 B4
Wagrowiec PL .76 B2
Wahlsdorf D ...74 C2
Wahlstedt D...64 C3
Wahrenholz D .73 B3
Waiblingen D..94 C1
Waidhaus D....95 B4
Waidhofen an der Thaya A......97 C3
Waidhofen an der Ybbs A 110 B1
Waimes B......80 B2
Wainfleet All Saints UK...........41 B4
Waizenkirchen A............96 C1
Wakefield UK .. 40 B2
Wałbrzych PL .85 B4
Walchensee D 108 B2
Walchsee A ... 109 B3
Wałcz PL......75 A5
Wald CH..... 107 B3
Waldaschaff D .94 B1
Waldbach A... 110 B2
Waldböckelheim D............93 B3
Waldbröl D....81 B3
Waldeck D.....81 A5
Waldenburg D .83 B4
Waldfischbach-Burgalben D ..93 B3
Waldheim D...83 A5
Waldkappel D .82 A1
Waldkirch D .. 106 A2
Waldkirchen D .96 C1
Waldkirchen am Wesen A......96 C1
Waldkraiburg D 109 A3
Wald-Michelbach D............93 B4
Waldmohr D...93 B3
Waldmünchen D............95 B4
Waldring A ... 109 B3
Waldsassen D..95 A4
Waldshut D... 106 B3
Waldstatt CH. 107 B4
Waldwisse F ...92 B2
Walenstadt CH 107 B4
Walentynów PL...........87 A5
Walichnowy PL .86 A2
Walincourt F ...90 A3
Walkenried D..82 A2
Walkeringham UK...........40 B3
Wallasey UK ...38 A3
Walldürn D 94 B1
Wallenfells D ..82 B3
Wallenhorst D .71 B5
Wallers F......78 B3
Wallersdorf D .95 C4
Wallerstein D .94 C2
Wallingford UK .44 B2
Wallitz D......74 A1
Walls UK......33 A5
Wallsbüll D....64 B2
Walmer UK....45 B5
Walsall UK....40 C2
Walsrode D....72 B2
Waltenhofen D........... 107 B5
Waltershausen D............82 B2
Waltham Abbey UK...........45 B4
Waltham on the Wolds UK.....40 C3
Walton-on-Thames UK...........44 B3
Walton-on-the-Naze UK......45 B5
Wamba E..... 142 C2
Wanderup D...64 B2
Wandlitz D....74 B2
Wanfried D....82 A2
Wangen im Allgäu D 107 B4
Wangerooge D .71 A4

Wangersen D...72 A2
Wängi CH.....107 B3
Wanna D.......64 C1
Wansford UK...40 C3
Wantage UK...44 B2
Wanzleben D..73 B4
Waplewo PL...77 A5
Wapnica PL...75 A4
Wapno PL.....76 B2
Warburg D....81 A5
Wardenburg D.71 A5
Ware UK......44 B3
Waregem B....79 B3
Wareham UK...43 B4
Waremme B....79 B5
Waren D......74 A1
Warendorf D..71 C4
Warga NL.....70 A2
Warin D......65 C4
Wark UK......37 A4
Warka PL.....87 A5
Warkworth UK.37 A5
Warlubie PL..69 B3
Warminster UK.43 A4
Warnemünde
  D..........65 B5
Warnow D.....65 C4
Warnsveld NL..70 B3
Warrenpoint
  UK.........27 B4
Warrington UK.38 A4
Warsaw =
  Warszawa PL..77 B6
Warsingsfehn
  D..........71 A4
Warsow D.....73 A4
Warstein D...81 A4
Warszawa =
  Warsaw PL...77 B6
Warta PL.....86 A2
Wartberg A...110 B1
Warth A......107 B5
Warwick UK...44 A2
Warza D......82 B2
Wasbister UK..33 B3
Washington
  UK.........37 B5
Wąsosz PL....85 A4
Wasselonne F..93 C3
Wassen CH....107 C3
Wassenaar NL..70 B1
Wasserauen
  CH.........107 B4
Wasserburg D.108 A3
Wassertrüdingen
  D..........94 B2
Wassy F......91 C4
Wasungen D...82 B2
Watchet UK...43 A3
Waterford IRL..30 B1
Watergrasshill
  IRL........29 B3
Waterloo B...79 B4
Waterville IRL.29 C1
Watford UK...44 B3
Wathlingen D..72 B3
Watten
  F..........78 B2
  UK.........32 C3
Wattens A....108 B2
Watton UK....41 C4
Wattwil CH...107 B4
Waunfawr UK..38 A2
Wavignies F...90 B2
Wavre B......79 B4
Wearhead UK..37 B4
Wechadlow PL..87 B4
Wedel D......72 A2
Wedemark D...72 B2
Weedon Bec
  UK.........44 A2
Weener D.....71 A4
Weert NL.....80 A1
Weesp NL.....70 B2
Weeze D......80 A2
Weferlingen D.73 B4
Wegeleben D..82 A3
Weggis CH....106 B3
Węgierska-Górka
  PL.........99 B3
Węgliniec PL..84 A3
Węgorzyno PL..75 A4
Węgrzynice PL.75 B4
Wegscheid D..96 C1
Wehdel D.....72 A1
Wehr D.......106 B2
Weibersbrunn
  D..........94 B1
Weichering D..95 C3
Weida D......83 B4
Weiden D.....95 B4
Weidenberg D..95 B3
Weidenhain D..83 A4

Weidenstetten
  D..........94 C1
Weierbach D...93 B3
Weikersheim
  D..........94 B1
Weil D.......108 A1
Weil am Rhein
  D..........106 B2
Weilburg D...81 B4
Weil der Stadt
  D..........93 C4
Weilerswist D..80 B2
Weilheim
  Baden-Württemberg
  D..........94 C1
  Bayern D...108 B2
Weilmünster D.81 B4
Weiltensfeld
  A..........110 C1
Weimar D.....82 B3
Weinberg D...94 B2
Weinfelden
  CH.........107 B4
Weingarten
  Baden-Württemberg
  D..........93 B4
  Baden-Württemberg
  D..........107 B4
Weinheim D...93 B4
Weinstadt D..94 C1
Weismain D...82 B3
Weissbriach A 109 C4
Weissenbach
  A..........108 B1
Weissenberg D.84 A2
Weissenbrunn
  D..........82 B3
Weissenburg D.94 B2
Weissenfels D..83 A3
Weissenhorn D 94 C2
Weissenkirchen
  A..........97 C3
Weissensee D..82 A3
Weissenstadt
  D..........83 B3
Weisskirchen im
  Steiermark
  A..........110 B1
Weisstannen
  CH.........107 C4
Weisswasser D.84 A2
Weitendorf D..65 C5
Weitersfeld A..97 C3
Weitersfelden
  A..........96 C2
Weitnau D....107 B5
Wéitra A.....96 C2
Weiz A.......110 B2
Wejherowo PL..68 A3
Welkenraedt B..80 B1
Wellaune D...83 A4
Wellin B.....91 A5
Wellingborough
  UK.........44 A3
Wellington
  Somerset UK..43 B3
  Telford & Wrekin
  UK.........38 B4
Wellingtonbridge
  IRL........30 B2
Wells UK.....43 A4
Wells-next-the-Sea
  UK.........41 C4
Wels A.......109 A5
Welschenrohr
  CH.........106 B2
Welshpool UK..38 B3
Welver D.....81 A3
Welwyn Garden
  City UK.....44 B3
Welzheim D...94 C1
Welzow D.....84 A2
Wem UK.......38 B4
Wembury UK...42 B2
Wemding D....94 C2
Wenden D.....81 B3
Wendisch Rietz
  D..........74 B3
Wendlingen D..94 C1
Weng A.......110 B1
Weng bei Admont
  A..........110 B1
Wengen CH...106 C2
Wenigzell A..110 B2
Wennigsen D..72 B2
Wenns A......108 B1
Wenzenbach
  D..........95 B4
Weppersdorf
  A..........111 B3
Werben D.....73 B4
Werbig D.....74 C2
Werdau D.....83 B4

Werder D.....74 B1
Werdohl D....81 A3
Werfen A.....109 B4
Werkendam NL..79 A4
Werl D.......81 A3
Werlte D.....71 B4
Wermelskirchen
  D..........80 A3
Wermsdorf D..83 A4
Wernberg Köblitz
  D..........95 B4
Werne D......81 A3
Werneck D....94 B2
Werneuchen D..74 B2
Wernigerode
  D..........82 A2
Wertach D....108 B1
Wertheim D...94 B1
Wertingen D..94 C2
Weseke D.....80 A2
Wesel D......80 A2
Wesenberg D..74 A1
Wesendorf D..73 B3
Wesołowo PL..77 A5
Wesselburen D.64 B1
Wesseling D..80 B2
West Bridgford
  UK.........40 C2
West Bromwich
  UK.........40 C2
Westbury
  Shropshire UK.38 B4
  Wiltshire UK..43 A4
Westbury-on-
  Severn UK...39 C4
Westendorf A.108 B3
Westensee D..64 B2
Westerbork NL.71 B3
Westerburg D..81 B3
Westerhaar NL.71 B3
Westerholt D..71 A4
Westerkappeln
  D..........71 B4
Westerland D..64 B1
Westerlo B...79 A4
Westerstede D.71 A4
West Haddon
  UK.........44 A2
Westheim D...94 B2
Westhill UK...33 D4
Westkapelle
  B..........78 A3
  NL.........79 A3
West Kilbride
  UK.........34 C3
West Linton UK 35 C4
West Lulworth
  UK.........43 B4
West Mersea
  UK.........45 B4
Westminster
  UK.........44 B3
Weston UK....40 C1
Weston-super-Mare
  UK.........43 A4
Westport IRL..28 A2
Westruther UK.35 C5
West-Terschelling
  NL.........70 A2
Westward Ho!
  UK.........42 A2
West Woodburn
  UK.........37 A4
Wetheral UK..37 B4
Wetherby UK..40 B2
Wetter
  Hessen D....81 B4
  Nordrhein-
  Westfalen D..80 A3
Wetteren B...79 A3
Wettin D.....83 A3
Wettringen D..71 B4
Wetzikon CH..107 B3
Wetzlar D....81 B4
Wewelsfleth D.64 C2
Wexford IRL...30 B2
Weybridge UK.44 B3
Weyerbusch D..81 B3
Weyer Markt
  A..........110 B1
Weyersheim F..93 C3
Weyhe D......72 B1
Weyhill UK...44 B2
Weymouth UK..43 B4
Weyregg A...109 B4
Węzyska PL....75 B3
Whalton UK...37 A5
Whauphill UK..36 B2
Wheatley UK..44 B2
Whickham UK..37 B5
Whipsnade UK.44 B3
Whitburn UK..35 C4
Whitchurch

Whitchurch
  Hampshire UK.44 B2
  Herefordshire
  UK.........39 C4
  Shropshire UK.38 B4
White Bridge
  UK.........32 D2
Whitegate IRL..29 C3
Whitehaven UK 36 B3
Whitehead UK..27 B5
Whithorn UK..36 B2
Whitley Bay UK.37 A5
Whitstable UK..45 B5
Whittington UK 38 B4
Whittlesey UK..41 C3
Wiązów PL....85 B5
Wick UK......32 C3
Wickede D....81 A3
Wickford UK..45 B4
Wickham UK...44 C2
Wickham Market
  UK.........45 A5
Wicklow IRL...30 B2
Wicko PL.....68 A2
Widawa PL....86 A2
Widdrington
  UK.........37 A5
Widecombe in the
  Moor UK....42 B3
Widemouth UK.42 B2
Widnes UK....38 A4
Widuchowo PL.74 A3
Więcbork PL..76 A2
Wiefelstede D..71 A5
Wiehe D......82 A3
Wiehl D......81 B3
Wiek D.......66 B2
Większyce PL..86 B1
Wielbark PL...77 A5
Wiele PL.....68 B2
Wielen PL....75 B5
Wielgie
  Kujawsko-
  Pomorskie PL.77 B4
  Łódzkie PL...86 A2
  Mazowieckie
  PL.........77 B5
Wielgomłyny
  PL.........87 A3
Wielichowo PL.75 B5
Wieliczka PL..99 B4
Wielka Łąka PL.76 A3
Wielowies PL..86 B2
Wieluń PL....86 A2
Wien = Vienna
  A..........111 A3
Wiener Neustadt
  A..........111 B3
Wiepke D.....73 B4
Wierden NL...71 B3
Wieren D.....73 B3
Wieruszów PL.86 A2
Wierzbica
  Mazowieckie
  PL.........77 B6
  Mazowieckie
  PL.........87 A5
Wierzbie PL...86 A2
Wierzbięcin PL.75 A4
Wierzchowo
  PL.........75 A5
Wierzchucino
  PL.........68 A3
Wierzchy PL...86 A2
Wies A.......110 C2
Wiesau D.....95 B4
Wiesbaden D..81 B4
Wieselburg A.110 A2
Wiesen CH....107 C4
Wiesenburg D.73 B5
Wiesenfelden
  D..........95 B4
Wiesensteig D..94 C1
Wiesentheid D.94 B2
Wiesloch D...93 B4
Wiesmath A...111 B3
Wiesmoor D...71 A4
Wietmarschen
  D..........71 B4
Wietze D.....72 B2
Wigan UK.....38 A4
Wiggen CH...106 C2
Wigston UK...40 C2
Wigton UK....36 B3
Wijchen NL...80 A1
Wijhe NL.....70 B3
Wijk bij Duurstede
  NL.........70 C2
Wil CH.......107 B4
Wilamowice PL.99 B3
Wilczęta PL...69 A4
Wilczkowice PL.77 B4

Wilczna PL....76 B3
Wilczyn PL....76 B3
Wildalpen A..110 B1
Wildbad D....93 C4
Wildberg
  Baden-Württemberg
  D..........93 C4
  Brandenburg
  D..........74 B1
Wildegg CH...106 B3
Wildendürnbach
  A..........97 C4
Wildeshausen
  D..........72 B1
Wildon A....110 C2
Wilfersdorf A..97 C4
Wilhelmsburg
  A..........110 A2
  D..........74 A2
Wilhelmsdorf
  D..........107 B4
Wilhelmshaven
  D..........71 A5
Wilków PL....77 B5
Willebadessen
  D..........81 A5
Willebroek B..79 A4
Willgottheim F.93 C3
Willhermsdorf
  D..........94 B2
Willich D....80 A2
Willingen D...81 A4
Willington UK..37 B5
Willisau CH...106 B3
Wilmslow UK..40 B1
Wilsdruff D...83 A5
Wilster D....64 C2
Wilsum D.....71 B3
Wilton UK....44 B2
Wiltz L......92 B1
Wimborne Minster
  UK.........43 B5
Wimereux F...78 B1
Wimmenau F...93 C3
Wimmis CH....106 C2
Wincanton UK.43 A4
Winchcombe
  UK.........44 B2
Winchelsea UK.45 C4
Winchester UK.44 B2
Windermere
  UK.........36 B4
Windischeschenbach
  D..........95 B4
Windischgarsten
  A..........110 B1
Windorf D....96 C1
Windsbach D..94 B2
Windsor UK...44 B3
Wingene B....78 A3
Wingham UK...45 B5
Winkleigh UK..42 B3
Winklern A...109 C3
Winnenden D..94 C1
Winnica PL....77 B5
Winnigstedt D.73 B3
Winnweiler D..93 B3
Winschoten NL.71 A4
Winsen
  Niedersachsen
  D..........72 A3
  Niedersachsen
  D..........72 A3
Winsford UK..38 A4
Wińsko PL....85 A4
Winslow UK...44 B3
Winsum
  Friesland NL..70 A2
  Groningen NL..71 A3
Winterberg D..81 A4
Winterfeld D..73 B4
Winterswijk NL.71 C3
Winterthur
  CH.........107 B3
Wintzenheim
  F..........106 A2
Winzer D.....95 C5
Wipperdorf D..82 A2
Wipperfürth D.80 A3
Wirksworth
  UK.........40 B2
Wisbech UK...41 C4
Wischhafen D..64 C2
Wishaw UK....35 C4
Wisła PL.....98 B2
Wisła Wielka
  PL.........98 B2
Wislica PL....87 B4
Wismar D.....65 C4
Wisniewo PL...77 A5
Wiśniowa PL...99 B4
Wissant F....78 B1
Wissembourg F 93 B3

Wissen D.....81 B3
Witanowice PL..99 B3
Witham UK....45 B4
Withern UK...41 B4
Withernsea UK..41 B4
Witkowo PL...76 B2
Witmarsum NL.70 A2
Witney UK....44 B2
Witnica PL....75 B3
Witonia PL....77 B4
Witry-les-Reims
  F..........91 B4
Wittdün D....64 B1
Wittelsheim F. 106 B2
Witten D.....80 A3
Wittenberge D.73 B4
Wittenburg D..73 A4
Wittenheim F. 106 B2
Wittichenau D..84 A2
Wittighausen D 94 B1
Wittingen D...73 B3
Wittislingen D.94 C2
Wittlich D....92 B2
Wittmannsdorf
  A..........110 C2
Wittmund D...71 A4
Wittorf D....72 A2
Wittstock D...73 A5
Witzenhausen
  D..........82 A1
Wiveliscombe
  UK.........43 A3
Wivenhoe UK..45 B4
Władysławowo
  PL.........69 A3
Wleń PL......84 A3
Włocławek PL..77 B4
Włodawa PL...13 C5
Włodzimierzów
  PL.........87 A3
Włosień PL....84 A3
Włostow PL....87 B5
Włoszakowice
  PL.........75 C5
Włoszczowa
  PL.........87 B3
Wöbbelin D...73 A4
Woburn UK....44 B3
Wodzisław PL..87 B4
Wodzisław Śląski
  PL.........98 B2
Woerden NL...70 B1
Woerth F.....93 C3
Wohlen CH...106 B3
Woippy F.....92 B2
Wojcieszow PL.85 B3
Wojkowice
  Kościelne PL..86 B3
Wojnicz PL....99 B4
Woking UK....44 B3
Wokingham UK 44 B3
Wola Jachowa
  PL.........87 B4
Wola Niechcicka
  PL.........86 A3
Wolbórz PL....87 A3
Wolbrom PL...87 B3
Wołczyn PL...86 A2
Woldegk D....74 A2
Wolfach D....93 C4
Wolfegg D....107 B4
Wolfen D.....83 A4
Wolfenbüttel
  D..........73 B3
Wolfersheim D.81 B4
Wolfhagen D..81 A5
Wolfratshausen
  D..........108 B2
Wolfsberg A..110 C1
Wolfsburg D..73 B3
Wolf's Castle
  UK.........39 C2
Wolfshagen D.74 A2
Wolfstein D...93 B3
Wolfurt A...107 B4
Wolgast D....66 B2
Wolhusen CH. 106 B3
Wolin PL.....67 C3
Wołów PL.....85 A4
Wolsztyn PL...75 B5
Wolvega NL...70 B2
Wolverhampton
  UK.........40 C1
Wolverton UK.44 A3
Wombwell UK..40 B2

Woodbridge
  UK.........45 A5
Woodhall Spa
  UK.........41 B3
Woodstock UK.44 B2
Wookey Hole
  UK.........43 A4
Wool UK......43 B4
Woolacombe
  UK.........42 A2
Wooler UK....37 A4
Woolwich UK..45 B4
Wooperton UK.37 A5
Worb CH......106 C2
Worbis D.....82 A2
Worcester UK..39 B4
Wördern A....97 C4
Wörgl A......108 B3
Workington UK.36 B3
Worksop UK...40 B2
Workum NL....70 B2
Wörlitz D....83 A4
Wormer NL....70 B1
Wormhout F...78 B2
Wormit UK....35 B5
Worms D......93 B4
Worpswede D..72 A1
Wörrstadt D..93 B4
Wörschach A..110 B1
Worsley UK...38 A4
Wörth
  Bayern D....93 B5
  Bayern D....95 B4
  Bayern D....95 C4
  Rheinland-Pfalz
  D..........93 B4
Worthing UK..44 C3
Woudsend NL..70 B2
Woumen B....78 A2
Woźniki PL....86 B3
Wragby UK....41 B3
Wrangle UK...41 B4
Wręczyca Wlk.
  PL.........86 B2
Wredenhagen
  D..........73 A5
Wremen D.....72 A1
Wrentham UK..45 A5
Wrexham UK...38 A3
Wriedel D....72 A3
Wriezen D....74 B3
Wrist D......64 C2
Wróblewo
  Mazowieckie
  PL.........77 B5
  Wielkopolskie
  PL.........75 B5
Wrocki PL....69 B4
Wrocław PL...85 A5
Wronki PL....75 B5
Wroxham UK...41 C5
Września PL...76 B2
Wrzosowo PL..67 B4
Wschowa PL...85 A4
Wulfen D.....80 A3
Wülfen D.....83 A3
Wulkau D.....73 B5
Wünnenberg D.81 A4
Wünsdorf D...74 B2
Wunsiedel D..95 A4
Wunstorf D...72 B2
Wuppertal D..80 A3
Wurmannsquick
  D..........95 C4
Würselen D...80 B2
Wurzbach D...82 B3
Würzburg D...94 B1
Wurzen D.....83 A4
Wust D.......74 B1
Wusterhausen
  D..........73 B5
Wusterwitz D..73 B5
Wustrau-Altfriesack
  D..........74 B1
Wustrow D....66 B1
Wye UK.......45 B4
Wygiełdów PL..87 A5
Wyk D........64 B1
Wykroty PL...84 A3
Wylye UK.....43 A5
Wymiarki PL...84 A3
Wymondham
  UK.........41 C5
Wyrzysk PL...76 A2
Wyśmierzyce
  PL.........87 A4
Wysoka
  Dolnośląskie
  PL.........85 A3

Wysoka continued
Wielkopolskie
PL........76 A2
Wyszanów PL..86 A2
Wyszogród PL..77 B5

X
Xanten D.......80 A2
Xanthi GR.....188 B3
Xarrë AL......182 D2
Xátiva E......159 C3
Xeraco E......159 B3
Xert E........153 B4
Xerta E.......153 B4
Xertigny F....105 A5
Xilagani GR..183 C7
Xilokastro GR.184 A3
Xinzo de Limia
E............140 B3
Xixón = Gijón
E............140 A3
Xove E........140 A3
Xubia E.......140 A2
Xunqueira de
Ambía E......140 B3
Xunqueira de
Espadañedo
E............140 B3
Xylophagou
CY...........181 B2

Y
Yablanitsa BG.. 17 D6
Yağcılar TR....186 C3
Yahyalı TR.....23 B8
Yakoruda BG.. 183 A5
Yalova TR......187 B4
Yalvaç TR......189 A6
Yambol BG.....17 D7
Yampil UA.....13 D8
Yaniskoski
RUS..........193 D12
Yantarnyy RUS..69 A4
Yarbasan TR...186 D3
Yarcombe UK...43 B3
Yaremcha UA ..13 D6
Yarm UK........37 B5
Yarmouth UK ..44 C2
Yarrow UK.....35 C4
Yasinya UA....17 A6
Yatağan TR....188 B3
Yate UK........43 A4
Yatton UK......43 A4
Yavoriv UA....13 D5
Yaxley UK......41 C3
Yazıca TR......187 B6
Yazıköy TR....188 C2
Ybbs A.........110 A2
Ybbsitz A......110 B1
Ydby DK........58 B1
Yddal N........46 B2
Ydes F.........116 B2
Yealmpton UK .42 B3
Yebra de Basa
E............145 B3
Yecla E........159 C2
Yecla de Yeltes
E............149 B3
Yelsk BY.......13 C6
Yelverton UK ..42 B2
Yena RUS......197 B14
Yenice
Ankara TR 23 B7
Aydın TR.......188 B3
Çanakkale TR. 186 C2
Edirne TR 183 C8
Yenifoça TR...186 D1
Yeniköy TR....186 D4
Yeniköy Plaji
TR...........186 D4
Yenipazar TR. 188 B3
Yenişarbademli
TR...........189 B6
Yenişehir TR . 187 B4
Yenne F........118 B2
Yeovil UK......43 B4
Yepes E........151 C4
Yerköy TR......23 B8
Yerólakkos
CY...........181 A2

Yeroskipos CY 181 B1
Yerseke NL.....79 A4
Yerville F......89 A4
Yeşildağ TR ... 189 B6
Yeşilhisar TR...23 B8
Yeşilköy TR ... 186 B3
Yeşilova TR... 189 B4
Yeşilyurt TR...188 A3
Yeste E........164 A2
Yezerishche BY ..9 E6
Y Felinheli UK ..38 A2
Ygos-St-Saturnin
F............128 C2
Ygrande F......104 C1
Yialousa CY ... 181 A3
Yığılca TR.....187 B6
Yli-Ii FIN.......197 D8
Yli-Kärppä
FIN..........197 D8
Yli-Muonia
FIN..........196 A6
Ylitornio FIN . 196 C6
Ylivieska FIN ..3 D9
Ylläsjärvi FIN.. 196 B7
Ymonville F... 103 A3
Yngsjö S.......63 C2
York UK........40 B2
Youghal IRL....29 C4
Yoğuntaş TR .. 186 A2
Yozgat TR......23 B8
Yport F........89 A4
Ypres = Ieper B..78 B2
Yssingeaux F.. 117 B4
Ystad S........66 A2
Ystalyfera UK ..39 C3
Ystebrød N.....52 B1
Ystradgynlais
UK...........39 C3
Ytre Arna N....46 B2
Ytre Enebakk N .54 A2
Ytre Rendal N . 199 D8
Ytteran S......199 B11
Ytterhogdal
S............199 C11
Yttermalung S ..49 B5
Yunak TR.......187 D6
Yuncos E.......151 B4
Yunquera E ... 162 B3
Yunquera de
Henares E 151 B4
Yushkozero
RUS...........3 D13
Yverdon-les-Bains
CH...........106 C1
Yvetot F.......89 A4
Yvignac F..... 101 A3
Yvoir B........79 B4
Yvonand CH .. 106 C1
Yxnerum S......56 B2
Yzeure F.......104 C2

Z
Zaamslag NL....79 A3
Zaanstad NL....70 B1
Žabalj SRB ... 126 B2
Zabar H........113 A4
Zabari SRB ... 127 C3
Zabiče SLO.... 123 B3
Zabierzów PL...87 B3
Ząbki PL.......77 B6
Ząbkowice Śląskie
PL............85 B4
Zablaće HR.... 138 B1
Žabljak MNE .. 139 B5
Zabok HR...... 124 A1
Zaborek PL.....87 B4
Zabor PL.......75 C4
Żabowo PL.....75 A4
Zabrdje BIH... 125 C4
Zábřeh CZ......97 B4
Zabreže SRB.. 127 C2
Ząbrowo PL.....67 C4
Zabrze PL......86 B2
Zabrzeź PL.....99 B4
Zacharo GR.... 184 B2
Zadar HR.......137 A4
Zadzim PL......86 A2
Zafarraya E ... 163 B3
Zafferana Etnea
I.............177 B4
Zafra E........155 C4
Žaga SLO...... 122 A2
Zagajica SRB . 127 C3
Żagań PL.......84 A3

Zaglav HR.....137 B4
Zaglavak SRB . 127 D1
Zagnańsk PL...87 B4
Zagora GR 183 D5
Zagorá SLO 110 C2
Zagoričani
BIH..........138 B3
Zagorje SLO... 123 A4
Zagórów PL.....76 B2
Zagradje SRB . 127 C2
Zagreb HR.....124 B1
Zagrilla E 163 A3
Zagvozd HR...138 B3
Zagwiździe PL..86 B1
Zagyvarékas
H............113 B4
Zagyvaróna
H............113 A3
Zahara E.......162 B2
Zahara de los
Atunes E 162 B2
Zahinos E 155 C4
Zahna D........83 A4
Záhony H.......16 A5
Zähringen D ...106 B2
Záhřadná D....73 A4
Zahrensdorf D .73 A3
Zaidín E.......153 A4
Zaječar SRB... 16 D5
Zákamenné SK ..99 B3
Zákány H...... 124 A2
Zákányszék
H............126 A1
Zakliczyn PL...99 B4
Zakopane PL...99 B3
Zakroczym PL...77 B5
Zakrzew PL.....87 A5
Zakrzewo PL....76 B3
Zakupy CZ......84 B2
Zakynthos GR. 184 B1
Zalaapáti H....111 C4
Zalabaksa H...111 C3
Zalaegerszeg
H............111 C3
Zalakomár H...111 C4
Zalakoppány
H............111 C4
Zalalövö H....111 C3
Zalamea de la
Serena E 156 B2
Zalamea la Real
E............161 B3
Zalaszentgrót
H............111 C4
Zalaszentiván
H............111 C3
Zalău RO.......17 B5
Zalavár H......111 C4
Zalcsie PL.....86 A3
Zaldibar E.....143 A4
Žalec SLO.....123 A4
Zalesie PL.....77 A5
Zalewo PL......69 B4
Zalishchyky UA 13 D6
Zalla E........143 A3
Zaltbommel NL .79 A5
Zamárdi H 112 C1
Zamarte PL.....68 B2
Zamberk CZ 85 B4
Zambra E......163 A3
Zambugueira do
Mar P........160 B1
Zámoly H 112 B2
Zamora E......149 A4
Zamość PL.....13 C5
Zamość PL......86 A3
Zams A........108 B1
Zandhoven B ...79 A4
Žandov CZ......84 B2
Zandvoort NL...70 B1
Zangliveri GR . 183 C5
Zánka H.......111 C4
Zaorejas E 152 B1
Zaovine SRB .. 127 D1
Zapadnaya Dvina
RUS...........9 D8
Zapfend D......94 A2
Zapole PL......86 A2
Zapolyarnyy
RUS..........193 C14
Zapponeta I ... 171 B3
Zaprešić HR.. 124 B1
Zaragoza E.....153 A3
Zarasai LT.....13 A7
Zarautz E......144 A1
Zarcilla de Ramos
E............164 B3
Zaręby PL......77 A6

Žarki PL........86 B3
Zarko GR......182 D4
Žarnovica SK....98 C2
Zarnow PL......87 A4
Zarnowiec PL...68 A3
Zaroñie CZ.....97 B4
Žarów PL.......85 B4
Zarren B.......78 A2
Zarrentin D ...73 A3
Žary PL........84 A3
Zarza Capilla
E............156 B2
Zarza de Alange
E............156 B1
Zarza de Granadilla
E............149 B3
Zarza de Tajo
E............151 B4
Zarzadilla de
Totana E 164 B3
Zarza la Mayor
E............155 B4
Zarzuela del Monte
E............150 B3
Zarzuela del Pinar
E............151 A3
Zas E..........140 A2
Zasavica SRB . 127 C1
Zasieki PL.....84 A2
Zásmuky CZ....96 B3
Žatec CZ.......83 B5
Zaton HR......139 C4
Zatonie PL.....84 A3
Zator PL.......99 A3
Zauchwitz D ...74 B2
Zavala BIH.....139 C3
Zavalje BIH....124 C1
Zavattarello I . 120 C2
Zavidovići
BIH..........139 A4
Zavlaka SRB...127 C1
Zawady PL.....77 C5
Zawadzkie PL..86 B2
Zawdy PL.......86 A2
Zawidów PL....84 A3
Zawidz PL......77 B4
Zawiercie PL...86 B3
Zawoja PL......99 B3
Zawonia PL....85 A5
Žažina HR.....124 B2
Zázrivá SK.....99 B3
Zbarazh UA....13 D6
Zbąszyń PL.....75 B4
Zbąszynek PL..75 B4
Zbehy SK.......98 C2
Zbiersk PL.....76 C3
Zbiroh CZ......96 B1
Zblewo PL......69 B3
Zbójno PL......77 A4
Zbrachlin PL...76 A3
Zbraslav CZ....96 B2
Zbraslavice CZ ..97 B3
Ždala HR......124 A3
Ždánice CZ.....98 B1
Ždár nad Sázavou
CZ............97 B3
Zdbice PL......75 A5
Zdenci HR..... 125 B3
Ždiar SK.......99 B4
Zdice CZ.......96 B1
Zdirec nad
Doubravou
CZ............97 B3
Zdolbuniv UA.. 13 C7
Zdounky CZ....98 B1
Ždrelo SRB ... 127 C3
Zduńska Wola
PL............86 A2
Zduny
Łódzkie PL.....77 B4
Wielkopolskie
PL............85 A5
Ždáry PL.......87 A4
Zdziechowice
Opolskie PL....86 A2
Wielkopolskie
PL............76 B2
Zdziszowice PL .86 B2
Zeberio E......143 A4
Žebrák CZ......96 B1
Zebreira P.....155 B3
Zebrzydowa PL .84 A3
Zechlin D......74 A1
Zechlinerhütte
D............74 A1
Zederhaus A ...109 B4
Žednik SRB... 126 B1

Zeebrugge B....78 A3
Zegrze PL......77 B6
Zehdenick D ...74 B2
Zehren D.......83 A5
Zeil D.........94 A2
Zeilarn D......95 C4
Zeist NL.......70 B2
Zeithain D 83 A5
Zeitz D........83 A4
Želatava CZ....97 B3
Želazno PL.....68 A2
Zele B.........79 A4
Zelenoborskiy
RUS...........3 C13
Zelenogorsk
RUS...........9 B6
Zelenograd
RUS...........9 D10
Zelenogradsk
RUS..........12 A4
Železná Ruda
CZ............96 B1
Železnice CZ...84 B3
Železnik SRB .. 127 C2
Železniki SLO . 123 A3
Železný Brod
CZ............84 B3
Zelhem NL.....71 B3
Želiezovce SK . 112 A2
Želkowo PL.....68 A2
Zell
CH...........106 B2
Baden-Württemberg
D............93 C4
Baden-Württemberg
D............106 B2
Rheinland-Pfalz
D............92 A3
Zella-Mehlis D ..82 B2
Zell am See A.. 109 B3
Zell am Ziller
A............108 B2
Zell an der Pram
A............96 C1
Zell bei Zellhof
A............96 C2
Zellerndorf A ..97 C3
Zellingen D 94 B1
Želovce SK.....112 A3
Zelów PL.......86 A3
Zeltweg A......110 B1
Zelzate B.......79 A3
Zemberovce SK .98 C2
Zembrzyce PL...99 B3
Zemianske-
Kostol'any SK ..98 C2
Zemitz D.......66 C2
Zemné SK..... 112 B1
Zemst B........79 B4
Zemun SRB.... 127 C2
Zemunik Donji
HR...........137 A4
Zenica BIH.... 139 A3
Zennor UK.....42 B1
Žepa BIH......139 B5
Žepče BIH..... 139 A4
Zepponami I... 168 A2
Zerbst D.......73 C5
Zerf D.........92 B2
Zerind RO......17 B5
Zerkow PL......76 B2
Zermatt CH ... 119 A4
Zernez CH.....107 C5
Zerpen-schleuse
D............74 B2
Zestoa E......144 A1
Zetel D........71 A4
Zeulenroda D .. 83 B3
Zeven D........72 A2
Zevenaar NL...70 C3
Zevenbergen
NL...........79 A4
Zévio I........121 B4
Zeytinbaği TR. 186 B3
Zeytindağ TR . 186 D2
Zgierz PL......86 A3
Zgorzelec PL...84 A3
Zgošča BIH.... 139 A4
Zhabinka BY...13 B6
Zharkovskiy RUS. 9 E8
Zhashkiv UA...13 D9
Zhlobin BY....13 B9
Zhmerynka UA. 13 D8
Zhodzina BY...13 A8
Zhytomyr UA...13 C8
Žiar nad Hronom
SK............98 C2

Zicavo F.......180 B2
Zickhusen D ...65 C4
Zidani Most
SLO..........123 A4
Ziddorf D......73 A5
Židlochovice
CZ............97 B4
Ziębice PL.....85 B5
Ziegendorf D ...73 A4
Ziegenrück D ..83 B3
Zielenec
Dolnośląskie
PL............85 B4
Žrnovica HR.... 138 B2
Zielona E......156 B2
Zielona Góra
PL............75 C4
Zieluń-Osada
PL............77 A4
Ziemetshausen
D............94 C2
Zierenberg D ..81 A5
Zierikzee NL...79 A3
Ziersdorf A 97 C3
Zierzow D......73 A4
Ziesar D.......73 B5
Ziesendorf D ..65 C5
Ziethen D......74 B2
Žihle CZ.......96 A1
Žilina SK......98 B2
Ziltendorf D ...74 B3
Zimandu Nou
RO...........126 A3
Zimna Woda
PL............77 A5
Zimnicea RO ...17 D6
Zinal CH...... 119 A4
Zinasco I...... 120 B2
Zingst D.......66 B1
Zinkgruvan S . 55 B6
Zinkovy CZ.....96 B1
Zinnowitz D ...66 B2
Zirc H........112 B1
Žiri SLO......123 A3
Zirl A.........108 B2
Zirndorf D.....94 B2
Zirovnica SRB . 127 C3
Žirovnice CZ...97 B3
Zisterdorf A ...97 C4
Žitište SRB ... 126 B2
Zitsa GR.......182 D2
Zittau D.......84 B2
Živaja HR..... 124 B2
Živinice BIH... 139 A4
Zlatar HR..... 124 A2
Zlatar Bistrica
HR...........124 A2
Zlaté Hory CZ...85 B5
Zlaté Klasy SK. 111 A4
Zlaté Moravce
SK............98 C2
Zlatna Ostrove
SK........... 112 B1
Zlatniky SK....98 C2
Zlatograd BG . 183 B7
Zlatibič SLO... 123 B3
Zlín CZ........98 B1
Złocieniec PL...75 A5
Złoczew PL.....86 A2
Zlonice CZ.....84 B2
Złotniki Kujawskie
PL............76 B3
Złotoryja PL...85 A3
Złoty Stok PL...85 B4
Zlutice CZ.....83 B5
Zmajevac BIH . 124 C2
Žmigród PL.....85 A4
Zmijavci HR... 138 B3
Žminj HR.......122 B2
Znin PL........76 B2
Znojmo CZ......97 C4
Zöblitz D.......83 B5
Zocca I........135 A3
Zoetermeer NL .70 B1
Zofingen CH ... 106 B2
Zogno I........120 B2
Zohor SK.......97 C4
Zolochiv UA...13 D6
Zomba H......112 C2
Zomergem B ...79 A3
Zoñán E.......141 A3

Zonguldak TR. 187 A6
Zonhoven B....79 B5
Zonza F........180 B2
Zörbig D.......83 A4
Zorita E........156 A2
Žory PL........98 A2
Zossen D.......74 B2
Zottegem B 79 B3
Zoutkamp NL...71 A3
Zovi Do BIH ... 139 B4
Zreče SLO.....123 A4
Zrenjanin SRB. 126 B2
Žrnovica HR... 138 B2
Zručnad Sazavou
CZ............97 B3
Zsadány H.....113 C5
Zsámbék H 112 B2
Zsámbok H....112 B3
Zsana H.......126 A1
Zschopau D....83 B5
Zuberec SK.....99 B3
Zubieta E......144 A2
Zubiri E.......144 B2
Zubtsov RUS....9 D9
Zucaina E......153 B3
Zudar D........66 B2
Zuera E........144 C3
Zufre E........161 B3
Zug CH........107 B3
Zuheros E......163 A3
Zuidhorn NL...71 A3
Zuidlaren NL...71 A3
Zuidwolde NL. 71 B3
Zújar E........164 B2
Žukowo PL.....69 A3
Žuljana HR.....138 C3
Žulová CZ.......85 B5
Zülpich D......80 B2
Zumaia E......144 A1
Zumárraga E . 143 A4
Zundert NL.....79 A4
Zungri I.......175 C1
Županja HR ... 125 B4
Zurgena E......164 B2
Zürich CH.....107 B3
Žuromin PL.....77 A4
Zurzach CH ... 106 B3
Zusmarshausen
D............94 C2
Zusow D........65 C4
Züssow D.......66 C2
Žuta Lovka
HR...........123 C4
Zutphen NL....70 B3
Žužemberk
SLO..........123 B3
Zvenyhorodka
UA...........13 D9
Zvikovské Podhradí
CZ............96 B2
Zvolen SK......99 C3
Zvolenská Slatina
SK............99 C3
Zvornik BIH... 139 A5
Zwartsluis NL...70 B3
Zweibrücken D .93 B3
Zweisimmen
CH...........106 C2
Zwettl A........97 C3
Zwettl an der Rodl
A.............96 C2
Zwickau D......83 B4
Zwiefalten D . 107 A4
Zwierzyn PL....75 B4
Zwierzyno PL...69 A4
Zwiesel D......96 B1
Zwieselstein
A............108 C2
Zwoleń PL......87 A5
Zwolle NL......70 B3
Zwönitz D......83 B4
Zydowo
Wielkopolskie
PL............76 B2
Zachodnio-
Pomorskie PL . 68 A1
Żytno PL.......86 B3
Żywiec PL......99 B3
Zyyi CY........181 B2